A Compendium Of Orthodox S[ervices]

Volume 1

To the glory of God.

Version 1v7

Changelog: Version 1v6   Minor spelling corrections.

Changelog: Version 1v7   Changed "will" to "shall", this is more accurate for "thee/thou".

Index

Index Of Volume 2

"The Compendium is a magnificent undertaking that will help all those who wish to know about our Orthodox Church, the structure and order of its worship, and its rich spiritual treasures.

I am happy to give this work my formal commendation for use for consultative purposes, since a deeper understanding and appreciation of the Orthodox Ethos is essential not only for our Faithful and for Academia but also for those who are responsible for the worship of our Church being carried out in an orderly, dignified and spiritual fashion."

His Eminence Gregorios, Archbishop of Thyateira and Great Britain.
12th April 2018.

"Concerning the two volume compendium of church services. I am sure that this publication will prove of very great value to all Orthodox - parishes, monasteries and individual Christians - who use the English language in their worship. I shall certainly wish to buy a copy, and I will gladly make it known to others."

+ Metropolitan Kallistos of Diokleia
27th June 2018.

Foreword

For Whom Is This Book?

In any traditional Greek Orthodox church, at the Readers stand are many shelves of books. Many of these contain variables for any of the services that may occur in any given day. Others contain the services themselves in varying degrees of accessibility. A complete set of books would probably exceed 6 feet in length and cost over £2,500 in 2018 money. They will all be in Ancient Greek. If yours is an old Greek parish these books may have been donated by a rich parishioner in the past or by bequest. Then they remain on the shelves for generations of Readers. This volume will extend that set by another couple of inches, just in case they want to do a service in English.

In the West. Orthodoxy is seeing something of a revival and many new parishes are English-speaking. Books in Ancient Greek are of no use. However there are no complete sets of services in English ready to buy. Readers often find themselves searching the internet for services, and hence there is little or no unity between parishes as to the texts. There are two exceptions; first the Divine Liturgy of Saint John Chrysostom as set out in the translation by Fr Ephrem Lash and committee in the informally titled "Blue Book". This is now out of print and secondhand copies may be found for astronomical prices. The replacement "Red Book" was more of a solo venture by Fr Ephrem, and though still distributed suffers from an eccentric layout lending increased difficulty in a linear use. Sometimes one must skip pages backwards or forwards, and this is often confusing. However the text itself is authorised by His All Holiness Patriarch Bartholomew and forms the basis for the Divine Liturgies herein included, and in the companion volume The Divine Liturgy Of St John Chrysostom In Ancient Greek, English and Welsh. These texts aim to ensure a linear "from beginning to end" flow in all services.

The second exception is the outstanding collection of services by the protestant Isabel Florence Hapgood from 1906, a composite of Greek and Byzantine practices as used in America at that time, compiled as an academic exercise and not intended for liturgical use. A copy of Hapgood has been indispensable for any English-speaking parish for its astonishing array of services. There are still items therein that still may not be found on the internet. However it is also out of print and hard to find. Sadly it also suffers from an incomprehensible layout. Often the first two words of a prayer will be quoted and the expectation that the user knows the rest.

This volume then is an attempt to be an "instant set" of the most used services that any English-speaking Reader would need. It comprises most of those that the author has been called upon to deliver over 12 years. It may be followed by another volume containing rarer services. In many of these newer English speaking parishes most people are adult converts and often someone is thrown onto the Readers stand and expected to cope with no training whatsoever. As a result these big-hearted and well-meaning people are working it out for themselves. Consequently their self teaching inevitably misses parts and services can end up as a mix of correct parts, bits from other services, things that they were told by someone else, half remembering, and also ignorant of the use of variables, leading to pared down services that become Protestant-like in their sparse presentation. This volume shall also have accompanying notes intended to aid those out of their depth to deliver a more rounded set of services.

Nearly all services have variables. Very rarely does a service have no changes at all. Pascha is one notable exception. Therefore each service shall be preceded by a line *[noting which variables to prepare]*. All Readers should familiarise themselves with each service before it used. Preferably the day before one should go through the service next to be used and ensure that all variables are to hand. Often this means recourse to the <u>Festal Menaion</u> (the nine fixed Great Feasts) or <u>Triodion</u> - both of which excellent versions exist courtesy of Metropolitan Kallistos and Mother Mary – and a <u>Pentecostarion</u> (such as that published by Holy Transfiguration Monastery in Boston).

How To Sing

Up to about 800 AD those attending Church would sing together. Each small paragraph or even sentence is an "ymnoi" - an aid to remembrance; translated into English as "hymn". Loosely from this point there was more emphasis on the chorus taking the lead. Increasing influence from the East of the Byzantine Empire led to one man, the Psaltis – a singer with an excellent voice taking over the majority of the vocals (excepting the Priests' parts). This became known as the "cult of the Psaltis", but "cult" is not used in the extreme sense as in the West, but gentler. For example those baptised Orthodox take on the name of the saint and pray to him or her for support. They are then in that "cult".

In the Russian Church the emperor Peter the Great had an eye to the West and desired to lessen the Slavic peasants demeanour in favour of Westernisation. He introduced a beard tax to encourage his Orthodox subjects to shave. He appreciated Western choral pieces such as Bach and encouraged the great Russian composers, such as Tchaikovsky to write similar beautiful pieces or complete Liturgies. This was an effort to emphasise the Church as a performance. Today Russian practise has not changed from that, but it has been going on so long that they feel now that it is normal. For this reason it is important for each parish to advertise in which tradition they are. A Russian, expecting great majesty and beauty, is going to be disappointed upon walking into a Greek church and finding a more homespun form of chanting. A Greek entering a Russian church shall surely enjoy the magnificent singing, but will feel sidelined because many of the peoples prayers are missing and there seems to be no way to join in. Even the "Lord have mercy's" are done chorally with no way for the congregation to know the music.

The Antiochan Church followed the Greek pattern but in recent centuries have incorporated bits that they like from the Russians. Other jurisdictions tend to either Greek or Russian usage with regional variations.

It is best to think of these styles as not being in competition but more rather like the way that different families do the same things. Do you recall as, when a child, you went on a sleepover and for the first time you were exposed to how another family did things? Then you came home horrified and reported to your parents "but they brushed their teeth BEFORE putting on their pyjamas, and that's just SO WRONG". All Orthodox jurisdictions have their own patterns. These are small 't' traditions and cause diversity not division. In all cases where differing traditions are mentioned there is no judgement involved whatsoever, the differences are noted for reference only and the understanding that one well versed in one tradition should keep that knowledge for that tradition and accept that the other has a new set of rules.

It is worth noting that "Russian" really does indicate an ethnic preference. "Greek" is an unfortunate English word indicating the multicultural nature of the Byzantine Empire, whose language was Greek. The Greek

Orthodox Patriarch in Constantinople is head of a conglomerate of Churches, including those of Greece and Cyprus. It would be far more technically correct to address him as the Ecumenical Patriarch and the accompanying tradition as Byzantine. Let us treat "Greek" as a substitute for "Byzantine" in all cases except when dealing specifically with language.

For those who have seen old Greek plays, such as Sophocles, you will recall that the protagonist takes centre stage against a chorus. The function of the chorus is to spell out to the audience what is going on and what the protagonist is thinking. "I am going to war" he may sing, "and I am the bravest of all soldiers". The chorus then chant as one behind him to us that "he is actually quite frightened and has not yet earned the rank of warrior." This chorus is clearly not a choir. It is not their job to take centre stage and sing songs to us, as in Italian opera. They shall not entertain us with the songs of a choir that breaks up the action.

These chorus' are still extant in the Greek / Byzantine Church tradition. A Reader (who should be so tonsured) will have prepared the service with the variables and shall direct the chorus in the manner of a director. He shall indicate "sing that" by judicious use of a pointing finger. The Russian tradition is clearly that of a Choir who sing to, and on behalf of, the congregation.

There are several rules as to Greek singing. In no particular order these include:

- No musical instruments. Human voices only.

- No polyphony. We do not use harmony as in bass, tenor, alto and soprano. All singing is done solo or in unison. We do make use (if possible) of an ison, that is a bass note that keeps on the key currently in use. This key may change during the piece. A multi-tasking Reader will be able to motion with his hand whether the ison is about to go up or down. In some cases, where spare men are not available, but enthusiastic women are able to lend support to a grateful Reader, an alto may do the ison to good effect.

- No worldly tunes may be used. All the music must be for church use only.

- There is no stave music. The Church has been going a lot longer than Western Notation and formally uses a system called "neumes". These look like short hand squiggles above the text. There is no requirement to learn these for English speaking parishes as the system is translated below into something more familiar to a Western musician.

- In the Russian tradition they have 8 tones. However the word "tone" is used loosely as they quite clearly mean "tune". If tone 1 is that used for the current service then you can be assured that you are going to hear that two line tune used extensively over the next couple of hours. Fr Ephraim Lash points out that one of those tunes is <u>Greensleeves</u>.

- The Trisagion prayers are those on the first page of most services. If one service is to immediately follow another then these prayers need not be repeated. The section starting *"O come let us worship God our King."* indicates that a Psalm is to follow and may be used as a starting point when chaining services together. Some services have more Trisagion within them, these should be kept.

- When a musician reads music they follow the staves and interpret what the composer laid down. In modern popular Blues and Rock music there is much use made of extemporisation, that is the lead guitarist will "jam" along over the top of an established rhythm and set of key changes, such a 12 bar in *Em7*. He has his basic tone for the music, as laid down by the backing band. He has his structure, for example a Rock piece will be in 4/4 time with the emphasis on the 1st and 3rd beat. Funk and Reggae has its emphasis on the 2nd beat. He also knows what key to play, so his jamming then uses the scale of that key and he will work out various series of notes and groups that go well together. He will often learn his own jamming for a particular song in order to reproduce it at subsequent concerts. This gives the indication that he is playing a tune, but as you can see it is not quite that. It is certainly not the melody of the song.

- This extemporisation is what we do in the Greek Church. We use a system called "Tagis". When something positive is in the sentence we go up, when it is something bad we go down. If it is a name or a quote we start high and clear and slow and gradually return to the speed and pitch of that used before a quote or name. Let us take the:

Kontakion Of The Resurrection

When Thou went down to death, O immortal life, then Thou slew Hell with the lightning flash of Thy Godhead; but when from the depths below the earth Thou raised the dead, all the Powers in the heavens cried out: "Giver of life, Christ our God, glory to Thee."

This would be something like:

			life,	Thou			of Thy
When Thou went down to		immortal	then	slew	with the lightning flash		
	death, O			Hell			
Godhead;							
	but when from the		Thou raised		all the Powers in the		
		depths below the earth	the dead,				
	(slower) "Giver	life, Christ our God, glory to					
heavens cried out:	of		Thee".				

It is easier to understand what is meant by the above after having heard it. This is clearly a simplistic version as there are only 3 notes used.

- Each syllable should have one note, there should be no long drawn out notes and one word going on for ages. In many ethnic Greek churches the cult of the Psaltis is still going strong and in unfortunate circumstances is being attempted by an elderly member of the parish who is trying to do the soaring vocals of a great singer, but the listener, hearing the long drawn out wavering note, including panting for breath, may become confused as to whether the single word is really still going on or we are now actually listening to the Readers dying death rattle.

- In most usage each note shall be next to the one preceding it. Interval jumps may be used if starting a new phrase or some similar break.

- As we are reading prose, not verse, there may be times at which a sentence is not going to fit an extemporised tune. In this case it is absolutely fine to give one or two syllables an extra beat to make everything fit.

- This author is keen to promote the pre 800 AD tradition of congregational singing. In this case there are times when one must draw breath. At that moment one does not wish the congregation to come in with their bit before one is done. Audio cues may be employed, such as not resolving a sentence when breath is required, but ending the line high, drawing breath, then resuming with the next phrase and finally resolving when you are really done. This is used during the prokeimenon. Example:

  Reader: The Lord is my Light and My salvation: whom shall I fear? ← all on one note.

  People: *The Lord is my Light and My salvation: whom shall I fear?* ← congregation replies on same note

  Reader: The Lord is the Protector of my [go high] life: [breathe] of whom shall I be afraid? [resolve to root]

  People: *The Lord is my Light and My salvation: whom shall I fear?*

  Reader: The Lord is my Light and My salvation [go high as a cue] | *People:* whom shall I fear? [resolve]

- Psalms are sung, prayers are read on a single note chant. However when several prayers are read in succession, such as during the <u>Pre-Communion Canon</u>, it helps the people if you go up on the last few words. This then cues the people to join in the final "Amen".
- In some services there is a tight interchange between the Reader and the one or more member of the chorus, perhaps a sentence each. In this case it may add to the presentation to refrain from resolving at the end of your phrase and let your singing partner pick up from there and then he or she may resolve. A bit of practice is a good idea.
- In the Greek / Byzantine tradition "tone" is used to indicate similar to "tone of voice". If you say something in an angry tone of voice, this does not dictate the notes that you use, or their order, but rather your inflections. There are 8 or 9 tones, depending on how you count them, by tone number or rhythm number:

Tone	Rhythmic	Scale(s)	Tonic note / Ison	Dominant notes
1	Heirmological	Diatonic	D	G
1	Sticheraic	Diatonic	D	F
2	Heirmological	Soft or Hard Chromatic	G/E	E/A
2	Sticheraic	Soft Chromatic	G	E,C
3	Heirmological	Enharmonic	F	A,D,C
3	Sticheraic	Enharmonic	F	A,D,C
4	Heirmological	Diatonic/Soft Chromatic	E	G
4	Sticheraic	Diatonic	E	D,G
Plagal 1	Heirmological	Diatonic	A	C
Plagal 1	Sticheraic	Diatonic	D	A,G
Plagal 2	Heirmological	Soft Chromatic	G	E,C
Plagal 2	Sticheraic	Hard Chromatic	D	G,A
Grave	Heirmological	Enharmonic	F	Bb,G,C
Grave	Sticheraic	Enharmonic	F	Bb,G,C
Plagal 4	Heirmological	Diatonic	C or F	G,E or A,G
Plagal 4	Sticheraic	Diatonic	C	G,E
Papadicon	Idiomelismatic			

| **Diatonic** | Scale of C-ish. (Not the scales of F or Dm). | C, D, Eb, F, G, A, Bb, C. |
| **Tones:** | 1st, 4th, Plagal 1st, Plagal 4th and Papadic Grave. | |

| **Enharmonic** | Scale of F. | F, G, A, A#, C, D, E, F. |
| **Tones:** | 3rd and Grave. | |

| **Soft Chromatic** | Scale of G-ish. | C, Db, *(E, F, G, Ab, B, C.)* D, Eb |
| **Tones:** | Second, 4th, Plagal Second. | *(Usual range)*. E is the harmonic. |

| **Hard Chromatic** | Scale of D-ish. | D, Eb, F##, G, A, Bb, C##, D. |
| **Tones:** | Plagal 2nd, Bits of Second (for emphasis). | |

Papadicon

Used to cover the priest doing some long work (hence the root "papa"). Extemporise using the relevant tone from above. Usually this is only half a verse so you may need to draw out notes, but make sure words are still intelligible and properly pronounced.

Most often used during the Cherubikon. As that is a short hymn and the priest needs a long time to prepare and start Communion it may be repeated many times. Doing it quick will result in repeating it many tens of times. Doing it as slow as possible shall result in fewer repetitions. Don't end up in a death rattle, and if possible use the same tune each week as this will allow the people to join in.

During the Paschal service there is a point wherein the priest needs to move from the back of the church all the way to the front and the only thing that the Reader has to fill that gap is one "Amen".

- Like our rock guitarist above the Reader chooses phrases from the scale and extemporises up and down it.
- These scales are those used to give that authentic "Persian wail". However any "odd" note such as F## may be substituted for F#. It is often difficult for the Western ear to insert those quarter notes and it is fine to adjust the scale to make it more suitable for a Western taste. My parish has mostly Western converts so we made the decision to use the simpler Western scales for everything.
- Frequent repetition of any hymn, such as each Sunday, works well if delivered in the same way, especially if it is something that the people are supposed to sing. As there are about 3,000 hymns that means that we could say that there are 3,000 tunes. A lot of people are not natural musicians and so, when designing a part for the people to sing, try to keep it simple. As the hymns are short often a simple 3 note tune will be easy to recall.
- Use of minor and major keys is advised to reflect positive or contemplative parts of the service. For example the pensive Cherubikon (before Communion) *"We, who in a mystery represent the Cherubim and sing the thrice holy hymn to the life giving Trinity. Let us now lay aside every care of this life."* works well in a minor key. The subsequent celebratory *"We have seen the true Light, we have received the heavenly Spirit, We have found the true Faith, as we worship the undivided Trinity. For the Trinity has saved us."* works well as a declarative in a major key.

- If you don't understand all of this it really don't worry about it. Do your best to keep singing. Ideally the man or woman acting as Reader should be an experienced singer, able to project and lead the people with a strong voice for their parts. Some time spend jamming in a band or playing jazz would be a valuable asset. Those formally trained, for example classical pianists, have more of a head start than most people, but lack the natural extemporisation skills used by a Reader.

- The services in this book make calls to other books for variables. At the very lowest level if you follow the services in this book without any variables and do it chanting all on one note, then that is a service done and you have glorified God. As you learn you can incorporate more and more.

- Here are the tones as used in this book:

Tone 1	*Magnificent, happy and earthy.*	*C, D, Eb, F, G, A, Bb, C.*
Tone 2	*Majesty, gentleness, hope, repentance and sadness.*	*E, F, G, Ab, B, C.*
Tone 3	*Arrogant, brave, and mature atmosphere.*	*F, G, A, A#, C, D, E, F.*
Tone 4	*Festive, joyous and expressing deep piety.*	*C, D, Eb, F, G, A, Bb, C.*
Tone 5	*Stimulating, dancing, and rhythmical.*	*C, D, Eb, F, G, A, Bb, C.*
Tone 6	*Rich texture, funeral, sorrowful.*	*D, Eb, F##, G, A, Bb, C##, D.*
Tone 7	*Manly character and strong melody.*	*F, G, A, A#, C, D, E, F.*
Tone 8	*Humility, tranquillity, repose, suffering, pleading. Papadic.*	*C, D, Eb, F, G, A, Bb, C.*

- If you were pleading with someone, or in suffering (tone 8) your voice would go high. Hence anything sung in tone 8 should be substantially higher up the scale than the other tones. Most Theotokia are in tone 8.

- Arrogant people tend to shout in deep voices for authority. When using tone 3 go low and sound bossy.

- If you are dancing you need quite a snappy beat. Tone 4 should have a definite rhythm.

- Use the scales as you are able. Otherwise just use the words to give you an idea of what you should sound like.

- If you were able to follow all of the above and be completely technically-competent there would always be that one person who says "Well, I've been to Greece and you don't sound like them." The nature of the complaint would appear to be "you don't sound like you are singing in Greek". Of course not, Greek and English have completely different intonations.

- Between Russian, Greek and other traditions operating in an English-speaking environment a certain amount of homogenisation is inevitable due to the cadence and rhythms of English. An English-sounding Orthodoxy is already growing up, and is not in opposition to, but a companion to, the sounds of the old countries.

- "Halleluiah" is a Hebrew word that means "Praise you the Lord". It starts many Psalms.

- Most importantly, you don't need to sound like anyone else. You will always sounds first and foremost like yourself. Use that to glorify God and to help your parishioners to glorify God. Pray that your voice be a conduit to the worship of God and not the centre of attention. Give the people space to say their parts: Let the people pray!

- In this Compendium the Doxology contains marks "/" and "\". These are key changes for the benefit of whosoever sings the ison.
- When preparing the service it is helpful to make sure that you have all of the variables ready.

Mnemonic For Service Preparation

F	Feasts	
O	Octoechos	
M	Menaion	
P	Pentecostarion	(5.5 months of Easter to Pentecost and Sunday after)
T	Triodion	(The weeks approaching and including Lent)
E	Eothinón	(cycle of Gospels - 11 accounts of the resurrection)

The Nine Fixed Feasts

September 8th	Birth Of The Theotokos.
September 14th	Exaltation Of The Cross.
November 21st	Entry Of The Theotokos Into The Temple.
December 25th	Nativity Of Our Lord.
January 6th	Theophany - The Baptism Of Christ And Blessing Of The Waters.
February 2nd	Meeting Of Our Lord In The Temple.
March 25th	Annunciation.
August 6th	Transfiguration Of Our Lord.
August 15th	Dormition Of The Theotokos.

Credits

A great debt is owed to Fr Luke Holden who directed most of the Priests services for live use in church at Llanelli and Swansea. Using his many bookshelves full of resources services were put together as he directed.

Authorisation

With the blessings of Their Eminences Archbishop Gregorios and Metropolitan Kallistos of the Greek Orthodox Archdiocese of Thyateira and Great Britain.

Charles "Harry" Harrison / Xaralambous Zantis

Echelefechan Martin Sant, Silian.

orthodoxsilian@gmail.com

1st February 2018.

Sunday

The services on Sunday are Resurrectional in nature and are an exception to the general tone of services during the week, which tend towards the penitential. The Six Psalms of Orthros are a good example of this and all speak of events in Jesus' life, before they happened.

If there is no Priest, but there is a Deacon, he is permitted to carry out most of the functions of a Priest in his absence, but may not serve the Eucharist. Hence there is no Divine Liturgy without a Priest. A Typika may be served instead.

If there are no clergy there are many Readers services, especially during the week. Monastics are not clergy unless especially ordained, so from the monasteries arises a whole range of services to be done without a priest. Note the heading of services in this book for guidance.

Some Christians have so arranged their lives to be pseudo-monastic. They don't have a family at home, they don't have a TV, their income or job is such that they have ample time for many hours of prayer each day, they have their own private chapel in one room or in the garden and they say the daily sets of services as would a monk. They should be part of a parish and attend weekly services as much as possible. Such people should seek the guidance of their priest as no one should undertake such a venture outside of the structure of the church. If the priest has not the knowledge to guide such a person then they should undertake together to find someone well suited who may offer guidance and guidelines. An idea of a prayer rule could be:

Daily Sequence Of Services

Ordinary days:

Morning	Midnight, Matins. First, Third, Sixth Hours.
Evening	Ninth Hour, Vespers, Compline.

Weekdays during Lent:

Morning	Midnight, Matins, First, Third, Sixth, Ninth Hours. Vespers.
Evening	Great Compline.

All Night Vigil. E.g. The Eve of Christmas, Theophany or the Annunciation:

Morning	Midnight.
Afternoon	Ninth Hour, Vespers, Compline.
Early night	Vespers, Compline, Matins, First Hour.

Those with families or a more worldly-facing life should not undertake monastic services at home. A married person is already in service to their partner and their example of a holy Orthodox life is their light to the world. Families should pray together and such prayers are included near the back of this book.

These Sunday services are in order of how they should be performed during the day. The Orthodox day runs from sunset to sunset, so technically Sunday starts on Saturday evening. Thus Saturdays Great Vespers is the first service of Sunday. However for the sake of newcomers whose is a day from midnight to midnight, this Sunday starts in the morning. Further in the book are services whose name reflects the Orthodox day, they also bear comments as to their place in the modern idea of day. It can be confusing keeping both days and as much guidance is given as possible.

Given that the day runs from sunset to sunset this means that for the evening services such as Vespers or Compline, variables such as Troparia or Kontakia are taken from the next day. e.g. A service on the evening of the 15th shall use the variables from the 16th.

The Divine Liturgy

Concentrating on the Divine Liturgy for Sunday there are three versions herein. The people should use the first version, the Acolytes should use the second (or the Acolyte Guide). These two first texts do not have the long prayers said by the Priest, thus they may be used during the Liturgies of Ss John Chrysostom, James and Basil. The Divine Liturgy For Clergy includes those long prayers so is only usable during the Liturgy of St John. The appropriate Liturgy should be used for those other times of the year when St John is not used, such as Lent.

"Liturgy" means the "work of the people" so it is worth remembering that the service is a journey to the Eucharist. It is also a three-way song to God between the Priest, the Reader and the people. The first half is "The Service of the Word" and the Reader has a greater part to play. The second half is "The Service of the Bread" and the emphasis shifts to the song between the Priest and the people. The Reader is still there providing a strong lead, but not drowning out the people.

To avoid slowing the service Troparia of the season may be substituted for the Third Antiphon (processional) and the Troparia of the Saints of the Day may be sung as normal after the Priests following entrance in the Sanctuary. Around 3 Seasonal Troparia are enough to cover the procession. Any more may be put at the start of the following group. If there are not enough then sing the Beatitudes instead and do all the Troparia after the entrance.

Except for major feasts when no Troparia for the Saints of the Day should be sung, and in some cases the Troparia for the Temple is also skipped.

There is some discussion over the directions to the Priest to say some long prayers starting "mystagogos" and later parts "ektophonia". Respectively these mean "mystically" and "loud". This pairing implies that "mystically" means "quiet", but that is not at all the meaning. If these prayers are done in a low voice the people miss the benefit of them. Some Priests are aware of this and have taken to saying the Mystical prayers in a normal voice, then adding some emphasis to the parts marked "loud". This works well as an audio cue to the Reader, chorus and people that it is nearly time for them to do provide their part.

During Communion itself the Priest says a prayer over each Communicant, and they should stay in place before him until he has completed, upon which they say "Amen" and move to the side.

[Priest puts on the Epitrachelion and stands in front of the Holy Table:]

Priest: Blessed is our God, always, now and for ever, and to the ages of ages.

People: *Amen.*

[Priest blesses the incense and begins to cense the sanctuary and the whole church as usual.]

Reader:

O come let us worship God our King.

O come let us worship and fall down before Christ, our King and God.

O come let us worship and fall down before Christ Himself, our King and our God.

Psalm 19

May the Lord hear you in the day of trouble; may the name of the God of Jacob shield you. May he send thee His help from the holy place, and support you from Zion. May He remember thine every sacrifice, and accept with favour thine whole burnt offering. May the Lord give thee thine hearts desire, and fulfil thine every purpose. We shall rejoice in Thy salvation, and be magnified in the name of our the Lord our God. May the Lord fulfil all thine petitions. Now I know that the Lord has saved his Christ. He shall hear him from his holy heaven; in mighty acts is the salvation of his right hand. Some put their trust in chariots and some in horses, but we shall call on the name of the Lord our God. They were fettered and fell, but we have risen and been set upright. Lord, save the king, and hear us on the day we call upon you.

Psalm 20

The king shall rejoice in Thy power, O Lord, he shall exult exceedingly in Thy salvation. Thou gavest him his hearts desire; Thou didst not deny him the request of his lips. For Thou camest to meet him with blessings of goodness; Thou placed a crown of precious stones upon his head. He asked Thee for life, and Thou gavest him length of days for age on age. Great is his glory because of Thy salvation; Thou shall place on him glory and majesty. For Thou shall give him blessing for age on age, and make him glad with the joy of Thy countenance. For the king puts his hope in the Lord, and through the mercy of the Most High he shall not be shaken. May Thy hand light upon all Thy enemies, and Thy right hand find out all who hate Thee. Thou wilt make them like a blazing oven at the time of Thy presence. The Lord shall confound them in his wrath and fire shall devour them. Thou wilt destroy their offspring from the earth, and their seed from among the children of mankind. Because they intended evils against Thee, and devised plans by which they can in no way succeed. For Thou wilt put them to flight; among Thy remnants Thou wilt prepare their presence. Be exalted, Lord, in Thy power; we shall sing and praise Thy mighty acts.

The Trisagion Prayers

Glory be to the Father, and to the Son, and to the Holy Spirit;

Both now and forever, and unto the ages of ages. Amen.

Holy God, Holy Mighty, Holy Immortal, have mercy on us. **(x3)**

Glory be to the Father, and to the Son, and to the Holy Spirit;

Both now and forever, and unto the ages of ages. Amen.

O Most Holy Trinity, have mercy on us.

O Lord, cleanse us from our sins.

O Master, pardon our iniquities.

O Holy One, visit and heal our infirmities, for Thy names sake.

Lord have mercy. **(x3)**

Glory be to the Father, and to the Son, and to the Holy Spirit;

Both now and forever, and unto the ages of ages. Amen.

[Priest stands beneath the Polyeleos to say this conclusion.]

People: *Our Father, who art in heaven, hallowed be Thy name. Thy Kingdom come. Thy will be done, on earth as it is in heaven. Give us this day our daily bread; and forgive us our trespasses, as we forgive those who trespass against us; and lead us not into temptation, but deliver us from the evil one.*

Priest: For Thine is the kingdom, the power, and the glory, of the Father, and the Son and the Holy Spirit, both now and forever, and to the ages of ages.

People: Amen.

[Priest enters sanctuary, puts away the censer and stands in front of the Holy Table.]

Apolytikion Of The Exaltation Of The Holy Cross

Tone 1   *Magnificent, happy and earthy.*   C, D, Eb, F, G, A, Bb, C.

Reader: O Lord, save Thy people and bless Thine inheritance. Grant victories to the Orthodox Christians over their adversaries. And by virtue of Thy Cross, preserve Thy commonwealth.

Chorus: *Glory be to the Father, and to the Son, and to the Holy Spirit;*

Kontakion Of The Holy And Life Giving Cross

Tone 4   Festive, joyous and expressing deep piety.   C, D, Eb, F, G, A, Bb, C.

Reader: As Thou wast voluntarily crucified for our sake, grant mercy to those who are called by Thy Name. Make all Orthodox Christians glad by Thy power, granting them victories over their adversaries, by bestowing on them the invincible trophy, Thy weapon of peace.

Chorus: *Both now and forever, and unto the ages of ages. Amen.*

Theotokion

O Dread Champion who cannot be put to shame, do not despise our petitions, O Good One. All praised Mother of God establish the commonwealth of the Orthodox, save thy people and give them victory from heaven, for thou gavest birth to God, O only blessed one.

Little Litany

Priest: Have mercy on us, O God, according to Thy great mercy. We pray Thee, hear us and have mercy.

People: *Lord have mercy.* **(x3)**

Priest: For Thou, O God, art merciful, and lovest mankind, and to Thee we give glory, to the Father, the Son and the Holy Spirit, both now and for ever and unto the ages of ages.

People: *Amen. Holy Father, bless!*

The Six Psalms

[These should be read by one reader, not divided between several. They are one of the gerontika, that is the parts normally read by the Superior, and should be allocated to a senior person, such a visiting priest. All should remain standing during the Six Psalms.]

Priest: Glory to the holy, consubstantial, life giving and undivided Trinity, always, now and for ever, and to the ages of ages.

People: *Amen.*

Doxology – excerpt Glory to God in the highest and on earth peace good will toward men.

Psalm 50 – excerpt O Lord, open my lips, and my mouth shall proclaim Thy praise.

[Priest comes from the Altar and during the Six Psalms reads the Twelve Morning Prayers.]

Psalm 3

Lord, how they have increased who trouble me. Many are they who rise up against me. Many are they who say of me, "There is no help for him in God." But Thou, O Lord, art a shield for me, my glory and the One Who lifts up my head. I cried to the Lord with my voice, and He heard me from His holy hill. I lay down and slept; I awoke, for the Lord sustained me. I shall not be afraid of ten thousands of people who have set themselves against me all around. Arise, O Lord; save me, O my God. For Thou hast struck all mine enemies on the cheekbone; Thou hast broken the teeth of the ungodly. Salvation belongs to the Lord. Thy blessing is upon Thy people.

Chorus: *I lay down and slept; I awoke, for the Lord sustained me.*

Psalm 37

O Lord, do not rebuke me in Thy wrath, nor chasten me in Thy hot displeasure. For Thine arrows deeply pierce me, and Thine hand presses me down. There is no soundness in my flesh because of Thine anger, Nor is there any health in my bones because of my sin. For mine iniquities have gone over my head; like a heavy burden they are too heavy for me. My wounds are foul and festering because of my foolishness. I am troubled, I am bowed down greatly; I go mourning all the day long. For my loins are full of inflammation, and there is no soundness in my flesh. I am feeble and severely broken; I groan because of the turmoil of my heart. Lord, all my desire is before Thee; and my sighing is not hidden from Thee. My heart pants, my strength fails me; as for the light of mine eyes, it also has gone from me. My loved ones and my friends stand aloof from my plague, and my kinsmen stand afar off. Those also who seek my life lay snares for me; those who seek my hurt speak of destruction, and plan deception all the day long. But I, like a deaf man, do not hear; and I am like a mute who does not open his mouth. Thus I am like a man who does not hear, and in whose mouth is no response. For in Thee, O Lord, I hope; Thou wilt hear, O Lord my God. For I said, "Hear me, lest they rejoice over me, lest, when my foot slips, they magnify themselves against me." For I am ready to fall, and my sorrow is continually before me. For I shall declare mine iniquity; I shall be in anguish over my sin. But mine enemies are vigorous, and they are strong; and those who wrongfully hate me have multiplied. Those also who render evil for good, they are mine adversaries, because I follow what is good. Do not forsake me, O Lord; O my God, be not far from me. Make haste to help me, O Lord, my salvation.

Chorus: *Do not forsake me, O Lord; O my God, be not far from me.*
Make haste to help me, O Lord, my salvation.

Psalm 62

O God, Thou art my God; early shall I seek Thee; my soul thirsts for Thee; My flesh longs for Thee in a dry and thirsty land where there is no water. So I have looked for Thee in the sanctuary, to see Thy power and Thy glory. Because Thy loving kindness is better than life, my lips shall praise Thee. Thus I shall bless Thee while I live; I shall lift up my hands in Thy name. My soul shall be satisfied as with marrow and fatness, and my mouth shall praise Thee with joyful lips. When I remember Thee on my bed, I meditate on Thee in the night watches. Because Thou hast been my help, therefore in the shadow of Thy wings I shall rejoice. My soul follows close behind Thee; Thy right hand upholds me. But those who seek my life, to destroy it, shall go into the lower parts of the earth. They shall fall by the sword; they shall be a portion for jackals. But the king shall rejoice in God; everyone who swears by Him shall glory; but the mouth of those who speak lies shall be stopped.

Chorus: *I meditate on Thee in the night watches.*

   Because Thou hast been my help, therefore in the shadow of Thy wings I shall rejoice.

After The Psalm

Glory be to the Father, and to the Son, and to the Holy Spirit;
Both now and forever, and unto the ages of ages. Amen.

Halleluiah, Halleluiah, Halleluiah. Glory to Thee, O God. **(x3)**
Lord have mercy. **(x3)**

Glory be to the Father, and to the Son, and to the Holy Spirit;
Both now and forever, and unto the ages of ages. Amen.

Psalm 87

O Lord, God of my salvation, I have cried out day and night before Thee. Let my prayer come before Thee; incline Thine ear to my cry. For my soul is full of troubles, and my life draws near to the grave. I am counted with those who go down to the pit; I am like a man who has no strength, Adrift among the dead, like the slain who lie in the grave, whom Thou rememberest no more, and who are cut off from Thine hand. Thou hast laid me in the lowest pit, in darkness, in the depths. Thy wrath lies heavy upon me, and Thou hast afflicted me with all Thy waves. Thou hast put away mine acquaintances far from me; Thou hast made me an abomination to them; I am shut up, and I cannot get out; Mine eye wastes away because of affliction. Lord, I have called daily upon Thee; I have stretched out my hands to Thee. Willest Thou work wonders for the dead? Shall the dead arise and praise Thee? Shall Thy loving kindness be declared in the grave? Or Thy faithfulness in the place of destruction? Shall Thy wonders be known in the dark? And Thy righteousness in the land of forgetfulness? But to Thee I have cried out, O Lord, and in the morning my prayer comes before Thee. Lord, why dost Thou cast off my soul? Why dost Thou hide Thy face from me? I have been afflicted and ready to die from my youth up; I suffer Thy terrors; I am distraught. Thy fierce wrath has gone over me; Thy terrors have cut me off. They came around me all day long like water; they engulfed me altogether. Loved one and friend Thou hast put far from me, and mine acquaintances into darkness.

Chorus: *O Lord, God of my salvation, I have cried out day and night before Thee.*

   Let my prayer come before Thee; incline Thine ear to my cry.

Psalm 102

Bless the Lord O my soul; and all that is within me, bless His holy name. Bless the Lord O my soul, and forget not all His benefits: Who forgives all thine iniquities, Who heals all thy diseases, Who redeems thy life from destruction, Who crowns thee with loving kindness and tender mercies, Who satisfies thy mouth with good things, so that thine youth is renewed like the eagles. The Lord executes righteousness and justice for all who are oppressed. He made known His ways to Moses, His acts to the children of Israel. The Lord is merciful and gracious, slow to anger, and abounding in mercy. He shall not always strive with us, nor shall He keep His anger forever. He has not dealt with us according to our sins, nor punished us according to our iniquities. For as the heavens are high above the earth, so great is His mercy toward those who fear Him; As far as the east is from the west, so far has He removed our transgressions from us. As a father pities his children, so the Lord pities those who fear Him. For He knows our frame; He remembers that we are dust. As for man, his days are like grass; as a flower of the field, so he flourishes. For the wind passes over it, and it is gone, and its place remembers it no more. But the mercy of the Lord is from everlasting to everlasting on those who fear Him, and His righteousness to childrens children, To such as keep His covenant, and to those who remember His commandments to do them. The Lord has established His throne in heaven, and His kingdom rules overall. Bless the Lord you His angels, who excel in strength, who do His word, heeding the voice of His word. Bless the Lord all you His hosts, you ministers of His, who do His pleasure. Bless the Lord all His works, in all places of His dominion. Bless the Lord O my soul.

Chorus: *Bless the Lord all His works, in all places of His dominion. Bless the Lord O my soul.*

Psalm 142

Hear my prayer, O Lord, give ear to my supplications. In Thy faithfulness answer me, and in Thy righteousness. Do not enter into judgement with Thy servant, for in Thy sight no one living is righteous. For the enemy has persecuted my soul; he has crushed my life to the ground; he has made me dwell in darkness, like those who have long been dead. Therefore my spirit is overwhelmed within me; my heart within me is distressed. I remember the days of old; I meditate on all Thy works; I muse on the work of Thine hands. I spread out my hands to Thee; my soul longs for Thee like a thirsty land. Answer me speedily, O Lord; my spirit fails. Do not hide Thy face from me, lest I be like those who go down into the pit. Cause me to hear Thy loving kindness in the morning, for in Thee do I trust; cause me to know the way in which I should walk, for I lift up my soul to Thee. Deliver me, O Lord, from mine enemies; in Thee I take shelter. Teach me to do Thy shall, for Thou art my God; Thy Spirit is good. Lead me in the land of uprightness. Revive me, O Lord, for Thy names sake. For Thy righteousness' sake bring my soul out of trouble. In Thy mercy cut off mine enemies, and destroy all those who afflict my soul; for I am Thy servant.

Chorus: *In Thy justice hear me, O Lord; and do not enter into judgement with Thy servant.* **(x2)**
           Thy good Spirit shall guide me in an upright land.

After The Psalm

Glory be to the Father, and to the Son, and to the Holy Spirit;
Both now and forever, and unto the ages of ages. Amen.

Halleluiah, Halleluiah, Halleluiah. Glory to Thee, O God. **(x3)**

[Priest kisses the icon of the Lord and stands in front of the Holy Doors.]

Litany Of Peace

Priest: In peace, let us pray to the Lord.

People: *Lord, have mercy.*

Priest: For the peace from on high and for the salvation of our souls, let us pray to the Lord.

People: *Lord, have mercy.*

Priest: For the peace of the whole world, for the welfare of the holy Churches of God, and for the union of all, let us pray to the Lord.

People: *Lord, have mercy.*

Priest: For this holy house, and for those who enter it with faith, reverence and the fear of God, let us pray to the Lord.

People: *Lord, have mercy.*

Priest: For our Archbishop Nikitas, for the honoured order of presbyters, for the diaconate in Christ, for all the clergy and the people, let us pray to the Lord.

People: *Lord, have mercy.*

Priest: For our Sovereign Lady, Queen Elizabeth, the Royal Family, her Government, and all in authority, let us pray to the Lord.

People: *Lord, have mercy.*

Priest: For this parish, city, town and village, and for the faithful who dwell in them, let us pray to the Lord.

People: *Lord, have mercy.*

Priest: For favourable weather, an abundance of the fruits of the earth, and temperate seasons, let us pray to the Lord.

People: *Lord, have mercy.*

Priest: For those who travel by land, air or water, for the sick, the suffering, for those in captivity, and for their safety and salvation, let us pray to the Lord.

People: *Lord, have mercy.*

Priest: For our deliverance from all affliction, wrath, danger and constraint, let us pray to the Lord.

People: *Lord, have mercy.*

Priest: Help us, save us, have mercy on us, and keep us, O God, by Thy grace.

People: *Lord, have mercy.*

Priest: Commemorating our all holy, pure, most blessed and glorious Lady, Mother of God and Ever Virgin Mary, with all the Saints, let us entrust ourselves and one another and our whole life to Christ our God.

People: *To Thee, O Lord.*

Priest: For to Thee belongest all glory, honour and worship, to the Father, the Son and the Holy Spirit, both now and for ever, and unto the ages of ages.

People: *Amen.*

God Is The Lord

People: *God is the Lord and has revealed Himself to us. Blessed is He who comes in the Name of the Lord.*

Reader: Give thanks to the Lord, for He is good; and His steadfast love endures forever.

People: *God is the Lord and has revealed Himself to us. Blessed is He who comes in the Name of the Lord.*

Reader: All nations surrounded me; in the Name of the Lord, I withstood them.

People: *God is the Lord and has revealed Himself to us. Blessed is He who comes in the Name of the Lord.*

Reader: This is the Lords doing and is marvellous in our eyes.

People: *God is the Lord and has revealed Himself to us. Blessed is He who comes in the Name of the Lord.*

[Sunday]　　　　　**Troparion Of The Resurrection**

　Tone 4　　　*Festive, joyous and expressing deep piety.*　　　　*C, D, Eb, F, G, A, Bb, C.*

Having learned the joyful message of the Resurrection from the angel, the women Disciples cast from them their parental condemnation, and proudly broke the news to the Disciples, saying, Death has been spoiled. Christ God is risen, granting the world Great Mercy.

[Monday]　　　　　**St Michael And All Angels**

　Tone 4　　　*Festive, joyous and expressing deep piety.*　　　　*C, D, Eb, F, G, A, Bb, C.*

O Commanders of Sabaoth, We who are unworthy beseech you ceaselessly that you wouldst encompass us with the shelter of your prayers and cover us beneath the wings of your immaterial glory. We fall down before you crying out: *"Protect us from all harm, O Princes of the powers on high."*

[Tuesday]　　　　　**Forerunner And Baptist John**

　Tone 2　　　*Majesty, gentleness, hope, repentance and sadness.*　　　　*E, F, G, Ab, B, C.*

The memory of the righteous is worthy of praise, But thou, O Forerunner, are well pleased by the Lords own witness. Thou wast revealed as greater than the prophets, For thou baptised in the waters Him whom they foretold. Therefore, having fought and suffered for the Truth, thou proclaimed to those in the tombs the Gospel of the incarnate God, Who takest away the sins of the world and grantest us great mercy.

[Wednesday]　　　　　**Holy And Life Giving Cross**

　Tone 2　　　*Majesty, gentleness, hope, repentance and sadness.*　　　　*E, F, G, Ab, B, C.*

O Lord, save Thy people, And bless Thine inheritance. Grant victories to the Orthodox Christians over their adversaries. And by virtue of Thy Cross, Preserve Thy habitation.

[Thursday]　　　　　**Holy Apostles And St Nicholas**

　Tone 3　　　*Arrogant, brave, and mature atmosphere.*　　　　*F, G, A, A#, C, D, E, F.*

O holy Apostles, intercede with our merciful God to grant our souls forgiveness of our sins.

[Friday]   **Holy And Life Giving Cross**

Tone 1   *Magnificent, happy and earthy.*   *C, D, Eb, F, G, A, Bb, C.*

O Lord, save Thy people, And bless Thine inheritance. Grant victories to the Orthodox Christians over their adversaries. And by virtue of Thy Cross, Preserve Thy habitation.

[Saturday]   **The Theotokos, All Saints, The Faithful Departed**

Tone 2   *Majesty, gentleness, hope, repentance and sadness.*   *E, F, G, Ab, B, C.*

Apostles, martyrs, and prophets, Holy hierarchs, saints and righteous, Having fought the good fight and kept the Faith, Thou hast boldness toward the Saviour. Intercede for us with Him for He is good, and pray that He may save our souls.

Reader: Lord have mercy. **(x3)**

Chorus: *Glory be to the Father, and to the Son, and to the Holy Spirit;*
              Both now and forever, and unto the ages of ages. Amen.

Halleluiah, Halleluiah, Halleluiah. Glory to Thee, O God. **(x3)**
Lord have mercy. **(x3)**

              Glory be to the Father, and to the Son, and to the Holy Spirit;
              Both now and forever, and unto the ages of ages. Amen.

Ekphoneses 1

Priest: For Thine is the might and Thine is the kingdom, the power, and the glory, of the Father, and the Son and   the Holy Spirit, both now and forever, and to the ages of ages.
People: *Amen.*

Ekphoneses 2

Priest: For Thou, O God, art good and love mankind, and to Thee we give glory, to the Father, the Son and the Holy Spirit, both now and for ever, and unto the ages of ages.
People: *Amen.*

The Evlogitaria For The Departed

Tone 5   *Stimulating, dancing, and rhythmical.*   *C, D, Eb, F, G, A, Bb, C.*

Chorus: *Blessed art Thou, O Lord, teach me Thy statutes.*

[Saturday]

Reader: The Chorus of Saints has found the source of life and the door of Paradise; may I too find the way through repentance; I am the lost sheep, call me back, O Saviour, and save me.

Chorus: *Blessed art Thou, O Lord, teach me Thy statutes.*

Reader: Ye, O Holy Martyrs, who proclaimed the Lamb of God, and like lambs were slain, and have been taken over to the unending life which knows no ageing, plead with Him to grant us abolition of our debts.

Chorus: *Blessed art Thou, O Lord, teach me Thy statutes.*

Reader: All you who trod in life the hard and narrow way; all you who took the Cross as a yoke, and followed me in faith, come, enjoy that heavenly rewards and crowns which I have prepared for you.

Chorus: *Blessed art Thou, O Lord, teach me Thy statutes.*

Reader: I am an image of Thine ineffable glory, though I bear the marks of offences; take pity on Thy creature, Master, and with compassion cleanse me; and give me the longed for homeland, making me once again a citizen of Paradise.

Chorus: *Blessed art Thou, O Lord, teach me Thy statutes.*

Reader: Of old Thou formed me from nothing and honoured me with Thy divine image, but because I transgressed Thy commandment, Thou returned me to the earth from which I was taken; bring me back to Thy likeness, my ancient beauty.

Chorus: *Blessed art Thou, O Lord, teach me Thy statutes.*

Reader: Give rest, O God, to Thy servants, and settle them in Paradise, where the Chorus' of the Saints and all the Just shine out like beacons; give rest to Thy servants who have fallen asleep, overlooking all their offences.

Chorus: *Glory be to the Father, and to the Son, and to the Holy Spirit;*

Triadikon

Let us devoutly hymn the threefold light of the one Godhead as we cry: Holy art Thou, the Father without beginning, the Son likewise without beginning and the divine Spirit; enlighten us who worship Thee in faith, and snatch us from the everlasting fire.

Chorus: *Both now and forever, and unto the ages of ages. Amen.*

Theotokion

Hail, honoured one, who bore God in the flesh for the salvation of all; through thee the human race has found salvation; through thee may we find Paradise, O pure and blessed Mother of God.

Chorus: *Halleluiah. Halleluiah. Halleluiah. Glory to Thee, O God.* **(x3)**

Psalm 50

Have mercy on me, O God, according to Thy great mercy; and according to the multitude of Thy compassions blot out my transgression. Wash me thoroughly from mine iniquity, and cleanse me from my sin. For I acknowledge mine iniquity, and my sin is ever before me. Against Thee, Thee only have I sinned, and done evil in Thy sight, that Thou mayest be found just when Thou speakest, and victorious when Thou art judged. For behold, I was conceived in iniquity, and in sin my mother bore me. For behold, Thou hast loved truth; Thou hast made known to me the hidden and secret things of Thy wisdom. Thou shalt sprinkle me with hyssop, and I shall be made clean; Thou shalt wash me, and I shalt be whiter than snow. Make me to hear joy and gladness; that the humbled bones may rejoice. Turn Thy face away from my sins, and blot out all mine iniquities.

Create in me a clean heart, O God, and renew a steadfast spirit within me. Cast me not away from Thy presence, and take not Thy Holy Spirit from me. Restore to me the joy of Thy salvation, and establish me with Thy governing Spirit. I shall teach transgressors Thy ways, and the ungodly shall turn back to Thee. Deliver me from blood guiltiness, O God, the God of my salvation; my tongue shall joyfully declare Thy righteousness. Lord, open my lips, and my mouth shall declare Thy praise. For if Thou hadst desired sacrifice, I would give it; Thou dost not delight in burned offerings. A sacrifice to God is a broken spirit; God shall not despise a broken and a humbled heart. Do good, O Lord, in Thy good pleasure to Zion, and let the walls of Jerusalem be builded. Then Thou shalt be pleased with a sacrifice of righteousness, with oblation and whole burned offerings. Then shall they offer bulls on Thine altar.

Ode 1

Chorus: *Let us sing to the Lord, for he is greatly glorified.*

Reader: Let us sing to the Lord, for He is greatly glorified; horse and rider he has cast into the sea. Helper and protector he has become for my salvation; He is my God and I shall glorify him; my fathers God and I shall exalt Him. The Lord shatters wars, the Lord is his name; Pharaohs chariots and army He has cast into the sea. With the deep He covered them; they sank to the bottom like a stone. Then the leaders of Edom and the rulers of the Moabites hastened; trembling took hold of them; all the inhabitants of Canaan melted away. Let fear and trembling fall upon them; by the greatness of Thine arm let them be turned to stone. Till Thy people pass over, O Lord; till Thy people, whom Thou hast purchased, pass over. The sanctuary which Thou hast made, Lord; which Thy hands have prepared. The Lord reigns over the ages and for ever and ever; for Pharaohs horse went with the chariots and horsemen into the sea. But the children of Israel walked on dry land in the midst of the sea.

Chorus: *Glory be to the Father, and to the Son, and to the Holy Spirit;*
Both now and forever, and unto the ages of ages. Amen.

Ode 3

Chorus: *Holy art Thou, O Lord, and my spirit sings Thy praise.*

Reader: My heart is established in the Lord, my spirit is exalted in my God; my mouth derides my enemies, I rejoice in Thy salvation. There is none holy like the Lord, and none righteous like our God. Do not boast or talk so very proudly; let no arrogance come from your mouths. For the Lord is a God of knowledge; and God prepares his ways. He grants the prayers of him who prays; and blesses the years of the righteous. The Lord shall weaken his adversary; the Lord is holy. Let not the wise man boast of his wisdom, nor the powerful boast of his power, nor the wealthy boast of his wealth. But let him who boasts boast of this; of understanding and knowing the Lord; and of executing judgement and righteousness in the midst of the earth. The Lord has gone up to the heavens and thundered; being righteous He shall judge the ends of the earth. He shall give strength to our kings; and exalt the horn of his anointed ones.

Chorus: *Glory be to the Father, and to the Son, and to the Holy Spirit;*
Both now and forever, and unto the ages of ages. Amen.

Short Litany

Priest: Again and again in peace, let us pray to the Lord.

People: *Lord, have mercy.*

Priest: Help us, save us, have mercy on us, and keep us, O God, by Thy grace.

People: *Lord, have mercy.*

Priest: Commemorating our all holy, pure, most blessed and glorious Lady, Mother of God and Ever Virgin Mary, with all the Saints, let us entrust ourselves and one another and our whole life to Christ our God.

People: *To Thee, O Lord.*

Priest: For Thou art our God, and to Thee we give glory, to the Father, the Son and the Holy Spirit, both now and for ever, and unto the ages of ages.

People: *Amen.*

Ode 4

Chorus: *Glory to Thy power O Lord.*

Reader: O Lord, I heard Thy report and was afraid; Lord I considered Thy works and was amazed. When my soul is troubled, in anger Thou wilt remember mercy. God shall come from Teman; and the Holy One from a shady, wooded mountain. His glory covered the heavens; and the earth was full of his praise. For the fig tree shall not bear fruit, nor shall there be produce on the vines. The labour of the olive shall deceive, and the fields yield no food. The sheep have failed from lack of fodder, and there shall be no oxen at the mangers. Yet I shall rejoice in the Lord; I shall be joyful in God my Saviour. The Lord is my strength; He shall perfectly station my feet. And he puts me on high places; for me to conquer with His song.

Chorus: *Glory be to the Father, and to the Son, and to the Holy Spirit;*
Both now and forever, and unto the ages of ages. Amen.

Ode 5

Chorus: *O Lord our God give us peace.*

Reader: From nightfall my spirit is awake for Thee, O God; for Thy commandments are a light upon the earth. Learn righteousness, inhabitants of the earth. Let the impious be taken away, that he may not see the glory of the Lord. O Lord Thy hand was lifted up and they knew it not; but once they know they shall be ashamed. Jealousy shall seize an untaught people; and now fire devours their adversaries. Bring evils upon them, O Lord, bring evils upon them; the glorious ones of the earth. O Lord in affliction we remembered Thee, with a little affliction Thou hast chastised us. As the woman in labour draws near the time of her delivery and cries out in her labour; so have we been to Thy beloved. We shall not fall, but they shall fall, the inhabitants of the earth. The dead shall arise and those in the graves shall be raised; and those in the earth shall rejoice. For the dew which comes from Thee is healing for them; but the land of the impious shall perish.

Chorus: *Glory be to the Father, and to the Son, and to the Holy Spirit;*
Both now and forever, and unto the ages of ages. Amen.

Ode 6

Chorus: *As Thou didst for the prophet Jonah, save us, O Lord.*

Reader: For Thou cast me into the deep, into the heart of the seas, and the floods surrounded me; all Thy billows and Thy waves passed over me. Yet I shall look again toward Thy holy temple. The waters encompassed me, even to my soul; the deep closed around me. I went down to the moorings of the mountains; the earth with its bars closed behind me forever; yet Thou hast brought up my life from the pit, O Lord, my God. My prayer went up to Thee, into Thy holy temple. Those who regard worthless idols forsake their own Mercy. I shall pay what I have vowed, for my salvation.

Chorus: *Glory be to the Father, and to the Son, and to the Holy Spirit;*
Both now and forever, and unto the ages of ages. Amen.

Short Litany

Priest: Again and again in peace, let us pray to the Lord.

People: *Lord, have mercy.*

Priest: Help us, save us, have mercy on us, and keep us, O God, by Thy grace.

People: *Lord, have mercy.*

Priest: Commemorating our all holy, pure, most blessed and glorious Lady, Mother of God and Ever Virgin Mary, with all the Saints, let us entrust ourselves and one another and our whole life to Christ our God.

People: *To Thee, O Lord.*

Priest: For Thou art the King of peace and the Saviour of our souls, and to Thee we give glory, to the Father, the Son and the Holy Spirit, both now and for ever, and unto the ages of ages.

People: Amen.

Ode 7

Chorus: Our God and the God of our fathers, blessed art Thou.

Reader: Blessed art Thou, O Lord, the God of our fathers; and praised and glorified is Thy Name for ever more. For Thou art righteous in all that Thou hast done for us. And all Thy works are true, and Thy ways are right, and all Thy judgements are true; and judgements of truth Thou hast executed in all that Thou hast brought upon us. And upon Jerusalem the city of our fathers.

Reader:	**Chorus:**
Blessed art Thou, O Lord, God of our fathers;	*and to be praised and highly exalted forever.*
And blessed is Thy glorious, holy name;	*and to be highly praised and highly exalted forever.*
Blessed art Thou in the temple of Thy holy glory;	*and to be extolled and highly glorified forever.*
Blessed art Thou, who sittest upon Cherubim and lookest upon the deeps;	
	and to be praised and highly exalted forever.
Blessed art Thou upon the throne of Thy kingdom;	*and to be extolled and highly exalted forever.*
Blessed art Thou in the firmament of heaven;	*and to be sung and glorified forever.*

Chorus: Glory be to the Father, and to the Son, and to the Holy Spirit;
Both now and forever, and unto the ages of ages. Amen.

Ode 8

Chorus: Praise the Lord his works and exalt him above all for ever.

Reader: Bless the Lord all you works of the Lord, praise the Lord, and exalt him above all for ever. Bless the Lord Angels of the Lord, praise the Lord, and exalt him above all for ever. Bless the Lord all you waters above the heavens, all you powers of the Lord, praise the Lord, and exalt him above all for ever. Bless the Lord sun and moon, stars of heaven, praise the Lord, and exalt him above all for ever. Bless the Lord all you birds of the air, beasts and cattle, praise the Lord, and exalt him above all for ever. Bless the Lord you sons of men. Let Israel bless the Lord, praise the Lord, and exalt him above all for ever. Bless the Lord priests of the Lord and servants of the Lord, praise the Lord, and exalt him above all for ever. Bless the Lord spirits and souls of the righteous, holy and humble of heart, praise the Lord, and exalt him above all for ever. Bless the Lord Ananias, Azarias and Misael, praise the Lord, and exalt him above all for ever. Bless the Lord Apostles, Prophets and Martyrs, praise the Lord, and exalt him above all for ever. We bless The Father, Son and Holy Spirit, we praise the Lord, and exalt him above all for ever.

Chorus: Glory be to the Father, and to the Son, and to the Holy Spirit;

Both now and forever, and unto the ages of ages. Amen.

Reader: We praise, bless and worship the Lord, praising and exalting him above all for ever.

Priest: The Mother of God and Mother of the Light in hymns let us honour and magnify.

[Priest censes the whole sanctuary and church as usual.]

The Magnificat

Chorus: *A maiden mother hymns her Son and God; In hymns Gods Mother now we magnify.*

Reader: Greater in honour than the Cherubim and beyond compare more glorious than the Seraphim; without corruption thou gavest birth to God the Word, truly the Theotokos, we magnify thee.

My soul magnifies the Lord, and my spirit has rejoiced in God my Saviour. For He has regarded the lowly state of His maidservant; for behold, henceforth all generations shall call me blessed. For He who is mighty has done great things for me, and holy is His name. And His mercy is on those who fear Him from generation to generation. He has shown strength with His arm; he has scattered the proud in the imagination of their hearts. He has put down the mighty from their thrones, and exalted the lowly. He has filled the hungry with good things, and the rich He has sent empty away. He has helped His servant Israel, in remembrance of His mercy, as He spoke to our fathers, to Abraham and to his seed forever.

Ode 9

Chorus: *Zachariah blesses the birth of his child.*

Reader: Blessed be the God of Israel, for he has visited and redeemed his people. And has raised up a horn of salvation for us in the house of his servant David. As he spoke by the mouth of his holy prophets, who have been since the world began. Salvation from our enemies and from the hand of all who hate us. To perform the mercy promised to our fathers, and to remember his holy covenant. The oath which he swore to our father Abraham, to grant us that without fear we, being delivered from the fear of our enemies. Might serve him in holiness and righteousness before him all the days of our life. And thou, child, shall be called the prophet of the Highest, for thou wilt go before the Lord to prepare his ways. To give knowledge of salvation to his people by the forgiveness of their sins through the tender mercy of our God. By which the Dayspring from on high has visited us, to appear to those who sit in darkness and in the shadow of death. To guide our feet into the way of peace.

Chorus: *Glory be to the Father, and to the Son, and to the Holy Spirit;*
Both now and forever, and unto the ages of ages. Amen.

Reader: *[Archangel Gabriel:* It is truly right to call thee blessed, who gavest birth to God, ever-blessed and God-obedient the Mother of our God.*]* Greater in honour than the Cherubim and beyond compare more glorious than the Seraphim; without corruption thou gavest birth to God the Word, truly the Mother of God, we magnify thee.

Short Litany

Priest: Again and again in peace, let us pray to the Lord.

People: *Lord, have mercy.*

Priest: Help us, save us, have mercy on us, and keep us, O God, by Thy grace.

People: *Lord, have mercy.*

Priest: Commemorating our all holy, pure, most blessed and glorious Lady, Mother of God and Ever Virgin Mary, with all the Saints, let us entrust ourselves and one another and our whole life to Christ our God.

People: *To Thee, O Lord.*

Priest: For all the Powers of heaven praise Thee, and to Thee we give glory, to the Father, the Son and the Holy Spirit, both now and for ever, and unto the ages of ages.

People: *Amen.*

Exapostilaria For Weekdays

[When none is appointed in the Monaion]

[Monday]

   Tone 3   *Arrogant, brave, and mature atmosphere.*   *F, G, A, A#, C, D, E, F.*

As God Thou adorned the heavens with stars, and through Thine Angels Thou leadest the whole earth to the light, O Creator of all things save those who hymn Thee.

Theotokion

O Sweetness of the Angels, joy of the afflicted, protectress of Christians, Virgin Mother of the Lord, help me and deliver me from eternal tortures.

[Tuesday]

   Tone 3   *Arrogant, brave, and mature atmosphere.*   *F, G, A, A#, C, D, E, F.*

Let us all hymn John the Forerunner and Baptist of the Saviour, Prophet among the Prophets, nurseling of the desert, offspring of Elisabeth.

Theotokion

O Sweetness of the Angels, joy of the afflicted, protectress of Christians, Virgin Mother of the Lord, help me and deliver me from eternal tortures.

[Wednesday, Friday]

   Tone 2   *Majesty, gentleness, hope, repentance and sadness.*   *E, F, G, Ab, B, C.*

The Cross is the guardian of the whole world; the Cross is the beauty of the Church; the Cross is the strength of kings; the Cross is the support of the faithful; the Cross is the glory of Angels and the wound of demons.

Theotokion For The Cross

Standing by Thy Cross, she who bore Thee without seed lamenting cried out, *"Alas sweetest child, how hast Thou set from my sight? How hast Thou been numbered among the dead?"*

[Thursday]

Tone 2   Majesty, gentleness, hope, repentance and sadness.   *E, F, G, Ab, B, C.*

Having sped to every place beneath the sun, Thou proclaimedest the holy incarnation of Christ from a Virgin, truly turning the nations from error, enlightening them and teaching all to honour the holy Trinity, O Apostles of the Saviour.

Tone 2   Majesty, gentleness, hope, repentance and sadness.   *E, F, G, Ab, B, C.*

Let us all praise the chief shepherd and high priest, Nicholas the leader of the people of Myra; for many men he saved who were to die unjustly; and he appeared to the King in a dream with Avlavios, abolishing the unjust decree.

Theotokion

Tone 2   Majesty, gentleness, hope, repentance and sadness.   *E, F, G, Ab, B, C.*

Mary, censer of purest gold, having become the vessel of the uncontainable Trinity; in whom the Father was well pleased, the Son dwelt, and the all holy Spirit, having overshadowed thee, showed thee, O Maiden, to be Mother of God.

[Saturday]

As God Thou hast power over the living and the dead, and through Thine Angels Thou leadest the whole earth to the light, O Creator of all things save those who sing Thy praise.

Theotokion

In thee we boast, Mother of God, and thou we have as advocate before God: stretch out thine invincible hand and trounce our foes, send forth thy help to thy servants from the holy place.

Lauds - The Praises
Psalm 148

Praise the Lord. Praise the Lord from the heavens; praise Him in the heights. Praise Him, all His angels; praise Him, all His hosts. Praise Him, sun and moon; praise Him, all you stars of light. Praise Him, you heavens of heavens, and you waters above the heavens. Let them praise the name of the Lord, for He commanded and they were created. He has also established them forever and ever; He has made a decree that shall not pass away. Praise the Lord from the earth, you great sea creatures and all the depths; Fire and hail, snow and clouds; stormy wind, fulfilling His word; Mountains and all hills; fruitful trees and all cedars; Beasts and all cattle; creeping things and flying fowl; Kings of the earth and all peoples; princes and all judges of the earth; Both young men and maidens; old men and children. Let them praise the name of the Lord, for His name alone is exalted; His glory is above the earth and heaven. And He has exalted the horn of His people, the praise of all His saints - of the children of Israel, a people near to Him. Praise the Lord.

Psalm 149

Praise the Lord. Sing to the Lord a new song, and His praise in the congregation of saints. Let Israel rejoice in their Maker; let the children of Zion be joyful in their King. Let them praise His name with the dance; let them sing praises to Him with the timbrel and harp. For the Lord takes pleasure in His people; He shall beautify the humble with salvation. Let the saints be joyful in glory; let them sing aloud on their beds. Let the high praises of God be in their mouth, and a two edged sword in their hand, To execute vengeance on the nations, and punishments on the peoples; To bind their kings with chains, and their nobles with fetters of iron; To execute on them the written judgement; this honour have all His saints. Praise the Lord.

Psalm 150

Praise the Lord. Praise God in His sanctuary; praise Him in His mighty firmament. Praise Him for His mighty acts; praise Him according to His excellent greatness. Praise Him with the sound of the trumpet; praise Him with the lute and harp. Praise Him with the timbrel and dance; praise Him with stringed instruments and flutes. Praise Him with loud cymbals; praise Him with high sounding cymbals. Let everything that has breath praise the Lord. Praise the Lord.

After The Psalm

Glory be to the Father, and to the Son, and to the Holy Spirit;
Both now and forever, and unto the ages of ages. Amen.

To Thee glory is due, Lord our God, and to Thee we give glory, Father, Son and Holy Spirit, both now and for ever, and unto the ages of ages. Amen.

Lesser Doxology

Glory to God, Who has shown us the Light. Glory to God in the highest, and on earth, peace, good will toward men. We praise Thee. We bless Thee. We worship Thee. We glorify Thee and give thanks to Thee for Thy great glory. O Lord God, Heavenly King, God the Father Almighty. O Lord, the Only Begotten Son, Jesus Christ, and the Holy Spirit. \

O Lord God, Lamb of God, Son of the Father, Who takes away the sins of the world, have mercy on us. Thou, Who takes away the sins of the world, receive our prayer. Thou, Who sittest at the right hand of God the Father, have mercy on us. /

For Thou alone art holy, and Thou alone art Lord. Thou alone, O Lord Jesus Christ, are most high in the glory of God the Father. Amen. I shall give thanks to Thee every day and praise Thy Name forever and ever. Lord, Thou hast been our refuge from generation to generation. I said, *"Lord, have mercy on me. Heal my soul, for I have sinned against Thee."* \

Lord, I flee to Thee. Teach me to do Thy will, for Thou art my God. For with Thee is the fountain of Life, and in Thy light we shall see light. Continue Thy loving kindness to those who know Thee. Vouchsafe, O Lord, to keep us this day without sin. Blessed art Thou, O Lord, the God of our fathers, and praised and glorified is Thy Name forever. Amen. Let Thy mercy be upon us, O Lord, even as we have set our hope on Thee. Blessed art Thou, O Master; teach me Thy statutes. Blessed art Thou, O Lord; enlighten me with Thy commandments. Blessed art Thou, O Holy One; make me to understand Thy precepts. Thy mercy endures forever, O Lord. Do not despise the works of Thine hands. To Thee belongs worship, to Thee belongs praise, to Thee belongs glory: to the Father and to the Son and to the Holy Spirit, both now and forever and unto the ages of ages. Amen. \

Litany Of Fervent Intercession

Priest: Let us complete our morning prayer to the Lord.

People: *Lord, have mercy.*

Priest: Help us, save us, have mercy on us and keep us, O God, by Thy grace.

People: *Lord, have mercy.*

Priest: That the whole day may be perfect, holy, peaceful and sinless, let us ask of the Lord.

People: *Grant this, O Lord.*

Priest: An angel of peace, a faithful guide, a guardian of our souls and bodies, let us ask of the Lord.

People: *Grant this, O Lord.*

Priest: Pardon and forgiveness of our sins and offences, let us ask of the Lord.

People: *Grant this, O Lord.*

Priest: Things good and profitable for our souls, and peace for the world, let us ask of the Lord.

People: *Grant this, O Lord.*

Priest: That we may live out the rest of our days in peace and repentance, let us ask of the Lord.

People: *Grant this, O Lord.*

Priest: A Christian end to our life, painless, unashamed and peaceful, and a good defence before the dread judgement seat of Christ, let us ask.

People: *Grant this, O Lord.*

Priest: Commemorating our all holy, pure, most blessed and glorious Lady, Mother of God and Ever Virgin Mary, with all the Saints, let us entrust ourselves and one another and our whole life to Christ our God.

People: *To Thee, O Lord.*

Priest: For Thou art a God of mercy, compassion and love towards mankind, and to Thee we give glory, to the Father, the Son and the Holy Spirit, both now and for ever, and unto the ages of ages.

People: *Amen.*

Priest: Peace be with you.

People: And with thy spirit.

Priest: Let us bow our heads to the Lord.

People: To Thee, O Lord.

Prayer At The Bowing Of Heads

Priest *[soto voce]*: Holy Lord, dwelling on high and beholding things below and, with Thine eye that observes all, keeping watch over the whole creation, to Thee we have bowed the neck of our soul and body, and we beseech Thee, O Holy of Holies: Stretch forth Thine invisible hand from Thy holy dwelling and bless us all. And, as Thou art good and lovest mankind, pardon us if we have sinned in anything, voluntarily or involuntarily, granting us Thy blessings both of this world and of the world above.

Priest *[aloud]*: For Thine it is to have mercy and to save us, O our God, and to Thee we give glory, to the Father, the Son and the Holy Spirit, now and for ever, and to the ages of ages.

People: Amen.

[Then the Aposticha from the Paraklitiki, with the following verses, from Monday to Friday.]

Reader: Verse 1:   We have been filled in the morning with Thy mercy, Lord, we have rejoiced and been glad. In all our day let us be glad, in return for the days when Thou hast humbled us, for the years wherein we saw evils. And look on Thy servants and on the work of Thy hands and guide their children.

Chorus: Verse 2:   *And may the splendour of the Lord our God be upon us, and direct the work of our hands for us, and direct the work of our hands.*

[Saturday]

Verse 1:   Blessed art those whom Thou hast chosen and taken, O Lord; they shall dwell in Thy courts.

Verse 2:   Their souls shall dwell among good things.

Verse 3:   And their memorial is from age to age.

> *Glory be to the Father, and to the Son, and to the Holy Spirit;*
> *Both now and forever, and unto the ages of ages. Amen.*

[The Idiomel, if there is one.]

Priest: It is good to give thanks to the Lord, to sing praises to Thy name, O Most High. To declare Thy love in the morning and Thy truth every night.

Reader: Holy God, Holy Strong, Holy Immortal, have mercy on us. **(x3)**

> *Glory be to the Father, and to the Son, and to the Holy Spirit;*
> *Both now and forever, and unto the ages of ages. Amen.*

O Most Holy Trinity, have mercy on us.

O Lord, cleanse us from our sins.

O Master, pardon our iniquities.

O Holy One, visit and heal our infirmities, for Thy names sake.

Lord have mercy. **(x3)**

Glory be to the Father, and to the Son, and to the Holy Spirit;
Both now and forever, and unto the ages of ages. Amen.

People:　*Our Father, Who art in Heaven, hallowed be Thy Name. Thy Kingdom come, Thy will be done, on earth as it is in Heaven. Give us this day our daily bread, and forgive us our trespasses, as we forgive those who trespass against us; and lead us not into temptation, but deliver us from the evil one.*

Priest:　For Thine is the kingdom, the power, and the glory, of the Father, and the Son and the Holy Spirit, both now and forever, and to the ages of ages.

People:　*Amen.*

Glory be to the Father, and to the Son, and to the Holy Spirit;
Both now and forever, and unto the ages of ages. Amen.

Great Litany

Priest:　Have mercy on us, O God, according to Thy great mercy, we pray Thee, hear us and have mercy.

People:　*Lord, have mercy.* **(x3)**

Priest:　Also we pray for our Sovereign Lady, Queen Elizabeth, the royal family, her Government and all in authority.

People:　*Lord, have mercy.* **(x3)**

Priest:　Also we pray for our Archbishop Nikitas, the Priests, Deacons and all our brotherhood in Christ.

People:　*Lord, have mercy.* **(x3)**

Priest:　Also we pray for mercy, life, peace, health, salvation, visitation, pardon and forgiveness of sins for the servants of God, all devout and Orthodox Christians, the benefactors, helpers, worshippers and pilgrims in this holy parish; *[and for the servants of God N. & N.]*, and all who have asked for our prayers, unworthy though we are.

People:　*Lord, have mercy.* **(x3)**

Priest:　Also we pray for the blessed and ever remembered founders of this holy parish, and for all our departed brothers and sisters, Orthodox believers, who have gone to their rest before us and who here and in all the world lie asleep in the Lord; *[and for the servants of God N. & N.]*, and that they may be pardoned all their offences, both voluntary and involuntary.

People:　*Lord, have mercy.* **(x3)**

Priest:　Also we pray for those serve, or who have served in this holy parish, and for all our brothers and sisters of the monastic order, who await Thy great and rich mercy.

People: *Lord, have mercy.* **(x3)**

Priest: For Thou, O God, art merciful, and love mankind, and to Thee we give glory, to the Father, the Son and the Holy Spirit, now and for ever, and to the ages of ages.

People: *Amen.*

Priest: Wisdom.

Reader: Holy Father, bless.

Priest: Blessed is He Who Is, Christ our true God, always, now and for ever, and to the ages of ages.

People: *Amen.*

Reader: May the Lord God strengthen the holy and pure faith of devout and orthodox Christians, with his holy Church and this sacred parish, to ages of ages.

Priest: Most holy Mother of God, save us.

Reader: Greater in honour than the Cherubim and beyond compare more glorious than the Seraphim; without corruption thou gavest birth to God the Word, truly the Theotokos, we magnify thee.

[Prepare Synaxarion and Katabasia]

Trisagion

Reader: Through the prayers of our holy fathers, Lord Jesus Christ our God, have mercy on us and save us.

People: *Amen. Glory to Thee, O Lord, glory to Thee.*

Reader: O Heavenly King, Comforter, Spirit of Truth, Who art everywhere present and fillest all things, Treasury of blessings and Giver of life: Come and abide in us and cleanse us from every impurity and save our souls, O Good One.

Holy God, Holy Mighty, Holy Immortal, have mercy on us. **(x3)**

Glory be to the Father, and to the Son, and to the Holy Spirit;
Both now and forever, and unto the ages of ages. Amen.

O Most Holy Trinity, have mercy on us.

O Lord, cleanse us from our sins.

O Master, pardon our iniquities.

O Holy One, visit and heal our infirmities, for Thy names sake.

Lord have mercy. **(x3)**

Glory be to the Father, and to the Son, and to the Holy Spirit;
Both now and forever, and unto the ages of ages. Amen.

People: *Our Father, Who art in Heaven, hallowed be Thy Name. Thy Kingdom come, Thy will be done, on earth as it is in Heaven. Give us this day our daily bread, and forgive us our trespasses, as we forgive those who trespass against us; and lead us not into temptation, but deliver us from the evil one.*

Reader: Through the prayers of our holy fathers, Lord Jesus Christ our God, have mercy on us and save us.

People: *Amen.*

Lord, have mercy. **(x12)**

Glory be to the Father and to the Son and to the Holy Spirit;
Both now and forever and unto the ages of ages. Amen.

Come, let us worship God, our King.

Come, let us worship and fall down before Christ, our King and our God.

Come, let us worship and fall down before Christ Himself, our King and our God.

Psalm 19

The Lord hear thee in the day of affliction; the name of the God of Jacob defend thee. Let Him send forth unto thee help from His sanctuary, and out of Zion let Him help thee. Let Him remember every sacrifice of thine, and thy whole burnt offering let Him fatten. The Lord grant thee according to thy heart, and fulfil all thy purposes. We shall rejoice in Thy salvation, and in the name of the Lord our God shall we be magnified. The Lord fulfil all thy requests. Now have I known that the Lord hath saved His anointed one; He shall hearken unto him out of His holy heaven; in mighty deeds is the salvation of His right hand. Some trust in chariots, and some in horses, but we shall call upon the name of the Lord our God. They have been fettered and have fallen, but we are risen and are set upright. O Lord, save the king, and hearken unto us in the day when we call upon Thee.

Psalm 120 - An Ode of Ascents.

I have lifted up mine eyes to the mountains, from whence cometh my help. My help cometh from the Lord, Who hath made heaven and the earth. Give not thy foot unto moving, and may He not slumber that keepeth thee. Behold, He shall not slumber nor shall He sleep, He that keepeth Israel. The Lord shall keep thee; the Lord is thy shelter at thy right hand. The sun shall not burn thee by day, nor the moon by night. The Lord shall keep thee from all evil, the Lord shall guard thy soul. The Lord shall keep thy coming in and thy going out, from henceforth and for evermore.

After The Psalm

Glory be to the Father and to the Son and to the Holy Spirit,
Both now and forever and unto the ages of ages. Amen.

Halleluiah, Halleluiah, Halleluiah. Glory to Thee, O God. **(x3)**
Lord have mercy. **(x3)**

Glory be to the Father and to the Son and to the Holy Spirit;
Both now and forever and unto the ages of ages. Amen.

Reader: Through the prayers of our holy fathers, Lord Jesus Christ our God, have mercy on us and save us.
People: *Amen.*

Troparion Of The Holy And Life Giving Cross

Tone 2 Majesty, gentleness, hope, repentance and sadness.   *E, F, G, Ab, B, C.*
O Lord, save Thy people, And bless Thine inheritance. Grant victories to the Orthodox Christians over their adversaries. And by virtue of Thy Cross, Preserve Thy habitation.

Glory be to the Father, and to the Son, and to the Holy Spirit;

Kontakion Of The Holy And Life Giving Cross

Tone 4   Festive, joyous and expressing deep piety.   *C, D, Eb, F, G, A, Bb, C.*

As Thou wast voluntarily crucified for our sake, Grant mercy to those who are called by Thy Name. Make all Orthodox Christians glad by Thy power, Granting them victories over their adversaries, By bestowing on them the invincible trophy, Thy weapon of peace.

Both now and forever, and unto the ages of ages. Amen.

Kontakion For Ordinary Sundays

Tone 2   Majesty, gentleness, hope, repentance and sadness.   *E, F, G, Ab, B, C.*

O protection of Christians that cannot be put to shame, mediation unto the Creator most constant, O despise not the suppliant voices of those who have sinned; but be thou quick, O good one, to come unto our aid, who in faith cry unto thee: Hasten to intercession, and speed thou to make supplication, thou who dost ever protect, O Theotokos, them that honour thee.

Reader: Through the prayers of our holy fathers, Lord Jesus Christ our God, have mercy on us and save us.
People: Amen.

Doxology – excerpt Glory to God in the highest and on earth peace good will toward men. **(x3)**

Psalm 50 – excerpt O Lord, open my lips, and my mouth shall proclaim Thy praise. **(x2)**

Psalm 3

Lord, how they have increased who trouble me. Many are they who rise up against me. Many are they who say of me, "There is no help for him in God." But Thou, O Lord, art a shield for me, my glory and the One Who lifts up my head. I cried to the Lord with my voice, and He heard me from His holy hill. I lay down and slept; I awoke, for the Lord sustained me. I shall not be afraid of ten thousands of people who have set themselves against me all around. Arise, O Lord; save me, O my God. For Thou hast struck all mine enemies on the cheekbone; Thou hast broken the teeth of the ungodly. Salvation belongs to the Lord. Thy blessing is upon Thy people.

Psalm 37

O Lord, do not rebuke me in Thy wrath, nor chasten me in Thy hot displeasure. For Thine arrows deeply pierce me, and Thine hand presses me down. There is no soundness in my flesh because of Thine anger, Nor is there any health in my bones because of my sin. For mine iniquities have gone over my head; like a heavy burden they are too heavy for me. My wounds are foul and festering because of my foolishness. I am troubled, I am bowed down greatly; I go mourning all the day long. For my loins are full of inflammation, and there is no soundness in my flesh. I am feeble and severely broken; I groan because of the turmoil of my heart. Lord, all my desire is before Thee; and my sighing is not hidden from Thee. My heart pants, my strength fails me; as for the light of mine eyes, it also has gone from me. My loved ones and my friends stand aloof from my plague, and my kinsmen stand afar off. Those also who seek my life lay snares for me; those who seek my hurt speak of destruction, and plan deception all the day long. But I, like a deaf man, do not hear; and I am like a mute who does not open his mouth. Thus I am like a man who does not hear, and in whose mouth is no response. For in Thee, O Lord, I hope; Thou wilt hear, O Lord my God. For I said, "*Hear me, lest they rejoice over me, lest, when my foot slips, they magnify themselves against me.*" For I am ready to fall, and my sorrow is continually before me. For I shall declare mine iniquity; I shall be in anguish over my sin. But mine enemies are vigorous, and they are strong; and those who wrongfully hate me have multiplied. Those also who render evil for good, they are mine adversaries, because I follow what is good. Do not forsake me, O Lord; O my God, be not far from me. Make haste to help me, O Lord, my salvation.

Psalm 62

O God, Thou art my God; early shall I seek Thee; my soul thirsts for Thee; My flesh longs for Thee in a dry and thirsty land where there is no water. So I have looked for Thee in the sanctuary, to see Thy power and Thy glory. Because Thy loving kindness is better than life, my lips shall praise Thee. Thus I shall bless Thee while I live; I shall lift up my hands in Thy name. My soul shall be satisfied as with marrow and fatness, and my mouth shall praise Thee with joyful lips. When I remember Thee on my bed, I meditate on Thee in the night watches. Because Thou hast been my help, therefore in the shadow of Thy wings I shall rejoice. My soul follows close behind Thee; Thy right hand upholds me. But those who seek my life, to destroy it, shall go into the lower parts of the earth. They shall fall by the sword; they shall be a portion for jackals. But the king shall rejoice in God; everyone who swears by Him shall glory; but the mouth of those who speak lies shall be stopped.

After The Psalm

Glory be to the Father and to the Son and to the Holy Spirit,
Both now and forever and unto the ages of ages. Amen.
Halleluiah, Halleluiah, Halleluiah. Glory to Thee, O God. **(x3)**
Lord have mercy. **(x3)**

Glory be to the Father, and to the Son, and to the Holy Spirit;
Both now and forever, and unto the ages of ages. Amen.

Psalm 87

O Lord, God of my salvation, I have cried out day and night before Thee. Let my prayer come before Thee; incline Thine ear to my cry. For my soul is full of troubles, and my life draws near to the grave. I am counted with those who go down to the pit; I am like a man who has no strength, Adrift among the dead, like the slain who lie in the grave, whom Thou rememberest no more, and who are cut off from Thine hand. Thou hast laid me in the lowest pit, in darkness, in the depths. Thy wrath lies heavy upon me, and Thou hast afflicted me with all Thy waves. Thou hast put away mine acquaintances far from me; Thou hast made me an abomination to them; I am shut up, and I cannot get out; Mine eye wastes away because of affliction. Lord, I have called daily upon Thee; I have stretched out my hands to Thee. Willest Thou work wonders for the dead? Shall the dead arise and praise Thee? Shall Thy loving kindness be declared in the grave? Or Thy faithfulness in the place of destruction? Shall Thy wonders be known in the dark? And Thy righteousness in the land of forgetfulness? But to Thee I have cried out, O Lord, and in the morning my prayer comes before Thee. Lord, why dost Thou cast off my soul? Why dost Thou hide Thy face from me? I have been afflicted and ready to die from my youth up; I suffer Thy terrors; I am distraught. Thy fierce wrath has gone over me; Thy terrors have cut me off. They came around me all day long like water; they engulfed me altogether. Loved one and friend Thou hast put far from me, and mine acquaintances into darkness.

Psalm 102

Bless the Lord O my soul; and all that is within me, bless His holy name. Bless the Lord O my soul, and forget not all His benefits: Who forgives all thine iniquities, Who heals all thy diseases, Who redeems thy life from destruction, Who crowns thee with loving kindness and tender mercies, Who satisfies thy mouth with good things, so that thine youth is renewed like the eagles. The Lord executes righteousness and justice for all who are oppressed. He made known His ways to Moses, His acts to the children of Israel. The Lord is merciful and gracious, slow to anger, and abounding in mercy. He shall not always strive with us, nor shall He keep His anger forever. He has not dealt with us according to our sins, nor punished us according to our iniquities. For as the heavens are high above the earth, so great is His mercy toward those who fear Him; As far as the east is from the west, so far has He removed our transgressions from us. As a father pities his children, so the Lord pities those who fear Him. For He knows our frame; He remembers that we are dust. As for man, his days are like grass; as a flower of the field, so he flourishes. For the wind passes over it, and it is gone, and its place remembers it no more. But the mercy of the Lord is from everlasting to everlasting on those who fear Him, and His righteousness to childrens children, To such as keep His covenant, and to those who remember His commandments to do them. The Lord has established His throne in heaven, and His kingdom rules overall. Bless the Lord you His angels, who excel in strength, who do His word, heeding the voice of His word. Bless the Lord all you His hosts, you ministers of His, who do His pleasure. Bless the Lord all His works, in all places of His dominion. Bless the Lord O my soul.

Psalm 142

Lord, hear my prayer; in Thy truth give ear to my supplications; in Thy righteousness hear me. Enter not into judgement with Thy servant, for no one living is justified in Thy sight. For the enemy has pursued my soul; he has crushed my life to the ground. He has made me to dwell in darkness, like those that have long been dead, and my spirit within me is overwhelmed; my heart within me is distressed. I remembered the days of old, I meditated on all Thy works, I pondered on the creations of Thine hands. I stretched forth my hands to Thee; my soul longs for Thee like a thirsty land. Lord, hear me quickly; my spirit fails. Turn not Thy face away from me, lest I be like those who go down into the pit. Let me hear Thy mercy in the morning; for in Thee have I put my trust. Lord, teach me to know the way wherein I should walk; for I lift up my soul to Thee. Rescue me, Lord, from mine enemies, to Thee have I fled for refuge. Teach me to do Thy will, for Thou art my God. Thy good Spirit shall lead me on a level path. Lord, for Thy names sake Thou shalt preserve my life. In Thy righteousness Thou shalt bring my soul out of trouble, and in Thy mercy Thou shalt utterly destroy my enemies. And Thou shalt destroy all those who afflict my soul, for I am Thy servant.

After The Psalm

Glory be to the Father and to the Son and to the Holy Spirit,

Both now and forever and unto the ages of ages. Amen.

Halleluiah, Halleluiah, Halleluiah. Glory to Thee, O God. **(x3)**

O God our Hope, O Lord, glory to Thee.

Lord, have mercy. **(x12)**

Reader: Through the prayers of our holy fathers, Lord Jesus Christ our God, have mercy on us and save us.

People: Amen.

God Is The Lord

People: God is the Lord and has revealed Himself to us. Blessed is He who comes in the Name of the Lord.

Reader: Give thanks to the Lord, for He is good; and His steadfast love endures forever.

People: God is the Lord and has revealed Himself to us. Blessed is He who comes in the Name of the Lord.

Reader: All nations surrounded me; in the Name of the Lord, I withstood them.

People: God is the Lord and has revealed Himself to us. Blessed is He who comes in the Name of the Lord.

Reader: I shall not die, but live, and recount the deeds of the Lord.

People: God is the Lord and has revealed Himself to us. Blessed is He who comes in the Name of the Lord.

Reader: The stone that the builders rejected has become the chief cornerstone.

This is the Lords doing and is marvellous in our eyes.

People: God is the Lord and has revealed Himself to us. Blessed is He who comes in the Name of the Lord.

Resurrectional Apolytikion

Tone 3   Arrogant, brave, and mature atmosphere.   *F, G, A, A#, C, D, E, F.*

Let the heavens rejoice and the earth be glad, for the Lord hath done a mighty act with His own arm. He hath trampled down death by death, and became the first born from the dead. He hath delivered us from the depths of Hades, granting the world the Great Mercy.

Theotokion

Tone 8   Humility, tranquillity, repose, suffering, pleading.   *C, D, Eb, F, G, A, Bb, C.*

To Thee, the Champion Leader, we Thy servants dedicate a feast of victory and of thanksgiving as ones rescued out of sufferings, O Theotokos: but as Thou art one with might, which is invincible, from all dangers that can be, do Thou deliver us, that we may cry to Thee: Rejoice, Thou Bride Unwedded.

Lord, have mercy. **(x12)**

Reader: Through the prayers of our holy fathers, Lord Jesus Christ our God, have mercy on us and save us.

People: *Amen.*

Evlogitária Of The Resurrection

Tone 5   Stimulating, dancing, and rhythmical.   C, D, Eb, F, G, A, Bb, C.

Chorus: *Blessed art Thou, O Lord, teach me Thy statutes.*

Reader: The assembly of angels was amazed, beholding Thee, a man among the dead, yet O Saviour destroying the stronghold of death, and with Thyself raising up Adam, and freeing all from Hades.

Chorus: *Blessed art Thou, O Lord, teach me Thy statutes.*

Reader: 'Why mingle you myrrh with tears of pity, O you women disciples?' Thus the radiant angel within the tomb addressed the myrrh bearing women. 'Behold the tomb and understand, for the Saviour has risen from the tomb.'

Chorus: *Blessed art Thou, O Lord, teach me Thy statutes.*

Reader: Very early the myrrh bearing women hastened, unto thy tomb, lamenting. But the angel stood before them and said: 'The time for lamentation is passed! Weep not! But tell of the resurrection to the apostles.'

Chorus: *Blessed art Thou, O Lord, teach me Thy statutes.*

Reader: The myrrh bearing women, with myrrh came to Thy tomb, O Saviour, made ready. But the angel addressed them saying, 'Why seek you the living among the dead? For as God He is risen from the tomb!'

Chorus: *Glory be to the Father and to the Son and to the Holy Spirit,*

Reader: Let us all worship the Father, and His Son, and the Holy Spirit; the Holy Trinity, one in essence; crying with the Seraphim: Holy, Holy, Holy art Thou, O Lord.

Chorus: *Both now and forever and unto the ages of ages. Amen.*

Reader: In bringing forth the Giver of Life, thou hast delivered Adam from Sin, O Virgin, and hast brought joy to Eve instead of sorrow. Man thus fallen from life, hath thereunto been restored by Him who of thee was incarnate, both God and man.

Chorus: *Halleluiah, Halleluiah, Halleluiah! Glory to Thee, O God.* **(x3)**

Lord, have mercy. **(x12)**

Reader: Through the prayers of our holy fathers, Lord Jesus Christ our God, have mercy on us and save us.

People: *Amen.*

Paschal Hypakoe

Tone 4   Festive, joyous and deep piety.   C, D, Eb, F, G, A, Bb, C.

They who were with Mary came before the dawn, found the stone rolled away from the sepulchre, and heard the angels say unto them, Why seek thee Him as man with the dead, Who dwells in light eternal? Behold the grave wrappings; make haste and declare to the world that the Lord is risen, and has caused death to die; for

He is the Son of God, the Saviour of mankind.

Anabathmoi

Chorus: *From my youth up many passions have warred against me. But do thou help and save me, O my Saviour.* **(x2)**

Reader: You who hate Zion shall be put to confusion of the Lord; like grass in the fire shall you be withered up. **(x2)**

Chorus: *Glory be to the Father and to the Son and to the Holy Spirit,*

Reader: Through the Holy Spirit it is every soul quickened and exalted in purity and made resplendent by the Triune Unity in mystic holiness.

Chorus: *Both now and forever and unto the ages of ages. Amen.*

Reader: Through the Holy Spirit the channels and streams of grace overflow, showering all creation with invigorating life.

Resurrection Ode

Reader: Let us who have beheld the Resurrection of Christ, worship our Holy Lord Jesus, Who is alone without sin. We worship Thy Cross, O Christ, and praise and glorify Thy Holy Resurrection. For Thou art our God, and we know none other beside Thee, and we call upon Thy Name. Come, all you faithful, let us worship Christs' Holy Resurrection, for behold, through the Cross, joy has come to the whole world. We praise His Resurrection, and forever glorify the Lord. He endured the Cross for us, and by death destroyed Death.

Psalm 50

Have mercy on me, O God, according to Thy great mercy; and according to the multitude of Thy compassions blot out my transgression. Wash me thoroughly from mine iniquity, and cleanse me from my sin. For I acknowledge mine iniquity, and my sin is ever before me. Against Thee, Thee only have I sinned, and done evil in Thy sight, that Thou mayest be found just when Thou speakest, and victorious when Thou art judged. For behold, I was conceived in iniquity, and in sin my mother bore me. For behold, Thou hast loved truth; Thou hast made known to me the hidden and secret things of Thy wisdom. Thou shalt sprinkle me with hyssop, and I shall be made clean; Thou shalt wash me, and I shalt be whiter than snow. Make me to hear joy and gladness; that the humbled bones may rejoice. Turn Thy face away from my sins, and blot out all mine iniquities.

Create in me a clean heart, O God, and renew a steadfast spirit within me. Cast me not away from Thy presence, and take not Thy Holy Spirit from me. Restore to me the joy of Thy salvation, and establish me with Thy governing Spirit. I shall teach transgressors Thy ways, and the ungodly shall turn back to Thee. Deliver me from blood guiltiness, O God, the God of my salvation; my tongue shall joyfully declare Thy righteousness. Lord, open my lips, and my mouth shall declare Thy praise. For if Thou hadst desired sacrifice, I would give it; Thou dost not delight in burned offerings. A sacrifice to God is a broken spirit; God shall not despise a broken and a humbled heart. Do good, O Lord, in Thy good pleasure to Zion, and let the walls of Jerusalem be builded. Then Thou shalt be pleased with a sacrifice of righteousness, with oblation and whole burned offerings. Then shall they offer bulls on Thine altar.

After The Psalm

Chorus: *Glory be to the Father and to the Son and to the Holy Spirit;*

Reader: At the prayers of the Apostles, O Saviour, save us.

Chorus: *Both now and forever and unto the ages of ages. Amen.*

Reader: At the prayers of the Mother of God, O Saviour, save us.

Jesus having risen from the grave, as he foretold. Has granted us life everlasting, and great mercy.

Lord, have mercy. **(x40)**

Reader: Through the prayers of our holy fathers, Lord Jesus Christ our God, have mercy on us and save us.

People: Amen.

The Synaxarion For Today *(The Prologue Of Ohrid)*

[Ending with]

Reader: Through the prayers of Thy Saints, O Christ our God, have mercy on us.

People: *Amen.*

Katabasia

[Insert seasonal Katabasia Odes 1-8 from Katavasiae, Volume 2, page 688.]

The Magnificat (Luke 1:46-55).

Reader: My soul magnifies the Lord, and my spirit has rejoiced in God my Saviour.

Chorus: Greater in honour than the Cherubim and beyond compare more glorious than the Seraphim; without corruption thou gavest birth to God the Word, truly the Theotokos, we magnify thee.

Reader: For He has regarded the lowly state of His maidservant; for behold, henceforth all generations shall call me blessed.

Chorus: Greater in honour than the Cherubim and beyond compare more glorious than the Seraphim; without corruption thou gavest birth to God the Word, truly the Theotokos, we magnify thee.

Reader: For He who is mighty has done great things for me, and holy is His name. And His mercy is on those who fear Him from generation to generation.

Chorus: Greater in honour than the Cherubim and beyond compare more glorious than the Seraphim; without corruption thou gavest birth to God the Word, truly the Theotokos, we magnify thee.

Reader: He has shown strength with His arm; he has scattered the proud in the imagination of their hearts.

Chorus: *Greater in honour than the Cherubim and beyond compare more glorious than the Seraphim; without corruption thou gavest birth to God the Word, truly the Theotokos, we magnify thee.*

Reader: He has put down the mighty from their thrones, and exalted the lowly. He has filled the hungry with good things, and the rich He has sent empty away.

Chorus: *Greater in honour than the Cherubim and beyond compare more glorious than the Seraphim; without corruption thou gavest birth to God the Word, truly the Theotokos, we magnify thee.*

Reader: He has helped His servant Israel, in remembrance of His mercy, as He spoke to our fathers, to Abraham and to his seed forever.

Chorus: *Greater in honour than the Cherubim and beyond compare more glorious than the Seraphim; without corruption thou gavest birth to God the Word, truly the Theotokos, we magnify thee.*

[Insert seasonal Katabasia Ode 9 from Katavasiae, Volume 2, page 688.]

Lord, have mercy. **(x12)**

Reader: Through the prayers of our holy fathers, Lord Jesus Christ our God, have mercy on us and save us.
People: *Amen.*
Reader: Holy is the Lord our God. **(x3)**

Chorus: *Exalt you the Lord our God, and worship at His footstool. O Lord, save Thy people and bless Thine inheritance. Feed them, and lift them up forever.*

Exaposteilárion
[for the end of the canon, to match the Eothinón]

Idiomelismatic.

Reader: When Mary said, "They have taken away my Lord," Simon Peter and the other disciple, the anointed of Christ whom Jesus loved, went quickly to the grave. They came and found the grave clothes in the tomb, together with the napkin which had covered his head lying near them. Therefore they waited until they also had seen the Christ.

Chorus: *Glory be to the Father and to the Son and to the Holy Spirit,*

Tone 3   Arrogant, brave, and mature atmosphere.   *F, G, A, A#, C, D, E, F.*

Reader: The Saviour, who is grace and truth, has appeared in the streams of the Jordan and enlightened those who sleep in darkness and shadow. For the Light which no one can approach has come and been revealed.

Chorus: *Both now and forever and unto the ages of ages. Amen.*

The Gospel - Eothinón [This one for Week 7]

Reader: The Reading is From The Holy Gospel According To John 20:1-10.

People: *Glory to Thee, O Lord, glory to Thee.*

Reader: On the first day of the week Mary Magdalene came to the tomb early, while it was still dark, and saw that the stone had been taken away from the tomb. So she ran, and went to Simon Peter and the other disciple, the one whom Jesus loved, and said to them, "They have taken the Lord out of the tomb, and we do not know where they have laid him." Peter then came out with the other disciple, and they went toward the tomb. They both ran, but the other disciple outran Peter and reached the tomb first; and stooping to look in, he saw the linen cloths lying there, but he did not go in. Then Simon Peter came, following him, and went into the tomb; he saw the linen cloths lying, and the napkin, which had been on his head, not lying with the linen cloths but rolled up in a place by itself. Then the other disciple, who reached the tomb first, also went in, and he saw and believed; for as yet they did not know the scripture, that he must rise from the dead. Then the disciples went back to their homes.

People: *Glory to Thee, O Lord, glory to Thee.*

Lauds - The Praises
Psalm 148

Reader: Praise the Lord. Praise the Lord from the heavens; praise Him in the heights. Praise Him, all His angels; praise Him, all His hosts. Praise Him, sun and moon; praise Him, all you stars of light. Praise Him, you heavens of heavens, and you waters above the heavens. Let them praise the name of the Lord, for He commanded and they were created. He has also established them forever and ever; He has made a decree that shall not pass away. Praise the Lord from the earth, you great sea creatures and all the depths; Fire and hail, snow and clouds; stormy wind, fulfilling His word; Mountains and all hills; fruitful trees and all cedars; Beasts and all cattle; creeping things and flying fowl; Kings of the earth and all peoples; princes and all judges of the earth; Both young men and maidens; old men and children. Let them praise the name of the Lord, for His name alone is exalted; His glory is above the earth and heaven. And He has exalted the horn of His people, the praise of all His saints - of the children of Israel, a people near to Him. Praise the Lord.

Psalm 149

Reader: Praise the Lord. Sing to the Lord a new song, and His praise in the congregation of saints. Let Israel rejoice in their Maker; let the children of Zion be joyful in their King. Let them praise His name with the dance; let them sing praises to Him with the timbrel and harp. For the Lord takes pleasure in His people; He shall beautify the humble with salvation. Let the saints be joyful in glory; let them sing aloud on their beds. Let the high praises of God be in their mouth, and a two edged sword in their hand, To execute vengeance on the nations, and punishments on the peoples; To bind their kings with chains, and their nobles with fetters of iron. To execute on them the written judgement.

Chorus: *Almighty Lord, Thou suffered the cross and death, and rose from the dead. We glorify Thy resurrection.*

Reader: This honour have all His saints. Praise the Lord.

Chorus: *O Christ, Thou hast rescued us by Thy cross from the ancient curse and suppressed by Thy death the Devil who was tyrannising our nature. Thou hast filled everything with joy by Thy resurrection. Therefore we cry out to Thee, "O Lord, risen from the dead, glory be to Thee".*

Psalm 150

Reader: Praise the Lord. Praise God in His sanctuary; praise Him in His mighty firmament.

Chorus: *O Christ, Thou hast rescued us by Thy cross from the ancient curse and suppressed by Thy death the Devil who was tyrannising our nature. Thou hast filled everything with joy by Thy resurrection. Therefore we cry out to Thee, "O Lord, risen from the dead, glory be to Thee".*

Reader: Praise Him for His mighty acts; praise Him according to His excellent greatness.

Chorus: *O Christ our Saviour, lead us into Thy truth through Thy cross and rescue us from the snares of the enemy; Thou hast risen from the dead. O Lord, Lover of the human race, extend Thine arm and, at the prayers of Thy saints, raise us who have fallen because of sin.*

Reader: Praise Him with the sound of the trumpet; praise Him with the lute and harp.

Chorus: *O uniquely fathered Word of God, in Thy love for the human race Thou camest to earth without leaving the bosom of the Father. Thou becamest truly man, so that Thou could suffer the cross and death in the flesh, although Thou art without passion in Divinity. Thou hast granted the human race immortality by Thy resurrection, for Thou alone art all powerful.*

Reader: Praise Him with the timbrel and dance; praise Him with stringed instruments and flutes. Praise Him with loud cymbals; praise Him with high sounding cymbals. Let everything that has breath praise the Lord. Praise the Lord.

Chorus: *A great and fearful mystery has been accomplished. The Master of all is baptised by a servant for the purification of all mortal men.* **(x2)**

Psalm 113

Reader: The sea saw and fled; Jordan was turned back.

Chorus: *The voice of the Father was heard as it cried, "The Man who is being baptised in the flesh in Jordans stream is my dear Son."*

Reader: O sea, what happened to thee that thou fleddest and thee, O Jordan, that thou turnest back?

Chorus: *The ranks of the angels sang in amazement when they saw their Master in the form of a servant as he was baptised in the river.*

Chorus: *Glory be to the Father and to the Son and to the Holy Spirit;*

Doxastikón Of The Eothinón Of The Week

Tone 7 Manly character and strong melody.   *F, C, A, A#, C, D, E, F.*

Reader: O Mary, why didst thou stand at the grave to see the dawn and break of day? Thy mind was covered with a great darkness and thou asked him, "Where have they placed Jesus?" See how the disciples went quickly to the tomb, believed his resurrection because of the clothes and the napkin lying in the grave, and remembered what was predicted about him in the Scriptures. O Christ, Giver of life, we have believed through them and, together with them, also praise thee.

Chorus: *Both now and forever and unto the ages of ages. Amen.*

Theotokíon *[at the end of Lauds]*

Tone 2 Majesty, gentleness, hope, repentance and sadness.   *E, F, G, Ab, B, C.*

Reader: O Virgin Theotokos, thou art most blessed, for through the One who was born of thee, Hades has been captured and Adam recalled. The curse has been annulled, and Eve set free. Death has been slain, so we are given life. Blessed is Christ our God, whose good will it was. Glory to Thee.

Great Doxology

Glory to God, Who has shown us the Light. Glory to God in the highest, and on earth, peace, good will toward men. We praise Thee. We bless Thee. We worship Thee. We glorify Thee and give thanks to Thee for Thy great glory. O Lord God, Heavenly King, God the Father Almighty. O Lord, the Only Begotten Son, Jesus Christ, and the Holy Spirit. \

O Lord God, Lamb of God, Son of the Father, Who takes away the sins of the world, have mercy on us. Thou, Who takes away the sins of the world, receive our prayer. Thou, Who sittest at the right hand of God the Father, have mercy on us. /

For Thou alone art holy, and Thou alone art Lord. Thou alone, O Lord Jesus Christ, are most high in the glory of God the Father. Amen. I shall give thanks to Thee every day and praise Thy Name forever and ever, Lord. Every day shall I bless Thee and praise Thy name forever, and to the ages of ages. Amen. \

Vouchsafe, O Lord, to keep us this day without sin. Blessed art Thou, O Lord, the God of our fathers, and praised and glorified is Thy Name forever. Amen. Let Thy mercy be upon us, O Lord, even as we have set our hope on Thee.

Blessed art Thou, O Master; teach me Thy statutes.

Blessed art Thou, O Lord; enlighten me with Thy commandments.

Blessed art Thou, O Holy One; make me to understand Thy precepts.

Lord, Thou hast been our refuge from generation to generation. I said, *"Lord, have mercy on me. Heal my soul, for I have sinned against Thee."* \

Lord, I flee to Thee for refuge. Teach me to do Thy will, for Thou art my God. For with Thee is the fountain of Life, and in Thy light we shall see light. Continue Thy loving kindness to those who know Thee.

Holy God, Holy Strong, Holy Immortal, have mercy on us.

Holy God, Holy Strong, Holy Immortal, have mercy on us.

Holy God, Holy Strong, Holy Immortal, have mercy on us.

Glory be to the Father, and to the Son, and to the Holy Spirit;

Both now and ever, and unto the ages of ages. Amen.

Holy Immortal, have mercy on us.

Holy God, Holy Strong, Holy Immortal, have mercy on us.

Today salvation has come into the world. Let us sing to Him who rose from the tomb, the Author of our life. For, destroying death by death, he has given us the victory and His great mercy. \

Lord, have mercy. **(x40)**

Reader: Through the prayers of our holy fathers, Lord Jesus Christ our God, have mercy on us and save us.
People: Amen.

Dismissal

Confirm, O God, the holy Orthodox Faith and Orthodox Christians unto the ages of ages. Amen.

Greater in honour than the Cherubim and beyond compare more glorious than the Seraphim; without corruption thou gavest birth to God the Word, truly the Theotokos, we magnify thee.

Lord, have mercy. **(x3)**

Reader: Through the prayers of our holy fathers, Lord Jesus Christ our God, have mercy on us and save us.
People: Amen.

[Now the 1ˢᵗ , 3ʳᵈ, 6ᵗʰ and 9ᵗʰ Hours, then Typika]

Proskomede

[Before the Divine Liturgy.]

• *The priest that desireth to celebrate the Divine Mysteries must first be at peace with all, have nothing against anyone, and insofar as is within his power, keep his heart from evil thoughts, be continent from the evening before, and be vigilant until the time of divine service. When the time is come, he goeth into the temple, in company with the deacon, and together thy make three reverences towards the east before the holy doors.*

• *If a priest serve without a deacon, the words of the deacon in the Proskomede, and during the Liturgy before the Gospel, and his response:* Holy Father, bless, *and:* Pierce Master, *and:* It is time to act,... *are NOT said, but only the Ekteniae and the Order of the Prothesis.*

• *If many priests concelebrate, in the performance of the Proskomede, only one priest may serve and say what is set forth; but of the rest of the celebrants, none shall say the Proskomede separately.*

Deacon: Bless, Master.

Priest: Blessed is our God, always, now and ever, and unto the ages of ages.

Deacon: Amen. Glory to Thee, our God, glory to Thee.

O Heavenly King, Comforter, Spirit of Truth, Who art everywhere present and fillest all things, Treasury of good things and Giver of life: Come and dwell in us, and cleanse us of all impurity, and save our souls, O Good One.

Holy God, Holy Mighty, Holy Immortal, have mercy on us. **(x3)**

Glory be to the Father, and to the Son, and to the Holy Spirit;
Both now and forever, and unto the ages of ages. Amen.

O Most Holy Trinity, have mercy on us.

O Lord, cleanse us from our sins.

O Master, pardon our iniquities.

O Holy One, visit and heal our infirmities, for Thy name's sake.

Lord have mercy. **(x3)**

Glory be to the Father and to the Son and to the Holy Spirit;
Both now and forever, and unto the ages of ages. Amen.

Our Father, Who art in Heaven, hallowed be Thy Name. Thy Kingdom come, Thy will be done, on earth as it is in Heaven. Give us this day our daily bread, and forgive us our trespasses, as we forgive those who trespass against us; and lead us not into temptation, but deliver us from the evil one.

Priest: For Thine is the kingdom, and the power, and the glory: of the Father, and of the Son, and of the Holy Spirit; now and ever, and unto ages of ages.

Deacon: *Amen.*

Priest: Have mercy on us, O Lord, have mercy on us; for, at a loss for any defense, this prayer do we sinners offer unto Thee as Master, have mercy on us.

Deacon: *Glory be to the Father and to the Son and to the Holy Spirit;*

Priest: Lord, have mercy on us; for we have hoped in Thee, be not angry with us greatly, neither remember our iniquities; but look upon us now as Thou art compassionate, and deliver us from our enemies; for Thou art our God, and we Thy people; all are the works of Thy hands, and we call upon Thy name.

Deacon: *Both now and forever, and unto the ages of ages. Amen.*

Priest: The door of compassion open unto us, O blessed Theotokos, for hoping in thee, let us not perish; through thee may we be delivered from adversities; for thou art the salvation of the Christian race.

Deacon: Lord, have mercy. **(x12)**

[They approach and kiss the icon of Christ, saying:]

Both: We venerate Thine immaculate Icon, O Good One, asking the forgiveness of our failings, O Christ God; for of Thine Own will Thou wast well-pleased to ascend the Cross in the flesh, that Thou mightest deliver from slavery to the enemy those whom Thou hadst fashioned. Wherefore, we cry to Thee thankfully: Thou didst fill all things with joy, O our Saviour, when Thou camest to save the world.

[They approach and kiss the icon of the Theotokos, saying the Troparion:]

Both: As thou art a well spring of compassion, vouchsafe mercy unto us, O Theotokos. Look upon a sinful people; show forth, as always, thy power. For hoping in thee we cry "Rejoice!" to thee, as once did Gabriel, the Supreme Commander of the Bodiless Hosts.

[They approach and kiss the icon of the Forerunner, saying:]

Both: The just is remembered with praises, but for you, O Forerunner, the Lords testimony suffices. For you were revealed as more praiseworthy than the prophets, because you were found worthy to baptise in running streams the One that they had proclaimed. Therefore with joy you struggled bravely for the truth, and preached to those in Hades a God who had appeared to those in the flesh, who takes away the sin of the world and grants us His great mercy.

[With bowed head:]

Priest: O Lord, stretch forth Thy hand from Thy holy place on high, and strengthen me for this, Thine appointed service; that standing uncondemned before Thy dread altar, I may celebrate the bloodless ministry. For Thine is the power and the glory unto the ages of ages. Amen.

Remit, pardon, forgive, O God, our offenses, both voluntary and involuntary, in deed and word, in knowledge and ignorance, by day and by night, in mind and thought; forgive us all things, for Thou art good and the Lover of mankind.]

[They bow to the chorus, and go into the sanctuary:]

Both: I shall go into Thy house; I shall worship toward Thy holy temple in fear of Thee. O Lord, guide me in the way of Thy righteousness; because of mine enemies, make straight my way before Thee. For in their mouth there is no truth; their heart is vain. Their throat is an open sepulchre, with their tongues have they spoken deceitfully; judge them, O God. Let them fall down on account of their own devisings; according to the multitude of their ungodliness, cast them out, for they have embittered Thee, O Lord. And let all them be glad that hope in Thee; they shall ever rejoice, and Thou shalt dwell among them. And all shall glory in Thee that love Thy name, for Thou shalt bless the righteous, O Lord, as with a shield of Thy good pleasure hast Thou crowned us.

[Three bows before the Holy Table and kiss the Holy Gospel and the Holy Table.
Each kisseth the cross thereon as he putteth on his vestments.
Then each taketh his sticharion in his hands, and reverence thrice toward the east, whilst, to each other:]

Both: O God, cleanse me a sinner and have mercy on me.

[Deacon cometh to the priest, holding in his right hand the sticharion with the orarion, and bowing his head:]

Deacon: Bless, Master, the sticharion with the orarion.

Priest: Blessed is our God always, now and ever, and unto the ages of ages.

[Deacon kisses Priests hand, goeth to one side of the sanctuary, putteth on the sticharion, praying thus:]

Deacon: My soul shall rejoice in the Lord, for He hath clothed me in the garment of salvation, and with the vesture of gladness hath He covered me; He hath placed a crown upon me as on a bridegroom, and He hath adorned me as a bride with comeliness.

[Kissing the orarion, he placeth it on the left shoulder. Putting the epimanikia on the hands, with the right cuff:]

Deacon: Thy right hand, O Lord, is glorified in strength; Thy right hand, O Lord, hath shattered enemies, and in the multitude of Thy glory hast Thou ground down the adversaries.

[With the left:]

Deacon: Thy hands have made me and fashioned me; give me understanding and I shall learn Thy commandments.

[Going to the prothesis Deacon prepareth the holy things. The holy diskos he placeth on the left side; the chalice on the right; and the rest [the spoon and spear, etc.] with them.]

[Priest takes the sticharion in the left hand, and bowing thrice toward the east, he signeth it with the Cross:]

Priest: Blessed is our God, always, now and ever, and unto the ages of ages. Amen.

[Then he vesteth himself:]

Priest: My soul shall rejoice in the Lord, for He hath clothed me in the garment of salvation, and with the vesture of gladness hath He covered me; He hath placed a crown upon me as on a bridegroom, and He hath adorned me as a bride with comeliness.

[Taking the epitrachelion and signing it, he putteth it on:]

Priest: Blessed is God Who poureth out His grace upon His priests, like unto the oil of myrrh upon the head, which runneth down upon the beard, upon the beard of Aaron, which runneth down to the fringe of his raiment.

[Taking the zoen and girding himself:]

Priest: Blessed is God, Who girded me with power, and hath made my path blameless, Who maketh my feet like the feet of a hart, and setteth me upon high places.

[Putting the epimanikia on the hands, with the right cuff:]

Priest: Thy right hand, O Lord, is glorified in strength; Thy right hand, O Lord, hath shattered enemies, and in the multitude of Thy glory hast Thou ground down the adversaries.

[With the left:]

Priest: Thy hands have made me and fashioned me; give me understanding and I shall learn Thy commandments.

[Taking the epigonation, if he have it, and having blessed and kissed it:]

Priest: Gird Thy sword upon Thy thigh, O Mighty One, in Thy comeliness and Thy beauty, and bend Thy bow, and proceed prosperously, and be king, because of truth and meekness and righteousness, and Thy right hand shall guide Thee wondrously, always now and ever, and unto the ages of ages. Amen.

[Taking the Phelonion, and having blessed and kissed it:]

Priest: Thy Priests, O Lord, shall be clothed with righteousness, and Thy saints with rejoicing shall rejoice, always, now and ever, and unto the ages of ages. Amen.

[He goes to the prothesis; they wash their hands:]

Both: I shall wash my hands in innocency and I shall compass Thine altar, O Lord, that I may hear the voice of Thy praise and tell of all Thy wondrous works. O Lord, I have loved the beauty of Thy house, and the place where Thy glory dwelleth. Destroy not my soul with the ungodly, nor my life with men of blood, in whose hands are iniquities; their right hand is full of bribes. But as for me, in mine innocence have I walked; redeem me, O Lord, and have mercy on me. My foot hath stood in uprightness; in the congregations shall I bless Thee, O Lord.

[Making three reverences before the table of oblation:]

Both: O God, cleanse me a sinner and have mercy on me.

Thou hast redeemed us from the curse of the law by Thy precious Blood. Having been nailed to the Cross and pierced with a spear, Thou hast poured forth immortality upon mankind. O our Saviour, glory to Thee.

Deacon: Bless, Master.

Priest: Blessed is our God, always, now and ever, and unto the ages of ages.

Deacon: Amen.

[Priest taketh a prosphoron in his left hand, and in his right hand the holy spear, and making therewith the sign of the Cross thrice over the seal of the prosphoron:]

Priest: In remembrance of our Lord and God and Saviour, Jesus Christ. **(x3)**

[He thrusteth the spear into the right side of the seal and cuts:]

Priest: He was led as a sheep to the slaughter.

[Deacon holding also his orarion in his hand and reverently gazes at the Mystery.]

[And into the left side:]

Priest: And as a blameless lamb before his shearer is dumb, so He openeth not His mouth.

[Into the upper side of the seal:]

Priest: In His lowliness His judgment was taken away.

[Into the lower side:]

Priest: And who shall declare His generation?

Deacon: Take away, Master.

[Priest thrusts the holy spear obliquely into the right side of the prosphoron, then taketh away the holy bread:]

Priest: For His life is taken away from the earth.

[Priest lays it inverted on the holy diskos.]

Deacon: Sacrifice Master.

[Priest sacrificeth it cruciformly:]

Priest: Sacrificed is the Lamb of God, that taketh away the sin of the world, for the life and salvation of the world.

[Priest turneth upward the other side, which hath the sign of the Cross:]

Deacon: Pierce, Master.

[Priest pierces also in the right side with the spear:]

Priest: One of the soldiers with a spear pierced His side, and forthwith came there out blood and water. And he that saw it bare record, and his record is true.

[Deacon takes wine and water:]

Deacon: Bless, Master, the holy union.

[Priest blesseth it, saying:]

Priest: Blessed is the union of Thy Holy Ones, always, now, and ever, and unto the ages of ages. Amen.

[Priest poureth wine together with water into the holy chalice. Taking in his hand a second prosphoron:]

Priest: In Honour and remembrance of our most blessed Lady, the Theotokos and Ever Virgin Mary, through whose intercessions do Thou, O Lord, receive this sacrifice upon Thy most heavenly altar.

[Priest taketh out a particle, he placeth it on the right side of the Holy Bread, near its center:]

Priest: At Thy right hand stood the queen, arrayed in a vesture of inwoven gold, adorned in varied colours.

[Taking the third prosphoron:]

Priest: Of the honourable glorious Prophet, Forerunner and Baptist John.

[Taking the first particle, he placeth it on the left side of the holy bread, making the beginning of the first row:]

Priest: Of the holy glorious prophets: Moses and Aaron, Elijah and Elisha, David and Jesse; of the Holy Three Children, of Daniel the Prophet, and of all the holy prophets.

[Taking a particle, he placeth it below the first, in the proper order:]

Priest: Of the holy glorious and all praised Apostles Peter and Paul, and of all the other holy apostles.

[He placeth the third particle below the second, completing the first row:]

Priest: Of our fathers among the saints, the holy hierarchs: Basil the Great, Gregory the Theologian, and John Chrysostom; Athanasius and Cyril of Alexandria; Nicholas of Myra in Lycia; Michael of Kiev; Peter, Alexis, Jonah, Philip, Hermogenes, and Tikhon of Moscow; Nicetas of Novgorod; Leontius of Rostov, and of all the holy hierarchs.

[Taking a fourth particle, he placeth it near the first particle, making the beginning of the second row:]

Priest: Of the holy Apostle, Protomartyr and Archdeacon Stephen; the holy Great martyrs Demetrius, George, Theodore the Tyro, Theodore Stratelates, and of all the holy martyrs; and of the martyred women: Thecla, Barbara, Cyriaca, Euphemia and Paraskeve, Catherine, and of all the holy martyred women.

[Taking a fifth particle, he placeth it below the first which is at the beginning of the second row:]

Priest: Of our holy and God bearing fathers: Anthony, Euthymius, Sabbas, Onuphrius, Athanasius of Athos, Anthony and Theodosius of the Caves, Sergius of Radonezh, Barlaam of Hutyn, and of all the holy fathers; and of the holy mothers: Pelagia, Theodosia, Anastasia, Eupraxia, Febronia, Theodula, Euphrosyne, Mary of Egypt, and of all the holy mothers.

[Taking out a sixth particle, he placeth it below the second particle, in completion of the second row:]

Priest: Of the saints and wonder workers, the Unmercenaries: Cosmas and Damian, Cyrus and John, Panteleimon and Hermolaus, and of all the holy Unmercenaries.

[Taking out a seventh particle, he placeth it at the top, making the beginning of the third row:]

Priest: Of the holy and righteous Ancestors of God, Joachim and Anna; of Saint(s) *N. (N.)*, whose temple *it is and whose day it is;* of the holy Equals-of–the-apostles Methodius and Cyril, teachers of the Slavs; of the holy Equal of the Apostles Grand Prince Vladimir, and all the saints, through whose intercessions do Thou visit us, O God.

[He placeth the eighth particle below the first, in the proper order:

If the liturgy be of John Chrysostom:]

    Priest: Of our father among the saints John Chrysostom, Archbishop of Constantinople.

[If the liturgy be of Basil the Great:]

    Priest: Of our father among the saints, Basil the Great, archbishop of Caesarea in Cappadocia.

[Taking out a ninth particle, he placeth it at the end of the third row, completing it.

Then taking a fourth prosphoron:]

Priest: Remember, O Master, Lover of mankind, the Most Holy Orthodox Patriarchs, our Great Lord and Father, His Holiness, Patriarch <u>Bartholomew</u>; our lord the Very Most Reverend Archbishop <u>Nikitas</u> whose diocese it is; the honourable priesthood, the deaconate in Christ and all the priestly order, *(if in a monastery:* Archimandrite *or* Abbot *N.)* and all our brethren whom in Thy compassion, Thou has called into Thy communion, O All good Master.

[Taking out a particle, he placeth it below the holy bread. He commemorateth those that are in authority:]

Priest: Remember, O Lord, those who are in authority, and the armed forces.

[Commemorating those that are living, by name, and at each name he taketh out a particle:]

Priest: Remember, O Lord, *N.*

[Taking out a particle he placeth it below the holy bread. Taking a fifth prosphoron:]

Priest: In commemoration and for the remission of sins of the most holy patriarchs; of Orthodox and pious kings and pious queens; and of the blessed founders of this holy temple *(if it be a monastery:* this holy monastery).

[Commemorating the departed, by name: the bishop that ordained him (if he be among the departed), and others, whomsoever he will. At each name he taketh out a particle:]

Priest: Remember, O Lord, *N.*

          And of all our Orthodox fathers and brethren who have departed in the hope of resurrection, life eternal, and communion with Thee, O Lord, Lover of mankind.

[He taketh out another particle:]

Priest: Remember, O Lord, also mine unworthiness, and pardon me every transgression, both voluntary and involuntary.

[He taketh out a particle and the sponge. He gathereth the particles together on the diskos below the holy bread, so that they be secure, and none of them fall off.]

[Deacon takes the censer and having placed incense therein:]

Deacon: Bless the censer, Master. Let us pray to the Lord.

Prayer Of The Censer

Priest: Incense do we offer unto Thee, O Christ our God, as an odour of spiritual fragrance; accepting it upon Thy most heavenly altar, do Thou send down upon us the grace of Thy Most Holy Spirit.

Deacon: Let us pray to the Lord.

[Priest, having censed the star cover, placeth it over the holy bread:]

Priest: And the star came and stood over where the young Child was.

Deacon: Let us pray to the Lord.

[Priest, having censed the first veil, covereth the holy bread and the diskos:]

Priest: The Lord is King, He is clothed with majesty; the Lord is clothed with strength and He hath girt Himself. For He established the world which shall not be shaken. Thy throne is prepared of old; Thou art from everlasting. The rivers have lifted up, O Lord, the rivers have lifted up their voices. The rivers shall lift up their waves, at the voices of many waters. Wonderful are the surgings of the sea, wonderful on high is the Lord. Thy testimonies are made very sure. Holiness becometh Thy house, O Lord, unto length of days.

Deacon: Let us pray to the Lord. Cover Master.

[Priest, having censed the second veil, covereth the holy chalice:]

Priest: Thy virtue hath covered the heavens, O Christ, and the earth is full of Thy praise.

Deacon: Let us pray to the Lord. Cover Master.

[Priest, having censed the aer, covereth both the holy diskos and the holy chalice:]

Priest: Shelter us with the shelter of Thy wings, and drive away from us every enemy and adversary. Make our life peaceful, O Lord, have mercy on us, and on Thy world, and save our souls, for Thou art good and the Lover of mankind.

[Taking the censer, the priest censeth the prothesis:]

Priest: Blessed is our God Who is thus well pleased, glory to Thee. **(x3)**

Deacon: Always now and forever, and unto the ages of ages. Amen.

Both: *[Bow.]* **(x3)**

[Taking the censer:]

Deacon: For the precious gifts offered, let us pray to the Lord.

Prayer Of Oblation

Priest: O God, our God, Who didst send forth the Heavenly Bread, the food of the whole world, our Lord and God, Jesus Christ, the Saviour and Redeemer and Benefactor Who blesseth and sanctifieth us: Do Thou Thyself bless this offering, and accept it upon Thy most heavenly altar. As Thou art good and the Lover of mankind, remember those that offer it, and those for whose sake it was offered; and keep us uncondemned in the ministry of Thy Divine Mysteries. For hallowed and glorified is Thy most honourable and majestic Name, of the Father, and of the Son, and of the Holy Spirit, now and ever, and unto the ages of ages. Amen.

Dismissal

Priest: Glory to Thee, O Christ God, our hope, glory to Thee.

Deacon: *Glory be to the Father, and to the Son, and to the Holy Spirit;*

Both now and forever, and unto the ages of ages. Amen.

Lord, have mercy. **(x3)**

Holy Father, Bless.

Priest: May Christ our true God, [*Sundays:* Who rose from the dead] through the intercessions of His most pure Mother; of our father among the saints

[*if the Liturgy of St John:*] John Chrysostom, Archbishop of Constantinople;

[*if the Liturgy of St Basil:*] Basil the Great, Archbishop of Caesarea in Cappadocia;

and of all the saints, have mercy on us and save us, for He is good and the Lover of mankind.

Deacon: Amen.

[Deacon censeth the holy offerings then the Holy Table round about cruciformly:]

Deacon: *[soto voce]* In the grave bodily, but in hades with Thy soul as God; in paradise with the thief, and on the throne with the Father and the Spirit wast Thou Who fillest all things, O Christ the inexpressible.

[Deacon censes the sanctuary and the whole temple, he entereth again into the holy altar, and having again censed the Holy Table, and the Priest. Whilst:]

Psalm 50

Deacon: Have mercy on me, O God, according to Thy great mercy; and according to the multitude of Thy compassions blot out my transgression. Wash me thoroughly from mine iniquity, and cleanse me from my sin. For I acknowledge mine iniquity, and my sin is ever before me. Against Thee, Thee only have I sinned, and done evil in Thy sight, that Thou mayest be found just when Thou speakest, and victorious when Thou art judged. For behold, I was conceived in iniquity, and in sin my mother bore me. For behold, Thou hast loved truth; Thou hast made known to me the hidden and secret things of Thy wisdom. Thou shalt sprinkle me with hyssop, and I shall be made clean; Thou shalt wash me, and I shall be whiter than snow. Make me to hear joy and gladness; that the humbled bones may rejoice. Turn Thy face away from my sins, and blot out all mine iniquities.

Create in me a clean heart, O God, and renew a steadfast spirit within me. Cast me not away from Thy presence, and take not Thy Holy Spirit from me. Restore to me the joy of Thy salvation, and establish me with Thy governing Spirit. I shall teach transgressors Thy ways, and the ungodly shall turn back to Thee. Deliver me from blood guiltiness, O God, the God of my salvation; my tongue shall joyfully declare Thy righteousness. Lord, open my lips, and my mouth shall declare Thy praise. For if Thou hadst desired sacrifice, I would give it; Thou dost not delight in burnt offerings. A sacrifice to God is a broken spirit; God shall not despise a broken and a humbled heart. Do good, O Lord, in Thy good pleasure to Zion, and let the walls of Jerusalem be builded. Then Thou shalt be pleased with a sacrifice of righteousness, with oblation and whole burned offerings. Then shall they offer bulls on Thine altar.

[Deacon putteth aside the censer in its place, and approacheth the priest.
Standing together before the Holy Table, they bow down thrice. Whilst:]

Both: *[soto voce]* O Heavenly King, Comforter, Spirit of Truth, Who art everywhere present and fillest all things, Treasury of good things and Giver of life: Come and dwell in us, and cleanse us of all impurity, and save our souls, O Good One.

Glory to God in the highest, and on earth peace, good will among men. **(x3)**
O Lord, Thou shalt open my lips, and my mouth shall declare Thy praise. **(x2)**

[Priest kisseth the Holy Gospel, and the deacon the Holy Table.
Deacon bows his head to the priest, and holding his orarion with three fingers of his right hand:]

Deacon: It is time for the Lord to act. Master, bless.

[Priest, signs Deacon with the Cross:]

Priest: Blessed is our God, always, now and ever, and unto the ages of ages.

Deacon: Amen. Pray for me, Master.

Priest: May the Lord direct thy steps.

Deacon: Remember me, holy Master.

Priest: May the Lord God remember thee in His kingdom always now and ever and unto the ages of ages.

Deacon: Amen.

[Deacon bows, kisseth Priests hand and Holy Table and goeth out by the north door, because the Holy Doors are not opened until the Entry.

Standing in the usual place, directly before the holy doors, he boweth reverently, thrice.]

Deacon: *[soto voce]* O Lord, Thou shalt open my lips, and my mouth shall declare Thy praise.

[aloud] Holy Father, bless.

[Priest beginneth the Liturgy:]

Priest: Blessed is the kingdom….

Canon Of Preparation For Holy Communion

With A Priest

Reader: Holy Father, bless.

Priest: Blessed be the kingdom of the Father and of the Son and of the Holy Spirit;

Both now and unto the ages of ages.

People: Amen.

Without A Priest

Reader: In the Name of the Father and of the Son and of the Holy Spirit. Amen.

Glory to Thee, our God, glory to Thee.

From Pascha To Ascension (40 days)

All: Christ is risen from the dead, trampling down death by death,

and upon those in the tombs bestowing life.

Russian Kristos voss kreysyey iz myert vikh. Smyertee oh smyert poh prav.

Ee sooshim vogrow byekh zhivawt darowvav.

Greek Χριστὸς ἀνέστη ἐκ νεκρῶν, θανάτῳ θάνατον πατήσας,

καὶ τοῖς ἐν τοῖς μνήμασι, ζωὴν χαρισάμενος.

If not Pascha

O Heavenly King, the Comforter, the Spirit of Truth; who art everywhere present and fillest all things; Treasury of blessings, and giver of life: come and abide in us, and cleanse us from every impurity, and save our souls, O Good One.

The Trisagion Prayers

Holy God, Holy Mighty, Holy Immortal, have mercy on us. **(x3)**

Glory be to the Father, and to the Son, and to the Holy Spirit;
Both now and forever, and unto the ages of ages. Amen.

O Most Holy Trinity, have mercy on us.

O Lord, cleanse us from our sins.

O Master, pardon our iniquities.

O Holy One, visit and heal our infirmities, for Thy names sake.

Lord have mercy. **(x3)**

Glory be to the Father, and to the Son, and to the Holy Spirit;
Both now and forever, and unto the ages of ages. Amen.

People: *Our Father, who art in heaven, hallowed be Thy name. Thy Kingdom come. Thy will be done, on earth as it is in heaven. Give us this day our daily bread; and forgive us our trespasses, as we forgive those who trespass against us; and lead us not into temptation, but deliver us from the evil one.*

Priest: For Thine is the kingdom, the power, and the glory, of the Father, and the Son and the Holy Spirit, both now and forever, and to the ages of ages.

People: *Amen.*

Lord have mercy. **(x12)**

O come let us worship God our King.

O come let us worship and fall down before Christ, our King and God.

O come let us worship and fall down before Christ Himself, our King and our God.

Psalm 22

The Lord is my shepherd; I shall not want. He maketh me to lie down in green pastures: He leadeth me beside the still waters. He restoreth my soul: He leadeth me in the paths of righteousness for His names sake. Yea, though I walk through the valley of the shadow of death, I shall fear no evil: for Thou art with me; Thy rod and thy staff they comfort me. Thou preparest a table before me in the presence of mine enemies: Thou anointest my head with oil; my cup runneth over. Surely goodness and mercy shall follow me all the days of my life: and I shall dwell in the house of the Lord for ever.

Psalm 23

The earth is the Lords and all that is in it, the world and all who dwell in it. He has set it on the seas, and prepared it on the rivers. Who shall ascend the mountain of the Lord, or who shall stand in His holy place? He who has clean hands and a pure heart, who has not set his mind on vanity or deceitfully sworn to his neighbour. He shall receive a blessing from the Lord, and mercy from God his Saviour. These are the kind who seek the Lord, who seek the face of the God of Jacob. Lift up your gates, you princes, and be lifted up, you eternal doors, and the King of Glory shall enter in. Who is this King of Glory? The Lord strong and mighty, the Lord mighty in battle. Lift up your gates, you princes, and be lifted up, you eternal doors, and the King of Glory shall enter in. Who is this King of Glory? The Lord of Hosts; He is the King of Glory.

Psalm 115

I believed and so I spoke; but I was deeply humiliated. I said in my madness: *"Every man is a liar."* What shall I give in return to the Lord for all that He has given me? I shall receive the cup of salvation and call on the Name of the Lord. I shall pay my vows to the Lord in the presence of all His people. Precious in the sight of the Lord is the death of His Saints.

O Lord, I am Thy slave; I am Thy slave and son of Thy handmaiden. Thou hast broken my bonds asunder. I shall offer Thee the sacrifice of praise, and shall pray in the Name of the Lord. I shall pay my vows to the Lord in the presence of all His people, in the courts of the Lords house, in the midst of thee, O Jerusalem.

After The Psalm

Glory be to the Father, and to the Son, and to the Holy Spirit;

Both now and forever, and unto the ages of ages. Amen.

Halleluiah, Halleluiah, Halleluiah. Glory to Thee, O God. **(x3)**

Lord, have mercy. **(x3)**

Ode 1

Eirmos From Psalm 50

Tone 2   Majesty, gentleness, hope, repentance and sadness.   E, F, G, Ab, B, C.

Come, O you people, let us sing a song to Christ our God, Who divided the sea, and made a way for the nation which He had brought up out of the bondage of Egypt; for He is glorious.

Chorus: *Create in me a clean heart, O God, and renew a right spirit within me.*

Troparia

May Thy holy Body be for me the bread of eternal life, O gracious Lord, and may Thy precious Blood be a remedy for my many forms of sickness.

Chorus: *Cast me not away from Thy Face, and take not Thy Holy Spirit from me.*

Defiled by misguided deeds, wretched as I am, I am unworthy, O Christ, to partake of Thine immaculate Body and divine Blood, but make me worthy of them.

Chorus: *Glory be to the Father, and to the Son, and to the Holy Spirit;*

              Both now and forever, and unto the ages of ages. Amen.

Theotokion

O blessed Bride of God, O good land which produced the unploughed Corn which saves the world, grant that I may be saved by eating it.

Ode 3

Eirmos

By establishing me on the rock of faith, Thou hast given me power over mine enemies, and my spirit rejoices when I sing: There is none holy as our God, and none good but Thee, O Lord.

Chorus: *Create in me a clean heart, O God, and renew a right spirit within me.*

Troparia

Grant me, O Christ, tear drops to cleanse the dross from my heart, that, purified and with a good conscience, I may come with fear and faith, O Lord, to the communion of Thy divine gifts.

Chorus: *Cast me not away from Thy Face, and take not Thy Holy Spirit from me.*

May Thine immaculate Body and divine Blood be for the forgiveness of my transgressions, for communion with the Holy Spirit and for Eternal Life, O Lover of men, and for estrangement from passions and sorrows.

Chorus: *Glory be to the Father, and to the Son, and to the Holy Spirit;*

Both now and forever, and unto the ages of ages. Amen.

Theotokion

O all holy Lady, Altar of the Bread of Life, which for mercys sake came down from on high and gave new life to the world, make even me, who am unworthy, worthy now with fear to eat it and live.

Ode 4

Eirmos

From a Virgin didst Thou come, not as an Ambassador, nor as an Angel, but the very Lord Himself incarnate, and didst save me, the whole man. Therefore I cry to Thee: Glory to Thy power, O Lord.

Chorus: *Create in me a clean heart, O God, and renew a right spirit within me.*

Troparia

O most merciful One. Who wast incarnate for us, Thou didst will to be slain as a Sheep for the sins of men; therefore I implore Thee to blot out my offences.

Chorus: *Cast me not away from Thy Face, and take not Thy Holy Spirit from me.*

Heal the wounds of my soul, O Lord, and wholly sanctify me, and make me worthy, O Lord, to partake of Thy divine mystical Supper, wretched as I am.

Chorus: *Glory be to the Father, and to the Son, and to the Holy Spirit;*

Both now and forever, and unto the ages of ages. Amen.

Theotokion

O Lady, intercede for me also, with Him Who came from thy womb, and keep me, thy slave, pure and blameless that I may be sanctified by obtaining the spiritual pearl.

Ode 5

Eirmos

Giver of light and Sovereign Creator of the worlds, guide us in the light of Thy commandments, for we know no other God than Thee.

Chorus: *Create in me a clean heart, O God, and renew a right spirit within me.*

Troparia

As Thou didst foretell, O Christ, let it be to Thy wicked servant. Abide in me as Thou didst promise; for lo, I am eating Thy divine Body and drinking Thy Blood.

Chorus: *Cast me not away from Thy Face, and take not Thy Holy Spirit from me.*

O Word of God, and God, may the live coal of Thy Body be for the enlightenment of me who am darkened, and may Thy Blood be the cleansing of my sinful soul.

Chorus: *Glory be to the Father, and to the Son, and to the Holy Spirit;*
            Both now and forever, and unto the ages of ages. Amen.

Theotokion

O Mary, Mother of God, holy tabernacle of the scent of Heaven, make me by Thy prayers, a chosen vessel, that I may partake of the Sacrament of thy Son.

Ode 6

Eirmos

Whirled about in the abyss of sin, I appeal to the unfathomable abyss of Thy compassion: Raise me up from corruption, O God.

Chorus: *Create in me a clean heart, O God, and renew a right spirit within me.*

Troparia

O Saviour, sanctify my mind, soul, heart and body, and grant me uncondemned, O Lord, to approach the fearful Mysteries.

Chorus: *Cast me not away from Thy Face, and take not Thy Holy Spirit from me.*

Grant estrangement from passions, and the assistance of Thy grace, and assurance of life by the communion of Thy Holy Mysteries, O Christ.

Chorus: *Glory be to the Father, and to the Son, and to the Holy Spirit;*
            Both now and forever, and unto the ages of ages. Amen.

Theotokion

O Holy Word of God and God, sanctify the whole of me as I now approach Thy divine Mysteries, by the prayers of Thy Holy Mother.

Chorus: *Lord, have mercy.* **(x3)**

Glory be to the Father, and to the Son, and to the Holy Spirit;

Both now and forever, and unto the ages of ages. Amen.

Kontakion

Disdain me not to receive now, O Christ, the Bread which is Thy Body and Thy divine Blood, and to partake, O Lord, of Thy most pure and dread Mysteries, wretched as I am, and may it not be to me for judgement, but for eternal and immortal life.

Ode 7

Eirmos

The wise children did not adore the golden idol, but went themselves into the flame and defied the pagan gods. They prayed in the midst of the flame, and an Angel bedewed them: The prayer of thy lips has been heard.

Chorus: *Create in me a clean heart, O God, and renew a right spirit within me.*

Troparia

May the communion of Thine immortal Mysteries, the source of all goodness, O Christ, be to me light and life and dispassion and the means of progress and proficiency in divine virtue, O only Good One, that I may glorify Thee.

Chorus: *Cast me not away from Thy Face, and take not Thy Holy Spirit from me.*

That I may be redeemed from passions, enemies, wants, and every sorrow, I now draw near with trembling, love and reverence, O Lover of men, to Thine immortal and divine Mysteries, singing to Thee: Blessed art Thou, O God of our fathers.

Chorus: *Glory be to the Father, and to the Son, and to the Holy Spirit;*

Both now and forever, and unto the ages of ages. Amen.

Theotokion

O thou who art full of Divine Grace and gavest birth incomprehensibly to the Saviour Christ, I thy servant, unclean as I am, now beseech thee, O pure one: Cleanse me who now wish to approach the immaculate Mysteries, from all defilement of body and spirit.

Ode 8

Eirmos

Sing of the acts of God Who descended into the fiery furnace with the Hebrew children, and changed the flame into dew, and exalt Him as Lord throughout all ages.

Chorus: *Create in me a clean heart, O God, and renew a right spirit within me.*

Troparia

Grant me, who am desperate, to be a participant now of Thy heavenly, dread and holy Mysteries, O Christ, and of Thy divine Mystical Supper, O my Saviour and God.

Chorus: *Cast me not away from Thy Face, and take not Thy Holy Spirit from me.*

I fly for refuge to Thy compassion, O Good One, and I cry to Thee with fear: Abide in me, O Saviour, and I in Thee as Thou saidst; for lo, confiding in Thy mercy, I eat Thy Body and drink Thy Blood.

Chorus: *Glory be to the Father, and to the Son, and to the Holy Spirit;*
  Both now and forever, and unto the ages of ages. Amen.

I tremble, taking fire, lest I should burn as wax and hay. O dread Mystery. O Divine Compassion. How can I who am clay partake of the divine Body and Blood and become incorruptible.

Ode 9

Eirmos: The Son of the Eternal Father, God and Lord, has appeared to us incarnate of a Virgin, to enlighten those in darkness, and to gather the dispersed; therefore the all hymned Mother of God we magnify.

Chorus: *Create in me a clean heart, O God, and renew a right spirit within me.*

Troparia

The Lord is good. O taste and see! For of old He became like us for us, and once offered Himself as a sacrifice to His Father and is perpetually slain, sanctifying communicants.

Chorus: *Cast me not away from Thy Face, and take not Thy Holy Spirit from me.*

May I be sanctified in body and soul, O Lord; may I be enlightened and saved; may I become by the communion of the Holy Mysteries Thy dwelling, having Thee with the Father and the Spirit living within me, O most merciful Benefactor.

Chorus: *Glory be to the Father, and to the Son, and to the Holy Spirit;*

May Thy most precious Body and Blood, my Saviour, be to me as fire and light, consuming the fuel of sin and burning the thorns of my passions, enlightening the whole of me to adore Thy Divinity.

Chorus: *Both now and forever, and unto the ages of ages. Amen.*

Theotokion

O Lady, God took flesh of thy pure blood. Therefore, all generations sing to thee, and throngs of heavenly minds glorify thee. For through thee we have clearly seen Him Who is Lord of all united essentially with mankind.

Preparatory Prayers For Holy Communion

Troparion

Overlook my faults, O Lord Who wast born of a Virgin, and purify my heart, and make it a temple for Thy spotless Body and Blood. Let me not be rejected from Thy presence, O Thou, Who hast infinitely great mercy.

Chorus: *Glory be to the Father, and to the Son, and to the Holy Spirit;*

How can I who am unworthy dare to come to the communion of Thy Holy Things? For even if I should dare to approach Thee with those who are worthy, my garment betrays me, for it is not a festal robe, and I shall cause the condemnation of my sinful soul. Cleanse, O Lord, the pollution from my soul, and save me, as the Lover of men.

Chorus: *Both now and forever, and unto the ages of ages. Amen.*

Great is the multitude of my sins, O Mother of God. To thee, O pure one, I flee and implore salvation. Visit my sick and feeble soul and intercede with Thy Son and our God, that He may grant me forgiveness for the terrible things I have done, O thou who alone art blessed.

[During Lent:]

When Thy glorious Disciples were enlightened at the Supper by the feet washing, then impious Judas was darkened with the disease of avarice, and he delivered Thee, the Just Judge, to lawless judges. See O lover of money, this man, through money came to hang himself. Flee the insatiable desire which dared to do such things to the Master. O Lord, Who art good towards all, glory to Thee.

Lord, have mercy. **(x40)**

First Prayer Of St Basil The Great

O Sovereign Lord Jesus Christ our God, source of life and immortality, Who art the Author of all creation, visible and invisible, the equally everlasting and co-eternal Son of the eternal Father. Who, through the excess of Thy goodness, didst in those days assume our flesh and wast crucified for us, ungrateful and ignorant as we were, and didst cause through Thine own Blood the restoration of our nature that had been marred by sin. O immortal King, accept the repentance even of me a sinner, and incline Thine ear to me and hear my words. For I have sinned, O Lord, I have sinned against heaven and before Thee, and I am not worthy to gaze on the height of Thy glory; for I have provoked Thy goodness by transgressing Thy commandments and not obeying Thine orders. But Thou, O Lord, in Thy forbearance, patience, and great mercy, hast not given me up to be destroyed with my sins; but Thou awaitest my complete conversion. For Thou, O Lover of men, hast said through Thy Prophet that Thou desirest not the death of the sinner, but that he should return to Thee and live. For Thou dost not will, O Lord, that the work of Thy hands should be destroyed, neither dost Thou delight in the destruction of men, but Thou desirest that all should be saved and come to a knowledge of the Truth. Therefore, though I am unworthy both of heaven and earth, and even of this transient life, since I have completely succumbed to sin and am a slave to pleasure and have defaced Thine image, yet being Thy work and creation, wretch that I am, even I do not despair of my salvation and dare to draw near to Thy boundless compassion.

So receive even me, O Christ Lover of men, as the harlot, as the thief, as the publican, and as the prodigal; and take from me the heavy burden of my sins, Thou Who takest away the sin of the world, Who healest mens sicknesses, Who callest the weary and heavy laden to Thyself and givest them rest; for Thou camest not to call the righteous but sinners to repentance. And purify me from all defilement of flesh and spirit. Teach me to achieve perfect holiness in the fear of Thee, that with the clear witness of my conscience I may receive the portion of Thy holy Things and be united with Thy holy Body and Blood, and have Thee dwelling and remaining in me with the Father and Thy Holy Spirit.

And, O Lord Jesus Christ, my God, let not the communion of Thine immaculate and life giving Mysteries be to me for condemnation nor let it make me sick in body or soul through my unworthily partaking of them; but grant me till my last breath to receive without condemnation the portion of Thy holy Things, for communion with the Holy Spirit, as a provision for eternal life, and as an acceptable defence at Thy dread tribunal, so that I too with all Thine elect may become a partaker of Thy pure joys which Thou hast prepared for those who love Thee, O Lord; in whom Thou art glorified throughout the ages. Amen.

First Prayer Of St John Chrysostom

O Lord my God, I know that I am not worthy or sufficient that Thou shouldest come under the roof of the house of my soul, for all is desolate and fallen, and Thou hast not with me a place fit to lay Thy head. But as from the highest heaven Thou didst humble Thyself for our sake, so now conform Thyself to my humility. And as Thou didst consent to lie in a cave and in a manger of dumb beasts, so also consent to lie in the manger of my unspiritual soul and to enter my defiled body. And as Thou didst not disdain to enter and dine with sinners in the house of Simon the Leper, so consent also to enter the house of my humble soul which is leprous and sinful. And as Thou didst not reject the woman, who was a harlot and a sinner like me, when she approached and touched Thee, so also be compassionate with me, a sinner, as I approach and touch Thee, and let the live coal of Thy most holy Body and precious Blood be for the sanctification and enlightenment and strengthening of my humble soul and body, for a relief from the burden of my many sins, for a protection from all diabolical practices, for a restraint and a check on my evil and wicked way of life, for the mortification of passions, for the keeping of Thy commandments, for an increase of Thy divine grace, and for the advancement of Thy Kingdom. For it is not insolently that I draw near to Thee, O Christ my God, but as taking courage from Thine unutterable goodness, and that I may not by long abstaining from Thy communion become a prey to the spiritual wolf.

Therefore, I pray Thee, O Lord, Who alone art holy, sanctify my soul and body, my mind and heart, my emotions and affections, and wholly renew me. Root the fear of Thee in my members, and make Thy sanctification indelible in me. Be also my helper and defender, guide my life in peace, and make me worthy to stand at Thy right hand with Thy Saints: through the prayers and intercessions of Thine immaculate Mother, of Thy ministering Angels, of the immaculate Powers and of all the Saints who have ever been pleasing to Thee. Amen.

Prayer Of St Symeon The Translator

O only pure and sinless Lord, Who through the ineffable compassion of Thy love for men didst assume our whole nature through the pure and virgin blood of her who supernaturally conceived Thee by the coming of the Divine Spirit and by the will of the Eternal Father. O Christ Jesus, Wisdom and Peace and Power of God, Who in Thine assumption of our nature didst suffer Thy life giving and saving Passion, the Cross, the Nails, the Spear, and Death, mortify all the deadly passions of my body. Thou Who in Thy burial didst spoil the dominions of hell, bury with good thoughts my evil schemes and scatter the spirits of wickedness. Thou Who by Thy life giving Resurrection on the third day didst raise up our fallen first Parent, raise me up who am sunk in sin and suggest to me ways of repentance. Thou Who by Thy glorious Ascension didst deify our nature which Thou hadst assumed and didst honour it by Thy session at the right hand of the Father, make me worthy by partaking of Thy holy Mysteries of a place at Thy right hand amongst those who are saved. Thou Who by the descent of the Spirit, the Paraclete, didst make Thy holy Disciples worthy vessels, make me also a recipient of His coming. Thou Who art to come again to judge the World with justice, grant me also to meet Thee on the clouds, my Maker and Creator, with all Thy Saints, that I may unendingly glorify and praise Thee with Thine Eternal Father and Thine all holy and good and life creating Spirit, both now and for ever, and unto the ages of ages. Amen.

First Prayer Of St John Damascene

O Sovereign Lord Jesus Christ our God, Who alone hast authority to forgive men their sins, overlook in Thy goodness and love for men all mine offences whether committed with knowledge or in ignorance, and make me worthy to receive without condemnation Thy divine, glorious, spotless, and life giving Mysteries, not for punishment, nor for an increase of sins, but for purification and sanctification and as a pledge of the life and kingdom to come, as a protection and help, and for the destruction of enemies, and for the blotting out of my many transgressions. For Thou art a God of mercy and compassion and love for men, and to Thee we send up the glory, with the Father and the Holy Spirit, both now and forever, and unto the ages of ages. Amen.

Second Prayer Of St Basil The Great

I know, O Lord, that I partake of Thine immaculate Body and precious Blood unworthily, and that I am guilty, and eat and drink judgement to myself by not discerning the Body and Blood of Thee my Christ and God. But taking courage from Thy compassion I approach Thee, for Thou hast said: "He who eats My Flesh and drinks My Blood abides in Me and I in him." Therefore have compassion, O Lord, and do not make an example of me, a sinner, but deal with me according to Thy mercy; and let these Holy Things be for my healing and purification and enlightenment and protection and salvation and sanctification of body and soul, for the turning away of every fantasy and all evil practice and diabolical activity subconsciously working in my members, for confidence and love towards Thee, for reformation of life and security, for an increase of virtue and perfection, for fulfilment of the commandments, for communion with the Holy Spirit, as a provision for eternal life, and as an acceptable defence at Thy dread Tribunal, not for judgement or for condemnation.

Prayer Of St Symeon The New Theologian

From sullied lips, from an abominable heart, from an unclean tongue, out of a polluted soul, receive my prayer, O my Christ. Reject me not, nor my words, nor my ways, nor even my shamelessness, but give me courage to say what I desire, my Christ. And even more, teach me what to do and say. I have sinned more than the harlot who, on learning where Thou wast lodging, bought myrrh, and dared to come and anoint Thy feet, my Christ, my Lord and my God. As Thou didst not repulse her when she drew near from her heart, neither, O Word, abominate me, but grant me Thy feet to clasp and kiss, and with a flood of tears as with most precious myrrh to dare to anoint them.

Wash me with my tears and purify me with them, O Word. Forgive my sins and grant me pardon. Thou knowest the multitude of my evil doings, thou knowest also my wounds, and Thou seest my bruises. But also Thou knowest my faith, and Thou beholdest my willingness, And Thou hearest my sighs. Nothing escapes Thee, my God, my Maker, my Redeemer, Not even a tear drop, nor part of a drop. Thine eyes know what I have not achieved, And in Thy book things not yet done are written by Thee. See my depression, see how great is my trouble, and all my sins take from me, O God of all, that with a clean heart, trembling mind and contrite spirit I may partake of Thy pure and all holy Mysteries by which all who eat and drink Thee with sincerity of heart are quickened and deified.

For Thou, my Lord, hast said: "Whoever eats My Flesh and drinks My Blood abides in Me and I in Him." Wholly true is the Word of my Lord and God. For whoever partakes of Thy divine and deifying Gifts certainly is not alone, But is with Thee, my Christ, Light of the Triune Sun that illumines the world. And that I may not remain alone without Thee, the Giver of Life, My Breath, my Life, My Joy, The Salvation of the world, Therefore I have drawn near to Thee as Thou seest, with tears and with a contrite spirit.

Ransom of my offences, I beseech Thee to receive me, and that I may partake without condemnation Of Thy life giving and perfect Mysteries, that Thou mayest remain as Thou hast said with me, thrice wretched as I am, lest the tempter may find me without Thy grace and craftily seize me, and having deceived me, may seduce me from Thy deifying words. Therefore I fall at Thy feet and fervently cry to Thee: as Thou receivedst the Prodigal and the Harlot who drew near to Thee, So have compassion and receive me, the profligate and the prodigal, as with contrite spirit I now draw near to Thee. I know, O Saviour, that no other has sinned against Thee as I, nor has done the deeds that I have committed. But this again I know that not the greatness of my offences nor the multitude of my sins surpasses the great patience of my God, and His extreme love for men. With the oil of compassion those who fervently repent Thou dost purify and enlighten and makest them children of the light, sharers of Thy Divine Nature. And Thou dost act most generously, for what is strange to angels and to the minds of men often Thou tellest to them as to Thy true friends. These things make me bold, my Christ, these things give me wings, and I take courage from the wealth of Thy goodness to us. Rejoicing and trembling at once, I who am straw partake of fire and, strange wonder, I am ineffably bedewed. Like the bush of old that burnt without being consumed.

Therefore with thankful mind, and with thankful heart, and with thankfulness in all the members of my soul and body, I worship and magnify and glorify Thee, my God, for Thou art blessed, both now and throughout the ages. Amen.

Second Prayer Of St John Chrysostom

I am not worthy, O Lord and Master, that Thou shouldest enter under the roof of my soul; but since Thou in Thy love for men dost will to dwell in me, I take courage and approach. Thou commandest: I shall open wide the doors which Thou alone didst create, that Thou mayest enter with love as is Thy nature, enter and enlighten my darkened thought. I believe that Thou wilt do this, for Thou didst not banish the Harlot who approached Thee with tears, nor didst Thou reject the Publican who repented, nor didst Thou drive away the Thief who acknowledged Thy Kingdom, nor didst Thou leave the repentant persecutor Paul to himself; but all who had been brought to Thee by repentance Thou didst set in the company of Thy friends, O Thou Who alone art blessed always; both now and to endless ages. Amen.

Third Prayer Of St John Chrysostom

Lord Jesus Christ my God, remit, forgive, absolve and pardon the sins, offences and transgressions which I, Thy sinful, useless and unworthy servant have committed from my youth, up to the present day and hour, whether with knowledge or in ignorance, whether by words or deeds or intentions or thoughts, and whether by habit or through any of my senses. And through the intercession of her who conceived Thee without seed, the immaculate and ever virgin Mary Thy Mother, my only sure hope and protection and salvation, make me worthy without condemnation to receive Thy pure, immortal, life giving and dread Mysteries, for forgiveness of sins and for eternal life, for sanctification and enlightenment and strength and healing and health of soul and body, and for the blotting out and complete destruction of my evil reasonings and intentions and prejudices and nocturnal fantasies of dark evil spirits. For Thine is the kingdom and the power and the glory and the honour and the worship, with the Father and the Holy Spirit; both now and forever, and to the ages of ages. Amen.

Second Prayer Of St John Damascene

I stand before the doors of Thy sanctuary, yet I do not put away my terrible thoughts. But O Christ our God, Who didst justify the Publican, and have mercy on the Canaanite woman, and didst open the gates of Paradise to the Thief, open to me the depths of Thy love for men, and as I approach and touch Thee, receive me like the Harlot and the woman with an issue of blood. For the one easily received healing by touching the hem of Thy garment, and the other by clasping Thy sacred feet obtained release from her sins. And I, in my pitiableness, dare to receive Thy whole Body. Let me not be burnt, but receive me even as these; enlighten the senses of my soul, and burn the stains of my sins: through the intercessions of her who bore Thee without seed, and of the Heavenly Powers, for Thou art blessed to the ages of ages. Amen.

Fourth Prayer Of St John Chrysostom

I believe, Lord, and I confess that Thou art truly the Christ, the Son of the living God, Who came into the world to save sinners, of whom I am first. Also I believe that this is indeed Thy most pure Body, and this indeed Thy precious Blood. Therefore I beseech Thee, have mercy on me and forgive me my offences, voluntary and involuntary, in word and in deed, in knowledge and in ignorance, and count me worthy to partake uncondemned of Thy most pure Mysteries for forgiveness of sins and for eternal life. Amen.

Lines Of St Symeon The Translator

See, to divine Communion I draw near; My Maker, burn me not as I partake. For Thou art fire consuming the unworthy; But therefore make me clean from every stain. Of Thy mystical supper, Son of God, receive me today as a communicant; for I shall not tell of the Mystery to Thine enemies; I shall not give Thee a kiss like Judas; but like the thief I confess Thee. Remember me, Lord, in Thy kingdom.

Tremble, O man, when thou seest the deifying Blood, For it is a coal that burns the unworthy. The Body of God both deifies and nourishes; It deifies the spirit and wondrously nourishes the mind.

Troparia

Thou hast ravished me with longing, O Christ, and with Thy divine love Thou hast changed me. But burn up with spiritual fire my sins and make me worthy to be filled with delight in Thee, that I may leap for joy, O gracious Lord, and magnify Thy two comings.

Into the splendour of Thy Saints how shall I who am unworthy enter? For if I dare to enter the bride chamber, my vesture betrays me, for it is not a wedding garment, and as a prisoner I shall be cast out by the Angels. Cleanse my soul from pollution and save me, O Lord, in Thy love for men.

Master, lover of mankind, Lord Jesus Christ, my God, let not these Holy Mysteries be for my condemnation because of my unworthiness, but rather for the cleansing and sanctification of both soul and body, and as a pledge of the life and kingdom to come. It is good for me to cleave to God, to place in the Lord the hope of my salvation.

Through the prayers of our holy Fathers, Lord Jesus Christ our God, have mercy upon us and save us.
All: Amen.

[When Priest draws back the Holy Curtains:]

Great Doxology

Glory to God, Who has shown us the Light. Glory to God in the highest, and on earth, peace, good will toward men. We praise Thee. We bless Thee. We worship Thee. We glorify Thee and give thanks to Thee for Thy great glory. O Lord God, Heavenly King, God the Father Almighty. O Lord, the Only Begotten Son, Jesus Christ, and the Holy Spirit. \

O Lord God, Lamb of God, Son of the Father, Who takes away the sins of the world, have mercy on us. Thou, Who takes away the sins of the world, receive our prayer. Thou, Who sittest at the right hand of God the Father, have mercy on us. /

For Thou alone art holy, and Thou alone art Lord. Thou alone, O Lord Jesus Christ, are most high in the glory of God the Father. Amen. I shall give thanks to Thee every day and praise Thy Name forever and ever, Lord. Every day shall I bless Thee and praise Thy name forever, and to the ages of ages. Amen. \

Vouchsafe, O Lord, to keep us this day without sin. Blessed art Thou, O Lord, the God of our fathers, and praised and glorified is Thy Name forever. Amen. Let Thy mercy be upon us, O Lord, even as we have set our hope on Thee.

Blessed art Thou, O Master; teach me Thy statutes.

Blessed art Thou, O Lord; enlighten me with Thy commandments.

Blessed art Thou, O Holy One; make me to understand Thy precepts.

Lord, Thou hast been our refuge from generation to generation. I said, *"Lord, have mercy on me. Heal my soul, for I have sinned against Thee."* \

Lord, I flee to Thee for refuge. Teach me to do Thy will, for Thou art my God. For with Thee is the fountain of Life, and in Thy light we shall see light. Continue Thy loving kindness to those who know Thee.

Holy God, Holy Strong, Holy Immortal, have mercy on us.

Holy God, Holy Strong, Holy Immortal, have mercy on us.

Holy God, Holy Strong, Holy Immortal, have mercy on us.

Glory be to the Father, and to the Son, and to the Holy Spirit;

Both now and forever, and unto the ages of ages. Amen.

Holy Immortal, have mercy on us.

Holy God, Holy Strong, Holy Immortal, have mercy on us.

Today salvation has come into the world. Let us sing to Him who rose from the tomb, the Author of our life. For, destroying death by death, he has given us the victory and His great mercy. \

The Divine Liturgy Of Saint John Chrysostom For The People

Deacon: Holy Father, Bless.

Priest: Blessed is the kingdom of the Father, and of the Son and of the Holy Spirit;

Both now and forever, and unto the ages of ages.

People: Amen.

The Litany of Peace

Deacon: In peace let us pray to the Lord.

People: Lord, have mercy.

Deacon: For the peace from above and the salvation of our souls, let us pray to the Lord.

People: Lord, have mercy.

Deacon: For the peace of the whole world, the welfare of the holy churches of God, and for the union of all, let us pray to the Lord.

People: Lord, have mercy.

Deacon: For this holy house, and for those who enter it with faith, reverence and the fear of God, let us pray to the Lord.

People: Lord, have mercy.

Deacon: For all devout and Orthodox Christians, let us pray to the Lord.

People: Lord, have mercy.

Deacon: For our Archbishop Nikitas, for the honoured order of presbyters, for the diaconate in Christ, for all the clergy and the people, let us pray to the Lord.

People: Lord, have mercy.

Deacon: For our Sovereign Lady, Queen Elizabeth, the Royal family, our Government, and all in authority, let us pray to the Lord.

People: Lord, have mercy.

Deacon: For this [city/town/village], and for every city, town and village, and for the faithful who dwell in them, let us pray to the Lord.

People: Lord, have mercy.

Deacon: For favourable weather, an abundance of the fruits of the earth and temperate seasons, let us pray to the Lord.

People: Lord, have mercy.

Deacon: For those who travel by land, air or water, for the sick, the suffering, for those in captivity, and for their safety and salvation, let us pray to the Lord.

People: Lord, have mercy.

Deacon: For our deliverance from all affliction, wrath, danger and constraint, let us pray to the Lord.

People: Lord, have mercy.

Deacon: Help us, save us, have mercy on us, and keep us, O God, by Thy grace.

People: Lord, have mercy.

Deacon: Commemorating our all holy, pure, most blessed and glorious Lady, Mother of God and Ever Virgin Mary, with all the Saints, let us entrust ourselves and one another, and our whole life to Christ our God.

People: *To Thee, O Lord.*

Priest: For to Thee belongs all glory, honour and worship, to the Father, the Son, and the Holy Spirit, both now and forever, and unto the ages of ages.

People: *Amen.*

The First Antiphon

[May change – follow the Reader.]

Reader: Bless the Lord, O my soul, and all that is within me bless His holy Name.

People: *At the prayers of the Mother of God, O Saviour, save us.*

Reader: Bless the Lord, O my soul, and forget not all His benefits.

People: *At the prayers of the Mother of God, O Saviour, save us.*

Reader: The Lord has prepared His throne in Heaven, and His kingdom rules over all.

People: *At the prayers of the Mother of God | O Saviour, save us.*

Short Litany

Deacon: Again and again, in peace let us pray to the Lord.

People: *Lord, have mercy.*

Deacon: Help us, save us, have mercy on us and keep us, O God, by Thy grace.

People: *Lord, have mercy.*

Deacon: Commemorating our all holy, pure, most blessed and glorious Lady, Mother of God and Ever Virgin Mary, with all the Saints, let us entrust ourselves and one another, and our whole life to Christ our God.

People: *To Thee, O Lord.*

Priest: For Thine is the might, and Thine the kingdom, the power and the glory, of the Father, the Son and the Holy Spirit, both now and forever, and unto the ages of ages.

People: *Amen.*

The Second Antiphon from Psalm 145

[May change – follow the Reader.]

Reader: Praise the Lord, O my soul; while I live I shall praise the Lord.

While I have any being I shall praise my God.

People: *Save us, O Son of God, risen from the dead. Save us who sing to Thee: Halleluiah.*

Reader: Blessed is he whose help is the God of Jacob, whose hope is in the Lord their God.

People: *Save us, O Son of God, risen from the dead. Save us who sing to Thee: Halleluiah.*

Reader: The Lord shall be king for ever; Thy God, O Zion, shall reign throughout all generations.

People: *Save us, O Son of God, risen from the dead. Save us who sing to Thee: Halleluiah.*

Reader: Glory to the Father and to the Son and to the Holy Spirit.

Chorus: Both now and ever, and unto the ages of ages. Amen.

Reader: Only begotten Son and Word of God, Who, being immortal, accepted for our salvation to take flesh from the Holy Mother of God and Ever Virgin Mary and without change became man. Thou wert crucified, Christ God, by death trampling on death, being one of the Holy Trinity, glorified with the Father and the Holy Spirit: Save us.

Short Litany

Deacon: Again and again, in peace let us pray to the Lord.

People: *Lord, have mercy.*

Deacon: Help us, save us, have mercy on us and keep us, O God, by Thy grace.

People: *Lord, have mercy.*

Deacon: Commemorating our all holy, pure, most blessed and glorious Lady, Mother of God and Ever Virgin Mary, with all the Saints, let us entrust ourselves and one another, and our whole life to Christ our God.

People: *To Thee, O Lord.*

Priest: For Thou, O God, art good and love mankind, and to Thee we give glory, to the Father, the Son and the Holy Spirit, both now and forever, and unto the ages of ages.

People: *Amen.*

The Third Antiphon – The Beatitudes

[may change – follow the Reader]

People:

In Thy Kingdom. Remember us, O Lord, when Thou comest in Thy Kingdom.

Blessed are the poor in spirit, for theirs is the Kingdom of Heaven.

Blessed are the mourners, for they shall be comforted.

Blessed are the meek, for they shall inherit the earth.

Blessed are those who hunger and thirst for righteousness, for they shall be satisfied.

Blessed are the merciful, for they shall obtain mercy.

Blessed are the pure in heart, for they shall see God.

Blessed are the peacemakers, for they shall be called the children of God.

Blessed are those who are persecuted for righteousness' sake, for theirs is the Kingdom of Heaven.

Blessed are you when men revile and persecute you and say all manner of evil against you falsely and on My account.

Rejoice and be exceeding glad, for great is thy reward in Heaven.

The Little Entrance

Deacon: *[soto voce]* Master, bless the Holy Entrance.

Priest: *[soto voce]* Blessed is the Entrance to Thy Holy place; Both now and forever, and unto the ages of ages.

Deacon: Wisdom, stand upright!

Reader: Come let us worship and bow down before Christ.

People: *Save us, O Son of God, risen from the dead. Save us who sing to Thee: Halleluiah.*

[Sit for the **Troparia** *and* **Kontakia***. This educational section is to help us to remember the saints.]*

Deacon: Let us pray to the Lord.

People: *Lord have mercy.*

Priest: For Thou, our God, art Holy, and to Thee we give glory, to the Father and to the Son and to the Holy Spirit, both now and forever ...

Deacon: .... And to the ages of ages.

People: *Amen.*

The Trisagion

People: Holy God, Holy Strong, Holy Immortal, have mercy on us. **(x3)**

Glory be to the Father, and to the Son, and to the Holy Spirit;

Both now and forever, and unto the ages of ages. Amen.

Holy Immortal, have mercy on us.

Deacon: Dynamis!

People: Holy God, Holy Strong, Holy Immortal, have mercy on us.

The Apostle

Deacon: Let us attend.

Priest: Peace be with you all.

People: *And with thy spirit.*

Deacon: Wisdom!

Reader: *[The Prokeimenon]*

Deacon: Wisdom!

Reader: The Reading is from the book of ...

Deacon: Let us attend.

Reader: *[Reads the Apostle.]*

Priest: Peace be to thee who readest.

Reader: And with thy spirit.

Halleluiarion

People: *Halleluiah, Halleluiah, Halleluiah.*

Reader: [Response of the week.]

People: *Halleluiah, Halleluiah, Halleluiah.*

Reader: [Response of the week.]

People: *Halleluiah, Halleluiah, Halleluiah.*

The Gospel

Deacon: *[soto voce]* Bless, Father, the reader of the Gospel of the holy Apostle and Evangelist N.

Priest: *[soto voce]* May God, through the intercessions of the holy and glorious Apostle and Evangelist, *N.*, grant thee to announce the glad tidings with great power, for the fulfilment of the Gospel of His beloved Son, our Lord Jesus Christ.

Deacon: Amen.

Priest: Wisdom, stand upright! Let us listen to the Holy Gospel. Peace be with you all.

People: *And with thy spirit.*

Deacon: The Reading is from the Holy Gospel according to *N.*

People: *Glory to Thee, O Lord, glory to Thee.*

Priest: Let us attend.

Deacon: *[reads the Gospel.]*

Priest: Peace be with you who read.

People: *Glory to Thee, O Lord, glory to Thee.*

*[If no catechumens present skip to next page - **The Liturgy of the Faithful**.]*

The Litany Of Fervent Supplication

Deacon: Let us all say with our whole soul, and with our whole mind let us say:

People: *Lord, have mercy.*

Deacon: Lord Almighty, God of our Fathers, we pray Thee, hearest and have mercy.

People: *Lord, have mercy.*

Deacon: Have mercy on us, O God, according to Thy great mercy, we pray Thee; hear us and have mercy.

People: *Lord, have mercy.* **(x3)**

Deacon: Also we pray for our Archbishop Nikitas.

People: *Lord, have mercy.* **(x3)**

Deacon: For our Sovereign Lady, Queen Elizabeth, the Royal family, our Government, and all in authority, let us pray to the Lord.

People: *Lord, have mercy.* **(x3)**

Deacon: Also we pray for mercy, life, peace, health, salvation, visitation, pardon and forgiveness of sins for the servants of God, all devout and Orthodox Christians, those who dwell in or visit this city or town and parish, the wardens and members of this church and their families *[and the servants of God N and N – names given before the service]* and all who have asked for our prayers, unworthy though we are.

People: *Lord, have mercy.* **(x3)**

Deacon: Also we pray for the blessed and ever remembered founders of this holy church, and for all our brothers and sisters who have gone to their rest before us, and who lie here asleep in the true faith; and for the Orthodox everywhere *[and the servants of God N and N – (names given before the service)]* and that they may be pardoned all their offences, both voluntary and involuntary.

People: *Lord, have mercy.* **(x3)**

Deacon: Also we pray for those who bring offerings, those who care for the beauty of this holy and venerable house, for those who labour in its service, for those who sing, and for the people here present, who await Thy great and rich mercy.

People: *Lord, have mercy. (x3)*

Priest: For Thou, O God, art merciful and love mankind, and to Thee we givest glory, to the Father, the Son and the Holy Spirit, both now and forever, and unto the ages of ages.

People: *Amen.*

The Litany Of The Catechumens

Deacon: Catechumens, pray to the Lord.

People: *Lord, have mercy.*

Deacon: Believers, let us pray for the Catechumens;

People: *Lord, have mercy.*

Deacon: That the Lord shall have mercy on them;

People: *Lord, have mercy.*

Deacon: Instruct them in the Word of Truth;

People: *Lord, have mercy.*

Deacon: Reveal to them the gospel of righteousness;

People: *Lord, have mercy.*

Deacon: Unite them to His Holy, Catholic and Apostolic Church.

People: *Lord, have mercy.*

Deacon: Save them, have mercy on them, help them and keep them, O God, by Thy grace.

People: *Lord, have mercy.*

Deacon: Catechumens, bow thine heads to the Lord.

People: *To Thee, O Lord.*

Priest: That with us they may glorify Thine all honoured and majestic Name, of the Father, the Son, and the Holy Spirit, both now and forever, and unto the ages of ages.

People: *Amen.*

Deacon: As many as are Catechumens depart. Catechumens depart. All Catechumens depart. Let no Catechumen remain, but only the faithful.

The Liturgy Of The Faithful

Deacon: As many as are believers: again and again in peace, let us pray to the Lord.

People: *Lord, have mercy.*

Deacon: Help us, save us, have mercy on us and keep us, O God, by Thy grace.

People: *Lord, have mercy.*

Deacon: Wisdom!

Priest: For to Thee belongs all glory, honour and worship, to the Father, and to the Son, and to the Holy Spirit, both now and forever, and unto the ages of ages.

People: *Amen.*

Deacon: Again and again, in peace let us pray to the Lord.

People: *Lord, have mercy.*

Deacon: Help us, save us, have mercy on us and keep us, O God, by Thy grace.

People: *Lord, have mercy.*

Deacon: Wisdom. *[enter sanctuary]*

Priest: That being always guarded by Thy might, we may give glory to the Father, and to the Son, and to the Holy Spirit, now and ever, and to the ages of ages.

People: *Amen.*

The Cherubic Hymn

(Sung slow until the Entry.)

Chorus: We, who in a mystery represent the Cherubim and sing the thrice holy hymn to the life giving Trinity. Let us now lay aside every care of this life.

The Great Entrance

Priest: May the Lord God remember you all in His Kingdom; Always now and forever and to the ages of ages.

People: *Amen.*

Remember us, Lord, when Thou comest in Thy kingdom. **(x3)**

Amen.

Cherubic Hymn Resumed

[Repeat until censing finished.]

Chorus: For we are about to receive the King of all, invisibly escorted by the angelic hosts. Halleluiah, Halleluiah, Halleluiah.

Litany Of The Precious Gifts

Deacon: Let us complete our prayer to the Lord.

People: *Lord, have mercy.*

Deacon: For the Precious Gifts that have been offered, let us pray to the Lord.

People: *Lord, have mercy.*

Deacon: For this holy house, and for those who enter it with faith, reverence and the fear of God, let us pray to the Lord.

People: *Lord, have mercy.*

Deacon: For our deliverance from all affliction, wrath, danger and constraint, let us pray to the Lord.

People: *Lord, have mercy.*

Deacon: Help us, save us, have mercy on us and keep us, O God, by Thy grace.

People: *Lord, have mercy.*

Deacon: That the whole day may be perfect, holy, peaceful and sinless, let us ask of the Lord.

People: *Grant this, O Lord.*

Deacon: For an Angel of peace, a faithful guide and guardian of our souls and bodies, let us ask of the Lord.

People: *Grant this, O Lord.*

Deacon: For the pardon and forgiveness of our sins and offences, let us ask of the Lord.

People: *Grant this, O Lord.*

Deacon: Things that are good and profitable for our souls, and for peace in the world, let us ask of the Lord.

People: *Grant this, O Lord.*

Deacon: That we may live out the rest of our days in peace and repentance, let us ask of the Lord.

People: *Grant this, O Lord.*

Deacon: For a Christian end to our life, painless, unashamed and peaceful, and a good defence at the dread judgement seat of Christ, let us ask.

People: *Grant this, O Lord.*

Deacon: Commemorating our all holy, pure, most blessed and glorious Lady, Mother of God and Ever Virgin Mary, with all the Saints, let us entrust ourselves and one another, and our whole life to Christ our God.

People: *To Thee, O Lord.*

Prayer Of Offering

Priest: Through the compassion of Thine only begotten Son, with whom Thou art blessed, with the all holy and good and life creating Spirit, both now and forever and unto the ages of ages.

People: *Amen.*

Priest: Peace be with you all.

People: *And with thy spirit.*

Deacon: Let us love one another that with one mind we may confess:

People: *Father, Son, and Holy Spirit, Trinity consubstantial and undivided.*

The Creed

Deacon: The Doors! The Doors! With Wisdom let us attend!

The Symbol of Faith

People: I believe in one God, Father, Almighty, Maker of heaven and earth, and of all things visible and invisible.

And in one Lord Jesus Christ, the only begotten Son of God, begotten from the Father before all ages; Light from Light, true God from true God; begotten not made; consubstantial with the Father, through Him all things were made. For our sake and for our salvation He came down from Heaven, and was incarnate from the Holy Spirit and the Virgin Mary and became man. He was crucified for us under Pontius Pilate, and suffered and was buried. He rose again on the third day in accordance with the Scriptures, and ascended into Heaven, and is seated at the right hand of the Father. He is coming again in glory to judge the living and the dead. And His kingdom shall have no end.

And in the Holy Spirit, the Lord, the Giver of life; Who proceeds from the Father; Who together with Father and Son is worshipped and glorified; Who spoke through the prophets. In One, Holy, Catholic, and Apostolic Church. I confess one baptism for the forgiveness of sins. I await the resurrection of the dead, And the life of the age to come. Amen.

The Holy Oblation

Deacon: Let us stand with awe, let us stand with fear, let us attend, that we may offer the Holy Sacrifice in peace. *[enter Sanctuary]*

People: *Mercy and Peace, a Sacrifice of Praise.*

Priest: The grace of Our Lord Jesus Christ, and the Love of God the Father, and the Communion of the Holy Spirit be with you all.

People: *And with thy spirit.*

Priest: Let our hearts be on high.

People: *We have them with the Lord.*

Priest: Let us give thanks to the Lord.

People: *It is right and fitting to worship Father, Son, and Holy Spirit, the Trinity consubstantial and undivided.*

Priest: … Singing, crying, shouting the triumphal hymn and saying:

People: *Holy, holy holy, Lord Sabaoth; heaven and earth are full of Thy glory. Hosanna in the highest. Blessed is He Who comes in the Name of the Lord. Hosanna in the highest.*

Priest: Take, eat. This is My Body, Which is broken for ye, for the forgiveness of sins.

People: *Amen.*

Priest: Drink from this all of ye. This is My Blood of the New Covenant, Which is shed for ye, and for many, for the forgiveness of sins.

People: *Amen.*

Priest: Offering Thee Thine own of Thine own – in all things and for all things.

People: *We praise Thee, we bless Thee, we thank Thee, O Lord, and we pray to Thee, our God.*

The Consecration

Priest: Above all for our most holy, most pure, most blessed and glorious Lady, Mother of God, and Ever Virgin Mary.

People: *It is truly right to call thee blessed, who gave birth to God, ever blessed and most pure Virgin and Mother of our God. Greater in honour than the Cherubim and beyond compare more glorious than the Seraphim; without corruption thou gavest birth to God the Word, truly the Theotokos, we magnify thee.*

Priest: First of all remember, Lord, our Archbishop Nikitas and grant that he may serve Thy Holy Church in peace, safety, honour, health and length of days, rightly proclaiming the word of Thy truth.

People: *Amen.*

Priest: Remember too, Lord, those whom each one has in mind, and each and all.

People: *And each and all.*

Priest: And grant that with one voice and one heart we may praise and glorify Thine all honoured and majestic Name, of the Father, the Son, and the Holy Spirit, both now and forever, and unto the ages of ages.

People: *Amen.*

Priest: And may the mercies of our Great God, and Saviour Jesus Christ, be with you all.

People: *And with thy spirit.*

Litany Of The Lords Prayer

Deacon: Having commemorated all the Saints, again and again in peace, let us pray to the Lord.

People: *Lord, have mercy.*

Deacon: For the Precious Gifts that have been offered and sanctified, let us pray to the Lord.

People: *Lord, have mercy.*

Deacon: That our God, who loves mankind, having accepted them on His holy and immaterial altar above the heavens, as an aroma of spiritual fragrance, may send down upon us in return His divine grace and the gift of His Holy Spirit, let us pray to the Lord.

People: *Lord, have mercy.*

Deacon: For our deliverance from all affliction, wrath, danger and constraint, let us pray to the Lord.

People: *Lord, have mercy.*

Deacon: Help us, save us, have mercy on us and keep us, O God, by Thy grace.

People: *Lord, have mercy.*

Deacon: That the whole day may be perfect, holy, peaceful, and sinless, let us ask of the Lord.

People: *Grant this, O Lord.*

Deacon: An Angel of peace, a faithful guide and guardian of our souls and bodies, let us ask of the Lord.

People: *Grant this, O Lord.*

Deacon: Pardon and forgiveness of our sins and offences, let us ask of the Lord.

People: *Grant this, O Lord.*

Deacon: Things good and profitable for our souls, and peace for the world, let us ask of the Lord.

People: *Grant this, O Lord.*

Deacon: That we may live out the rest of our days in peace and repentance, let us ask of the Lord.

People: *Grant this, O Lord.*

Deacon: A Christian end to our life, painless, unashamed and peaceful, and for a good defence at the dread judgement seat of Christ, let us ask.

People: *Grant this, O Lord.*

Deacon: Having asked for the unity of the Faith, and the communion of the Holy Spirit, let us entrust ourselves and one another, and our whole life to Christ our God.

People: *To Thee, O Lord.*

Priest: And count us worthy, O Lord, with boldness and without condemnation to dare to call upon Thee, the Heavenly God, as Father, and say:

The Lords Prayer

People: *Our Father, Who art in heaven, hallowed be Thy Name.*

Thy Kingdom come, Thy will be done on earth, as it is in heaven.

Give us this day our daily bread.

And forgive us our trespasses as we forgive those who trespass against us.

And lead us not into temptation; but deliver us from the evil one.

Priest: For Thine is the kingdom, the power, and the glory, of the Father, and the Son and the Holy Spirit, both now and ever, and to the ages of ages.

People: *Amen.*

Priest: Peace be with you all.

People: *And with thy spirit.*

Deacon: Let us bow down our heads to the Lord.

People: *To Thee, O Lord.*

Priest: … Through the grace and compassion and love for men of Thine only begotten Son, with Whom Thou art blessed, and Thine all holy and good and life creating Spirit, both now and forever, and unto the ages of ages.

People: *Amen.*

The Elevation

Deacon: Let us attend.

Priest: The Holy Things for the holy.

People: *One is holy, one is Lord, Jesus Christ, to the glory of God the Father. Amen.*

Chorus: Praise the Lord from Heaven, praise Him in the Heights. Halleluiah. Halleluiah. Halleluiah.

(The clergy now partake of Communion within the Altar.)

Prayers Said By The Clergy Before Communion.

[In Place Of A Communion Hymn, Chant the following. Deep and slow.]

1. I believe, Lord, and I confess that Thou art truly the Christ, the son of the living God, who came into the world to save sinners, of whom I am first. Also I believe that this is indeed Thy most pure Body, and this indeed Thy precious Blood. Therefore I beseech Thee, have mercy on me and forgive me my offences, voluntary and involuntary, in word and in deed, in knowledge and in ignorance, and count me worthy to partake uncondemned of Thy most pure Mysteries for forgiveness of sins and for eternal life. Amen.

2. See, to divine Communion I draw near; My Maker, burn me not as I partake. For Thou art fire, consuming the unworthy; But therefore make me clean from every stain.

3. Of Thy mystical supper, Son of God, receive me today as a communicant; for I shall not tell of the Mystery to Thine enemies; I shall not give Thee a kiss like Judas; but like the thief I confess Thee. Remember me, Lord, in Thy kingdom.

4.   Master, lover of mankind, Lord Jesus Christ, my God, let not these Holy Mysteries be for my condemnation because of my unworthiness, but rather for the cleansing and sanctification of both soul and body, and as a pledge of the life and kingdom to come. It is good for me to cleave to God, to place in the Lord the hope of my salvation.

5.   Let not the Communion of Thy holy Mysteries, Lord, be to me for judgement or condemnation, but for healing of soul and body.

[Then sing Psalm 32. The refrain is:
People: *For he spoke, and it was done; he commanded, and it stood fast.]*

The Communion of the People.

[Deacon takes the chalice and exits via Holy Doors.]
Deacon: With fear of God, with faith and love, draw near.
People: *Blessed is He Who comes in the Name of the Lord. The Lord is God and has appeared to us.*
[Deacon hands the chalice to the Priest.]

[Whilst there is a queue sing the following, deep and slow.]
Reader: Of Thy mystical supper, Son of God, receive me today as a communicant; for I shall not tell of the Mystery to Thine enemies. I shall not give Thee a kiss like Judas; But like the thief I confess Thee.
|: Remember me, Lord, in Thy kingdom. :|

Priest: The Servant of God *N*, partakes of the Precious and Holy Body and Blood of our Lord and God and Saviour Jesus Christ, for the remission of his/her sins, and for life eternal.
[When all have been communicated:]
Priest: O God, save Thy people, and bless Thine inheritance.
People: *We have seen the true Light, we have received the heavenly Spirit, We have found the true Faith, as we worship the undivided Trinity. For the Trinity has saved us.*

Priest: Always, now and ever, and to the ages of ages.
People: *Amen. Let our mouth be filled with Thy praise, O Lord, that we may sing of Thy glory, For Thou hast counted us worthy to partake of Thine Holy Mysteries. Keep us in Thy holiness that we may meditate on Thy righteousness all the day long. Halleluiah. Halleluiah. Halleluiah.*

Thanksgiving And Dismissal

Deacon: Stand up! Having received the divine, holy, pure, immortal, heavenly, life giving and dread Mysteries of Christ, let us give worthy thanks to the Lord.
People: *Lord, have mercy.*
Deacon: Help us, save us, have mercy on us and keep us, O God, by Thy grace.
People: *Lord, have mercy.*

Deacon: Having asked that the whole day may be perfect, holy, peaceful and sinless, let us entrust ourselves and one another, and our whole life to Christ our God.

People: *To Thee, O Lord.*

Priest: For Thou art our sanctification, and to Thee we give glory, to the Father, the Son, and the Holy Spirit, both both now and forever, and unto the ages of ages.

People: *Amen.*

Priest: Let us depart in peace.

People: *In the Name of the Lord.*

Deacon: Let us pray to the Lord.

People: *Lord, have mercy.*

Prayer Behind The Ambo

Priest: O Lord, Thou blessest those who bless Thee, and sanctify those who put their trust in Thee: Save Thy people and bless Thine inheritance. Preserve the fullness of Thy churches; sanctify those who love the beauty of Thy House; glorify them with Thy divine power, and forsake not us who put our hope in Thee. Grant peace to Thy world, to Thy Church, to Thy Priests, to all God fearing rulers, and to all Thy people. For every blessing and every perfect gift is from above and comes down from Thee, the Father of Lights. And to Thee we give glory and thanksgiving and worship, to the Father, the Son, and the Holy Spirit, now and ever and to the ages of ages.

People: *Amen.*

Blessed be the Name of the Lord from this time forth and for evermore. **(x3)**

Priest: May the blessing of the Lord and His mercy be upon ye, by His grace and love for mankind, always, both now and forever, and unto the ages of ages.

People: *Amen.*

Dismissal

Priest: Glory to Thee, O Christ, our God and our hope, glory to Thee.

Reader: *Glory be to the Father, and to the Son, and to the Holy Spirit;*

Both now and forever, and unto the ages of ages. Amen.

Lord, have mercy. **(x3)**

Holy Father, bless!

Priest: May *(Sundays: He Who rose from the dead)* Christ our true God, through the prayers of His most holy Mother, by the power of the precious and life giving Cross, through the protection of the honoured, Bodiless powers of Heaven, through the intercessions of the honoured, glorious prophet, forerunner and baptist John, of the holy, all praised and glorious Apostles, of the holy, glorious and triumphant Martyrs, of our venerable and God bearing Fathers and Mothers who have shone forth in the ascetic life, of our Father among the Saints, John Chrysostom, Archbishop of Constantinople, of the holy and righteous ancestors of God, Joachim and Anna, of *[Saint of your parish]* to whom the church is dedicated, of Saint *N* whose memory we celebrate today, and of all the Saints, have mercy on us and save us, for He is good and loves mankind.

People:	*Amen.*
Priest:	Through the prayers of our holy fathers, Lord Jesus Christ, our God, have mercy on us.
People:	*Amen.*
Priest:	May the Holy Trinity protect you all.
Reader:	O Lord, protect the one who blesses us and sanctifies us, for many years.
Priest:	Come forward to receive the Antidoron.

The Divine Liturgy Of Saint John Chrysostom For Acolytes

Prepare incense = This means: scrape the old incense off the charcoal to the side, prod the charcoal back into life and drop some new incense (4 or 5 bits) on the top.

Instructions in boxes and italics are for the acolytes.

Remember that when you have given the incense to the Priest that he shall want to give it back to you in a minute. When you take it back hold it and kiss his hand before he releases it.

Before The Service Starts

Light the charcoal and put on incense.

Light all the candles: by the icons, on the Holy Table etc.

If Father has already prepared the bread then cut the remaining loaf into chunks for the Eucharist

Deacon: Father, Bless.

Priest: Blessed is the kingdom of the Father, and of the Son and of the Holy Spirit;

Both now and forever, and unto the ages of ages.

People: Amen.

The Litany of Peace

Deacon: In peace let us pray to the Lord.

People: Lord, have mercy.

Deacon: For the peace from above and the salvation of our souls, let us pray to the Lord.

People: Lord, have mercy.

Deacon: For the peace of the whole world, the welfare of the holy churches of God, and for the union of all, let us pray to the Lord.

People: Lord, have mercy.

Deacon: For this holy house, and for those who enter it with faith, reverence and the fear of God, let us pray to the Lord.

People: Lord, have mercy.

Deacon: For all devout and Orthodox Christians, let us pray to the Lord.

People: Lord, have mercy.

Deacon: For our Archbishop Nikitas, for the honoured order of presbyters, for the diaconate in Christ, for all the clergy and the people, let us pray to the Lord.

People: Lord, have mercy.

Deacon: For our Sovereign Lady, Queen Elizabeth, the Royal family, our Government, and all in authority, let us pray to the Lord.

People: Lord, have mercy.

Deacon: For this [city/town/village], and for every city, town and village, and for the faithful who dwell in them, let us pray to the Lord.

People: Lord, have mercy.

Deacon: For favourable weather, an abundance of the fruits of the earth and temperate seasons, let us pray to the Lord.

People: *Lord, have mercy.*

Deacon: For those who travel by land, air or water, for the sick, the suffering, for those in captivity, and for their safety and salvation, let us pray to the Lord.

People: *Lord, have mercy.*

Deacon: For our deliverance from all affliction, wrath, danger and constraint, let us pray to the Lord.

People: *Lord, have mercy.*

Deacon: Help us, save us, have mercy on us, and keep us, O God, by Thy grace.

People: *Lord, have mercy.*

Deacon: Commemorating our all holy, pure, most blessed and glorious Lady, Mother of God and Ever Virgin Mary, with all the Saints, let us entrust ourselves and one another, and our whole life to Christ our God.

People: *To Thee, O Lord.*

Priest: For to Thou belongest all glory, honour and worship, to the Father, the Son, and the Holy Spirit, both now and forever, and unto the ages of ages.

People: *Amen.*

The First Antiphon

[May change – follow the Reader.]

Reader: Bless the Lord, O my soul, and all that is within me bless His holy Name.

People: *At the prayers of the Mother of God, O Saviour, save us.*

Reader: Bless the Lord, O my soul, and forget not all His benefits.

People: *At the prayers of the Mother of God, O Saviour, save us.*

Reader: The Lord has prepared His throne in Heaven, and His kingdom rules over all.

People: *At the prayers of the Mother of God | O Saviour, save us.*

Short Litany

Deacon: Again and again, in peace let us pray to the Lord.

People: *Lord, have mercy.*

Deacon: Help us, save us, have mercy on us and keep us, O God, by Thy grace.

People: *Lord, have mercy.*

Deacon: Commemorating our all holy, pure, most blessed and glorious Lady, Mother of God and Ever Virgin Mary, with all the Saints, let us entrust ourselves and one another, and our whole life to Christ our God.

People: *To Thee, O Lord.*

Priest: For Thine is the might, and Thine the kingdom, the power and the glory, of the Father, the Son and the Holy Spirit, both now and forever, and unto the ages of ages.

People: *Amen.*

The Second Antiphon from Psalm 145

[May change – follow the Reader.]

Reader: Praise the Lord, O my soul; while I live I shall praise the Lord;

While I have any being I shall praise my God.

People: *Save us, O Son of God, risen from the dead. Save us who sing to Thee: Halleluiah.*

Reader: Blessed is he whose help is the God of Jacob, whose hope is in the Lord their God.

People: *Save us, O Son of God, risen from the dead. Save us who sing to Thee: Halleluiah.*

Reader: The Lord shall be king for ever; thy God, O Zion, shall reign throughout all generations.

People: *Save us, O Son of God, risen from the dead. Save us who sing to Thee: Halleluiah.*

---

1) Light the tall candle stand for the procession.

2) After you return from the procession put out that candle.

Reader: Glory be to the Father and to the Son and to the Holy Spirit.

Chorus: Both now and ever, and unto the ages of ages. Amen.

Reader: Only begotten Son and Word of God, Who, being immortal, accepted for our salvation to take flesh from the Holy Mother of God and Ever Virgin Mary and without change became man. Thou wert crucified, Christ God, by death trampling on death, being one of the Holy Trinity, glorified with the Father and the Holy Spirit: Save us.

Little Litany

Deacon: Again and again, in peace let us pray to the Lord.

People: *Lord, have mercy.*

Deacon: Help us, save us, have mercy on us and keep us, O God, by Thy grace.

People: *Lord, have mercy.*

Deacon: Commemorating our all holy, pure, most blessed and glorious Lady, Mother of God and Ever Virgin Mary, with all the Saints, let us entrust ourselves and one another, and our whole life to Christ our God.

People: *To Thee, O Lord.*

Priest: For Thou, O God, art good and lovest mankind, and to Thee we give glory, to the Father, the Son and the Holy Spirit, both now and forever, and unto the ages of ages.

People: *Amen.*

The Third Antiphon – The Beatitudes

[may change – follow the Reader]

People:

In Thy Kingdom. Remember us, O Lord, when Thou comest into Thy Kingdom.

Blessed are the poor in spirit, for theirs is the Kingdom of Heaven.

Blessed are the mourners, for they shall be comforted.

Blessed are the meek, for they shall inherit the earth.

Blessed are those who hunger and thirst for righteousness, for they shall be satisfied.

Blessed are the merciful, for they shall obtain mercy.

Blessed are the pure in heart, for they shall see God.

Blessed are the peacemakers, for they shall be called the children of God.

Blessed are those who are persecuted for righteousness' sake, for theirs is the Kingdom of Heaven.

Blessed are you when men revile and persecute you and say all manner of evil against you falsely and on My account.

Rejoice and be exceedingly glad, for great is thy reward in Heaven.

The Little Entrance

Deacon: *[soto voce]* Master, bless the Holy Entrance.

Priest: *[soto voce]* Blessed is the Entrance to Thy Holy place; both now and forever, and unto the ages of ages.

Deacon: Wisdom, stand upright!

Reader: Come let us worship and bow down before Christ.

People: *Save us, O Son of God, risen from the dead. Save us who sing to Thee: Halleluiah.*

*[Here are sung the appointed **Troparia** and **Kontakia**.]*

Deacon: Let us pray to the Lord.

People: *Lord have mercy.*

Priest: For Thou, our God, art Holy, and to Thee we give glory, to the Father and to the Son and to the Holy Spirit, both now and forever ...

Deacon: .... And to the ages of ages.

People: *Amen.*

Prepare incense.

The Trisagion

Reader: Holy God, Holy Strong, Holy Immortal, have mercy on us. **(x3)**

Glory be to the Father, and to the Son, and to the Holy Spirit,

Both now and forever, and to the ages of ages. Amen.

Holy Immortal, have mercy on us.

Deacon: Dynamis!

Reader: Holy God, Holy Strong, Holy Immortal, have mercy on us.

The Apostle

Deacon: Let us attend.

Priest: Peace be with you all.

Reader   And with thy spirit.

Deacon: Wisdom! The Prokeimenon.

Incense to Priest.

Deacon: Wisdom!

Reader: The Reading is from the book of *N.*

Deacon: Let us attend.

Reader: *[Reads the Apostle.]*

Priest: Peace be to thee who reads.

Reader: And with thy spirit.

People: *Halleluiah, Halleluiah, Halleluiah.*

Reader: [Response of the week.]

People: *Halleluiah, Halleluiah, Halleluiah.*

Reader: [Response of the week.]

People: *Halleluiah, Halleluiah, Halleluiah.*

Be ready to receive back the incense.

The Gospel

Deacon: *[soto voce]* Bless, Father, the reader of the Gospel of the holy Apostle and Evangelist N.

Priest: *[soto voce]* May God, through the intercessions of the holy and glorious Apostle and Evangelist, *N.*, grant thee to announce the glad tidings with great power, for the fulfilment of the Gospel of His beloved Son, our Lord Jesus Christ.

Deacon: Amen.

Priest: Wisdom, stand upright! Let us listen to the Holy Gospel. Peace be with you all.

People: *And with thy spirit.*

---

1) If your priest uses a Bible lectern place, it in front of the Holy Doors now.

2) Light the tall candle stand and place it in front of the Holy Doors. Historically it popped over the top
*   of the Bible so the priest could read, not halfway down the church.*

Deacon: The Reading is from the Holy Gospel of *N.*

People: *Glory to Thee, O Lord, glory to Thee.*

Priest: Let us attend.

Deacon: *[reads the Gospel.]*

Priest: Peace be with thou who reads.

People: *Glory to Thee, O Lord, glory to Thee.*

After the Priest has finished reading, he motions everyone to sit down for his sermon.

3) Remove the lectern then the tall candle.

After the Priest finishes his sermon.

4) Prepare incense to give to the Priest.

*[If no catechumens are present skip to **The Cherubic Hymn**.]*

The Litany Of Fervent Supplication

Deacon: Let us all say with our whole soul, and with our whole mind let us say:

People: *Lord, have mercy.*

Deacon: Lord Almighty, God of our Fathers, we pray Thee, hear and have mercy.

People: *Lord, have mercy.*

Deacon: Have mercy on us, O God, according to Thy great mercy, we pray Thee; hear us and have mercy.

People: *Lord, have mercy.* **(x3)**

Deacon: Also we pray for our Archbishop Nikitas.

People: *Lord, have mercy.* **(x3)**

Deacon: For our Sovereign Lady, Queen Elizabeth, the Royal family, our Government, and all in authority, let us pray to the Lord.

People: *Lord, have mercy.* *(x3)*

Deacon: Also we pray for mercy, life, peace, health, salvation, visitation, pardon and forgiveness of sins for the servants of God, all devout and Orthodox Christians, those who dwell in or visit this city or town and parish, the wardens and members of this church and their families *[and the servants of God N and N – names given before the service]* and all who have asked for our prayers, unworthy though we are.

People: *Lord, have mercy.* *(x3)*

Deacon: Also we pray for the blessed and ever remembered founders of this holy church, and for all our brothers and sisters who have gone to their rest before us, and who lie here asleep in the true faith; and for the Orthodox everywhere *[and the servants of God N and N – (names given before the service)]* and that they may be pardoned all their offences, both voluntary and involuntary.

People: *Lord, have mercy.* *(x3)*

Deacon: Also we pray for those who bring offerings, those who care for the beauty of this holy and venerable house, for those who labour in its service, for those who sing, and for the people here present, who await Thy great and rich mercy.

People: *Lord, have mercy.* *(x3)*

Priest: For Thou, O God, art merciful and love mankind, and to Thee we give glory, to the Father, the Son and the Holy Spirit, both now and forever, and unto the ages of ages.

People: *Amen.*

The Litany Of The Catechumens

Deacon: Catechumens, pray to the Lord.

People: *Lord, have mercy.*

Deacon: Believers, let us pray for the Catechumens;

People: *Lord, have mercy.*

Deacon: That the Lord shall have mercy on them;

People: *Lord, have mercy.*

Deacon: Instruct them in the Word of Truth;

People: *Lord, have mercy.*

Deacon: Reveal to them the gospel of righteousness;

People: *Lord, have mercy.*

Deacon: Unite them to His Holy, Catholic and Apostolic Church.

People: *Lord, have mercy.*

Deacon: Save them, have mercy on them, help them and keep them, O God, by Thy grace.

People: *Lord, have mercy.*

Deacon: Catechumens, bow thine heads to the Lord.

People: *To Thee, O Lord.*

Priest: That with us they may glorify Thine all honoured and majestic Name, of the Father, the Son, and the Holy Spirit, both now and forever, and unto the ages of ages.

People: *Amen.*

Deacon: As many as are Catechumens depart. Catechumens depart. All Catechumens depart. Let no Catechumen remain, but only the faithful.

The Liturgy Of The Faithful

Deacon: As many as are believers: again and again in peace, let us pray to the Lord.

People: *Lord, have mercy.*

Deacon: Help us, save us, have mercy on us and keep us, O God, by Thy grace.

People: *Lord, have mercy.*

Deacon: Wisdom!

Priest: For to Thee belongs all glory, honour and worship, to the Father, and to the Son, and to the Holy Spirit, both now and forever, and unto the ages of ages.

People: *Amen.*

Deacon: Again and again, in peace let us pray to the Lord.

People: *Lord, have mercy.*

Deacon: Help us, save us, have mercy on us and keep us, O God, by Thy grace.

People: *Lord, have mercy.*

Deacon: Wisdom. *[enter sanctuary]*

Priest: That being always guarded by Thy might, we may give Glory be to the Father, and to the Son, and to the Holy Spirit, Both now and forever, and to the ages of ages.

People: Amen.

[If no catechumens are present skip to here.]

The Cherubic Hymn

(Sung slow until the Entry.)

Chorus: We, who in a mystery represent the Cherubim and sing the thrice holy hymn to the life giving Trinity. Let us now lay aside every care of this life.

---

1) Prepare incense.

When the Priest puts the aer over his shoulders:

2) Light tall candle stand for procession.

3) After you return from the procession put out that candle.

4) Prepare incense to give to the Priest.

The Great Entrance

Priest: May the Lord God remember you all in His Kingdom;

Always now and forever and to the ages of ages.

People: *Amen. Remember us, Lord, when Thou comest in Thy kingdom.* **(x3)** *Amen.*

Cherubic Hymn Resumed

Chorus: For we are about to receive the King of all, invisibly escorted by the angelic hosts.

Halleluiah, Halleluiah, Halleluiah. *[Repeat until censing is finished.]*

Litany Of The Precious Gifts

Deacon: Let us complete our prayer to the Lord.

People: *Lord, have mercy.*

Deacon: For the Precious Gifts that have been offered, let us pray to the Lord.

People: *Lord, have mercy.*

Deacon: For this holy house, and for those who enter it with faith, reverence and the fear of God, let us pray to the Lord.

People: *Lord, have mercy.*

Deacon: For our deliverance from all affliction, wrath, danger and constraint, let us pray to the Lord.

People: *Lord, have mercy.*

Deacon: Help us, save us, have mercy on us and keep us, O God, by Thy grace.

People: *Lord, have mercy.*

Deacon: That the whole day may be perfect, holy, peaceful and sinless, let us ask of the Lord.

People: *Grant this, O Lord.*

Deacon: For an Angel of peace, a faithful guide and guardian of our souls and bodies, let us ask of the Lord.

People: *Grant this, O Lord.*

Deacon: For the pardon and forgiveness of our sins and offences, let us ask of the Lord.

People: *Grant this, O Lord.*

Deacon: Things that are good and profitable for our souls, and for peace in the world, let us ask of the Lord.

People: *Grant this, O Lord.*

Deacon: That we may live out the rest of our days in peace and repentance, let us ask of the Lord.

People: *Grant this, O Lord.*

Deacon: For a Christian end to our life, painless, unashamed and peaceful, and a good defence at the dread judgement seat of Christ, let us ask.

People: *Grant this, O Lord.*

Deacon: Commemorating our all holy, pure, most blessed and glorious Lady, Mother of God and Ever Virgin Mary, with all the Saints, let us entrust ourselves and one another, and our whole life to Christ our God.

People: *To Thee, O Lord.*

Prayer Of Offering

Priest: Through the compassion of Thine only begotten Son, with whom Thou art blessed, with the all holy and good and life creating Spirit, both now and forever and unto the ages of ages.

People: *Amen.*

Priest: Peace be with you all.

People: *And with thy spirit.*

Deacon: Let us love one another that with one mind we may confess:

People: *Father, Son, and Holy Spirit, Trinity consubstantial and undivided.*

The Creed

Deacon: The Doors! The Doors! With Wisdom let us attend!

The Symbol of Faith

People: I believe in one God, Father, Almighty, Maker of heaven and earth, and of all things visible and invisible.

And in one Lord Jesus Christ, the only begotten Son of God, begotten from the Father before all ages; Light from Light, true God from true God; begotten not made; consubstantial with the Father, through Him all things were made. For our sake and for our salvation He came down from Heaven, and was incarnate from the Holy Spirit and the Virgin Mary and became man. He was crucified for us under Pontius Pilate, and suffered and was buried. He rose again on the third day in accordance with the Scriptures, and ascended into Heaven, and is seated at the right hand of the Father. He is coming again in glory to judge the living and the dead. And His kingdom shall have no end.

And in the Holy Spirit, the Lord, the Giver of life; Who proceeds from the Father; Who together with Father and Son is worshipped and glorified; Who spoke through the prophets. In One, Holy, Catholic, and Apostolic Church. I confess one baptism for the forgiveness of sins. I await the resurrection of the dead, And the life of the age to come. Amen.

The Holy Oblation

Deacon: Let us stand with awe, let us stand with fear, let us attend, that we may offer the Holy Sacrifice in peace. *[enter Sanctuary]*

People: *Mercy and Peace, a Sacrifice of Praise.*

Priest: The grace of Our Lord Jesus Christ, and the Love of God the Father, and the Communion of the Holy Spirit be with you all.

People: *And with thy spirit.*

Priest: Let our hearts be on high.

People: *We have them with the Lord.*

Priest: Let us give thanks to the Lord.

People: *It is right and fitting to worship Father, Son, and Holy Spirit, Trinity consubstantial and undivided.*

Priest: … Singing, crying, shouting the triumphal hymn and saying:

People: *Holy, holy holy, Lord Sabaoth; heaven and earth are full of Thy glory. Hosanna in the highest. Blessed is He Who comes in the Name of the Lord. Hosanna in the highest.*

Prepare incense.

Priest: Take, eat. This is My Body, Which is broken for you, for the forgiveness of sins.

People: *Amen.*

Priest: Drink from this all of you. This is My Blood of the New Covenant, Which is shed for you, and for many, for the forgiveness of sins.

People: *Amen.*

Priest: Offering Thee Thine own of Thine own – in all things and for all things.

People: *We praise Thee, we bless Thee, we thank Thee, O Lord, and we pray to Thee, our God.*

Priest: Amen, Amen, Amen. *(And a small quiet prayer).*

Incense to the Priest.

The Consecration

Priest: Above all for our most holy, most pure, most blessed and glorious Lady, Mother of God, and Ever Virgin Mary.

Reader: It is truly right to call Thee blessed, who gave birth to God, ever blessed and most pure Virgin and Mother of our God. Greater in honour than the Cherubim and beyond compare more glorious than the Seraphim; without corruption thou gavest birth to God the Word, truly the Theotokos, we magnify thee.

Priest: First of all remember, Lord, our Archbishop Nikitas and grant that he may serve Thy Holy Church in peace, safety, honour, health and length of days, rightly proclaiming the word of Thy truth.

People: *Amen.*

Priest: Remember too, Lord, those whom each one has in mind, and each and all.

People: *And each and all.*

> 1) *Have the bread ready.*
>
> Priest says a small quiet prayer ending with "...rich mercies".
>
> 2) *Bread to the Priest.*

Priest: And grant that with one voice and one heart we may praise and glorify Thine all honoured and majestic Name, of the Father, the Son, and the Holy Spirit, both now and forever, and unto the ages of ages.

People: Amen.

Priest: And may the mercies of our Great God, and Saviour Jesus Christ, be with you all.

People: And with thy spirit.

Litany Of The Lords Prayer

Deacon: Having commemorated all the Saints, again and again in peace, let us pray to the Lord.

People: Lord, have mercy.

Deacon: For the Precious Gifts that have been offered and sanctified, let us pray to the Lord.

People: Lord, have mercy.

> 1) *If no flask of hot water is available, put on the kettle.*
>
> 2) *The collection is taken. Be ready to receive the plate of money at your door.*
>
> 3) *Offer the plate to the Priest for blessing.*
>
> 4) *Put the plate somewhere safe where it won't be kicked over.*

Deacon: That our God, who loves mankind, having accepted them on His holy and immaterial altar above the heavens, as an aroma of spiritual fragrance, may send down upon us in return His divine grace and the gift of His Holy Spirit, let us pray to the Lord.

People: Lord, have mercy.

Deacon: For our deliverance from all affliction, wrath, danger and constraint, let us pray to the Lord.

People: Lord, have mercy.

Deacon: Help us, save us, have mercy on us and keep us, O God, by Thy grace.

People: Lord, have mercy.

Deacon: That the whole day may be perfect, holy, peaceful, and sinless, let us ask of the Lord.

People: Grant this, O Lord.

Deacon: An Angel of peace, a faithful guide and guardian of our souls and bodies, let us ask of the Lord.

People: Grant this, O Lord.

Deacon: Pardon and forgiveness of our sins and offences, let us ask of the Lord.

People: Grant this, O Lord.

Deacon: Things good and profitable for our souls, and peace for the world, let us ask of the Lord.

People: Grant this, O Lord.

Deacon: That we may live out the rest of our days in peace and repentance, let us ask of the Lord.

People: *Grant this, O Lord.*

Deacon: A Christian end to our life, painless, unashamed and peaceful, and for a good defence at the dread judgement seat of Christ, let us ask.

People: *Grant this, O Lord.*

Deacon: Having asked for the unity of the Faith, and the communion of the Holy Spirit, let us entrust ourselves and one another, and our whole life to Christ our God.

People: *To Thee, O Lord.*

Priest: And count us worthy, O Lord, with boldness and without condemnation to dare to call upon Thee, the Heavenly God, as Father, and say:

The Lords Prayer

People: *Our Father, who art in heaven, hallowed be Thy name. Thy Kingdom come. Thy will be done, on earth as it is in heaven. Give us this day our daily bread; and forgive us our trespasses, as we forgive those who trespass against us; and lead us not into temptation, but deliver us from the evil one.*

Priest: For Thine is the kingdom, the power, and the glory, of the Father, and the Son and the Holy Spirit, Both now and forever, and to the ages of ages.

People: *Amen.*

Priest: Peace be with you all.

People: *And with thy spirit.*

Deacon: Let us bow our heads to the Lord.

People: *To Thee, O Lord.*

Priest: Through the grace and compassion and love for men of Thine only begotten Son, with Whom Thou art blessed, and Thine all holy and good and life creating Spirit, both now and forever, and unto the ages of ages.

People: *Amen.*

The Elevation

Have the hot water ready.

Deacon: Let us attend.

Priest: The Holy Things for the holy.

People: *One is holy, one is Lord, Jesus Christ, to the glory of God the Father. Amen.*

Chorus: Praise the Lord from Heaven, praise Him in the Heights. Halleluiah. Halleluiah. Halleluiah.

(The clergy now partake of Communion within the Altar.)

1) *Hot water to the Priest.*

2) *Light the tall candle stand and place it in front of the Holy Doors.*

3) *When the Priest moves to the centre holding the wine, remove the candle stand.*

4) *Stand to the right side of the Priest holding the tray of bread.*

5) When communion is finished and you are back in your place, prepare the incense.

Prayers Said By The Clergy Before Communion.

[Before The Communion Hymn, Chant the following. Deep and slow.]

1.   I believe, Lord, and I confess that Thou art truly the Christ, the son of the living God, who came into the world to save sinners, of whom I am first. Also I believe that this is indeed Thy most pure Body, and this indeed Thy precious Blood. Therefore I beseech Thee, have mercy on me and forgive me my offences, voluntary and involuntary, in word and in deed, in knowledge and in ignorance, and count me worthy to partake uncondemned of Thy most pure Mysteries for forgiveness of sins and for eternal life. Amen.

2.   See, to divine Communion I draw near; My Maker, burn me not as I partake. For Thou art fire, consuming the unworthy; But therefore make me clean from every stain.

3.   Of Thy mystical supper, Son of God, receive me today as a communicant; for I shall not tell of the Mystery to Thine enemies; I shall not give Thee a kiss like Judas; but like the thief I confess Thee. Remember me, Lord, in Thy kingdom.

4.   Master, lover of mankind, Lord Jesus Christ, my God, let not these Holy Mysteries be for my condemnation because of my unworthiness, but rather for the cleansing and sanctification of both soul and body, and as a pledge of the life and kingdom to come. It is good for me to cleave to God, to place in the Lord the hope of my salvation.

5.   Let not the Communion of Thy holy Mysteries, Lord, be to me for judgement or condemnation, but for healing of soul and body.

[Then sing Psalm 32. The refrain is:

People: *For he spoke, and it was done; he commanded, and it stood fast.]*

The Communion of the People.

[Deacon takes the chalice and exits via Holy Doors.]

Deacon: With fear of God, with faith and love, draw near.

People: *Blessed is He Who comes in the Name of the Lord. The Lord is God and has appeared to us.*

[Deacon hands the chalice to the Priest.]

[Whilst there is a queue sing the following, deep and slow.]

Reader: Of Thy mystical supper, Son of God, receive me today as a communicant;

For I shall not tell of the Mystery to Thine enemies; I shall not give Thee a kiss like Judas;

But like the thief I confess Thee. |: Remember me, Lord, in Thy kingdom. :|

Priest: The Servant of God *N*, partakes of the Precious and Holy Body and Blood of our Lord and God and Saviour Jesus Christ, for the remission of his/her sins, and for life eternal.

[When all have communed:]

Priest: O God, save Thy people, and bless Thine inheritance.

People: *We have seen the true Light, we have received the heavenly Spirit. We have found the true Faith, as we worship the undivided Trinity. For the Trinity has saved us.*

Incense to the Priest.

Priest: Always, now and ever, and to the ages of ages.

People: *Amen.*

People: *Let our mouth be filled with Thy praise, O Lord, that we may sing of Thy glory, for Thou hast counted us worthy to partake of Thy Holy Mysteries. Keep us in Thy holiness that we may meditate on Thy righteousness all the day long. Halleluiah. Halleluiah. Halleluiah.*

Thanksgiving And Dismissal

Deacon: Stand upright! Having received the divine, holy, pure, immortal, heavenly, life creating and dread Mysteries of Christ, let us give worthy thanks to the Lord.

People: *Lord, have mercy.*

Deacon: Help us, save us, have mercy on us and keep us, O God, by Thy grace.

People: *Lord, have mercy.*

Deacon: Having asked that the whole day may be perfect, holy, peaceful and sinless, let us entrust ourselves and one another, and our whole life to Christ our God.

People: *To Thee, O Lord.*

Priest: For Thou art our sanctification, and to Thee we give glory, to the Father, the Son, and the Holy Spirit, both both now and forever, and unto the ages of ages.

People: *Amen.*

Priest: Let us depart in peace.

People: *In the Name of the Lord.*

Deacon: Let us pray to the Lord.

People: *Lord, have mercy.*

Prayer Behind The Ambo

Priest: O Lord, Thou blessest those who bless Thee, and sanctify those who put their trust in Thee: Save Thy people and bless Thine inheritance. Preserve the fullness of Thy churches; sanctify those who love the beauty of Thy House; glorify them with Thy divine power, and forsake not us who put our hope in Thee. Grant peace to Thy world, to Thy Church, to Thy Priests, to all God fearing rulers, and to all Thy people. For every blessing and every perfect gift is from above and comes down from Thee, the Father of Lights. And to Thee we give glory and thanksgiving and worship, to the Father, the Son, and the Holy Spirit, now and ever and to the ages of ages.

People: *Amen. Blessed be the Name of the Lord from this time forth and for evermore.* **(x3)**

Priest: May the blessing of the Lord and His mercy be upon you, by His grace and love for mankind, always, both now and forever, and unto the ages of ages.

People: *Amen.*

Priest: Glory to Thee, O Christ, our God and our hope, glory to Thee.

Reader: *Glory be to the Father, and to the Son, and to the Holy Spirit,*

          Both now and forever, and to the ages of ages. Amen.

          Lord, have mercy. **(x3)**

          Holy Father, bless!

Priest: May *(Sundays: He Who rose from the dead)* Christ our true God, through the prayers of His most holy Mother, by the power of the precious and life giving Cross, through the protection of the honoured, Bodiless powers of Heaven, through the intercessions of the honoured, glorious prophet, forerunner and baptist John, of the holy, all praised and glorious Apostles, of the holy, glorious and triumphant Martyrs, of our venerable and God bearing Fathers and Mothers who have shone forth in the ascetic life, of our Father among the Saints, John Chrysostom, Archbishop of Constantinople, of the holy and righteous ancestors of God, Joachim and Anna, of *[Saints ...]* to whom the church is dedicated, of Saints *N* whose memory we celebrate today, and of all the Saints, have mercy on us and save us, for He is good and loves mankind.

People: *Amen.*

Priest: Through the prayers of our holy fathers, Lord Jesus Christ, our God, have mercy on us.

Priest: May the Holy Trinity protect you all.

Reader: O Lord, protect the one who blesses us and sanctifies us, for many years.

With the tray of antidoron (bread) stand to the left of the Priest.

Priest: Come forward to receive the antidoron.

Divine Liturgy Guide For Acolytes

Prepare incense = This means: scrape the old incense off the charcoal to the side, prod the charcoal back into life and drop some new incense (4 or 5 bits) on the top.

Instructions in italics are for the acolytes.

Remember that when you have given the incense to the Priest that he shall want to give it back to you in a minute.

Before The Service Starts

Light the charcoal and put on incense.

Light all the candles: by the icons, on the Holy Table etc.

During the Service

People: Save us, O Son Of God, risen from the dead. Save us who sing to you, Halleluiah.

Priest: ... Again and again in peace, let us pray to the Lord.

1) Light the tall candle stand for the procession.

2) After you return from the procession put out that candle.

Reader: Holy God, Holy Strong, Holy Immortal **(x3)**

1) Prepare incense.

Priest: Wisdom. The Prokeimenon.

2) Incense to Priest.

People: Halleluiah, Halleluiah, Halleluiah. **(x3)**

3) Be ready to receive the incense back.

Priest: Wisdom. Stand upright. Let us listen to the Holy Gospel. Peace be with you all.

1) Light the tall candle stand and place it in front of the Holy Doors.

After the Priest has finished reading, he motions everyone to sit down for his sermon.

2) Remove the tall candle.

After the Priest finishes his sermon.

3) Prepare incense to give to the Priest.

Reader: "We who in a mystery". *(The long slow hymn.)*

1) Prepare incense.

When Priest puts a small cape over his shoulders.

2) Light tall candle stand for procession.

3) After you return from the procession put out that candle.

4) Prepare incense to give to the Priest.

Reader: Holy, holy, holy. Lord of hosts ...

1) Prepare incense.

Priest: Amen, Amen, Amen. (And a small quiet prayer).

2) Incense to the Priest.

People: And each and all.

3) Have the bread ready.

Priest does a small quiet prayer ending with "...rich mercies".

4) Bread to the Priest.

Priest: For the precious gifts here set forth and sanctified, let us pray to the Lord.

1) Here the collection is taken. Be ready to receive the plate of money at your side door.

2) Offer the plate to the Priest for blessing.

3) Put the plate somewhere safe where it won't be kicked over.

People: One is Holy, one is Lord: Jesus Christ, to the glory of God the Father. Amen.

1) Have the hot water ready.

People: Praise the Lord from heaven, praise him in the highest. Halleluiah, Halleluiah, Halleluiah.

2) Hot water to the Priest.

Reader: (Long slow prayers in a deep voice, starting:) "I believe, Lord, and I confess"

1) Light the tall candle stand and place it in front of the Holy Doors.

2) When the Priest moves to the centre holding the wine, remove the candle stand.

3) Stand to the right side of the Priest holding the tray of bread.

4) When communion is finished and you are back in your seat, Prepare the incense.

People: We have seen the true light.

1) Incense to the Priest.

Reader: O Lord protect the one who blesses us and sanctifies us, for many years.

2) With the tray of antidoron (bread) stand to the left of the Priest.

The Divine Liturgy Of Saint John Chrysostom For Clergy

[Instruction in italics and square brackets are for the clergy.]

Instructions in boxes are for Acolytes.

Before The Service Starts

Light the charcoal and put on incense.

Light all the candles: by the icons, on the Holy Table etc.

If Father has already prepared the bread then cut the loaf into chunks.

[Priest blesses deacon.

Deacon exits North door and stands in front of Holy Doors. 3 bows and:]

Deacon: Father, Bless.

Priest: Blessed is the kingdom of the Father, and of the Son and of the Holy Spirit;

Both now and forever, and unto the ages of ages.

People: Amen.

The Litany of Peace

Deacon: In peace let us pray to the Lord.

People: Lord, have mercy.

Deacon: For the peace from above and the salvation of our souls, let us pray to the Lord.

People: Lord, have mercy.

Deacon: For the peace of the whole world, the welfare of the holy churches of God, and for the union of all, let us pray to the Lord.

People: Lord, have mercy.

Deacon: For this holy house, and for those who enter it with faith, reverence and the fear of God, let us pray to the Lord.

People: Lord, have mercy.

Deacon: For all devout and Orthodox Christians, let us pray to the Lord.

People: Lord, have mercy.

Deacon: For our Archbishop Nikitas, for the honoured order of presbyters, for the diaconate in Christ, for all the clergy and the people, let us pray to the Lord.

People: Lord, have mercy.

Deacon: For our Sovereign Lady, Queen Elizabeth, the Royal family, our Government, and all in authority, let us pray to the Lord.

People: Lord, have mercy.

Deacon: For this *[city/town/village]*, and for every city, town and village, and for the faithful who dwell in them, let us pray to the Lord.

People: *Lord, have mercy.*

Deacon: For favourable weather, an abundance of the fruits of the earth and temperate seasons, let us pray to the Lord.

People: *Lord, have mercy.*

Deacon: For those who travel by land, air or water, for the sick, the suffering, for those in captivity, and for their safety and salvation, let us pray to the Lord.

People: *Lord, have mercy.*

Deacon: For our deliverance from all affliction, wrath, danger and constraint, let us pray to the Lord.

People: *Lord, have mercy.*

Deacon: Help us, save us, have mercy on us, and keep us, O God, by Thy grace.

People: *Lord, have mercy.*

Deacon: Commemorating our all holy, pure, most blessed and glorious Lady, Mother of God and Ever Virgin Mary, with all the Saints, let us entrust ourselves and one another, and our whole life to Christ our God.

People: *To Thee, O Lord.*

Priest: *[soto voce]*Lord, our God, whose might is beyond compare and whose glory is beyond understanding, whose mercy is without measure and whose love for mankind is beyond all telling, look upon us and upon this holy house, Master, according to Thy loving kindness, and bestow upon us and on those who pray with us Thine acts of rich mercy and compassion.

[aloud] For to Thee belongs all glory, honour and worship, to the Father, the Son, and the Holy Spirit, both now and forever, and unto the ages of ages.

People: *Amen.*

[During the following the Deacon bows and goes to stand in front of the Theotokos, looking to Christ, orarion in 3 fingers of the right hand.]

The First Antiphon

[May change – follow the Reader.]

Reader: Bless the Lord, O my soul, and all that is within me bless His holy Name.

People: *At the prayers of the Mother of God, O Saviour, save us.*

Reader: Bless the Lord, O my soul, and forget not all His benefits.

People: *At the prayers of the Mother of God, O Saviour, save us.*

Reader: The Lord has prepared His throne in Heaven, and His kingdom rules over all.

People: *At the prayers of the Mother of God | O Saviour, save us.*

[Deacon returns to usual place for:]

Short Litany

Deacon: Again and again, in peace let us pray to the Lord.

People: *Lord, have mercy.*

Deacon: Help us, save us, have mercy on us and keep us, O God, by Thy grace.

People: *Lord, have mercy.*

Deacon: Commemorating our all holy, pure, most blessed and glorious Lady, Mother of God and Ever Virgin Mary, with all the Saints, let us entrust ourselves and one another, and our whole life to Christ our God.

People: *To Thee, O Lord.*

Priest: *[Soto voce]* Lord our God, save Thy people and bless Thine inheritance; protect the fullness of Thy Church, sanctify those who love the beauty of Thy house, glorify them in return by Thy divine power, and do not forsake us who hope in Thee.

      [aloud] For Thine is the might, and Thine the kingdom, the power and the glory, of the Father, the Son and the Holy Spirit, both now and forever, and unto the ages of ages.

People: *Amen.*

The Second Antiphon from Psalm 145

[May change – follow the Reader.]

Reader: Praise the Lord, O my soul; while I live I shall praise the Lord;

      While I have any being I shall praise my God.

People: *Save us, O Son of God, risen from the dead. Save us who sing to Thee: Halleluiah.*

Reader: Blessed is he whose help is the God of Jacob, whose hope is in the Lord their God.

People: *Save us, O Son of God, risen from the dead. Save us who sing to Thee: Halleluiah.*

Reader: The Lord shall be king for ever; Thy God O Zion, shall reign throughout all generations.

People: *Save us, O Son of God, risen from the dead. Save us who sing to Thee: Halleluiah.*

Reader: Glory be to the Father and to the Son and to the Holy Spirit.

Chorus: *Both now and ever, and unto the ages of ages. Amen.*

Reader: Only begotten Son and Word of God, Who, being immortal, accepted for our salvation to take flesh from the Holy Mother of God and Ever Virgin Mary and without change became man. Thou wast crucified, Christ God, by death trampling on death, being one of the Holy Trinity, glorified with the Father and the Holy Spirit: Save us.

[Deacon to usual place for:]

Short Litany

Deacon: Again and again, in peace let us pray to the Lord.

People: *Lord, have mercy.*

Deacon: Help us, save us, have mercy on us and keep us, O God, by Thy grace.

People: *Lord, have mercy.*

Deacon: Commemorating our all holy, pure, most blessed and glorious Lady, Mother of God and Ever Virgin Mary, with all the Saints, let us entrust ourselves and one another, and our whole life to Christ our God.

People: *To Thee, O Lord.*

Light the tall candle stand for the procession.

Priest: *[soto voce]*Thou hast given us grace to make these common and united prayers, and have promised that when two or three agree in Thy name Thou wilt grant their requests, fulfil now the petitions of Thy servants as is expedient, granting us in this present age the knowledge of Thy truth and in the age to come eternal life.

[aloud] For Thee, O God, are good and love mankind, and to Thee we give glory, to the Father, the Son and the Holy Spirit, both now and forever, and unto the ages of ages.

People: Amen.

[Deacon enters by South door.

Priest and Deacon stand in front of Holy Table, make 3 bows.

Priest gives Holy Gospel to Deacon who kisses Priests hand.

Both exit via North door, circle and end with bowed heads.]

The Third Antiphon – The Beatitudes

[may change – follow the Reader]

People:

In Thy Kingdom. Remember us, O Lord, when Thou comest into Thy Kingdom.

Blessed are the poor in spirit, for theirs is the Kingdom of Heaven.

Blessed are the mourners, for they shall be comforted.

Blessed are the meek, for they shall inherit the earth.

Blessed are those who hunger and thirst for righteousness, for they shall be satisfied.

Blessed are the merciful, for they shall obtain mercy.

Blessed are the pure in heart, for they shall see God.

Blessed are the peacemakers, for they shall be called the children of God.

Blessed are those who are persecuted for righteousness' sake, for theirs is the Kingdom of Heaven.

Blessed art thou when men revile and persecute thee and say all manner of evil against thee falsely and on My account.

Rejoice and be exceedingly glad, for great is thy reward in Heaven.

The Little Entrance

Deacon: *[soto voce]*Let us pray to the Lord.

Priest: *[soto voce]*Master, Lord our God, Thou hast set orders and armies of Angels and Archangels in heaven to minister to Thy glory; grant that, with our entrance, holy Angels may enter, concelebrating with us, and with us glorifying Thy goodness. For to Thee belongest all glory, honour and worship, to the Father, the Son and the Holy Spirit, both now and forever, and to the ages of ages. Amen.

Deacon: *[soto voce]* Master, bless the Holy Entrance.

[Priest blesses Holy Doors.]

Priest: *[soto voce]* Blessed is the Entrance to Thy Holy place; both now and forever, and unto the ages of ages. Amen.

[Priest kisses Gospel.

Deacon stands in the middle in front of the Priest, raises Gospel and:]

Deacon: Wisdom, stand upright!

[Deacon then Priest enters via Holy Doors and places Gospel on Holy Table.]

If Not Pascha

Reader: Come let us worship and bow down before Christ.

People: *Save us, O Son of God, risen from the dead. Save us who sing to Thee: Halleluiah.*

During Pascha

Reader: Bless God in the Church; the Lord from the fountains of Israel.

People: *Save us, O Son of God, risen from the dead. Save us who sing to Thee: Halleluiah.*

---

*[Here are sung the appointed **Troparia** and **Kontakia**.]*

Deacon: Let us pray to the Lord.

People: *Lord have mercy.*

Priest: *[Soto voce]* Holy God, at rest in the holy place, hymned by the Seraphim with the thrice holy song, glorified by the Cherubim and worshipped by every heavenly Power, out of non existence Thou broughtest the universe into being and created male and female according to Thine image and likeness, adorning them with every gift of Thy grace. Thou givest wisdom and understanding to those who ask, and Thou do not rejectest the sinner, but for our salvation Thou hast established repentance. Thou hast counted us, Thy humble and unworthy servants, worthy to stand at this time before the glory of Thy Holy Altar, and to offer Thee due worship and praise. Accept, Master, the thrice holy Hymn even from the mouth of us sinners, and visit us in Thy goodness. Pardon us every offence, voluntary and involuntary; sanctify our souls and bodies, and grant that we may worship Thee in holiness all the days of our life; at the prayers of the holy Mother of God and of all the Saints who have been well pleasing to Thee in every age.

[Deacon goes to Holy Doors and faces the people.]

Priest: *[aloud]* For Thee, our God, are Holy, and to Thee we give glory, to the Father and to the Son and to the Holy Spirit, both now and forever …

Deacon: …. And to the ages of ages.

People: *Amen.*

Prepare incense.

[Priest and Deacon join in the following, making 3 bows before the Holy Table.]

The Trisagion

People: Holy God, Holy Strong, Holy Immortal, have mercy on us. **(x3)**

Glory be to the Father, and to the Son, and to the Holy Spirit,

Both now and forever, and to the ages of ages. Amen.

Holy Immortal, have mercy on us.

Deacon: Dynamis!

People: Holy God, Holy Strong, Holy Immortal, have mercy on us.

Deacon: Master, command.

[Deacon and Priest go to the throne. On the way:]

Priest: Blessed is he who comes in the name of the Lord.

Deacon: Master, bless the Throne on high.

Priest: Blessed art Thou on the throne of glory of Thy Kingdom, who are seated upon the Cherubim, always, now and for ever, and to the ages of ages. Amen.

[Deacon exits via Holy Doors and stands in front for:]

The Apostle

Deacon: Let us attend.

Priest: Peace be with you all.

Reader And with thy spirit.

Deacon: Wisdom! The Prokeimenon.

Incense to Priest.

Deacon: Wisdom!

Reader: The Reading is from the book of ...

Deacon: Let us attend.

Reader: *[Reads the Apostle.]*

Priest: Peace be to thou who readest.

Reader: And with thy spirit.

[During the following the Deacon asks the Priests blessing over the censer.

Censes the Gospel, all around the Holy Table, whole Sanctuary, Priest.

Exits via Holy Doors, stands there and censes the main icons and the people.]

People: *Halleluiah, Halleluiah, Halleluiah.*

Reader: [Response of the week.]

People: *Halleluiah, Halleluiah, Halleluiah.*

Reader: [Response of the week.]

People: *Halleluiah, Halleluiah, Halleluiah.*

Prayer Of The Gospel

Priest: *[Soto voce]* Master, Lover of mankind, make the pure light of Thy divine knowledge shine in our hearts and open the eyes of our mind to understand the message of Thy Gospel. Implant in us the fear of Thy blessed commandments, so that, having trampled down all carnal desires, we may change to a spiritual way of life, thinking and doing all things that are pleasing to Thee. For Thou art the illumination of our souls and bodies, Christ God, and to Thee we give glory, together with Thy Father who is without beginning, and Thine all holy, good and life creating Spirit, Both now and for ever, and unto the ages of ages. Amen.

Be ready to receive back the incense from the Deacon.

[Deacon finishes censing. Approaches Priest, holds orarion with tips of fingers, points to Gospel, bows head and says:]

Deacon: *[soto voce]* Bless, Father, the reader of the Gospel of the holy Apostle and Evangelist N.

Priest: *[soto voce]* May God, through the intercessions of the holy and glorious Apostle and Evangelist, *N.*, grant thee to announce the glad tidings with great power, for the fulfilment of the Gospel of His beloved Son, our Lord Jesus Christ.

Deacon: Amen.

[Deacon bows to Priest, takes Gospel out via Holy Doors to Ambo.
Priest goes to Holy doors, faces the people and:]

Priest: Wisdom, stand upright! Let us listen to the Holy Gospel. Peace be with you all.

People: *And with thy spirit.*

1.   *Light the tall candle stand and place it in front of the Holy Doors.*

Deacon: The Reading is from the Holy Gospel of *N.*

People: *Glory to Thee, O Lord, glory to Thee.*

Priest: Let us attend.

Deacon: *[reads the Gospel.]*

Priest: Peace be with thee who read.

People: *Glory to Thee, O Lord, glory to Thee.*

[Priest takes Gospel from Deacon, kisses it and blesses the people with it. Then replaces it on the Holy Table.]

After the reading, the Priest motions everyone to sit down for his sermon.

2)   *Remove the tall candle.*

After the Priest finishes his sermon.

3)   *Prepare incense to give to the Priest.*

[If no catechumens are present skip to <u>The Cherubic Hymn.</u>]

[Deacon to usual place for:]

The Litany Of Fervent Supplication

Deacon: Let us all say with our whole soul, and with our whole mind let us say:

People: *Lord, have mercy.*

Deacon: Lord Almighty, God of our Fathers, we pray Thee, hear and have mercy.

People: *Lord, have mercy.*

Deacon: Have mercy on us, O God, according to Thy great mercy, we pray Thee; hear and have mercy.

People: *Lord, have mercy.* **(x3)**

Deacon: Also we pray for our Archbishop Nikitas.

People: *Lord, have mercy.* **(x3)**

Deacon: For our Sovereign Lady, Queen Elizabeth, the Royal family, our Government, and all in authority, let us pray to the Lord.

People: *Lord, have mercy.* **(x3)**

Deacon: Also we pray for mercy, life, peace, health, salvation, visitation, pardon and forgiveness of sins for the servants of God, all devout and Orthodox Christians, those who dwell in or visit this city or town and parish, the wardens and members of this church and their families *[and the servants of God N and N – names given before the service]* and all who have asked for our prayers, unworthy though we are.

People: *Lord, have mercy.* **(x3)**

Deacon: Also we pray for the blessed and ever remembered founders of this holy church, and for all our brothers and sisters who have gone to their rest before us, and who lie here asleep in the true faith; and for the Orthodox everywhere *[and the servants of God N and N – (names given before the service)]* and that they may be pardoned all their offences, both voluntary and involuntary.

People: *Lord, have mercy.* **(x3)**

Deacon: Also we pray for those who bring offerings, those who care for the beauty of this holy and venerable house, for those who labour in its service, for those who sing, and for the people here present, who await Thy great and rich mercy.

People: *Lord, have mercy.* **(x3)**

Priest: *[Soto voce]* Lord, our God, accept this fervent supplication from Thy servants, and have mercy on us according to the multitude of Thy mercy, and send down Thy pity on us and on all Thy people, who await Thy rich mercy.

Priest: *[aloud]* For Thou, O God, art merciful and love mankind, and to Thee we give glory, to the Father, the Son and the Holy Spirit, both now and forever, and unto the ages of ages.

People: *Amen.*

The Litany Of The Catechumens

Deacon: Catechumens, pray to the Lord.

People: *Lord, have mercy.*

Deacon: Believers, let us pray for the Catechumens;

People: *Lord, have mercy.*

Deacon: That the Lord shall have mercy on them;

People: *Lord, have mercy.*

Deacon: Instruct them in the Word of Truth;

People: *Lord, have mercy.*

Deacon: Reveal to them the gospel of righteousness;

People: *Lord, have mercy.*

Deacon: Unite them to His Holy, Catholic and Apostolic Church.

People: *Lord, have mercy.*

Deacon: Save them, have mercy on them, help them and keep them, O God, by Thy grace.

People: *Lord, have mercy.*

Deacon: Catechumens, bow thine heads to the Lord.

People: *To Thee, O Lord.*

Priest: *[Soto voce]* Lord, our God, dwelling on high and beholding things below, who for the salvation of mankind sent forth Thine only begotten Son, our Lord and God, Jesus Christ, look upon Thy servants the catechumens, who have bowed their necks to Thee and count them worthy in due time of the washing of rebirth, the forgiveness of sins and the garment of incorruption, unite them to Thy holy, Catholic and Apostolic Church, and number them with Thy chosen flock.

Priest: *[aloud]* That with us they may glorify Thine all honoured and majestic Name, of the Father, the Son, and the Holy Spirit, both now and forever, and unto the ages of ages.

People: *Amen.*

Deacon: As many as are Catechumens depart. Catechumens depart. All Catechumens depart. Let no Catechumen remain, but only the faithful.

The Liturgy Of The Faithful

Deacon: As many as are believers: again and again in peace, let us pray to the Lord.

People: *Lord, have mercy.*

Deacon: Help us, save us, have mercy on us and keep us, O God, by Thy grace.

People: *Lord, have mercy.*

Deacon: Wisdom!

First Prayer Of The Faithful

[Priest unfolds Antimension.]

Priest: *[Soto voce]* We thank Thee, Lord, God of the powers of heaven, for counting us worthy to stand even now before Thy holy altar and humbly seek Thy compassion for our sins and for those committed in ignorance by the people. Receive our supplication, O God; make us worthy to offer Thee prayers and entreaties and unbloody sacrifices for all of Thy people. And enable us, whom Thou hast appointed to this Thy ministry by the power of Thy Holy Spirit, to invoke Thee at every time and place without blame and without condemnation, with the witness of a pure conscience, so that Thou mayest hear us and be merciful to us in the abundance of Thy goodness.

Priest: *[aloud]* For to Thee belongest all glory, honour and worship, to the Father, and to the Son, and to the Holy Spirit, both now and forever, and unto the ages of ages.

People: *Amen.*

Deacon: Again and again, in peace let us pray to the Lord.

People: *Lord, have mercy.*

Deacon: Help us, save us, have mercy on us and keep us, O God, by Thy grace.

People: *Lord, have mercy.*

Deacon: Wisdom. *[enter sanctuary]*

Second Prayer Of The Faithful

Priest: *[Soto voce]* Again and many times we fall down before Thee and beseech Thee, who art good and the lover of mankind, that heeding our prayer Thou wilt cleanse out souls and bodies from every defilement of flesh and spirit, and shall grant us to stand without guilt or condemnation before Thy holy altar. Give also to those who pray with us the grace of progress in right living, in faith and spiritual understanding. Grant that always worshipping Thee with fear and love, they may partake of Thy holy Mysteries without guilt or condemnation, and be counted worthy of Thy heavenly kingdom.

[Resume here if no catechumens present.]

Priest: *[aloud]* That being always guarded by Thy might, we may give Glory be to the Father, and to the Son, and to the Holy Spirit, Both now and forever, and to the ages of ages.

People: *Amen.*

The Cherubic Hymn

(Sung slowly until the Entry.)

Chorus: We, who in a mystery represent the Cherubim and sing the thrice holy hymn to the life giving Trinity. Let us now lay aside every care of this life.

1)	Prepare incense.

[During the above the Priest is in front of The Holy Table and:]

Prayer Of The Cherubic Hymn

Priest: *[Soto voce]* No one bound by worldly desires and pleasures is worthy to approach, draw near or minister to Thee, the King of glory. To serve Thee is great and awesome even for the heavenly powers. But because of Thine ineffable and immeasurable love for us, Thou becamest man without alteration or change. Thou hast served as our High Priest, and as Lord of all, and have entrusted to us the celebration of this liturgical sacrifice without the shedding of blood.

For Thou alone, Lord our God, rulest over all things in heaven and on earth. Thou art seated on the throne of the Cherubim, the Lord of the Seraphim and the King of Israel. Thou alone art holy and dwell among Thy saints. Thou alone art good and ready to hear. Therefore, I implore Thee, look upon me, Thy sinful and unworthy servant, and cleanse my soul and heart from evil consciousness. Enable me by the power of Thy Holy Spirit so that, vested with the grace of priesthood, I may stand before Thy holy Table and celebrate the mystery of Thy holy and pure Body and Thy precious Blood.

To Thee I come with bowed head and pray: do not turn Thy face away from me or reject me from among Thy children, but make me, Thy sinful and unworthy servant, worthy to offer to Thee these gifts. For Thou, Christ our God, art the Offerer and the Offered, the One who receives and is distributed, and to Thee we give glory, together with Thine eternal Father and Thy holy, good and life creating Spirit, now and forever and to the ages of ages. Amen.

/	**Priest:**	*[Soto voce]* We, who in a mystery represent the Cherubim and sing the
/		thrice holy hymn to the life giving Trinity. Let us now lay aside every care of this life.
(x3)	**Deacon:**	*[Soto voce]* For we are about to receive the King of all, invisibly
\		escorted by the angelic hosts. Halleluiah, Halleluiah, Halleluiah.
\		

[Priest/Deacon censes the Gospel, all around the Holy Table, whole Sanctuary.
Exits via Holy Doors, stands there and censes the main icons and the people.]

On Sundays

Priest or Deacon: *[Soto voce]*   Having beheld the resurrection of Christ, let us worship the holy Lord Jesus, the only Sinless One. We venerate Thy cross, O Christ, and we praise and glorify Thy holy resurrection. Thou art our God. We know no other than Thee, and we call upon Thy name. Come, all faithful, let us venerate the holy resurrection of Christ. For behold, through the cross joy has come to all the world. Blessing the Lord always, let us praise His resurrection. For enduring the cross for us, he destroyed death by death.

If Not Sunday

Come let us worship and bow down before Christ. **(x3)**

[Continuing With:]

Psalm 50

Have mercy on me, O God, according to Thy great mercy; and according to the multitude of Thy compassions blot out my transgression. Wash me thoroughly from mine iniquity, and cleanse me from my sin. For I acknowledge mine iniquity, and my sin is ever before me. Against Thee, Thee only have I sinned, and done evil in Thy sight, that Thee mayest be found just when Thou speakest, and victorious when Thou art judged. For behold, I was conceived in iniquity, and in sin my mother bore me. For behold, Thou hast loved truth; Thou hast made known to me the hidden and secret things of Thy wisdom. Thou shalt sprinkle me with hyssop, and I shall be made clean; Thou shalt wash me, and I shall be whiter than snow. Make me to hear joy and gladness; that the humbled bones may rejoice. Turn Thy face away from my sins, and blot out all my iniquities.

Create in me a clean heart, O God, and renew a steadfast spirit within me. Cast me not away from Thy presence, and take not Thy Holy Spirit from me. Restore to me the joy of Thy salvation, and establish me with Thy governing Spirit. I shall teach transgressors Thy ways, and the ungodly shall turn back to Thee. Deliver me from blood guiltiness, O God, the God of my salvation; my tongue shall joyfully declare Thy righteousness. Lord, open my lips, and my mouth shall declare Thy praise. For if Thou hadst desired sacrifice, I would give it; Thou dost not delight in burnt offerings. A sacrifice to God is a broken spirit; God shall not despise a broken and a humbled heart.

[Enter Sanctuary; put away censer.
Deacon and Priest to front of Holy Table, 3 bows and Troparia of Compunction. Both kiss the Antimension and the Holy Table, bow, turn to people and bow to them saying:]
Deacon / Priest: Forgive me.

[At Prothesis, 3 bows, kiss covered Holy Gifts, saying:]
Deacon / Priest: God cleanse me a sinner.
Deacon: Master, lift up.
[Priest lifts Aer and places it on the shoulders of the Deacon, saying:]
Priest: Lift up thine hands to the holy place and bless the Lord.
[Priest takes covered Paten and reverently gives it to the Deacon.
Priest holds covered Chalice.]

When the Priest puts the aer over his or the Deacons shoulders:
2)   *Light tall candle stand for procession.*
3)   *Procession from North doors round to Holy Doors.*

The Great Entrance

Priest: May the Lord God remember you all in His Kingdom;
            Always now and forever and to the ages of ages.
Deacon: May the Lord God remember you all in His Kingdom;
            Always now and forever and to the ages of ages.
People: *Amen.*
            Remember us, Lord, when Thou comest in Thy kingdom. **(x3)** *Amen.*

4)   *After returning from the procession put out that candle.*

Cherubic Hymn Resumed

Chorus: For we are about to receive the King of all, invisibly escorted by the angelic hosts. Halleluiah, Halleluiah, Halleluiah.

[Repeat until censing finishes.]

[Deacon and Priest enter via Holy Doors.

Deacon stands to the right of the Holy Table and as the Priest enters says:]

Deacon: May the Lord God remember thy priesthood in His Kingdom, always, now and forever, and to the ages of ages.

Priest: May the Lord God remember thy diaconate in His Kingdom, always, now and forever, and to the ages of ages.

[Priest places Chalice on the Holy Table, takes the Paten and places it to the left of the Chalice.]

Priest: The noble Joseph, taking down Thy most pure Body from the Tree, wrapped it in a clean shroud with sweet spices and laid it for burial in a new grave.

[Priest takes covers from Paten and Chalice and lays them to one side.

Takes Aer from Deacons shoulders, holds it around the censer and lays it over the Chalice and Paten.

Censes the Gifts three times as:]

Deacon: Do good, Master.

Priest: Do good, O Lord, in Thy good pleasure to Zion, and let the walls of Jerusalem be builded. Then Thou shalt be pleased with a sacrifice of righteousness, with oblation and whole burned offerings. Then shall they offer bulls on Thine altar.

[Censer away.]

Priest: *[to Deacon]*   Remember me my brother and fellow celebrant.

Deacon: *[to Priest]* May the Lord God remember thy priesthood in His Kingdom, always, now and forever, and to the ages of ages.

[Deacon bows head, holding orarion in 3 fingers of right hand and says to Priest:]

Deacon: Pray for me, Holy Master.

Priest: The Holy Spirit shall come upon thee, and the power of the Most High shall overshadow thee.

Deacon: The Spirit Himself shall concelebrate with us all the days of our life. Remember me, holy Master.

Priest: May the Lord God remember thee in His Kingdom, always, now and forever, and to the ages of ages.

Deacon: Amen.

[Deacon kisses Priests hand, goes out to usual place and:]

Litany Of The Precious Gifts

Deacon: Let us complete our prayer to the Lord.

People: *Lord, have mercy.*

Deacon: For the Precious Gifts that have been offered, let us pray to the Lord.

People: *Lord, have mercy.*

Deacon: For this holy house, and for those who enter it with faith, reverence and the fear of God, let us pray to the Lord.

People: *Lord, have mercy.*

Deacon: For our deliverance from all affliction, wrath, danger and constraint, let us pray to the Lord.

People: *Lord, have mercy.*

Deacon: Help us, save us, have mercy on us and keep us, O God, by Thy grace.

People: *Lord, have mercy.*

Deacon: That the whole day may be perfect, holy, peaceful and sinless, let us ask of the Lord.

People: *Grant this, O Lord.*

Deacon: For an Angel of peace, a faithful guide and guardian of our souls and bodies, let us ask of the Lord.

People: *Grant this, O Lord.*

Deacon: For the pardon and forgiveness of our sins and offences, let us ask of the Lord.

People: *Grant this, O Lord.*

Deacon: Things that are good and profitable for our souls, and for peace in the world, let us ask of the Lord.

People: *Grant this, O Lord.*

Deacon: That we may live out the rest of our days in peace and repentance, let us ask of the Lord.

People: *Grant this, O Lord.*

Deacon: For a Christian end to our life, painless, unashamed and peaceful, and a good defence at the dread judgement seat of Christ, let us ask.

People: *Grant this, O Lord.*

Deacon: Commemorating our all holy, pure, most blessed and glorious Lady, Mother of God and Ever Virgin Mary, with all the Saints, let us entrust ourselves and one another, and our whole life to Christ our God.

People: *To Thee, O Lord.*

Prayer Of The Proskomide

Priest: *[Soto voce]* Lord, God Almighty, Thou alone art holy. Thou accepted a sacrifice of praise from those who call upon Thee with their whole heart. Receive also the prayer of us sinners and let it reach Thy holy altar. Enable us to bring before Thee gifts and spiritual sacrifices for our sins and for the transgressions of the people. Make us worthy to find grace in Thy presence so that our sacrifice may be pleasing to Thee and that Thy good and gracious Spirit may abide with us, with the gifts here presented, and with all Thy people.

Priest: *[aloud]* Through the compassion of Thine only begotten Son, with whom Thou art blessed, with the all holy and good and life creating Spirit, both now and forever and unto the ages of ages.

People: *Amen.*

Priest: Peace be with you all.

People: *And with thy spirit.*

Deacon: Let us love one another that with one mind we may confess:

People: *Father, Son, and Holy Spirit, Trinity consubstantial and undivided.*

[Priest bows 3 times and kisses the Aer over the Gifts, saying:]

Priest: *[Soto voce]* I love Thee, Lord, my strength. The Lord is my firm foundation, my refuge and my deliverer.

[Deacon bows and kisses the Cross on his orarion.

If concelebrating, Priests kiss.]

Senior Priest: Christ is in our midst.

Junior Priest: He is and shall be.

[Deacons do likewise.]

[During below Priest waves Aer above the Gifts.

At "Ascended into heaven" he kisses the central Cross of the Aer, folds it and places it on the covers.]

The Creed

Deacon: The Doors! The Doors! With Wisdom let us attend!

The Symbol of Faith

I believe in one God, Father, Almighty, Maker of heaven and earth, and of all things visible and invisible.

And in one Lord Jesus Christ, the only begotten Son of God, begotten from the Father before all ages; Light from Light, true God from true God; begotten not made; consubstantial with the Father, through Him all things were made. For our sake and for our salvation He came down from Heaven, and was incarnate from the Holy Spirit and the Virgin Mary and became man. He was crucified for us under Pontius Pilate, and suffered and was buried. He rose again on the third day in accordance with the Scriptures, and ascended into Heaven, and is seated at the right hand of the Father. He is coming again in glory to judge the living and the dead. And His kingdom shall have no end.

And in the Holy Spirit, the Lord, the Giver of life; Who proceeds from the Father; Who together with Father and Son is worshipped and glorified; Who spoke through the prophets. In One, Holy, Catholic, and Apostolic Church. I confess one baptism for the forgiveness of sins. I await the resurrection of the dead, And the life of the age to come. Amen.

The Holy Oblation

Deacon: Let us stand with awe, let us stand with fear, let us attend, that we may offer the Holy Sacrifice in peace.

[enter Sanctuary]

People: *Mercy and Peace, a Sacrifice of Praise.*

Priest: The grace of Our Lord Jesus Christ, and the Love of God the Father, and the Communion of the Holy Spirit be with you all.

People: And with thy spirit.

[Priest raises his hands.]

Priest: Let our hearts be on high.

People: We have them with the Lord.

[Priest faces east.]

Priest: Let us give thanks to the Lord.

People: It is right and fitting to worship Father, Son, and Holy Spirit, the Trinity consubstantial and undivided.

Priest: [Soto voce]   It is proper and right to sing to Thee, bless Thee, praise Thee, thank Thee and worship Thee in all places of Thy dominion; for Thou art God ineffable, beyond comprehension, invisible, beyond understanding, existing forever and always the same; Thee and Thine only begotten Son and Thy Holy Spirit. Thou broughtest us into being out of nothing, and when we fell, Thou raised us up again. Thou didst not cease doing everything until Thou led us to heaven and granted us Thy kingdom to come. For all these things we thank Thee and Thine only begotten Son and Thy Holy Spirit; for all things that we know and do not know, for blessings seen and unseen that have been bestowed upon us. We also thank Thee for this liturgy which Thou art pleased to accept from our hands, even though Thou art surrounded by thousands of Archangels and tens of thousands of Angels, by the Cherubim and Seraphim, six winged, many eyed, soaring aloft upon their wings,

Priest: [aloud]   … Singing, crying, shouting the triumphal hymn and saying:

People: Holy, holy holy, Lord Sabaoth; heaven and earth are full of Thy glory.
                   Hosanna in the highest. Blessed is He Who comes in the Name of the Lord.
                   Hosanna in the highest.

Prepare incense and charcoal.

[Deacon takes the Star from the Paten, makes the sign of the Cross over the Paten, kisses it and puts it aside.]

Priest: [Soto voce]   Together with these blessed powers, merciful Master, we also proclaim and say: Thou art holy and most holy, Thee and Thine only begotten Son and Thy Holy Spirit. Thou art holy and most holy, and sublime is Thy glory. Thou so loved Thy world that Thou gavest Thine only begotten Son so that whoever believes in Him should not perish, but have eternal life. He came and fulfilled the divine plan for us. On the night when He was delivered up, or rather when He gave Himself up for the life of the world, He took bread in His holy, pure, and blameless hands, gave thanks, blessed, sanctified, broke it and gave it to His holy Disciples and Apostles, saying:

Priest: [aloud]   Take, eat. This is My Body, Which is broken for ye, for the forgiveness of sins.

People: Amen.

Priest: [Soto voce]   Likewise, after supper, He took the cup, saying:

Priest: *[aloud]* Drink from this all of ye. This is My Blood of the New Covenant, Which is shed for ye, and for many, for the forgiveness of sins.

People: Amen.

Priest: *[Soto voce]* Remembering, therefore, this command of the Saviour, and all that came to pass for our sake, the cross, the tomb, the resurrection on the third day, the ascension into heaven, the enthronement at the right hand of the Father, and the second, glorious coming again,

[Priest crosses his hands and elevates Chalice and Paten.]

Priest: *[aloud]* Offering Thee Thine own of Thine own – in all things and for all things.

People: We praise Thee, we bless Thee, we thank Thee, O Lord, and we pray to Thee, our God.

Priest: *[Soto voce]* Once again we offer to Thee this spiritual worship without the shedding of blood, and we ask, pray, and entreat Thee: send down Thy Holy Spirit upon us and upon these gifts here set forth.

[Deacon points to the Holy Bread with his orarion and:]

Deacon: *[Soto voce]* Master, bless the Holy Bread.

[Priest stands upright and blesses the Holy Bread whilst:]

Priest: *[Soto voce]* And make this bread the precious Body of Thy Christ.

Deacon: Amen.

[Deacon points to Chalice with orarion and:]

Deacon: *[Soto voce]* Master, bless the holy cup.

[Priest blesses Chalice and:]

Priest: *[Soto voce]* And that which is in this cup the precious Blood of Thy Christ.

Deacon: Amen.

[Deacon points to both and:]

Deacon: *[Soto voce]* Master, bless them both.

[Priest blesses both and:]

Priest: *[Soto voce]* Changing them by Thy Holy Spirit.

Deacon: Amen, Amen, Amen.

[Both bow low.]

Priest: *[Soto voce]* So that they may be to those who partake of them for vigilance of soul, forgiveness of sins, communion of Thy Holy Spirit, fulfilment of the kingdom of heaven, confidence before Thee, and not in judgement or condemnation. Again, we offer this spiritual worship for those who repose in the faith, forefathers, fathers, patriarchs, prophets, apostles, preachers, evangelists, martyrs, confessors, ascetics, and for every righteous spirit made perfect in faith.

The Consecration

Priest: *[aloud]* Above all for our most holy, most pure, most blessed and glorious Lady, Mother of God, and Ever Virgin Mary.

People: *It is truly right to call thee blessed, who gave birth to God, ever blessed and most pure Virgin and Mother of our God. Greater in honour than the Cherubim and beyond compare more glorious than the Seraphim; without corruption thou gavest birth to God the Word, truly the Theotokos, we magnify thee.*

[Priest gives censer to Deacon, who censes around the Holy Table and quietly recites the names of the dead.]

Priest: *[Soto voce]*   For Saint John the prophet, forerunner, and baptist; for the holy glorious and most honourable Apostles; for Saint(s) N, whose memory we commemorate today; and for all Thy saints, through whose supplications, O God, bless us. Remember also all who have fallen asleep in the hope of resurrection unto eternal life. *(names of the dead).* And grant them rest, our God, where the light of Thy countenance shines. Again, we ask Thee, Lord, remember all Orthodox bishops who rightly teach the word of Thy truth, all presbyters, all deacons in the service of Christ, and every one in holy orders. We also offer to Thee this spiritual worship for the whole world, for the holy, catholic, and apostolic Church, and for those living in purity and holiness. And for all those in public service; permit them, Lord, to serve and govern in peace that through the faithful conduct of their duties we may live peaceful and serene lives in all piety and holiness.

Priest: *[aloud]* First of all remember, Lord, our Archbishop Nikitas and grant that he may serve Thy Holy Church in peace, safety, honour, health and length of days, rightly proclaiming the word of Thy truth.

People: *Amen.*

[Deacon stands at the Holy doors and recites the names of the living and:]

Deacon: Remember too, Lord, those whom each one has in mind, and each and all.

People: *And each and all.*

1)	Have the bread ready.

Priest: Remember, Lord, the city in which we live, every city and country, and the faithful who dwell in them. Remember, Lord, the travellers, the sick, the suffering, and the captives, granting them protection and salvation. Remember, Lord, those who do charitable work, who serve in Thy Holy Church, and who care for the poor. And send upon us all Thy rich mercies.

2)	Bread to the Priest.

Priest: *[aloud]* And grant that with one voice and one heart we may praise and glorify Thine all honoured and majestic Name, of the Father, the Son, and the Holy Spirit, both now and forever, and unto the ages of ages.

People: *Amen.*

[Priest blesses the people.]

Priest: And may the mercies of our Great God, and Saviour Jesus Christ, be with you all.

People: *And with thy spirit.*

[Deacon to usual place.]

THE PREPARATION FOR HOLY COMMUNION
Litany Of The Lords Prayer

Deacon: Having commemorated all the Saints, again and again in peace, let us pray to the Lord.

People: *Lord, have mercy.*

Deacon: For the Precious Gifts that have been offered and sanctified, let us pray to the Lord.

People: *Lord, have mercy.*

1)   *If no flask of hot water is available, put on the kettle.*

2)   *The collection is taken. Be ready to receive the plate of money at your door.*

3)   *Offer the plate to the Priest for blessing.*

4)   *Put the plate somewhere safe where it won't be kicked over.*

Deacon: That our God, who loves mankind, having accepted them on His holy and immaterial altar above the heavens, as an aroma of spiritual fragrance, may send down upon us in return His divine grace and the gift of His Holy Spirit, let us pray to the Lord.

People: *Lord, have mercy.*

Deacon: For our deliverance from all affliction, wrath, danger and constraint, let us pray to the Lord.

People: *Lord, have mercy.*

Deacon: Help us, save us, have mercy on us and keep us, O God, by Thy grace.

People: *Lord, have mercy.*

Deacon: That the whole day may be perfect, holy, peaceful, and sinless, let us ask of the Lord.

People: *Grant this, O Lord.*

Deacon: An Angel of peace, a faithful guide and guardian of our souls and bodies, let us ask of the Lord.

People: *Grant this, O Lord.*

Deacon: Pardon and forgiveness of our sins and offences, let us ask of the Lord.

People: *Grant this, O Lord.*

Deacon: For things good and profitable for our souls, and peace for the world, let us ask of the Lord.

People: *Grant this, O Lord.*

Deacon: That we may live out the rest of our days in peace and repentance, let us ask of the Lord.

People: *Grant this, O Lord.*

Deacon: A Christian end to our life, painless, unashamed and peaceful, and for a good defence at the dread judgement seat of Christ, let us ask.

People: *Grant this, O Lord.*

Deacon: Having asked for the unity of the Faith, and the communion of the Holy Spirit, let us entrust ourselves and one another, and our whole life to Christ our God.

People: *To Thee, O Lord.*

Priest: *[Soto voce]*   We entrust to Thee, loving Master, our whole life and hope, and we ask, pray, and entreat: make us worthy to partake of Thy heavenly and awesome Mysteries from this holy and spiritual Table with a clear conscience; for the remission of sins, forgiveness of transgressions, communion of the Holy Spirit, inheritance of the kingdom of heaven, confidence before Thee, and not in judgement or condemnation.

Priest: *[aloud]* And count us worthy, O Lord, with boldness and without condemnation to dare to call upon Thee, the Heavenly God, as Father, and to say:

The Lords Prayer

People: *Our Father, Who art in heaven, hallowed be Thy Name.*

            Thy Kingdom come, Thy will be done on earth, as it is in heaven.

            Give us this day our daily bread.

            And forgive us our trespasses as we forgive those who trespass against us.

            And lead us not into temptation; but deliver us from the evil one.

Priest: For Thine is the kingdom, the power, and the glory, of the Father, and the Son and the Holy Spirit, Both now and forever, and to the ages of ages.

People: *Amen.*

Priest: Peace be with you all.

People: *And with thy spirit.*

Deacon: Let us bow our heads to the Lord.

People: *To Thee, O Lord.*

Priest: *[Soto voce]*   We give thanks to Thee, invisible King. By Thy infinite power Thee created all things and by Thy great mercy Thou broughtest everything from nothing into being. Master, look down from heaven upon those who have bowed their heads before Thee; they have bowed not before flesh and blood but before Thee the awesome God. Therefore, Master, guide the course of our life for our benefit according to the need of each of us. Sail with those who sail; travel with those who travel; and heal the sick, Physician of our souls and bodies.

Priest: Through the grace and compassion and love for men of Thine only begotten Son, with Whom Thou art blessed, and Thine all holy and good and life creating Spirit, both now and forever, and unto the ages of ages.

People: *Amen.*

Priest: *[Soto voce]* Lord Jesus Christ, our God, hear us from Thy holy dwelling place and from the glorious throne of Thy kingdom. Thou art enthroned on high with the Father and are also invisibly present among us. Come and sanctify us, and let Thy pure Body and precious Blood be given to us by Thy mighty hand and through us to all Thy people.

[Priest and Deacon in usual place bow three times and:]

Priest and Deacon: *[Soto voce]* God, cleanse me a sinner.

The Elevation

Deacon: Let us attend.

Priest: The Holy Things for the holy.

People: *One is holy, one is Lord, Jesus Christ, to the glory of God the Father. Amen.*

Have the hot water ready.

Communion Of The Clergy And The People

Chorus: Praise the Lord from Heaven, praise Him in the Heights. Halleluiah. Halleluiah. Halleluiah.

[Deacon enters and ties orarion in a cross and moves to right side of Priest.]

Deacon: Master, break the Holy Bread.

[Priest divides the Lamb into four parts and:]

Priest: The Lamb of God is broken and distributed; broken but not divided. He is forever eaten yet is never consumed, but He sanctifies those who partake of Him.

[Priest arranges them on the Paten in the form of a Cross:

IC

NI   KA

XC

Deacon points to Chalice with orarion and:]

Deacon: Master, fill the Holy Cup.

[Priest takes **IC** *and makes the Cross with it over Chalice and places it therein and:]*

Priest: The fullness of the Holy Spirit.

Deacon: Amen.

Hot water to the Deacon.

Deacon: Master, bless the hot water.

[Priest blesses it and:]

Priest: Blessed is the fervour of Thy saints, now and forever and to the ages of ages. Amen.

[Deacon pours hot water into Chalice in a crosswise and:]

Deacon: The warmth of the Holy Spirit. Amen.

---

1)	Light the tall candle stand and place it in front of the Holy Doors.

Prayers Said By The Clergy Before Communion.

[Before The Communion Hymn, Chant the following. Deep and slow.]

Reader:

1.   I believe, Lord, and I confess that Thou art truly the Christ, the son of the living God, who came into the world to save sinners, of whom I am first. Also I believe that this is indeed Thy most pure Body, and this indeed Thy precious Blood. Therefore I beseech Thee, have mercy on me and forgive me my offences, voluntary and involuntary, in word and in deed, in knowledge and in ignorance, and count me worthy to partake uncondemned of Thy most pure Mysteries for forgiveness of sins and for eternal life. Amen.

2.   See, to divine Communion I draw near; My Maker, burn me not as I partake. For Thou art fire, consuming the unworthy; But therefore make me clean from every stain.

3.   Of Thy mystical supper, Son of God, receive me today as a communicant; for I shall not tell of the Mystery to Thine enemies; I shall not give Thee a kiss like Judas; but like the thief I confess Thee. Remember me, Lord, in Thy kingdom.

4.   Master, lover of mankind, Lord Jesus Christ, my God, let not these Holy Mysteries be for my condemnation because of my unworthiness, but rather for the cleansing and sanctification of both soul and body, and as a pledge of the life and kingdom to come. It is good for me to cleave to God, to place in the Lord the hope of my salvation.

5.   Let not the Communion of Thy holy Mysteries, Lord, be to me for judgement or condemnation, but for healing of soul and body.

[Then sing Psalm 32. The refrain is:

People: For He spoke, and it was done; He commanded, and it stood fast.]

[Priest asks forgiveness of those in the Altar and the rest of the Church. Goes to the Holy Table and:]

Priest: Behold, I approach Christ, our immortal King and God.

*[Priest takes **XC** and:]*

Priest: The precious and most holy Body of our Lord, God, and Saviour Jesus Christ is given to me *N* the priest (and monk), for the forgiveness of my sins and for eternal life.

[Priest reverently eats the Holy Bread, wipes hands over Paten with sponge and:]

Priest: Deacon, draw near.

Deacon: Behold I draw near to Christ, our immortal King and God. Grant me, the unworthy Deacon (and monk) *N* communion, Master of the precious and all holy Body of our Lord and God and Saviour, Jesus Christ, for the forgiveness of my sins and for eternal life.

[Deacon kisses Priests hand, goes to back of the Holy Table, eats the Holy Bread.]
[Priest takes Chalice with red Communion cloth and:]

Priest: To me, the unworthy Priest (and monk) *N* is granted Communion of the precious and all Holy Blood of our Lord and Saviour, Jesus Christ, for the forgiveness of my sins and for eternal life.

[Priest drinks 3 times from Chalice, wipes his lips and the Chalice with the cloth, and kisses the Chalice and:]

Priest: This has touched my lips, taking away my transgressions and cleansing my sins. Deacon, again draw near.

[Deacon wipes his hand over the Paten with the sponge, approaches and:]

Deacon: Behold, again I draw near to Christ, our immortal King and God. Grant me Communion, Master, of the precious and all Holy Blood of our Lord and God and Saviour, Jesus Christ, for the forgiveness of my sins and for eternal life.

[Priest takes Chalice and Communicates the Deacon 3 times and:]

Priest: To thee the devout Deacon (and monk) *N* is granted Communion of the precious and all Holy Blood of our Lord and God and Saviour, Jesus Christ, for the forgiveness of thy sins and for eternal life. This has touched thy lips, it shall take away thine iniquities and cleanse thy sins.

[Deacon divides **NI** *and* **KA** *into small pieces and places them in the Chalice, then covers it with the Communion cloth. Lays the spoon on the covered Chalice.]*
[The Holy doors are opened and Priest hands Chalice to Deacon.

The Communion of the People.

2)	*When the Deacon moves to the centre holding the wine, remove the candle.*
3)	*Stand to the right side of the Priest holding the tray of bread.*
4)	*When communion is finished and you are back in your place, prepare incense.*

[Deacon takes the Chalice and exits via Holy Doors.]

Deacon: With the fear of God, with faith and love, draw near.

People: *Blessed is He Who comes in the Name of the Lord. The Lord is God and has appeared to us.*

[Deacon hands the chalice to the Priest.]
[Whilst there is a queue sing the following, deep and slow.]

If Not Pascha

Reader: Of Thy mystical supper, Son of God, receive me today as a communicant;

For I shall not tell of the Mystery to Thine enemies;

I shall not give Thee a kiss like Judas; but like the thief I confess Thee.

|: Remember me, Lord, in Thy kingdom. :|

If Pascha

Receive the Body of Christ, taste from the fount of immortality. Halleluiah, Halleluiah, Halleluiah.

[As dispensing Communion:]

Priest: The Servant of God *N*, partakes of the Precious and Holy Body and Blood of our Lord and God and Saviour Jesus Christ, for the remission of his/her sins, and for life eternal.

[When all have been communicated Priest hands Chalice to Deacon who replaces it on the Holy Table. Priest blesses the people and:]

Priest: O God, save Thy people, and bless Thine inheritance.

People: *We have seen the true Light, we have received the heavenly Spirit, we have found the true Faith, as we worship the undivided Trinity. For the Trinity has saved us.*

[Deacon holds Paten above Chalice and wipes ALL crumbs and:]

Deacon: Wash away, Lord, by Thy Holy Blood the sins of Thy servants here remembered, through the prayers of the Mother of God and of all of Thy saints. Amen. Master, exalt.

Incense to the Priest.

[Priest censes Chalice 3 times, each time saying:]

Priest: Be exalted, O God, above the heavens. Let Thy glory be over all the earth.

[Priest gives Paten, Covers and the Star to the Deacon, who shows them to the people, goes behind Holy Table to Prothesis. Unties orarion. Priest bows, takes Chalice and:]

Priest: *[Soto voce]* Blessed is our God.

[Priest turns to people and shows the Chalice and:]

Priest: *[aloud]* Always, now and ever, and to the ages of ages.

People: *Amen.*

People: Let our mouth be filled with Thy praise, O Lord, that we may sing of Thy glory, For Thou hast counted us worthy to partake of Thy Holy Mysteries. Keep us in Thy holiness that we may meditate on Thy righteousness all the day long. Halleluiah. Halleluiah. Halleluiah.

[Deacon places Chalice on Prothesis, returns to Holy Table, checks for crumbs and folds Antimension. Deacon goes to usual place and:]

Thanksgiving And Dismissal

Deacon: Stand upright! Having received the divine, holy, pure, immortal, heavenly, life creating and dread Mysteries of Christ, let us give worthy thanks to the Lord.

People: *Lord, have mercy.*

Deacon: Help us, save us, have mercy on us and keep us, O God, by Thy grace.

People: *Lord, have mercy.*

Deacon: Having asked that the whole day may be perfect, holy, peaceful and sinless, let us entrust ourselves and one another, and our whole life to Christ our God.

People: *To Thee, O Lord.*

Priest: *[Soto voce]* We thank Thee, loving Master, benefactor of our souls, that on this day Thou hast made us worthy once again of Thy heavenly and immortal Mysteries. Direct our ways in the right path, establish us firmly in Thy fear, guard our lives, and make our endeavours safe, through the prayers and supplications of the glorious Theotokos and Ever Virgin Mary and of all Thy saints.

[Priest makes the sign of the Cross with the Gospel over the folded Antimension and:]

Priest: *[aloud]* For Thou art our sanctification, and to Thee we give glory, to the Father, the Son, and the Holy Spirit, both both now and forever, and unto the ages of ages.

People: *Amen.*

Priest: Let us depart in peace.

People: *In the Name of the Lord.*

Deacon: Let us pray to the Lord.

People: *Lord, have mercy.*

Prayer Behind The Ambo

Priest: O Lord, Thou blessest those who bless Thee, and sanctify those who put their trust in Thee: Save Thy people and bless Thine inheritance. Preserve the fullness of Thy Church; sanctify those who love the beauty of Thy House; glorify them with Thy divine power, and forsake not us who put our hope in Thee. Grant peace to Thy world, to Thy churches, to Thy Priests, to all God fearing rulers, and to all Thy people. For every blessing and every perfect gift is from above and comes down from Thee, the Father of Lights. And to Thee we give glory and thanksgiving and worship, to the Father, the Son, and the Holy Spirit, now and ever and to the ages of ages.

People: *Amen.*

Blessed be the Name of the Lord from this time forth and for evermore. **(x3)**

[Priest returns to Prothesis and:]

Priest: *[Soto voce]* Christ our God, Thou art the fulfilment of the Law and the prophets. Thou hast fulfilled all the dispensation of the Father. Fill our hearts with joy and gladness always, now and forever and to the ages of ages. Amen.

Deacon: Let us pray to the Lord.

People: *Lord, have mercy.*

[Deacon enters via North door, asks a blessing of the Priest and goes to Prosthesis, consumes the contents of the Chalice and purifies it and tidies the Holy Vessels.]

[Priest exits via Holy Doors and blesses the people and:]

Priest: May the blessing of the Lord and His mercy be upon you, by His grace and love for mankind, always, both now and forever, and unto the ages of ages.

People: *Amen.*

Priest: Glory to Thee, O Christ, our God and our hope, glory to Thee.

Reader: Glory be to the Father, and to to Son, and to the Holy Spirit, both now and for ever, both and to the ages of ages. Amen.

   Lord, have mercy. **(x3)**

   Holy Father, bless!

Priest: May *(Sundays: He Who rose from the dead)* Christ our true God, through the prayers of His most holy Mother, by the power of the precious and life giving Cross, through the protection of the honoured, Bodiless powers of Heaven, through the intercessions of the honoured, glorious prophet, forerunner and baptist John, of the holy, all praised and glorious Apostles, of the holy, glorious and triumphant Martyrs, of our venerable and God bearing Fathers and Mothers who have shone forth in the ascetic life, of our Father among the Saints, John Chrysostom, Archbishop of Constantinople, of the holy and righteous ancestors of God, Joachim and Anna, of *[Saint of your parish]* to whom the church is dedicated, of Saint N whose memory we celebrate today, and of all the Saints, have mercy on us and save us, for He is good and loves mankind.

People: *Amen.*

Priest: Through the prayers of our holy fathers, Lord Jesus Christ, our God, have mercy on us.

People: *Amen.*

[Priest blesses people and:]

Priest: May the Holy Trinity protect you all.

Reader: O Lord, protect the one who blesses us and sanctifies us, for many years.

With the tray of antidoron (bread) stand to the left of the Priest.

Priest: Come forward to receive the Antidoron.

   [To each recipient:]

   May the blessing and mercy of the Lord come upon you.

[If no Deacon then at this point Priest drains and cleans the Chalice, tidies up and disrobes. Bows to the Holy Table, gives thanks for all things and departs.]

The Koinonikon (short version) is the paragraph or sentence sung whilst the people Commune. However Communion starts for the clergy before the Holy Doors are opened and the summons to the people is made. The Koinonikon (long version) is sung to cover this gap. This one comes from before 800 AD and is a call and response with the people. It may be plain chanted or sung. In this parish the peoples refrain goes:

C B A   B C   B A   B C

For He spoke, and it was done; He commanded, and it stood fast.

Reader: Rejoice in the Lord, O you righteous: praise is comely for the upright.

People: *For He spoke, and it was done; He commanded, and it stood fast.*

Reader: Praise the Lord with the harp and on the ten stringed lyre.

People: *For He spoke, and it was done; He commanded, and it stood fast.*

Reader: Sing unto Him a new song; play skilfully with a loud noise.

People: *For He spoke, and it was done; He commanded, and it stood fast.*

Reader: For the word of the Lord is right; and all His works are done in truth.

People: *For He spoke, and it was done; He commanded, and it stood fast.*

Reader: He loves righteousness and judgement. The earth is full of the goodness of the Lord.

People: *For He spoke, and it was done; He commanded, and it stood fast.*

Reader: By the word of the Lord were the heavens made;
And all the host of them by the breath of His mouth.

People: *For He spoke, and it was done; He commanded, and it stood fast.*

Reader: He gathers the waters of the sea together in a heap. He puts the depth into storehouses.

People: *For He spoke, and it was done; He commanded, and it stood fast.*

Reader: Let all the earth fear the Lord. Let all the people of the world revere Him.

People: *For He spoke, and it was done; He commanded, and it stood fast.*

Reader: The Lord brings the counsel of the heathen to nought:
He makes the devices of the people of none effect.

People: *For He spoke, and it was done; He commanded, and it stood fast.*

Reader: The counsel of the Lord stands for ever; the thoughts of His heart to all generations.

People: *For He spoke, and it was done; He commanded, and it stood fast.*

Reader: Blessed is the nation whose God is the Lord:

And the people whom He has chosen for His own inheritance.

People: *For He spoke, and it was done; He commanded, and it stood fast.*

Reader: The Lord looks from heaven; He beholds all the sons of men.

People: *For He spoke, and it was done; He commanded, and it stood fast.*

Reader: From the place of His habitation, He looks on all the inhabitants of the earth.

People: *For He spoke, and it was done; He commanded, and it stood fast.*

Reader: He fashions their hearts alike; He considers all their works.

People: *For He spoke, and it was done; He commanded, and it stood fast.*

Reader: No king is saved by the size of his army. A mighty man is not delivered by much strength.

People: *For He spoke, and it was done; He commanded, and it stood fast.*

Reader: A horse is a vain thing for safety; despite all its great strength it cannot save.

People: *For He spoke, and it was done; He commanded, and it stood fast.*

Reader: Behold, the eye of the Lord is upon them that fear Him. Upon them that hope in His mercy.

People: *For He spoke, and it was done; He commanded, and it stood fast.*

Reader: To deliver their soul from death, and to keep them alive in famine.

People: *For He spoke, and it was done; He commanded, and it stood fast.*

Reader: Our souls wait for the Lord: He is our help and our shield.

People: *For He spoke, and it was done; He commanded, and it stood fast.*

Reader: For our heart shall rejoice in Him, because we trusted in His Holy Name.

People: *For He spoke, and it was done; He commanded, and it stood fast.*

Reader: Let Thine mercy, O Lord, be upon us, according as we hope in Thee.

People: *For He spoke, and it was done; He commanded, and it stood fast.*

All: For He spoke, and it was done; He commanded, and it stood fast.

Prayer Of The Prothesis

[In the skevophylakion.]

Priest: Glory to the Father and to the Son and to the Holy Spirit, the one, simple and undivided Trinity, that unites and sanctifies us through itself, and brings peace to our lives, now and for ever, and to the ages of ages. Amen.

Priest: *[soto voce]:* Defiled as I am by many sins, do not utterly reject me, Master, Lord, our God. For see, I draw near to this divine and heavenly mystery, not as though I were worthy, but, looking to your goodness, I raise my voice to you, 'God, be merciful to me, a sinner. For I have sinned against heaven and before you, and I am not worthy to lift up my eyes to this your sacred and spiritual Table, on which your only begotten Son, our Lord Jesus Christ, is mystically set forth as a sacrifice by me, a sinner stained by every defilement. Therefore I bring you this supplication, that your Spirit, the Advocate, may be sent down to me, strengthening and preparing me for this ministry. And grant that without condemnation the word that has been declared by you may be proclaimed by me to the people in Christ Jesus our Lord, with whom you are blessed, together with your all holy, good, life giving and consubstantial Spirit, now and for ever, and to the ages of ages. Amen.

[Before the Holy Doors, as the clergy are about to make the Entrance.]

Priest: *[aloud]:* Glory to the Father and to the Son and to the Holy Spirit, the triple and single light of the one Godhead, that exists singly in Trinity and is divided without division. For the one God is Trinity, whose glory the heavens declare, while earth proclaims His dominion, the sea His might and every physical and immaterial creature his greatness. For to Him belongs all glory, honour, might, greatness and magnificence, now and for ever, and to the ages of ages.

People: Amen.

Prayers Of The Enarxis

Priest: *[aloud]:* Benefactor and King of the ages, and Fashioner of all creation, accept your Church, which approaches you through your Christ. Fulfil what is profitable for each, bring all to perfection, and make us worthy of the grace of your sanctification, gathering us together in your Holy, Catholic and Apostolic Church, which you gained by the blood of your only begotten Son, our Lord and saviour, Jesus Christ, with whom you are blessed and glorified, together with your all holy, good and life giving Spirit, now and forever, and to the ages of ages.

Deacon: Amen.

Priest: Peace be with you all.

People: And with thy spirit.

Deacon: Let us pray to the Lord.

People: Lord, have mercy.

Prayer Of The Incense At The Entrance

Priest: *[aloud]*: O God, who accepted the gifts of Abel, the sacrifices of Noah and Abraham, the incense of Aaron and Zachary, accept from the hands of us sinners this incense for a sweet fragrance and forgiveness of our sins and those of all your people. For you are blessed and to you belongs glory, to the Father with your only begotten Son and your all holy, good and life giving Spirit, now and for ever, and to the ages of ages.

[Deacon censes and:]

Deacon: Only begotten Son and Word of God, who, being immortal, accepted for our salvation to take flesh from the holy Mother of God and Ever Virgin Mary, and without change became man; you were crucified, Christ God, by death trampling on death, being one of the Holy Trinity, glorified with the Father and the Holy Spirit: save us!

Reader: *[Troparion for the Entrance of the clergy with the holy Gospel.]*

Reader: Only begotten Son and Word of God, who, being immortal, accepted for our salvation to take flesh from the holy Mother of God and Ever Virgin Mary, and without change became man; you were crucified, Christ God, by death trampling on death, being one of the Holy Trinity, glorified with the Father and the Holy Spirit: save us!

[When at the middle of the church, where a vima [platform] has been set up, they place the holy Gospel on it, and go towards the sanctuary.]

[standing in front of the holy Doors]

Priest *[aloud]*: Almighty God, Lord, whose name is great, who give us entrance to the Holy of Holies through the coming of your only begotten Son, our Lord and God and Saviour, Jesus Christ, we entreat and implore your goodness. Since we are full of fear and trembling as we are about to stand before your holy altar, send forth your good grace upon us, sanctify our souls, bodies and spirits and change our thoughts to true devotion, so that, with a pure conscience, we may offer you gifts, presents, fruits, for the removal of our sins, for the forgiveness of all your people, by the grace and love for humankind of your only begotten Son, with whom you are blessed, together with your all holy, good and life giving Spirit, now and for ever, and to the ages of ages.

People: Amen.

[Priest: enters the sanctuary.]

[Deacon faces the People]

Deacon: In peace, let us pray to the Lord.

People: Lord, have mercy.

Deacon: For the peace from on high, Gods love for humankind, and the salvation of our souls, let us pray to the Lord.

People: Lord, have mercy.

Deacon: For the peace of the whole world and the union of all the holy churches of God, let us pray to the Lord.

People: *Lord, have mercy.*

Deacon: For the salvation and of our most holy Father and Archbishop Gregory, all the clergy and Christ loving people, let us pray to the Lord.

People: *Lord, have mercy.*

Deacon: For the forgiveness of our sins and pardon of our offences, and for us to be delivered from all affliction, wrath, danger, constraint and assault of enemies, let us pray to the Lord.

People: *Lord, have mercy.*

Deacon: Let us call to mind our most holy, pure, most glorious and blessed Lady, Mother of God and Ever Virgin Mary, of the holy, glorious Prophet, Forerunner and Baptist John, of the holy, godlike and all praised Apostles, of the glorious Prophets and victorious Martyrs and all the holy and just, that by their prayers and intercessions we may all find mercy.

People: *Lord, have mercy.*

[bowing and quiet]

The Prayer of the Trisagion

Priest: Compassionate and merciful, long suffering, most merciful and true Lord, look down from your holy dwelling place, hearken to us, your, supplicants, and deliver us from every trial and temptation, both diabolic and human. Do not deprive us of your help, nor bring upon us heavier chastisement than we are able to bear. For we are not capable of conquering what opposes us, while you, Lord, have power to save us from all adversities. Save us, O God, from the difficulties of this world in accordance with your goodness, so that, having entered your holy altar with a pure conscience, we may, without condemnation, offer you with the heavenly Powers the blessed and thrice holy hymn, and have accomplished the divine ministry that is well pleasing to you, we may be found worthy of eternal life.

Priest: *[aloud]* For holy are you, Lord our God, and you dwell and take your rest in the holy place, and to you we offer glory and the thrice holy hymn, to Father, Son and Holy Spirit, now and for ever, and to the ages of ages.

People: *Amen.*

Holy God, Holy Strong, Holy Immortal, have mercy on us. **(x3)**

> *Glory to the Father, and to the Son, and to the Holy Spirit.*
>
> *Both now and for ever, and unto the ages of ages. Amen.*

Holy Immortal, have mercy on us.

Deacon: Dynamis.

People: Holy God, holy Strong, holy Immortal, have mercy on us.

Priest: Peace be with you all.

People: *And with thy spirit.*

Deacon: Wisdom. The Prokeimenon.

Reader: *[the Prokeimenon]*

Deacon: Wisdom.

Reader: *[title of the Apostle]*

Deacon: Let us attend.

Reader: *[the Apostle]*

Priest: Peace be with you who read.

Reader: And with thy spirit.

People: *Halleluiah.* **(x3)**

[While the Halleluiah is being sung, the Deacon takes the censer, receives the Priests blessing, and comes out and censes the holy Gospel.]

The Prayer of the Incense

Priest: *[soto voce]* To you, Lord our God, who are filled with all fragrance and joy, we offer you this incense from the things that you have given us. Let it then, we beg you, be taken up from our poor hands to your holy altar above the heavens for an odour of sweetness and forgiveness of our sins and those of all your people, by the grace and compassion and love for humankind of your only begotten Son, with whom you are blessed, together with your all holy, good and life giving Spirit, now and for ever, and to the ages of ages. Amen.

Deacon: Let us all say, Lord, have mercy.

People: *Lord, have mercy.*

Deacon: Almighty, heavenly Lord, the God of our fathers, we pray you, hear us.

People: *Lord, have mercy.*

Deacon: For the peace of the whole world and union of all the Holy Church, we pray you, hear us.

People: *Lord, have mercy.*

Deacon: For the salvation and assistance of our most holy father and Archbishop Nikitas, all the clergy and the Christ loving people, we pray you, hear us.

People: *Lord, have mercy.*

Deacon: For our sovereign Lady, Queen Elizabeth, the Royal family, her government and all in authority, we pray you, hear us.

People: *Lord, have mercy.*

Deacon: For this city, for every city, town and village, we pray you, hear us.

People: *Lord, have mercy.*

Deacon: For our deliverance from all affliction, wrath, danger, constraint, captivity, bitter death, and our iniquities, we pray you, hear us.

People: *Lord, have mercy.*

Deacon: For the people here present and who await your great and rich mercy, we implore you, have compassion and mercy.

People: *Lord, have mercy.*

Deacon: O God, save your people and bless your inheritance. Visit your world with mercy and pity. Exalt the horn of Christians by the power of the precious and life giving Cross, at the intercession of our all pure and blessed Lady, Mother of God, of the Forerunner, your Apostles and all your Saints, we implore you, most merciful Lord, hear us as we pray, and have mercy.

People: *Lord, have mercy.* **(x3)**

Prayer Before The Holy Gospel

Priest: *[soto voce]*:   Master, Lover of humankind, make the pure light of your divine knowledge shine in our hearts and open the eyes of our mind to understand the message of your Gospel. Implant in us the fear of your blessed commandments, so that, having trampled down all carnal desires, we may change to a spiritual way of life, thinking and doing all things that are pleasing to you.

Priest: *[aloud]*:   For you are the glad tidings, enlightenment, Saviour and guardian of our souls and bodies, O God, and to you we give glory, together with your only begotten Son, and your all holy Spirit, now and for ever, and to the ages of ages.

People: *Amen.*

Deacon: Stand upright. Let us listen to the holy Gospel.

Priest: Peace be with you all.

People: *And with thy spirit.*

Deacon: The reading is from the holy Gospel according to N.

People: *Glory to you, Lord. Glory to you.*

Priest: Let us attend.

Deacon: *[The Holy Gospel]*

Priest: Peace be with you who reads.

People: *Glory to you, Lord. Glory to you.*

Priest: *[Gives the sermon]*

[Standing in front of the holy Door, facing the People.]

Deacon: Let us be devoutly attentive. In peace let us pray to the Lord.

People: *Lord, have mercy.*

Deacon: For the peace of the whole world and the union of all the Holy Church, let us pray to the Lord.

People: *Lord, have mercy.*

Deacon: For the salvation and assistance of our most holy Archbishop N., of all the clergy and the Christ loving people, let us pray to the Lord.

People: *Lord, have mercy.*

Deacon: For forgiveness of our sins and pardon of our offences, and for our deliverance from all affliction, wrath, danger and constraint, assault of enemies, let us pray to the Lord.

People: *Lord, have mercy.*

Deacon: That the day that we pass through may be perfect, holy, peaceful and sinless, let us all ask of the Lord.

People: *Grant this, O Lord.*

Deacon: An angel of peace, a faithful guide, a guardian of our souls and bodies, let us ask of the Lord.

People: *Grant this, O Lord.*

Deacon: Pardon and forgiveness of our sins and offences, let us ask of the Lord.

People: *Grant this, O Lord.*

Deacon: Things good and profitable for our souls, and peace for the world, let us ask of the Lord.

People: *Grant this, O Lord.*

Deacon: That we may live out the rest of our days in peace and good health, let us ask of the Lord.

People: *Grant this, O Lord.*

Deacon: A Christian end to our life, painless, unashamed and peaceful, and a good defence before the fearsome and dread judgement seat of Christ, let us ask.

People: *Grant this, O Lord.*

Deacon: Commemorating our all holy, pure, most glorious and blessed Lady, Mother of God and Ever Virgin Mary, of the holy, glorious, Prophet, Forerunner and Baptist, John, of the godlike and all praised Apostles, glorious Prophets and triumphant Martyrs with all the Holy and Just, let us entrust ourselves and one another and our whole life to Christ our God.

People: *To you, O Lord.*

Prayer After The Holy Gospel

Priest: *[soto voce]*: You have made your divine and saving words resound for us, O God, enlighten the souls of us sinners to understand the things that have been read, so that we may be seen to be not only hearers of the spiritual songs, but also doers of good deeds, maintaining a faith without pretence, a life without blame, conduct without reproach,

Priest: *[aloud]*: In Christ Jesus our Lord, with whom you are blessed and glorified, together with your all holy, good and life giving Spirit, now and for ever, and to the ages of ages.

People: *Amen.*

Priest: Peace be with you all.

People: *And with thy spirit.*

Deacon: Let us bow our heads to the Lord.

People: *To you, O Lord.*

Priest: *[bowing and quiet]*: Good Master, giver of life and bestower of good things, who give mortals the blessed hope of eternal life, our Lord Jesus Christ, count us worthy also to accomplish this ministry in holiness, for the enjoyment of the blessedness to come.

Priest: *[aloud]*: That being always guarded by your might, and guided to the light of truth, we may give glory and thanksgiving to you, Father, Son and Holy Spirit, now and for ever, and to the ages of ages.

People: *Amen.*

Deacon: Let us chant in the peace of Christ.

Deacon: Let none of the catechumens; none of the uninitiated; none of those who cannot pray with us. Recognize one another. The doors! Let all stand upright.

Singers *[slow]*: Let all mortal flesh keep silent, and with fear and trembling stand. Ponder nothing earthly minded, Let all mortal flesh keep silent, and with fear and trembling stand. Ponder nothing earthly minded, for the King of kings and Lord of lords advances to be slain and given as food to the faithful. Before him go the Chorus' of Angels, with every rule and authority, the many eyed Cherubim and the six winged Seraphim, veiling their sight and crying out the hymn: Halleluiah, Halleluiah, Halleluiah.

[The holy Gifts are placed on the holy Altar and before they are covered with the Cloud.]

The Prayer Of The Prothesis

Priest: God, our God, who sent forth the heavenly Bread, the food of the whole world, our Lord and God Jesus Christ, as our Saviour, Redeemer and Benefactor, to bless and sanctify us; bless this Offering, and receive it on your altar above the heavens. In your goodness and love for humankind be mindful of those who have offered it, and those for whom they have offered it, and grant all their requests that are for their salvation; and as we celebrate your divine mysteries keep us without condemnation. For sanctified and glorified is your all honoured and majestic name, of the Father, the Son and the Holy Spirit, now and for ever, and to the ages of ages. Amen.

[Priest: censes the holy Gifts.]

Priest: Master almighty, King of glory, the God who knows all things before they come to be, be present with us as we call upon you at this holy time, and redeem us from the shame of transgressions. Cleanse our mind and our thoughts from foul desires, worldly deception and every operation of the devil, and accept from the hand of us sinners this incense for an odour of sweet fragrance, as you accepted the offering of Abel and Noah, Aaron and Samuel and all your holy ones, delivering us from every evil deed, and keeping us safe to be always well pleasing to you, and to worship and glorify you, our Father, and your only begotten Son and your all holy Spirit, now and for ever, and to the ages of ages. Amen.

Deacon: In Gods wisdom, let us attend.

[Priest covers the holy Gifts with the Cloud.]

The Symbol Of Faith

Priest: I believe in one God.

People: I believe in one God, Father, Almighty, Maker of heaven and earth, and of all things visible and invisible.

And in one Lord, Jesus Christ, the only begotten Son of God, begotten from the Father before all ages, Light from Light, true God from true God, begotten not made, consubstantial with the Father, through him all things were made. For our sake and for our salvation he came down from heaven, and was incarnate from the Holy Spirit and the Virgin Mary and became man. He was crucified also for us under Pontius Pilate, and suffered and was buried; he rose again on the third day, in accordance with the Scriptures, and ascended into heaven and is seated at the right hand of the Father. He is coming again in glory to judge the living and the dead, and his kingdom shall have no end.

And in the Holy Spirit, the Lord, the Giver of life, who proceeds from the Father, who together with Father and Son is worshipped and glorified; who spoke through the Prophets. In one Holy, Catholic and Apostolic Church. I confess one Baptism for the forgiveness of sins. I await the resurrection of the dead and the life of the age to come. Amen.

The Prayer Of The Kiss

Priest: *[soto voce]* God and Master of all, lover of humankind, make us, unworthy though we are, worthy of this hour, so that, cleansed of all deceit and hypocrisy, we may be united to one another by the bond of peace and love, confirmed by the sanctification of your divine knowledge through your only begotten Son, our Lord Jesus Christ, with whom you are blessed, together with your all holy, good and life giving Spirit, now and for ever, and to the ages of ages. Amen.

Deacon: Let us stand with awe. In peace let us pray to the Lord.

People: *Lord, have mercy.*

Priest: *[aloud]*   For you are a God of peace, mercy, love, compassion and love for humankind, with your only begotten Son and your all holy Spirit, now and for ever, and to the ages of ages.

People: *Amen.*

Priest: Peace be with you all.

People: *And with thy spirit.*

Deacon: Let us greet one another with a holy kiss.

Deacon: Let us bow down our heads to the Lord.

People: *To you, O Lord.*

Priest: *[bowing and quiet]*   O only Lord and merciful God, who dwell in the highest and look upon lowly things, send forth your good grace upon those who have bowed their necks before your holy altar, and seek the spiritual gifts that come from you, and bless us all with every spiritual that cannot be taken away.

Priest: *[aloud]*   For your name, of the Father, the Son and the Holy Spirit, is to be praised, worshipped and supremely glorified, now and for ever, and to the ages of ages.

People: *Amen.*

[To the Priest]

Deacon: Holy Father, bless.

[A prayer for those present.]

Priest: The Lord shall bless us all, serve with us and make us worthy of taking our stand at his holy altar and of the coming of his holy Spirit, now and always, and to the ages of ages.

[Priest: signs the holy Gifts]

Priest: *[soto voce]*

- Glory to God in the highest and peace on earth, goodwill. **(x3)**
- Lord, you shall open my lips and my mouth shall proclaim your praise. **(x3)**
- Let my mouth be filled with your praise, that I may sing your glory, all day long your majesty. **(x3)**
- Of Father, Son and Holy Spirit, now and for ever, and to the ages of ages. Amen.

[Bowing to left and right; melodiously.]

Priest: *[aloud]* Magnify the Lord with me, and let us praise his name together.

People: *The Holy Spirit shall come upon you, and the power of the Most High shall overshadow you.*

Priest: May the Lord remember you in the kingdom of heaven, always, now and for ever, and to the ages of ages.

Deacon: In peace, let us pray to the Lord.

People: *Lord, have mercy.*

Deacon: Save us, have mercy one us, have pity on us and keep us, O God, by your grace.

People: *Lord, have mercy.*

Deacon: For the peace from on high, Gods love for humankind, and the salvation of our souls, let us pray to the Lord.

People: *Lord, have mercy.*

Deacon: For the peace of the whole world and the union of all the holy churches, let us pray to the Lord.

People: *Lord, have mercy.*

Deacon: For this holy house, and for the Catholic and Apostolic Church, from the ends of the earth and to its furthest bounds, let us pray to the Lord.

People: *Lord, have mercy.*

Deacon: For the safety and salvation and assistance of our most holy Father and Archbishop Nikitas, all the clergy and Christ loving people, let us pray to the Lord.

People: *Lord, have mercy.*

Deacon: For our Sovereign Lady, Queen Elizabeth, the Royal Family, her government, and all in authority, let us pray to the Lord.

People: *Lord, have mercy.*

Deacon: For this city, for every city, town and village, and for those who dwell in them with Orthodox faith and reverence for God, for their peace and security, let us pray to the Lord.

People: *Lord, have mercy.*

Deacon: For those who bring offerings, those who care for the beauty of the Holy Church of God, and who remember the poor, the widows and orphans, foreigners, strangers and those in need, and those who have asked us to remember them in our prayers, let us pray to the Lord.

People: *Lord, have mercy.*

Deacon: For those in old age and incapacity, the sick, the suffering, those troubled by unclean spirits, and for their speedy healing from God and for their safety and salvation, let us pray to the Lord.

People: *Lord, have mercy.*

Deacon: For those who pass their lives in virginity, purity and asceticism, and in holy wedlock, and for our venerable fathers, mothers and brethren who struggle on mountains, in caves, and in the hollows of the earth, let us pray to the Lord.

People: *Lord, have mercy.*

Deacon: For those who travel by land, air or water, for Christians who are far from home, for those our brethren in captivity and exile, in prisons and bitter slavery, and for the peaceful return of each one to their own home with joy, let us pray to the Lord.

People: *Lord, have mercy.*

Deacon: For those who are present here and who pray with us at this holy time and at every moment, fathers, mothers and brethren, for their zeal, toil and readiness, let us pray to the Lord.

People: *Lord, have mercy.*

Deacon: And for every Christian soul that is afflicted and distressed, and in need of Gods mercy and help; for the return of those who have been led astray, the health of the sick, the liberation of prisoners, and the repose of our fathers, mothers and brethren who have gone to their rest before us, let us pray to the Lord.

People: *Lord, have mercy.*

Deacon: For the forgiveness of our sins and the pardon of our offences, for our deliverance from all affliction, wrath, anger and constraint, and from the assault of nations, let us pray to the Lord.

People: *Lord, have mercy.*

Deacon: More intensely, for favourable weather, peaceful rains, good dews, abundant harvests, fair seasons, and for the crowning of the year, let us pray to the Lord.

People: *Lord, have mercy.*

Deacon: For our prayer to be heard and to be acceptable before God, and that he send down to us his rich mercies and acts of compassion, and for us all to be found worthy of his kingdom, let us fervently pray.

People: *Lord, have mercy.*

Deacon: Commemorating our all holy, pure, most glorious and blessed Lady, Mother of God and Ever Virgin Mary, of the holy and blessed John, the glorious Prophet, Forerunner and Baptist, of the holy Apostles, of Stephen the Archdeacon and Protomartyr, of Moses, Aaron, Elijah, Elishah, Samuel, David, Daniel, the Prophets and of the Holy and Just, that by their prayers and intercessions we may all find mercy.

People: *Lord, have mercy.*

Deacon: And for the precious and heavenly, ineffable, immaculate, glorious, fearsome, divine gifts, here set forth, and for the salvation of our honoured father and Priest, who presides and offers them, let us entreat the Lord our God.

People: *Lord, have mercy.* **(x3)**

The Prayer Of Offering Of St James

Priest: *[bowing and quiet]* Master and Lord, who visit us in mercy and compassion and have granted us, humble sinners and your unworthy servants the grace to stand at your holy Altar and to offer to you this dread sacrifice without shedding of blood for our own sins and those committed in ignorance by the people, look on me, your unprofitable servant and wipe away my transgressions through your compassion and purify my lips and my heart from every defilement of flesh and spirit, and banish from me every base and unseemly thought, and enable me for this ministry by the power of your all holy Spirit, and accept me through your goodness as I approach your holy altar, and be well pleased, Lord, for these gifts to be acceptable that are offered through our hands, being gracious to my weaknesses, and do not cast me away from your presence. Do not despise my unworthiness, but have mercy on me, O God, in accordance with your great mercy and according to the abundance of your compassion disregard my offences, so that, coming into the presence of your glory with condemnation, I may be found worthy of the protection of your only begotten Son and the illumination of your all holy Spirit, but as your servant may I find grace, mercy and forgiveness of sins both in this present age and in the age to come. Yes, Master almighty and all powerful, listen to my supplication and grant me reprieve from my evil deeds, for it is you who work all in all, and in all things we seek from you your help and assistance and that of your only begotten Son and your good, life giving and consubstantial Spirit, now and for ever, and to the ages of ages. Amen.

Prayer Of Saint Denys The Areopagite

O God, who through your great and ineffable love for humankind sent out your only begotten Son into the world that he might turn back the sheep that had gone astray, do not turn us sinners away as we undertake for you this dread sacrifice without shedding of blood, for we do not trust in our own righteousness but in your loving mercy, through which you acquire our race. And now too we implore and beseech your goodness that this mystery, which is performed through us for salvation, may not become a cause of condemnation for your people, but be for the wiping away of sins, renewal of souls and bodies, and for your good pleasure, God and Father, for you are a God who loves humankind and to you belongs glory, Father, Son and Holy Spirit, now and for ever, and to the ages of ages. Amen.

The Prayer Of The Veil

We thank you, Lord our God, that you have given us the freedom of entry into the holy place by the blood of Jesus, inaugurating for us a new and living way through the veil of his flesh. Having therefore been counted worthy to enter the place where your glory dwells, and to be within the veil, and to look upon the Holy of Holies, we fall down before your goodness, Master. Have mercy on us, for we are filled with fear and trembling as we are about to stand at your holy altar and to offer to you this dread sacrifice without shedding of blood for our sins and those committed in ignorance by the people. Send forth your good grace upon us, O God, and sanctify our souls and bodies and spirits, and change our thoughts towards true religion, that with a pure conscience we may offer you mercy, peace, a sacrifice of praise. And having uncovered the veils of the mysteries that symbolically surround this sacred rite, show us clearly, and fill our spiritual vision with your boundless light; and having cleansed our poverty from all defilement of flesh and spirit, make it worthy of this dread and fearful presence.

Priest: *[aloud]* By the mercy and compassion and love for humankind of your only begotten Son, with whom you are blessed, together with all holy, good and life giving Spirit, now and for ever and to the ages of ages.

People: Amen.

Priest: And unveiling the coverings of the mysteries which in symbol surround this sacred rite, show them to us clearly and fill the eyes of our minds with your incomprehensible light, and purifying our poverty from every defilement of flesh and spirit, make it worthy of this dread and fearful presence, because you are a God of surpassing compassion and mercy, and to you we give glory and thanksgiving, Father, Son and holy Spirit, now and for ever, and to the ages of ages. Amen.

Priest: Peace be with you all.

People: And with thy spirit.

Deacon: Let us stand with awe. Let us devoutly stand. Let us stand with fear of God and with compunction. Let us attend, that we may offer the holy oblation to God in peace.

People: *Mercy, peace, a sacrifice of praise.*

Priest: The love of God the Father, the grace of our Lord and God and Saviour Jesus Christ, and the communion and gift of the Holy Spirit, be with you all.

People: *And with thy spirit.*

Priest: Let our mind and hearts be on high.

People: *We have them with the Lord.*

Priest: Let us give thanks to the Lord.

People: *It is right and fitting.*

Priest: *[bowing and quiet]* Truly it is right and fitting, proper and necessary, to praise you, to hymn you, to bless you, to worship you, to glorify you, to give thanks to you, Fashioner of every creature, visible and invisible, the Treasury of the eternal good things, the Source of life and immortality, the God and Master of all, whose praise is sung by the heavens and the heavens of heavens and all their powers, the sun and the moon and the whole Chorus of stars, earth, sea and all that they contain; the heavenly Jerusalem, festival of the chosen, church of the first born, who are inscribed in heaven; spirits of the Just and of Prophets, souls of Martyrs and Apostles; Angels, Archangels, Thrones, Dominions, Principalities, Authorities and dread Powers, the many eyed Cherubim and the six winged Seraphim, that with two wings cover their faces, with two their feet and with two they fly, as they cry out to one another with unceasing voices and with never silent hymns of glory,

Priest: *[aloud]* With radiant voices singing the triumphant hymn of your majestic glory, shouting, glorifying, crying aloud and saying.

People: *Holy, holy, holy, Lord Sabaoth. Heaven and earth are full of your glory. Hosanna in the highest. Blessed is he who comes in the name of the Lord. Hosanna in the highest.*

[Standing and signing the holy things.]

Priest: *[soto voce]* Holy are you, King of the ages, Lord and giver of all holiness. Holy too is your only begotten Son, our Lord and Saviour Jesus Christ, through whom you made all things. Holy too is your all holy Spirit, who searches all things, and your depths, God and Father.

[Bowing he continues]

Priest: *[soto voce]:* Holy are you, all powerful, fearsome, good, tender hearted, compassionate to what you fashioned. You made humankind from earth, according to your image and likeness, granting it the enjoyment of Paradise. But when it transgressed your commandment and fell away, you do not forsake or abandon it, O Good One, but chastened it as a compassionate Father, called it through the Law, tutored it through the Prophets. Finally you sent your only begotten Son, our Lord Jesus Christ, forth into the world, to come and renew and raise up your image. He came down from heaven and was incarnate from the Holy Spirit and Mary the holy Ever Virgin and Mother of God, lived among mortals and disposed all things for the salvation of our race. When he, the one without sin, was about to accept for us sinners his voluntary and life giving death through a cross, on the night he was given up, or rather gave himself up, for the life and salvation of the world.

[Priest: takes the bread and signs it.]

Priest: *[soto voce]:*   Taking bread in his holy, immaculate and unblemished and immortal hands, looking up heaven and showing it to you, his God and Father, giving thanks, blessing, sanctifying and breaking it, he shared it among his holy and blessed Disciples and Apostles, saying:

[Priest: replaces the bread.]

Priest: *[aloud]:* Take, eat. This is my body which is broken and distributed for you for the forgiveness of sins.

People: Amen.

[Priest: takes the cup and signs it.]

Priest: *[soto voce]:*   Likewise after supper, taking the cup and mixing wine and water, gazing up to heaven and showing it to you, his God and Father, giving thanks, blessing, sanctifying, filling it with the Holy Spirit, he shared it among his holy and blessed Disciples and Apostles, saying:

[Priest: puts down the cup.]

Priest: *[aloud]:* Drink from this all of you. This is my blood of the new covenant, which is poured out and distributed for you and for many for the forgiveness of sins.

People: Amen.

Priest: *[soto voce]:*   Do this in memory of me. For as often as you eat this bread and drink this cup, you proclaim the death of the Son of Man, and confess his resurrection, until he comes.

Deacon: We believe and confess.

People: *Your death, Lord, we proclaim, and your resurrection we confess.*

[Priest: signs the Gifts and bows.]

Priest: *[soto voce]:*   Therefore, we sinners too, remembering his life giving sufferings and the saving Cross, his death and burial, and resurrection from the dead on the third day, his ascension into heaven and sitting at your right hand, his God and Father, and his second, glorious and fearsome coming, when he comes in glory to judge the living and the dead, when he shall render to each according to their works.

Priest: Spare us, O Lord! **(x3)**.

Priest: Or rather according to his compassion, offer to you, Master, this dread sacrifice without shedding of blood, asking that you do not act towards us according to our sins, but that, according to your kindness and ineffable love for humankind, setting aside and wiping out the record of the debt against us your suppliants, you would grant us your heavenly and eternal gifts, which eye has not seen, nor ear heard, nor has it entered the human heart the things that you have prepared, O God, for those who love you. And do not reject your people because of me and because of my sins, O Lord who love humankind.

Priest: *[soto voce]:*   Your people and your Church entreat you. **(x3)**

People: *Have mercy on us, Lord God, the Father, the Almighty.* **(x3)**

Priest: *[soto voce]:*   Have mercy on us, Lord God, the Father, the Almighty. Have mercy on us, God our Saviour. Have mercy on us, O God, in accordance with your great mercy, and send forth upon these holy gifts, here set forth, your all holy Spirit, *(bowing)* the Lord and giver of life, enthroned with you, God and Father, and your only begotten Son, co reigning, consubstantial and co eternal, who spoke by the Law and the Prophets and by your New Covenant, who came down in the form of a dove upon our Lord Jesus Christ in the river Jordan, and rested upon him, who came down upon your holy Apostles in the form of fiery tongues in the upper room of holy and glorious Zion on the day of Pentecost. *(Standing up)* Your same all holy Spirit, Lord, send down on us and on these gifts here set forth,

Priest: *[aloud]*: That having come by his holy, good and glorious presence, he may sanctify this bread and make it the holy body of Christ,

People: Amen.

Priest: And this Cup the precious blood of Christ,

People: Amen.

[Priest: signs the holy Gifts.]

Priest: *[soto voce]*: That they may become for all those who partake of them for forgiveness of sins and everlasting life. For sanctification of souls and bodies. For a fruitful harvest of good works. For the strengthening of your holy, Catholic and Apostolic Church, which you founded on the rock of the faith, so that the gates of Hell might not prevail against it, delivering it from every heresy and from the scandals caused by those who work iniquity, and from the enemies who arise and attack it, until the consummation of the age.

All clergy: Amen.

[Priest: signs the Gifts and bows.]

Priest: We make this offering to you, Master, for your holy places also, which you glorified by the divine Epiphany of your Christ, and by the visitation of your all holy Spirit, especially for the holy and glorious Zion, the mother of all the Churches; and for your holy, Catholic and Apostolic Church throughout the whole inhabited world. Richly bestow on it now too, Master, the gifts of your all holy Spirit.

People: Remember, Lord our God.

Priest: Remember, Lord, also our holy fathers and bishops in your Church, who throughout the inhabited world rightly proclaim the word of truth.

People: Remember, Lord our God.

Priest: Especially our holy father, our most holy Archbishop N., all his clergy and priesthood, grant him an honoured old age, preserve him for many years, as he shepherds your people in all true religion and reverence.

People: Remember, Lord our God.

Priest: Remember, Lord, the honourable order of presbyters here and everywhere, the diaconate in Christ, all the rest of the ministers, every order in the Church and our brotherhood in Christ and the whole Christ loving people.

People: Remember, Lord our God.

Priest: Remember, Lord, the priests present with us at this holy time before your holy altar for the offering of the holy sacrifice without shedding of blood, and give to them and us a word by the opening of our mouth to the glory and praise of your all holy name.

People: *Remember, Lord our God.*

Priest: Remember, Lord, also according to the multitude of your mercy and acts of compassion, me, your lowly, sinful and unworthy servant, and visit me with mercy and compassion. Deliver and free me from those who persecute me, Lord, Lord of Powers. And though sin has multiplied in me, your grace shall abound even more.

People: *Remember, Lord our God.*

Priest: Remember, Lord, the deacons who stand round your holy altar and them a life without reproach, preserve their diaconate unstained and grant them good standing.

People: *Remember, Lord our God.*

Priest: Remember, Lord, the holy city of you our God, the queen of cities, every city, town and village, and those who with Orthodox faith and devotion dwell in them, and their peace and security.

People: *Remember, Lord our God.*

Priest: Remember, Lord, our Sovereign Lady, Queen Elizabeth, the Royal Family, her government and all in authority, and all her household. Set in order her counsels, that we may live a quiet life in all piety and reverence.

People: *Remember, Lord our God.*

Priest: Remember, Lord, those who travel by land, sea and air, Christians who live far from home, those in bondage and prisons, those in captivity and exile, those in mines and in tortures and bitter slavery, our fathers, mothers and brethren, and a peaceful return for each of them to their own homes.

People: *Remember, Lord our God.*

Priest: Remember, Lord, those in old age and incapacity, the sick, the suffering, those troubled by unclean spirits, and for their speedy healing from God and for their safety and salvation.

People: *Remember, Lord our God.*

Priest: Remember, Lord, every Christian soul that is afflicted and distressed, and in need of Gods mercy and help, and the return of those who have been led astray.

People: *Remember, Lord our God.*

Priest: Remember, Lord, those who pass their lives in virginity, purity and asceticism, and in holy wedlock, and for our venerable fathers, mothers and brethren who struggle on mountains, in caves, and in the hollows of the earth, and Orthodox communities in every place and for our community in Christ in this place.

People: *Remember, Lord our God.*

Priest: Remember, Lord, our father, mothers and brethren who labour and serve for the sake of your holy Name.

People: *Remember, Lord our God.*

Priest: Remember, Lord, all for their good. Have mercy on all, Master. Be reconciled with us all. Give peace to the multitudes of your people. Disperse scandals; put an end to wars; ends the schisms of the churches; speedily dissolve the uprisings of heresies; throw down the pride of the nations; exalt the horn of Christians; grant us your peace and your love, O God, our Saviour, the hope of all the ends of the earth.

People: *Remember, Lord our God.*

Priest: Remember, Lord, seasonable weather, gentle showers, fair dews, abundant harvests, perfect seasons and the crowning of the year with your goodness. For the eyes of all hope on you, and you give them their food in due season; you open your hand and fill every living being with your good pleasure.

People: *Remember, Lord our God.*

Priest: Remember, Lord, those who have brought and those who bring offerings in the Holy Church of God, those who remember the poor, and those who have asked us to remember them in our prayers.

People: *Remember, Lord our God.*

Priest: Also be pleased to remember, Lord, those too who have brought offerings today for your holy altar, and those for whom each has brought them, or whom each one has in mind, and those whose names are now read to you.

People: *Remember, Lord our God.*

Priest: Remember, Lord, our parents, friends, relatives and brethren *[Names here[.*

People: *Remember, Lord our God.*

Priest: All these Orthodox remember, Lord, those we have remembered and those we have not. Give them heavenly things in return for things earthly, incorruptible for corruptible, everlasting for temporary, in accordance with the promise of your Christ, for you have the authority of life and death.

People: *Remember, Lord our God.*

Priest: Also be pleased to remember, Lord, those who have been well pleasing to you from the beginning of time, generation by generation, holy Fathers, Mothers, Patriarchs, Prophets, Apostles, Martyrs, Confessors, Teachers, Ascetics, and every righteous spirit, made perfect in faith.

People: *Remember, Lord our God.*

Priest: Hail, full of grace, the Lord is with you. Blessed are you among women, and blessed is the fruit of your womb, for you gave birth to the Saviour of our souls.

People: *Remember, Lord our God.*

Priest: Especially our all holy and blessed, immaculate Lady, Mother of God and Ever Virgin Mary,

People: *Remember, Lord our God.*

Priest: The holy, glorious Prophet, Forerunner and Baptist John, the holy Apostles and Evangelists, the holy Prophets, Patriarchs and Righteous ones, the holy Martyrs and Confessors and all the Saints, not because we are worthy to commemorate their blessedness, but that they too, as they stand before your dread and terrible judgement seat, may in return remember our wretchedness.

People: *Remember, Lord our God.*

Priest: Remember all these, O Lord, the God of spirits and all flesh, those Orthodox, we have remembered and those we have not. Give them rest in the land of the living, in your kingdom, in the delight of Paradise, in the bosom of Abraham, Isaac and Jacob, our holy Fathers, whence pain, grief and sighing have fled away, where the light of your face watches and shines out for ever. And make the ending of our lives Christian, well pleasing, sinless and in peace, Lord, gathering us under the feet of your chosen ones, when you wish and as you wish, only with shame and transgressions, through your only begotten Son, our Lord and God and Saviour Jesus Christ, for he is only one without sin who has appeared upon earth.

People: *Remember, Lord our God.*

Deacon: And for the peace and stability of the whole world and of the holy churches of God, and those for whom each has made offerings or whom they have in mind and for the people here present, and for all people.

People: *Remember, Lord our God.*

Priest: Through whom for us and for them, for you Master are a good God and a Master who loves humankind:

People: *Remember, Lord our God.*

People: Remit, forgive, pardon, O God, our transgressions, voluntary and involuntary, in knowledge and in ignorance.

People: *Remember, Lord our God.*

Priest: By the grace, compassion and love for humankind of your Christ, with whom you are blessed and glorified with your all holy, good and life giving Spirit, now and for ever, and to the ages of ages.

People: *Amen.*

Priest: Peace be with you all.

People: *And with thy spirit.*

Deacon: Again and again and at all times, in peace let us pray to the Lord.

People: *Lord, have mercy.*

Deacon: For the precious, heavenly, glorious, divine gifts here set forth and sanctified, to the Lord our God let us pray.

People: *Lord, have mercy.*

Deacon: That the Lord our God, having accepted them on his holy and spiritual Altar above the heavens, as a savour of spiritual fragrance, may send down upon us in return his divine grace and the gift of the all holy Holy Spirit, let us pray.

People: *Lord, have mercy.*

Deacon: Having asked for the unity of the faith and the communion of the all holy Spirit, let us entrust ourselves and one another and our whole life to Christ, our God.

People: *To you, O Lord.*

Priest: *[bowing and quiet]*: O God and Father of our Lord and God and Saviour, Jesus Christ, the Lord whose name is exalted, the blessed nature, the unstinting goodness, the God and Master of all things, the One who Exists, blessed to the ages of ages, enthroned upon the Cherubim, glorified by the Seraphim, before whom stand thousands and thousands, and tens of thousands of armies Angels and Archangels, accept as sweet fragrance the gifts, offerings and fruits here presented to you, by the grace of your Christ and the visitation of your all holy Spirit. Sanctify also, Master, our souls and bodies and spirits. Touch our minds and search out our consciences. Cast out from us every evil thought, every impure idea, every base desire and memory, every unseemly word, all envy, pride and hypocrisy, every lie, every deceit, every worldly temptation, all greed, all vainglory, all wickedness, all wrath, all anger, all malice, all blasphemy, and all sloth, every movement of flesh and spirit that is alien to the will of your holiness.

Priest *[aloud]*: And count us worthy, Master, Lord who love humankind, with boldness and without condemnation, with a pure heart, enlightened soul, face unashamed, lips that are sanctified to dare to call upon you, the holy God in heaven, as Father, and to say:

People: *Our Father, who art in heaven, hallowed be Thy name. Thy Kingdom come. Thy will be done, on earth as it is in heaven. Give us this day our daily bread; and forgive us our trespasses, as we forgive those who trespass against us; and lead us not into temptation, but deliver us from the evil one.*

Priest *[soto voce]*: And do not lead us into temptation that we cannot endure, Lord, Lord of powers, who know our weakness, but deliver us from the evil one and from his works, and from all his influence and guile, for the sake of your holy Name, that has been invoked upon our lowliness.

Priest: *[aloud]*: For yours is the Kingdom, the power and the glory, of the Father, the Son and the Holy Spirit, now and for ever, and to the ages of ages.

People: *Amen.*

Priest: Peace be with you all.

People: *And with thy spirit.*

Deacon: Let us bow down our heads to the Lord.

People: *To you, O Lord.*

Priest: *[bowing and soto voce]*: We, your servants, Lord, have bowed our necks to you before your holy altar, awaiting rich mercies from you. Send forth to us now, Master, your rich grace and blessing, and sanctify our souls and bodies and spirits, that we may become worthy communicants and partakers of your holy mysteries for forgiveness and everlasting life.

Priest: *[aloud]*: For you, our God, are to be worshipped and glorified, with your only begotten Son and your all holy Spirit, now and for ever, and to the ages of ages.

People: *Amen.*

Priest: And the grace and mercies of the holy, consubstantial, uncreated, indivisible and adored Trinity shall be with us all.

People: *And with your spirit.*

Deacon: Let us attend.

[Priest: signs and raises the Bread.]

Priest: *[soto voce]*:   Holy Lord, who rest in the holy place, make us holy by the word of your grace and the coming of your all holy Spirit. For you said, Master, 'Be holy, because I, the Lord your God, am holy'.

God beyond understanding, Word, consubstantial with the Father and the Holy Spirit, co-eternal and inseparable, accept from me, a sinner, with the Cherubim and Seraphim, this pure hymn among your holy sacrifices without shedding of blood, as I cry out and say:

Priest: *[aloud]*: The Holy Things for the holy.

People: *One is holy, one is Lord: Jesus Christ, to the glory of God the Father, with the Holy Spirit, to whom be glory to the ages of ages.*

[Priest: breaks the bread and holds one half in his right hand and one in his left. He dips that in his right in the chalice.]

Priest: *[aloud]*: The union of the all holy Body and precious Blood of our Lord and God and Saviour Jesus Christ.

[He signs the part in his left hand and swaps, holding the two parts. He signs the other part. Then joining the two parts and dipping the other two of the extremities in the chalice and signing the remaining breads, he says at each dipping the word of union and at once begins to divide and first of all he places one part in each single chalice.]

Priest: *[aloud]:* It has been united and sanctified and perfected, in the name of the Father, the Son and the Holy Spirit.

[Then he makes double parts for each of the clergy and dips them in the chalice.
After the completion of the Glory.]

Deacon: In the peace of the Lord let us sing.

Koinoinikon: Taste and see that the Lord is good. Halleluiah.

Deacon: Holy Father, bless.

Priest: God is blessed, who blesses and sanctifies you that divide in the fear of God, and all who are about to communicate in faith.

All clergy: Amen.

[When the Priest: is about to communicate:]

Priest: Master, Christ our God, the heavenly Bread, the food of the whole world, I have sinned against heaven and before you, and I am not worthy to partake of your holy and immaculate mysteries. But through goodness and ineffable long suffering, make me worthy, without condemnation and shame, to partake of your all holy Body and your precious Blood for forgiveness of sins and everlasting life.

[Then he communicates and distributes to the clergy.]

[The Deacon raises the chalice.]

Deacon: Master, bless.

Priest: Glory to God, who has sanctified and sanctifies us all.

Priest and Deacon: Be exalted to the heavens, O God, and your glory into all the earth, and your kingdom abides to the ages of ages.

Priest: Blessed is the name of the Lord our God to the ages of ages.

Deacon: With fear of God and faith, draw near.

[Signing the faithful, as he gives communion.]

Priest: The holy Body of our Lord and God and Saviour Jesus Christ is distributed to the faithful for forgiveness and everlasting life.

[Communion is traditionally given under the two kinds separately.
As he gives the consecrated Bread:]

Priest: The Body of Christ.

Communicant: Amen.

[For the Cup:]

Priest: The Blood of Christ. The Cup of salvation.

Communicant: Amen.

People: *Fill my mouth with your praise, O Lord, fill my lips with joy, that I may raise a hymn to your glory.* [Whilst he censes the Holy Things.]

The Prayer Of Incense

Priest: *[soto voce]* We thank you, Saviour, God of all things, for all the good things you have granted us, and for the communion of your holy and immaculate mysteries, and we offer you this incense, as we ask: Guard us under the shelter of your wings, and count us worthy even until our last breath to partake of your holy things, for the sanctification of our souls and bodies, and for inheritance of the kingdom of heaven, for you, O God, are our sanctification, and to you we give glory and thanksgiving, to the Father, the Son and the Holy Spirit.

Deacon: We thank you, Christ our God, that you have counted us worthy to partake of your Body and Blood for forgiveness of sins and everlasting life. Keep, we entreat, without condemnation, as you are good and love humankind.

Another Prayer Of The Incense

Priest: You have made us glad, O God, by union with you, and we offer you incense of gratitude, fruit of our lips, as we confess your grace. Let it ascend, O God, and not descend empty, but grant too the pure and lasting myron of the sweet fragrance of your all holy Spirit. Fill our mouths with praise and our lips with gladness and our hearts with joy and delight in Christ Jesus our Lord, with whom you are blessed with your all holy Spirit, now and for ever and to the ages of ages.

Deacon: Again and again at all times, in peace let us pray to the Lord.

People: *Lord, have mercy.*

Deacon: That the communion of his holy Gifts may become for us an averting of every evil thing, provision for the journey of eternal life, for the communion and gift of the Holy Spirit, let us pray.

People: *Lord, have mercy.*

Deacon: Commemorating our all holy, pure, most glorious and blessed Lady, Mother of God and Ever Virgin Mary, with all the Saints and Just, let us entrust ourselves and one another and our whole life to Christ our God.

People: *To you, O Lord.*

Priest: *[soto voce]* O God, who through great and ineffable compassion, have condescended to the weakness of your servants, and counted us worthy to partake of this heavenly table, do not condemn us sinners for communicating of your immaculate mysteries, but preserve us, O Good One, in your sanctification, so that, becoming worthy of your all holy Spirit, we may find a part and lot with all the Saints from the beginning, who have been well pleasing to you, in the light of your face, through the compassion of your only begotten Son, our Lord and God and Saviour Jesus Christ, with whom you are blessed and glorified, with your all holy, good and life giving Spirit, now and for ever, and to the ages of ages.

Priest: *[aloud]* For blessed and sanctified and glorified is your all honoured and majestic holy Name, of the Father, the Son and the Holy Spirit, now and for ever, and to the ages of ages.

People: Amen.

Priest: Peace be with you all.

People: And with thy spirit.

Deacon: Let us bow our heads to the Lord.

People: To you, O Lord.

Priest: *[soto voce]*:   O God great and wonderful, look upon your servants, for to you we have bent our necks, and stretch out your mighty hand, that is filled with blessings, and bless your people and preserve your inheritance, that we may always at every moment glorify you, our only living and true God, the holy and consubstantial Trinity, Father, Son, and Holy Spirit.

Priest: *[aloud]*:   For to you belong and are due from us all, all glory, honour, worship and thanksgiving, Father, Son and Holy Spirit, now and for ever, and to the ages of ages.

People: Amen.

Deacon: In the peace of Christ, let us go forth.

People: In the name of the Lord. Holy Father, bless.

Priest: You have given us sanctification, Master, by the communion of the all holy Body and precious Blood of your only begotten Son, our Lord and God and Saviour Jesus Christ. Give us too the grace of your good Spirit and keep us blameless in the faith and guide to perfect son ship and redemption and the everlasting enjoyment to come, for you and your only begotten Son and your all holy Spirit are our sanctification and enlightenment, O God, now and for ever and to the ages.

Advancing from power to power, and having completed in your church the whole divine ministry, we now ask you also, Lord our God, count us worthy of your perfect love for humankind. Make straight our way, root us in your fear, have mercy on us all, and declare us worthy of your heavenly kingdom in Christ Jesus our Lord, with whom you are blessed and glorified, with your all holy, good and life giving Spirit, now and for ever, and to the ages of ages.

Deacon: May we be guarded in the peace of Christ.

Priest: Blessed is God, who blesses and sanctifies, protects and gives peace, and preserves the life of us all through the communion of his holy, immaculate and life giving mysteries, which we have been counted worthy to receive, always, now and for ever, and to the ages of ages.

People: Amen.

Thanksgiving After Holy Communion

Verses Of Admonition

Whenever thou hast had Communion of the life giving and transcendent gifts, at once give praise and offer heartfelt thanks, and from thy soul say fervently to God:

Glory to Thee, O God. **(x3)**

Prayer Of Saint Basil The Great

Master, Christ God, King of the ages, and Creator of all things, I thank Thee for all the good things Thou hast given me, and for Communion in Thy most pure and life giving Mysteries. Therefore I pray Thee, O Good One, Lover of Mankind: guard me under Thy protection and in the shadow of Thy wings; and grant that until my last breath I may share worthily and with a pure conscience as Thy holy things for forgiveness of sins and everlasting life. For Thou art the Bread of life, the source of sanctification, the giver of blessings; and to Thee we give glory, with the Father and the Holy Spirit, both now and forever, and to the ages of ages. Amen.

Anonymous

I thank Thee, Lord my God, because Thou hast not rejected me a sinner, but have counted me worthy to be a communicant of Thy holy things. I thank Thee, because Thou hast counted me, the unworthy, worthy to share in Thy most pure and heavenly gifts. But, Master, Lover of Mankind, who died for our sake and rose again, and gave us these Thine awe inspiring and life giving Mysteries, for the well being and sanctification of our souls and bodies, grant these gifts may bring me also healing of soul and body, the repelling of every adversary, the enlightenment of the eyes of my heart, peace of my spiritual powers, faith unashamed, love without pretence, fullness of wisdom, the keeping of Thy commandments, increase of Thine divine grace and the gaining of Thy Kingdom that preserved through them by Thy sanctification, I may always remember but for Thee, our Master and Benefactor. And so, when I leave this present life in the hope of life eternal, I shall find everlasting repose where the sound of those who feast is unceasing, and the delight of those who see the ineffable beauty of Thy face is unbounded. For Thou art the true desire and the inexpressible joy of those who love, Christ, our God, and all creation hymns Thee to the ages. Amen.

Prayer Of Saint Symeon The Translator

Thou who willingly givest me Thy flesh for food, Who are a fire consuming the unworthy. Do not burn me up, my Maker; But penetrate the structure of my limbs; All my joints, my inner parts, my heart. Burn up the thorns of all my offences, purify my soul and sanctify my mind. Strengthen my knees, together with my bones. Enlighten the five fold simpleness of my senses. Nail down the whole of me with fear of Thee. Always protect, guard, and keep me from every soul destroying deed and word. Hallow me, purify me, bring me to harmony, And give me beauty, understanding, light. Show me to be Thy dwelling, the Spirits house alone, and no longer the dwelling place of sin. That by the entrance of Communion, every evil doer, every passion may flee from me, Thy house, as from a fire. As intercessors I bring Thee all the Saints, the Companies of the Bodiless Hosts, Thy Forerunner, the wise Apostles, and with them Thy most pure and holy Mother. Accept their prayers, O my compassionate Christ, and make Thy worshipper a child of light. For Thou alone art the sanctification of our souls, O Good One, and their brightness. And fittingly to Thee, as to our God and Master, We all give praise and glory every day.

Anonymous

May Thy Holy Body, Lord Jesus Christ our God, bring me eternal life, and Thy Precious Blood for forgiveness of sins. May this Eucharist bring me joy, health and gladness; and at Thy dread Second Coming make me, a sinner, worthy to stand at the right hand of Thy glory, at the prayers of Thine all pure Mother and of all Thy Saints. Amen.

To The Most Holy Mother Of God

All holy Lady, Mother of God, the light of my darkened soul, my hope, protection, refuge, comfort, joy, I thank thee, because thou hast made me, the unworthy, worthy to become a partaker in the most pure Body and precious Blood of thy Son. But, O thou who gavest birth to the true Light, enlighten the spiritual eyes of my heart; thou who barest the Source of Immortality, give life to me, who have been slain by sin, thou the compassionate Mother of the merciful God, have mercy on me and give me compunction and contrition in my heart, humility in my ideas, and the release from the imprisonment of my thoughts. And count me worthy, until my last breath, to receive without condemnation the sanctification of the most pure Mysteries, for healing of soul and body; and grant me tears of repentance and thanksgiving, to praise and glorify thee all the days of my life.

For thou art blessed and glorified to the ages. Amen. **(x3)**

Song Of Symeon

Priest: Lord, now lettest Thou Thy servant depart in peace, according to Thy word, for mine eyes have seen Thy salvation, which Thou hast prepared before the face of all peoples; a light of revelation for the Gentiles, and the glory of Thy people Israel.

Reader: Holy God, Holy Strong, Holy Immortal, have mercy on us. **(x3)**

Glory be to the Father, and to the Son, and to the Holy Spirit;
Both now and forever, and unto the ages of ages. Amen.

O Most Holy Trinity, have mercy on us.

O Lord, cleanse us from our sins.

O Master, pardon our iniquities.

O Holy One, visit and heal our infirmities, for Thy names sake.

Lord, have mercy. **(x3)**

Glory be to the Father, and to the Son, and to the Holy Spirit;
Both now and forever, and unto the ages of ages. Amen.

People: *Our Father, who art in heaven, hallowed be Thy name. Thy Kingdom come. Thy will be done, on earth as it is in heaven. Give us this day our daily bread; and forgive us our trespasses, as we forgive those who trespass against us; and lead us not into temptation, but deliver us from the evil one.*

Priest: For Thine is the kingdom, the power and the glory, of the Father, and of the Son, and of the Holy Spirit, now and forever, and to the ages of ages.

People: *Amen.*

During Dormition & Lent (But not Palm Sunday):

Apolytikion Of St Basil

Thy voice resounded throughout the world that received the Word by which, in godly manner, thou taughtest dogma, clarified the nature of beings, and set in order the character of people. Venerable Father Basil, Royal Priesthood, intercede to Christ God to grant us Great Mercy.

Glory be to the Father, and to the Son, and to the Holy Spirit.

Kontakion Of Saint Basil

Even as a youth thou served the Lord, O wise one, belabouring thy body with prayer and vigil. Because thou wert shown to be a precious vessel of the Holy Spirit, He established thee as a pastor of his church which thou tended well. And as such thou departed to the Lord whom thou loved. We pray to thee to remember us who keep thy memory with faith, that all may shout unto thee: "Rejoice, O most honourable Basil."

Both now and forever, and to the ages of ages. Amen.

If Not Lent:

Apolytikion Of St John Chrysostom

The grace which shone forth from thy mouth like a torch of flame enlightened the whole earth; it laid up for the world the treasures of freedom from avarice; it showed us the height of humility. But as thou trainest us by thy words, Father John Chrysostom, intercede with Christ God, the Word, that our souls may be saved.

Glory be to the Father, and to the Son, and to the Holy Spirit.

Kontakion Of St John Chrysostom

Thou receivedst divine grace from heaven, and through thy lips thou teachest us all to worship our God in Trinity, venerable John Chrysostom, wholly blessed. Fittingly we praise thee, for thou art a teacher, who makes clear things divine.

Both now and forever, and to the ages of ages. Amen.

Theotokion

At the prayers of all Thy Saints and of the Mother of God, grant us Thy peace, Lord, and have mercy on us, for thou alone art compassionate.

Lord, have mercy. **(x12)**

Glory be to the Father, and to the Son, and to the Holy Spirit;
Both now and forever, and unto the ages of ages. Amen.

Greater in honour than the Cherubim and beyond compare more glorious than the Seraphim; without corruption thou gavest birth to God the Word, truly the Theotokos, we magnify thee.

Holy Father, Bless.

Priest: May God take pity on us and bless us, and shed the light of his countenance on us, and have mercy on us.

People: Amen.

Priest: Glory to Thee, Christ God, our hope, Glory to Thee.

Reader: *Glory be to the Father and to the Son and to the Holy Spirit;*

Both now and forever, and unto the ages of ages. Amen.

Lord have mercy. **(x3)**

Holy Father, Bless.

Priest: May *(on Sundays: he who rose from the dead)* Christ our true God, through the prayers of his all pure and Holy Mother; of the holy, glorious and all praised Apostles *[of Saint N, Patron of this church]* of Saint N, whose memory we keep today], of our father amongst the Saints John Chrysostom, Archbishop of Constantinople, and of all the Saints, have mercy on us and save us, for He is good and loves mankind.

Priest or Reader:

Through the prayers of our Holy Fathers, Lord Jesus Christ our God, have mercy on us and save us.

All: Amen.

[For a Sunday, without the Divine Liturgy.]

Deacon: Holy Father, Bless.

Priest: Blessed is the kingdom of the Father, and of the Son, and of the Holy Spirit, now and ever, and to the ages of ages.

People: *Amen.*

The Litany of Peace

Deacon: In peace let us pray to the Lord.

People: *Lord, have mercy.*

Deacon: For the peace from above and the salvation of our souls, let us pray to the Lord.

People: *Lord, have mercy.*

Deacon: For peace in the whole world, the welfare of the holy churches of God, and the union of all men, let us pray to the Lord.

People: *Lord, have mercy.*

Deacon: For this holy Temple, and for those who enter it with faith, reverence and the fear of God, let us pray to the Lord.

People: *Lord, have mercy.*

Deacon: For the Most Holy Orthodox Patriarchs, for His Eminence Nikitas, for the honourable Priesthood, the Diaconate in Christ, and for all the clergy and the people, let us pray to the Lord.

People: *Lord, have mercy.*

Deacon: For our Country, our Sovereign Prince, our Government, and all in seats of authority, let us pray to the Lord.

People: *Lord, have mercy.*

Deacon: For this City, and for every city and land, and for those who live in them by faith, let us pray to the Lord.

People: *Lord, have mercy.*

Deacon: For seasonable weather, the abundance of the fruits of the earth and peaceful times, let us pray to the Lord.

People: *Lord, have mercy.*

Deacon: For those who are travelling by land, air and water, for the sick, the suffering, for prisoners and captives, and for their salvation, let us pray to the Lord.

People: *Lord, have mercy.*

Deacon: That He shall deliver us from all tribulation, anger, danger, and want, let us pray to the Lord.

People: *Lord, have mercy.*

Deacon: Help us, save us, have mercy on us, and keep us, O God, by Thy grace.

People: *Lord, have mercy.*

Deacon: Remembering our most holy, most pure, most blessed and glorious Lady, Mother of God and Ever Virgin Mary, with all the Saints, let us entrust ourselves and each other, and all our life to Christ our God.

People: *To You, O Lord.*

Priest: For to Thee belongs all glory, honour and adoration, to the Father, and to the Son, and to the Holy Spirit, now and ever, and to the ages of ages.

People: *Amen.*

The First Antiphon - Psalm 102

Reader: Bless the Lord, O my soul. Blessed are You, O Lord. Bless the Lord, O my soul, and all that is within me bless His holy name. Bless the Lord, O my soul, and forget not all that He has done for you. He is gracious to all your iniquities, Who heals all your infirmities. Who redeems your life from corruption. Who crowns you with mercy and compassion. Who fulfils your desire with good things; your youth shall be renewed as the eagles. The Lord performs deeds of mercy, and executes judgement for all them that are wronged. He has made His ways known to Moses, to the sons of Israel the things that He has willed. Compassionate and merciful is the Lord, long suffering and plenteous in mercy. Not unto the end shall He be angered, neither to eternity shall He be wroth. Not according to our iniquities has He dealt with us, neither according to our sins has He rewarded us. For according to the height of heaven from the earth, the Lord has made His mercy to prevail over them that fear Him. As far as the east is from the west, so far has He removed our iniquities from us, Like as a father has compassion upon his sons, so has the Lord had compassion upon them that fear Him. For He knows whereof we are made, He has remembered that we are dust. As for man, his days are as the grass; as a flower of the field, so shall he blossom forth. For when the wind is passed over it, then it shall be gone, and no longer shall it know the place thereof. But the mercy of the Lord is from eternity, even to eternity, upon them that fear Him. And His righteousness is upon sons of sons, upon them that keep His testament and remember His commandments to do them. The Lord in heaven has prepared His throne, and His kingdom rules over all. Bless the Lord, all you His angels, mighty in strength, that perform His word, to hear the voice of His words. Bless the Lord, all you His hosts, His ministers that do His will. Bless the Lord, all you His works, in every place of His dominion.

Glory be to the Father, and to the Son, and to the Holy Spirit.

Short Litany

Deacon: Again and again, in peace let us pray to the Lord.

People: *Lord, have mercy.*

Deacon: Help us, save us, have mercy on us and keep us, O God, by Thy grace.

People: *Lord, have mercy.*

Deacon: Remembering our most holy, most pure, most blessed and glorious Lady, Mother of God and Ever Virgin Mary, with all the Saints, let us entrust ourselves and each other, and all our life to Christ our God.

People: *To You, O Lord.*

Priest: For Thine is the dominion, Thine the kingdom, the power and the glory, of the Father, and of the Son, and of the Holy Spirit, now and ever, and to the ages of ages.

People: *Amen.*

The Second Antiphon - Psalm 145

Reader: Praise the Lord, O my soul. I shall praise the Lord in my life, I shall chant to my God for as long as I have my being. Trust not in princes, in the sons of men, in whom there is no salvation. His spirit shall go forth, and he shall return to his earth. In that day all his thoughts shall perish. Blessed is he of whom the God of Jacob is his help, whose hope is in the Lord his God. Who has made heaven and earth, the sea and all that is therein. Who keeps truth unto eternity, Who executes judgement for the wronged, Who gives food unto the hungry. The Lord looses the fettered; the Lord makes wise the blind; the Lord sets aright the fallen; the Lord loves the righteous; The Lord preserves the proselytes. He shall adopt for His own the orphan and widow, and the way of sinners shall He destroy. The Lord shall be king to eternity; thy God, O Zion, to generation and generation.

Both now and forever, and unto the ages of ages. Amen.

Reader: O Only begotten Son and Word of God, Who is immortal, Yet did deign for our salvation To be incarnate of the holy Theotokos and ever virgin Mary, And without change become man, And was crucified, O Christ God, trampling down death by death, Thou Who art one of the Holy Trinity, Glorified with the Father and the Holy Spirit, save us.

Little Litany

Deacon: Again and again, in peace let us pray to the Lord.

People: *Lord, have mercy.*

Deacon: Help us, save us, have mercy on us and keep us, O God, by Thy grace.

People: *Lord, have mercy.*

Deacon: Remembering our most holy, most pure, most blessed and glorious Lady, Mother of God and Ever Virgin Mary, with all the Saints, let us entrust ourselves and each other, and all our life to Christ our God.

People: *To You, O Lord.*

Priest: For You, O God, are good and love mankind, and to Thee we give glory, to the Father, and to the Son, and to the Holy Spirit, now and forever, and to the ages of ages.

People: *Amen.*

Third Antiphon - The Beatitudes

[may change – follow the Reader]

People:

In Thy Kingdom, remember us, O Lord, when Thou comest in Thy kingdom.

Blessed are the poor in spirit, for theirs is the kingdom of heaven.

Blessed are they that mourn, for they shall be comforted.

Blessed are the meek, for they shall inherit the earth.

Blessed are they that hunger and thirst after righteousness, for they shall be satisfied.

Blessed are the merciful, for they shall obtain mercy.

Blessed are the pure in heart, for they shall see God.

Blessed are the peacemakers, for they shall be called the children of God.

Blessed are they that are persecuted for righteousness' sake, for theirs is the kingdom of heaven.

Blessed are you when men shall revile you, and persecute you, and shall say all manner of evil against you falsely for My sake.

Rejoice and be glad, for great is your reward in heaven.

Reader: *Glory be to the Father, and to the Son, and to the Holy Spirit.*

Both now and forever, and unto the ages of ages. Amen.

Trisagion

Reader: Holy God, Holy Mighty, Holy Immortal have mercy on us. **(x3)**

Glory be to the Father, and to the Son, and to the Holy Spirit.

Both now and forever, and unto the ages of ages. Amen.

Holy Immortal have mercy on us.

Holy God, Holy Mighty, Holy Immortal have mercy on us.

The Apostle

Deacon: Let us attend.

Priest: Peace be with you all.

Reader: And with thy spirit.

Deacon: Wisdom! The Prokeimenon.

Reader: *[The Prokeimenon of the day.]*

Deacon: Wisdom!

Reader: The Reading is from the book of ...

Deacon: Let us attend.

Reader: *[The Epistle of the day.]*

Priest: Peace be to you who reads.

Reader: And with thy spirit.

People: *[Halleluiahs of the day.]*

The Gospel

Deacon: *[soto voce]* Bless, Father, the reader of the Gospel of the Apostle and Evangelist *N.*

Priest: *[soto voce]* May God, through the intercessions of the holy and glorious Apostle and Evangelist, *N.*, grant thee to announce the glad tidings with great power, for the fulfilment of the Gospel of His beloved Son, our Lord Jesus Christ.

Deacon: Amen.

Priest: Wisdom, stand upright! Let us listen to the Holy Gospel. Peace be with you all.

People: *And with thy spirit.*

Deacon:	The Reading is from the Holy Gospel of *N.*
People:	*Glory to You, O Lord, glory to You.*
Priest:	Let us attend.
Deacon:	*[reads the Gospel.]*
Priest:	Peace to thee who has announced the glad tidings.
People:	*Glory to You, O Lord, glory to You.*
Reader:	Remember us, O Lord, when Thou comest in Thy kingdom.
	Remember us, O Master, when Thou comest in Thy kingdom.
	Remember us, O Holy One, when Thou comest in Thy kingdom.
Reader:	The heavenly Chorus praises Thee and says:
People:	*Holy, Holy, Holy, Lord of Sabaoth; heaven and earth are full of Thy glory.*
Reader:	Come unto Him, and be enlightened, and your faces shall not be ashamed.
	The heavenly Chorus praises Thee and says:
People:	*Holy, Holy, Holy, Lord of Sabaoth; heaven and earth are full of Thy glory.*
Reader:	Glory be to the Father, and to the Son, and to the Holy Spirit. The Chorus of holy angels and archangels, with all the heavenly hosts, praises Thee and says:
People:	*Holy, Holy, Holy, Lord of Sabaoth; heaven and earth are full of Thy glory.*
Reader:	Both now and forever, and unto the ages of ages. Amen.

The Creed

I believe in one God, the Father Almighty, Maker of heaven and earth and of all things visible and invisible.

And in one Lord Jesus Christ, the Son of God, the Only begotten, begotten of the Father before all ages; Light of Light, true God of true God; begotten, not made; of one essence with the Father, by Whom all things were made; Who for us men and for our salvation came down from heaven, and was incarnate of the Holy Spirit and the Virgin Mary, and became man; And was crucified for us under Pontius Pilate, and suffered and was buried; And arose again on the third day according to the Scriptures; And ascended into the heavens, and sits at the right hand of the Father; And shall come again, with glory, to judge both the living and the dead; Whose kingdom shall have no end.

And in the Holy Spirit, the Lord, the Giver of life; Who proceeds from the Father; Who together with the Father and the Son is worshipped and glorified; Who spoke by the prophets. In One, Holy, Catholic, and Apostolic Church. I confess one baptism for the remission of sins. I look for the resurrection of the dead, And the life of the age to come. Amen.

Reader: Forgive, remit, pardon, O God, our sins, both voluntary and involuntary, in deed and word, in knowledge or in ignorance, committed by day or by night, in mind and in thought. Forgive us them all, for Thou art good and the Lover of mankind.

The Lords Prayer

People: *Our Father, Who art in heaven, hallowed be Thy name. Thy kingdom come, Thy will be done, on earth as it is in heaven. Give us this day our daily bread, and forgive us our trespasses, as we forgive those who trespass against us; and lead us not into temptation, but deliver us from the evil one.*

Priest: For Thine is the kingdom, the power, and the glory, of the Father, and of the Son, and of the Holy Spirit, both now and forever, and to the ages of ages.

People: *Amen.*

Reader: O protection of Christians, that cannot be put to shame; mediation unto the Creator most constant: O despise not the suppliant voices of those who have sinned, but be Thou quick, O good one, to come unto our aid, who in faith cry to you. Hasten to intercession, and speed Thou to make supplication, Thou who dost ever protect, O Theotokos, them that honour Thee.

Lord, have mercy. **(x40)**

Priest: O All Holy Trinity, consubstantial Might, Kingdom undivided, Source of all good, be gracious to me, a sinner, establish and give understanding to my heart, and take away from me every defilement. Enlighten my mind that I may continually glorify, hymn and worship Thee and say: One is Holy, One is Lord, Jesus Christ, to the Glory of God the Father.

Reader: *Amen.*

Blessed be the name of the Lord, from this time forth and for evermore. **(x3)**

Glory be to the Father, and to the Son, and to the Holy Spirit.
Both now and forever, and unto the ages of ages. Amen.

Psalm 33

Reader:

• I shall bless the Lord at all times, His praise shall continually be in my mouth. In the Lord shall my soul be praised; let the meek hear and be glad.

• O Magnify the Lord with me, and let us exalt His name together. I sought the Lord, and He heard me, and delivered me from all my tribulations.

• Come unto Him, and be enlightened, and your faces shall not be ashamed. This poor man cried, and the Lord heard him, and saved him out of all his tribulations.

• The angel of the Lord shall encamp round about them that fear Him, and shall deliver them. O Taste and see that the Lord is good; blessed is the man that hopes in Him.

• O Fear the Lord, all you His saints; for there is no want to them that fear Him. Rich men have turned poor and gone hungry; but they that seek the Lord shall not be deprived of any good thing.

• Come you children, hearken unto me; I shall teach you the fear of the Lord. What man is there that desires life, who loves to see good days?

• Keep thy tongue from evil, and your lips from speaking guile. Turn away from evil and do good; seek peace, and pursue it.

• The eyes of the Lord are upon the righteous, and His ears are opened unto their supplication. The face of the Lord is against them that do evil, utterly to destroy the remembrance of them from the earth.

• The righteous cried, and the Lord heard them, and He delivered them out of all their tribulations. The Lord is nigh unto them that are of a contrite heart, and He shall save the humble of spirit.

• Many are the tribulations of the righteous, and the Lord shall deliver them out of them all. The Lord keeps all their bones, not one of them shall be broken.

• The death of sinners is evil, and they that hate the righteous shall do wrong. The Lord shall redeem the souls of His servants, and none of them shall do wrong that hope in Him.

Reader: *Glory be to the Father, and to the Son, and to the Holy Spirit.*

Both now and forever, and unto the ages of ages. Amen.

Megalynarion

Priest: Wisdom.

Reader: It is truly meet to bless you, the Theotokos, ever blessed and most blameless, and mother of our God.

Priest: Most Holy Theotokos, save us.

Reader: Greater in honour than the Cherubim and beyond compare more glorious than the Seraphim; without corruption thou gavest birth to God the Word, truly the Theotokos, we magnify thee.

Dismissal

Priest: Glory to you, O Christ our God and our Hope, glory to you.

Reader: *Glory be to the Father, and to the Son, and to the Holy Spirit.*

Both now and forever, and unto the ages of ages. Amen.

Lord, have mercy. **(x3)**

Holy Father, Bless!

Priest: May Christ, Our true God, through the intercessions of His all immaculate and all blameless holy Mother, of the holy and righteous ancestors of God, Joachim and Anna, of *[the saints of the day]* whose memory we celebrate today, and of all the saints; have mercy on us and save us, for He is a good God and loves mankind.

People: *Amen.*

Priest: Through the prayers of our Holy Fathers, Lord Jesus Christ our God, have mercy on us and save us.

People: *Amen.*

[To celebrate the Divine Liturgy without a priest. Divine Liturgy Variables required.]

The Trisagion Prayers

Reader: Through the prayers of our holy Fathers, O Lord Jesus Christ our God, have mercy on us.

People: *Amen. Glory to Thee, our God, glory to Thee.*

Reader: O Heavenly King, Comforter, Spirit of Truth, Who art everywhere present and fillest all things, Treasury of blessings and Giver of life: Come and abide in us and cleanse us from every impurity and save our souls, O Good One.

Holy God, Holy Mighty, Holy Immortal, have mercy on us. **(x3)**

> *Glory be to the Father and to the Son and to the Holy Spirit;*
> *Both now and forever, and unto the ages of ages. Amen.*

O Most Holy Trinity, have mercy on us.

O Lord, cleanse us from our sins.

O Master, pardon our iniquities.

O Holy One, visit and heal our infirmities, for Thy names sake.

Lord have mercy. **(x3)**

> *Glory be to the Father and to the Son and to the Holy Spirit;*
> *Both now and forever, and unto the ages of ages. Amen.*

Our Father, Who art in Heaven, hallowed be Thy Name. Thy Kingdom come, Thy will be done, on earth as it is in Heaven. Give us this day our daily bread, and forgive us our trespasses, as we forgive those who trespass against us; and lead us not into temptation, but deliver us from the evil one. Amen.

Lord, have mercy. **(x12)**

> *Glory be to the Father and to the Son and to the Holy Spirit.*
> *Both now and ever and to the ages of ages, Amen.*

Come, let us worship God, our King.

Come, let us worship and fall down before Christ, our King and our God.

Come, let us worship and fall down before Christ Himself, our King and our God.

The First Antiphon - Psalm 102

Bless the Lord, O my soul; blessed art Thou, O Lord. Bless the Lord O my soul; and all that is within me, bless His holy name. Bless the Lord O my soul, and forget not all His benefits: Who forgives all thine iniquities, Who heals all thy diseases, Who redeems thy life from destruction, Who crowns thee with loving kindness and tender mercies, Who satisfies thy mouth with good things, so that thine youth is renewed like the eagles. The Lord executes righteousness and justice for all who are oppressed. He made known His ways to Moses, His acts to the children of Israel. The Lord is merciful and gracious, slow to anger, and abounding in mercy. He shall not always strive with us, nor shall He keep His anger forever. He has not dealt with us according to our sins, nor punished us according to our iniquities. For as the heavens are high above the earth, so great is His mercy toward those who fear Him; As far as the east is from the west, so far has He removed our transgressions from us. As a father pities his children, so the Lord pities those who fear Him. For He knows our frame; He remembers that we are dust. As for man, his days are like grass; as a flower of the field, so he flourishes. For the wind passes over it, and it is gone, and its place remembers it no more. But the mercy of the Lord is from everlasting to everlasting on those who fear Him, and His righteousness to childrens children, To such as keep His covenant, and to those who remember His commandments to do them. The Lord has established His throne in heaven, and His kingdom rules overall. Bless the Lord you His angels, who excel in strength, who do His word, heeding the voice of His word. Bless the Lord all you His hosts, you ministers of His, who do His pleasure. Bless the Lord all His works, in all places of His dominion. Bless the Lord O my soul.

Glory be to the Father, and to the Son, and to the Holy Spirit.
Both now and forever, and unto the ages of ages. Amen.

Bless the Lord, O my soul, and all that is within me bless His holy name; blessed art Thou, O Lord.

The Second Antiphon

Glory be to the Father, and to the Son, and to the Holy Spirit.

Praise the Lord, O my soul. I shall praise the Lord in my life, I shall chant unto my God for as long as I have my being. Trust you not in princes, in the sons of men, in whom there is no salvation. His spirit shall go forth, and he shall return unto his earth. In that day all his thoughts shall perish. Blessed is he of whom the God of Jacob is his help, whose hope is in the Lord his God, Who has made heaven and the earth, the sea and all that is therein. Who keeps truth to eternity, Who executes judgement for the wronged, Who giveth food unto the hungry. The Lord looses the fettered; the Lord makes wise the blind; the Lord sets aright the fallen; the Lord loves the righteous; the Lord preserves the proselytes. He shall adopt for His own the orphan and widow, and the way of sinners shall He destroy. The Lord shall be king to eternity; Thy God, O Zion, to generation and generation.

Both now and forever, and unto the ages of ages. Amen.

O only begotten Son and Word of God, Who, being immortal, accepted for our salvation to take flesh from the Mother of God and Ever Virgin Mary, and without change became man; Thou wast crucified, Christ God, by death trampling on death, being one of the Holy Trinity, glorified with the Father and the Holy Spirit, save us.

Third Antiphon

[Troparia of the day are read between these verses. NOT Kontakia.]

In Thy Kingdom. Remember us, O Lord, when Thou comest in Thy Kingdom.
Blessed are the poor in spirit, for theirs is the Kingdom of Heaven.

[Troparion 1]

Blessed are the mourners, for they shall be comforted.
Blessed are the meek, for they shall inherit the earth.

[Troparion 2]

Blessed are those who hunger and thirst for righteousness, for they shall be satisfied.
Blessed are the merciful, for they shall obtain mercy.

[Troparion 3]

Blessed are the pure in heart, for they shall see God.
Blessed are the peacemakers, for they shall be called the children of God.
Blessed are those who are persecuted for righteousness' sake, for theirs is the Kingdom of Heaven.
Blessed are you when men revile and persecute you and say all manner of evil against you falsely and on My account.
Rejoice and be exceeding glad, for great is thy reward in Heaven.

Glory be to the Father, and to the Son, and to the Holy Spirit.
Both now and forever, and unto the ages of ages. Amen.

Entry Hymn

[Sundays]
Reader: O come let us worship and fall down before Christ.
People: *Save us, O Son of God, risen from the dead. Save us who sing to Thee: Halleluiah.*
[Weekdays]
Reader: O come let us worship and fall down before Christ.
People: *Save us, O Son of God, Who art wondrous in the saints. Save us who sing to Thee: Halleluiah.*

[A feast of the Theotokos]

Reader: O come let us worship and fall down before Christ.

People: *At the prayers of the Mother of God, O Saviour, save us: Halleluiah.*

Troparia

[The remaining appointed Troparia of the day. NOT Kontakia.]

[Penultimate Troparion for the Dedication of the Church:]

Glory be to the Father, and to the Son, and to the Holy Spirit.

[if your church is to St Martin:]

Troparion Of St Martin

Tone 4   *Festive, joyous and expressing deep piety.*   *C, D, Eb, F, G, A, Bb, C.*

In signs and in miracles thou wast renowned throughout Gaul. By grace and adoption thou art a light for the world, O Martin, blessed of God. Alms deeds and compassion filled thy life with their splendours. Teaching and wise counsel were thy riches and treasures, which thou dispensest freely to those who honour thee.

Both now and forever, and unto the ages of ages. Amen.

Trisagion

Holy God, Holy Strong, Holy Immortal have mercy on us. (**x3**)

Glory be to the Father and to the Son and to the Holy Spirit;

Both now and forever, and unto the ages of ages. Amen.

Holy Immortal have mercy on us.

Holy God, Holy Strong, Holy Immortal have mercy on us.

Prokeimenon

[The prokeimenon of the day]

Epistle

Reader: The reading is from the letter of the blessed apostle St ... to ...

Hallelujarion

People: *Halleluiah, Halleluiah, Halleluiah.*

Reader: [Response of the week.]

People: *Halleluiah, Halleluiah, Halleluiah.*

Reader: [Response of the week.]

People: *Halleluiah, Halleluiah, Halleluiah.*

Gospel

Reader: The Reading is from the Holy Gospel according to ...

People: *Glory to Thee, O Lord, glory to Thee.*

Reader: *[The Gospel is plain chanted].*

People: *Glory to Thee, O Lord, glory to Thee.*

Chorus: *Remember us, Lord, when Thou comest in Thy kingdom.* **(x3)**

Reader: The heavenly Chorus praises Thee and says:

Holy, Holy, Holy; Lord Sabaoth; heaven and earth are full of Thy glory.

Stichos: *Come to Him, and be enlightened and thy faces shall not be ashamed.*

Reader: The heavenly Chorus praises Thee and says:

Holy, Holy, Holy; Lord Sabaoth; heaven and earth are full of Thy glory.

Stichos: *Glory be to the Father, and to the Son, and to the Holy Spirit.*

Reader: The Chorus of Holy angels and archangels, with all the heavenly hosts praises Thee and says:

Holy, Holy, Holy, Lord of Sabaoth; heaven and earth are full of Thy glory.

Stichos: *Both now and forever, and unto the ages of ages. Amen.*

The Symbol Of Faith

I believe in one God, Father, Almighty, Maker of heaven and earth, and of all things visible and invisible.

And in one Lord Jesus Christ, the only begotten Son of God, begotten from the Father before all ages; Light from Light, true God from true God; begotten not made; consubstantial with the Father, through Him all things were made. For our sake and for our salvation He came down from Heaven, and was incarnate from the Holy Spirit and the Virgin Mary and became man. He was crucified for us under Pontius Pilate, and suffered and was buried. He rose again on the third day in accordance with the Scriptures, and ascended into Heaven, and is seated at the right hand of the Father. He is coming again in glory to judge the living and the dead. And His kingdom shall have no end.

And in the Holy Spirit, the Lord, the Giver of life; Who proceeds from the Father; Who together with the Father and the Son is worshipped and glorified; Who spoke through the prophets. In One, Holy, Catholic, and Apostolic Church. I confess one baptism for the forgiveness of sins. I await the resurrection of the dead, And the life of the age to come. **Amen.**

Reader: Remit, pardon, forgive, O God, our offences, both voluntary and involuntary, in deed and word, in knowledge and ignorance, by day and by night, in mind and thought; forgive us all things, for Thou art good and the Lover of mankind.

People: *Our Father, Who art in heaven, hallowed be Thy name. Thy kingdom come, Thy will be done, on earth as it is in heaven. Give us this day our daily bread, and forgive us our trespasses, as we forgive those who trespass against us; and lead us not into temptation, but deliver us from the evil one.*

Reader: O Lord Jesus Christ, Son of God, have mercy on us.

People: *Amen.*

[Penultimate Kontakion for the Dedication of the Church]

Glory be to the Father, and to the Son, and to the Holy Spirit.

Kontakion Of St Martin *[if your church is to St Martin]*

Tone 8   *Humility, tranquillity, repose, suffering, pleading.*   *C, D, Eb, F, G, A, Bb, C.*

As a devoted man of God, thou proclaimest His mysteries, and as a seer of the Trinity, thou sheddest your blessings on the Occident. By thy prayers and entreaties, O adornment of Tours and glory of all the Church, Preserve us, O Saint Martin, and save all who praise thy memory.

Both now and forever, and unto the ages of ages. Amen.

Reader: Lord, have mercy. **(x12)**

O All Holy Trinity, the consubstantial dominion, the indivisible Kingdom, and cause of every Good: Show Thy good will even unto me a sinner; make steadfast my heart and grant it understanding, and take away mine every defilement; enlighten my mind that I may glorify, hymn, worship, and say:

People: *One is Holy, One is Lord, Jesus Christ, to the Glory of God the Father. Amen.*

Reader: *Glory be to the Father and to the Son and to the Holy Spirit;*

Both now and forever, and unto the ages of ages. Amen.

Psalm 33

I shall bless the Lord at all times, His praise shall continually be in my mouth. In the Lord shall my soul be praised; let the meek hear and be glad. O magnify the Lord with me, and let us exalt His name together. I sought the Lord, and He heard me, and delivered me from all my tribulations. Come unto Him, and be enlightened, and thy faces shall not be ashamed. This poor man cried, and the Lord heard him, and saved him out of all his tribulations. The angel of the Lord shall encamp round about them that fear Him, and shall deliver them. O taste and see that the Lord is good; blessed is the man that hopes in Him. O fear the Lord, all you His saints; for there is no want to them that fear Him. Rich men have turned poor and gone hungry; but they that seek the Lord shall not be deprived of any good thing. Come you children, hearken unto me; I shall teach you the fear of the Lord. What man is there that desires life, who loves to see good days? Keep thy tongues from evil, and thy lips from speaking guile. Turn away from evil, and do good; seek peace, and pursue it. The eyes of the Lord are upon the righteous, and His ears are opened unto their supplication. The face of the Lord is against them that do evil, utterly to destroy the remembrance of them from the earth. The righteous cried, and the Lord heard them, and He delivered them out of all their tribulations. The Lord is nigh unto them that are of a contrite heart, and He shall save the humble of spirit. Many are the tribulations of the righteous, and the Lord shall deliver them out of them all. The Lord keeps all their bones, not one of them shall be broken. The death of sinners is evil, and they that hate the righteous shall do wrong. The Lord shall redeem the souls of His servants, and none of them shall do wrong that hope in Him.

Megalynarion

[Archangel Gabriel: It is truly right to call thee blessed, who gavest birth to God, ever-blessed and God-obedient the Mother of our God.] Greater in honour than the Cherubim and beyond compare more glorious than the Seraphim; without corruption thou gavest birth to God the Word, truly the Mother of God, we magnify thee.

Glory be to the Father and to the Son and to the Holy Spirit;

Both now and forever, and unto the ages of ages. Amen.

Lord, have mercy. **(x3)**

Dismissal

[Sunday]

Thou that didst rise from the dead, O Lord Jesus Christ, Son of God, for the sake of the prayers of Thy most pure Mother, of our holy and God bearing fathers, of [St Martin], of _____ *(saints of the day)*, and of all the saints, have mercy on us and save us, for Thou art good and the Lover of mankind.

People: *Amen.*

[Weekdays]

O Lord Jesus Christ, Son of God, for the sake of the prayers of Thy most pure Mother, of our holy and God bearing fathers, of [St Martin], of _____ *(saints of the day)*, and of all the saints, have mercy on us and save us, for Thou art good and the Lover of mankind.

People: *Amen.*

The Synaxarion For Today *(The Prologue Of Ohrid)*

Tone 5   Stimulating, dancing, and rhythmical.   *C, D, Eb, F, G, A, Bb, C.*

We who are walled about by the cross are ranged against the enemy, not fearing his devices and ambushes, for the proud one has been destroyed and trampled underfoot by the power of Christ crucified on the Tree.

Dismissal

Reader: *Glory be to the Father and to the Son and to the Holy Spirit;*

Both now and forever, and unto the ages of ages. Amen.

Preserve our most holy Archbishop Nikitas and all Orthodox Christians, O Lord, for many years.

Lord, have mercy. **(x3)**

Through the prayers of our holy Fathers, O Lord Jesus Christ our God, have mercy on us and save us.

People: *Amen.*

Litya To Bless Bread Or Kolyva Offered In Honour Of A Saint
Also For The Blessing Of Phanouropita

[The bread or kolyva is placed in front of the Icon of Christ on the templom (eikonostasion) with a lit candle.]

If the blessing is to take place <u>during the Divine Liturgy</u>, after the Prayer behind the Ambon.

Apolytikion And Kontakion Of The Saint Of The Day

[insert here]

Apolytikion Of St Phanourios

Tone 4   Festive, joyous and expressing deep piety.   *C, D, Eb, F, G, A, Bb, C.*

A heavenly song of praise is chanted radiantly upon the earth; the company of Angels now joyfully celebrateth an earthly festival, and from on high with hymns they praise thy contests, and from below the Church doth proclaim the Heavenly glory which thou hast found by thy labours and struggles, O glorious Phanourios.

Glory be to the Father and to the Son and to the Holy Spirit.

Kontakion Of St Phanourios

Ione 3   Arrogant, brave, and mature atmosphere.   *F, G, A, A#, C, D, E, F.*

Thou didst save the Priests from an ungodly captivity, and didst break their bonds by Divine power, O godly minded one; thou didst bravely shame the audacity of the tyrants, and didst gladden the orders of the Angels, O Great Martyr. Wherefore, we honour thee, O divine warrior, glorious Phanourios.

Both now and forever and unto the ages of ages. Amen.

Priest: Let us pray to the Lord.

People: *Lord, have mercy.*

[The priest then stands in the midst of the Holy Doors, turned slightly towards the Icon of Christ, and censes the bread or kolyva as he says the following:]

Priest: O Lord, Jesus Christ, the Heavenly Bread, the munificent Bestower of the food that abideth unto eternity, the Giver of good things, Who through Elias didst cause miraculous sustenance to gush forth, the Hope of the hopeless, the Help of the helpless, and the Salvation of our souls: Bless these gifts and those who have offered them unto Thee, to Thy glory and in honour of *[Name of the Saint]*.

Grant, O Good One, unto those who have prepared these gifts *[names of the donors]* all Thine earthly and Heavenly good things. Gladden them in joy with Thy countenance, and show them the paths to salvation. Be swift to fulfil the requests of their hearts and their every wish, guiding them to the doing of Thy commandments, that in gladness and rejoicing they may forever hymn and glorify Thy most honourable and majestic Name, by the intercessions of the Most blessed Theotokos, of the holy, glorious *[Name of the Saint]* and of all Thy Saints.

People: Amen.

Chorus: *Blessed be the Name of The Lord.*

[Continue the rest of Divine Liturgy.]

If The Blessing Is To Take Place Outside Of The Divine Liturgy.

Priest: Blessed is our God, always, now and ever, and unto the ages of ages.

People: *Amen.*

Priest: O Heavenly King, the Comforter, the Spirit of Truth; who art everywhere present and fillest all things; Treasury of blessings, and giver of life: come and abide in us, and cleanse us from every impurity, and save our souls, O Good One.

The Trisagion Prayers

Reader: Holy God, Holy Mighty, Holy Immortal, have mercy on us. **(x3)**

Glory be to the Father, and to the Son, and to the Holy Spirit;
Both now and forever, and unto the ages of ages. Amen.

O Most Holy Trinity, have mercy on us.

O Lord, cleanse us from our sins.

O Master, pardon our iniquities.

O Holy One, visit and heal our infirmities, for Thy names sake.

Lord have mercy. **(x3)**

Glory be to the Father, and to the Son, and to the Holy Spirit;
Both now and forever, and unto the ages of ages. Amen.

People: *Our Father, who art in heaven, hallowed be Thy name. Thy Kingdom come. Thy will be done, on earth as it is in heaven. Give us this day our daily bread; and forgive us our trespasses, as we forgive those who trespass against us; and lead us not into temptation, but deliver us from the evil one.*

Priest: For Thine is the kingdom, the power, and the glory, of the Father, and the Son and the Holy Spirit, both now and forever, and to the ages of ages.

People: *Amen.*

The Apolytikion and Kontakion of the Saint

[insert here]

The Dismissal

Priest: Establish, O God, the holy Orthodox Faith of Orthodox Christians to the ages of ages.

Reader: Greater in honour than the Cherubim and beyond compare more glorious than the Seraphim; without corruption thou gavest birth to God the Word, truly the Theotokos, we magnify thee.

Glory be to the Father, and to the Son, and to the Holy Spirit;
Both now and forever, and unto the ages of ages. Amen.

Lord have mercy. **(x3)**

People: *Holy Father, bless!*

Priest: O Lord Jesus Christ, Son of God, for the sake of the prayers of Thy most pure Mother, of our holy and God bearing fathers, of *[St Martin – or the patron of your parish]*, of _____ *(saints of the day)*, and of all the saints, have mercy on us and save us, for Thou art good and the Lover of mankind.

People: *Amen.*

Priest: Bless our most holy Archbishop Nikitas, the faithful of this holy place; and all Orthodox Christians. Preserve us, O Lord, for many years.

People: *Amen.*

Priest: Through the prayers of our holy Fathers; O Lord Jesus Christ our God; have mercy on us and save us.

People: *Amen.*

Prayer For Kolyva – In Commemoration Of A Saint

O Lord, who brought all things to completion by Thy word, and ordered the earth to product fruits of all kinds for our enjoyment and nourishment; who showed Daniel and the three youths to be healthier through seeds and pulses than those who had fed sumptuously in Babylon; do Thou, all loving King, bless these seeds, mixed with different fruits. And sanctify those who partake of them. For they have been offered by Thy servants for Thy glory, and in honour of Saint *N*, and in memory of those who have been made perfect in death in the Orthodox faith.   Grant also, loving Lord, to those who have prepared these things and who celebrate this memorial, all their requests which are for their salvation and the enjoyment of Thy eternal blessings; at the prayers of our all pure Lady, the Mother of God and Ever Virgin Mary, of Saint *N*, whose memory we celebrate, and of all Thy saints.

For it is Thou who blessest and sanctifiest all things, Christ our God, and to Thee we give glory, together with Thy Father who is without beginning, and Thy all holy, good and life giving Spirit, both now and forever and to the ages of ages.

People: *Amen.*

Blessing Of The 5 Loaves - Artoklasia

[artos = bread, klasis = breaking.]

Prayer Before Preparing The Artoklasia Bread

Lord, please help us to prepare this Artoklasia which I am about to begin and bring it to completion according to Thy will so that we can pray for the well being of our loved ones whose names we are about to offer and so that we can share the blessing of these five loaves with the faithful who join us in asking for Thy great mercy and Divine grace. Amen.

[Service held at the end of Vespers, Orthros and increasingly at the end of the Divine Liturgy, though it would be better to be held after the Doxology before the Liturgy.

If Done After The Divine Liturgy	*Straight after the Prayer behind the Ambo.*
If Done After Vespers	*Straight after the Apolytikia of Vespers.*
If Done After Orthros	*Straight after the Doxology.*

The loaves are donated together with wine and oil for saint name days, anniversaries, etc. The bread shall be eaten and the wine used for Holy Communion and the oil for the lamps. Non Greek traditions may consume all three.

They are placed on a little table in front of the Holy Doors.

*The **Troparion of the Saint being remembered** is sung whilst the clergy move to the table, facing east.]*

The Litany

Deacon: Have mercy on us, O God, according to Thy great mercy, we pray you, hear us and have mercy.

People: *Lord, have mercy.* **(x3)**

Deacon: Also we pray for all all devout and Orthodox Christians.

People: *Lord, have mercy.* **(x3)**

Deacon: Also we pray for our Archbishop Nikitas.

People: *Lord, have mercy.* **(x3)**

Deacon: For our Sovereign Lady, Queen Elizabeth, the Royal family, our Government, and all in authority, let us pray to the Lord.

People: *Lord, have mercy.* **(x3)**

Deacon: Also we pray for mercy, life, peace, health, salvation, visitation, pardon and forgiveness of sins for the servants of God, who celebrate this holy feast, and of the servants of God *[Names of those who offered the loaves].*

People: *Lord, have mercy.* **(x3)**

People: *Lord, have mercy.* **(x12)** *[softly during:]*

Deacon: Also we pray for the protection of this holy Church, this city and every city, town and village from plague, famine, earthquake, flood, fire, sword, invasion by enemies, civil war and sudden death; and that our good God, who lovest mankind, shall be merciful, kindly and easily entreated, turn away and dispel all wrath and disease stirred up against us, and deliver us from His just threat that hangs over us, and have mercy on us.

Deacon: Also we pray that the Lord, our God, shall hear the voice of supplication of us sinners, and have mercy on us.

People: *Lord, have mercy.* **(x3)**

Priest: Hear us, O God, our Saviour, the hope of all the ends of the Earth and of those far off on the sea; and have mercy on us. For Thou, O God, art merciful, and lovest mankind, and to Thee we givest glory, to the Father, to the Son and to the Holy Spirit, both now and forever, and unto the ages of ages.

People: *Amen.*

Priest: Peace be with you all.

People: *And with thy spirit.*

Deacon: Let us bow our heads to the Lord.

People: *To Thee, O Lord.*

Priest: Most merciful Master, Lord Jesus Christ, our God, through the prayers of our all our Lady, Mother of God and Ever Virgin Mary; by the power of the precious and life giving Cross; through the protection of the honoured Bodiless Powers of heaven; through the intercessions of the honoured, glorious Prophet, Forerunner and Baptist John; of the holy, glorious and all praised Apostles; of our Fathers among the saints, great hierarchs and ecumenical teachers, Basil the Great, Gregory the Theologian and John Chrysostom; of our Father among the saints Nicholas of Myra in Lycia, the wonder worker, of the holy and glorious [St David, the patron of Wales (or) Great Martyr George the Victor, the patron saint of England]; of the holy, glorious and triumphant Martyrs; of our venerable and God bearing Forebears of God, Joachim and Anna, of Saint *N*, whose memory we are celebrating, and of all Thy Saints; **make** our supplication acceptable; **grant** us the forgiveness of our offences; **shelter** us in the shelter of Thy wings; **drive** from us every foe and enemy; **make** our life peaceful, Lord, have mercy on us and on Thy world, and save our souls, for Thou art good and lovest mankind.

[Priest censes the loaves in the form of a cross, going round the 4 sides of the table. The Deacon or candle bearer circles opposite him, whilst the Priest or the People chant:]

People: Virgin Mother of God, hail Mary, full of grace, the Lord is with thee, blessed art thou among women; and blessed is the fruit of your womb; for you gave birth to Saviour of our souls.

Deacon: Let us pray to the Lord.

People: *Lord, have mercy.*

[Priest takes a loaf and makes the sign of the Crossover it with his right hand and says:]

Prayer Of The Breaking Of The bread

Priest: *[aloud]* Lord, Jesus Christ, our God, who blessed the five loaves in the desert, and from them fed five thousand, bless these loaves also, this wheat, wine and oil, and multiply them in this city *[or town or village]* and in all Thy world, and sanctify Thy faithful servants who partake of them. For it is Thou who blesses and sanctifies all things, Christ, our God, and to Thee we give glory, with Thine Father who is without beginning, and Thine all holy, good and life creating Spirit, both now and forever and unto the ages of ages.

People: *Amen.*

[Priest and Deacon kiss a loaf and return to the Sanctuary, whist:]

Priest and Deacon: The rich have become poor and hungry, whilst those who seek the Lord shall not lack any good thing.

Chorus: *The rich have become poor and hungry, whilst those who seek the Lord shall not lack any good thing.* **(x2)**

Deacon: Let us pray to the Lord.

People: *Lord, have mercy.*

[Priest in front of the Holy Doors, facing west and:]

Priest: May the blessing of the Lord and His mercy come upon you all, by His grace and love for mankind, always now and forever, and to the ages of ages.

People: *Amen.*

If Done After The Divine Liturgy   *Return to the Liturgy at:*

"Blessed be the name of the Lord from this time forth and forever more".

If Done After Vespers   *[Carry straight on.]*

If Done After Orthros   *[Carry straight on.]*

Dismissal

Priest: Glory to Thee, O Christ, our God and our hope, glory to Thee.

Reader: *Glory be to the Father, and to the Son, and to the Holy Spirit;*

Both now and forever, and unto the ages of ages. Amen.

Lord, have mercy. **(x3)**

Holy Father, bless!

Priest: May *(Sundays: He Who rose from the dead)* Christ our true God, through the prayers of His most holy Mother, by the power of the precious and life giving Cross, through the protection of the honoured, Bodiless powers of Heaven, through the intercessions of the honoured, glorious prophet, forerunner and baptist John, of the holy, all praised and glorious Apostles, of the holy, glorious and triumphant Martyrs, of our venerable and God bearing Fathers and Mothers who have shone forth in the ascetic life, of our Father among the Saints, John Chrysostom, Archbishop of Constantinople, of the holy and righteous ancestors of God, Joachim and Anna, of *[Saint of your parish]* to whom the church is dedicated, of Saint *N* whose memory we celebrate today, and of all the Saints, have mercy on us and save us, for He is good and loves mankind.

People: *Amen.*

Priest: Through the prayers of our holy fathers, Lord Jesus Christ, our God, have mercy on us.

People: *Amen.*

[if not joined to another service start here.]

Trisagion

Priest: Blessed is our God always, now and forever, and unto the ages of ages.

People: *Amen.*

Priest: O Heavenly King, Comforter, Spirit of Truth, Who art everywhere present and fillest all things, Treasury of blessings and Giver of life: Come and abide in us and cleanse us from every impurity and save our souls, O Good One.

Reader: Holy God, Holy Mighty, Holy Immortal, have mercy on us. **(x3)**

Glory be to the Father, and to the Son, and to the Holy Spirit;

Both now and forever, and unto the ages of ages. Amen.

O Most Holy Trinity, have mercy on us.

O Lord, cleanse us from our sins.

O Master, pardon our iniquities.

O Holy One, visit and heal our infirmities, for Thy names sake.

Lord have mercy. **(x3)**

Glory be to the Father, and to the Son, and to the Holy Spirit;

Both now and forever, and unto the ages of ages. Amen.

People: *Our Father, Who art in Heaven, hallowed be Thy Name. Thy Kingdom come, Thy will be done, on earth as it is in Heaven. Give us this day our daily bread, and forgive us our trespasses, as we forgive those who trespass against us; and lead us not into temptation, but deliver us from the evil one.*

Priest: For Thine is the Kingdom, and the power, and the glory; of the Father, and of the Son, and of the Holy Spirit, now and ever, and unto the ages of ages.

People: *Amen.*

Reader: Lord, have mercy. **(x3)**

Glory be to the Father, and to the Son, and to the Holy Spirit;

Both now and forever, and unto the ages of ages. Amen.

[if joined to another service start here.]

Tone 4   Festive, joyous and expressing deep piety.   *C, D, Eb, F, G, A, Bb, C.*

With the spirits of the righteous made perfect Give rest to the soul of Thy servant*[s]*, O Saviour; And keep it safe in that life of blessedness that is lived with Thee, O Lover of mankind. In the place of Thy rest, O Lord, Where all Your Saints repose, Give rest also to the soul*[s]* of Thy servant*[s]*, For Thou alone art immortal.

Glory be to the Father and to the Son and to the Holy Spirit;

Thou art our God Who went down to Hades to loose the pains of the dead that were there; Give rest also to the soul*[s]* of Your servant*[s]*, O Saviour.

Both now and forever and unto the ages of ages. Amen.

O Virgin, alone pure and immaculate, who ineffably bore God, intercede for the salvation of the soul*[s]* of your servant*[s]*.

[All days]
Deacon: Have mercy on us. O God, according to Thy great mercy; we pray Thee, hear us and have mercy.
People: *Lord, have mercy.* **(x3)**

[Saturdays]
Deacon: Also we pray for blessed memory and eternal rest for all devout and Orthodox Christians who have fallen asleep before us in the hope of resurrection; Rulers, Patriarchs, Bishops, Priests, Deacons, Monks, Nuns, Parents, Grandparents, Great Grandparents and Ancestors, our children, brothers and sisters, and relatives, those from the beginning until the last, and that they may be pardoned every offence, both voluntary and involuntary.
People: *Lord, have mercy.* **(x3)**

[All days]
Deacon: Again we pray for the repose of the soul of the servant of God *(Name[s])*, who *has / have* fallen asleep, and for the forgiveness of *his / her / their* every transgression, voluntary and involuntary.
People: *Lord, have mercy.* **(x3)**
Deacon: Let the Lord God establish *his / her / their* soul*[s]* where the righteous repose.
People: *Lord, have mercy.* **(x3)**
Deacon: The mercies of God, the Kingdom of the Heavens, and the remission of *his / her / their* sins, let us ask of Christ, our immortal King and our God.
People: *Grant this, O Lord.*

Prayer For Kolyva

Priest: O Lord, who brought all things to completion by Thy word, and ordered the earth to product fruits of all kinds for our enjoyment and nourishment; who showed Daniel and the three youths to be healthier through seeds and pulses than those who had fed sumptuously in Babylon; do Thou, all loving King, bless these seeds, mixed with different fruits. And sanctify those who partake of them. For they have been offered by Thy servants for Thy glory, and in honour of Saint *N*, and in memory of those who have been made perfect in death in the Orthodox faith. Grant also, loving Lord, to those who have prepared these things and who celebrate this memorial, all their requests which are for their salvation and the enjoyment of Thy eternal blessings; at the prayers of our all pure Lady, the Mother of God and Ever Virgin Mary, of Saint *N*, whose memory we celebrate, and of all Thy saints. For it is Thou who blessest and sanctifiest all things, Christ our God, and to Thee we give glory, together with Thy Father who is without beginning, and Thy all holy, good and life giving Spirit, both now and forever and to the ages of ages.

People: Amen.

Deacon: Let us pray to the Lord.

People: Lord have mercy.

Priest: O God of all spirits and of every flesh, Who did tread down death and overcome the devil, bestowing life on this Thy world, to the soul of this Thy servant *(Name[s])*, departed this life, do Thee Thyself, O Lord, give rest in a place of fight, in a place of green pasture, in a place of refreshment, from where pain and sorrow and mourning have fled away. Every sin by *him / her / them* committed in thought, word, or deed, do Thou as our Good and Loving God forgive; seeing that there is no man who shall live and sin not, for Thou alone art without sin. Thy righteousness is an everlasting righteousness, and Thy Law is truth. For Thou art the Resurrection, the Life, and the Repose of Thy servant *(Name[s])*, departed this life, O Christ our God; and to Thee do we send up glory, with Thine Eternal Father and Thine All Holy, Good and Life creating Spirit; both now and forever, and unto the ages of ages.

People: Amen.

Priest: Glory to Thee, O Christ our God and our Hope; glory to Thee.

Reader: *Glory be to the Father and to the Son and to the Holy Spirit;*

Both now and forever and unto the ages of ages. Amen.

Lord have mercy. **(x3)**

Holy Father, Bless.

Priest: May Christ our true God, Who rose from the dead, have mercy on us; He Who as Immortal King has authority over both the dead and the living. Through the intercessions of His spotless, pure and holy Mother; of the holy, glorious, and all praiseworthy Apostles, of our venerable and God bearing Fathers; of the holy and glorious forefathers Abraham, Isaac and Jacob; of His holy and just friend Lazarus, who lay in the grave four days; and of all the Saints; establish the soul*[s]* of His servant *(Name[s])*, departed from us, establish in the tents of the righteous; give *him / her / them* rest in the bosom of Abraham; and number *him / her / them* among the righteous,; and have mercy on us and save us, for He is good and loves mankind.

Give eternal rest in blessed falling asleep, O Lord, to the soul*[s]* of Thy departed servant*[s]* *(Name[s])*, and make *his / her / their* memory eternal.

People: Memory eternal. **(x3)**

Priest: Through the prayers of our holy Fathers, Lord Jesus Christ, our God, have mercy on us and save us.

People: Amen.

These are mostly Readers services, that is, without a Priest and suitable for monasteries and non family settings. They are mostly pared down services of those with a Priest.

As these are mostly Readers prayers no clergy are required and so one may apportion different people to different parts e.g. a Psalm for each person present, working round and round those present with the most accomplished person there present acting as director.

In these services we often encounter repetition of "Lord, have mercy" in either **(x3)**, **(x12)**, **(x40)**. These take the place of an ektenia or litany that would have been led by a Priest at that point. So we are answering and condoning prayers that the Priest would have said.

- Lord, have mercy. **(x3)**
  is in place of a Little Litany of only 3 short prayers ending with a commemoration of the Theotokos.
- Lord, have mercy. **(x12)**
  is in place of an Augmented Litany. This is a short litany, but the people reply "Lord, have mercy" 3 times after each prayer.
- Lord, have mercy. **(x40)**
  is in place of a Long Litany of 40 prayers.

These should be said in groups of threes. They should not be gabbled. Another way of involving the people in the worship is to set these to a tune. Recalling that tunes for the people must work for all levels and so be simple. One that works well is on 5 notes.

Lord, have mercy. (x3)

C	D	E	D C
Lord have mercy.	Lord have mercy.	Lord have mercy.	

Lord, have mercy. (x12)

C	D	E	D C	D	E	D C
Lord have mercy.	Lord have mercy.	Lord have mercy.	Lord have mercy.	Lord have mercy.	Lord have mercy.	
G	F	E	D G	F	E	D C
Lord have mercy.	Lord have mercy.	Lord have mercy.	Lord have mercy.	Lord have mercy.	Lord have mercy.	

Lord, have mercy. (x40)

C	D	E	D C	D	E	D C
Lord have mercy.	Lord have mercy.	Lord have mercy.	Lord have mercy.	Lord have mercy.	Lord have mercy.	

G	F	E	D G	F	E	D
Lord have mercy.	Lord have mercy.	Lord have mercy.	Lord have mercy.	Lord have mercy.	Lord have mercy.	

Repeat all of the above 3 times to take you to 36, then:

C	D	E	D C	D C
Lord have mercy.	Lord have mercy.	Lord have mercy.	Lord have mercy.	

The very last one should be slower, this is a cue to the people that we are ending.

The Russians, again with their eye to a beautiful presentation, may have other groupings, such as x30 or x50. This is mostly to do with their musical tradition rather than reflecting certain litanies.

Services, such as Orthros, have several Psalms. It is accepted practice to sing all of them each day. In other places they are distributed throughout the week. Follow whichever practice with which you feel comfortable and have the time. Treat the *[days in brackets]* as a guide only.

In a monastic, or pseudo-monastic setting it would appear that the times of the services should exactly follow the headings. i.e.:

5:00	Orthros	12:00	6th Hour	19:00	Small Compline
6:00	1st Hour	15:00	9th Hour		
9:00	3rd Hour	18:00	Vespers		

However they are often grouped:

8:00   Orthros, 1st Hour, 3rd Hour, 6th Hour (maybe the 9th Hour).

    Then the monastics attend to their duties for the day, or the pseudo-monastic goes to work for the day.

18:00   (maybe the 9th Hour here), Vespers, Small Compline, an akathist if appropriate.

It is not about adopting a hard and fast rule that makes life impossible, it is about adopting a prayer rule that can work for a long time and thereby enriches your life. Here at St Martins the author works from 7:00-9:00, then again from 12:00-14:00. Hence the morning group of services is done about 9:00. The evenings are easier.

Those who chant in the churches should refrain from forcing their nature to yell, but also from saying anything else that is unsuitable for the church. Canon LXXV of the Sixth Ecumenical Synod.

Readers Daily Orthros

[Daily Gospel required.]

Trisagion

Reader: In the Name of the Father and of the Son and of the Holy Spirit.

People: Amen. Glory to Thee, our God, glory to Thee.

Reader: O Heavenly King, Comforter, Spirit of Truth, Who art everywhere present and fillest all things, Treasury of blessings and Giver of life: Come and abide in us and cleanse us from every impurity and save our souls, O Good One.

Holy God, Holy Mighty, Holy Immortal, have mercy on us. **(x3)**

Glory be to the Father, and to the Son, and to the Holy Spirit;
Both now and forever, and unto the ages of ages. Amen.

O Most Holy Trinity, have mercy on us.

O Lord, cleanse us from our sins.

O Master, pardon our iniquities.

O Holy One, visit and heal our infirmities, for Thy names sake.

Lord have mercy. **(x3)**

Glory be to the Father, and to the Son, and to the Holy Spirit;
Both now and forever, and unto the ages of ages. Amen.

People: *Our Father, Who art in Heaven, hallowed be Thy Name. Thy Kingdom come, Thy will be done, on earth as it is in Heaven. Give us this day our daily bread, and forgive us our trespasses, as we forgive those who trespass against us; and lead us not into temptation, but deliver us from the evil one. Amen.*

Reader: Lord, have mercy. **(x3)**

Glory be to the Father, and to the Son, and to the Holy Spirit;
Both now and forever, and unto the ages of ages. Amen.

Come, let us worship God, our King.

Come, let us worship and fall down before Christ, our King and our God.

Come, let us worship and fall down before Christ Himself, our King and our God.

Doxology – excerpt Glory to God in the highest and on earth peace good will toward men.

Psalm 50 – excerpt O Lord, open my lips, and my mouth shall proclaim Thy praise.

[Monday, Sunday]   **Psalm 3**

Lord, how they have increased who trouble me. Many are they who rise up against me. Many are they who say of me, "There is no help for him in God." But Thou, O Lord, art a shield for me, my glory and the One Who lifts up my head. I cried to the Lord with my voice, and He heard me from His holy hill. I lay down and slept; I awoke, for the Lord sustained me. I shall not be afraid of ten thousands of people who have set themselves against me all around. Arise, O Lord; save me, O my God. For Thou hast struck all mine enemies on the cheekbone; Thou hast broken the teeth of the ungodly. Salvation belongs to the Lord. Thy blessing is upon Thy people.

[Tuesday, Sunday]   **Psalm 37**

O Lord, do not rebuke me in Thy wrath, nor chasten me in Thy hot displeasure. For Thine arrows deeply pierce me, and Thine hand presses me down. There is no soundness in my flesh because of Thine anger, Nor is there any health in my bones because of my sin. For mine iniquities have gone over my head; like a heavy burden they are too heavy for me. My wounds are foul and festering because of my foolishness. I am troubled, I am bowed down greatly; I go mourning all the day long. For my loins are full of inflammation, and there is no soundness in my flesh. I am feeble and severely broken; I groan because of the turmoil of my heart. Lord, all my desire is before Thee; and my sighing is not hidden from Thee. My heart pants, my strength fails me; as for the light of mine eyes, it also has gone from me. My loved ones and my friends stand aloof from my plague, and my kinsmen stand afar off. Those also who seek my life lay snares for me; those who seek my hurt speak of destruction, and plan deception all the day long. But I, like a deaf man, do not hear; and I am like a mute who does not open his mouth. Thus I am like a man who does not hear, and in whose mouth is no response. For in Thee, O Lord, I hope; Thou wilt hear, O Lord my God. For I said, "*Hear me, lest they rejoice over me, lest, when my foot slips, they magnify themselves against me.*" For I am ready to fall, and my sorrow is continually before me. For I shall declare mine iniquity; I shall be in anguish over my sin. But mine enemies are vigorous, and they are strong; and those who wrongfully hate me have multiplied. Those also who render evil for good, they are mine adversaries, because I follow what is good. Do not forsake me, O Lord; O my God, be not far from me. Make haste to help me, O Lord, my salvation.

[Wednesday, Sunday]   **Psalm 62**

O God, Thou art my God; early shall I seek Thee; my soul thirsts for Thee; My flesh longs for Thee in a dry and thirsty land where there is no water. So I have looked for Thee in the sanctuary, to see Thy power and Thy glory. Because Thy loving kindness is better than life, my lips shall praise Thee. Thus I shall bless Thee while I live; I shall lift up my hands in Thy name. My soul shall be satisfied as with marrow and fatness, and my mouth shall praise Thee with joyful lips. When I remember Thee on my bed, I meditate on Thee in the night watches. Because Thou hast been my help, therefore in the shadow of Thy wings I shall rejoice. My soul follows close behind Thee; Thy right hand upholds me. But those who seek my life, to destroy it, shall go into the lower parts of the earth. They shall fall by the sword; they shall be a portion for jackals. But the king shall rejoice in God; everyone who swears by Him shall glory; but the mouth of those who speak lies shall be stopped.

[Thursday, Sunday] **Psalm 87**

O Lord, God of my salvation, I have cried out day and night before Thee. Let my prayer come before Thee; incline Thine ear to my cry. For my soul is full of troubles, and my life draws near to the grave. I am counted with those who go down to the pit; I am like a man who has no strength, Adrift among the dead, like the slain who lie in the grave, whom Thou rememberest no more, and who are cut off from Thine hand. Thou hast laid me in the lowest pit, in darkness, in the depths. Thy wrath lies heavy upon me, and Thou hast afflicted me with all Thy waves. Thou hast put away mine acquaintances far from me; Thou hast made me an abomination to them; I am shut up, and I cannot get out; Mine eye wastes away because of affliction. Lord, I have called daily upon Thee; I have stretched out my hands to Thee. Willest Thou work wonders for the dead? Shall the dead arise and praise Thee? Shall Thy loving kindness be declared in the grave? Or Thy faithfulness in the place of destruction? Shall Thy wonders be known in the dark? And Thy righteousness in the land of forgetfulness? But to Thee I have cried out, O Lord, and in the morning my prayer comes before Thee. Lord, why dost Thou cast off my soul? Why dost Thou hide Thy face from me? I have been afflicted and ready to die from my youth up; I suffer Thy terrors; I am distraught. Thy fierce wrath has gone over me; Thy terrors have cut me off. They came around me all day long like water; they engulfed me altogether. Loved one and friend Thou hast put far from me, and mine acquaintances into darkness.

[Friday, Sunday] **Psalm 102**

Bless the Lord O my soul; and all that is within me, bless His holy name. Bless the Lord O my soul, and forget not all His benefits: Who forgives all thine iniquities, Who heals all thy diseases, Who redeems thy life from destruction, Who crowns thee with loving kindness and tender mercies, Who satisfies thy mouth with good things, so that thine youth is renewed like the eagles. The Lord executes righteousness and justice for all who are oppressed. He made known His ways to Moses, His acts to the children of Israel. The Lord is merciful and gracious, slow to anger, and abounding in mercy. He shall not always strive with us, nor shall He keep His anger forever. He has not dealt with us according to our sins, nor punished us according to our iniquities. For as the heavens are high above the earth, so great is His mercy toward those who fear Him; As far as the east is from the west, so far has He removed our transgressions from us. As a father pities his children, so the Lord pities those who fear Him. For He knows our frame; He remembers that we are dust. As for man, his days are like grass; as a flower of the field, so he flourishes. For the wind passes over it, and it is gone, and its place remembers it no more. But the mercy of the Lord is from everlasting to everlasting on those who fear Him, and His righteousness to childrens children, To such as keep His covenant, and to those who remember His commandments to do them. The Lord has established His throne in heaven, and His kingdom rules overall. Bless the Lord you His angels, who excel in strength, who do His word, heeding the voice of His word. Bless the Lord all you His hosts, you ministers of His, who do His pleasure. Bless the Lord all His works, in all places of His dominion. Bless the Lord O my soul.

[Saturday, Sunday] **Psalm 142**

Lord, hear my prayer; in Thy truth give ear to my supplications; in Thy righteousness hear me. Enter not into judgement with Thy servant, for no one living is justified in Thy sight. For the enemy has pursued my soul; he has crushed my life to the ground. He has made me to dwell in darkness, like those that have long been dead, and my spirit within me is overwhelmed; my heart within me is distressed. I remembered the days of old, I meditated on all Thy works, I pondered on the creations of Thine hands. I stretched forth my hands to Thee; my soul longs for Thee like a thirsty land. Lord, hear me quickly; my spirit fails. Turn not Thy face away from me, lest I be like those who go down into the pit. Let me hear Thy mercy in the morning; for in Thee have I put my trust. Lord, teach me to know the way wherein I should walk; for I lift up my soul to Thee. Rescue me, Lord, from mine enemies, to Thee have I fled for refuge. Teach me to do Thy will, for Thou art my God. Thy good Spirit shall lead me on a level path. Lord, for Thy names sake Thou shalt preserve my life. In Thy righteousness Thou shalt bring my soul out of trouble, and in Thy mercy Thou shalt utterly destroy my enemies. And Thou shalt destroy all those who afflict my soul, for I am Thy servant.

After The Psalm

> Glory be to the Father and to the Son and to the Holy Spirit,
> Both now and forever and unto the ages of ages. Amen.

Halleluiah, Halleluiah, Halleluiah. Glory to Thee, O God. **(x3)**

Commemoration Of The Living

• O Lord Jesus Christ our God, Who for the sake of Thine eternal mercy and loving kindness became man, and suffered crucifixion and death for the salvation of all; Who rose from the dead and ascended into heaven, and sittest on the right hand of the Father, where Thou hearest the prayers of all who call upon Thee humbly and with their whole heart: incline Thine ear to us, and hearken to the prayer that Thine unworthy servants offer as a spiritual sacrifice for all Thy people.

• Remember first of all Thy Holy, Catholic and Apostolic Church, that Thou hast purchased with Thy precious blood. Strengthen it, multiply it, keep it in peace, and do not allow the gates of hell to stand against it. Heal the schisms of the churches, stop the raging of the heathen, root out and cleanse all heresies, destroying them by the power of Thy Holy Spirit.

• Have mercy, O Lord, upon our Royal family, our ministers, and all in civil authority, and save them, together with the armed forces of our country. Give them peace and continual victory over injustice and evil in all places. May they keep Thy holy Church secure, that all Thy people may live calm and ordered lives in Thy sight, in true faith and prayer, with godly deeds.

• Have mercy, O Lord, upon the Orthodox patriarchs and archbishops, the metropolitans and bishops, the priests and deacons, and the whole order of Thy Churchs clergy. Save them whom Thou hast established to feed Thy flock, and by their prayers have mercy on us sinners, and save us.

• Have mercy, O Lord, on our spiritual fathers, mothers, brothers, sisters and children, and save them, and by their holy prayers forgive us our transgressions.

- Have mercy, O Lord, on our parents, and save them, together with our brothers and sisters, our children, our relatives and our friends. Grant them Thy blessing both here and in the life to come.

- Have mercy, O Lord, on the old and the young, the needy, the orphans and widows, and all who are in sickness and sorrow, distress and affliction, oppression and captivity, in prison and confinement. Save them, together with Thy servants who are under persecution for Thy sake and for the sake of the Orthodox faith. Remember them, visit them, strengthen and comfort them, and by Thy power grant them speedy relief, freedom and deliverance.

- Have mercy, O Lord, on all who travel, and save all those who are sent on duty: our fathers, mothers, brothers, sisters and children, all our loved ones and all Orthodox Christians.

- Have mercy, O Lord, on our enemies: save all those who envy us, wish us evil or deal unjustly with us. May they not perish because of us sinners. Enlighten, O Lord, with the truth of Thy holy wisdom all who have gone astray from the Orthodox faith, led by destructive heresies, and unite them once more to Thy Holy Catholic and Apostolic Church.

*[List the names of the **Living** to be remembered in Prayer. Use your Prayer list.]*

Commemoration Of The Departed

- Remember, O Lord, those who have departed this life: all Orthodox patriarchs, archbishops, metropolitans, bishops and all who served Thee in the priesthood and ministry of the Church and in the monastic order, and grant them rest with Thy saints in Thine eternal kingdom.

- Remember, O Lord, the souls of Thy servants now fallen asleep: our parents, family and friends. Forgive them all their sins, committed knowingly or unknowingly; grant them Thy kingdom, a portion in Thine eternal blessing and the enjoyment of Thine unending life.

- Remember, O Lord, all who have fallen asleep in the hope of the resurrection and of eternal life: our fathers, mothers, brothers, sisters and children, all our loved ones and Orthodox Christians throughout the world. Place them with Thy saints before the light of Thy countenance and have mercy on us, for Thou art good and lovest mankind.

*[List the names of the **Departed** to be remembered in Prayer.]*

God Is The Lord

People: *God is the Lord and has revealed Himself to us. Blessed is He who comes in the Name of the Lord.*

Reader: Give thanks to the Lord, for He is good; and His steadfast love endures forever.

People: *God is the Lord and has revealed Himself to us. Blessed is He who comes in the Name of the Lord.*

Reader: All nations surrounded me; in the Name of the Lord, I withstood them.

People: *God is the Lord and has revealed Himself to us. Blessed is He who comes in the Name of the Lord.*

Reader: I shall not die, but live, and recount the deeds of the Lord.

People: *God is the Lord and has revealed Himself to us. Blessed is He who comes in the Name of the Lord.*

Reader: The stone that the builders rejected has become the chief cornerstone.

This is the Lords doing and is marvellous in our eyes.

People: *God is the Lord and has revealed Himself to us. Blessed is He who comes in the Name of the Lord.*

[Sunday] ### Troparion Of The Resurrection

   Tone 4   Festive, joyous and expressing deep piety.   *C, D, Eb, F, G, A, Bb, C.*

Having learned the joyful message of the Resurrection from the angel, the women Disciples cast from them their parental condemnation, and proudly broke the news to the Disciples, saying, Death has been spoiled. Christ God is risen, granting the world Great Mercy.

[Monday] ### St Michael And All Angels

   Tone 4   Festive, joyous and expressing deep piety.   *C, D, Eb, F, G, A, Bb, C.*

O Commanders of Sabaoth, We who are unworthy beseech you ceaselessly that you wouldst encompass us with the shelter of your prayers and cover us beneath the wings of your immaterial glory. We fall down before you crying out: *"Protect us from all harm, O Princes of the powers on high."*

[Tuesday] ### Forerunner And Baptist John

   Tone 2   Majesty, gentleness, hope, repentance and sadness.   *E, F, G, Ab, B, C.*

The memory of the righteous is worthy of praise, But thou, O Forerunner, are well pleased by the Lords own witness. Thou wast revealed as greater than the prophets, For thou baptised in the waters Him whom they foretold. Therefore, having fought and suffered for the Truth, thou proclaimed to those in the tombs the Gospel of the incarnate God, Who takest away the sins of the world and grantest us great mercy.

[Wednesday] ### Holy And Life Giving Cross

   Tone 2   Majesty, gentleness, hope, repentance and sadness.   *E, F, G, Ab, B, C.*

O Lord, save Thy people, And bless Thine inheritance. Grant victories to the Orthodox Christians over their adversaries. And by virtue of Thy Cross, Preserve Thy habitation.

[Thursday] ### Holy Apostles And St Nicholas

   Tone 3   Arrogant, brave, and mature atmosphere.   *F, G, A, A#, C, D, E, F.*

O holy Apostles, intercede with our merciful God to grant our souls forgiveness of our sins.

[Friday] ### Holy And Life Giving Cross

   Tone 1   Magnificent, happy and earthy.   *C, D, Eb, F, G, A, Bb, C.*

O Lord, save Thy people, And bless Thine inheritance. Grant victories to the Orthodox Christians over their adversaries. And by virtue of Thy Cross, Preserve Thy habitation.

[Saturday] ### The Theotokos, All Saints, The Faithful Departed

   Tone 2   Majesty, gentleness, hope, repentance and sadness.   *E, F, G, Ab, B, C.*

Apostles, martyrs, and prophets, Holy hierarchs, saints and righteous, Having fought the good fight and kept the Faith, Thou hast boldness toward the Saviour. Intercede for us with Him for He is good, and pray that He may save our souls.

Prokeimenon Of The Day

Reader: The Prokeimenon.

[Sunday]   [Refer To Variables.]

[Monday]   ## Prokeimenon From Psalm 103

   Tone 4   Festive, joyous and expressing deep piety.   *C, D, Eb, F, G, A, Bb, C.*

Reader: He makest his angels spirits and His ministers a flame of fire.

People: *He makest his angels spirits and His ministers a flame of fire.*

Reader: Bless the Lord O my soul. O Lord my God, Thou art very great.

People: *He makest his angels spirits and His ministers a flame of fire.*

Reader: He makest his angels spirits | and His ministers a flame of fire.

[Tuesday]   ## Prokeimenon From Psalm 63

   Tone 7   Manly character and strong melody.   *F, G, A, A#, C, D, E, F.*

Reader: The righteous shall rejoice in the Lord, and shall hope in Him.

People: *The righteous shall rejoice in the Lord, and shall hope in Him.*

Reader: Hear my voice, O God, when I pray to Thee.

People: *The righteous shall rejoice in the Lord, and shall hope in Him.*

Reader: The righteous shall rejoice in the Lord | and shall hope in Him.

[Wednesday]   ## Prokeimenon From The Magnificat

   Tone 3   Arrogant, brave, and mature atmosphere.   *F, G, A, A#, C, D, E, F.*

Reader: My soul magnifies the Lord, and my spirit rejoices in God my Saviour.

People: *My soul magnifies the Lord, and my spirit rejoices in God my Saviour.*

Reader: For He has regarded the lowly state of His handmaiden;

   For behold, henceforth all generations shall call me blessed.

People: *My soul magnifies the Lord, and my spirit rejoices in God my Saviour.*

Reader: My soul magnifies the Lord | and my spirit rejoices in God my Saviour.

[Thursday]   ## Prokeimenon From Psalm 18

   Tone 8   Humility, tranquillity, repose, suffering, pleading.   *C, D, Eb, F, G, A, Bb, C.*

Reader: Their proclamation has gone out into all the earth and their words to the end of the universe.

People: *Their proclamation has gone out into all the earth and their words to the end of the universe.*

Reader: The heavens are telling the glory of God; and the firmament proclaims His handiwork.

People: *Their proclamation has gone out into all the earth and their words to the end of the universe.*

Reader: Their proclamation has gone out into all the earth | and their words to the end of the universe.

[Friday]   **Prokeimenon From Psalm 98**

   Tone 7   Manly character and strong melody.   *F, G, A, A#, C, D, E, F.*

Reader: Extol the Lord our God; worship at His footstool, for it is holy.

People: *Extol the Lord our God; worship at His footstool, for it is holy.*

Reader: The Lord reigns; let the peoples tremble.

People: *Extol the Lord our God; worship at His footstool, for it is holy.*

Reader: Extol the Lord our God | worship at His footstool, for it is holy.

[Saturday]   **Prokeimenon From Psalm 31**

   Tone 8   Humility, tranquillity, repose, suffering, pleading.   *C, D, Eb, F, G, A, Bb, C.*

Reader: Be glad in the Lord and rejoice, O you righteous.

People: *Be glad in the Lord and rejoice, O you righteous.*

Reader: Blessed is he whose transgression is forgiven, whose sin is covered.

People: *Be glad in the Lord and rejoice, O you righteous.*

Reader: Be glad in the Lord and rejoice | O you righteous.

Let Every Breath Praise The Lord

Let every breath praise the Lord. Praise God in His sanctuary.

Praise Him in His mighty firmament. Let every breath praise the Lord.

The Daily Gospel

The Reading is From The Holy Gospel According To ...

People: *Glory to Thee, O Lord, glory to Thee.*

Reader: *[Read The Gospel For The Day.]*

People: *Glory to Thee, O Lord, glory to Thee.*

Psalm 50

Have mercy on me, O God, according to Thy great mercy; and according to the multitude of Thy compassions blot out my transgression. Wash me thoroughly from mine iniquity, and cleanse me from my sin. For I acknowledge mine iniquity, and my sin is ever before me. Against Thee, Thee only have I sinned, and done evil in Thy sight, that Thou mayest be found just when Thou speakest, and victorious when Thou art judged. For behold, I was conceived in iniquity, and in sin my mother bore me. For behold, Thou hast loved truth; Thou hast made known to me the hidden and secret things of Thy wisdom. Thou shalt sprinkle me with hyssop, and I shall be made clean; Thou shalt wash me, and I shalt be whiter than snow. Make me to hear joy and gladness; that the humbled bones may rejoice. Turn Thy face away from my sins, and blot out all mine iniquities.

Create in me a clean heart, O God, and renew a steadfast spirit within me. Cast me not away from Thy presence, and take not Thy Holy Spirit from me. Restore to me the joy of Thy salvation, and establish me with Thy governing Spirit. I shall teach transgressors Thy ways, and the ungodly shall turn back to Thee. Deliver me from blood guiltiness, O God, the God of my salvation; my tongue shall joyfully declare Thy righteousness. Lord, open my lips, and my mouth shall declare Thy praise. For if Thou hadst desired sacrifice, I would give it; Thou dost not delight in burned offerings. A sacrifice to God is a broken spirit; God shall not despise a broken and a humbled heart. Do good, O Lord, in Thy good pleasure to Zion, and let the walls of Jerusalem be builded. Then Thou shalt be pleased with a sacrifice of righteousness, with oblation and whole burned offerings. Then shall they offer bulls on Thine altar.

After The Psalm

Glory be to the Father and to the Son and to the Holy Spirit;
Both now and forever and unto the ages of ages. Amen.

Halleluiah, Halleluiah, Halleluiah. Glory to Thee, O God. **(x3)**

Lord, have mercy. **(x3)**

The Canon Of Biblical Odes
Ode 1

[Sunday]   **The Song Of Moses** (Exodus 15:1-18).

I shall sing to the Lord, for He has triumphed gloriously. The horse and its rider He has thrown into the sea. The Lord is my strength and song, and He has become my salvation; He is my God, and I shall praise Him; my fathers God, and I shall exalt him. The Lord is a man of war; the Lord is His name. Pharaohs chariots and his army He has cast into the sea; his chosen captains also are drowned in the Red Sea. The depths have covered them; they sank to the bottom like a stone. Thy right hand, O Lord, has become glorious in power; Thy right hand, O Lord, has dashed the enemy in pieces. And in the greatness of Thine excellence Thou hast overthrown those who rose against Thee; Thou sent forth Thy wrath that consumed them like stubble. And with the blast of Thy nostrils the waters were gathered together; the floods stood upright like a heap; and the depths congealed in the heart of the sea. The enemy said, "I shall pursue, I shall overtake, I shall divide the spoil; my desire shall be satisfied on them. I shall draw my sword, my hand shall destroy them." Thou blewest with Thy wind, the sea covered them; they sank like lead in the mighty waters. Who is like Thee O Lord, among the gods? Who is likest unto Thou, glorious in holiness, fearful in praises, doing wonders? Thou stretched out Thy right hand; the earth swallowed them. Thou in Thy mercy have led forth the people whom Thou hast redeemed; Thou hast guided them in Thy strength to Thy holy habitation. The people shall hear and be afraid; sorrow shall take hold of the inhabitants of Palestine. Then the chiefs of Edom shall be dismayed; the mighty men of Moab, trembling shall take hold of them; all the inhabitants of Canaan shall melt away. Fear and dread shall fall on them; by the greatness of Thine arm they shall be as still as a stone, till Thy people pass over, O Lord, till the people pass over whom Thou hast purchased. Thou wilt bring them in and plant them in the mountain of Thine inheritance, in the place, O Lord, that Thou hast made for Thine own dwelling, the sanctuary, O Lord, that Thine hands have established. The Lord shall reign forever and ever.

Ode 2

[Monday]   **The Song Of Moses** (Deuteronomy 32:1-43).

Give ear, O heavens, and I shall speak; and hear, O earth, the words of my mouth. Let my teaching drop as the rain, my speech distil as the dew, as raindrops on the tender herb, and as showers on the grass. For I proclaim the name of the Lord: ascribe greatness to our God. He is the Rock, His work is perfect; for all His ways are justice, a God of truth and without injustice; righteous and upright is He. They have corrupted themselves; they are not His children, because of their blemish: a perverse and crooked generation. Do thou thus deal with the Lord, O foolish and unwise people? Is He not thy Father, who bought thee? Has He not made thee and established thee? Remember the days of old, consider the years of many generations. Ask thy father, and he shall show thee; thine elders, and they shall tell thee: When the Most High divided their inheritance to the nations, when He separated the sons of Adam, He set the boundaries of the peoples according to the number of the children of Israel.

For the Lords portion is His people; Jacob is the place of His inheritance. He found him in a desert land and in the wasteland, a howling wilderness; He encircled him, He instructed him, He kept him as the apple of His eye. As an eagle stirs up its nest, hovers over its young, spreading out its wings, taking them up, carrying them on its wings. So the Lord alone led him, and there was no foreign god with him. He made him ride in the heights of the earth, that he might eat the produce of the fields; He made him to draw honey from the rock, and oil from the flinty rock; curds from the cattle, and milk of the flock, with fat of lambs; and rams of the breed of Bashan, and goats, with the choicest wheat; and thou drankest wine, the blood of the grapes. But Jeshurun grew fat and kicked; thou grewest fat, thou grewest thick, thou art covered with fat; then he forsook God who made him, and scornfully esteemed the Rock of his salvation. They provoked Him to jealousy with foreign gods; with abominations they provoked Him to anger. They sacrificed to demons, not to God, to gods they did not know, to new gods, new arrivals that thy fathers did not fear. Of the Rock who begot thee, thou art unmindful, and have forgotten the God who fathered thee. And when the Lord saw it, He spurned them, because of the provocation of His sons and His daughters. And He said: "I shall hide My face from them, I shall see what their end shall be, for they are a perverse generation, children in whom is no faith. They have provoked Me to jealousy by what is not God; they have moved Me to anger by their foolish idols. But I shall provoke them to jealousy by those who are not a nation; I shall move them to anger by a foolish nation. For a fire is kindled in My anger, and shall burn to the lowest hell; it shall consume the earth with her increase, and set on fire the foundations of the mountains. I shall heap disasters upon them; I shall spend Mine arrows upon them. They shall be wasted with hunger, devoured by pestilence and bitter destruction; I shall also send against them the teeth of beasts, with the poison of serpents of the dust. The sword shall destroy outside; there shall be terror within for the young man and virgin, the nursing child and the man of grey hairs. I would have said, "I shall dash them in pieces, I shall make the memory of them to cease from among men, Had I not feared the wrath of the enemy, lest their adversaries should misunderstand, lest they should say, "Our hand is high; and it is not the Lord who has done all this."

For they are a nation void of counsel, nor is there any understanding in them. Oh, that they were wise, that they understood this, that they would consider their latter end. How could one chase a thousand, and two put ten thousand to flight, unless their Rock had sold them, and the Lord had surrendered them? For their rock is not like our Rock, even our enemies themselves being judges. For their vine is of the vine of Sodom and of the fields of Gomorrah; their grapes are grapes of gall, their clusters are bitter. Their wine is the poison of serpents, and the cruel venom of cobras. "Is this not laid up in store with Me, sealed up among My treasures? Vengeance is Mine, and recompense; their foot shall slip in due time; for the day of their calamity is at hand, and the things to come hasten upon them." For the Lord shall judge His people and have compassion on His servants, when He seest that their power is gone, and there is no one remaining, bond or free. He shall say: "Where are their gods, the rock in which they sought refuge? Who ate the fat of their sacrifices, and drank the wine of their drink offering? Let them rise and help thee, and be thy refuge." Now see that I, even I, am He, and there is no God besides Me; I kill and I make alive; I wound and I heal; nor is there any who can deliver from My hand. For I lift My hand to heaven, and say, "As I live forever, If I whet My glittering sword, and My hand takest hold on judgement, I shall render vengeance to Mine enemies, and repay those who hate Me. I shall make Mine arrows drunk with blood, and My sword shall devour flesh, with the blood of the slain and the captives, from the heads of the leaders of the enemy." Rejoice, O Gentiles, with His people; for He shall avenge the blood of His servants, and render vengeance to His adversaries; He shall provide atonement for His land and His people.

Ode 3

[Tuesday]   **The Song Of Hannah.** (1 Reigns 2:1-10).

And Hannah prayed and said: "My heart rejoices in the Lord; my horn is exalted in the Lord. I smile at my enemies, because I rejoice in Thy salvation. There is none holy like the Lord, for there is none besides Thee, nor is there any rock like our God." Talk no more so very proudly; let no arrogance come from thy mouth, for the Lord is the God of knowledge; and by Him actions are weighed. The bows of the mighty men are broken, and those who stumbled are girded with strength. Those who were full have hired themselves out for bread, and those who were hungry have ceased to hunger. Even the barren has borne seven, and she who has many children has become feeble. The Lord killest and makest alive; He brings down to the grave and bringeth up. The Lord maketh poor and maketh rich; He bringeth low and lifteth up. He raiseth the poor from the dust and lifteth the beggar from the ash heap, to set them among princes and make them inherit the throne of glory. For the pillars of the earth are the Lords and He hast set the world upon them. He shall guard the feet of His saints but the wicked shall be silent in darkness. For by strength no man shall prevail. The adversaries of the Lord shall be broken in pieces; from heaven He shall thunder against them. The Lord shall judge the ends of the earth. He shall give strength to His king and exalt the horn of His anointed

Ode 4

[Wednesday]   **The Song Of Habbakuk** (Habbakuk 3:2-19).

O Lord, I have heard Thy speech and was afraid; O Lord, revive Thy work in the midst of the years. In the midst of the years make it known; in wrath remember mercy. God came from Teman, the Holy One from Mount Paran. His glory covered the heavens, and the earth was full of His praise. His brightness was like the light; He had rays flashing from His hand, and there His power was hidden. Before Him went pestilence, and fever followed at His feet. He stood and measured the earth; He looked and startled the nations. And the everlasting mountains were scattered, the perpetual hills bowed. His ways are everlasting. I saw the tents of Cushan in affliction; the curtains of the land of Midian trembled. O Lord, wast Thou displeased with the rivers, was Thine anger against the rivers, was Thy wrath against the sea, that Thou rode on Thy horses, Thy chariots of salvation? Thy bow was made quite ready; oaths were sworn over Thine arrows. Thou divided the earth with rivers. The mountains saw Thee and trembled; the overflowing of the water passed by. The deep uttered its voice, and lifted its hands on high. The sun and moon stood still in their habitation; at the light of Thine arrows they went, at the shining of Thy glittering spear. Thou marched through the land in indignation; Thou trampled the nations in anger. Thou went forth for the salvation of Thy people, for salvation with Thine Anointed. Thou struck the head from the house of the wicked, by laying bare from foundation to neck. Thou thrust through with his own arrows the head of his villages. They came out like a whirlwind to scatter me; their rejoicing was like feasting on the poor in secret. Thou walked through the sea with Thy horses, through the heap of great waters. When I heard, my body trembled; my lips quivered at the voice; rottenness entered my bones; and I trembled in myself, that I might rest in the day of trouble. When He comes up to the people, He shall invade them with his troops. Though the fig tree may not blossom, nor fruit be on the vines; though the labour of the olive may fail, and the fields yield no food; though the flock be cut off from the fold, and there be no herd in the stalls - yet I shall rejoice in the Lord, I shall joy in the God of my salvation. The Lord God is my strength; he shall make my feet like deer's feet, and He shall make me walk on my high hills.

Ode 5

[Thursday]   **The Song Of Isaiah** (Isaiah 26:9-21).

My spirit seeks Thee very early in the morning, O God, for Thy commandments are a light on the earth: learn righteousness, you that dwell upon the earth. For the ungodly one is put down: no one who shall not learn righteousness on the earth shall be able to do the truth: let the ungodly be taken away, that he see not the glory of the Lord. O Lord, Thine arm is exalted, yet they knew it not: but when they know they shall be ashamed: jealousy shall seize upon an untaught nation, and now fire shall devour the adversaries. O Lord our God, give us peace: for Thou hast rendered to us all things. O Lord our God, take possession of us: O Lord, we know not any other beside Thee: we name Thy name. But the dead shall not see life, neither shall physicians by any means raise them up: therefore Thou hast brought wrath upon them, and slain them, and hast taken away every male of them. Bring more evils upon them, O Lord; Bring more evils on the glorious ones of the earth. Lord, in affliction I remembered Thee; Thy chastening was to us with small affliction. And as a woman in travail draws nigh to be delivered, and cries out in her pain; so have we been to Thy beloved. We have conceived, O Lord, because of Thy fear, and have been in pain, and have brought forth the breath of Thy salvation, that we have wrought upon the earth: we shall not fall, but all that dwell upon the land shall fall. The dead shall rise, and they that are in the tombs shall be raised, and they that are in the earth shall rejoice:

for the dew from Thee is healing to them: but the land of the ungodly shall perish. Go, my people, enter into thy closets, shut thy door, hide thyself for a little season, until the anger of the Lord have passed away. For behold, the Lord is bringing wrath from His holy place upon the dwellers on the earth: the earth also shall disclose her blood, and shall not cover her slain.

Ode 6

[Friday]   **The Song Of Jonah** (Jonah 2:1-9).

Then Jonah prayed to the Lord his God from the fishes belly. And he said: I cried out to the Lord because of mine affliction, and He answered me. Out of the belly of Sheol I cried, and Thou heard my voice. For Thou cast me into the deep, into the heart of the seas, and the floods surrounded me; all Thy billows and Thy waves passed over me. Then I said, "I have been cast out of Thy sight; yet I shall look again toward Thy holy temple." The waters encompassed me, even to my soul; the deep closed around me; weeds were wrapped around my head. I went down to the moorings of the mountains; the earth with its bars closed behind me forever; yet Thou hast brought up my life from the pit, O Lord, my God. When my soul fainted within me, I remembered the Lord; and my prayer went up to Thee, into Thy holy temple. Those who regard worthless idols forsake their own Mercy. But I shall sacrifice to Thee with the voice of thanksgiving; I shall pay what I have vowed. Salvation is of the Lord.

Ode 7

[Saturday]   **The Prayer Of Azariah And The 3 Youths** (Daniel 3:26-45, 52-56).

Blessed art Thou, O Lord, God of our fathers, and worthy of praise; and Thy name is glorified forever. For Thou art just in all that Thou hast done to us, and all Thy works are true and Thy ways right, and all Thy judgements are truth. Thou hast executed true judgements in all that Thou hast brought upon us and upon Jerusalem, the holy city of our fathers, for in truth and justice Thou hast brought all this upon us because of our sins. For we have sinfully and lawlessly departed from Thee, and have sinned in all things and have not obeyed Thy commandments; We have not observed them or done them, as Thou hast commanded us that it might go well with us. So all that Thou hast brought upon us, and all that Thou hast done to us, Thou hast done in true judgement.

Thou hast given us into the hands of lawless enemies, most hateful rebels, and to an unjust king, the most wicked in all the world. And now we cannot open our mouths; shame and disgrace have befallen Thy servants and worshippers. For Thy names sake do not give us up utterly, and do not break Thy covenant, And do not withdraw Thy mercy from us, for the sake of Abraham Thy beloved and for the sake of Isaac Thy servant and Israel Thy holy one, To whom Thou didst promise to make their descendants as many as the stars of heaven and as the sand on the shore of the sea.

For we, O Lord, have become fewer than any nation, and are brought low this day in all the world because of our sins. And at this time there is no prince, or prophet, or leader, no burned offering, or sacrifice, or oblation, or incense, no place to make an offering before thee or to find mercy. Yet with a contrite heart and a humble spirit may we be accepted, as though it were with burned offerings of rams and bulls, and with tens of thousands of fat lambs; Such may our sacrifice be in Thy sight this day, and may we wholly follow Thee, for there shall be no shame for those who trust in Thee.

And now with all our heart we follow Thee, we fear Thee and seek Thy face. Do not put us to shame, but deal with us in Thy forbearance and in Thine abundant mercy. Deliver us in accordance with Thy marvellous works, and give glory to Thy name, O Lord. Let all who do harm to Thy servants be put to shame; Let them be disgraced and deprived of all power and dominion, and let their strength be broken. Let them know that Thou art the Lord, the only God, glorious over the whole world."

- Blessed art Thou, O Lord, God of our fathers; and to be praised and highly exalted forever.
- And blessed is Thy glorious, holy name; and to be highly praised and highly exalted forever.
- Blessed art Thou in the temple of Thy holy glory; and to be extolled and highly glorified forever.
- Blessed art Thou, who sittest upon Cherubim and lookest upon the deeps; and to be praised and highly exalted forever.
- Blessed art Thou upon the throne of Thy kingdom; and to be extolled and highly exalted forever.
- Blessed art Thou in the firmament of heaven; and to be sung and glorified forever.

Ode 8

[Sunday]   **The Song Of The Three Holy Youths** (Daniel 3:57-90).

- Bless the Lord all works of the Lord; Sing praise to Him and highly exalt Him for ever.
- Bless the Lord you heaven; Sing praise to Him and highly exalt Him for ever.
- Bless the Lord you angels of the Lord; Sing praise to Him and highly exalt Him for ever.
- Bless the Lord all waters above the heaven; Sing praise to Him and highly exalt Him for ever.
- Bless the Lord all powers; Sing praise to Him and highly exalt Him for ever.
- Bless the Lord sun and moon; Sing praise to Him and highly exalt Him for ever.
- Bless the Lord stars of heaven; Sing praise to Him and highly exalt Him for ever.
- Bless the Lord rain and dew; Sing praise to Him and highly exalt Him for ever.
- Bless the Lord all winds; Sing praise to Him and highly exalt Him for ever.
- Bless the Lord fire and heat; Sing praise to Him and highly exalt Him for ever.
- Bless the Lord winter cold and summer heat; Sing praise to Him and highly exalt Him for ever.
- Bless the Lord dews and snows; Sing praise to Him and highly exalt Him for ever.
- Bless the Lord nights and days; Sing praise to Him and highly exalt Him for ever.
- Bless the Lord light and darkness; Sing praise to Him and highly exalt Him for ever.
- Bless the Lord ice and cold; Sing praise to Him and highly exalt Him for ever.
- Bless the Lord frosts and snows; Sing praise to Him and highly exalt Him for ever.
- Bless the Lord lightnings and clouds; Sing praise to Him and highly exalt Him for ever.
- Let the earth bless the Lord; Sing praise to Him and highly exalt Him forever.
- Bless the Lord mountains and hills; Sing praise to Him and highly exalt Him for ever.
- Bless the Lord all things that grow on the earth; Sing praise to Him and highly exalt Him for ever.
- Bless the Lord you springs; Sing praise to Him and highly exalt Him for ever.
- Bless the Lord seas and rivers; Sing praise to Him and highly exalt Him for ever.

- Bless the Lord you whales and all creatures that move in the waters;

> Sing praise to Him and highly exalt Him for ever.

- Bless the Lord all birds of the air;   Sing praise to Him and highly exalt Him for ever.
- Bless the Lord all beasts and cattle;   Sing praise to Him and highly exalt Him for ever.
- Bless the Lord you sons of men;   Sing praise to Him and highly exalt Him for ever.
- Bless the Lord O Israel;   Sing praise to Him and highly exalt Him for ever.
- Bless the Lord you priests of the Lord;   Sing praise to Him and highly exalt Him for ever.
- Bless the Lord you servants of the Lord;   Sing praise to Him and highly exalt Him for ever.
- Bless the Lord spirits and souls of the righteous;   Sing praise to Him and highly exalt Him for ever.
- Bless the Lord you who are holy and humble in heart;

> Sing praise to Him and highly exalt Him for ever.

- Bless the Lord Hananiah, Azariah, and Mishael;   Sing praise to Him and highly exalt Him for ever.
- For He has rescued us from Hades and saved us from the hand of death; and delivered us from the midst of the burning fiery furnace;   From the midst of the fire He has delivered us.
- Give thanks to the Lord, for He is good.   For His mercy endureth forever.
- Bless Him all who worship the Lord God of gods;

> Sing praises to Him and gives thanks to Him, for His mercy endureth forever.

Ode 9 - Part 1

[Daily]   **The Magnificat** (Luke 1:46-55).

Greater in honour than the Cherubim and beyond compare more glorious than the Seraphim; without corruption thou gavest birth to God the Word, truly the Theotokos, we magnify thee.

My soul magnifies the Lord, and my spirit has rejoiced in God my Saviour. For He has regarded the lowly state of His maidservant; for behold, henceforth all generations shall call me blessed. For He who is mighty has done great things for me, and holy is His name. And His mercy is on those who fear Him from generation to generation. He has shown strength with His arm; he has scattered the proud in the imagination of their hearts. He has put down the mighty from their thrones, and exalted the lowly. He has filled the hungry with good things, and the rich He has sent empty away. He has helped His servant Israel, in remembrance of His mercy, as He spoke to our fathers, to Abraham and to his seed forever.

Ode 9 - Part 2

[Daily]   **The Song Of Zechariah** (Luke 1:68-79).

Blessed is the Lord God of Israel, for He has visited and redeemed His people, and has raised up a horn of salvation for us in the house of His servant David. As He spoke by the mouth of His holy prophets, who have been since the world began. That we should be saved from our enemies and from the hand of all who hate us. To perform the mercy promised to our fathers and to remember His holy covenant. The oath that He swore to our father Abraham: To grant us that we, being delivered from the hand of our enemies, might serve Him without fear; in holiness and righteousness before Him all the days of our life. And thou, child, shall be called the prophet of the Highest. For thou wilt go before the face of the Lord to prepare His ways, to give knowledge of salvation to His people by the remission of their sins through the tender mercy of our God; with which the Dayspring from on high has visited us. To give light to those who sit in darkness and the shadow of death, to guide our feet into the way of peace.

Kontakia

[Sunday]   **Kontakion Of The Resurrection**

Tone 2   Majesty, gentleness, hope, repentance and sadness.   *E, F, G, Ab, B, C.*

When Thou submitted Thyself to death, O Thou deathless and immortal one, then Thou destroyed Hell with Thy Godly power, and when Thou raised the dead from beneath the earth, all the powers of heaven cried aloud to Thee: O Christ, Thou giver of life, glory to Thee.

[Monday]   **Kontakion Of St Michael And All Angels**

Tone 2   Majesty, gentleness, hope, repentance and sadness.   *E, F, G, Ab, B, C.*

You Princes and Leaders of the armies of God, Servants of the Divine Glory and guides of men. Ask whatever is good for us and for bountiful mercy, O Commanders of Sabaoth.

[Tuesday]   **Kontakion Of The Forerunner And Baptist John**

Tone 2   Majesty, gentleness, hope, repentance and sadness.   *E, F, G, Ab, B, C.*

O Prophet of God and Forerunner of Grace, thy head has blossomed from the earth as a most sacred rose. We are ever being healed, For as of old, thou preachest repentance to the world.

[Wednesday]   **Kontakion Of The Holy And Life Giving Cross**

Tone 4   Festive, joyous and expressing deep piety.   *C, D, Eb, F, G, A, Bb, C.*

As Thou wast voluntarily crucified for our sake, Grant mercy to those who are called by Thy Name. Make all Orthodox Christians glad by Thy power, Granting them victories over their adversaries, By bestowing on them the invincible trophy, Thy weapon of peace.

[Thursday]   **Kontakion Of The Holy Apostles And St Nicholas**

Tone 3   Arrogant, brave, and mature atmosphere.   *F, G, A, A#, C, D, E, F.*

Thou hast taken, O Lord, the firm and divinely inspired preachers, the holy apostles, into rest and the enjoyment of Thy blessings. For Thou hast accepted their labours and death above every burned offering, O Thou Who alone know the secrets of our hearts.

[Friday]   **Kontakion Of The Holy And Life Giving Cross**

Tone 4   Festive, joyous and expressing deep piety.   *C, D, Eb, F, G, A, Bb, C.*

As Thou wast voluntarily crucified for our sake, Grant mercy to those who are called by Thy name. Make all Orthodox Christians glad by Thy power, Granting them victories over their adversaries, By bestowing on them the invincible trophy, Thy weapon of peace.

[Saturday]   **Kontakion Of The Theotokos, All Saints, The Faithful Departed**

With the saints give rest, O Christ, To the souls of Thy servants Where sickness and sorrow are no more, Neither sighing, but life everlasting.

Lauds - The Praises

[Monday, Thursday, Sunday]   **Psalm 148**

Praise the Lord. Praise the Lord from the heavens; praise Him in the heights. Praise Him, all His angels; praise Him, all His hosts. Praise Him, sun and moon; praise Him, all you stars of light. Praise Him, you heavens of heavens, and you waters above the heavens. Let them praise the name of the Lord, for He commanded and they were created. He has also established them forever and ever; He has made a decree that shall not pass away. Praise the Lord from the earth, you great sea creatures and all the depths; Fire and hail, snow and clouds; stormy wind, fulfilling His word; Mountains and all hills; fruitful trees and all cedars; Beasts and all cattle; creeping things and flying fowl; Kings of the earth and all peoples; princes and all judges of the earth; Both young men and maidens; old men and children. Let them praise the name of the Lord, for His name alone is exalted; His glory is above the earth and heaven. And He has exalted the horn of His people, the praise of all His saints - of the children of Israel, a people near to Him. Praise the Lord.

[Tuesday, Friday, Sunday]   **Psalm 149**

Praise the Lord. Sing to the Lord a new song, and His praise in the congregation of saints. Let Israel rejoice in their Maker; let the children of Zion be joyful in their King. Let them praise His name with the dance; let them sing praises to Him with the timbrel and harp. For the Lord takes pleasure in His people; He shall beautify the humble with salvation. Let the saints be joyful in glory; let them sing aloud on their beds. Let the high praises of God be in their mouth, and a two edged sword in their hand, To execute vengeance on the nations, and punishments on the peoples; To bind their kings with chains, and their nobles with fetters of iron; To execute on them the written judgement; this honour have all His saints. Praise the Lord.

[Wednesday, Saturday, Sunday]   **Psalm 150**

Praise the Lord. Praise God in His sanctuary; praise Him in His mighty firmament. Praise Him for His mighty acts; praise Him according to His excellent greatness. Praise Him with the sound of the trumpet; praise Him with the lute and harp. Praise Him with the timbrel and dance; praise Him with stringed instruments and flutes. Praise Him with loud cymbals; praise Him with high sounding cymbals. Let everything that has breath praise the Lord. Praise the Lord.

After The Psalm

Glory be to the Father and to the Son and to the Holy Spirit;
Both now and forever and unto the ages of ages. Amen.

Halleluiah, Halleluiah, Halleluiah. Glory to Thee, O God. **(x3)**

Lesser Doxology

Glory to God, Who has shown us the Light. Glory to God in the highest, and on earth, peace, good will toward men. We praise Thee. We bless Thee. We worship Thee. We glorify Thee and give thanks to Thee for Thy great glory. O Lord God, Heavenly King, God the Father Almighty. O Lord, the Only Begotten Son, Jesus Christ, and the Holy Spirit. \

O Lord God, Lamb of God, Son of the Father, Who takes away the sins of the world, have mercy on us. Thou, Who takes away the sins of the world, receive our prayer. Thou, Who sittest at the right hand of God the Father, have mercy on us. /

For Thou alone art holy, and Thou alone art Lord. Thou alone, O Lord Jesus Christ, are most high in the glory of God the Father. Amen. I shall give thanks to Thee every day and praise Thy Name forever and ever. Lord, Thou hast been our refuge from generation to generation. I said, *"Lord, have mercy on me. Heal my soul, for I have sinned against Thee."* \

Lord, I flee to Thee. Teach me to do Thy will, for Thou art my God. For with Thee is the fountain of Life, and in Thy light we shall see light. Continue Thy loving kindness to those who know Thee. Vouchsafe, O Lord, to keep us this day without sin. Blessed art Thou, O Lord, the God of our fathers, and praised and glorified is Thy Name forever. Amen. Let Thy mercy be upon us, O Lord, even as we have set our hope on Thee. Blessed art Thou, O Master; teach me Thy statutes. Blessed art Thou, O Lord; enlighten me with Thy commandments. Blessed art Thou, O Holy One; make me to understand Thy precepts. Thy mercy endures forever, O Lord. Do not despise the works of Thine hands. To Thee belongs worship, to Thee belongs praise, to Thee belongs glory: to the Father and to the Son and to the Holy Spirit, both now and forever and unto the ages of ages. Amen. \

Morning Prayer Of The Last Elders Of Optina

O Lord, grant that I may meet all that this coming day brings to me with spiritual tranquillity. Grant that I may fully surrender myself to Thy holy Will. At every hour of this day, direct and support me in all things. Whatsoever news may reach me in the course of the day, teach me to accept it with a calm soul and firm conviction that all is subject to Thy holy will. Direct my thoughts and feelings in all my words and actions. In all unexpected occurrences, do not let me forget that all is sent down from Thee. Grant that I may deal straightforwardly and wisely with every member of my family, neither embarrassing nor saddening anyone. O Lord, grant me the strength to endure the fatigue of the coming day and all the events that take place during it. Direct my will and teach me to pray, to believe, to hope, to be patient, to forgive, and to love. Amen.

Most holy God, we pray and beseech Thee, give each of us a pure heart and a way of speaking that befits the faith we profess; grant us uprightness of purpose, powers of reasoning unhindered by passions, conduct that becometh those who fear Thee, and perfect knowledge of Thy commandments; may we enjoy health in body and in spirit. Grant us a life of peace, genuine faith and living hope, sincere charity and bountiful generosity, patience that knows no bounds and the light of Thy truth to proclaim Thy goodness to us, that for ever and in all things placing our trust only in Thee, we may abound in every good work, and that in Christ Thy gifts may increase in every soul. For to Thee belongest all glory, honour and majesty, Father, Son and Holy Spirit, now and forever and unto the ages of ages. Amen.

Dismissal

Confirm, O God, the holy Orthodox Faith and Orthodox Christians unto the ages of ages. Amen.

Most holy Theotokos, save us. Greater in honour than the Cherubim and beyond compare more glorious than the Seraphim; without corruption thou gavest birth to God the Word, truly the Theotokos, we magnify thee.

Glory to Thee, O Christ, our God and our hope, glory to Thee.

Glory be to the Father and to the Son and to the Holy Spirit;
Both now and forever and unto the ages of ages. Amen.

Lord, have mercy. **(x3)**

Through the prayers of our holy fathers, Lord Jesus Christ our God, have mercy on us and save us. **Amen.**

[With or without a Priest. His sayings in brackets.]

[If preceded by Matins then start at "Come let us worship…"]

The Trisagion Prayers

In the Name of the Father, and of the Son, and of the Holy Spirit. Amen.

Glory to Thee, our God, glory to Thee.

O Heavenly King, the Comforter, the Spirit of Truth; who art everywhere present and fillest all things; Treasury of blessings, and giver of life: come and abide in us, and cleanse us from every impurity, and save our souls, O Good One.

Holy God, Holy Mighty, Holy Immortal, have mercy on us. **(x3)**

> *Glory be to the Father and to the Son and to the Holy Spirit;*
> *Both now and forever and unto the ages of ages. Amen.*

O Most Holy Trinity, have mercy on us.

O Lord, cleanse us from our sins.

O Master, pardon our iniquities.

O Holy One, visit and heal our infirmities, for Thy names sake.

Lord have mercy. **(x3)**

> *Glory be to the Father and to the Son and to the Holy Spirit;*
> *Both now and forever and unto the ages of ages. Amen.*

Our Father, who art in heaven, hallowed be Thy name. Thy Kingdom come. Thy will be done, on earth as it is in heaven. Give us this day our daily bread; and forgive us our trespasses, as we forgive those who trespass against us; and lead us not into temptation, but deliver us from the evil one.

[Priest: For Thine is the kingdom, the power and the glory, of the Father, the Son and the Holy Spirit, both now and for ever, and unto the ages of ages.]

People: Amen.

Lord have mercy. **(x12)**

> *Glory be to the Father and to the Son and to the Holy Spirit;*
> *Both now and forever and unto the ages of ages. Amen.*

Come, let us worship God, our King.

Come, let us worship and fall down before Christ, our King and our God.

Come, let us worship and fall down before Christ Himself, our King and our God.

[Monday, Thursday, Sunday]   **Psalm 5**

Unto my words give ear, O Lord, hear my cry. Attend unto the voice of my supplication, O my King and my God; for unto Thee shall I pray, O Lord. In the morning shalt Thou hear my voice. In the morning shall I stand before Thee, and Thou shalt look upon me; for not a God that willest iniquity art Thou. He that worketh evil shall not dwell near Thee nor shall transgressors abide before Thine eyes. Thou hast hated all them that work iniquity; Thou shalt destroy all them that speak a lie. A man that is bloody and deceitful shall the Lord abhor. But as for me, in the multitude of Thy mercy shall I go into Thy house; I shall worship toward Thy holy temple in fear of Thee. O Lord, guide me in the way of Thy righteousness; because of mine enemies, make straight my way before Thee, For in their mouth there is no truth; their heart is vain. Their throat is an open sepulchre, with their tongues have they spoken deceitfully; judge them, O God. Let them fall down on account of their own devisings; according to the multitude of their ungodliness, cast them out, for they have embittered Thee, O Lord. And let all them be glad that hope in Thee; they shall rejoice, and Thou shalt dwell among them. And all shall glory in Thee that love Thy name, for Thou shalt bless the righteous. O Lord, as with a shield of Thy good pleasure hast Thou crowned us.

[Tuesday, Friday, Sunday]   **Psalm 89**

Lord, Thou hast been our refuge in generation and generation. Before the mountains came to be and the earth was formed and the world, even from everlasting to everlasting art Thou. Turn not man away unto lowliness; yea, Thou hast said: Turn back you sons of men. For a thousand years in Thine eyes, O Lord, are but as yesterday that is past, and as a watch in the night. Things of no account shall their years be; in the morning like grass shall man pass away. In the morning shall he bloom and pass away. In the evening shall he fall and grow withered and dry. For we have fainted away in Thy wrath, and in Thine anger have we been troubled. Thou hast set our iniquities before us; our lifespan is in the light of Thy countenance. For all our days are faded away, and in Thy wrath are we fainted away; our years have, like a spider, spun out their tale. As for the days of our years, in their span, they be threescore years and ten. And if we be in strength, mayhap fourscore years; and what is more than these is toil and travail. For mildness is come upon us, and we shall be chastened. Who knoweth the might of Thy wrath? And out of fear of Thee, who can recount Thine anger? So make Thy right hand known to me, and to them that in their heart are instructed in wisdom. Return, O Lord; how long? And be Thou entreated concerning Thy servants. We were filled in the morning with Thy mercy, O Lord, and we rejoiced and were glad. In all our days, let us be glad for the days wherein Thou didst humble us, for the years wherein we saw evils. And look upon Thy servants, and upon Thy works, and do Thou guide their sons. And let the brightness of the Lord our God be upon us, and the works of our hands do Thou guide aright upon us, yea, the works of our hands do Thou guide aright.

Of mercy and judgement shall I sing to Thee, O Lord; I shall chant and have understanding in a blameless path. When wilt Thou come unto me? I have walked in the innocence of my heart in the midst of my house. I have no unlawful thing before mine eyes; the workers of transgressions I have hated. A crooked heart hath not cleaved unto me; as for the wicked man who turned from me, I knew him not. Him that privily talked against his neighbour did I drive away from me. With him whose eye was proud and his heart insatiate, I did not eat. Mine eyes were upon the faithful of the land, that they might sit with me; the man that walked in the blameless path, he ministered unto me. The proud doer dwelt not in the midst of my house; the speaker of unjust things prospered not before mine eyes. In the morning I slew all the sinners of the land, utterly to destroy out of the city of the Lord all them that work iniquity.

After The Psalm

Glory be to the Father, and to the Son, and to the Holy Spirit;

Both now and forever, and unto the ages of ages. Amen.

Halleluiah, Halleluiah, Halleluiah. Glory to Thee, O God. **(x3)**

Lord, have mercy. **(x3)**

If there are two troparia, we say the first one here. If not, we continue:

Glory be to the Father, and to the Son, and to the Holy Spirit;

And we say the second troparion, if any, or the only troparion. Then:

Both now and forever, and unto the ages of ages. Amen.

Theotokion

What shall we call thee, O thou who art full of grace? Heaven, for from thee hast dawned forth the Sun of Righteousness. Paradise, for from thee hath blossomed forth the flower of immortality. Virgin, for thou hast remained incorrupt. Pure Mother, for thou hast held in thy holy embrace the Son, the God of all. Do thou entreat Him to save our souls.

Psalm Verse

Order my steps in Thy Word, and so shall no wickedness have dominion over me. Deliver me from the wrongful dealings of men, and so shall I keep Thy commandments. Show the light of Thy countenance upon Thy servant, and teach me Thy commandments. Let my mouth be filled with Thy praise, O Lord, that I may sing of Thy glory and honour all day long.

Holy God, Holy Mighty, Holy Immortal, have mercy on us. **(x3)**

Glory be to the Father and to the Son and to the Holy Spirit;

Both now and forever and unto the ages of ages. Amen.

O Most Holy Trinity, have mercy on us.

O Lord, cleanse us from our sins.

O Master, pardon our iniquities.

O Holy One, visit and heal our infirmities, for Thy names sake.

Lord have mercy. **(x3)**

Glory be to the Father and to the Son and to the Holy Spirit;
Both now and forever and unto the ages of ages. Amen.

Our Father, who art in heaven, hallowed be Thy name. Thy Kingdom come. Thy will be done, on earth as it is in heaven. Give us this day our daily bread; and forgive us our trespasses, as we forgive those who trespass against us; and lead us not into temptation, but deliver us from the evil one.

[Priest: For Thine is the kingdom, the power and the glory, of the Father, the Son and the Holy Spirit, both now and for ever, and unto the ages of ages.]

People: *Amen.*

O Lord, Jesus Christ, Son of God, have mercy on us and save us. Amen.

[Sunday] **Kontakion Of The Resurrection**

Tone 8 *Humility, tranquillity, repose, suffering, pleading.* *C, D, Eb, F, G, A, Bb, C.*

When Thou went down to death, O immortal life, then Thou slew Hell with the lightning flash of Thy Godhead; but when from the depths below the earth Thou raised the dead, O Christ God, proclaiming *"Rejoice"* to the myrrh bearing women, granting peace to Thine apostles and bestowing resurrection to the fallen.

[Monday] **Kontakion Of St Michael And All The Angels**

Tone 2 *Majesty, gentleness, hope, repentance and sadness.* *E, F, G, Ab, B, C.*

You Princes and Leaders of the armies of God, Servants of the Divine Glory and guides of men. Ask whatever is good for us and for bountiful mercy, O Commanders of Sabaoth.

[Tuesday] **Kontakion Of The Forerunner And Baptist John**

Tone 2 *Majesty, gentleness, hope, repentance and sadness.* *E, F, G, Ab, B, C.*

O Prophet of God and Forerunner of Grace, thy head has blossomed from the earth as a most sacred rose. We are ever being healed, for as of old, thou preachest repentance to the world.

[Wednesday] **Kontakion Of The Holy And Life Giving Cross**

Tone 4 *Festive, joyous and expressing deep piety.* *C, D, Eb, F, G, A, Bb, C.*

As Thou wast voluntarily crucified for our sake, grant mercy to those who are called by Thy Name. Make all Orthodox Christians glad by Thy power, granting them victories over their adversaries, by bestowing on them the invincible trophy, Thy weapon of peace.

[Thursday]   Kontakion Of The Holy Apostles And St Nicholas

Tone 3   Arrogant, brave, and mature atmosphere.   *F, G, A, A#, C, D, E, F.*

Thou hast taken O Lord the firm and divinely inspired preachers, the holy apostles into rest and the enjoyment of Thy blessings. For Thou hast accepted their labours and death above every burned offering. O Thou Who alone knows the secrets of our hearts.

[Friday]   Kontakion Of The Holy And Life Giving Cross

Tone 4   Festive, joyous and expressing deep piety.   *C, D, Eb, F, G, A, Bb, C.*

As Thou wast voluntarily crucified for our sake, grant mercy to those who are called by Thy Name. Make all Orthodox Christians glad by Thy power, granting them victories over their adversaries, by bestowing on them the invincible trophy, Thy weapon of peace.

[Saturday]   Kontakion Of The Theotokos, The Saints & The Faithful Departed

Tone 2   Majesty, gentleness, hope, repentance and sadness.   *E, F, G, Ab, B, C.*

With the saints give rest, O Christ, to the souls of Thy servants, where sickness and sorrow are no more. Neither sighing, but life everlasting.

Lord, have mercy. **(x40)**

The Prayer Of The Hours

At all times and in every hour, Thou art worshipped and glorified in heaven and on earth, Christ our God. Long in patience, great in mercy and compassion, Thou lovest the righteous and showest mercy to sinners. Thou callest all to salvation through the promise of good things to come. Lord, receive our prayers at the present time. Direct our lives according to Thy commandments. Sanctify our souls. Purify our bodies. Set our minds aright. Cleanse our thoughts, and deliver us from all sorrow, evil and distress. Surround us with Thy holy angels, that, guarded and guided by their host, we may arrive at the unity of the faith and the understanding of Thine Ineffable glory. For Thou art blessed unto the ages of ages. Amen.

The Prayer Of The First Hour

O Christ, the True Light, Who enlightenest and sanctifiest every man that cometh into the world: Let the Light of Thy countenance be signed upon us, that in it we may see the Unapproachable Light, and guide our steps in the doing of Thy commandments, through the intercessions of Thy most pure Mother, and of all Thy saints. Amen.

Order my steps in Thy Word, and so shall no wickedness have dominion over me. Deliver me from the wrongful dealings of men, and so shall I keep Thy commandments. Show the light of Thy countenance upon Thy servant, and teach me Thy commandments. Let my mouth be filled with Thy praise, O Lord, that I may sing of Thy glory and honour all day long.

Kontakion For The Annunciation

Tone 8   *Humility, tranquillity, repose, suffering, pleading.*   *C, D, Eb, F, G, A, Bb, C.*

To Thee, the Champion Leader, we Thy servants dedicate a feast of victory and of thanksgiving as ones rescued out of sufferings, O Theotokos: but as Thou art one with might, which is invincible, from all dangers that can be, do Thou deliver us, that we may cry to Thee: Rejoice, Thou Bride Unwedded.

Glory be to the Father and to the Son and to the Holy Spirit;
Both now and forever and unto the ages of ages. Amen.

Dismissal

[with a Priest]

Priest: Glory to you, Christ God, our hope, glory to you.

Reader: *Glory be to the Father, and to the Son, and to the Holy Spirit;*

Both now and forever, and unto the ages of ages. Amen.

Lord, have mercy. **(x3)**

People: *Holy Father, bless.*

Priest: May God take pity on us and bless us; show the light of His countenance on us and have mercy on us.

People: *Amen.*

Priest: Christ, the true light, who enlightenest and hallowest everyone who comest into the world, may the light of Thy countenance be signed upon us, that in it we may see Thine unapproachable light; and direct our steps to the doing of Thy commandments; at the intercessions of Thy most pure Mother and of all Thy Saints.

People: *Amen.*

Priest: May Christ our true God, at the prayers of His most pure and spotless Mother; of the holy, glorious and all praised Apostles; of the holy, glorious and triumphant Martyrs; of our venerable and God bearing Fathers; of Saint *N [patron]*; *[of Saints N & N, whose memory we celebrate;]* of the holy and righteous forebears of God, Joachim and Anna, and of all the Saints, have mercy and save us, for He is good and lovest mankind.

People: *Amen.*

[without a priest]

Lord, have mercy. **(x3)**

Glory be to the Father and to the Son and to the Holy Spirit;
Both now and forever and unto the ages of ages. Amen.

Greater in honour than the Cherubim and beyond compare more glorious than the Seraphim; without corruption thou gavest birth to God the Word, truly the Theotokos, we magnify thee.

Through the prayers of our holy fathers, O Lord Jesus Christ our God, have mercy on us and save us. Amen.

O Lord Jesus Christ, Son of God, for the sake of the prayers of Thy most pure Mother, our holy and God bearing fathers, and of all the saints, have mercy on us and save us, for Thou art good and the Lover of mankind. Amen.

[After each Hour during Lent and the first day of the Lesser Fasts. NOT during Great Week.]

Come, let us worship God, our King.

Come, let us worship and fall down before Christ, our King and our God.

Come, let us worship and fall down before Christ Himself, our King and our God.

[Monday, Thursday, Sunday] **Psalm 45**

God is our refuge and power, very much a helper in afflictions that befall us. Therefore we shall not fear, when the earth is troubled and mountains be transposed in hearts of seas. Their waters roared and were troubled; the mountains were troubled by his force.

The rivers strong currents make glad the city of God; the Most High sanctified his refuge. God is in its midst; it shall not be shaken; God shall help it in the morning. Nations were troubled, kingdoms tilted; he gave forth his voice; the earth was shaken. The Lord of hosts is with us; our supporter is the God of Jacob.

Come, see the works of the Lord, what feats He put on the earth, cancelling wars to the ends of the earth; he shall shatter bow and break armour, and he shall burn shields with fire. "Relax, and know that I am God. I shall be exalted among the nations; I shall be exalted in the earth." The Lord of hosts is with us; our supporter is the God of Jacob.

[Tuesday, Friday, Sunday] **Psalm 91**

It is good to acknowledge the Lord and to make music to Thy name, O Most High, in order to declare Thy mercy in the morning and Thy truth every night on a ten stringed harp, with an ode on a lyre, because Thee, O Lord, made me glad by Thy work, and at the deeds of Thy hands I shall rejoice.

How were Thy deeds extolled, O Lord. Thy thoughts reached great depth. A foolish man shall not know, and a stupid one shall not understand these things. When the sinners sprang up like grass also all who practice lawlessness popped up so that they may be destroyed forever and ever. But Thou art most high forever, O Lord, because, look, Thine enemies, O Lord, because, look, Thine enemies shall perish and all those who practice lawlessness shall be scattered.

And my horn shall be exalted like a unicorns, and mine old age with thick oil. And mine eye looked at mine enemies, and among those who keep rising against me, doing evil, mine ear shall hear. A righteous one shall flourish like a palm, and like a cedar in Lebanon he shall increase. Planted in the house of the Lord, in the courts of our God, they shall flourish. In prosperous old age they shall still increase, and they shall be living in comfort, to declare that the Lord my God is upright, and there is no injustice in him.

[Wednesday, Saturday, Sunday] **Psalm 92**

The Lord became king; He was robed in majesty; the Lord was robed in power and girded himself. Indeed, He made firm the world, that it shall not be shaken; Thy throne is prepared from then on; from everlasting Thou art. The streams lifted up, O Lord; the streams lifted up their voices. Due to the voices of many waters wondrous are the billows of the sea; wondrous on high is the Lord. Thy testimonies were made very sure; sanctity befits Thy house, O Lord, unto length of days.

After The Psalm

Glory be to the Father, and to the Son, and to the Holy Spirit;
Both now and forever, and unto the ages of ages. Amen.

Halleluiah, Halleluiah, Halleluiah. Glory to Thee, O God. **(x3)**

Lord, have mercy. **(x3)**

Holy God, Holy Mighty, Holy Immortal, have mercy on us. **(x3)**

Glory be to the Father, and to the Son, and to the Holy Spirit;
Both now and forever, and unto the ages of ages. Amen.

O Most Holy Trinity, have mercy on us.
O Lord, cleanse us from our sins.
O Master, pardon our iniquities.
O Holy One, visit and heal our infirmities, for Thy names sake.

Lord have mercy. **(x3)**

Glory be to the Father, and to the Son, and to the Holy Spirit;
Both now and forever, and unto the ages of ages. Amen.

Our Father, who art in heaven, hallowed be Thy name. Thy Kingdom come. Thy will be done, on earth as it is in heaven. Give us this day our daily bread; and forgive us our trespasses, as we forgive those who trespass against us; and lead us not into temptation, but deliver us from the evil one.

O Lord, Jesus Christ, Son of God, have mercy on us and save us. Amen.

[Sunday] **Kontakion Of The Resurrection**

Tone 8   Humility, tranquillity, repose, suffering, pleading.   C, D, Eb, F, G, A, Bb, C.

When Thou went down to death, O immortal life, then Thou slew Hell with the lightning flash of Thy Godhead; but when from the depths below the earth Thou raised the dead, O Christ God, proclaiming *"Rejoice"* to the myrrh bearing women, granting peace to Thine apostles and bestowing resurrection to the fallen.

[Monday] **Kontakion Of St Michael And All The Angels**

Tone 2   Majesty, gentleness, hope, repentance and sadness.   E, F, G, Ab, B, C.

You Princes and Leaders of the armies of God, Servants of the Divine Glory and guides of men. Ask whatever is good for us and for bountiful mercy, O Commanders of Sabaoth.

[Tuesday]   **Kontakion Of The Forerunner And Baptist John**

Tone 2   Majesty, gentleness, hope, repentance and sadness.   *E, F, G, Ab, B, C.*

O Prophet of God and Forerunner of Grace, thy head has blossomed from the earth as a most sacred rose. We are ever being healed, for as of old, thou preachest repentance to the world.

[Wednesday]   **Kontakion Of The Holy And Life Giving Cross**

Tone 4   Festive, joyous and expressing deep piety.   *C, D, Eb, F, G, A, Bb, C.*

As Thou wast voluntarily crucified for our sake, grant mercy to those who are called by Thy Name. Make all Orthodox Christians glad by Thy power, granting them victories over their adversaries, by bestowing on them the invincible trophy, Thy weapon of peace.

[Thursday]   **Kontakion Of The Holy Apostles And St Nicholas**

Tone 3   Arrogant, brave, and mature atmosphere.   *F, G, A, A#, C, D, E, F.*

Thou hast taken O Lord the firm and divinely inspired preachers the holy apostles into rest and the enjoyment of Thy blessings. For Thou hast accepted their labours and death above every burned offering. Thou who alone knows the secrets of our hearts.

[Friday]   **Kontakion Of The Holy And Life Giving Cross**

Tone 4   Festive, joyous and expressing deep piety.   *C, D, Eb, F, G, A, Bb, C.*

As Thou wast voluntarily crucified for our sake, grant mercy to those who are called by Thy Name. Make all Orthodox Christians glad by Thy power, granting them victories over their adversaries, by bestowing on them the invincible trophy, Thy weapon of peace.

[Saturday]   **Kontakion Of The Theotokos, The Saints & The Faithful Departed**

Tone 2   Majesty, gentleness, hope, repentance and sadness.   *E, F, G, Ab, B, C.*

With the saints give rest, O Christ, to the souls of Thy servants, where sickness and sorrow are no more. Neither sighing, but life everlasting.

Lord, have mercy. **(x40)**

The Prayer Of The Hours

At all times and in every hour, Thou art worshipped and glorified in heaven and on earth, Christ our God. Long in patience, great in mercy and compassion, Thou lovest the righteous and showest mercy to sinners. Thou callest all to salvation through the promise of good things to come. Lord, receive our prayers at the present time. Direct our lives according to Thy commandments. Sanctify our souls. Purify our bodies. Set our minds aright. Cleanse our thoughts, and deliver us from all sorrow, evil and distress. Surround us with Thy holy angels, that, guarded and guided by their host, we may arrive at the unity of the faith and the understanding of Thine ineffable glory. For Thou art blessed to the ages of ages. Amen.

Prayer Of St Ephrem The Syrian To The Most Holy Spirit

O Lord, Heavenly King, Comforter, Spirit of Truth, have compassion and mercy on Thy sinful servant and pardon mine unworthiness, and forgive me all the sins that I have humanly committed today, and not only humanly but even worse than a beast - my voluntary sins, known and unknown, from my youth and from evil suggestions, and from my brazenness, and from boredom. If I have sworn by Thy Name or blasphemed it in thought, blamed or reproached anyone, or in mine anger have detracted or slandered anyone, or grieved anyone, or if I have become angry about anything, or have told a lie, if I have slept unnecessarily, or if a beggar has come to me and I despised or neglected him, or if I have troubled my brother or quarrelled with him, or if I have condemned anyone, or have boasted, or have been proud, or lost my temper with anyone, or if when standing in prayer my mind has been distracted by the glamour of this world, or if I have had depraved thoughts or have overeaten, or have drunk excessively, or have laughed frivolously, or have thought evil, or have seen the attraction of someone and been wounded by it in my heart, or said indecent things, or made fun of my brothers sin when mine own faults are countless, or been neglectful of prayer, or have done some other wrong that I cannot remember - for I have done all this and much more - have mercy, my Lord and Creator, on me Thy wretched and unworthy servant, and absolve and forgive and deliver me in Thy goodness and love for men, so that, lustful, sinful and wretched as I am, I may lie down and sleep and rest in peace. And I shall worship, praise and glorify Thy most honourable Name, with the Father and His only begotten Son, now and ever, and for all ages. Amen.

Dismissal

Lord, have mercy. **(x3)**

Glory be to the Father, and to the Son, and to the Holy Spirit;
Both now and forever, and unto the ages of ages. Amen.

Greater in honour than the Cherubim and beyond compare more glorious than the Seraphim; without corruption thou gavest birth to God the Word, truly the Theotokos, we magnify thee.

Through the prayers of our holy fathers, O Lord Jesus Christ our God, have mercy on us and save us. Amen.

The Trisagion Prayers

In the Name of the Father, and of the Son, and of the Holy Spirit. Amen.

Glory to Thee, our God, glory to Thee.

O Heavenly King, the Comforter, the Spirit of Truth; who art everywhere present and fillest all things; Treasury of blessings, and giver of life: come and abide in us, and cleanse us from every impurity, and save our souls, O Good One.

Holy God, Holy Mighty, Holy Immortal, have mercy on us. **(x3)**

Glory be to the Father and to the Son and to the Holy Spirit;

Both now and forever and unto the ages of ages. Amen.

O Most Holy Trinity, have mercy on us.

O Lord, cleanse us from our sins.

O Master, pardon our iniquities.

O Holy One, visit and heal our infirmities, for Thy names sake.

Lord have mercy. **(x3)**

Glory be to the Father and to the Son and to the Holy Spirit;

Both now and forever and unto the ages of ages. Amen.

Our Father, who art in heaven, hallowed be Thy name. Thy Kingdom come. Thy will be done, on earth as it is in heaven. Give us this day our daily bread; and forgive us our trespasses, as we forgive those who trespass against us; and lead us not into temptation, but deliver us from the evil one.

[**Priest:** For Thine is the kingdom, the power and the glory, of the Father, the Son and the Holy Spirit, both now and for ever, and unto the ages of ages.]

People: *Amen.*

Lord have mercy. **(x12)**

Glory be to the Father and to the Son and to the Holy Spirit;

Both now and forever and unto the ages of ages. Amen.

Come, let us worship God, our King.

Come, let us worship and fall down before Christ, our King and our God.

Come, let us worship and fall down before Christ Himself, our King and our God.

Hearken, O Lord, unto my righteousness, attend unto the voice of my supplication. Give ear unto my prayer, which cometh not from deceitful lips. From before Thy face let my judgement come forth, let mine eyes behold uprightness. Thou hast proved my heart, Thou hast visited it in the night, Thou hast tried me by fire, and unrighteousness was not found in me. That my mouth may not speak of the works of men, for the sake of the words of Thy lips have I kept the ways that are hard. Set my footsteps in Thy paths, that my steps may not be shaken. I have cried for Thou hast hearkened unto me, O God. Incline Thine ear unto me, and hearken unto my words. Let Thy mercies be made wonderful, O Thou that savest them that hope in Thee. From them that have resisted Thy right hand, keep me, O Lord, as the apple of Thine eye. In the shelter of Thy wings wilt Thou shelter me, from the face of the ungodly which have oppressed me. Mine enemies have surrounded my soul, they have enclosed themselves with their own fat, their mouth hath spoken pride. They that have cast me out have now encircled me, they have set their eyes to look askance on the earth. They have taken me as might a lion ready for his prey, and as might a lions whelp that dwelleth in hiding. Arise, O Lord, overtake them and trip their heels; deliver my soul from ungodly men, Thy sword from the enemies of Thy hand. O Lord, from Thy few do Thou separate them from the earth in their life; yea, with Thy hidden treasures hath their belly been filled. They have satisfied themselves with swine and have left the remnants to their babes. But as for me, in righteousness shall I appear before Thy face; I shall be filled when Thy glory is made manifest to me.

Unto Thee, O Lord, have I lifted up my soul. O my God, in Thee have I trusted; let me never be put to shame, nor let mine enemies laugh me to scorn. Yea, let none that wait on Thee be put to shame; let them be ashamed which are lawless without a cause. Make Thy ways, O Lord, known unto me and teach me Thy paths. Lead me in Thy truth and teach me, for Thou art God my Saviour; for on Thee have I waited all the day long. Remember Thy compassions, O Lord, and Thy mercies, for they are from everlasting. The sins of my youth and mine ignorances remember not; according to Thy mercy remember Thou me, for the sake of Thy goodness, O Lord. Good and upright is the Lord; therefore shall He set a law for them that sin in the way. He shall guide the meek in judgement, He shall teach the meek His ways. All the ways of the Lord are mercy and truth, unto them that seek after His covenant and His testimonies. For the sake of Thy name, O Lord, be gracious unto my sin; for it is great. Who is the man that feareth the Lord? He shall set him a law in the way which he hath chosen. His soul shall dwell among good things, and his seed shall inherit the earth. The Lord is the strength of them that fear Him, and His covenant shall be manifested unto them. Mine eyes are ever toward the Lord, for He it is that shall draw my feet out of the snare. Look upon me, and have mercy on me; for I am one only begotten and poor. The afflictions of my heart are multiplied; bring me out from my necessities. Behold my lowliness and my toil, and forgive all my sins. Look upon mine enemies, for they are multiplied, and with an unjust hatred have they hated me. Keep my soul and rescue me; let me not be put to shame, for I have hoped in Thee. The innocent and the upright have cleaved unto me, for I waited on Thee, O Lord. Redeem Israel, O God, out of all his afflictions.

Have mercy on me, O God, according to Thy great mercy; and according to the multitude of Thy compassions blot out my transgression. Wash me thoroughly from mine iniquity, and cleanse me from my sin. For I acknowledge mine iniquity, and my sin is ever before me. Against Thee, Thee only have I sinned, and done evil in Thy sight, that Thou mayest be found just when Thou speakest, and victorious when Thou art judged. For behold, I was conceived in iniquity, and in sin my mother bore me. For behold, Thou hast loved truth; Thou hast made known to me the hidden and secret things of Thy wisdom. Thou shalt sprinkle me with hyssop, and I shall be made clean; Thou shalt wash me, and I shalt be whiter than snow. Make me to hear joy and gladness; that the humbled bones may rejoice. Turn Thy face away from my sins, and blot out all mine iniquities.

Create in me a clean heart, O God, and renew a steadfast spirit within me. Cast me not away from Thy presence, and take not Thy Holy Spirit from me. Restore to me the joy of Thy salvation, and establish me with Thy governing Spirit. I shall teach transgressors Thy ways, and the ungodly shall turn back to Thee. Deliver me from blood guiltiness, O God, the God of my salvation; my tongue shall joyfully declare Thy righteousness. Lord, open my lips, and my mouth shall declare Thy praise. For if Thou hadst desired sacrifice, I would give it; Thou dost not delight in burned offerings. A sacrifice to God is a broken spirit; God shall not despise a broken and a humbled heart. Do good, O Lord, in Thy good pleasure to Zion, and let the walls of Jerusalem be builded. Then Thou shalt be pleased with a sacrifice of righteousness, with oblation and whole burned offerings. Then shall they offer bulls on Thine altar.

After The Psalm

Glory be to the Father, and to the Son, and to the Holy Spirit;
Both now and forever, and unto the ages of ages. Amen.
Halleluiah, Halleluiah, Halleluiah. Glory to Thee, O God. **(x3)**
Lord, have mercy. **(x3)**

If there are two troparia, we say the first one here. If not, we continue:
Glory be to the Father, and to the Son, and to the Holy Spirit;
And we say the second troparion, if any, or the only troparion. Then:
Both now and forever, and unto the ages of ages. Amen.

Theotokion

O Theotokos; thou art the true vine that hath blossomed forth for us the Fruit of Life. Thee do we supplicate: Intercede, O Lady, together with the holy apostles, that our souls find mercy.

Psalm Verse

Blessed is the Lord God, blessed is the Lord day by day; the God of our salvation shall prosper us along the way; our God is the God of salvation.
Holy God, Holy Mighty, Holy Immortal, have mercy on us. **(x3)**

Glory be to the Father and to the Son and to the Holy Spirit;

Both now and forever and unto the ages of ages. Amen.

O Most Holy Trinity, have mercy on us.

O Lord, cleanse us from our sins.

O Master, pardon our iniquities.

O Holy One, visit and heal our infirmities, for Thy names sake.

Lord have mercy. **(x3)**

Glory be to the Father and to the Son and to the Holy Spirit;

Both now and forever and unto the ages of ages. Amen.

Our Father, who art in heaven, hallowed be Thy name. Thy Kingdom come. Thy will be done, on earth as it is in heaven. Give us this day our daily bread; and forgive us our trespasses, as we forgive those who trespass against us; and lead us not into temptation, but deliver us from the evil one.

[**Priest:** For Thine is the kingdom, the power and the glory, of the Father, the Son and the Holy Spirit, both now and for ever, and unto the ages of ages.]

People: Amen.

Reader: O Lord, Jesus Christ, Son of God, have mercy on us and save us.

People: Amen.

[Sunday]   **Kontakion Of The Resurrection**

  Tone 8   Humility, tranquillity, repose, suffering, pleading.   *C, D, Eb, F, G, A, Bb, C.*

When Thou went down to death, O immortal life, then Thou slewest Hell with the lightning flash of Thy Godhead; but when from the depths below the earth Thou raised the dead, O Christ God, proclaiming *"Rejoice"* to the myrrh bearing women, granting peace to Thine apostles and bestowing resurrection to the fallen.

[Monday]   **Kontakion Of St Michael And All The Angels**

  Tone 2   Majesty, gentleness, hope, repentance and sadness.   *E, F, G, Ab, B, C.*

You Princes and Leaders of the armies of God, Servants of the Divine Glory and guides of men. Ask whatever is good for us and for bountiful mercy, O Commanders of Sabaoth.

[Tuesday]   **Kontakion Of The Forerunner And Baptist John**

  Tone 2   Majesty, gentleness, hope, repentance and sadness.   *E, F, G, Ab, B, C.*

O Prophet of God and Forerunner of Grace, thy head has blossomed from the earth as a most sacred rose. We are ever being healed, for as of old, thou preachest repentance to the world.

[Wednesday] **Kontakion Of The Holy And Life Giving Cross**

Tone 4   Festive, joyous and expressing deep piety.   *C, D, Eb, F, G, A, Bb, C.*

As Thou wast voluntarily crucified for our sake, grant mercy to those who are called by Thy Name. Make all Orthodox Christians glad by Thy power, granting them victories over their adversaries, by bestowing on them the invincible trophy, Thy weapon of peace.

*[Thursday]   **Kontakion Of The Holy Apostles And St Nicholas***

Tone 3   Arrogant, brave, and mature atmosphere.   *F, G, A, A#, C, D, E, F.*

Thou hast taken O Lord the firm and divinely inspired preachers the holy apostles into rest and the enjoyment of Thy blessings. For Thou hast accepted their labours and death above every burned offering. Thou who alone knows the secrets of our hearts.

*[Friday]   **Kontakion Of The Holy And Life Giving Cross***

Tone 4   Festive, joyous and expressing deep piety.   *C, D, Eb, F, G, A, Bb, C.*

As Thou wast voluntarily crucified for our sake, grant mercy to those who are called by Thy Name. Make all Orthodox Christians glad by Thy power, granting them victories over their adversaries, by bestowing on them the invincible trophy, Thy weapon of peace.

*[Saturday]   **Kontakion Of The Theotokos, The Saints & The Faithful Departed***

Tone 2   Majesty, gentleness, hope, repentance and sadness.   *E, F, G, Ab, B, C.*

With the saints give rest, O Christ, to the souls of Thy servants, where sickness and sorrow are no more. Neither sighing, but life everlasting.

Lord, have mercy. **(x40)**

The Prayer Of The Hours

At all times and in every hour, Thou art worshipped and glorified in heaven and on earth, Christ our God. Long in patience, great in mercy and compassion, Thou lovest the righteous and showest mercy to sinners. Thou callest all to salvation through the promise of good things to come. Lord, receive our prayers at the present time. Direct our lives according to Thy commandments. Sanctify our souls. Purify our bodies. Set our minds aright. Cleanse our thoughts, and deliver us from all sorrow, evil and distress. Surround us with Thy holy angels, that, guarded and guided by their host, we may arrive at the unity of the faith and the understanding of Thine ineffable glory. For Thou art blessed unto the ages of ages. Amen.

The Prayer Of The Third Hour

Blessed be the Lord God. Blessed be the Lord day by day. May the God of our salvation prosper us, for He is our God, the God of our salvation.

The Prayer Of St Mardarius [of December 13th]

O Master God, the Father Almighty, O Lord, the only begotten Son, Jesus Christ, and O Holy Spirit, one Godhead, one Power: Have mercy on me a sinner, and by the judgements which Thou knowest, save me, Thine unworthy servant; for blessed art Thou unto the ages of ages. Amen.

Theotokion

Seeing that we have no boldness on account of our many sins, do thou beseech Him that was born of thee, O Virgin Theotokos for the supplication of a mother availeth much to win the Masters favour. Disdain not the prayers of sinners, O all pure one, for merciful and mighty to save is He Who deigned also to suffer for our sake.

Psalm Verse

Let Thy compassions quickly go before us, O Lord, for we are become exceedingly poor. Help us, O God our Saviour, for the sake of the glory of Thy name. O Lord, deliver us and be gracious unto our sins for Thy names sake.

The Prayer Of St Basil The Great

O God and Lord of Hosts, and Maker of all Creation, Who, by the tender compassion of Thy mercy that transcendeth comprehension, didst send down Thine only begotten Son, our Lord Jesus Christ, for the salvation of our race, and by His precious Cross didst tear asunder the handwriting of our sins, and thereby didst triumph over the principalities and powers of darkness: Do Thou Thyself, O Master, Lover of mankind, accept also from us sinners these prayers of thanksgiving and entreaty, and deliver us from every destructive and dark transgression, and from all enemies, both visible and invisible, that seek to do us evil. Nail down our flesh with the fear of Thee, and incline not our hearts unto words or thoughts of evil, but pierce our souls with longing for Thee, so that ever looking to Thee, and being guided by Thy Light as we behold Thee, the unapproachable and everlasting Light, we may send up unceasing praise and thanksgiving unto Thee, the Unoriginate Father, with Thine Only begotten Son, and Thine All Holy and good and life creating Spirit, now and ever, and unto the ages of ages. Amen.

Dismissal

[with a Priest]

Priest: Glory to you, Christ God, our hope, glory to you.

Reader: *Glory be to the Father, and to the Son, and to the Holy Spirit;*

Both now and forever, and unto the ages of ages. Amen.

Lord, have mercy. **(x3)**

People: *Holy Father, bless.*

Priest: May God take pity on us and bless us; show the light of His countenance on us and have mercy on us.

People: *Amen.*

Priest: Christ, the true light, who enlightenest and hallowest everyone who comest into the world, may the light of Thy countenance be signed upon us, that in it we may see Thine unapproachable light; and direct our steps to the doing of Thy commandments; at the intercessions of Thy most pure Mother and of all Thy Saints.

People: Amen.

Priest: May Christ our true God, at the prayers of His most pure and spotless Mother; of the holy, glorious and all praised Apostles; of the holy, glorious and triumphant Martyrs; of our venerable and God bearing Fathers; of Saint *N [patron]*; *[of Saints N & N, whose memory we celebrate;]* of the holy and righteous forebears of God, Joachim and Anna, and of all the Saints, have mercy and save us, for He is good and lovest mankind.

People: Amen.

[without a Priest]

Lord, have mercy. **(x3)**

Glory be to the Father and to the Son and to the Holy Spirit;
Both now and forever and unto the ages of ages. Amen.

Greater in honour than the Cherubim and beyond compare more glorious than the Seraphim; without corruption thou gavest birth to God the Word, truly the Theotokos, we magnify thee.

Through the prayers of our holy fathers, O Lord Jesus Christ our God, have mercy on us and save us. Amen.

O Lord Jesus Christ, Son of God, for the sake of the prayers of Thy most pure Mother, our holy and God bearing fathers, and of all the saints, have mercy on us and save us, for Thou art good and the Lover of mankind. Amen.

[After each Hour during Lent and the first day of the Lesser Fasts.]

Come, let us worship God, our King.

Come, let us worship and fall down before Christ, our King and our God.

Come, let us worship and fall down before Christ Himself, our King and our God.

[Monday, Thursday, Sunday]   **Psalm 29**

I shall exalt Thee, O Lord, because Thou upheld me and did not gladden mine enemies over me. O Lord my God I cried to Thee and Thou healed me. O Lord, Thou brought up my soul from Hades; Thou savest me from those that go down into a pit. Make music to the Lord, O you His devout, and acknowledge the mentioning of His holiness, because wrath is in His fury and life in His will. Weeping shall lodge for the evening, and rejoicing comes with the morning. But as for me, I said in my prosperity, "I shall never be shaken." O Lord, by Thy will, Thou furnished my beauty with power, but Thou turned away Thy face, and I became troubled. To Thee, O Lord, I shall cry, and to my God I shall petition: "What profit is there in my blood, when I go down to corruption? Surely dust shall not acknowledge Thee or tell of Thy truth?" The Lord heard and had mercy on me; the Lord became my helper. Thou turned my mourning into a dance for me; Thou tore my sackcloth and girded me with gladness so that my glory may make music to Thee and I shall not be stunned. O Lord my God, I shall acknowledge Thee forever.

[Tuesday, Friday, Sunday]   **Psalm 31**

Happy are those whose lawless behaviour was forgiven and whose sins were covered over. Happy the man whose sin the Lord shall not reckon, and in his mouth there is no deceit. Because I kept silence, my bones grew old from my crying all day long. Because day and night Thy hand was heavy upon me, I was turned to wretchedness when a thorn was stuck in me. My sin I made known and my lawlessness I did not cover; I said, "I shall declare to the Lord against myself my lawlessness" and Thou forgavest the impiety of my sin.

Over this, every devout person shall pray to Thee at an appropriate time, but at a flood of many waters, these shall not reach him. Thou art my refuge from affliction that besets me - mine enjoyment, redeem me from those that encircle me. I shall instruct you and teach you in this way in which you should go; I shall fix mine eyes upon ye. Do not be like horse and mule, who have no understanding; with bridle and muzzle squeeze their jaws when they do not come near to Thee. Many are the scourges of the sinner, but mercy shall surround him that hopeth in the Lord. Be glad in the Lord, and rejoice, O righteous, and boast, all you upright in heart.

[Wednesday, Saturday, Sunday]   **Psalm 60**

Listen to my petition, O God; pay attention to my prayer. From the ends of the earth I cried to Thee, when my heart was weary. On a rock Thou exalted me. Thou guided me, because Thou became my hope, a tower of strength from before an enemy. I shall sojourn in Thy refuge forever, find shelter in the shelter of Thy wings. Because Thou, O God, Thou listened to my vows, Thou gave a heritage to those who fear Thy name. Thou shall add days to a kings days, his years until days of generation and generation. He shall remain forever before God; his mercy and truth, who shall seek out? So I shall make music to Thy name forever and ever, that I pay my vows day after day.

After The Psalm

Glory be to the Father, and to the Son, and to the Holy Spirit;
Both now and forever, and unto the ages of ages. Amen.

Halleluiah, Halleluiah, Halleluiah. Glory to Thee, O God. **(x3)**

Lord, have mercy. **(x3)**

Holy God, Holy Mighty, Holy Immortal, have mercy on us. **(x3)**

Glory be to the Father, and to the Son, and to the Holy Spirit;
Both now and forever, and unto the ages of ages. Amen.

O Most Holy Trinity, have mercy on us.

O Lord, cleanse us from our sins.

O Master, pardon our iniquities.

O Holy One, visit and heal our infirmities, for Thy names sake.

Lord have mercy. **(x3)**

Glory be to the Father, and to the Son, and to the Holy Spirit;
Both now and forever, and unto the ages of ages. Amen.

Our Father, who art in heaven, hallowed be Thy name. Thy Kingdom come. Thy will be done, on earth as it is in heaven. Give us this day our daily bread; and forgive us our trespasses, as we forgive those who trespass against us; and lead us not into temptation, but deliver us from the evil one.

O Lord, Jesus Christ, Son of God, have mercy on us and save us. Amen.

[Sunday]   **Kontakion Of The Resurrection**

Tone 8   Humility, tranquillity, repose, suffering, pleading.   *C, D, Eb, F, G, A, Bb, C.*

When Thou went down to death, O immortal life, then Thou slew Hell with the lightning flash of Thy Godhead; but when from the depths below the earth Thou raised the dead, O Christ God, proclaiming 'Rejoice' to the myrrh bearing women, granting peace to Thine apostles and bestowing resurrection to the fallen.

[Monday]   **Kontakion Of St Michael And All The Angels**

Tone 2   Majesty, gentleness, hope, repentance and sadness.   *E, F, G, Ab, B, C.*

You Princes and Leaders of the armies of God, Servants of the Divine Glory and guides of men. Ask whatever is good for us and for bountiful mercy, O Commanders of Sabaoth.

[Tuesday]   **Kontakion Of The Forerunner And Baptist John**

Tone 2   Majesty, gentleness, hope, repentance and sadness.   *E, F, G, Ab, B, C.*

O Prophet of God and Forerunner of Grace, Thine head has blossomed from the earth as a most sacred rose. We are ever being healed, for as of old, thou preachest repentance to the world.

[Wednesday]   **Kontakion Of The Holy And Life Giving Cross**

Tone 4   Festive, joyous and expressing deep piety.   *C, D, Eb, F, G, A, Bb, C.*

As Thou wast voluntarily crucified for our sake, grant mercy to those who are called by Thy Name. Make all Orthodox Christians glad by Thy power, granting them victories over their adversaries, by bestowing on them the invincible trophy, Thy weapon of peace.

[Thursday]   **Kontakion Of The Holy Apostles And St Nicholas**

Tone 3   Arrogant, brave, and mature atmosphere.   *F, G, A, A#, C, D, E, F.*

Thou hast taken O Lord the firm and divinely inspired preachers the holy apostles into rest and the enjoyment of Thy blessings. For Thou hast accepted their labours and death above every burned offering. Thou who alone knows the secrets of our hearts.

[Friday]   **Kontakion Of The Holy And Life Giving Cross**

Tone 4   Festive, joyous and expressing deep piety.   *C, D, Eb, F, G, A, Bb, C.*

As Thou wast voluntarily crucified for our sake, grant mercy to those who are called by Thy Name. Make all Orthodox Christians glad by Thy power, granting them victories over their adversaries, by bestowing on them the invincible trophy, Thy weapon of peace.

[Saturday]   **Kontakion Of The Theotokos, The Saints And The Faithful Departed**

Tone 2   Majesty, gentleness, hope, repentance and sadness.   *E, F, G, Ab, B, C.*

With the saints give rest, O Christ, to the souls of Thy servants, where sickness and sorrow are no more. Neither sighing, but life everlasting.

Lord, have mercy. **(x40)**

The Prayer Of The Hours

At all times and in every hour, Thou art worshipped and glorified in heaven and on earth, Christ our God. Long in patience, great in mercy and compassion, Thou lovest the righteous and showest mercy to sinners. Thou callest all to salvation through the promise of good things to come. Lord, receive our prayers at the present time. Direct our lives according to Thy commandments. Sanctify our souls. Purify our bodies. Set our minds aright. Cleanse our thoughts, and deliver us from all sorrow, evil and distress. Surround us with Thy holy angels, that, guarded and guided by their host, we may arrive at the unity of the faith and the understanding of Thine ineffable glory. For Thou art blessed to the ages of ages. Amen.

Prayer Of St Ephrem The Syrian To The Most Holy Spirit

O Lord, Heavenly King, Comforter, Spirit of Truth, have compassion and mercy on Thy sinful servant and pardon mine unworthiness, and forgive me all the sins that I have humanly committed today, and not only humanly but even worse than a beast - my voluntary sins, known and unknown, from my youth and from evil suggestions, and from my brazenness, and from boredom. If I have sworn by Thy Name or blasphemed it in thought, blamed or reproached anyone, or in mine anger have detracted or slandered anyone, or grieved anyone, or if I have become angry about anything, or have told a lie, if I have slept unnecessarily, or if a beggar has come to me and I despised or neglected him, or if I have troubled my brother or quarrelled with him, or if I have condemned anyone, or have boasted, or have been proud, or lost my temper with anyone, or if when standing in prayer my mind has been distracted by the glamour of this world, or if I have had depraved thoughts or have overeaten, or have drunk excessively, or have laughed frivolously, or have thought evil, or have seen the attraction of someone and been wounded by it in my heart, or said indecent things, or made fun of my brothers sin when mine own faults are countless, or been neglectful of prayer, or have done some other wrong that I cannot remember - for I have done all this and much more - have mercy, my Lord and Creator, on me Thy wretched and unworthy servant, and absolve and forgive and deliver me in Thy goodness and love for men, so that, lustful, sinful and wretched as I am, I may lie down and sleep and rest in peace. And I shall worship, praise and glorify Thy most honourable Name, with the Father and His only begotten Son, now and ever, and for all ages. Amen.

Dismissal

Lord, have mercy. (x3)

Glory be to the Father, and to the Son, and to the Holy Spirit;
Both now and forever, and unto the ages of ages. Amen.

Greater in honour than the Cherubim and beyond compare more glorious than the Seraphim; without corruption thou gavest birth to God the Word, truly the Theotokos, we magnify thee.

Through the prayers of our holy fathers, O Lord Jesus Christ our God, have mercy on us and save us. Amen.

The Trisagion Prayers

In the Name of the Father, and of the Son, and of the Holy Spirit. Amen.

Glory to Thee, our God, glory to Thee.

O Heavenly King, the Comforter, the Spirit of Truth; who art everywhere present and fillest all things; Treasury of blessings, and giver of life: come and abide in us, and cleanse us from every impurity, and save our souls, O Good One.

Holy God, Holy Mighty, Holy Immortal, have mercy on us. **(x3)**

Glory be to the Father and to the Son and to the Holy Spirit;
Both now and forever and unto the ages of ages. Amen.

O Most Holy Trinity, have mercy on us.

O Lord, cleanse us from our sins.

O Master, pardon our iniquities.

O Holy One, visit and heal our infirmities, for Thy names sake.

Lord have mercy. **(x3)**

Glory be to the Father and to the Son and to the Holy Spirit;
Both now and forever and unto the ages of ages. Amen.

Our Father, who art in heaven, hallowed be Thy name. Thy Kingdom come. Thy will be done, on earth as it is in heaven. Give us this day our daily bread; and forgive us our trespasses, as we forgive those who trespass against us; and lead us not into temptation, but deliver us from the evil one.

[Priest: For Thine is the kingdom, the power and the glory, of the Father, the Son and the Holy Spirit, both now and for ever, and unto the ages of ages.]

People: *Amen.*

Lord have mercy. **(x12)**

Glory be to the Father and to the Son and to the Holy Spirit;
Both now and forever and unto the ages of ages. Amen.

Come, let us worship God, our King.

Come, let us worship and fall down before Christ, our King and our God.

Come, let us worship and fall down before Christ Himself, our King and our God.

[Monday, Thursday, Sunday] **Psalm 53**

Save me, O God, by Thy name, and vindicate me by Thy strength. Hear my prayer, O God; give ear to the words of my mouth. For strangers have risen up against me, and oppressors have sought after my life; they have not set God before them. Behold, God is my helper; the Lord is with those who uphold my life. He shall repay mine enemies for their evil. Cut them off in Thy truth. I shall freely sacrifice to Thee; I shall praise Thy name, O Lord, for it is good. For He has delivered me out of all trouble; and mine eye has seen its desire upon mine enemies.

[Tuesday, Friday, Sunday] **Psalm 54**

Give ear to my prayer, O God, and do not hide Thyself from my supplication. Attend to me, and hear me; I am restless in my complaint, and moan noisily because of the voice of the enemy, because of the oppression of the wicked; for they bring down trouble upon me, and in wrath they hate me. My heart is severely pained within me, and the terrors of death have fallen upon me. Fearfulness and trembling have come upon me, and horror has overwhelmed me. And I said, "Oh, that I had wings like a dove. For then I would fly away and be at rest. Indeed, I would wander far off, and remain in the wilderness. I would hasten mine escape from the windy storm and tempest." Destroy, O Lord, and divide their tongues, for I have seen violence and strife in the city. Day and night they go around it on its walls; iniquity and trouble are also in the midst of it. Destruction is in its midst; deceit and guile do not depart from its streets.

For it is not an enemy who reproaches me; then I could bear it. Nor is it one who hates me who has magnified himself against me; then I could hide from him. But it was thee, a man mine equal, my companion and mine acquaintance. We took sweet counsel together, and walked to the house of God in the throng. Let death seize them; let them go down alive into hell, for wickedness is in their dwellings and among them.

As for me, I shall call upon God, and the Lord shall save me. Evening and morning and at noon I shall pray, and cry aloud, and He shall hear my voice. He has redeemed my soul in peace from the battle which was against me, for there were many against me. God shall hear, and afflict them, even He who abides from of old. Because they do not change, therefore they do not fear God.

This man has put forth his hands against those who were at peace with him; he has broken his covenant. The words of his mouth were smoother than butter, but war was in his heart; his words were softer than oil, yet they were drawn swords.

Cast thy burden on the Lord, and He shall sustain ye; He shall never permit the righteous to be moved. But Thou, O God, shall bring them down to the pit of destruction; bloodthirsty and deceitful men shall not live out half their days; but I shall trust in Thee.

He who dwells in the secret place of the Most High shall abide under the shadow of the Almighty. I shall say of the Lord, *"He is my refuge and my fortress; My God, in Him I shall trust."* Surely He shall deliver thee from the snare of the fowler and from the perilous pestilence. He shall cover thee with His feathers, and under His wings thou shalt take refuge; His truth shall be thy shield and buckler. You shall not be afraid of the terror by night, nor of the arrow that flies by day, Nor of the pestilence that walks in darkness, nor of the destruction that lays waste at noonday. A thousand may fall at thy side, and ten thousand at thy right hand; but it shall not come near thee. Only with thine eyes shalt thou look, and see the reward of the wicked. Because thou hast made the Lord, Who is my refuge, even the Most High, thy habitation.

No evil shall befall thee, nor shall any plague come near thy dwelling; For He shall give His angels charge over thee, to keep thee in all thy ways. They shall bear thee up in their hands, lest thou dashest thy foot against a stone. Thou shalt tread upon the lion and the cobra, the young lion and the serpent thou shalt trample under foot. Because he has set his love upon Me, therefore I shall deliver him; I shall set him on high, because he has known My name. He shall call upon Me, and I shall answer him; I shall be with him in trouble; I shall deliver him and honour him. With long life shall I satisfy him, and show him My salvation.

After The Psalm

Glory be to the Father, and to the Son, and to the Holy Spirit;
Both now and forever, and unto the ages of ages. Amen.

Halleluiah, Halleluiah, Halleluiah! Glory to Thee, O God. **(x3)**
Lord, have mercy. **(x3)**

Troparia

[Daily]   **Troparion For The Noon Office**

Tone 2   Majesty, gentleness, hope, repentance and sadness.   *E, F, G, Ab, B, C.*

O Thou who on the sixth day and hour nailed to the cross the sin which rebellious Adam committed in Paradise. Tear asunder also the bond of our iniquities, O Christ our God, and save us.

Glory be to the Father, and to the Son, and to the Holy Spirit;

[Sunday]   **Troparion Of The Resurrection**

Tone 6   Rich texture, funeral character, sorrowful tone.   *D, Eb, F##, G, A, Bb, C##, D.*

When Mary stood at Thy grave looking for Thy sacred body, angelic powers shone above Thy revered tomb, and the soldiers who were to keep guard became as dead men. Thou led hades captive and wast not tempted thereby. Thou didst meet the Virgin and didst give life to the world. Thou who art risen from the dead, O Lord, glory to Thee.

[Monday] **Troparion Of St Michael And All Angels**

Tone 4   *Festive, joyous and expressing deep piety.*   *C, D, Eb, F, G, A, Bb, C.*

O Commanders of Sabaoth, We who are unworthy beseech you ceaselessly that you wouldst encompass us with the shelter of your prayers and cover us beneath the wings of your immaterial glory. We fall down before you crying out: *"Protect us from all harm, O Princes of the powers on high."*

[Tuesday] **Troparion Of The Forerunner And Baptist John**

Tone 2   *Majesty, gentleness, hope, repentance and sadness.*   *E, F, G, Ab, B, C.*

The memory of the righteous is worthy of praise. But thou, O Forerunner, are well pleased by the Lords own witness. Thou wast revealed as greater than the prophets, For thou baptised in the waters Him whom they foretold. Therefore, having fought and suffered for the Truth, thou proclaimed to those in the tombs the Gospel of the incarnate God, Who takes away the sins of the world and grants us great mercy.

[Wednesday] **Troparion Of The Holy And Life Giving Cross**

Tone 1   *Magnificent, happy and earthy.*   *C, D, Eb, F, G, A, Bb, C.*

O Lord, save Thy people and bless Thine inheritance. Grant victories to the Orthodox Christians over their adversaries. And by virtue of Thy Cross, preserve Thy commonwealth.

[Thursday] **Troparion Of The Holy Apostles And St Nicholas**

Tone 3   *Arrogant, brave, and mature atmosphere.*   *F, G, A, A#, C, D, E, F.*

O holy Apostles, intercede with our merciful God to grant our souls forgiveness of our sins.

[Friday] **Troparion Of The Holy And Life Giving Cross**

Tone 1   *Magnificent, happy and earthy.*   *C, D, Eb, F, G, A, Bb, C.*

O Lord, save Thy people and bless Thine inheritance. Grant victories to the Orthodox Christians over their adversaries. And by virtue of Thy Cross, preserve Thine commonwealth.

[Saturday] **Troparion Of The Theotokos, All Saints And The Faithful Departed**

Tone 2   *Majesty, gentleness, hope, repentance and sadness.*   *E, F, G, Ab, B, C.*

Apostles, martyrs, and prophets, holy hierarchs, saints and the righteous. Having fought the good fight and kept the faith, you have boldness toward the Saviour. Intercede for us with Him for He is good, and pray that He may save our souls.

Both now and forever, and unto the ages of ages. Amen.

Theotokion

Since there is no boldness in us because of the multitude of our sins, O Virgin Theotokos, intercede with the Son Whom thou hast borne, for the entreaty of a mother has great power to win the favour of the Master. Do not despise the prayers of sinners, O all venerable Lady, for He Who took upon Himself to suffer for our sake is merciful and strong to save.

Psalm Verse

Let Thy tender mercies, O Lord, speedily go before us, for we have become exceedingly poor. Help us, O God of our salvation, for the glory of Thy Name, O Lord, deliver us and purge our sins for Thy Names sake.

[Sunday]   **Kontakion Of The Resurrection**

Tone 8   Humility, tranquillity, repose, suffering, pleading.   *C, D, Eb, F, G, A, Bb, C.*

When Thou went down to death, O immortal life, then Thou slew Hell with the lightning flash of Thy Godhead; but when from the depths below the earth Thou raised the dead, O Christ God, proclaiming *"Rejoice"* to the myrrh bearing women, granting peace to Thine apostles and bestowing resurrection to the fallen.

[Monday]   **Kontakion Of St Michael And All The Angels**

Tone 2   Majesty, gentleness, hope, repentance and sadness.   *E, F, G, Ab, B, C.*

You Princes and Leaders of the armies of God, Servants of the Divine Glory and guides of men. Ask whatever is good for us and for bountiful mercy, O Commanders of Sabaoth.

[Tuesday]   **Kontakion Of The Forerunner And Baptist John**

Tone 2   Majesty, gentleness, hope, repentance and sadness.   *E, F, G, Ab, B, C.*

O Prophet of God and Forerunner of Grace, thy head has blossomed from the earth as a most sacred rose. We are ever being healed, for as of old thou preachest repentance to the world.

[Wednesday]   **Kontakion Of The Holy And Life Giving Cross**

Tone 4   Festive, joyous and expressing deep piety.   *C, D, Eb, F, G, A, Bb, C.*

As Thou wast voluntarily crucified for our sake, grant mercy to those who are called by Thy Name. Make all Orthodox Christians glad by Thy power, granting them victories over their adversaries, by bestowing on them the invincible trophy, Thy weapon of peace.

[Thursday]   **Kontakion Of The Holy Apostles And St Nicholas**

Tone 3   Arrogant, brave, and mature atmosphere.   *F, G, A, A#, C, D, E, F.*

Thou hast taken O Lord, the firm and divinely inspired preachers, the holy apostles into rest and the enjoyment of Thy blessings. For Thou hast accepted their labours and death above every burned offering, Thou alone knowest the secrets of our hearts.

[Friday]   **Kontakion Of The Holy And Life Giving Cross**

Tone 4   Festive, joyous and expressing deep piety.   *C, D, Eb, F, G, A, Bb, C.*

As Thou wast voluntarily crucified for our sake, grant mercy to those who are called by Thy Name. Make all Orthodox Christians glad by Thy power, granting them victories over their adversaries, by bestowing on them the invincible trophy, Thy weapon of peace.

[Saturday]   **Kontakion Of The Theotokos, The Saints & The Faithful Departed**

Tone 2   Majesty, gentleness, hope, repentance and sadness.   *E, F, G, Ab, B, C.*

With the saints give rest, O Christ, to the souls of Thy servants, where sickness and sorrow are no more. Neither sighing, but life everlasting.

Lord, have mercy. **(x40)**

The Prayer Of The Hours

At all times and in every hour, Thou art worshipped and glorified in heaven and on earth, Christ our God. Long in patience, great in mercy and compassion, Thou lovest the righteous and showest mercy to sinners. Thou callest all to salvation through the promise of good things to come. Lord, receive our prayers at the present time. Direct our lives according to Thy commandments. Sanctify our souls. Purify our bodies. Set our minds aright. Cleanse our thoughts, and deliver us from all sorrow, evil and distress. Surround us with Thy holy angels, that, guarded and guided by their host, we may arrive at the unity of the faith and the understanding of Thine ineffable glory. For Thou art blessed unto the ages of ages. Amen.

Prayer Of The Sixth Hour

Let Thy tender mercies speedily go before us, O Lord, for we have become very poor. Help us, O God our Saviour, for the glory of Thy Name: O Lord, deliver us and cleanse our sins for Thy Names sake.

Prayer Of St Basil The Great

O God, Lord of hosts and Maker of all creation, Who in Thy great compassion and mercy sent down Thine only begotten Son, our Lord Jesus Christ, for the redemption of mankind and by His precious Cross destroyed the record of our sins, triumphing over the source and power of darkness: O Lord and Lover of mankind, accept also the thanksgiving and fervent prayers of us sinners. Deliver us from every dark and harmful transgression and from all the visible and invisible enemies that seek to destroy us. Nail our flesh to the fear of Thee, and do not incline our hearts to deceitful words or thoughts, but wound our souls with love for Thee. That always looking to Thee, guided by Thy light, and seeing Thee, the eternal and ineffable Light, we may give Thee unceasing praise and thanksgiving: to the Father without beginning, with Thine only begotten Son and Thine all holy, good and life creating Spirit, both now and forever and unto the ages of ages. Amen.

Dismissal

[with a Priest]

Priest: Glory to you, Christ God, our hope, glory to you.

Reader: *Glory be to the Father, and to the Son, and to the Holy Spirit;*

               Both now and forever, and unto the ages of ages. Amen.

               Lord, have mercy. **(x3)**

People: *Holy Father, bless.*

Priest: May God take pity on us and bless us; show the light of His countenance on us and have mercy on us.

People: *Amen.*

Priest: Christ, the true light, who enlightenest and hallowest everyone who comest into the world, may the light of Thy countenance be signed upon us, that in it we may see Thine unapproachable light; and direct our steps to the doing of Thy commandments; at the intercessions of Thy most pure Mother and of all Thy Saints.

People: *Amen.*

Priest: May Christ our true God, at the prayers of His most pure and spotless Mother; of the holy, glorious and all praised Apostles; of the holy, glorious and triumphant Martyrs; of our venerable and God bearing Fathers; of Saint *N [patron]*; *[of Saints N & N, whose memory we celebrate;]* of the holy and righteous forebears of God, Joachim and Anna, and of all the Saints, have mercy and save us, for He is good and lovest mankind.

People: *Amen.*

[without a Priest]

Lord, have mercy. **(x3)**

> *Glory be to the Father and to the Son and to the Holy Spirit;*
> *Both now and forever and unto the ages of ages. Amen.*

Greater in honour than the Cherubim and beyond compare more glorious than the Seraphim; without corruption thou gavest birth to God the Word, truly the Theotokos, we magnify thee.

Through the prayers of our holy fathers, O Lord Jesus Christ our God, have mercy on us and save us. Amen.

O Lord Jesus Christ, Son of God, for the sake of the prayers of Thy most pure Mother, our holy and God bearing fathers, and of all the saints, have mercy on us and save us, for Thou art good and the Lover of mankind. Amen.

Inter Hour Of The 6th Hour - Mesorion

[After each Hour during Lent and the first day of the Lesser Fasts.]

Come, let us worship God, our King.

Come, let us worship and fall down before Christ, our King and our God.

Come, let us worship and fall down before Christ Himself, our King and our God.

[Monday, Thursday, Sunday]   **Psalm 55**

Have mercy on me, O Lord, because a person trampled on me; all day long, while fighting, he afflicted me; mine enemies trampled on me all day long, because many are they that fight against me from on high. By day I shall be afraid; I shall hope in Thee. In God I shall commend my words; in God I hoped; I shall not fear what flesh may do to me.

All day long they would make my words loathsome; all their thoughts against me are for evil. They shall sojourn and hide; my heel they shall watch, as they waited to have my soul. On no account wilt Thou save them; in wrath Thou wilt bring down peoples, O God.

My life I proclaimed to Thee; Thou put my tears before Thee, as also by Thy promise. Mine enemies shall turn back in the day when I call upon Thee. Look, I knew that Thou art my God. In God I shall praise with a word; in the Lord I shall praise with a statement. In God I hoped; I shall not fear what a person may do to me. In me, O God, are the vows of praise to Thee, which I shall pay, because Thou rescued my soul from death and my feet from slipperiness so that I may be pleasing before God in the light of the living.

[Tuesday, Friday, Sunday]   **Psalm 56**

Have mercy on me, O God; have mercy on me, because in Thee my soul trusts and in the shadow of Thy wings I shall hope until lawlessness passes by. I shall cry to God the Most High, to God who acts as my benefactor. He sent from heaven and saved me; he gave over to reproach those who were trampling on me. God sent forth his mercy and his truth, and he rescued my soul from among whelps. I slept, though troubled. As for sons of men - their teeth are a weapon and darts, and their tongue a sharp dagger. Be exalted to the heavens, O God, and to all the earth be Thy glory. A trap they prepared for my feet, and they bowed down my soul. They dug a hole in front of me, and they fell into it. My heart is ready, O God; my heart is ready. I shall sing and make music. Awake, my glory! Awake, O harp and lyre! I shall awaken at dawn. I shall acknowledge Thee O Lord among peoples; I shall make music to Thee among nations, because Thy mercy was magnified to the heavens and to the clouds Thy truth. Be exalted to the heavens O God, and to all the earth be Thy glory.

[Wednesday, Saturday, Sunday]   **Psalm 69**

O God, be attentive to help me; Lord, make haste to help me. Let them be ashamed and confounded who seek after my life. Let them be turned back and be ashamed who desire evil against me. Let them be turned back because of their shame who say to me: "Well done! Well done!" Let all those who seek Thee rejoice and be glad in Thee, O God, and let those who love Thy salvation say continually: Let the Lord be magnified. But as for me, I am poor and needy; O God help me. Thou art my help and my deliverer; Lord; do not delay.

After The Psalm

Glory be to the Father, and to the Son, and to the Holy Spirit;
Both now and forever, and unto the ages of ages. Amen.

Halleluiah, Halleluiah, Halleluiah. Glory to Thee, O God. **(x3)**
Lord, have mercy. **(x3)**

Holy God, Holy Mighty, Holy Immortal, have mercy on us. **(x3)**

Glory be to the Father, and to the Son, and to the Holy Spirit;
Both now and forever, and unto the ages of ages. Amen.

O Most Holy Trinity, have mercy on us.
O Lord, cleanse us from our sins.
O Master, pardon our iniquities.
O Holy One, visit and heal our infirmities, for Thy names sake.

Lord have mercy. **(x3)**

Glory be to the Father, and to the Son, and to the Holy Spirit;
Both now and forever, and unto the ages of ages. Amen.

Our Father, who art in heaven, hallowed be Thy name. Thy Kingdom come. Thy will be done, on earth as it is in heaven. Give us this day our daily bread; and forgive us our trespasses, as we forgive those who trespass against us; and lead us not into temptation, but deliver us from the evil one.

O Lord, Jesus Christ, Son of God, have mercy on us and save us. Amen.

[Sunday]   **Kontakion Of The Resurrection**
   Tone 8   Humility, tranquillity, repose, suffering, pleading.   *C, D, Eb, F, G, A, Bb, C.*
When Thou went down to death, O immortal life, then Thou slew Hell with the lightning flash of Thy Godhead; but when from the depths below the earth Thou raised the dead, O Christ God, proclaiming "Rejoice" to the myrrh bearing women, granting peace to Thy apostles and bestowing resurrection to the fallen.

[Monday]   **Kontakion Of St Michael And All The Angels**
   Tone 2   Majesty, gentleness, hope, repentance and sadness.   *E, F, G, Ab, B, C.*
You Princes and Leaders of the armies of God, Servants of the Divine Glory and guides of men. Ask whatever is good for us and for bountiful mercy, O Commanders of Sabaoth.

[Tuesday]   **Kontakion Of The Forerunner And Baptist John**

Tone 2   *Majesty, gentleness, hope, repentance and sadness.*   *E, F, G, Ab, B, C.*

O Prophet of God and Forerunner of Grace, Thy head has blossomed from the earth as a most sacred rose. We are ever being healed, for as of old, thou preachest repentance to the world.

[Wednesday]   **Kontakion Of The Holy And Life Giving Cross**

Tone 4   *Festive, joyous and expressing deep piety.*   *C, D, Eb, F, G, A, Bb, C.*

As Thou wast voluntarily crucified for our sake, grant mercy to those who are called by Thy Name. Make all Orthodox Christians glad by Thy power, granting them victories over their adversaries, by bestowing on them the invincible trophy, Thy weapon of peace.

[Thursday]   **Kontakion Of The Holy Apostles And St Nicholas**

Tone 3   *Arrogant, brave, and mature atmosphere.*   *F, G, A, A#, C, D, E, F.*

Thou hast taken O Lord the firm and divinely inspired preachers the holy apostles into rest and the enjoyment of Thy blessings. For Thou hast accepted their labours and death above every burned offering. Thou who alone knows the secrets of our hearts.

[Friday]   **Kontakion Of The Holy And Life Giving Cross**

Tone 4   *Festive, joyous and expressing deep piety.*   *C, D, Eb, F, G, A, Bb, C.*

As Thou wast voluntarily crucified for our sake, grant mercy to those who are called by Thy Name. Make all Orthodox Christians glad by Thy power, granting them victories over their adversaries, by bestowing on them the invincible trophy, Thy weapon of peace.

[Saturday]   **Kontakion Of The Theotokos, The Saints And The Faithful Departed**

Tone 2   *Majesty, gentleness, hope, repentance and sadness.*   *E, F, G, Ab, B, C.*

With the saints give rest, O Christ, to the souls of Thy servants, where sickness and sorrow are no more. Neither sighing, but life everlasting.

Lord, have mercy. **(x40)**

The Prayer Of The Hours

At all times and in every hour, Thou art worshipped and glorified in heaven and on earth, Christ our God. Long in patience, great in mercy and compassion, Thou lovest the righteous and showest mercy to sinners. Thou callest all to salvation through the promise of good things to come. Lord, receive our prayers at the present time. Direct our lives according to Thy commandments. Sanctify our souls. Purify our bodies. Set our minds aright. Cleanse our thoughts, and deliver us from all sorrow, evil and distress. Surround us with Thy holy angels, that, guarded and guided by their host, we may arrive at the unity of the faith and the understanding of Thine ineffable glory. For Thou art blessed to the ages of ages. Amen.

Prayer Of St Ephrem The Syrian To The Most Holy Spirit

O Lord, Heavenly King, Comforter, Spirit of Truth, have compassion and mercy on Thy sinful servant and pardon mine unworthiness, and forgive me all the sins that I have humanly committed today, and not only humanly but even worse than a beast - my voluntary sins, known and unknown, from my youth and from evil suggestions, and from my brazenness, and from boredom. If I have sworn by Thy Name or blasphemed it in thought, blamed or reproached anyone, or in mine anger have detracted or slandered anyone, or grieved anyone, or if I have become angry about anything, or have told a lie, if I have slept unnecessarily, or if a beggar has come to me and I despised or neglected him, or if I have troubled my brother or quarrelled with him, or if I have condemned anyone, or have boasted, or have been proud, or lost my temper with anyone, or if when standing in prayer my mind has been distracted by the glamour of this world, or if I have had depraved thoughts or have overeaten, or have drunk excessively, or have laughed frivolously, or have thought evil, or have seen the attraction of someone and been wounded by it in my heart, or said indecent things, or made fun of my brothers sin when mine own faults are countless, or been neglectful of prayer, or have done some other wrong that I cannot remember - for I have done all this and much more - have mercy, my Lord and Creator, on me Thy wretched and unworthy servant, and absolve and forgive and deliver me in Thy goodness and love for men, so that, lustful, sinful and wretched as I am, I may lie down and sleep and rest in peace. And I shall worship, praise and glorify Thy most honourable Name, with the Father and His only begotten Son, now and ever, and for all ages. Amen.

Dismissal

Lord, have mercy. **(x3)**

Glory be to the Father, and to the Son, and to the Holy Spirit;
Both now and forever, and unto the ages of ages. Amen.

Greater in honour than the Cherubim and beyond compare more glorious than the Seraphim; without corruption thou gavest birth to God the Word, truly the Theotokos, we magnify thee.

Through the prayers of our holy fathers, O Lord Jesus Christ our God, have mercy on us and save us. Amen.

The Trisagion Prayers

In the Name of the Father, and of the Son, and of the Holy Spirit. Amen.

Glory to Thee, our God, glory to Thee.

O Heavenly King, the Comforter, the Spirit of Truth; who art everywhere present and fillest all things; Treasury of blessings, and giver of life: come and abide in us, and cleanse us from every impurity, and save our souls, O Good One.

Holy God, Holy Mighty, Holy Immortal, have mercy on us. **(x3)**

Glory be to the Father and to the Son and to the Holy Spirit;

Both now and forever and unto the ages of ages. Amen.

O Most Holy Trinity, have mercy on us.

O Lord, cleanse us from our sins.

O Master, pardon our iniquities.

O Holy One, visit and heal our infirmities, for Thy names sake.

Lord have mercy. **(x3)**

Glory be to the Father and to the Son and to the Holy Spirit;

Both now and forever and unto the ages of ages. Amen.

Our Father, who art in heaven, hallowed be Thy name. Thy Kingdom come. Thy will be done, on earth as it is in heaven. Give us this day our daily bread; and forgive us our trespasses, as we forgive those who trespass against us; and lead us not into temptation, but deliver us from the evil one.

[**Priest:** For Thine is the kingdom, the power and the glory, of the Father, the Son and the Holy Spirit, both now and for ever, and unto the ages of ages.]

People: *Amen.*

Lord have mercy. **(x12)**

Glory be to the Father and to the Son and to the Holy Spirit;

Both now and forever and unto the ages of ages. Amen.

Come, let us worship God, our King.

Come, let us worship and fall down before Christ, our King and our God.

Come, let us worship and fall down before Christ Himself, our King and our God.

[Monday, Thursday, Sunday] **Psalm 83**

How beloved are Thy dwellings, O Lord of Hosts; my soul longeth and fainteth for the courts of the Lord. My heart and my flesh have rejoiced in the living God. For the sparrow hath found herself a house, and the turtle dove a nest for herself where she may lay her young, even in Thine altars, O Lord of Hosts, my King and my God. Blessed are they that dwell in Thy house; unto ages of ages shall they praise Thee. Blessed is the man whose help is from Thee; he hath made ascents in his heart, in the vale of weeping, in the place which he hath appointed. Yea, for the lawgiver shall give blessings; they shall go from strength to strength, the God of Gods shall be seen in Zion. O Lord of Hosts, hearken unto my prayer; give ear, O God of Jacob. O God, our defender, behold, and look upon the face of Thine anointed one. For better is one day in Thy court than thousands elsewhere. I have chosen rather to be an outcast in the house of my God than to dwell in the tents of sinners. For the Lord loveth mercy and truth, God shall give grace and glory; the Lord shall not withhold good things from them that walk in innocence. O Lord God of Hosts, blessed is the man that hopeth in Thee.

[Tuesday, Friday, Sunday] **Psalm 84**

Thou hast been gracious, O Lord, unto Thy land; Thou hast turned back the captivity of Jacob. Thou hast forgiven the iniquities of Thy people, Thou hast covered all their sins. Thou hast made all Thy wrath to cease, Thou hast turned back from the wrath of Thine anger. Turn us back, O God of our salvation, and turn away Thine anger from us. Wilt Thou be wroth with us unto the ages? Or wilt Thou draw out Thy wrath from generation to generation? O God, Thou wilt turn and quicken us, and Thy people shall be glad in Thee. Show us, O Lord, Thy mercy, and Thy salvation do Thou give unto us. I shall hear what the Lord God shall speak in me; for He shall speak to His people and to His saints and to them that turn their heart unto Him. Surely nigh unto them that fear Him is His salvation, that glory may dwell in our land. Mercy and truth are met together, righteousness and peace have kissed each other. Truth is sprung up out of the earth, and righteousness hath looked down from heaven. Yea, for the Lord shall give goodness, and our land shall yield her fruit. Righteousness shall go before him and shall set his footsteps in the way.

[Wednesday, Saturday, Sunday] **Psalm 85**

Bow down Thine ear, O Lord, and hearken unto me, for poor and needy am I. Preserve my soul, for I am holy; save Thy servant, O my God, that hopeth in Thee. Have mercy on me, O Lord, for unto Thee shall I cry all the day long; make glad the soul of Thy servant, for unto Thee have I lifted up my soul. For Thou, O Lord, art good and gentle, and plenteous in mercy unto all them that call upon Thee. Give ear, O Lord, unto my prayer, and attend unto the voice of my supplication. In the day of mine affliction have I cried unto Thee, for Thou hast heard me. There is none like unto Thee among the gods, O Lord, nor are there any works like unto Thy works. All the nations whom Thou hast made shall worship before Thee, O Lord, and shall glorify Thy name. For Thou art great and workest wonders; Thou alone art God. Guide me, O Lord, in Thy way, and I shall walk in Thy truth; let my heart rejoice that I may fear Thy name. I shall confess Thee, O Lord my God, with all my heart, and I shall glorify Thy name forever. For great is Thy mercy upon me, and Thou hast delivered my soul from the nethermost hades. O God, transgressors have risen up against me, and the assembly of the mighty hath sought after my soul, and they have not set Thee before them. But Thou, O Lord my God, art compassionate and merciful, long suffering and plenteous in mercy, and true. Look upon me and have mercy upon me; give Thy strength unto Thy servant, and save the son of Thy handmaiden. Work in me a sign unto good, and let them that hate me behold and be put to shame; for Thou, O Lord, hast helped me and comforted me.

After The Psalm

Glory be to the Father, and to the Son, and to the Holy Spirit;
Both now and forever, and unto the ages of ages. Amen.
Halleluiah, Halleluiah, Halleluiah. Glory to Thee, O God. **(x3)**
Lord, have mercy. **(x3)**

If there are two troparia, we say the first one here. If not, we continue:
Glory be to the Father, and to the Son, and to the Holy Spirit;
And we say the second troparion, if any, or the only troparion. Then:
Both now and forever, and unto the ages of ages. Amen.

Theotokion

O Thou Who for our sake wast born of a Virgin, and didst suffer crucifixion, O Good One, and didst despoil death by death, and, as God, didst reveal the resurrection: Disdain not them which Thou hast fashioned with Thine hand; show forth Thy love for mankind, O Merciful One; accept the Theotokos who gave Thee birth, who intercedeth for us; and do Thou, our Saviour, save a despairing people.

Psalm Verse

Do not forsake us utterly, for Thy Names sake, and do not destroy Thy covenant; and do not take Thy mercies from us, for the sake of Abraham whom Thou loved, and for the sake of Isaac, Thy servant, and of Israel, Thy holy one.

Holy God, Holy Mighty, Holy Immortal, have mercy on us. **(x3)**

Glory be to the Father and to the Son and to the Holy Spirit;
Both now and forever and unto the ages of ages. Amen.

O Most Holy Trinity, have mercy on us.
O Lord, cleanse us from our sins.
O Master, pardon our iniquities.
O Holy One, visit and heal our infirmities, for Thy names sake.

Lord have mercy. **(x3)**
Glory be to the Father and to the Son and to the Holy Spirit;

Both now and forever and unto the ages of ages. Amen.

Our Father, who art in heaven, hallowed be Thy name. Thy Kingdom come. Thy will be done, on earth as it is in heaven. Give us this day our daily bread; and forgive us our trespasses, as we forgive those who trespass against us; and lead us not into temptation, but deliver us from the evil one.

[Priest: For Thine is the kingdom, the power and the glory, of the Father, the Son and the Holy Spirit, both now and for ever, and unto the ages of ages.]

People: Amen.

O Lord, Jesus Christ, Son of God, have mercy on us and save us. Amen.

[Sunday] **Kontakion Of The Resurrection**

Tone 8 Humility, tranquillity, repose, suffering, pleading.   *C, D, Eb, F, G, A, Bb, C.*

When Thou went down to death, O immortal life, then Thou slewest Hell with the lightning flash of Thy Godhead; but when from the depths below the earth Thou raised the dead, O Christ God, proclaiming *"Rejoice"* to the myrrh bearing women, granting peace to Thine apostles and bestowing resurrection to the fallen.

[Monday] **Kontakion Of St Michael And All The Angels**

Tone 2 Majesty, gentleness, hope, repentance and sadness.   *E, F, G, Ab, B, C.*

You Princes and Leaders of the armies of God, Servants of the Divine Glory and guides of men. Ask whatever is good for us and for bountiful mercy, O Commanders of Sabaoth.

[Tuesday] **Kontakion Of The Forerunner And Baptist John**

Tone 2 Majesty, gentleness, hope, repentance and sadness.   *E, F, G, Ab, B, C.*

O Prophet of God and Forerunner of Grace, thine head has blossomed from the earth as a most sacred rose. We are ever being healed, for as of old, thou preachest repentance to the world.

[Wednesday] **Kontakion Of The Holy And Life Giving Cross**

Tone 4 Festive, joyous and expressing deep piety.   *C, D, Eb, F, G, A, Bb, C.*

As Thou wast voluntarily crucified for our sake, grant mercy to those who are called by Thy Name. Make all Orthodox Christians glad by Thy power, granting them victories over their adversaries, by bestowing on them the invincible trophy, Thy weapon of peace.

[Thursday] **Kontakion Of The Holy Apostles And St Nicholas**

Tone 3 Arrogant, brave, and mature atmosphere.   *F, G, A, A#, C, D, E, F.*

Thou hast taken, O Lord, the firm and divinely inspired preachers, the holy apostles into rest and the enjoyment of Thy blessings. For Thou hast accepted their labours and death above every burned offering. O Thou Who alone knows the secrets of our hearts.

[Friday] **Kontakion Of The Holy And Life Giving Cross**

Tone 4   Festive, joyous and expressing deep piety.   *C, D, Eb, F, G, A, Bb, C.*

As Thou wast voluntarily crucified for our sake, grant mercy to those who are called by Thy Name. Make all Orthodox Christians glad by Thy power, granting them victories over their adversaries, by bestowing on them the invincible trophy, Thy weapon of peace.

[Saturday]   **Kontakion Of The Theotokos, The Saints & The Faithful Departed**

Tone 2   Majesty, gentleness, hope, repentance and sadness.   *E, F, G, Ab, B, C.*

With the saints give rest, O Christ, to the souls of Thy servants, where sickness and sorrow are no more. Neither sighing, but life everlasting.

Lord, have mercy. **(x40)**

The Prayer Of The Hours

At all times and in every hour, Thou art worshipped and glorified in heaven and on earth, Christ our God. Long in patience, great in mercy and compassion, Thou lovest the righteous and showest mercy to sinners. Thou callest all to salvation through the promise of good things to come. Lord, receive our prayers at the present time. Dircot our livoc according to Thy commandments. Sanctify our souls. Purify our bodies. Set our minds aright. Cleanse our thoughts, and deliver us from all sorrow, evil and distress. Surround us with Thy holy angels, that, guarded and guided by their host, we may arrive at the unity of the faith and the understanding of Thine ineffable glory. For Thou art blessed unto the ages of ages. Amen.

The Prayer Of The Ninth Hour

Do not forsake us utterly, for Thy Names sake, and do not destroy Thy covenant; and do not take Thy mercies from us, for the sake of Abraham whom Thou loved, and for the sake of Isaac, Thy servant, and of Israel, Thy holy one.

The Prayer Of The Ninth Hour By St Basil The Great

O Master, Lord Jesus Christ our God, Who art long suffering in the face of our transgressions, and Who hast brought us even unto this present hour, wherein Thou didst hang upon the life giving tree, and didst make a way into paradise for the wise thief, and by death didst destroy death: Be gracious unto us sinners and Thine unworthy servants; for we have sinned and committed iniquity, and are not worthy to lift up our eyes and behold the height of heaven, for we have abandoned the way of Thy righteousness, and have walked in the desires of our hearts. But we beseech Thy boundless goodness: Spare us, O Lord, according to the multitude of Thy mercy and save us for Thy holy names sake; for our days were consumed in vanity. Rescue us from the hand of the adversary, and forgive us our sins, and mortify our carnal mind; that, putting aside the old man, we may be clad with the new, and live for Thee, our Master and Benefactor; and that thus by following in Thy commandments, we may attain to rest everlasting, wherein is the dwelling place of all them that rejoice. For Thou art indeed the true joy and gladness of them that love Thee, O Christ our God, and unto Thee we send up glory, with Thine Father Who has no beginning, and Thy Most holy and good and life creating Spirit, now and ever, and unto the ages of ages. Amen.

Dismissal

[with a Priest]

Priest: Glory to you, Christ God, our hope, glory to you.

Reader: *Glory be to the Father, and to the Son, and to the Holy Spirit;*

Both now and forever, and unto the ages of ages. Amen.

Lord, have mercy. **(x3)**

People: *Holy Father, bless.*

Priest: May God take pity on us and bless us; show the light of His countenance on us and have mercy on us.

People: *Amen.*

Priest: Christ, the true light, who enlightenest and hallowest everyone who comest into the world, may the light of Thy countenance be signed upon us, that in it we may see Thine unapproachable light; and direct our steps to the doing of Thy commandments; at the intercessions of Thy most pure Mother and of all Thy Saints.

People: *Amen.*

Priest: May Christ our true God, at the prayers of His most pure and spotless Mother; of the holy, glorious and all praised Apostles; of the holy, glorious and triumphant Martyrs; of our venerable and God bearing Fathers; of Saint *N [patron]*; *[of Saints N & N, whose memory we celebrate;]* of the holy and righteous forebears of God, Joachim and Anna, and of all the Saints, have mercy and save us, for He is good and lovest mankind.

People: *Amen.*

[without a Priest]

Lord, have mercy. **(x3)**

Glory be to the Father and to the Son and to the Holy Spirit;

Both now and forever and unto the ages of ages. Amen.

Greater in honour than the Cherubim and beyond compare more glorious than the Seraphim; without corruption thou gavest birth to God the Word, truly the Theotokos, we magnify thee.

Through the prayers of our holy fathers, O Lord Jesus Christ our God, have mercy on us and save us. Amen.

O Lord Jesus Christ, Son of God, for the sake of the prayers of Thy most pure Mother, our holy and God bearing fathers, and of all the saints, have mercy on us and save us, for Thou art good and the Lover of mankind. Amen.

[After each Hour during Lent and the first day of the Lesser Fasts.]

Come, let us worship God, our King.

Come, let us worship and fall down before Christ, our King and our God.

Come, let us worship and fall down before Christ Himself, our King and our God.

[Monday, Thursday, Sunday] **Psalm 112**

Halleluiah. Praise the Lord, O servants; praise the name of the Lord. May the name of the Lord be blessed from now on and forever more. From the suns rising to its setting, praise the name of the Lord! High is the Lord to all nations; to the heavens is his glory. Who is like the Lord our God, who resides on high, and looks upon that which is lowly in the sky and on the earth? It is He who raises a poor one from the ground, and from a rubbish heap He lifts a needy one, to make him sit with rulers, with rulers of His people. It is He who establishes a barren one in a home, a gladdened mother of children.

[Tuesday, Friday, Sunday] **Psalm 137**

I shall acknowledge Thee, O Lord, with my whole heart, because Thou heard the words of my mouth, and before angels I shall make music to Thee. I shall do obeisance toward Thy holy shrine and acknowledge Thy name for Thy mercy and for Thy truth, because Thou magnified Thy saying upon every name. In the day I call upon Thee, hearken to me quickly; Thou wilt care for me with power in my soul. Let all the kings of the earth acknowledge Thee, O Lord, because they heard all the words of Thy mouth. And let them sing in the ways of the Lord, because great is the glory of the Lord, because the Lord is high and he regards things that are lowly and things that are high He perceives from far away. If I walk in the midst of affliction, Thou wilt quicken me; against wrath of mine enemies Thou stretched out Thy hand, and Thy right hand saved me. The Lord shall repay on my behalf; O Lord, Thy mercy is forever. The works of Thy hands do not disregard.

[Wednesday, Saturday, Sunday] **Psalm 139**

Deliver me, O Lord, from an evil person; from an unjust man rescue me, whoever schemed acts of injustice in their heart; all day long they kept waging wars. They made their tongue sharp as a snakes; venom of vipers is under their lips. Guard me, O Lord, from a sinners hand; from unjust people deliver me - whoever schemed to trip up my steps. Arrogant ones hid a trap for me, and they stretched cords, traps for my feet; close to a path they set an obstacle for me. I said to the Lord, *"Thou art my God; give ear, O Lord, to the voice of my petition."* O Lord, Lord, power of my deliverance, Thou shaded my head in a day of battle. Do not hand me over, O Lord, to a sinner due to my desire; they schemed against me; do not abandon me, that they not be exalted. The head of their encirclement - mischief of their lips shall cover them. Coals shall fall on them; with fire Thou wilt throw them down; in misery they shall not bear up. A garrulous man shall not succeed in the land; evil shall hunt down an unjust man to corruption. I knew that the Lord would maintain the cause of the poor one and the case of the needy. But the righteous shall acknowledge Thy name, and the upright shall live together with Thy presence.

After The Psalm

Glory be to the Father, and to the Son, and to the Holy Spirit;
Both now and forever, and unto the ages of ages. Amen.

Halleluiah, Halleluiah, Halleluiah. Glory to Thee, O God. **(x3)**
Lord, have mercy. **(x3)**

Holy God, Holy Mighty, Holy Immortal, have mercy on us. **(x3)**

Glory be to the Father, and to the Son, and to the Holy Spirit;
Both now and forever, and unto the ages of ages. Amen.

O Most Holy Trinity, have mercy on us.
O Lord, cleanse us from our sins.
O Master, pardon our iniquities.
O Holy One, visit and heal our infirmities, for Thy names sake.

Lord have mercy. **(x3)**

Glory be to the Father, and to the Son, and to the Holy Spirit;
Both now and forever, and unto the ages of ages. Amen.

Our Father, who art in heaven, hallowed be Thy name. Thy Kingdom come. Thy will be done, on earth as it is in heaven. Give us this day our daily bread; and forgive us our trespasses, as we forgive those who trespass against us; and lead us not into temptation, but deliver us from the evil one.

O Lord, Jesus Christ, Son of God, have mercy on us and save us. Amen.

[Sunday]   **Kontakion Of The Resurrection**

    Tone 8   *Humility, tranquillity, repose, suffering, pleading.*   *C, D, Eb, F, G, A, Bb, C.*

When Thou went down to death, O immortal life, then Thou slew Hell with the lightning flash of Thy Godhead; but when from the depths below the earth Thou raised the dead, O Christ God, proclaiming 'Rejoice' to the myrrh bearing women, granting peace to Thine apostles and bestowing resurrection to the fallen.

[Monday]   **Kontakion Of St Michael And All The Angels**

    Tone 2   *Majesty, gentleness, hope, repentance and sadness.*   *E, F, G, Ab, B, C.*

You Princes and Leaders of the armies of God, Servants of the Divine Glory and guides of men. Ask whatever is good for us and for bountiful mercy, O Commanders of Sabaoth.

[Tuesday]   **Kontakion Of The Forerunner And Baptist John**

Tone 2   Majesty, gentleness, hope, repentance and sadness.   *E, F, G, Ab, B, C.*

O Prophet of God and Forerunner of Grace, thine head has blossomed from the earth as a most sacred rose. We are ever being healed, for as of old, thou preachest repentance to the world.

[Wednesday]   **Kontakion Of The Holy And Life Giving Cross**

Tone 4   Festive, joyous and expressing deep piety.   *C, D, Eb, F, G, A, Bb, C.*

As Thou wast voluntarily crucified for our sake, grant mercy to those who are called by Thy Name. Make all Orthodox Christians glad by Thy power, granting them victories over their adversaries, by bestowing on them the invincible trophy, Thy weapon of peace.

[Thursday]   **Kontakion Of The Holy Apostles And St Nicholas**

Tone 3   Arrogant, brave, and mature atmosphere.   *F, G, A, A#, C, D, E, F.*

Thou hast taken O Lord the firm and divinely inspired preachers the holy apostles into rest and the enjoyment of Thy blessings. For Thou hast accepted their labours and death above every burned offering. Thou who alone knows the secrets of our hearts.

[Friday]   **Kontakion Of The Holy And Life Giving Cross**

Tone 4   Festive, joyous and expressing deep piety.   *C, D, Eb, F, G, A, Bb, C.*

As Thou wast voluntarily crucified for our sake, grant mercy to those who are called by Thy Name. Make all Orthodox Christians glad by Thy power, granting them victories over their adversaries, by bestowing on them the invincible trophy, Thy weapon of peace.

[Saturday]   **Kontakion Of The Theotokos, The Saints And The Faithful Departed**

Tone 2   Majesty, gentleness, hope, repentance and sadness.   *E, F, G, Ab, B, C.*

With the saints give rest, O Christ, to the souls of Thy servants, where sickness and sorrow are no more. Neither sighing, but life everlasting.

Lord, have mercy. **(x40)**

The Prayer Of The Hours

At all times and in every hour, Thou art worshipped and glorified in heaven and on earth, Christ our God. Long in patience, great in mercy and compassion, Thou lovest the righteous and showest mercy to sinners. Thou callest all to salvation through the promise of good things to come. Lord, receive our prayers at the present time. Direct our lives according to Thy commandments. Sanctify our souls. Purify our bodies. Set our minds aright. Cleanse our thoughts, and deliver us from all sorrow, evil and distress. Surround us with Thy holy angels, that, guarded and guided by their host, we may arrive at the unity of the faith and the understanding of Thine ineffable glory. For Thou art blessed to the ages of ages. Amen.

Prayer Of St Ephrem The Syrian To The Most Holy Spirit

O Lord, Heavenly King, Comforter, Spirit of Truth, have compassion and mercy on Thy sinful servant and pardon mine unworthiness, and forgive me all the sins that I have humanly committed today, and not only humanly but even worse than a beast - my voluntary sins, known and unknown, from my youth and from evil suggestions, and from my brazenness, and from boredom. If I have sworn by Thy Name or blasphemed it in thought, blamed or reproached anyone, or in mine anger have detracted or slandered anyone, or grieved anyone, or if I have become angry about anything, or have told a lie, if I have slept unnecessarily, or if a beggar has come to me and I despised or neglected him, or if I have troubled my brother or quarrelled with him, or if I have condemned anyone, or have boasted, or have been proud, or lost my temper with anyone, or if when standing in prayer my mind has been distracted by the glamour of this world, or if I have had depraved thoughts or have overeaten, or have drunk excessively, or have laughed frivolously, or have thought evil, or have seen the attraction of someone and been wounded by it in my heart, or said indecent things, or made fun of my brothers sin when mine own faults are countless, or been neglectful of prayer, or have done some other wrong that I cannot remember - for I have done all this and much more - have mercy, my Lord and Creator, on me Thy wretched and unworthy servant, and absolve and forgive and deliver me in Thy goodness and love for men, so that, lustful, sinful and wretched as I am, I may lie down and sleep and rest in peace. And I shall worship, praise and glorify Thy most honourable Name, with the Father and His only begotten Son, now and ever, and for all ages. Amen.

Dismissal

Lord, have mercy. **(x3)**

Glory be to the Father, and to the Son, and to the Holy Spirit;
Both now and forever, and unto the ages of ages. Amen.

Greater in honour than the Cherubim and beyond compare more glorious than the Seraphim; without corruption thou gavest birth to God the Word, truly the Theotokos, we magnify thee.

Through the prayers of our holy fathers, O Lord Jesus Christ our God, have mercy on us and save us. Amen.

Daily Evening Services

The two main services for the end of the day are <u>Small Compline</u> and <u>Vespers</u>. Additional services are <u>Great Compline</u> and <u>Great Vespers</u>. There are seasonal variants for special occasions such as the <u>Kneeling Vespers for Pentecost</u> and others.

"Compline" is derived from "complete" referring to the completion of the day. But as there is no gap between days it is done straight after Vespers.

"Vespers" comes from "esperinos" and is about hope. The service includes Psalm 103 that is one of the seven creation stories in the Bible. The oldest Christian hymn is the Phos Ilarion, "O Gladsome Light". This is a great favourite of Orthodox Christians and many people have favourite tunes. If you don't know one, then do your best using the rules above. If there is an experienced Greek in your congregation see if they are able to teach you the one that they know.

O Gladsome Light

O Gladsome Light of the holy glory of the immortal Father; Heavenly holy, blessed Jesus Christ.

Now that we have come to the setting of the sun, and behold the Evening Light.

We praise God; Father, Son and Holy Spirit.

For meet it is at all time to worship Thee, with voices of praise;

O Son of God and Giver of Life. Therefore all the world doth glorify Thee.

Vespers starts with the church in darkness, only the Reader has a candle or small lamp to read by. When the Phos Ilarion is started all the lights in church should be switched on and candles lit. The hymn is about Christ, who brings His light to us: in the desert leading the Hebrews in exile as a column of fire, as the fire around the burning bush, as the star leading the magi to His own birth, in the Transfiguration on the top of Mount Tabor, as the eternal light or fire emanating from God that we perceive as judgement (from the book of Enoch), as the light to the world (Gospel of John), as the light that protects us from infernal darkness. Switching on all the lights serves as a reminder to us of the magnificence of Christ.

In the strictest traditions the Phos Ilarion marks the start of the new day, but in normal usage Vespers, then Compline, or one or the other is said at the end of the evening. As usual use the Priest or Readers version as appropriate.

The chanting that is done in churches is an entreaty towards God to be appeased for our sins. Whoever begs and prayerfully supplicates must have a humble and contrite manner; but to cry out manifests a manner that is audacious and irreverent. Canon LXXV of the Sixth Ecumenical Synod.

The Trisagion Prayers

Deacon: Holy Father, Bless.

Priest: Blessed is our God always, now and forever, and unto the ages of ages.

People: Amen.

Priest: O Heavenly King, Comforter, Spirit of Truth, Who art everywhere present and fillest all things, Treasury of blessings and Giver of life: Come and abide in us and cleanse us from every impurity and save our souls, O Good One.

Reader: Holy God, Holy Mighty, Holy Immortal, have mercy on us. **(x3)**

Glory be to the Father, and to the Son, and to the Holy Spirit;

Both now and forever, and unto the ages of ages. Amen.

O Most Holy Trinity, have mercy on us.

O Lord, cleanse us from our sins.

O Master, pardon our iniquities.

O Holy One, visit and heal our infirmities, for Thy names sake.

Lord have mercy. **(x3)**

Glory be to the Father and to the Son and to the Holy Spirit;

Both now and forever, and unto the ages of ages. Amen.

People: *Our Father, Who art in Heaven, hallowed be Thy Name. Thy Kingdom come, Thy will be done, on earth as it is in Heaven. Give us this day our daily bread, and forgive us our trespasses, as we forgive those who trespass against us; and lead us not into temptation, but deliver us from the evil one.*

Priest: For Thine is the Kingdom, and the power, and the glory; of the Father, and of the Son, and of the Holy Spirit, now and ever, and unto the ages of ages.

People: *Amen.*

Lord, have mercy. **(x12)**

Glory be to the Father and to the Son and to the Holy Spirit.

Both now and ever and to the ages of ages, Amen.

O come let us worship God our King.

O come let us worship and fall down before Christ our King and God.

O come let us worship and fall down before Christ Himself, our King and our God.

Glory be to the Father and to the Son and to the Holy Spirit.

Both now and ever and to the ages of ages, Amen.

Psalm 50

Have mercy on me, O God, according to Thy great mercy; and according to the multitude of Thy compassions blot out my transgression. Wash me thoroughly from mine iniquity, and cleanse me from my sin. For I acknowledge mine iniquity, and my sin is ever before me. Against Thee, Thee only have I sinned, and done evil in Thy sight, that Thou mayest be found just when Thou speakest, and victorious when Thou art judged. For behold, I was conceived in iniquity, and in sin my mother bore me. For behold, Thou hast loved truth; Thou hast made known to me the hidden and secret things of Thy wisdom. Thou shalt sprinkle me with hyssop, and I shall be made clean; Thou shalt wash me, and I shalt be whiter than snow. Make me to hear joy and gladness; that the humbled bones may rejoice. Turn Thy face away from my sins, and blot out all mine iniquities.

Create in me a clean heart, O God, and renew a steadfast spirit within me. Cast me not away from Thy presence, and take not Thy Holy Spirit from me. Restore to me the joy of Thy salvation, and establish me with Thy governing Spirit. I shall teach transgressors Thy ways, and the ungodly shall turn back to Thee. Deliver me from blood guiltiness, O God, the God of my salvation; my tongue shall joyfully declare Thy righteousness. Lord, open my lips, and my mouth shall declare Thy praise. For if Thou hadst desired sacrifice, I would give it; Thou dost not delight in burnt offerings. A sacrifice to God is a broken spirit; God shall not despise a broken and a humbled heart. Do good, O Lord, in Thy good pleasure to Zion, and let the walls of Jerusalem be builded. Then Thou shalt be pleased with a sacrifice of righteousness, with oblation and whole burned offerings. Then shall they offer bulls on Thine altar.

Psalm 69

O God, be attentive to help me; Lord, make haste to help me. Let them be ashamed and confounded who seek after my life. Let them be turned back and be ashamed who desire evil against me. Let them be turned back because of their shame who say to me: Well done! Well done! Let all those who seek you rejoice and be glad in you, O God, and let those who love your salvation say continually: Let the Lord be magnified. But as for me, I am poor and needy; O God help me. You are my help and my deliverer; Lord; do not delay.

Psalm 142

Lord, hear my prayer; in your truth give ear to my supplications; in your righteousness hear me. Enter not into judgement with your servant, for no one living is justified in your sight. For the enemy has pursued my soul; he has crushed my life to the ground. He has made me to dwell in darkness, like those that have long been dead, and my spirit within me is overwhelmed; my heart within me is distressed. I remembered the days of old, I meditated on all your works, I pondered on the creations of your hands. I stretched forth my hands to you; my soul longs for you like a thirsty land. Lord, hear me quickly; my spirit fails. Turn not your face away from me, lest I be like those who go down into the pit. Let me hear your mercy in the morning; for in you have I put my trust. Lord, teach me to know the way wherein I should walk; for I lift up my soul to you. Rescue me, Lord, from my enemies, to you have I fled for refuge. Teach me to do your will, for you are my God. Your good Spirit shall lead me on a level path. Lord, for your names sake you shall preserve my life. In your righteousness you shall bring my soul out of trouble, and in your mercy you shall utterly destroy mine enemies. And you shall destroy all those who afflict my soul, for I am your servant.

Lesser Doxology

Glory to God, Who has shown us the Light. Glory to God in the highest, and on earth, peace, good will toward men. We praise Thee. We bless Thee. We worship Thee. We glorify Thee and give thanks to Thee for Thy great glory. O Lord God, Heavenly King, God the Father Almighty. O Lord, the Only Begotten Son, Jesus Christ, and the Holy Spirit. \

O Lord God, Lamb of God, Son of the Father, Who takes away the sins of the world, have mercy on us. Thou, Who takes away the sins of the world, receive our prayer. Thou, Who sittest at the right hand of God the Father, have mercy on us. /

For Thou alone art holy, and Thou alone art Lord. Thou alone, O Lord Jesus Christ, are most high in the glory of God the Father. Amen. I shall give thanks to Thee every day and praise Thy Name forever and ever. Lord, Thou hast been our refuge from generation to generation. I said, *"Lord, have mercy on me. Heal my soul, for I have sinned against Thee."* \

Lord, I flee to Thee. Teach me to do Thy will, for Thou art my God. For with Thee is the fountain of Life, and in Thy light we shall see light. Continue Thy loving kindness to those who know Thee. Vouchsafe, O Lord, to keep us this day without sin. Blessed art Thou, O Lord, the God of our fathers, and praised and glorified is Thy Name forever. Amen. Let Thy mercy be upon us, O Lord, even as we have set our hope on Thee.

Blessed art Thou, O Master; teach me Thy statutes.

Blessed art Thou, O Lord; enlighten me with Thy commandments.

Blessed art Thou, O Holy One; make me to understand Thy precepts.

Thy mercy endures forever, O Lord. Do not despise the works of Thine hands. To Thee belongs worship, to Thee belongs praise, to Thee belongs glory: to the Father and to the Son and to the Holy Spirit, both now and forever and unto the ages of ages. Amen. \

The Symbol Of Faith

I believe in one God, Father, Almighty, Maker of heaven and earth, and of all things visible and invisible.

And in one Lord Jesus Christ, the only begotten Son of God, begotten from the Father before all ages; Light from Light, true God from true God; begotten not made; consubstantial with the Father, through Him all things were made. For our sake and for our salvation He came down from Heaven, and was incarnate from the Holy Spirit and the Virgin Mary and became man. He was crucified for us under Pontius Pilate, and suffered and was buried. He rose again on the third day in accordance with the Scriptures, and ascended into Heaven, and is seated at the right hand of the Father. He is coming again in glory to judge the living and the dead. And His kingdom shall have no end.

And in the Holy Spirit, the Lord, the Giver of life; Who proceeds from the Father; Who together with Father and Son is worshipped and glorified; Who spoke through the prophets. In One, Holy, Catholic, and Apostolic Church. I confess one baptism for the forgiveness of sins. I await the resurrection of the dead, And the life of the age to come. Amen.

[At this point a canon or akathist may be read.]

Reader: It is truly right to call you blessed, who gave birth to God, ever blessed and most pure Virgin and Mother of our God. Greater in honour than the Cherubim and beyond compare more glorious than the Seraphim; without corruption thou gavest birth to God the Word, truly the Theotokos, we magnify thee.

Troparion Of The Patron Saint Of The Church

[Sunday to Friday:] **Troparion Of St Martin** *(if your church is to St Martin)*

Tone 4   *Festive, joyous and expressing deep piety.*   C, D, Eb, F, G, A, Bb, C.

In signs and in miracles you were renowned throughout Gaul. By grace and adoption you are a light for the world, O Martin, blessed of God. Alms deeds and compassion filled your life with their splendours, Teaching and wise counsel were your riches and treasures, Which you dispense freely to those who honour you.

[Saturday:] **Troparion Of The Resurrection**

Tone 6   *Rich texture, funeral character, sorrowful tone.*   D, Eb, F##, G, A, Bb, C##, D.

When Mary stood at your grave looking for your sacred body, angelic powers shone above your revered tomb, and the soldiers who were to keep guard became as dead men. You led hades captive and were not tempted thereby. You did meet the Virgin and did give life to the world. You who are risen from the dead, O Lord, glory to You.

[Sunday:] **To The Angels**

Supreme Commanders of the Heavenly Hosts, we unworthy ones implore you that by your supplications you shall encircle us with the shelter of the wings of your immaterial glory, and guard us who fall down before you and fervently cry: Deliver us from dangers since you are the Marshals of the Hosts on high.

[Monday:] **To St John The Baptist**

The memory of the righteous is celebrated with hymns of praise, but the Lords testimony is sufficient for you, O Forerunner; for you have proved to be even more venerable than the prophets since you were granted to baptise in the running waters Him whom they proclaimed. Wherefore, having contested for the truth, you did rejoice to announce the good tidings even to those in Hades; that God has appeared in the flesh, taking away the sin of the world and granting us great mercy.

[Tuesday:] **Troparion Of The Holy And Life Giving Cross**

Tone 1   *Magnificent, happy and earthy.*   C, D, Eb, F, G, A, Bb, C.

Save, O Lord, your people, and bless your inheritance; grant to Orthodox Christians victory over their enemies; and by the power of your Cross do you preserve your commonwealth.

[Wednesday:] **To The Holy Apostles And St Nicholas**

Tone 4   *Festive, joyous and expressing deep piety.*   C, D, Eb, F, G, A, Bb, C.

O holy Apostles, intercede with the merciful God, that He grant to our souls forgiveness of offences.

Troparion Of The Holy And Life Giving Cross

Tone 1   Magnificent, happy and earthy.   *C, D, Eb, F, G, A, Bb, C.*

O Lord, save Thy people and bless Thine inheritance. Grant victories to the Orthodox Christians over their adversaries. And by virtue of Thy Cross, preserve Thine commonwealth.

[Sunday to Thursday:]

God of our fathers, you always treat us with leniency. Do not withdraw your mercy from us, but by the intercessions of our fathers, guide our life in peace.

With the blood of your martyrs throughout all the world, as if with purple and fine linen having been adorned, your Church, through them, cries out to you, Christ our God. Send down your mercies upon your people; grant peace to your commonwealth, and to our souls your great compassion.

Glory be to the Father, and to the Son, and to the Holy Spirit.

With your saints, O Christ, give rest to the souls of your servants, where there is no pain, nor sorrow, nor suffering, but life everlasting.

Both now and forever, and unto the ages of ages. Amen.

Through the intercessions of all your saints and the Theotokos, O Lord, grant us your peace, and have mercy upon us, only merciful one.

[Friday:]

O Apostles, Martyrs, and Prophets, Venerable and Righteous Ones; you that have accomplished a good work and kept the Faith, that have boldness before the Saviour; O Good Ones, intercede for us, we pray, that our souls be saved.

Glory be to the Father and to the Son, and to the Holy Spirit.

With your saints, O Christ, give rest to the souls of your servants, where there is no pain, nor sorrow, nor suffering, but life everlasting.

Both now and forever, and unto the ages of ages. Amen.

To you, O Lord, the Planter of creation, the world does offer the God bearing martyrs as the first fruits of nature. By their intercessions and through the Theotokos, preserve your Church, your commonwealth, in profound peace, O greatly merciful One.

[Sunday to Friday:]   **Kontakion Of The Resurrection**

Tone 2   Majesty, gentleness, hope, repentance and sadness.   *E, F, G, Ab, B, C.*

When you went down to death, O immortal life, then you slew Hell with the lightning flash of your Godhead; but when from the depths below the earth you raised the dead, all the Powers in the heavens cried out: Giver of life, Christ our God, glory to you.

Troparion Of The Saint Of The Day

[Omit if a feast of the Theotokos, an akathist or a great doxology:]

[From the Sunday of the Publican through Lent (except week 5);

And in the Holy Pentecost season on all days; until the Sunday of All Saints:]

Kontakion From The Pentecostarion

Tone 4   Festive, joyous and expressing deep piety.   *C, D, Eb, F, G, A, Bb, C.*

As with fine porphyry and royal purple, your Church has been adorned with your martyrs blood shed throughout all the world. She cries to you, O Christ God: "Send down your bounties on your people, grant peace to your habitation, and great mercy to our souls."

Reader: Lord, have mercy. **(x40)**

The Prayer Of The Hours

At all times and in every hour, Thou art worshipped and glorified in heaven and on earth, Christ our God. Long in patience, great in mercy and compassion, Thou lovest the righteous and showest mercy to sinners. Thou callest all to salvation through the promise of good things to come. Lord, receive our prayers at the present time. Direct our lives according to Thy commandments. Sanctify our souls. Purify our bodies. Set our minds aright. Cleanse our thoughts, and deliver us from all sorrow, evil and distress. Surround us with Thy holy angels, that, guarded and guided by their host, we may arrive at the unity of the faith and the understanding of Thine ineffable glory. For Thou art blessed to the ages of ages. Amen.

Lord have mercy. **(x3)**

Glory be to the Father, and to the Son, and to the Holy Spirit;
Both now and forever, and unto the ages of ages. Amen.

Greater in honour than the Cherubim and beyond compare more glorious than the Seraphim; without corruption thou gavest birth to God the Word, truly the Theotokos, we magnify thee.

Holy Father bless.

Priest: Through the prayers of our holy fathers, Lord Jesus Christ our God, have mercy on us and save us.

People: Amen.

[During Great Lent:]

Prayer Of St Ephrem The Syrian To The Most Holy Spirit

Priest: O Lord, Heavenly King, Comforter, Spirit of Truth, have compassion and mercy on your sinful servant and pardon my unworthiness, and forgive me all the sins that I have humanly committed today, and not only humanly but even worse than a beast - my voluntary sins, known and unknown, from my youth and from evil suggestions, and from my brazenness, and from boredom. If I have sworn by your Name or blasphemed it in thought, blamed or reproached anyone, or in my anger have detracted or slandered anyone, or grieved anyone, or if I have become angry about anything, or have told a lie, if I have slept unnecessarily, or if a beggar has come to me and I despised or neglected him, or if I have troubled my brother or quarrelled with him, or if I have condemned anyone, or have boasted, or have been proud, or lost my temper with anyone, or if when standing in prayer my mind has been distracted by the glamour of this world, or if I have had depraved thoughts or have overeaten, or have drunk excessively, or have laughed frivolously, or have thought evil, or have seen the attraction of someone and been wounded by it in my heart, or said indecent things, or made fun of my brothers sin when my own faults are countless, or been neglectful of prayer, or have done some other wrong that I cannot remember - for I have done all this and much more - have mercy, my Lord and Creator, on me your wretched and unworthy servant, and absolve and forgive and deliver me in your goodness and love for men, so that, lustful, sinful and wretched as I am, I may lie down and sleep and rest in peace. And I shall worship, praise and glorify your most honourable Name, with the Father and His only begotten Son, now and ever, and for all ages.

People: Amen.

Supplicatory Prayer To The Most Holy Theotokos

Paul, The Monk Of The Monastery Of Evergetis.

Priest or Reader: Spotless, undefiled, immaculate, unstained, pure Virgin, Lady and Bride of God, by your wondrous conceiving you united God the Word with human beings and joined the fallen nature of our race to heavenly things. You are the only hope of the hopeless, and the help of those oppressed. You are the ready protection of those who flee to you, and the refuge of all Christians. Do not spurn me an accused sinner, though I have made myself completely useless by my shameful thoughts, words and deeds and through indolence have become a slave to the pleasures of life. But as the Mother of God who loves all people, mercifully have compassion upon me a sinner and a prodigal and receive my prayer though it be offered to you by unclean lips. Entreat your Son and our Lord and Master, using your boldness as a mother, that he may open to me the loving mercy of his goodness, overlook my numberless transgressions, turn me to repentance, and make me an acceptable doer of His commandments. Always be near me, for you are merciful, compassionate and loving. Be my ardent help and protection in this present life, defending me from the assaults of adversaries and lead me to salvation. At the hour of my death, care for my miserable soul, and drive the dark visions of evil spirits from it. On the awesome day of judgement, save me from eternal punishment and make me an inheritor of the ineffable glory of your Son, our God. May this be my lot, my Lady, all Holy Theotokos, through your intercession and protection, by the grace and love of your only begotten Son, our Lord and God and Saviour, Jesus Christ, to whom belong all glory, honour and worship, together with his eternal Father, and all holy, righteous, and life creating Spirit, both now and forever, and unto the ages of ages.

People: *Amen.*

A Prayer To Our Lord Jesus Christ

[Antiochus, The Monk Of Pandektes.]

Priest: Grant us, Master, as we depart for sleep, rest for body and soul. Protect us from the gloom of sinful sleep and from all dark pleasures of the night. Calm the impulses of passion, and quench the fiery darts of evil that are treacherously cast against us. Restrain the turbulence of our flesh and lull all our earthly and mundane thoughts. Grant to us, O God, a watchful mind, prudent reason, a vigilant heart, and tranquil sleep, free from all evil dreams. Raise us up at the hour of prayer, strengthen us in your commandments, and keep unshaken within us the remembrance of your judgements. Grant us to glorify you all night long that we may praise and bless and glorify your all honourable and majestic name; of the Father and of the Son and of the Holy Spirit, both now and forever, and unto the ages of ages. Amen.

Most glorious, ever virgin, blessed Theotokos, present our prayers to your Son and our God, and plead with him, that through you, He may save our souls.

My hope is the Father, my refuge the Son, my protection the Holy Spirit: O Holy Trinity, glory to you.

Priest: Glory to Thee, O Christ our God, our hope, glory to Thee.

Reader: *Glory be to the Father, and to the Son, and to the Holy Spirit;*
Both now and forever, and unto the ages of ages. Amen.
Lord, have mercy. **(x3)**
Holy Father, bless.

Priest: May Christ our true God, through the intercessions of His most pure Mother, of our holy and God bearing fathers, and of all the saints, have mercy on us and save us, for He is good and the Lover of mankind.

People: *Amen.*

[When a priest is not present.]

The Trisagion Prayers

In the Name of the Father, and of the Son, and of the Holy Spirit. Amen.

Glory to Thee, our God, glory to Thee.

O Heavenly King, the Comforter, the Spirit of Truth; who art everywhere present and fillest all things; Treasury of blessings, and giver of life: come and abide in us, and cleanse us from every impurity, and save our souls, O Good One.

Holy God, Holy Mighty, Holy Immortal, have mercy on us. **(x3)**

> *Glory be to the Father and to the Son and to the Holy Spirit;*
> *Both now and forever, and unto the ages of ages. Amen.*

O Most Holy Trinity, have mercy on us.

O Lord, cleanse us from our sins.

O Master, pardon our iniquities.

O Holy One, visit and heal our infirmities, for Thy names sake.

Lord have mercy. **(x3)**

> *Glory be to the Father and to the Son and to the Holy Spirit;*
> *Both now and forever, and unto the ages of ages. Amen.*

Our Father, who art in heaven, hallowed be Thy name. Thy Kingdom come. Thy will be done, on earth as it is in heaven. Give us this day our daily bread; and forgive us our trespasses, as we forgive those who trespass against us; and lead us not into temptation, but deliver us from the evil one. Amen.

Lord have mercy. **(x12)**

> *Glory be to the Father and to the Son and to the Holy Spirit;*
> *Both now and forever, and unto the ages of ages. Amen.*

Come, let us worship God, our King.

Come, let us worship and fall down before Christ, our King and our God.

Come, let us worship and fall down before Christ Himself, our King and our God.

[Monday, Thursday, Sunday] **Psalm 50**

Have mercy on me, O God, according to Thy great mercy; and according to the multitude of Thy compassions blot out my transgression. Wash me thoroughly from mine iniquity, and cleanse me from my sin. For I acknowledge mine iniquity, and my sin is ever before me. Against Thee, Thee only have I sinned, and done evil in Thy sight, that Thou mayest be found just when Thou speakest, and victorious when Thou art judged. For behold, I was conceived in iniquity, and in sin my mother bore me. For behold, Thou hast loved truth; Thou hast made known to me the hidden and secret things of Thy wisdom. Thou shalt sprinkle me with hyssop, and I shall be made clean; Thou shalt wash me, and I shall be whiter than snow. Make me to hear joy and gladness; that the humbled bones may rejoice. Turn Thy face away from my sins, and blot out all mine iniquities. Create in me a clean heart, O God, and renew a steadfast spirit within me. Cast me not away from Thy presence, and take not Thy Holy Spirit from me. Restore to me the joy of Thy salvation, and establish me with Thy governing Spirit. I shall teach transgressors Thy ways, and the ungodly shall turn back to Thee. Deliver me from blood guiltiness, O God, the God of my salvation; my tongue shall joyfully declare Thy righteousness. Lord, open my lips, and my mouth shall declare Thy praise. For if Thou hadst desired sacrifice, I would give it; Thou dost not delight in burnt offerings. A sacrifice to God is a broken spirit; God shall not despise a broken and a humbled heart. Do good, O Lord, in Thy good pleasure to Zion, and let the walls of Jerusalem be builded. Then Thou shalt be pleased with a sacrifice of righteousness, with oblation and whole burned offerings. Then shall they offer bulls on Thine altar.

[Tuesday, Friday, Sunday] **Psalm 69**

O God, be attentive to help me; Lord, make haste to help me. Let them be ashamed and confounded who seek after my life. Let them be turned back and be ashamed who desire evil against me. Let them be turned back because of their shame who say to me: "Well done! Well done!" Let all those who seek Thee rejoice and be glad in Thee, O God, and let those who love Thy salvation say continually: "Let the Lord be magnified." But as for me, I am poor and needy; O God help me. Thou art my help and my deliverer; Lord; do not delay.

[Wednesday, Saturday, Sunday] **Psalm 142**

Lord, hear my prayer; in Thy truth give ear to my supplications; in Thy righteousness hear me. Enter not into judgement with Thy servant, for no one living is justified in Thy sight. For the enemy has pursued my soul; he has crushed my life to the ground. He has made me to dwell in darkness, like those that have long been dead, and my spirit within me is overwhelmed; my heart within me is distressed. I remembered the days of old, I meditated on all Thy works, I pondered on the creations of Thine hands. I stretched forth my hands to Thee; my soul longs for Thee like a thirsty land. Lord, hear me quickly; my spirit fails. Turn not Thy face away from me, lest I be like those who go down into the pit. Let me hear Thy mercy in the morning; for in Thee have I put my trust. Lord, teach me to know the way wherein I should walk; for I lift up my soul to Thee. Rescue me, Lord, from mine enemies, to Thee have I fled for refuge. Teach me to do Thy will, for Thou art my God. Thy good Spirit shall lead me on a level path. Lord, for Thy names sake Thou shalt preserve my life. In Thy righteousness Thou shalt bring my soul out of trouble, and in Thy mercy Thou shalt utterly destroy my enemies. And Thou shalt destroy all those who afflict my soul, for I am Thy servant.

Lesser Doxology

Glory to God, Who has shown us the Light. Glory to God in the highest, and on earth, peace, good will toward men. We praise Thee. We bless Thee. We worship Thee. We glorify Thee and give thanks to Thee for Thy great glory. O Lord God, Heavenly King, God the Father Almighty. O Lord, the Only Begotten Son, Jesus Christ, and the Holy Spirit. \

O Lord God, Lamb of God, Son of the Father, Who takes away the sins of the world, have mercy on us. Thou, Who takes away the sins of the world, receive our prayer. Thou, Who sittest at the right hand of God the Father, have mercy on us. /

For Thou alone art holy, and Thou alone art Lord. Thou alone, O Lord Jesus Christ, are most high in the glory of God the Father. Amen. I shall give thanks to Thee every day and praise Thy Name forever and ever. Lord, Thou hast been our refuge from generation to generation. I said, *"Lord, have mercy on me. Heal my soul, for I have sinned against Thee."* \

Lord, I flee to Thee. Teach me to do Thy will, for Thou art my God. For with Thee is the fountain of Life, and in Thy light we shall see light. Continue Thy loving kindness to those who know Thee. Vouchsafe, O Lord, to keep us this day without sin. Blessed art Thou, O Lord, the God of our fathers, and praised and glorified is Thy Name forever. Amen. Let Thy mercy be upon us, O Lord, even as we have set our hope on Thee.

Blessed art Thou, O Master; teach me Thy statutes.

Blessed art Thou, O Lord; enlighten me with Thy commandments.

Blessed art Thou, O Holy One; make me to understand Thy precepts.

Thy mercy endures forever, O Lord. Do not despise the works of Thine hands. To Thee belongs worship, to Thee belongs praise, to Thee belongs glory: to the Father and to the Son and to the Holy Spirit, both now and forever and unto the ages of ages. Amen. \

The Symbol Of Faith

I believe in one God, Father, Almighty, Maker of heaven and earth, and of all things visible and invisible.

And in one Lord Jesus Christ, the only begotten Son of God, begotten from the Father before all ages; Light from Light, true God from true God; begotten not made; consubstantial with the Father, through Him all things were made. For our sake and for our salvation He came down from Heaven, and was incarnate from the Holy Spirit and the Virgin Mary and became man. He was crucified for us under Pontius Pilate, and suffered and was buried. He rose again on the third day in accordance with the Scriptures, and ascended into Heaven, and is seated at the right hand of the Father. He is coming again in glory to judge the living and the dead. And His kingdom shall have no end.

And in the Holy Spirit, the Lord, the Giver of life; Who proceeds from the Father; Who together with Father and Son is worshipped and glorified; Who spoke through the prophets. In One, Holy, Catholic, and Apostolic Church. I confess one baptism for the forgiveness of sins. I await the resurrection of the dead, And the life of the age to come. Amen.

[Akathists may be inserted here.]

Stichera

[Sunday]   *Tone 8*   *Humility, tranquillity, repose, suffering, pleading.*   *C, D, Eb, F, G, A, Bb, C.*

Reader: Behold now, bless the Lord, all you servants of the Lord.

Stichos: You that stand in the house of the Lord, in the courts of the house of our God.

[Monday]   *Tone 4*   *Festive, joyous and expressing deep piety.*   *C, D, Eb, F, G, A, Bb, C.*

Reader: The Lord shall hearken unto me when I cry unto Him.

Stichos: When I called upon Thee, O God of my righteousness, Thou didst listen to me.

[Tuesday]   *Tone 1*   *Magnificent, happy and earthy.*   *C, D, Eb, F, G, A, Bb, C.*

Reader: Thy mercy, O Lord, shall pursue me all the days of my life.

Stichos: The Lord is my shepherd, and I shall not be in need.

         In a place of green pasture, there has He made me to dwell.

[Wednesday] *Tone 5*   *Stimulating, dancing, and rhythmical.*   *C, D, Eb, F, G, A, Bb, C.*

Reader: O God, in Thy name save me, and in Thy strength Thou judgest me.

Stichos: O God, hearken to my prayer, give ear to the words of my mouth.

[Thursday]   *Tone 6*   *Rich texture, funeral character, sorrowful tone.*   *D, Eb, F##, G, A, Bb, C##, D.*

Reader: My help comes from the Lord, who has made heaven and the earth.

Stichos: I lifted up mine eyes to the mountains, from where comes my help.

[Friday]   *Tone 7*   *Manly character and strong melody.*   *F, G, A, A#, C, D, E, F.*

Reader: O God, my helper art Thou, and Thy mercy shall go before me.

Stichos: Rescue me from mine enemies, O God. And from them that rise up against me redeem me.

[Saturday] *Tone 6*   *Rich texture, funeral character, sorrowful tone.*   *D, Eb, F##, G, A, Bb, C##, D.*

Reader: *The Lord is King, He is clothed with majesty.*

Stichos 1:   The Lord is clothed with strength and He has girded Himself.

Reader: *The Lord is King, He is clothed with majesty.*

Stichos 2:   For He established the world which shall not be shaken.

Reader: *The Lord is King, He is clothed with majesty.*

Stichos 3:   Holiness becomes Thy house, O Lord, to the length of days.

Reader: *[Archangel Gabriel:*   It is truly right to call thee blessed, who gavest birth to God, ever-blessed and God-obedient the Mother of our God.] Greater in honour than the Cherubim and beyond compare more glorious than the Seraphim; without corruption thou gavest birth to God the Word, truly the Mother of God, we magnify thee.

Holy God, Holy Mighty, Holy Immortal, have mercy on us. **(x3)**

Glory be to the Father and to the Son and to the Holy Spirit;

Both now and forever, and unto the ages of ages. Amen.

O Lord, Jesus Christ, Son of God, have mercy on us. Amen.

[Sunday to Friday]   **Troparion Of The Patron Saint [e.g. St Martin]**

Tone 4   Festive, joyous and expressing deep piety.   C, D, Eb, F, G, A, Bb, C.

In signs and in miracles thou wast renowned throughout Gaul. By grace and adoption thou art a light for the world, O Martin, blessed of God. Alms deeds and compassion filled thy life with their splendours. Teaching and wise counsel were thy riches and treasures, which thou dispense freely to those who honour thee.

The Troparion Of The Day

[Sunday]   **Troparion Of St Michael And All Angels**

Tone 4   Festive, joyous and expressing deep piety.   C, D, Eb, F, G, A, Bb, C.

O Commander of Sabaoth, we who are unworthy beseech Thee ceaselessly. That thou wouldst encompass us with the shelter of thy prayers and cover us beneath the wings of Thine immaterial glory. We fall down before Thee crying out: "Protect us from all harm, O prince of the powers on high."

[Monday]   **Troparion Of The Forerunner And Baptist John**

Tone 2   Majesty, gentleness, hope, repentance and sadness.   E, F, G, Ab, B, C.

The memory of the righteous is worthy of praise. But thou, O Forerunner, are well pleased by the Lords own witness. Thou wast revealed as greater than the prophets, For thou baptised in the waters Him whom they foretold. Therefore, having fought and suffered for the Truth, thou proclaimed to those in the tombs the Gospel of the incarnate God, Who takes away the sins of the world and grants us great mercy.

[Tuesday]   **Troparion Of The Holy And Life Giving Cross**

Tone 1   Magnificent, happy and earthy.   C, D, Eb, F, G, A, Bb, C.

O Lord, save Thy people and bless Thine inheritance. Grant victories to the Orthodox Christians over their adversaries. And by virtue of Thy Cross, preserve Thy commonwealth.

[Wednesday]   **To The Holy Apostles And St Nicholas**

Tone 4   Festive, joyous and expressing deep piety.   C, D, Eb, F, G, A, Bb, C.

O holy Apostles, intercede with our merciful God to grant our souls forgiveness of our sins.

[Thursday]   **Troparion Of The Holy And Life Giving Cross**

Tone 1   Magnificent, happy and earthy.   C, D, Eb, F, G, A, Bb, C.

O Lord, save Thy people and bless Thine inheritance. Grant victories to the Orthodox Christians over their adversaries. And by virtue of Thy Cross, preserve Thine commonwealth.

[Sunday to Thursday]

God of our fathers, Thou always treatest us with leniency. Do not withdraw Thy mercy from us, but by the intercessions of our fathers, guide our life in peace.

With the blood of Thy martyrs throughout all the world, as if with purple and fine linen having been adorned, Thy Church, through them, cries out to Thee, Christ our God. Send down Thy mercies upon Thy people; grant peace to Thy commonwealth, and to our souls Thy great compassion.

Glory be to the Father, and to the Son, and to the Holy Spirit.

With Thy saints, O Christ, give rest to the souls of Thy servants, where there is no pain, nor sorrow, nor suffering, but life everlasting.

Both now and forever, and unto the ages of ages. Amen.

Through the intercessions of all Thy saints and the Theotokos, O Lord, grant us Thy peace, and have mercy upon us, only merciful one.

[Friday]   **Troparion Of The Theotokos, All Saints And The Faithful Departed**

Tone 2   *Majesty, gentleness, hope, repentance and sadness.*   *E, F, G, Ab, B, C.*

Apostles, martyrs, and prophets, holy hierarchs, saints and the righteous. Having fought the good fight and kept the faith, You have boldness toward the Saviour. Intercede for us with Him for He is good, and pray that He may save our souls.

Glory be to the Father and to the Son, and to the Holy Spirit.

Kontakion Of The Theotokos, The Saints & The Faithful Departed

Tone 2   *Majesty, gentleness, hope, repentance and sadness.*   *E, F, G, Ab, B, C.*

With the saints give rest, O Christ, to the souls of Thy servants, where sickness and sorrow are no more. Neither sighing, but life everlasting.

Both now and forever, and unto the ages of ages. Amen.

To Thee, O Lord, the Planter of creation, the world does offer the God bearing martyrs as the first fruits of nature. By their intercessions and through the Theotokos, preserve Thy Church, Thy commonwealth in profound peace, greatly merciful One.

Kontakion Of The Resurrection

Tone 2   Majesty, gentleness, hope, repentance and sadness.   *E, F, G, Ab, B, C.*

When Thou went down to death, O immortal life, then Thou slew Hell with the lightning flash of Thy Godhead; but when from the depths below the earth Thou raised the dead, all the Powers in the heavens cried out: Giver of life, Christ our God, glory to Thee.

Troparion Of The Saint Of The Day

[From the Sunday of the Publican through Lent (except week 5);
And in the Holy Pentecost season on all days; until the Sunday of All Saints:]

Kontakion From The Pentecostarion

Tone 4   Festive, joyous and expressing deep piety.   *C, D, Eb, F, G, A, Bb, C.*

As with fine porphyry and royal purple, Thy Church has been adorned with Thy martyrs blood shed throughout all the world. She cries to Thee, O Christ God: "Send down Thy bounties on Thy people, grant peace to Thy commonwealth, and great mercy to our souls."

Reader: Lord, have mercy. **(x40)**

The Prayer Of The Hours

At all times and in every hour, Thou art worshipped and glorified in heaven and on earth, Christ our God. Long in patience, great in mercy and compassion, Thou lovest the righteous and showest mercy to sinners. Thou callest all to salvation through the promise of good things to come. Lord, receive our prayers at the present time. Direct our lives according to Thy commandments. Sanctify our souls. Purify our bodies. Set our minds aright. Cleanse our thoughts, and deliver us from all sorrow, evil and distress. Surround us with Thy holy angels, that, guarded and guided by their host, we may arrive at the unity of the faith and the understanding of Thine ineffable glory. For Thou art blessed to the ages of ages. Amen.

Lord have mercy. **(x3)**

Glory be to the Father and to the Son and to the Holy Spirit;
Both now and forever, and unto the ages of ages. Amen.

Greater in honour than the Cherubim and beyond compare more glorious than the Seraphim; without corruption thou gavest birth to God the Word, truly the Theotokos, we magnify thee.

Prayer Of St Ephrem The Syrian To The Most Holy Spirit

O Lord, Heavenly King, Comforter, Spirit of Truth, have compassion and mercy on Thy sinful servant and pardon mine unworthiness, and forgive me all the sins that I have humanly committed today, and not only humanly but even worse than a beast - my voluntary sins, known and unknown, from my youth and from evil suggestions, and from my brazenness, and from boredom. If I have sworn by Thy Name or blasphemed it in thought, blamed or reproached anyone, or in mine anger have detracted or slandered anyone, or grieved anyone, or if I have become angry about anything, or have told a lie, if I have slept unnecessarily, or if a beggar has come to me and I despised or neglected him, or if I have troubled my brother or quarrelled with him, or if I have condemned anyone, or have boasted, or have been proud, or lost my temper with anyone, or if when standing in prayer my mind has been distracted by the glamour of this world, or if I have had depraved thoughts or have overeaten, or have drunk excessively, or have laughed frivolously, or have thought evil, or have seen the attraction of someone and been wounded by it in my heart, or said indecent things, or made fun of my brothers sin when my own faults are countless, or been neglectful of prayer, or have done some other wrong that I cannot remember - for I have done all this and much more - have mercy, my Lord and Creator, on me Thy wretched and unworthy servant, and absolve and forgive and deliver me in Thy goodness and love for men, so that, lustful, sinful and wretched as I am, I may lie down and sleep and rest in peace. And I shall worship, praise and glorify Thy most honourable Name, with the Father and His only begotten Son, now and ever, and for all ages. Amen.

Supplicatory Prayer To The Most Holy Theotokos

Paul, The Monk Of The Monastery Of Evergetis.

Spotless, undefiled, immaculate, unstained, pure Virgin, Lady and Bride of God, by thy wondrous conceiving thou united God the Word with human beings and joined the fallen nature of our race to heavenly things. Thou art the only hope of the hopeless, and the help of those oppressed. Thou art the ready protection of those who flee to thee, and the refuge of all Christians. Do not spurn me an accused sinner, though I have made myself completely useless by my shameful thoughts, words and deeds and through indolence have become a slave to the pleasures of life. But as the Mother of God who loves all people, mercifully have compassion upon me a sinner and a prodigal and receive my prayer though it be offered to thee by unclean lips. Entreat thy Son and our Lord and Master, using thy boldness as a mother, that he may open to me the loving mercy of his goodness, overlook my numberless transgressions, turn me to repentance, and make me an acceptable doer of His commandments. Always be near me, for thou art merciful, compassionate and loving. Be mine ardent help and protection in this present life, defending me from the assaults of adversaries and lead me to salvation. At the hour of my death, care for my miserable soul, and drive the dark visions of evil spirits from it. On the awesome day of judgement, save me from eternal punishment and make me an inheritor of the ineffable glory of thy Son, our God. May this be my lot, my Lady, all Holy Theotokos, through thine intercession and protection, by the grace and love of thine only begotten Son, our Lord and God and Saviour, Jesus Christ, to whom belong all glory, honour and worship, together with his eternal Father, and all holy, righteous, and life creating Spirit, both now and forever, and unto the ages of ages. Amen.

A Prayer To Our Lord Jesus Christ

Antiochus, The Monk Of Pandektes.

Grant us, Master, as we depart for sleep, rest for body and soul. Protect us from the gloom of sinful sleep and from all dark pleasures of the night. Calm the impulses of passion, and quench the fiery darts of evil that are treacherously cast against us. Restrain the turbulence of our flesh and lull all our earthly and mundane thoughts. Grant to us, O God, a watchful mind, prudent reason, a vigilant heart, and tranquil sleep, free from all evil dreams. Raise us up at the hour of prayer, strengthen us in Thy commandments, and keep unshaken within us the remembrance of Thy judgements. Grant us to glorify Thee all night long that we may praise and bless and glorify Thine all honourable and majestic name; of the Father and of the Son and of the Holy Spirit, both now and forever, and unto the ages of ages. Amen.

Final Intercessions

Most glorious, ever virgin, blessed Theotokos, present our prayers to thy Son and our God, and plead with him, that through thee, He may save our souls.

Prayer Of Saint Ioannikios *(commemorated 4th November)*

My hope is the Father, my refuge the Son, my protection the Holy Spirit: O Holy Trinity, glory to Thee.

Glory be to the Father and to the Son and to the Holy Spirit;
Both now and forever, and unto the ages of ages. Amen.

Lord, have mercy. **(x3)**

My every hope I place in thee, Mother of God, keep me under thy protection.

O Lord Jesus Christ, Son of God, for the sake of the prayers of Thy most pure Mother, our holy and God bearing fathers, and of all the saints, have mercy on us and save us, for Thou art good and the Lover of mankind. Amen.

Remit, pardon, forgive, O God, our offences, both voluntary and involuntary, in deed and word, in knowledge and in ignorance, by day and by night, in mind and thought; forgive us all things, for Thou art good and the Lover of mankind. Amen.

O Lord, Lover of mankind, forgive them that hate and wrong us. Do good to them that do good. Grant our brethren and kindred their saving petitions and eternal life; visit the infirm and grant them healing. Guide those at sea. Journey with those who travel. Help Orthodox Christians in their tribulations. To those who serve and are kind to us grant remission of sins. On those who have charged us, the unworthy, to pray for them, have mercy according to Thy great mercy. Remember, Lord, our fathers and the brethren departed before us, and grant them rest where the light of Thy countenance shall shine upon them. Remember Lord, our brethren in captivity, and deliver them from every misfortune. Remember Lord, those who bear fruit and do good works in Thy holy Church and grant them their saving petitions and eternal life. Remember also Lord, us Thy lowly and sinful and unworthy servants, and enlighten our minds with the light of Thy knowledge and guide us in the way of Thy commandments; through the intercessions of our most pure Lady, the Theotokos and ever virgin Mary, and of all Thy saints, for blessed art Thou to the ages of ages. Amen.

Lord, have mercy. **(x3)**

Through the prayers of our holy fathers, Lord Jesus Christ our God, have mercy on us and save us. Amen.

[Daily and seasonal variables required.]

Trisagion Prayers

Priest: Blessed is our God, always, now and forever, and unto the ages of ages.

People: *Amen.*

Reader: Come, let us worship God, our King.

Come, let us worship and fall down before Christ, our King and our God.

Come, let us worship and fall down before Christ Himself, our King and our God.

Psalm 103

Of David. Concerning The Formation Of The World.

Bless the Lord, O my soul. O Lord my God, Thou hast been exceedingly magnified. Confession and majesty hast Thou put on, Who covered Thyself with light as with a garment, Who stretched out the heaven as it were a curtain; Who supports His chambers in the waters, Who appoints the clouds for His ascent, Who walks upon the wings of the winds, Who makes His angels spirits, and His ministers a flame of fire, Who establishes the earth in the sureness thereof; it shall not be turned back for ever and ever. The abyss like a garment is His mantle; upon the mountains shall the waters stand. At Thy rebuke they shall flee, at the voice of Thy thunder shall they be afraid.

The mountains rise up and the plains sink down to the place where Thou hast established them. Thou appointed a boundary that they shall not pass, neither return to cover the earth. He sends forth springs in the valleys; between the mountains shall the waters run. They shall give drink to all the beasts of the field; the wild asses shall wait to quench their thirst. Beside them shall the birds of the heaven lodge, from the midst of the rocks shall they give voice. He waters the mountains from His chambers; the earth shall be satisfied with the fruit of Thy works.

He causes the grass to grow for the cattle, and green herb for the service of men, To bring forth bread out of the earth; and wine makes glad the heart of man. To make his face cheerful with oil; and bread strengthens mans heart. The trees of the plain shall be satisfied, the cedars of Lebanon, which Thou hast planted. There shall the sparrows make their nests; the house of the heron is chief among them. The high mountains are a refuge for the harts, and so is the rock for the hares. He has made the moon for seasons; the sun knows his going down. Thou appointed the darkness, and there was the night, wherein all the beasts of the forest shall go abroad. Young lions roaring after their prey, and seeking their food from God. The sun arises, and they are gathered together, and they lay them down in their dens.

But man shall go forth unto his work, and to his labour until the evening. How magnified are Thy works, O Lord. In wisdom hast Thou made them all; the earth is filled with Thy creation. So is this great and spacious sea, therein are things creeping innumerable, small living creatures with the great. There go the ships; there this dragon, whom Thou hast made to play therein. All things wait on Thee, to give them their food in due season; when Thou gavest it to them, they shall gather it. When Thou opened Thy hand, all things shall be filled with goodness; when Thou turned away Thy face, they shall be troubled. Thou wilt take their spirit, and they shall cease; and to their dust shall they return. Thou wilt send forth Thy Spirit, and they shall be created; and Thou shalt renew the face of the earth.

Let the glory of the Lord be unto the ages; the Lord shall rejoice in His works. Who looks on the earth and makes it tremble, Who touches the mountains and they smoke. I shall sing unto the Lord throughout my life, I shall chant to my God for as long as I have my being. May my words be sweet unto Him, and I shall rejoice in the Lord. O that sinners would cease from the earth, and they that work iniquity, that they should be no more. Bless the Lord, O my soul. The sun knows his going down, Thou appointed the darkness, and there was the night. How magnified are Thy works, O Lord. In wisdom hast Thou made them all.

After The Psalm

Glory be to the Father and to the Son and to the Holy Spirit;
Both now and forever, and unto the ages of ages. Amen.
Halleluiah, Halleluiah, Halleluiah. Glory to Thee, O God. **(x3)**
O our God and our Hope, glory to Thee.

The Great Litany

Deacon: In peace, let us pray to the Lord.

People: *Lord, have mercy.*

Deacon: For the peace from above, and for the salvation of our souls, let us pray to the Lord.

People: *Lord, have mercy.*

Deacon: For the peace of the whole world, for the good estate of the holy churches of God, and for the union of all men, let us pray to the Lord.

People: *Lord, have mercy.*

Deacon: For this Holy House, and for those who with faith, reverence, and fear of God, enter therein, let us pray to the Lord.

People: *Lord, have mercy.*

Deacon: For our father and Archbishop Nikitas, for the venerable Priesthood, the Diaconate in Christ, for all the clergy and the people, let us pray to the Lord.

People: *Lord, have mercy.*

Deacon: For Her Majesty, the Queen, for the First Minister, for all civil authorities, and for our Armed Forces, let us pray to the Lord.

People: *Lord, have mercy.*

Deacon: That He shall aid them and grant them victory over every enemy and adversary, let us pray to the Lord.

People: *Lord, have mercy.*

Deacon: For this city, and for every city and land, and for the faithful who dwell therein, let us pray to the Lord.

People: *Lord, have mercy.*

Deacon: For healthful seasons, for abundance of the fruits of the earth, and for peaceful times, let us pray to the Lord.

People: *Lord, have mercy.*

Deacon: For travellers by sea, by land, and by air; for the sick and the suffering; for captives and their salvation, let us pray to the Lord.

People: *Lord, have mercy.*

Deacon: For our deliverance from all tribulation, wrath, danger, and necessity, let us pray to the Lord.

People: *Lord, have mercy.*

Deacon: Help us; save us; have mercy on us; and keep us, O God, by Thy grace.

People: *Lord, have mercy.*

Deacon: Calling to remembrance our all holy, immaculate, most blessed and glorious Lady Theotokos and ever virgin Mary, with all the Saints: let us commend ourselves and each other, and all our life unto Christ our God.

People: *To Thee, O Lord.*

Priest: For to Thou art due all glory, honour, and worship: to the Father, and to the Son, and to the Holy Spirit; Both now and forever and unto the ages of ages.

People: *Amen.*

Psalm 140

Chorus: Lord, I have cried to Thee: hear me. Hear me, O Lord.

Lord, I have cried to Thee: hear me. Receive the voice of my prayer.

When I call upon Thee, hear me, O Lord. Let my prayer arise as incense in Thy sight,

And let the lifting up of my hands be an evening sacrifice. Hear me, O Lord.

Kekragarion
Sticheroi From Psalm 140

• Set, O Lord, a watch before my mouth, and a door of enclosure round about my lips.

• Incline not my heart to words of evil, to make excuses for sins.

• Those that work iniquity; I shall not join with their number.

• The righteous man shall chasten me with mercy and reprove me; as for the oil of the sinner, let it not anoint my head.

• For yet more is my prayer in the presence of their pleasures; their judges have been swallowed up by the rock.

• They shall hear my words, for they be sweetened; as a clod of earth is broken upon the earth, so have their bones been scattered into hades.

• To Thee O Lord are mine eyes. In Thee have I hoped; take not my soul away.

• Keep me from the snare which they have laid for me, and from the stumbling blocks of them that work iniquity.

• The sinners shall fall into their own net; I am alone until I pass by.

Sticheroi From Psalm 141

- With my voice to the Lord have I cried, with my voice have I made supplication.

- I shall pour out before Him my supplications; my afflictions shall I declare before Him.

- When my spirit was fainting within me, then Thou knewest my paths.

- In this way wherein I have walked they hid for me a snare.

- I looked on my right hand, and beheld, and there was none that knew me.

- Flight has failed me, and there is none that watches out for my soul.

- I cried to Thee, O Lord; I said: Thou art my hope, my portion in the land of the living.

- Attend unto my supplication, for I am brought very low.

- Deliver me from them that persecute me, for they are stronger than I.

- 10. Bring my soul out of prison. That I may confess Thy name.

[daily or seasonal Troparia]

- 9.   The righteous shall patiently wait for me until Thou shalt reward me.

[daily or seasonal Troparia]

Sticheroi From Psalm 129

- 8   Out of the depths have I cried unto Thee, O Lord. O Lord, hear my voice.

[daily or seasonal Troparia]

- 7.   Let Thine ears be attentive to the voice of my supplication.

[daily or seasonal Troparia]

- 6.   If Thou should mark iniquities, O Lord; O Lord, who shall stand? For with Thee there is forgiveness.

[daily or seasonal Troparia]

- 5.   For Thy names sake have I patiently waited for Thee, O Lord; my soul has patiently waited for Thy word, my soul has hoped in the Lord.

[daily or seasonal Troparia]

- 4.   From the morning watch until night, from the morning watch let Israel hope in the Lord.

[daily or seasonal Troparia]

- 3.   For with the Lord there is mercy, and with Him is plenteous redemption; and He shall redeem Israel out of all his iniquities.

[daily or seasonal Troparia]

Sticheroi From Psalm 116

- 2.   O praise the Lord, all you nations; praise Him, all you peoples.

[daily or seasonal Troparia]

- 1.   For He has made His mercy to prevail over us, and the truth of the Lord abides forever.

[daily or seasonal Troparia]

Glory be to the Father and to the Son and to the Holy Spirit.

[Doxasticon – if available]

Both now and forever, and unto the ages of ages. Amen.

Theotokion

Tone 8   Humility, tranquillity, repose, suffering, pleading.   *C, D, Eb, F, G, A, Bb, C.*

Verily, the King of Heaven, for His love to mankind, didst appear on earth; and with men did He deal; for He took unto Himself a body from the pure Virgin. And from her did He issue in the adopted body, He being one Son, dual in Nature, not dual in Person. Wherefore, do we confess, preaching the truth that Christ our God is perfect God and perfect Man. Therefore, O Mother who hast no groom, beseech Him to have mercy upon our souls.

O Gladsome Light

O Gladsome Light of the holy glory of the immortal Father; Heavenly holy, blessed Jesus Christ.

Now that we have come to the setting of the sun, and behold the Evening Light.

We praise God; Father, Son and Holy Spirit.

For meet it is at all time to worship Thee, with voices of praise;

O Son of God and Giver of Life. Therefore all the world doth glorify Thee.

Prokeimenon

Priest: Peace be with you all.

People: *And with thy spirit.*

Priest: Wisdom! The Evening Prokeimenon.

[Sunday]   *Tone 8   Humility, tranquillity, repose, suffering, pleading.*   *C, D, Eb, F, G, A, Bb, C.*

Reader: Behold now, bless the Lord, all you servants of the Lord.

People: *Behold now, bless the Lord, all you servants of the Lord.*

Reader: You that stand in the house of the Lord, in the courts of the house of our God.

People: *Behold now, bless the Lord, all you servants of the Lord.*

Reader: Behold now, bless the Lord | *all you servants of the Lord.*

[Monday]   *Tone 4   Festive, joyous and expressing deep piety.*   *C, D, Eb, F, G, A, Bb, C.*

Reader: The Lord shall hearken unto me when I cry unto Him.

People: *The Lord shall hearken unto me when I cry unto Him.*

Reader: When I called upon Thee, O God of my righteousness; Thou didst hearken unto me.

People: *The Lord shall hearken unto me when I cry unto Him.*

Reader: The Lord shall hearken unto me | *when I cry unto Him.*

[Tuesday]   Tone 1   *Magnificent, happy and earthy.*   C, D, Eb, F, G, A, Bb, C.

Reader: Thy mercy, O Lord, shall pursue me all the days of my life.

People: *Thy mercy, O Lord, shall pursue me all the days of my life.*

Reader: The Lord is my shepherd, and I shall not want.

                    In a place of green pasture, there has He made me to dwell.

People: *Thy mercy, O Lord, shall pursue me all the days of my life.*

Reader: Thy mercy, O Lord | *shall pursue me all the days of my life.*

[Wednesday]   Tone 5 *Stimulating, dancing, and rhythmical.*   C, D, Eb, F, G, A, Bb, C.

Reader: O God, in Thy name save me, and in Thy strength Thou judgest me.

People: *O God, in Thy name save me, and in Thy strength Thou judgest me.*

Reader: O God, hearken to my prayer, give ear to the words of my mouth.

People: *O God, in Thy name save me, and in Thy strength Thou judgest me.*

Reader: O God, in Thy name save me | *and in Thy strength Thou judgest me.*

[Thursday]   Tone 6   *Rich texture, funeral, sorrowful.*   D, Eb, F##, G, A, Bb, C##, D.

Reader: My help comes from the Lord, who has made the heaven and the earth.

People: *My help comes from the Lord, who has made the heaven and the earth.*

Reader: I lifted up my eyes to the mountains from where comes my help.

People: *My help comes from the Lord, who has made the heaven and the earth.*

Reader: My help comes from the Lord | *who has made the heaven and the earth.*

[Friday]   Tone 7   *Manly character and strong melody.*   F, G, A, A#, C, D, E, F.

Reader: O God, my helper art Thou, and Thy mercy shall go before me.

People: *O God, my helper art Thou, and Thy mercy shall go before me.*

Reader: Rescue me from mine enemies, O God; and from them that rise up against me redeem me.

People: *O God, my helper art Thou, and Thy mercy shall go before me.*

Reader: O God, my helper art Thou | *and Thy mercy shall go before me.*

[Saturday]   Tone 6   *Rich texture, funeral, sorrowful.*   D, Eb, F##, G, A, Bb, C##, D.

Reader: The Lord is clothed with strength and He has girded Himself.

People: *The Lord is King, He is clothed with majesty.*

Reader: For He established the world which shall not be shaken.

People: *The Lord is King, He is clothed with majesty.*

Reader: Holiness becomes Thine house, O Lord, to the length of days.

People: *The Lord is King, He is clothed with majesty.*

Reader: The Lord is King | *He is clothed with majesty.*

Reader: Vouchsafe, O Lord, to keep us this evening without sin. Blessed art Thou, O Lord, the God of our fathers, and praised and glorified is Thy name unto the ages. Amen.

Let Thy mercy, O Lord, be upon us, according as we have hoped in Thee.

Blessed art Thou, O Lord, teach me Thy statutes.
Blessed art Thou, O Master, give me understanding of Thy statutes.
Blessed art Thou, O Holy One, enlighten me by Thy statutes.

O Lord, Thy mercy endures forever; disdain not the work of Thy hands. To Thee is due praise, to Thee is due song, to Thee is due glory, to the Father, and to the Son, and to the Holy Spirit; both now and forever, and unto the ages of ages. Amen.

The Litany Of Supplication

Deacon: Let us complete our evening prayer unto the Lord.

People: *Lord, have mercy.*

Deacon: Help us; save us; have mercy on us; and keep us, O God, by Thy grace.

People: *Lord, have mercy.*

Deacon: That the whole evening may be perfect, holy, peaceful and sinless, let us ask of the Lord.

People: *Grant this, O Lord.*

Deacon: An angel of peace, a faithful guide, a guardian of our souls and bodies, let us ask of the Lord.

People: *Grant this, O Lord.*

Deacon: Pardon and remission of our sins and transgressions, let us ask of the Lord.

People: *Grant this, O Lord.*

Deacon: All things good and profitable for our souls and peace for the world, let us ask of the Lord.

People: *Grant this, O Lord.*

Deacon: That we may complete the remaining time of our life in peace and repentance let us ask of the Lord.

People: *Grant this, O Lord.*

Deacon: A Christian ending to our life, painless, blameless, peaceful, and a good defence before the fearful judgement seat of Christ, let us ask of the Lord.

People: *Grant this, O Lord.*

Deacon: Calling to remembrance our all holy, immaculate, most blessed and glorious Lady Theotokos and ever virgin Mary, with all the Saints: let us commend ourselves and one another, and all our life to Christ our God.

People: *To Thee, O Lord.*

Priest: For Thou art a good God and lovest mankind, and to Thee we ascribe glory: to the Father, and to the Son, and to the Holy Spirit; both now and forever, and to the ages of ages.

People: *Amen.*

Priest: Peace be with you all.

People: And with thy spirit.

Deacon: Let us bow our heads unto the Lord.

People: To Thee, O Lord.

Priest: *[soto voce]*O Lord our God, Who did bow the heavens and come down for the salvation of mankind: Look upon Thy servants and Thine inheritance; for to Thee, the fearful Judge Who yet loves mankind, have Thine servants bowed their heads and submissively inclined their necks, awaiting not help from men but entreating Thy mercy and looking confidently for Thy salvation. Guard them at all times, both during this present evening and in the approaching night, from every foe, from all adverse powers of the devil, and from vain thoughts and from evil imaginations.

[aloud] Blessed and glorified be the might of Thy kingdom: of the Father, and of the Son, and of the Holy Spirit; both now and forever, and unto the ages of ages.

People: Amen.

The Aposticha From The Octoechos *(Triodion during Lent)* With These Stichoi

Stichos 1:

To Thee have I lifted up my eyes, to Thee that dwells in heaven. Behold, as the eyes of servants look at the hands of their masters, as the eyes of the handmaid look at the hands of her mistress, so do our eyes look to the Lord our God, until He take pity on us.

Stichos 2:

Have mercy on us, O Lord, have mercy on us, for greatly are we filled with abasement. Greatly has our soul been filled therewith; let reproach come upon them that prosper, and abasement on the proud.

Hymn Of Simeon The God Receiver

Reader: Lord, now lettest Thou Thy servant depart in peace, according to Thy word, for mine eyes have seen Thy salvation, which Thou hast prepared before the face of all peoples; a light of revelation for the Gentiles, and the glory of Thy people Israel.

Trisagion Prayers

Holy God, Holy Mighty, Holy Immortal, have mercy on us. **(x3)**

Glory be to the Father, and to the Son, and to the Holy Spirit;
Both now and forever, and unto the ages of ages. Amen.

O Most Holy Trinity, have mercy on us.

O Lord, cleanse us from our sins.

O Master, pardon our iniquities.

O Holy One, visit and heal our infirmities, for Thy names sake.

Lord have mercy. **(x3)**

> *Glory be to the Father and to the Son and to the Holy Spirit;*
> *Both now and forever, and unto the ages of ages. Amen.*

People: *Our Father, Who art in Heaven, hallowed be Thy Name. Thy Kingdom come, Thy will be done, on earth as it is in Heaven. Give us this day our daily bread, and forgive us our trespasses, as we forgive those who trespass against us; and lead us not into temptation, but deliver us from the evil one.*

Priest: For Thine is the kingdom, the power, and the glory, of the Father, and the Son and the Holy Spirit, both now and ever, and to the ages of ages.

People: *Amen.*

[Seasonal Apolytikion – if available]
> *Glory be to the Father and to the Son and to the Holy Spirit.*

[Seasonal Theotokion – if available]
> *Both now and forever, and unto the ages of ages. Amen.*

The Litany Of Fervent Supplication

Deacon: Let us all say with our whole soul, and with our whole mind let us say:

People: *Lord, have mercy.*

Deacon: Lord Almighty, God of our Fathers, we pray Thee, hearest and have mercy.

People: *Lord, have mercy.*

Deacon: Have mercy on us, O God, according to Thy great mercy, we pray Thee; hear us and have mercy.

People: *Lord, have mercy.* **(x3)**

Priest: Again we pray for mercy, life, peace health, salvation, and visitation for the servants of God *(names)*, and for the pardon and remission of their sins.

People: *Lord, have mercy.* **(x3)**

Deacon: Also we pray for our Archbishop Nikitas.

People: *Lord, have mercy.* **(x3)**

Deacon: For our Sovereign Lady, Queen Elizabeth, the Royal family, our Government, and all in authority, let us pray to the Lord.

People: *Lord, have mercy.* **(x3)**

Deacon: Also we pray for mercy, life, peace, health, salvation, visitation, pardon and forgiveness of sins for the servants of God, all devout and Orthodox Christians, those who dwell in or visit this city or town and parish, the wardens and members of this church and their families and all who have asked for our prayers, unworthy though we are.

People: *Lord, have mercy.* **(x3)**

Deacon: Also we pray for the blessed and ever remembered founders of this holy church, and for all our brothers and sisters who have gone to their rest before us, and who lie here asleep in the true faith; and for the Orthodox everywhere *[and the servants of God N and N – (names given before the service)]* and that they may be pardoned all their offences, both voluntary and involuntary.

People: *Lord, have mercy.* **(x3)**

Deacon: Also we pray for those who bring offerings, those who care for the beauty of this holy and venerable house, for those who labour in its service, for those who sing, and for the people here present, who await Thy great and rich mercy.

People: *Lord, have mercy.* **(x3)**

Priest: For Thou, O God, art merciful and love mankind, and to Thee we givest glory, to the Father, the Son and the Holy Spirit, both now and forever, and unto the ages of ages.

People: *Amen.*

The Dismissal

Deacon: Wisdom.

People: *Holy Father, bless.*

Priest: Christ our God, the Existing One, is blessed, always, now and forever, and unto the ages of ages.

People: *Amen.*

Reader: Preserve, O God, the holy Orthodox faith and all Orthodox Christians, unto the ages of ages.

People: *Amen.*

Priest: Most holy Theotokos, save us.

Reader: Greater in honour than the Cherubim and beyond compare more glorious than the Seraphim; without corruption thou gavest birth to God the Word, truly the Theotokos, we magnify thee.

Priest: Glory to Thee, O Christ, our God and our hope, glory to Thee.

Reader: Glory be to the Father, and to to Son, and to the Holy Spirit, both now and for ever, both and to the ages of ages.

People: *Amen.*

Lord, have mercy. **(x3)**

Holy Father, bless!

Priest: May He who rose from the dead, Christ our true God, through the prayers of His most holy Mother, by the power of the precious and life giving Cross, through the protection of the honoured, Bodiless powers of Heaven, through the intercessions of the honoured, glorious prophet, forerunner and baptist John, of the holy, all praised and glorious Apostles, of the holy, glorious and triumphant Martyrs, of our venerable and God bearing Fathers and Mothers who have shone forth in the ascetic life, of the holy and righteous ancestors of God, Joachim and Anna, of *[patronal saint(s)]* to whom the church is dedicated, of *[Saint N]* whose memory we celebrate today, and of all the Saints, have mercy on us and save us, for He is good and loves mankind.

People: *Amen.*

Priest: Through the prayers of our holy Fathers; O Lord Jesus Christ our God; have mercy on us and save us.

People: *Amen.*

[When a priest is not present. How many Troparia for today?]

Trisagion Prayers

Reader: In the Name of the Father and of the Son and of the Holy Spirit.

People: *Amen. Glory to Thee, our God, glory to Thee.*

Reader: O Heavenly King, Comforter, Spirit of Truth, Who art everywhere present and fillest all things, Treasury of blessings and Giver of life: Come and abide in us and cleanse us from every impurity and save our souls, O Good One.

Holy God, Holy Mighty, Holy Immortal, have mercy on us. **(x3)**

> *Glory be to the Father, and to the Son, and to the Holy Spirit;*
> *Both now and forever, and unto the ages of ages. Amen.*

O Most Holy Trinity, have mercy on us.

O Lord, cleanse us from our sins.

O Master, pardon our iniquities.

O Holy One, visit and heal our infirmities, for Thy names sake.

Lord have mercy. **(x3)**

> *Glory be to the Father and to the Son and to the Holy Spirit;*
> *Both now and forever, and unto the ages of ages. Amen.*

People: Our Father, Who art in Heaven, hallowed be Thy Name. Thy Kingdom come, Thy will be done, on earth as it is in Heaven. Give us this day our daily bread, and forgive us our trespasses, as we forgive those who trespass against us; and lead us not into temptation, but deliver us from the evil one. Amen.

Lord, have mercy. **(x3)**

> *Glory be to the Father and to the Son and to the Holy Spirit;*
> *Both now and forever and unto the ages of ages. Amen.*

Come, let us worship God, our King.

Come, let us worship and fall down before Christ, our King and our God.

Come, let us worship and fall down before Christ Himself, our King and our God.

Psalm 103

Of David. Concerning The Formation Of The World.

Bless the Lord, O my soul. O Lord my God, Thou hast been exceedingly magnified. Confession and majesty hast Thou put on, Who covered Thyself with light as with a garment, Who stretched out the heaven as it were a curtain; Who supports His chambers in the waters, Who appoints the clouds for His ascent, Who walks upon the wings of the winds, Who makes His angels spirits, and His ministers a flame of fire, Who establishes the earth in the sureness thereof; it shall not be turned back for ever and ever. The abyss like a garment is His mantle; upon the mountains shall the waters stand. At Thy rebuke they shall flee, at the voice of Thy thunder shall they be afraid.

The mountains rise up and the plains sink down to the place where Thou hast established them. Thou appointed a boundary that they shall not pass, neither return to cover the earth. He sends forth springs in the valleys; between the mountains shall the waters run. They shall give drink to all the beasts of the field; the wild asses shall wait to quench their thirst. Beside them shall the birds of the heaven lodge, from the midst of the rocks shall they give voice. He waters the mountains from His chambers; the earth shall be satisfied with the fruit of Thy works.

He causes the grass to grow for the cattle, and green herb for the service of men, To bring forth bread out of the earth; and wine makes glad the heart of man. To make his face cheerful with oil; and bread strengthens mans heart. The trees of the plain shall be satisfied, the cedars of Lebanon, which Thou hast planted. There shall the sparrows make their nests; the house of the heron is chief among them. The high mountains are a refuge for the harts, and so is the rock for the hares. He has made the moon for seasons; the sun knows his going down. Thou appointed the darkness, and there was the night, wherein all the beasts of the forest shall go abroad. Young lions roaring after their prey, and seeking their food from God. The sun arises, and they are gathered together, and they lay them down in their dens.

But man shall go forth unto his work, and to his labour until the evening. How magnified are Thy works, O Lord. In wisdom hast Thou made them all; the earth is filled with Thy creation. So is this great and spacious sea, therein are things creeping innumerable, small living creatures with the great. There go the ships; there this dragon, whom Thou hast made to play therein. All things wait on Thee, to give them their food in due season; when Thou gavest it to them, they shall gather it. When Thou opened Thy hand, all things shall be filled with goodness; when Thou turned away Thy face, they shall be troubled. Thou wilt take their spirit, and they shall cease; and to their dust shall they return. Thou wilt send forth Thy Spirit, and they shall be created; and Thou shalt renew the face of the earth.

Let the glory of the Lord be unto the ages; the Lord shall rejoice in His works. Who looks on the earth and makes it tremble, Who touches the mountains and they smoke. I shall sing unto the Lord throughout my life, I shall chant to my God for as long as I have my being. May my words be sweet unto Him, and I shall rejoice in the Lord. O that sinners would cease from the earth, and they that work iniquity, that they should be no more. Bless the Lord, O my soul. The sun knows his going down, Thou appointed the darkness, and there was the night. How magnified are Thy works, O Lord. In wisdom hast Thou made them all.

After The Psalm

Glory be to the Father and to the Son and to the Holy Spirit;

Both now and forever, and unto the ages of ages. Amen.

Halleluiah, Halleluiah, Halleluiah. Glory to Thee, O God. **(x3)**

Lord, have mercy. **(x12)**

Glory be to the Father and to the Son and to the Holy Spirit;

Both now and forever, and unto the ages of ages. Amen.

[Saturday]

Blessed is the man that has not walked in the counsel of the ungodly.   Halleluiah, Halleluiah, Halleluiah.

For the Lord knows the way of the righteous, and the way of the ungodly shall perish.

Halleluiah, Halleluiah, Halleluiah.

Serve the Lord with fear, and rejoice in Him with trembling.   Halleluiah, Halleluiah, Halleluiah.

Blessed are all that have put their trust in Him.   Halleluiah, Halleluiah, Halleluiah.

Arise, O Lord, save me, O my God.   Halleluiah, Halleluiah, Halleluiah.

Salvation is of the Lord, and Thy blessing is upon Thy people.   Halleluiah, Halleluiah, Halleluiah.

Glory be to the Father, and to the Son, and to the Holy Spirit;

Both now and forever, and unto ages of ages. Amen.   Halleluiah, Halleluiah, Halleluiah.

Halleluiah, Halleluiah, Halleluiah. Glory to Thee, O God. **(x3)**

Lord, have mercy. **(x3)**

Psalm 140

Chorus: Lord, I have cried to Thee: hear me. Hear me, O Lord.

Lord, I have cried to Thee: hear me. Receive the voice of my prayer.

When I call upon Thee, hear me, O Lord. Let my prayer arise as incense in Thy sight,

And let the lifting up of my hands be an evening sacrifice. Hear me, O Lord.

Kekragarion

Sticheroi From Psalm 140

29)   Set, O Lord, a watch before my mouth, and a door of enclosure round about my lips.

28)   Incline not my heart to words of evil, to make excuses for sins.

27)   Those that work iniquity; I shall not join with their number.

26)   The righteous man shall chasten me with mercy and reprove me; as for the oil of the sinner, let it not anoint my head.

25)   For yet more is my prayer in the presence of their pleasures; their judges have been swallowed up by the rock.

24) They shall hear my words, for they be sweetened; as a clod of earth is broken upon the earth, so have their bones been scattered into hades.

23) To Thee O Lord are mine eyes. In Thee have I hoped; take not my soul away.

22) Keep me from the snare which they have laid for me, and from the stumbling blocks of them that work iniquity.

21) The sinners shall fall into their own net; I am alone until I pass by.

Sticheroi From Psalm 141

20) With my voice to the Lord have I cried, with my voice have I made supplication.

19) I shall pour out before Him my supplications; my afflictions shall I declare before Him.

18) When my spirit was fainting within me, then Thou knewest my paths.

17) In this way wherein I have walked they hid for me a snare.

16) I looked on my right hand, and beheld, and there was none that knew me.

15) Flight has failed me, and there is none that watches out for my soul.

14) I cried to Thee, O Lord; I said: Thou art my hope, my portion in the land of the living.

13) Attend unto my supplication, for I am brought very low.

12) Deliver me from them that persecute me, for they are stronger than I.

11) Bring my soul out of prison.

10) That I may confess Thy name.

[daily or seasonal Troparia]

9) The righteous shall patiently wait for me until Thou shalt reward me.

[daily or seasonal Troparia]

Sticheroi From Psalm 129

8) Out of the depths have I cried unto Thee, O Lord. O Lord, hear my voice.

[daily or seasonal Troparia]

7) Let Thine ears be attentive to the voice of my supplication.

[daily or seasonal Troparia]

6) If Thou should mark iniquities, O Lord; O Lord, who shall stand? For with Thee there is forgiveness.

[daily or seasonal Troparia]

5) For Thy names sake have I patiently waited for Thee, O Lord; my soul has patiently waited for Thy word, my soul has hoped in the Lord.

[daily or seasonal Troparia]

4) From the morning watch until night, from the morning watch let Israel hope in the Lord.

[daily or seasonal Troparia]

3) For with the Lord there is mercy, and with Him is plenteous redemption; and He shall redeem Israel out of all his iniquities.

[daily or seasonal Troparia]

Sticheroi From Psalm 116

2)   O praise the Lord, all you nations; praise Him, all you peoples.

[daily or seasonal Troparia]

1)   For He has made His mercy to prevail over us, and the truth of the Lord abides forever.

[daily or seasonal Troparia]

Glory be to the Father and to the Son and to the Holy Spirit.

Both now and forever, and unto the ages of ages. Amen.

[Friday and Saturday]   **Dormition Dogmaticon**

   Tone 1   Magnificent, happy and earthy.   *C, D, Eb, F, G, A, Bb, C.*

At the sovereign command of God, the God bearing apostles were caught up from every place, and when they came to thine all pure body, from which life has come, they kissed it with love. The heavenly powers also came with their Master, and in awe escorted the body all pure and well pleasing to God. The body which had received God in the flesh; and with dignity they went before and cried out to the most high powers: *"Behold, the Queen of all and the maiden of God is coming."* Be lifted up, O gates! Receive her who is the Mother of the Everlasting Light. For through her was accomplished the salvation of all. We cannot gaze upon her, we cannot render her the honour which is her due; for her virtue surpasses all understanding. Therefore, O most pure Theotokos, who lives forever with thy Son, the life bearing King, pray to Him to preserve the new people of God, and to save them from every attack of the enemy; for we have acquired thine intercession, and we bless thee in beauty and light for ever.

[Sunday to Thursday]   **Theotokion From The Menaion**

   Tone 4   Festive, joyous and capable of expressing deep piety.   *C, D, Eb, F, G, A, Bb, C.*

O pure Virgin most graced of God, as the splendid and luminous palace of the Master, and as the shining cloud where from the spiritual light sprang up and brightly shone on the world, guide our soul and mind with thy light, O all blameless Maid; utterly destroy all the stumbling blocks laid by the deceiver; and make firm our understanding by thine entreaties on our behalf.

O Gladsome Light

O Gladsome Light of the holy glory of the immortal Father;

Heavenly holy, blessed Jesus Christ.

Now that we have come to the setting of the sun, and behold the Evening Light.

We praise God; Father, Son and Holy Spirit.

For meet it is at all time to worship Thee, with voices of praise;

O Son of God and Giver of Life. Therefore all the world doth glorify Thee.

Reader: The Prokeimenon.

[Sunday] Tone 8 *Humility, tranquillity, repose, suffering, pleading.* *C, D, Eb, F, G, A, Bb, C.*

Reader: Behold now, bless the Lord, all you servants of the Lord.

People: *Behold now, bless the Lord, all you servants of the Lord.*

Reader: You that stand in the house of the Lord, in the courts of the house of our God.

People: *Behold now, bless the Lord, all you servants of the Lord.*

Reader: Behold now, bless the Lord | *all you servants of the Lord.*

[Monday] Tone 4 *Festive, joyous and expressing deep piety.* *C, D, Eb, F, G, A, Bb, C.*

Reader: The Lord shall hearken unto me when I cry unto Him.

People: *The Lord shall hearken unto me when I cry unto Him.*

Reader: When I called upon Thee, O God of my righteousness; Thou didst hearken unto me.

People: *The Lord shall hearken unto me when I cry unto Him.*

Reader: The Lord shall hearken unto me | *when I cry unto Him.*

[Tuesday] Tone 1 *Magnificent, happy and earthy.* *C, D, Eb, F, G, A, Bb, C.*

Reader: Thy mercy, O Lord, shall pursue me all the days of my life.

People: *Thy mercy, O Lord, shall pursue me all the days of my life.*

Reader: The Lord is my shepherd, and I shall not want.

In a place of green pasture, there has He made me to dwell.

People: *Thy mercy, O Lord, shall pursue me all the days of my life.*

Reader: Thy mercy, O Lord | *shall pursue me all the days of my life.*

[Wednesday] Tone 5 *Stimulating, dancing, and rhythmical.* *C, D, Eb, F, G, A, Bb, C.*

Reader: O God, in Thy name save me, and in Thy strength Thou judgest me.

People: *O God, in Thy name save me, and in Thy strength Thou judgest me.*

Reader: O God, hearken to my prayer, give ear to the words of my mouth.

People: *O God, in Thy name save me, and in Thy strength Thou judgest me.*

Reader: O God, in Thy name save me | *and in Thy strength Thou judgest me.*

[Thursday] Tone 6 *Rich texture, funeral, sorrowful.* *D, Eb, F##, G, A, Bb, C##, D.*

Reader: My help comes from the Lord, who has made the heaven and the earth.

People: *My help comes from the Lord, who has made the heaven and the earth.*

Reader: I lifted up my eyes to the mountains from where comes my help.

People: *My help comes from the Lord, who has made the heaven and the earth.*

Reader: My help comes from the Lord | *who has made the heaven and the earth.*

[Friday]   *Tone 7*   *Manly character and strong melody.*   *F, G, A, A#, C, D, E, F.*

Reader: O God, my helper art Thou, and Thy mercy shall go before me.

People: *O God, my helper art Thou, and Thy mercy shall go before me.*

Reader: Rescue me from mine enemies, O God; And from them that rise up against me redeem me.

People: *O God, my helper art Thou, and Thy mercy shall go before me.*

Reader: O God, my helper art Thou | *and Thy mercy shall go before me.*

[Saturday]   *Tone 6*   *Rich texture, funeral, sorrowful.*   *D, Eb, F##, G, A, Bb, C##, D.*

Reader: The Lord is clothed with strength and He has girded Himself.

People: *The Lord is King, He is clothed with majesty.*

Reader: For He established the world which shall not be shaken.

People: *The Lord is King, He is clothed with majesty.*

Reader: Holiness becomes Thine house, O Lord, to the length of days.

Reader: The Lord is King | *He is clothed with majesty.*

*[**Scripture** readings for a **feast**:]*

Reader: The Reading is from _____.

Reader: Vouchsafe, O Lord, to keep us this evening without sin. Blessed art Thou, O Lord, the God of our fathers, and praised and glorified is Thy name unto the ages. Amen.

Let Thy mercy, O Lord, be upon us, according as we have hoped in Thee.

Blessed art Thou, O Lord, teach me Thy statutes.

Blessed art Thou, O Master, give me understanding of Thy statutes.

Blessed art Thou, O Holy One, enlighten me by Thy statutes.

O Lord, Thy mercy endures forever; disdain not the work of Thy hands. To Thee is due praise, to Thee is due song, to Thee is due glory, to the Father, and to the Son, and to the Holy Spirit; both now and forever, and unto the ages of ages. Amen.

Lord, have mercy. **(x12)**

Glory be to the Father, and to the Son, and to the Holy Spirit;

Both now and forever, and unto the ages of ages. Amen.

The Aposticha From The Octoechos (*Triodion during Lent*) **With These Stichoi**

Stichos 1:

To Thee have I lifted up my eyes, to Thee that dwells in heaven. Behold, as the eyes of servants look at the hands of their masters, as the eyes of the handmaid look at the hands of her mistress, so do our eyes look to the Lord our God, until He take pity on us.

Stichos 2:

Have mercy on us, O Lord, have mercy on us, for greatly are we filled with abasement. Greatly has our soul been filled therewith; let reproach come upon them that prosper, and abasement on the proud.

[Saturday]   **Resurrectional Apolytikion**

     Tone 1   *Magnificent, happy and earthy.*   *C, D, Eb, F, G, A, Bb, C.*

While the stone was sealed by the Jews, and the soldiers were guarding Thy most pure body, Thou didst arise on the third day, O Saviour, granting life to the world. For which cause the heavenly powers cried aloud to Thee O giver of life. Glory to Thy Resurrection O Christ, glory to Thy kingdom, glory to Thy providence, O Thou Who alone art the lover of mankind.

[Monday to Friday   ***Troparion of the saint.***

Or if a Great feast of the Lord ***Troparion of the feast.]***

Reader: Lord, now lettest Thou Thy servant depart in peace, according to Thy word, for mine eyes have seen Thy salvation, which Thou hast prepared before the face of all peoples; a light of revelation for the Gentiles, and the glory of Thy people Israel.

Holy God, Holy Mighty, Holy Immortal, have mercy on us. **(x3)**

     Glory be to the Father, and to the Son, and to the Holy Spirit;
     Both now and forever, and unto the ages of ages. Amen.

O Most Holy Trinity, have mercy on us.

O Lord, cleanse us from our sins.

O Master, pardon our iniquities.

O Holy One, visit and heal our infirmities, for Thy names sake.

Lord have mercy. **(x3)**

     Glory be to the Father and to the Son and to the Holy Spirit;
     Both now and forever, and unto the ages of ages. Amen.

People: *Our Father, Who art in Heaven, hallowed be Thy Name. Thy Kingdom come, Thy will be done, on earth as it is in Heaven. Give us this day our daily bread, and forgive us our trespasses, as we forgive those who trespass against us; and lead us not into temptation, but deliver us from the evil one.*

Reader: O Lord, Jesus Christ, Son of God, have mercy on us.

People: *Amen.*

Reader: Lord, have mercy. **(x40)**

Glory be to the Father, and to the Son, and to the Holy Spirit.
Both now and forever, and unto the ages of ages. Amen.

The Dismissal

Establish, O God, the holy Orthodox Faith of Orthodox Christians to the ages of ages.

Greater in honour than the Cherubim and beyond compare more glorious than the Seraphim; without corruption thou gavest birth to God the Word, truly the Theotokos, we magnify thee.

Glory be to the Father, and to the Son, and to the Holy Spirit;
Both now and forever, and unto the ages of ages. Amen.

Lord have mercy. **(x3)**

[Sunday:]

Thou that didst rise from the dead, O Lord Jesus Christ, Son of God, for the sake of the prayers of Thy most pure Mother, of our holy and God bearing fathers, *[of St Martin,]* of _____ *(saints of the day)*, and of all the saints, have mercy on us and save us, for Thou art good and the Lover of mankind. Amen.

[Monday to Saturday:]

O Lord Jesus Christ, Son of God, for the sake of the prayers of Thy most pure Mother, of our holy and God bearing fathers, *[of St Martin]*, of _____ *(saints of the day)*, and of all the saints, have mercy on us and save us, for Thou art good and the Lover of mankind. Amen.

Reader: Bless our most holy Archbishop Nikitas, the faithful of this holy place; And all Orthodox Christians. Preserve us, O Lord, for many years.

People: *Amen.*

Reader: Through the prayers of our holy Fathers; O Lord Jesus Christ our God; have mercy on us and save us.

People: *Amen.*

[If preceded by another service then start at "Come let us worship…"]

The Trisagion Prayers

In the Name of the Father, and of the Son, and of the Holy Spirit. Amen.

Glory to Thee, our God, glory to Thee.

O Heavenly King, the Comforter, the Spirit of Truth; who art everywhere present and fillest all things; Treasury of blessings, and giver of life: come and abide in us, and cleanse us from every impurity, and save our souls, O Good One.

Holy God, Holy Mighty, Holy Immortal, have mercy on us. **(x3)**

Glory be to the Father, and to the Son, and to the Holy Spirit;
Both now and forever, and unto the ages of ages. Amen.

O Most Holy Trinity, have mercy on us.

O Lord, cleanse us from our sins.

O Master, pardon our iniquities.

O Holy One, visit and heal our infirmities, for Thy names sake.

Lord have mercy. **(x3)**

Glory be to the Father, and to the Son, and to the Holy Spirit;
Both now and forever, and unto the ages of ages. Amen.

Our Father, who art in heaven, hallowed be Thy name. Thy Kingdom come. Thy will be done, on earth as it is in heaven. Give us this day our daily bread; and forgive us our trespasses, as we forgive those who trespass against us; and lead us not into temptation, but deliver us from the evil one. Amen.

Lord have mercy. **(x12)**

Glory be to the Father, and to the Son, and to the Holy Spirit;
Both now and forever, and unto the ages of ages. Amen.

Come, let us worship God, our King.

Come, let us worship and fall down before Christ, our King and our God.

Come, let us worship and fall down before Christ Himself, our King and our God.

Troparion To The Holy Trinity

Having arisen from sleep, we fall down before Thee, O blessed One, and sing to Thee, O Mighty One, the angelic hymn: Holy. Holy. Holy. art Thou O God; through the Theotokos, have mercy on us.

Glory be to the Father, and to the Son, and to the Holy Spirit;

Having raised me from my bed and from sleep, O Lord, enlighten my mind and heart, and open my lips that I might praise Thee, O Holy Trinity: Holy. Holy. Holy. art Thou O God; through the Theotokos, have mercy on us.

Both now and forever and to the ages of ages. Amen.

The Judge shall come suddenly and the acts of every man shall be revealed; but in the middle of the night we cry in fear: Holy. Holy. Holy. art Thou O God; through the Theotokos, have mercy on us.

Lord have mercy. **(x12)**

A Prayer To The Holy Trinity

Having arisen from sleep, I thank Thee, the Holy Trinity. In the abundance of Thy kindness and long patience, Thou hast not been angry with me for my laziness and sinfulness, nor hast Thou destroyed me in my lawlessness. Instead, in Thy usual love for mankind, Thou hast raised me as I lay in despair, that I might rise early and glorify Thy Reign. Enlighten now the eyes of my mind and open my lips, that I might learn of Thy words, understand Thy commandments, accomplish Thy will, hymn Thee in heart felt confession and praise Thine all holy name, of the Father and of the Son, and of the Holy Spirit, now and forever and to the ages of ages. Amen.

Another Prayer

Glory to Thee, O King, almighty God, because in Thine divine providence and love for mankind, Thou hast permitted me, sinner and unworthy, to rise from sleep and to gain entrance to Thine holy house. Accept, too, Lord, the voice of my supplication, as Thou dost that of Thine holy and spiritual Powers; and be well pleased for praise to be offered Thee with a pure heart and a spirit of humility from my sordid lips, that I too may become a companion of the wise virgins with the shining lamp of my soul and may glorify Thee, God the Word, glorified with the Father and the Spirit. Amen.

Psalm 50

Have mercy on me, O God, according to Thy great mercy; and according to the multitude of Thy compassions blot out my transgression. Wash me thoroughly from mine iniquity, and cleanse me from my sin. For I acknowledge mine iniquity, and my sin is ever before me. Against Thee, Thee only have I sinned, and done evil in Thy sight, that Thou mayest be found just when Thou speakest, and victorious when Thou art judged. For behold, I was conceived in iniquity, and in sin my mother bore me. For behold, Thou hast loved truth; Thou hast made known to me the hidden and secret things of Thy wisdom. Thou shalt sprinkle me with hyssop, and I shall be made clean; Thou shalt wash me, and I shalt be whiter than snow. Make me to hear joy and gladness; that the humbled bones may rejoice. Turn Thy face away from my sins, and blot out all mine iniquities.

Create in me a clean heart, O God, and renew a steadfast spirit within me. Cast me not away from Thy presence, and take not Thy Holy Spirit from me. Restore to me the joy of Thy salvation, and establish me with Thy governing Spirit. I shall teach transgressors Thy ways, and the ungodly shall turn back to Thee. Deliver me from blood guiltiness, O God, the God of my salvation; my tongue shall joyfully declare Thy righteousness. Lord, open my lips, and my mouth shall declare Thy praise. For if Thou hadst desired sacrifice, I would give it; Thou dost not delight in burned offerings. A sacrifice to God is a broken spirit; God shall not despise a broken and a humbled heart. Do good, O Lord, in Thy good pleasure to Zion, and let the walls of Jerusalem be builded. Then Thou shalt be pleased with a sacrifice of righteousness, with oblation and whole burned offerings. Then shall they offer bulls on Thine altar.

[Weekdays]

[Monday, Thursday]   **Second Stasis**

Thy hands have made me and fashioned me; give me understanding and I shall learn Thy commandments. They that fear Thee shall see me and be glad, for on Thy words have I set my hope. I have known, O Lord, that Thy judgements are righteousness, and with truth hast Thou humbled me. Let now Thy mercy be my comfort, according to Thy saying unto Thy servant. Let Thy compassions come upon me and I shall live, for Thy law is my meditation. Let the proud be put to shame, for unjustly have they transgressed against me; but as for me, I shall ponder on Thy commandments. Let those that fear Thee return unto me, and those that know Thy testimonies. Let my heart be blameless in Thy statutes, that I may not be put to shame. My soul fainteth for Thy salvation; on Thy words have I set my hope. Mine eyes are grown dim with waiting for Thine oracle; they say: When wilt Thou comfort me? For I am become like a wine skin in the frost; yet Thy statutes have I not forgotten. How many are the days of Thy servant? When wilt Thou execute judgement for me on them that persecute me? Transgressors have told me fables, but they are not like Thy law, O Lord. All Thy commandments are truth. Without a cause have men persecuted me; do Thou help me. They well nigh made an end of me on the earth; but as for me, I forsook not Thy commandments. According to Thy mercy quicken me, and I shall keep the testimonies of Thy mouth. For ever, O Lord, Thy word abideth in heaven. Unto generation and generation is Thy truth; Thou hast laid the foundation of the earth, and it abideth. By Thine ordinance doth the day abide, for all things are Thy servants. If Thy law had not been my meditation, then should I have perished in my humiliation. I shall never forget Thy statutes, for in them hast Thou quickened me.

[Tuesday, Friday]   **Middle**

I am Thine, save me; for after Thy statutes have I sought. Sinners have waited for me to destroy me; but Thy testimonies have I understood. Of all perfection have I seen the outcome; exceeding spacious is Thy commandment. O how I have loved Thy law, O Lord. the whole day long it is my meditation. Above mine enemies hast Thou made me wise in Thy commandment, for it is mine for ever. Above all that teach me have I gained understanding, for Thy testimonies are my meditation. Above mine elders have I received understanding, for after Thy commandments have I sought. From every way that is evil have I restrained my feet that I might keep Thy words. From Thy judgements have I not declined, for Thou hast set a law for me. How sweet to my palate are Thy sayings. more sweet than honey to my mouth. From Thy commandments have I gained understanding; therefore have I hated every way of unrighteousness. Thy law is a lamp unto my feet and a light unto my paths. I have sworn and resolved that I shall keep the judgements of Thy righteousness. I was humbled exceedingly; O Lord, quicken me according to Thy word. The free will offerings of my mouth be Thou now pleased to receive, O Lord, and teach me Thy judgements. My soul is in Thy hands continually, and Thy law have I not forgotten. Sinners have set a snare for me, yet from Thy commandment have I not strayed. I have inherited Thy testimonies for ever, for they are the rejoicing of my heart. I have inclined my heart to perform Thy statutes for ever for a recompense. Transgressors have I hated, but Thy law have I loved. My helper and my protector art Thou; on Thy words have I set my hope. Depart from me, you evil doers, and I shall search out the commandments of my God. Uphold me according to Thy saying and quicken me, and turn me not away in shame from mine expectation. Help me, and I shall be saved; and I shall meditate on Thy statutes continually. Thou hast set at nought all that depart from Thy statutes, for unrighteous is their inward thought. I have reckoned as transgressors all the sinners of the earth, therefore have I loved Thy testimonies. Nail down my flesh with the fear of Thee, for of Thy judgements am I afraid. I have wrought judgement and righteousness; O give me not up to them that wrong me. Receive Thy servant unto good, let not the proud falsely accuse me. Mine eyes have failed with waiting for Thy salvation, and for the word of Thy righteousness. Deal with Thy servant according to Thy mercy, and teach me Thy statutes. I am Thy servant; give me understanding, and I shall know Thy testimonies. It is time for the Lord to act; for they have dispersed Thy law. Therefore have I loved Thy commandments more than gold and topaz. Therefore I directed myself according to all Thy commandments; every way that is unrighteous have I hated. Wonderful are Thy testimonies; therefore hath my soul searched them out. The unfolding of Thy words shall give light and understanding unto babes. I opened my mouth and drew in my breath, for I longed for Thy commandments.

[Wednesday, Saturday]   **Third Stasis**

Look upon me and have mercy on me, according to the judgement of them that love Thy name. My steps do Thou direct according to Thy saying, and let no iniquity have dominion over me. Deliver me from the false accusation of men, and I shall keep Thy commandments. Make Thy face to shine upon Thy servant, and teach me Thy statutes. Mine eyes have poured forth streams of waters, because I kept not Thy law. Righteous art Thou, O Lord, and upright are Thy judgements. Thou hast ordained as Thy testimonies exceeding righteousness and truth. My zeal for Thee hath made me to pine away, because mine enemies have forgotten Thy words. Thine oracle is tried with fire to the uttermost, and Thy servant hath loved it. I am young and accounted as nothing, yet Thy statutes have I not forgotten. Thy righteousness is an everlasting righteousness, and Thy law is truth. Tribulations and necessities have found me, Thy commandments are my meditation. Thy testimonies are righteousness for ever; give me understanding and I shall live. I have cried with my whole heart; hear me, O Lord, and I shall seek after Thy statutes. I have cried unto Thee; save me, and I shall keep Thy testimonies. I arose in the dead of night and I cried; on Thy words have I set my hope. Mine eyes woke before the morning that I might meditate on Thy sayings. Hear my voice, O Lord, according to Thy mercy; according to Thy judgement, quicken me. They have drawn nigh that lawlessly persecute me, but from Thy law are they far removed. Near art Thou, O Lord, and all Thy ways are truth. From the beginning I have known from Thy testimonies that Thou hast founded them for ever. Behold my humiliation and rescue me, for Thy law have I not forgotten. Judge my cause and redeem me; for Thy words sake quicken me. Far from sinners is salvation, for they have not sought after Thy statutes. Thy compassions are many, O Lord; according to Thy judgement quicken me. Many are they that persecute me and afflict me; from Thy testimonies have I not declined. I beheld men acting foolishly and I pined away, because they kept not Thy sayings. Behold, how I have loved Thy commandments; O Lord, in Thy mercy, quicken me. The beginning of Thy words is truth, and all the judgements of Thy righteousness endure for ever. Princes have persecuted me without a cause, and because of Thy words my heart hath been afraid. I shall rejoice in Thy sayings as one that findeth great spoil. Unrighteousness have I hated and abhorred, but Thy law have I loved. Seven times a day have I praised Thee for the judgements of Thy righteousness. Much peace have they that love Thy law, and for them there is no stumbling block. I awaited Thy salvation, O Lord, and Thy commandments have I loved. My soul hath kept Thy testimonies and hath loved them exceedingly. I have kept Thy commandments and Thy testimonies, for all my ways are before Thee, O Lord. Let my supplication draw nigh before Thee, O Lord; according to Thine oracle give me understanding. Let my petition come before Thee, O Lord; according to Thine oracle deliver me. My lips shall pour forth a hymn when Thou hast taught me Thy statutes. My tongue shall speak of Thy sayings, for all Thy commandments are righteousness. Let Thy hand be for saving me, for I have chosen Thy commandments. I have longed for Thy salvation, O Lord, and Thy law is my meditation. My soul shall live and shall praise Thee, and Thy judgements shall help me. I have gone astray like a sheep that is lost; O seek Thy servant, for I have not forgotten Thy commandments.

Final Stasis

Glory be to the Father, and to the Son, and to the Holy Spirit;
Both now and forever and unto the ages of ages. Amen.

Halleluiah, Halleluiah, Halleluiah: Glory to Thee, O God. **(x3)**

Lord, have mercy. **(x3)**

[Saturday]

Kathisma 9

Psalm 64

A Canticle Of David: An Ode Sung By Jeremiah And Ezekiel
And The Captive People When They Were About To Depart

To Thee is due praise, O God, in Zion; and unto Thee shall a vow be rendered in Jerusalem. Hearken unto my prayer, for unto Thee shall all flesh come. The words of lawless men have overpowered us, but to our ungodliness shalt Thou be merciful. Blessed is he whom Thou hast chosen and hast taken to Thyself; he shall dwell in Thy courts. We shall be filled with the good things of Thy house; holy is Thy temple, wonderful in righteousness. Hearken unto us, O God our Saviour, Thou hope of all the ends of the earth and of them that be far off at sea, Who settest fast the mountains by Thy strength, Who art girded round about with power, Who troublest the hollow of the sea; as for the roar of its waves, who shall withstand them? The heathen shall be troubled, and the dwellers of the farthest regions shall be afraid at Thy signs; Thou shalt make the outgoings of the morning and the evening to delight. Thou hast visited the earth and abundantly watered her; Thou hast multiplied the means of enriching her. The river of God is filled with waters; Thou hast prepared their food, for thus is the preparation thereof. Do Thou make her furrows drunk with water, multiply her fruits; in her showers shall she be glad when she sprouteth forth. Thou shalt bless the crown of the year with Thy goodness, and Thy plains shall be filled with fatness. Enriched shall be the mountains of the wilderness, and the hills shall be girded with rejoicing. The rams of the flock have clothed themselves with fleece, and the valleys shall abound with wheat; they shall cry aloud, yea, they shall chant hymns unto Thee.

Psalm 65 - An Ode of Resurrection

Shout with jubilation unto the Lord all the earth; chant you unto His name, give glory in praise of Him. Say unto God: How awesome are Thy works. In the multitude of Thy power shall Thine enemies be proved false unto Thee. Let all the earth worship Thee and chant unto Thee; let them chant unto Thy name, O Most High. Come and see the works of the Lord, how awesome He is in His counsels, more than the sons of men. He turneth the sea into dry land; in the river shall they pass through on foot. There shall we rejoice in Him, in Him that is ruler in His sovereignty for ever. His eyes look upon the nations; let not them that embitter Him be exalted in themselves. O bless our God, you nations, and make the voice of His praise to be heard, Who hath established my soul in life, and permitteth not my feet to be shaken. For Thou hast proved us, O God, and by fire hast Thou tried us even as silver is tried by fire. Thou hast brought us into the snare, Thou hast laid afflictions upon our back, Thou madest men to mount upon our heads. We went through fire and water, and Thou didst bring us out into refreshment. I shall go into Thy house with a whole burned offering; to Thee shall I pay my vows which my lips pronounced and which my mouth had spoken in mine affliction. Whole burned offerings full of marrow shall I offer unto Thee, with incense and rams; oxen and goats shall I offer unto Thee. Come and hear, and I shall declare unto ye, all you that fear God, what things He hath done for my soul. Unto Him with my mouth have I cried, and I exalted Him with my tongue. If in my heart I regarded unrighteousness, let the Lord not hear me. Wherefore God hath hearkened unto me, He hath been attentive to the voice of my supplication. Blessed is God Who hath not turned away my prayer, nor His mercy away from me.

Psalm 66

God be gracious unto us and bless us, and cause His face to shine upon us and have mercy on us, That we may know upon the earth Thy way, among all the nations Thy salvation. Let the peoples give Thee praise, O God, let all the peoples praise Thee. Let the nations be glad and rejoice, for Thou shalt judge peoples with uprightness; and nations shalt Thou guide upon the earth. Let the peoples give Thee praise, O God, let all the peoples praise Thee; the earth hath yielded her fruit. Let God, our God, bless us; let God bless us, and let all the ends of the earth fear Him.

Stasis

Glory be to the Father, and to the Son, and to the Holy Spirit;
Both now and forever and unto the ages of ages. Amen.

Halleluiah, Halleluiah, Halleluiah: Glory to Thee, O God. **(x3)**
Lord, have mercy. **(x3)**

Psalm 67

Let God arise and let His enemies be scattered, and let them that hate Him flee from before His face. As smoke vanisheth, so let them vanish; as wax melteth before the fire, so let sinners perish at the presence of God. And let the righteous be glad; let them rejoice in the presence of God, let them delight in gladness. Sing unto God, chant unto His name; prepare you the way for Him that rideth upon the setting of the sun. Lord is His name; yea, rejoice before Him. Let them be troubled at His presence, Who is a father of orphans and a judge to the widows. God is in His holy place, God settleth the solitary in a house, Mightily leading forth them that were shackled, and likewise them that embitter Him, them that dwell in tombs. O God, when Thou wentest forth before Thy people, when Thou didst traverse the wilderness, The earth was shaken and the heavens dropped dew, at the presence of the God of Sinai, at the presence of the God of Israel. A rain freely given shalt Thou ordain, O God, for Thine inheritance; yea, it became weak, but Thou shalt restore it. Thy living creatures shall dwell therein; Thou hast prepared it in Thy goodness for the poor man, O God. The Lord shall give speech with great power to them that bring good tidings. He that is the King of the hosts of His beloved one shall divide the spoils for the beauty of the house. Even if you sleep among the lots, you shall have the wings of a dove covered with silver, and her pinions of sparkling gold. When He that is in the heavens ordaineth kings over her, they shall be made snow white in Selmon. The mountain of God is a butter mountain, a curdled mountain, a butter mountain. Why suppose you that there be other curdled mountains? This is the mountain wherein God is pleased to dwell, yea, for the Lord shall dwell therein to the end. The chariot host of God is ten thousandfold, yea, thousands of them that abound in number; the Lord is among them at Sinai, in His holy place. Thou hast ascended on high, Thou leddest captivity captive, Thou didst receive gifts among men (yea, for they were disobedient) that Thou mightest dwell there. Blessed is the Lord God, blessed is the Lord day by day; the God of our salvation shall prosper us along the way. Our God is the

God of salvation, and the pathways leading forth from death are those of the Lords Lord. But God shall crush the heads of His enemies, the hairy crown of them that continue in their trespasses. The Lord said: I shall return from Basan. I shall return in the deeps of the sea, That thy foot may be dipped in blood, yea, the tongue of thy dogs in that of thine enemies. Thy processionals have been seen, O God, the processionals of my God, of my King Who is in His sanctuary. Princes went before, and after them the chanters, in the midst of timbrel playing maidens. In congregations bless you God, the Lord from the well springs of Israel. Yonder is Benjamin the younger in rapture, the princes of Judah their rulers, the princes of Zabulon, the princes of Nephthalim. Give Thou command, O God, unto Thy hosts; strengthen, O God, this which Thou hast wrought in us. Because of Thy temple in Jerusalem, kings shall bring gifts unto Thee. Rebuke the wild beasts of the reed, that congregation of bulls among the heifers of the peoples, lest they exclude them that have been proved like silver. Scatter the nations that desire wars; ambassadors shall come out of Egypt; Ethiopia shall hasten to stretch out her hand unto God. You kingdoms of the earth, sing unto God; chant you unto the Lord, unto Him that rideth the heaven of heaven towards the dayspring. Lo, He shall utter with His voice a voice of power. Give you glory unto God; His magnificence is over Israel and His power is in the clouds. Wondrous is God in His saints; the God of Israel, He shall give power and strength unto His people. Blessed is God.

Stasis

Glory be to the Father, and to the Son, and to the Holy Spirit;
Both now and forever and unto the ages of ages. Amen.

Halleluiah, Halleluiah, Halleluiah: Glory to Thee, O God. **(x3)**
Lord, have mercy. **(x3)**

Psalm 68

Concerning Those Verses That Are to be Alternated. A Psalm of David.

Save me, O God, for the waters are come in unto my soul. I am stuck fast in the mire of the deep, and there is no sure standing. I am come into the deeps of the sea, and a tempest hath overwhelmed me. I am grown weary with crying, my throat is become hoarse; from my hoping in my God, mine eyes have failed me. They that hate me without a cause are multiplied more than the hairs of my head. Mine enemies are grown strong, they that persecute me unjustly; then did I restore that which I took not away. O God, Thou knowest my foolishness, and my transgressions are not hid from Thee. Let not them that wait on Thee be ashamed for my sake, O Lord, Thou Lord of hosts. Nor let them that seek after Thee be confounded for my sake, O God of Israel. Because for Thy sake I have borne reproach, shame hath covered my face. I am become a stranger unto my brethren, and an alien unto the sons of my mother. For the zeal of Thy house hath eaten me up, and the reproaches of them that reproach Thee are fallen on me. Yea, with fasting I covered my soul, and it was turned into a reproach for me. And I made sackcloth my clothing, and I became a proverb to them. And they prated against me, they that sit in the gates; and they made a song about me, they that drink wine. But as for me, with my prayer I cry unto Thee, O Lord; it is time for Thy good pleasure. O God, in the multitude of Thy mercy hearken unto me, in the truth of Thy salvation. Save me from the mire, that I be not stuck therein; let me be delivered from them that hate me and from the deeps of the waters. Let not the tempest of water overwhelm me, nor let the deep swallow me up, nor let the pit shut its mouth upon me. Hearken unto me, O Lord, for Thy mercy is good; according to the multitude of Thy compassions, look upon me. Turn not Thy countenance away from Thy servant, for I am afflicted; quickly hearken unto me. Attend unto my soul and deliver it; because of mine enemies, rescue me. For Thou knowest my reproach, my shame and my humiliation. Before Thee are all that afflict me; my soul hath awaited reproach and misery. And I waited for one that would grieve with me, but there was no one; and for them that would comfort me, but I found none. And they gave me gall for my food, and for my thirst they gave me vinegar to drink. Let their table before them be for a snare, for a recompense and for a stumbling block. Let their eyes be darkened that they may not see, and their back do Thou continually bow down. Pour out upon them Thy wrath, and let the fury of Thy wrath take hold upon them. Let their habitation be made desolate, and in their tents let there be none to dwell. For they persecuted him whom Thou hast smitten, and to the pain of my wounds have they added. Add iniquity to their iniquity, and let them not enter into Thy righteousness. Let them be blotted out of the book of the living, and with the righteous let them not be written. Poor and in sorrow am I; may Thy salvation, O God, be quick to help me. I shall praise the name of my God with an ode, I shall magnify Him with praise. And this shall please God more than a young calf that hath horns and hooves. Let beggars behold it and be glad; seek after God, and thy soul shall live. For the Lord hath hearkened unto the poor and hath not despised them that are fettered for His sake. Let the heavens and the earth praise Him, the sea and all the creeping things therein. For God shall save Zion, and the cities of Judea shall be builded; and they shall dwell therein and inherit it. And the seed of Thy servants shall possess it, and they that love Thy name shall dwell therein.

Psalm 69

Of David. In Remembrance. That the Lord May Save Me.

O God, be attentive to help me; Lord, make haste to help me. Let them be ashamed and confounded who seek after my life. Let them be turned back and be ashamed who desire evil against me. Let them be turned back because of their shame who say to me: "Well done. Well done." Let all those who seek Thee rejoice and be glad in Thee, O God, and let those who love Thy salvation say continually: "Let the Lord be magnified." But as for me, I am poor and needy; O God help me. Thou art my help and my deliverer; Lord; do not delay.

Final Stasis

Glory be to the Father, and to the Son, and to the Holy Spirit;
Both now and forever and unto the ages of ages. Amen.

Halleluiah, Halleluiah, Halleluiah: Glory to Thee, O God. **(x3)**

Lord, have mercy. **(x3)**

[End Saturday]

[Sunday]

Holy Trinity, one God, have mercy and save us.

Hymns To The Trinity

• It is truly right to praise the divine Trinity, the Father without beginning and Maker of all, the co-eternal Word, born without change from the Father before the ages, and the Holy Spirit, proceeding timelessly from the Father.

• It is truly right to glorify Thee, God the Word, at whom the Cherubim quail and tremble and whom the Powers of heaven glorify. Christ, the giver of life, who rose from the grave on the third day, with fear let us glorify.

• All those born from earth praise, and the Powers of heaven glorify the Unity in being in three Persons, that is worshipped by all the faithful.

• Christ, the giver of life, before whom the Cherubim quail and tremble and whom the hosts of Angels glorify, who was incarnate from the Virgin, with fear let us glorify.

• As befits God, let us all praise with songs inspired the Father and the Son and the divine Spirit, three personned might, one kingship and dominion.

• Immaculate Virgin, all creation seeing thy Son risen from the dead, as befits God, has been filled with unspeakable joy, as it glorifies him and honours thee.

Holy God, Holy Mighty, Holy Immortal, have mercy on us. **(x3)**

> *Glory be to the Father, and to the Son, and to the Holy Spirit;*
> *Both now and forever, and unto the ages of ages. Amen.*

O Most Holy Trinity, have mercy on us.

O Lord, cleanse us from our sins.

O Master, pardon our iniquities.

O Holy One, visit and heal our infirmities, for Thy names sake.

Lord have mercy. **(x3)**

> *Glory be to the Father, and to the Son, and to the Holy Spirit;*
> *Both now and forever, and unto the ages of ages. Amen.*

Our Father, Who art in Heaven, hallowed be Thy Name. Thy Kingdom come, Thy will be done, on earth as it is in Heaven. Give us this day our daily bread, and forgive us our trespasses, as we forgive those who trespass against us; and lead us not into temptation, but deliver us from the evil one.

O Lord, Jesus Christ, Son of God, have mercy on us. Amen.

Glory be to the Father, and to the Son, and to the Holy Spirit;
Both now and forever, and unto the ages of ages. Amen.

Greater in honour than the Cherubim and beyond compare more glorious than the Seraphim; without corruption thou gavest birth to God the Word, truly the Theotokos, we magnify thee.

Through the prayers of our holy fathers, O Lord Jesus Christ our God, have mercy on us. Amen.

Glory be to the Father, and to the Son, and to the Holy Spirit;
Both now and forever, and unto the ages of ages. Amen.

Lord, have mercy. **(x3)**

[End Sunday part]

[All days]   **The Symbol Of Faith**

I believe in one God, Father, Almighty, Maker of heaven and earth, and of all things visible and invisible.

And in one Lord Jesus Christ, the only begotten Son of God, begotten from the Father before all ages; Light from Light, true God from true God; begotten not made; consubstantial with the Father, through Him all things were made. For our sake and for our salvation He came down from Heaven, and was incarnate from the Holy Spirit and the Virgin Mary and became man. He was crucified for us under Pontius Pilate, and suffered and was buried. He rose again on the third day in accordance with the Scriptures, and ascended into Heaven, and is seated at the right hand of the Father. He is coming again in glory to judge the living and the dead. And His kingdom shall have no end.

And in the Holy Spirit, the Lord, the Giver of life; Who proceeds from the Father; Who together with Father and Son is worshipped and glorified; Who spoke through the prophets. In One, Holy, Catholic, and Apostolic Church. I confess one baptism for the forgiveness of sins. I await the resurrection of the dead, And the life of the age to come. Amen.

Holy God, Holy Mighty, Holy Immortal, have mercy on us. **(x3)**

Glory be to the Father, and to the Son, and to the Holy Spirit;
Both now and forever, and unto the ages of ages. Amen.

O Most Holy Trinity, have mercy on us.

O Lord, cleanse us from our sins.

O Master, pardon our iniquities.

O Holy One, visit and heal our infirmities, for Thy names sake.

Lord, have mercy. **(x3)**

Glory be to the Father, and to the Son, and to the Holy Spirit;
Both now and forever, and unto the ages of ages. Amen.

Our Father, Who art in Heaven, hallowed be Thy Name. Thy Kingdom come, Thy will be done, on earth as it is in Heaven. Give us this day our daily bread, and forgive us our trespasses, as we forgive those who trespass against us; and lead us not into temptation, but deliver us from the evil one.

O Lord, Jesus Christ, Son of God, have mercy on us. Amen.

[Saturdays]

O Uncreated Nature, the Creator of all things, open our lips, that we may proclaim Thy praise, as we cry out: Holy, Holy, Holy art Thou O God. Through the Theotokos, have mercy on us.

Glory be to the Father, and to the Son, and to the Holy Spirit;

Imitating the powers on high, we that are on the earth offer a hymn of victory to Thee, O Good One. Holy, Holy, Holy art Thou O God. Through the Theotokos, have mercy on us.

Both now and forever, and unto the ages of ages. Amen.

Having raised me from bed and from sleep. O Lord, enlighten my mind and my heart, and open Thou my lips, that I may praise Thee, O Holy Trinity. Holy, Holy, Holy art Thou O God. Through the Theotokos, have mercy on us.

Prayer Of St Eustratius

Thee do we bless, Thou Most High God and Lord of mercy, Who ever workest with us deeds great and unfathomable, glorious and extraordinary, whereof there is no number; Who hast given unto us sleep for rest from our infirmity, and for repose of our much toiling flesh. We thank Thee that Thou hast not destroyed us in our iniquities, but hast shown Thy wonted love for man, and though we were prostrate in despair, Thou hast raised us up to glorify Thy dominion. Wherefore, we beseech Thine incomparable goodness: Enlighten the eyes of our understanding and raise our mind from the heavy sleep of slothfulness. Open our mouth and fill it with Thy praise, that we may be able undistracted to sing and chant and give thanks unto Thee, Who art God glorified in all and by all, the unoriginate Father, with Thine Only begotten Son, and Thine All holy and good and life creating Spirit, now and ever and unto ages of ages. Amen.

[End Saturdays]

[Monday – Friday]
Kathisma 17
Psalm 118

Halleluiah. Blessed are the blameless in the way, who walk in the law of the Lord. Blessed are they that search out His testimonies; with their whole heart shall they seek after Him. For they that work iniquity have not walked in His ways. Thou hast enjoined Thy commandments, that we should keep them most diligently. Would that my ways were directed to keep Thy statutes. Then shall I not be ashamed, when I look on all Thy commandments. I shall confess Thee with uprightness of heart, when I have learned the judgements of Thy righteousness. I shall keep thy statutes; do not utterly forsake me. Wherewithal shall a young man correct his way? By keeping Thy words. With my whole heart have I sought after Thee, cast me not away from Thy commandments. In my heart have I hid Thy sayings that I might not sin against Thee. Blessed art Thou, O Lord, teach me Thy statutes. With my lips have I declared all the judgements of Thy mouth. In the way of Thy testimonies have I found delight, as much as in all riches.

On Thy commandments shall I ponder, and I shall understand Thy ways. On Thy statutes shall I meditate; I shall not forget Thy words. Give reward unto Thy servant, quicken me and I shall keep Thy words. O unveil mine eyes, and I shall perceive wondrous things out of Thy law. I am a sojourner on the earth, hide not from me Thy commandments. My soul hath longed to desire Thy judgements at all times. Thou hast rebuked the proud; cursed are they that decline from Thy commandments. Remove from me reproach and contempt, for after Thy testimonies have I sought. For princes sat and they spake against me, but Thy servant pondered on Thy statutes. For Thy testimonies are my meditation, and Thy statutes are my counsellors. My soul hath cleaved unto the earth; quicken me according to Thy word. My ways have I declared, and Thou hast heard me; teach me Thy statutes. Make me to understand the way of Thy statutes, and I shall ponder on Thy wondrous works.

My soul hath slumbered from despondency, strengthen me with Thy words. Remove from me the way of unrighteousness, and with Thy law have mercy on me. I have chosen the way of truth, and Thy judgements have I not forgotten. I have cleaved to Thy testimonies, O Lord; put me not to shame. The way of Thy commandments have I run, when Thou didst enlarge my heart. Set before me for a law, O Lord, the way of Thy statutes, and I shall seek after it continually. Give me understanding, and I shall search out Thy law, and I shall keep it with my whole heart. Guide me in the path of Thy commandments, for I have desired it. Incline my heart unto Thy testimonies and not unto covetousness. Turn away mine eyes that I may not see vanity, quicken Thou me in Thy way. Establish for Thy servant Thine oracle unto fear of Thee. Remove my reproach which I have feared, for Thy judgements are good. Behold, I have longed after Thy commandments; in Thy righteousness quicken me.

Let Thy mercy come also upon me, O Lord, even Thy salvation according to Thy word. So shall I give an answer to them that reproach me, for I have hoped in Thy words. And take not utterly out of my mouth the word of truth, for in Thy judgements have I hoped. So shall I keep Thy law continually, for ever, and unto the ages of ages. And I walked in spaciousness, for after Thy commandments have I sought. And I spake of Thy testimonies before kings, and I was not ashamed. And I meditated on Thy commandments which I have greatly loved. And I lifted up my hands to Thy commandments which I have loved, and I pondered on Thy statutes. Remember Thy words to Thy servant, wherein Thou hast made me to hope. This hath comforted me in my humiliation, for Thine oracle hath quickened me. The proud have transgressed exceedingly, but from Thy law have I not declined. I remembered Thy judgements of old, O Lord, and was comforted. Despondency took hold upon me because of the sinners who forsake Thy law. Thy statutes were my songs in the place of my sojourning. I remembered Thy name in the night, O Lord, and I kept Thy law. This hath happened unto me because I sought after Thy statutes. Thou art my portion, O Lord; I said that I would keep Thy law. I entreated Thy countenance with my whole heart: Have mercy on me according to Thy word. I have thought on Thy ways, and I have turned my feet back to Thy testimonies.

I made ready, and I was not troubled, that I might keep Thy commandments. The cords of sinners have entangled me, but Thy law have I not forgotten. At midnight I arose to give thanks unto Thee for the judgements of Thy righteousness. I am a partaker with all them that fear Thee, and with them that keep Thy commandments. The earth, O Lord, is full of Thy mercy; teach me Thy statutes. Thou hast dealt graciously with Thy servant, O Lord, according to Thy word. Goodness and discipline and knowledge teach Thou me, for in Thy commandments have I believed. Before I was humbled, I transgressed; therefore Thy saying have I kept. Thou art good, O Lord, and in Thy goodness teach me Thy statutes. Multiplied against me hath been the unrighteousness of the proud; but as for me, with my whole heart shall I search out Thy commandments. Curdled like milk is their heart; but as for me, in Thy law have I meditated. It is good for me that Thou hast humbled me, that I might learn Thy statutes. The law of Thy mouth is better to me than thousands of gold and silver.

Behold, the Bridegroom cometh at midnight, and blessed is that servant whom He shall find watching; but unworthy is he whom He shall find heedless. Beware, therefore, O my soul, lest thou be weighed down with sleep; lest thou be given up to death, and be shut out from the kingdom. But rouse thyself and cry: Holy, Holy, Holy art Thou, O God, through the Theotokos have mercy on us.

Glory be to the Father, and to the Son, and to the Holy Spirit;

Meditating on that terrible day, O my soul, watch, keeping thy lamp alight and filled with oil; for thou knowest not when unto thee shall come the voice saying: Behold the Bridegroom. Beware, therefore, my soul, lest thou fall into slumber and be left outside, knocking, as were the five virgins; but wakefully watch, that thou mayest come to meet Christ with good oil, and He shall bestow upon thee the divine chamber of His glory.

Both now and forever, and unto the ages of ages. Amen.

Theotokion

To thee, the unassailable wall, confirmation of salvation, O Virgin Theotokos, do we supplicate, to destroy the counsels of the enemies, to change the sorrows of thy people into joy, to protect thy city, to ensure victory for pious rulers, and to pray for the peace of the world; for thou, O Theotokos, art our hope.

[End weekdays part]

[All days]

Lord, have mercy. **(x40)**

The Prayer Of The Hours

At all times and in every hour, Thou art worshipped and glorified in heaven and on earth, Christ our God. Long in patience, great in mercy and compassion, Thou lovest the righteous and showest mercy to sinners. Thou callest all to salvation through the promise of good things to come. Lord, receive our prayers at the present time. Direct our lives according to Thy commandments. Sanctify our souls. Purify our bodies. Set our minds aright. Cleanse our thoughts, and deliver us from all sorrow, evil and distress. Surround us with Thy holy angels, that, guarded and guided by their host, we may arrive at the unity of the faith and the understanding of Thine ineffable glory. For Thou art blessed to the ages of ages. Amen.

Lord, have mercy. **(x3)**

Glory be to the Father, and to the Son, and to the Holy Spirit;
Both now and forever, and unto the ages of ages. Amen.

Greater in honour than the Cherubim and beyond compare more glorious than the Seraphim; without corruption thou gavest birth to God the Word, truly the Theotokos, we magnify thee.

[Great Lent, OR the first day of the Apostles' Fast, OR of Advent (if a weekday).]

The Prayer Of St Ephraim The Syrian

O Lord and Master of my life, give me not a spirit of idleness, despondency, ambition or vain talking.
prostration
But rather a spirit of purity, humility, patience and love, bestow on me Thy servant.
prostration
Yea, O Lord and King, grant me to see mine own faults and not to judge my brother, for blessed art Thou to the ages of ages. Amen. *prostration*

O God, cleanse me a sinner. *cross and bow* (x12)

O Lord and Master of my life, give me not a spirit of idleness, despondency, ambition or vain talking. But rather a spirit of purity, humility, patience and love, bestow on me Thy servant. Yea, O Lord and King, grant me to see mine own faults and not to judge my brother, for blessed art Thou to the ages of ages. Amen.

prostration

Prayer Of Saint Mardarios

O Sovereign Master, God the Father Almighty, O Lord the Only begotten Son, Jesus Christ, and Thou, O Holy Spirit, one Godhead, one Power, have mercy on me, a sinner; and by the judgements which Thou knowest, save me, Thine unworthy servant; for blessed art Thou unto ages of ages. Amen.

[End Lent]

[From September 22nd until Palm Sunday:]

Prayer Of Saint Basil The Great

O Lord Almighty, God of hosts and of all flesh, Who dwellest on high and lookest down on things that are lowly, Who searchest the heart and innermost being, and clearly foreknowest the secrets of men; O unoriginate and everlasting Light, with Whom is no variableness, neither shadow of turning: Do Thou, O Immortal King, receive our supplications which we, daring because of the multitude of Thy compassions, offer Thee at the present time from defiled lips; and forgive us our sins, in deed, word, and thought, whether committed by us knowingly or in ignorance, and cleanse us from every defilement of flesh and spirit. And grant us to pass through the whole night of this present life with watchful heart and sober thought, ever expecting the coming of the bright and appointed day of Thine Only begotten Son, our Lord and God and Saviour, Jesus Christ, whereon the Judge of all shall come with glory to reward each according to his deeds. May we not be found fallen and idle, but watching, and upright in activity, ready to accompany Him into the joy and divine palace of His glory, where there is the ceaseless sound of those that keep festival, and the unspeakable delight of those that behold the ineffable beauty of Thy countenance. For Thou art the true Light that enlightenest and sanctifiest all, and all creation doth hymn Thee unto the ages of ages. Amen.

Prayer Of Saint Basil

We bless Thee, O Most High God and Lord of mercy, Who ever doest with us things both great and inscrutable, both glorious and awesome, of which there is no measure; Who grantest to us sleep for rest from our infirmities, and relaxation from the labours of our much toiling flesh. We thank Thee that Thou hast not destroyed us with our iniquities, but hast shown Thy loving kindness to man as usual, and while we were lying in despair upon our beds, Thou hast raised us up that we might glorify Thy dominion. Wherefore, we implore Thy boundless goodness: Enlighten the eyes of our understanding and raise up our mind from the heavy sleep of indolence; open our mouth and fill it with Thy praise, that we may be able steadily to hymn and confess Thee, Who art God glorified in all and by all, the unoriginate Father, with Thine Only begotten Son, and Thine All holy and good and life creating Spirit, now and ever, and unto the ages of ages. Amen.

[End September 22nd until Palm Sunday]

[All days]
Prayer Of St Eustratius

Most highly do I magnify Thee, O Lord, for Thou didst take notice of my lowliness and hast not delivered me into the hands of mine enemies, but relieved my soul from wants. And now, O Master, let Thy hand shelter me and let Thy mercy descend upon me, for my soul is distracted and pained its departure from this my wretched and filthy body, lest the evil of the adversary overtake it and make it stumble into the darkness for the unknown and known sins amassed by me in this life. Be merciful unto me, O Master, and let not my soul see the dark countenances of evil spirits, but let it be received by angels bright and shining. Glorify Thy holy name and by Thy might set me before Thy divine judgement seat. When I am being judged, suffer not that the hand of the prince of this world should take hold of me to throw me, a sinner, into depths of Hades, but stand by me and be unto me a saviour and mediator, for these bodily torments gladden Thy servants. Have mercy, O Lord, on my soul defiled through passions of this life and receive it cleansed by penitence and confession, for blessed art Thou unto the ages of ages. Amen.

Psalm 120
An Ode of Ascents.

I have lifted up mine eyes to the mountains, from whence cometh my help. My help cometh from the Lord, Who hath made heaven and the earth. Give not thy foot unto moving, and may He not slumber that keepeth thee. Behold, He shall not slumber nor shall He sleep, He that keepeth Israel. The Lord shall keep thee; the Lord is thy shelter at thy right hand. The sun shall not burn thee by day, nor the moon by night. The Lord shall keep thee from all evil, the Lord shall guard thy soul. The Lord shall keep thy coming in and thy going out, from henceforth and for evermore.

Psalm 133
An Ode of Ascents.

Behold now, bless you the Lord, all you servants of the Lord. you that stand in the house of the Lord, in the courts of the house of our God, In the nights lift up thine hands unto the holies, and bless the Lord. The Lord bless thee out of Zion, He that made heaven and the earth.

After The Psalm
Glory be to the Father, and to the Son, and to the Holy Spirit;
Both now and forever, and unto the ages of ages. Amen.
Holy God, Holy Mighty, Holy Immortal, have mercy on us. **(x3)**

O Most Holy Trinity, have mercy on us.

O Lord, cleanse us from our sins.

O Master, pardon our iniquities.

O Holy One, visit and heal our infirmities, for Thy names sake.

Lord, have mercy. **(x3)**

Glory be to the Father, and to the Son, and to the Holy Spirit;
Both now and forever, and unto the ages of ages. Amen.

Our Father, Who art in heaven, hallowed be Thy Name. Thy Kingdom come, Thy will be done on earth, as it is in heaven. Give us this day our daily bread. And forgive us our trespasses as we forgive those who trespass against us. And lead us not into temptation; but deliver us from the evil one. Amen.

O Lord, Jesus Christ, Son of God, have mercy on us. Amen.

Tone 8   Humility, tranquillity, repose, suffering, pleading.   *C, D, Eb, F, G, A, Bb, C.*

Keep Thy servants in remembrance, O Lord, since Thou art good, and do Thou forgive their every sin in this life; for no man is without sin, except for Thee Who art able to grant rest even unto those that have departed hence.

O Thou Who by the depth of Thy wisdom dost provide all things out of love for man, and grantest unto all that which is profitable, O only Creator: grant rest, O Lord, to the souls of Thy servants; for in Thee have they placed their hope, O our Creator and Fashioner and God.

Glory be to the Father, and to the Son, and to the Holy Spirit;

With the Saints grant rest, O Christ, to the souls of Thy servants, where there is neither pain, nor sorrow, nor sighing, but life unending.

Both now and forever, and unto the ages of ages. Amen.

Theotokion

O Virgin Theotokos, all generations call thee blessed, for in thee He, the Uncontainable One, Christ our God, was pleased to be contained. Blessed are we also who have thee as protection, for day and night dost thou intercede for us, and the sceptres of the kingdom are strengthened by thine entreaties. Wherefore, with hymns we cry to thee: Rejoice, O Full of Grace, the Lord is with thee.

Lord, have mercy. **(x12)**

Remember, O Lord, our fathers and brethren that have fallen asleep in hope of the resurrection of eternal life, and all that have ended their days in piety and faith; and forgive their every transgression in which they have willingly or unwillingly transgressed in word or deed or thought. And make them to dwell in places of light, in places of verdure, in places of refreshment, where every pain, sorrow, and sighing is fled away, where the visitation of Thy countenance maketh glad all Thy Saints from ages past. Grant unto them and us Thy Kingdom, and participation in Thine ineffable and eternal good things, and the enjoyment of Thine endless and blessed life. For Thou art the Life, the Resurrection, and the Repose of Thy servants that have fallen asleep, O Christ our God, and unto Thee do we send up glory with Thy Father Who is without beginning, and Thine All holy and good and life creating Spirit, now and ever, and unto ages of ages. Amen.

Most glorious, Ever virgin, blessed Theotokos, present our prayer to thy Son and our God, and pray that through thee He would save our souls.

Prayer Of Saint Ioannikios

My hope is the Father, my refuge the Son, my shelter the Holy Spirit. O Holy Trinity, glory be to Thee.

Unto thee do I commit mine every hope, O Mother of God; guard me under thy shelter.

Glory be to the Father, and to the Son, and to the Holy Spirit;
Both now and forever, and unto the ages of ages. Amen.

Lord, have mercy. **(x3)**

Troparia

Tone 6   Rich texture, funereal character, sorrowful tone.   *D, Eb, F##, G, A, Bb, C##, D.*

Have mercy on us, Lord, have mercy on us; for we sinners, lacking all defence, offer Thee, as our Master, this supplication: have mercy on us.

Glory be to the Father, and to the Son, and to the Holy Spirit;

Lord, have mercy on us, for in Thee we have put our trust. Do not be very angry with us, nor remember our iniquities. But look on us now, as Thou art compassionate, and rescue us from our enemies. For Thou art our God, and we are Thine people; we are all the work of Thine hands, and we have called on Thy name.

Both now and forever, and unto the ages of ages. Amen.

Open the gate of compassion to us, blessed Mother of God; hoping in thee, may we not fail. Through thee may we be delivered from adversities, for thou art the salvation of the Christian race.

Glory be to the Father, and to the Son, and to the Holy Spirit;
Both now and forever, and unto the ages of ages. Amen.

Lord, have mercy. **(x3)**

O Lord Jesus Christ, Son of God, for the sake of the prayers of Thy most pure Mother, our holy and God bearing fathers, and all the saints, have mercy on us and save us, for Thou art good and the Lover of mankind. Amen.

Remit, pardon, forgive, O God, our offences, both voluntary and involuntary, in deed and word, in knowledge and ignorance, by day and by night, in mind and thought; forgive us all things, for Thou art good and the Lover of mankind. Amen.

O Lord, Lover of mankind, forgive them that hate and wrong us. Do good to them that do good. Grant our brethren and kindred their saving petitions and life eternal; visit the infirm and grant them healing. Guide those at sea. Journey with them that travel. Help Orthodox Christians to struggle. To them that serve and are kind to us grant remissions of sins. On them that have charged us, the unworthy, to pray for them, have mercy according to Thy great mercy. Remember, O Lord, our fathers and brethron departed before us, and grant them rest where the light of Thy countenance shall visit them. Remember, O Lord, our brethren in captivity, and deliver them from every misfortune. Remember, O Lord, those that bear fruit and do good works in Thy holy Church, and grant them their saving petitions and life eternal. Remember also, O Lord, us Thy lowly and sinful and unworthy servants, and enlighten our minds with the light of Thy knowledge, and guide us in the way of Thy commandments; through the intercessions of our most pure Lady, the Theotokos and Ever Virgin Mary, and of all Thy saints, for blessed art Thou unto the ages of ages. Amen.

Lord, have mercy. **(x3)**

Through the prayers of our holy Fathers, Lord Jesus Christ our God, have mercy on us. Amen.

Saturday

Various services that are usually done on the day before the Divine Liturgy.

The Pedalion or Rudder (the canons of the Church) forbid fasting on a Saturday evening in expectation of the Eucharist the next day. If in doubt about the "right" thing to do it is not a good idea to try and work it out for yourself, as often times the Church has instituted a procedure for historical reasons that are unknown to the lay person. It is always preferable to refer to The Pedalion for guidance.

There are 855 canons of the Church. These are accumulated from each Great and Holy Council. The first thing that each Council does is to ratify the previous Council and adopt its rulings. The purpose of each Council is defend Orthodoxy against some controversy at the time, not to introduce new teachings from nowhere. In the process of researching a point through the 855 canons one may find that an earlier Council was stricter about a point than a later Council. If this is a point that relates to you, you should seek the guidance of your immediate spiritual advisor.

Our own parish Priest is our first port of call. If he doesn't know he should be able to point you to someone who does. Our Priest is our family doctor, it is for him to refer us to a specialist. There are those who would go from Priest to Monk asking the same question until they receive the answer that they want. It is also worth remembering that a Monk is not a member of the clergy; they are Orthodox Christians working out their own salvation, though they may also be specialists. Clergy are sent to help us.

Those who chant should offer their psalmodies with great care to God, Who looks into the hidden recesses of the heart, i.e., into the psalmody and prayer that are done mentally in the heart rather than uttered in external cries. Canon LXXV of the Sixth Ecumenical Synod.

[Daily and seasonal variables required.]

Trisagion Prayers

Priest: Blessed is our God, always, now and forever, and unto the ages of ages.

People: *Amen.*

Reader: Come, let us worship God, our King.

Come, let us worship and fall down before Christ, our King and our God.

Come, let us worship and fall down before Christ Himself, our King and our God.

Psalm 103 - Of David. Concerning The Formation Of The World.

Bless the Lord, O my soul. O Lord my God, Thou hast been exceedingly magnified. Confession and majesty hast Thou put on, Who covered Thyself with light as with a garment, Who stretched out the heaven as it were a curtain; Who supports His chambers in the waters, Who appoints the clouds for His ascent, Who walks upon the wings of the winds, Who makes His angels spirits, and His ministers a flame of fire, Who establishes the earth in the sureness thereof; it shall not be turned back for ever and ever. The abyss like a garment is His mantle; upon the mountains shall the waters stand. At Thy rebuke they shall flee, at the voice of Thy thunder shall they be afraid.

The mountains rise up and the plains sink down to the place where Thou hast established them. Thou appointed a boundary that they shall not pass, neither return to cover the earth. He sends forth springs in the valleys; between the mountains shall the waters run. They shall give drink to all the beasts of the field; the wild asses shall wait to quench their thirst. Beside them shall the birds of the heaven lodge, from the midst of the rocks shall they give voice. He waters the mountains from His chambers; the earth shall be satisfied with the fruit of Thy works.

He causes the grass to grow for the cattle, and green herb for the service of men, To bring forth bread out of the earth; and wine makes glad the heart of man. To make his face cheerful with oil; and bread strengthens mans heart. The trees of the plain shall be satisfied, the cedars of Lebanon, which Thou hast planted. There shall the sparrows make their nests; the house of the heron is chief among them. The high mountains are a refuge for the harts, and so is the rock for the hares. He has made the moon for seasons; the sun knows his going down. Thou appointed the darkness, and there was the night, wherein all the beasts of the forest shall go abroad. Young lions roaring after their prey, and seeking their food from God. The sun arises, and they are gathered together, and they lay them down in their dens.

But man shall go forth unto his work, and to his labour until the evening. How magnified are Thy works, O Lord. In wisdom hast Thou made them all; the earth is filled with Thy creation. So is this great and spacious sea, therein are things creeping innumerable, small living creatures with the great. There go the ships; there this dragon, whom Thou hast made to play therein. All things wait on Thee, to give them their food in due season; when Thou gavest it to them, they shall gather it. When Thou opened Thy hand, all things shall be filled with goodness; when Thou turned away Thy face, they shall be troubled. Thou wilt take their spirit, and they shall cease; and to their dust shall they return. Thou wilt send forth Thy Spirit, and they shall be created; and Thou shalt renew the face of the earth.

Let the glory of the Lord be unto the ages; the Lord shall rejoice in His works. Who looks on the earth and makes it tremble, Who touches the mountains and they smoke. I shall sing unto the Lord throughout my life, I shall chant to my God for as long as I have my being. May my words be sweet unto Him, and I shall rejoice in the Lord. O that sinners would cease from the earth, and they that work iniquity, that they should be no more. Bless the Lord, O my soul. The sun knows his going down, Thou appointed the darkness, and there was the night. How magnified are Thy works, O Lord. In wisdom hast Thou made them all.

After The Psalm

Glory be to the Father and to the Son and to the Holy Spirit;
Both now and forever, and unto the ages of ages. Amen.

Halleluiah, Halleluiah, Halleluiah. Glory to Thee, O God. **(x3)**

The Great Litany

Deacon: In peace, let us pray to the Lord.

People: *Lord, have mercy.*

Deacon: For the peace from above, and for the salvation of our souls, let us pray to the Lord.

People: *Lord, have mercy.*

Deacon: For the peace of the whole world, for the good estate of the holy churches of God, and for the union of all men, let us pray to the Lord.

People: *Lord, have mercy.*

Deacon: For this Holy House, and for those who with faith, reverence, and fear of God, enter therein, let us pray to the Lord.

People: *Lord, have mercy.*

Deacon: For our father and Archbishop Nikitas, for the venerable Priesthood, the Diaconate in Christ, for all the clergy and the people, let us pray to the Lord.

People: *Lord, have mercy.*

Deacon: For Her Majesty, the Queen, for the First Minister, for all civil authorities, and for our Armed Forces, let us pray to the Lord.

People: *Lord, have mercy.*

Deacon: That He shall aid them and grant them victory over every enemy and adversary, let us pray to the Lord.

People: *Lord, have mercy.*

Deacon: For this city, and for every city and land, and for the faithful who dwell therein, let us pray to the Lord.

People: *Lord, have mercy.*

Deacon: For healthful seasons, for abundance of the fruits of the earth, and for peaceful times, let us pray to the Lord.

People: *Lord, have mercy.*

Deacon: For travellers by sea, by land, and by air; for the sick and the suffering; for captives and their salvation, let us pray to the Lord.

People: *Lord, have mercy.*

Deacon: For our deliverance from all tribulation, wrath, danger, and necessity, let us pray to the Lord.

People: *Lord, have mercy.*

Deacon: Help us; save us; have mercy on us; and keep us, O God, by Thy grace.

People: *Lord, have mercy.*

Deacon: Calling to remembrance our all holy, immaculate, most blessed and glorious Lady Theotokos and ever virgin Mary, with all the Saints: let us commend ourselves and each other, and all our life unto Christ our God.

People: *To Thee, O Lord.*

Priest: For to Thou art due all glory, honour, and worship: to the Father, and to the Son, and to the Holy Spirit; Both now and forever and unto the ages of ages.

People: *Amen.*

Psalm 140

Chorus: Lord, I have cried to Thee: hear me. Hear me, O Lord.

Lord, I have cried to Thee: hear me. Receive the voice of my prayer.

When I call upon Thee, hear me, O Lord. Let my prayer arise as incense in Thy sight,

And let the lifting up of my hands be an evening sacrifice. Hear me, O Lord.

Kekragarion
Sticheroi From Psalm 140

• Set, O Lord, a watch before my mouth, and a door of enclosure round about my lips.

• Incline not my heart to words of evil, to make excuses for sins.

• Those that work iniquity; I shall not join with their number.

• The righteous man shall chasten me with mercy and reprove me; as for the oil of the sinner, let it not anoint my head.

• For yet more is my prayer in the presence of their pleasures; their judges have been swallowed up by the rock.

• They shall hear my words, for they be sweetened; as a clod of earth is broken upon the earth, so have their bones been scattered into hades.

• To Thee O Lord are mine eyes. In Thee have I hoped; take not my soul away.

• Keep me from the snare which they have laid for me, and from the stumbling blocks of them that work iniquity.

• The sinners shall fall into their own net; I am alone until I pass by.

Sticheroi From Psalm 141

- With my voice to the Lord have I cried, with my voice have I made supplication.
- I shall pour out before Him my supplications; my afflictions shall I declare before Him.
- When my spirit was fainting within me, then Thou knewest my paths.
- In this way wherein I have walked they hid for me a snare.
- I looked on my right hand, and beheld, and there was none that knew me.
- Flight has failed me, and there is none that watches out for my soul.
- I cried to Thee, O Lord; I said: Thou art my hope, my portion in the land of the living.
- Attend unto my supplication, for I am brought very low.
- Deliver me from them that persecute me, for they are stronger than I.
- 10)   Bring my soul out of prison. That I may confess Thy name.

[daily or seasonal Troparia]

- 9)   The righteous shall patiently wait for me until Thou shalt reward me.

[daily or seasonal Troparia]

Sticheroi From Psalm 129

- 8) Out of the depths have I cried unto Thee, O Lord. O Lord, hear my voice.

[daily or seasonal Troparia]

- 7) Let Thine ears be attentive to the voice of my supplication.

[daily or seasonal Troparia]

- 6) If Thou should mark iniquities, O Lord; O Lord, who shall stand? For with Thee there is forgiveness.

[daily or seasonal Troparia]

- 5) For Thy names sake have I patiently waited for Thee, O Lord; my soul has patiently waited for Thy word, my soul has hoped in the Lord.

[daily or seasonal Troparia]

- 4) From the morning watch until night, from the morning watch let Israel hope in the Lord.

[daily or seasonal Troparia]

- 3) For with the Lord there is mercy, and with Him is plenteous redemption; and He shall redeem Israel out of all his iniquities.

[daily or seasonal Troparia]

Sticheroi From Psalm 116

- 2) O praise the Lord, all you nations; praise Him, all you peoples.

[daily or seasonal Troparia]

- 1) For He has made His mercy to prevail over us, and the truth of the Lord abides forever.

[daily or seasonal Troparia]

Glory be to the Father, and to the Son, and to the Holy Spirit;
Both now and forever, and unto the ages of ages. Amen.

Theotokion

Tone 8 Humility, tranquillity, repose, suffering, pleading. *C, D, Eb, F, G, A, Bb, C.*

Verily, the King of Heaven, for His love to mankind, didst appear on earth; and with men did He deal; for He took unto Himself a body from the pure Virgin. And from her did He issue in the adopted body, He being one Son, dual in Nature, not dual in Person. Wherefore, do we confess, preaching the truth that Christ our God is perfect God and perfect Man. Therefore, O Mother who hast no groom, beseech Him to have mercy upon our souls.

The Holy Entrance

[Whilst:]

Deacon: *[soto voce]* Let us pray to the Lord. Lord have mercy.

Priest: *[soto voce]* In the evening and in the morning and at noon we praise Thee, we bless Thee, we give thanks unto Thee, and we pray unto Thee, O Master of all, Lord Who lovest mankind; Direct our prayer as incense before Thee, and incline not our hearts unto words of thought of evil, but deliver us from all who seek after our souls. For unto Thee, O Lord, Lord are our eyes, and in Thee have we hoped. Put us not to shame, O our God. For unto Thee are due all glory, honour and worship, to the Father, the Son and the Holy Spirit, both now and forever, and to the ages of ages.

Deacon: Amen.

[Censing]

Deacon: *[soto voce]* Master, bless the Holy Entrance.

Priest: *[soto voce]* Blessed is the Entrance to Thy Holy place; both now and forever, and unto the ages of ages. Amen.

Deacon: *[aloud]* *Wisdom. Stand up!*

O Gladsome Light

O Gladsome Light of the holy glory of the immortal Father; Heavenly holy, blessed Jesus Christ.

Now that we have come to the setting of the sun, and behold the Evening Light.

We praise God; Father, Son and Holy Spirit. For meet it is at all time to worship Thee, with voices of praise; O Son of God and Giver of Life. Therefore all the world doth glorify Thee.

Prokeimenon

Priest: The Evening Prokeimenon.

[Saturday] Tone 6   *Rich texture, funeral, sorrowful.*   *D, Eb, F##, G, A, Bb, C##, D.*

Reader: The Lord is clothed with strength and He has girded Himself.

People: *The Lord is King, He is clothed with majesty.*

Reader: For He established the world which shall not be shaken.

People: *The Lord is King, He is clothed with majesty.*

Reader: Holiness becomes Thine house, O Lord, to the length of days.

People: *The Lord is King, He is clothed with majesty.*

Reader: The Lord is King | *He is clothed with majesty.*

The Litany Of Fervent Supplication

Deacon: Let us all say with our whole soul, and with our whole mind let us say:

People: *Lord, have mercy.*

Deacon: Lord Almighty, God of our Fathers, we pray Thee, hearest and have mercy.

People: *Lord, have mercy.*

Deacon: Have mercy on us, O God, according to Thy great mercy, we pray Thee; hear us and have mercy.

People: *Lord, have mercy.* **(x3)**

Deacon: Also we pray for our Archbishop Nikitas.

People: *Lord, have mercy.* **(x3)**

Deacon: For our Sovereign Lady, Queen Elizabeth, the Royal family, our Government, and all in authority, let us pray to the Lord.

People: *Lord, have mercy.* **(x3)**

Deacon: Also we pray for mercy, life, peace, health, salvation, visitation, pardon and forgiveness of sins for the servants of God, all devout and Orthodox Christians, those who dwell in or visit this city or town and parish, the wardens and members of this church and their families and all who have asked for our prayers, unworthy though we are.

People: *Lord, have mercy.* **(x3)**

Deacon: Also we pray for the blessed and ever remembered founders of this holy church, and for all our brothers and sisters who have gone to their rest before us, and who lie here asleep in the true faith; and for the Orthodox everywhere *[and the servants of God N and N – (names given before the service)]* and that they may be pardoned all their offences, both voluntary and involuntary.

People: *Lord, have mercy.* **(x3)**

Deacon: Also we pray for those who bring offerings, those who care for the beauty of this holy and venerable house, for those who labour in its service, for those who sing, and for the people here present, who await Thy great and rich mercy.

People: *Lord, have mercy.* **(x3)**

Priest: For Thou, O God, art merciful and love mankind, and to Thee we givest glory, to the Father, the Son and the Holy Spirit, both now and forever, and unto the ages of ages.

People: *Amen.*

Reader: Vouchsafe, O Lord, to keep us this evening without sin. Blessed art Thou, O Lord, the God of our fathers, and praised and glorified is Thy name unto the ages.

People: *Amen.*

Let Thy mercy, O Lord, be upon us, according as we have hoped in Thee.

Blessed art Thou, O Lord, teach me Thy statutes.

Blessed art Thou, O Master, give me understanding of Thy statutes.

Blessed art Thou, O Holy One, enlighten me by Thy statutes.

O Lord, Thy mercy endures forever; disdain not the work of Thy hands. To Thee is due praise, to Thee is due song, to Thee is due glory, to the Father, and to the Son, and to the Holy Spirit; both now and forever, and unto the ages of ages. Amen.

The Litany Of Supplication

Deacon: Let us complete our evening prayer unto the Lord.

People: *Lord, have mercy.*

Deacon: Help us; save us; have mercy on us; and keep us, O God, by Thy grace.

People: *Lord, have mercy.*

Deacon: That the whole evening may be perfect, holy, peaceful and sinless, let us ask of the Lord.

People: *Grant this, O Lord.*

Deacon: An angel of peace, a faithful guide, a guardian of our souls and bodies, let us ask of the Lord.

People: *Grant this, O Lord.*

Deacon: Pardon and remission of our sins and transgressions, let us ask of the Lord.

People: *Grant this, O Lord.*

Deacon: All things good and profitable for our souls and peace for the world, let us ask of the Lord.

People: *Grant this, O Lord.*

Deacon: That we may complete the remaining time of our life in peace and repentance, let us ask of the Lord.

People: *Grant this, O Lord.*

Deacon: A Christian ending to our life, painless, blameless, peaceful, and a good defence before the fearful judgement seat of Christ, let us ask of the Lord.

People: *Grant this, O Lord.*

Deacon: Calling to remembrance our all holy, immaculate, most blessed and glorious Lady Theotokos and ever virgin Mary, with all the Saints: let us commend ourselves and one another, and all our life to Christ our God.

People: *To Thee, O Lord.*

Priest: For Thou art a good God and lovest mankind, and to Thee we ascribe glory: to the Father, and to the Son, and to the Holy Spirit; both now and forever, and to the ages of ages.

People: *Amen.*

Priest: Peace be with you all.

People: *And with thy spirit.*

Deacon: Let us bow our heads unto the Lord.

People: *To Thee, O Lord.*

Priest: O Lord our God, Who did bow the heavens and come down for the salvation of mankind: Look upon Thy servants and Thine inheritance; for to Thee, the fearful Judge Who yet loves mankind, have Thine servants bowed their heads and submissively inclined their necks, awaiting not help from men but entreating Thy mercy and looking confidently for Thy salvation. Guard them at all times, both during this present evening and in the approaching night, from every foe, from all adverse powers of the devil, and from vain thoughts and from evil imaginations. Blessed and glorified be the might of Thy kingdom: of the Father, and of the Son, and of the Holy Spirit; both now and forever, and unto the ages of ages.

People: Amen.

The Aposticha From The Octoechos *(Triodion if Lent)* **With The Following Stichoi**

Stichos 1:

To Thee have I lifted up my eyes, to Thee that dwells in heaven. Behold, as the eyes of servants look at the hands of their masters, as the eyes of the handmaid look at the hands of her mistress, so do our eyes look to the Lord our God, until He take pity on us.

Stichos 2:

Have mercy on us, O Lord, have mercy on us, for greatly are we filled with abasement. Greatly has our soul been filled therewith; let reproach come upon them that prosper, and abasement on the proud.

Chorus: *The Lord is King, He is clothed with majesty.*

Reader: Let us glorify Christ risen from the dead; for He did take unto Himself a soul and a body; and He separated one from the other in the Passion, when His pure soul went down to Hades that He led captive; and the holy body saw no corruption in the grave, the body of the Redeemer, Saviour of our souls.

Chorus: *For He established the world which shall not be shaken.*

Reader: With psalms and songs of praise, O Christ, do we glorify Thy Resurrection from the dead, by which Thou didst deliver us from the rebellion of Hades. And since Thou art God, Thou didst grant us eternal life and the Great Mercy.

Chorus: *Holiness becomes Thine house, O Lord, to the length of days.*

Reader: O Lord of all, O incomprehensible One; O Maker of heaven and earth, when Thou didst suffer in Thy Passion on the Cross, Thou didst pour out for me passionlessness; and when Thou didst submit to burial and didst rise in glory, Thou didst raise Adam with Thee by a mighty hand. Wherefore, glory to Thy third day Resurrection by which Thou didst grant us eternal life and forgiveness of sins; for Thou alone art compassionate.

Glory be to the Father, and to the Son, and to the Holy Spirit;

[Daily Doxasticon – if available]

Both now and forever, and unto the ages of ages. Amen.

[Seasonal Doxasticon – if available]

Hymn Of Simeon The God Receiver

Reader: Lord, now lettest Thou Thy servant depart in peace, according to Thy word, for mine eyes have seen Thy salvation, which Thou hast prepared before the face of all peoples; a light of revelation for the Gentiles, and the glory of Thy people Israel.

Trisagion Prayers

Holy God, Holy Mighty, Holy Immortal, have mercy on us. **(x3)**

Glory be to the Father, and to the Son, and to the Holy Spirit;
Both now and forever, and unto the ages of ages. Amen.

O Most Holy Trinity, have mercy on us.

O Lord, cleanse us from our sins.

O Master, pardon our iniquities.

O Holy One, visit and heal our infirmities, for Thy names sake.

Lord have mercy. **(x3)**

Glory be to the Father and to the Son and to the Holy Spirit;
Both now and forever, and unto the ages of ages. Amen.

People: *Our Father, Who art in Heaven, hallowed be Thy Name. Thy Kingdom come, Thy will be done, on earth as it is in Heaven. Give us this day our daily bread, and forgive us our trespasses, as we forgive those who trespass against us; and lead us not into temptation, but deliver us from the evil one.*

Priest: For Thine is the kingdom, the power, and the glory, of the Father, and the Son and the Holy Spirit, both now and ever, and to the ages of ages.

People: *Amen.*

Resurrectional Apolytikion

Tone 8 Humility, tranquillity, repose, suffering, pleading.   *C, D, Eb, F, G, A, Bb, C.*

From the heights Thou didst descend, O compassionate One, and Thou didst submit to the three day burial, that Thou might deliver us from passion; Thou art our life and our Resurrection, O Lord, glory to Thee.

Glory be to the Father and to the Son and to the Holy Spirit;
Both now and forever, and unto the ages of ages. Amen.

Resurrectional Theotokion

Tone 1 Magnificent, happy, and earthy character.   *C, D, Eb, F, G, A, Bb, C.*

As Gabriel cried aloud unto thee: "Rejoice, O Virgin," with that cry did the Lord of all become incarnate in thee, O holy ark, as spake the righteous David; and thou wast revealed, as more spacious than the heavens, in that thou bore thy Creator. Wherefore, glory to Him Who abided in thee; glory to Him Who came from thee; glory to Him, Who through thy birth giving hath set us free.

The Dismissal

Deacon: Wisdom.

People: *Holy Father, bless.*

Priest: Christ our God, the Existing One, is blessed, always, now and forever, and unto the ages of ages.

People: *Amen.*

Reader: Preserve, O God, the holy Orthodox faith and all Orthodox Christians, unto the ages of ages.

People: *Amen.*

Priest: Most holy Theotokos, save us.

Reader: Greater in honour than the Cherubim and beyond compare more glorious than the Seraphim; without corruption thou gavest birth to God the Word, truly the Theotokos, we magnify thee.

Priest: Glory to Thee, O Christ, our God and our hope, glory to Thee.

Reader: Glory be to the Father, and to to Son, and to the Holy Spirit, both now and for ever, both and to the ages of ages.

People: *Amen.*

Lord, have mercy. **(x3)**

Holy Father, bless!

Priest: May He who rose from the dead, Christ our true God, through the prayers of His most holy Mother, by the power of the precious and life giving Cross, through the protection of the honoured, Bodiless powers of Heaven, through the intercessions of the honoured, glorious prophet, forerunner and baptist John, of the holy, all praised and glorious Apostles, of the holy, glorious and triumphant Martyrs, of our venerable and God bearing Fathers and Mothers who have shone forth in the ascetic life, of the holy and righteous ancestors of God, Joachim and Anna, of *[patronal saint(s)]* to whom the church is dedicated, of *[Saint N]* whose memory we celebrate today, and of all the Saints, have mercy on us and save us, for He is good and loves mankind.

People: *Amen.*

Priest: Through the prayers of our holy Fathers; O Lord Jesus Christ our God; have mercy on us and save us.

People: *Amen.*

[Without a Priest]

[Daily and seasonal variables required.]

Trisagion Prayers

Reader: In the Name of the Father and of the Son and of the Holy Spirit.

People: *Amen. Glory to Thee, our God, glory to Thee.*

Reader: O Heavenly King, Comforter, Spirit of Truth, Who art everywhere present and fillest all things, Treasury of blessings and Giver of life: Come and abide in us and cleanse us from every impurity and save our souls, O Good One.

Holy God, Holy Mighty, Holy Immortal, have mercy on us. **(x3)**

> *Glory be to the Father, and to the Son, and to the Holy Spirit;*
> *Both now and forever, and unto the ages of ages. Amen.*

O Most Holy Trinity, have mercy on us.

O Lord, cleanse us from our sins.

O Master, pardon our iniquities.

O Holy One, visit and heal our infirmities, for Thy names sake.

Lord have mercy. **(x3)**

> *Glory be to the Father and to the Son and to the Holy Spirit;*
> *Both now and forever, and unto the ages of ages. Amen.*

People: *Our Father, Who art in Heaven, hallowed be Thy Name. Thy Kingdom come, Thy will be done, on earth as it is in Heaven. Give us this day our daily bread, and forgive us our trespasses, as we forgive those who trespass against us; and lead us not into temptation, but deliver us from the evil one. Amen.*

Lord, have mercy. **(x12)**

> *Glory be to the Father and to the Son and to the Holy Spirit;*
> *Both now and forever and unto the ages of ages. Amen.*

Come, let us worship God, our King.

Come, let us worship and fall down before Christ, our King and our God.

Come, let us worship and fall down before Christ Himself, our King and our God.

Psalm 103

Of David. Concerning The Formation Of The World.

Bless the Lord, O my soul. O Lord my God, Thou hast been exceedingly magnified. Confession and majesty hast Thou put on, Who covered Thyself with light as with a garment, Who stretched out the heaven as it were a curtain; Who supports His chambers in the waters, Who appoints the clouds for His ascent, Who walks upon the wings of the winds, Who makes His angels spirits, and His ministers a flame of fire, Who establishes the earth in the sureness thereof; it shall not be turned back for ever and ever. The abyss like a garment is His mantle; upon the mountains shall the waters stand. At Thy rebuke they shall flee, at the voice of Thy thunder shall they be afraid.

The mountains rise up and the plains sink down to the place where Thou hast established them. Thou appointed a boundary that they shall not pass, neither return to cover the earth. He sends forth springs in the valleys; between the mountains shall the waters run. They shall give drink to all the beasts of the field; the wild asses shall wait to quench their thirst. Beside them shall the birds of the heaven lodge, from the midst of the rocks shall they give voice. He waters the mountains from His chambers; the earth shall be satisfied with the fruit of Thy works.

He causes the grass to grow for the cattle, and green herb for the service of men, To bring forth bread out of the earth; and wine makes glad the heart of man. To make his face cheerful with oil; and bread strengthens mans heart. The trees of the plain shall be satisfied, the cedars of Lebanon, which Thou hast planted. There shall the sparrows make their nests; the house of the heron is chief among them. The high mountains are a refuge for the harts, and so is the rock for the hares. He has made the moon for seasons; the sun knows his going down. Thou appointed the darkness, and there was the night, wherein all the beasts of the forest shall go abroad. Young lions roaring after their prey, and seeking their food from God. The sun arises, and they are gathered together, and they lay them down in their dens.

But man shall go forth unto his work, and to his labour until the evening. How magnified are Thy works, O Lord. In wisdom hast Thou made them all; the earth is filled with Thy creation. So is this great and spacious sea, therein are things creeping innumerable, small living creatures with the great. There go the ships; there this dragon, whom Thou hast made to play therein. All things wait on Thee, to give them their food in due season; when Thou gavest it to them, they shall gather it. When Thou opened Thy hand, all things shall be filled with goodness; when Thou turned away Thy face, they shall be troubled. Thou wilt take their spirit, and they shall cease; and to their dust shall they return. Thou wilt send forth Thy Spirit, and they shall be created; and Thou shalt renew the face of the earth.

Let the glory of the Lord be unto the ages; the Lord shall rejoice in His works. Who looks on the earth and makes it tremble, Who touches the mountains and they smoke. I shall sing unto the Lord throughout my life, I shall chant to my God for as long as I have my being. May my words be sweet unto Him, and I shall rejoice in the Lord. O that sinners would cease from the earth, and they that work iniquity, that they should be no more. Bless the Lord, O my soul. The sun knows his going down, Thou appointed the darkness, and there was the night. How magnified are Thy works, O Lord. In wisdom hast Thou made them all.

After The Psalm

Glory be to the Father and to the Son and to the Holy Spirit;
Both now and forever, and unto the ages of ages. Amen.

Halleluiah, Halleluiah, Halleluiah. Glory to Thee, O God. **(x3)**

Our Hope, O Lord, glory to Thee.

Lord, have mercy. **(x40)**

Through the prayers of our holy fathers, Lord Jesus Christ our God, have mercy on us and save us.
People: Amen.

Psalm 140

Chorus: Lord, I have cried to Thee: hear me. Hear me, O Lord.

Lord, I have cried to Thee: hear me. Receive the voice of my prayer.

When I call upon Thee, hear me, O Lord. Let my prayer arise as incense in Thy sight,

And let the lifting up of my hands be an evening sacrifice. Hear me, O Lord.

Kekragarion
Sticheroi From Psalm 140

• Set, O Lord, a watch before my mouth, and a door of enclosure round about my lips.

• Incline not my heart to words of evil, to make excuses for sins.

• Those that work iniquity; I shall not join with their number.

• The righteous man shall chasten me with mercy and reprove me; as for the oil of the sinner, let it not anoint my head.

• For yet more is my prayer in the presence of their pleasures; their judges have been swallowed up by the rock.

• They shall hear my words, for they be sweetened; as a clod of earth is broken upon the earth, so have their bones been scattered into hades.

• To Thee O Lord are mine eyes. In Thee have I hoped; take not my soul away.

• Keep me from the snare which they have laid for me, and from the stumbling blocks of them that work iniquity.

• The sinners shall fall into their own net; I am alone until I pass by.

Sticheroi From Psalm 141

• With my voice to the Lord have I cried, with my voice have I made supplication.

• I shall pour out before Him my supplications; my afflictions shall I declare before Him.

• When my spirit was fainting within me, then Thou knewest my paths.

- In this way wherein I have walked they hid for me a snare.

- I looked on my right hand, and beheld, and there was none that knew me.

- Flight has failed me, and there is none that watches out for my soul.

- I cried to Thee, O Lord; I said: Thou art my hope, my portion in the land of the living.

- Attend unto my supplication, for I am brought very low.

- Deliver me from them that persecute me, for they are stronger than I.

- 10. Bring my soul out of prison. That I may confess Thy name.

[daily or seasonal Troparia]

- 9. The righteous shall patiently wait for me until Thou shalt reward me.

[daily or seasonal Troparia]

Sticheroi From Psalm 129

- 8. Out of the depths have I cried unto Thee, O Lord. O Lord, hear my voice.

[daily or seasonal Troparia]

- 7. Let Thine ears be attentive to the voice of my supplication.

[daily or seasonal Troparia]

- 6. If Thou should mark iniquities, O Lord; O Lord, who shall stand? For with Thee there is forgiveness.

[daily or seasonal Troparia]

- 5. For Thy names sake have I patiently waited for Thee, O Lord; my soul has patiently waited for Thy word, my soul has hoped in the Lord.

[daily or seasonal Troparia]

- 4. From the morning watch until night, from the morning watch let Israel hope in the Lord.

[daily or seasonal Troparia]

- 3. For with the Lord there is mercy, and with Him is plenteous redemption; and He shall redeem Israel out of all his iniquities.

[daily or seasonal Troparia]

Sticheroi From Psalm 116

- 2. O praise the Lord, all you nations; praise Him, all you peoples.

[daily or seasonal Troparia]

- 1. For He has made His mercy to prevail over us, and the truth of the Lord abides forever.

[daily or seasonal Troparia]

Glory be to the Father and to the Son and to the Holy Spirit.

[Doxasticon – if available]

Both now and forever, and unto the ages of ages. Amen.

O Gladsome Light

O Gladsome Light of the holy glory of the immortal Father; Heavenly holy, blessed Jesus Christ.

Now that we have come to the setting of the sun, and behold the Evening Light.

We praise God; Father, Son and Holy Spirit.

For meet it is at all time to worship Thee, with voices of praise;

O Son of God and Giver of Life. Therefore all the world doth glorify Thee.

Prokeimenon

Reader: The Evening Prokeimenon.

[Saturday]

Tone 6   *Rich texture, funeral, sorrowful.*   *D, Eb, F##, G, A, Bb, C##, D.*

Reader: The Lord is clothed with strength and He has girded Himself.

People: *The Lord is King, He is clothed with majesty.*

Reader: For He established the world which shall not be shaken.

People: *The Lord is King, He is clothed with majesty.*

Reader: Holiness becomes Thine house, O Lord, to the length of days.

People: *The Lord is King, He is clothed with majesty.*

Reader: The Lord is King | *He is clothed with majesty.*

Lord, have mercy. **(x40)**

Through the prayers of our holy fathers, Lord Jesus Christ our God, have mercy on us and save us. Amen.

Reader: Vouchsafe, O Lord, to keep us this evening without sin. Blessed art Thou, O Lord, the God of our fathers, and praised and glorified is Thy name unto the ages. Amen.

Let Thy mercy, O Lord, be upon us, according as we have hoped in Thee.

Blessed art Thou, O Lord, teach me Thy statutes.

Blessed art Thou, O Master, give me understanding of Thy statutes.

Blessed art Thou, O Holy One, enlighten me by Thy statutes.

O Lord, Thy mercy endures forever; disdain not the work of Thy hands. To Thee is due praise, to Thee is due song, to Thee is due glory, to the Father, and to the Son, and to the Holy Spirit; both now and forever, and unto the ages of ages. Amen.

Lord, have mercy. **(x40)**

[Aposticha – if available]

Hymn Of Simeon The God Receiver

Reader: Lord, now lettest Thou Thy servant depart in peace, according to Thy word, for mine eyes have seen Thy salvation, which Thou hast prepared before the face of all peoples; a light of revelation for the Gentiles, and the glory of Thy people Israel.

Trisagion Prayers

Holy God, Holy Mighty, Holy Immortal, have mercy on us. **(x3)**

Glory be to the Father, and to the Son, and to the Holy Spirit;
Both now and forever, and unto the ages of ages. Amen.

O Most Holy Trinity, have mercy on us.

O Lord, cleanse us from our sins.

O Master, pardon our iniquities.

O Holy One, visit and heal our infirmities, for Thy names sake.

Lord have mercy. **(x3)**

Glory be to the Father and to the Son and to the Holy Spirit;
Both now and forever, and unto the ages of ages. Amen.

People: *Our Father, Who art in Heaven, hallowed be Thy Name. Thy Kingdom come, Thy will be done, on earth as it is in Heaven. Give us this day our daily bread, and forgive us our trespasses, as we forgive those who trespass against us; and lead us not into temptation, but deliver us from the evil one.*
O Lord, Jesus Christ, Son of God, have mercy on us. Amen.

Resurrectional Apolytikion

Tone 8 Humility, tranquillity, repose, suffering, pleading.   *C, D, Eb, F, G, A, Bb, C.*

From the heights Thou didst descend, O compassionate One, and Thou didst submit to the three day burial, that Thou might deliver us from passion; Thou art our life and our Resurrection, O Lord, glory to Thee.

Glory be to the Father and to the Son and to the Holy Spirit;

Resurrectional Theotokion

Tone 1 Magnificent, happy, and earthy character.   *C, D, Eb, F, G, A, Bb, C.*

As Gabriel cried aloud unto thee: "Rejoice, O Virgin," with that cry did the Lord of all become incarnate in thee, O holy ark, as spake the righteous David; and thou wast revealed, as more spacious than the heavens, in that thou bore thy Creator. Wherefore, glory to Him Who abided in thee; glory to Him Who came from thee; glory to Him, Who through thy birth giving hath set us free.

Both now and forever, and unto the ages of ages. Amen.

The Dismissal

Reader: Preserve, O God, the holy Orthodox faith and all Orthodox Christians, unto the ages of ages.

People: *Amen.*

Reader: Greater in honour than the Cherubim and beyond compare more glorious than the Seraphim; without corruption thou gavest birth to God the Word, truly the Theotokos, we magnify thee.

Glory be to the Father and to the Son and to the Holy Spirit;
Both now and forever, and unto the ages of ages. Amen.

Lord, have mercy. **(x3)**

Through the prayers of our holy Fathers; O Lord Jesus Christ our God; have mercy on us and save us.

People: *Amen.*

Occasional Services

This collection of services and prayers is done only from time to time. Some services or processions are only served once a year; as such it can be difficult to be well versed in them. Therefore it is of benefit to go through the service on the day before, as always looking for variables to be prepared, and planning movement of clergy and people and what may be sung to cover those.

During processions one may have an Apolytikion to sing, for example when processing from one interior wall of the Church to the next. Practising this beforehand you will soon see that this walk does not take long. Compare this with the time it takes to sing the hymn provided, it is probably longer. Therefore a slow procession shall be required to give you enough time to complete it.

The congregation usually should join the procession. For a number of reasons this may not happen; perhaps your Church is packed with people and there is no room for hundreds of people to shuffle around. Sometimes the people just don't know that they are supposed to join in, they all just watch the clergy and acolytes doing all the hard work. It may be worth warning some people beforehand to start things off by joining in the procession at the rear of the clergy.

Another point to consider is how long it takes a mass of people to process from one point to another. The line always stretches out, so even if you are going slow to give time to allow enough time to finish the hymn the people at the back shall still not be on point by the time the Priest starts his prayers. You may experiment with a compromise of moving slow enough to complete three quarters of the hymn, but having a sentence or so in hand to give the stragglers time to catch up. As the dynamics of each parish differs you will have to learn from the first time you do it and hone it from there.

[Apolytikion of the day and Kontakion of the Temple required.]

[The child stands facing the icon of Christ, if a boy, or the icon of the Theotokos, if a girl. The parents stand at the bottom of the steps. If the child is a baby the parents stand holding him / her.]

The Trisagion Prayers

Deacon: Holy Father, Bless.

Priest: Blessed is our God always, now and forever, and unto the ages of ages.

People: *Amen.*

Priest: O Heavenly King, Comforter, Spirit of Truth, Who art everywhere present and fillest all things, Treasury of blessings and Giver of life: Come and abide in us and cleanse us from every impurity and save our souls, O Good One.

Reader: Holy God, Holy Mighty, Holy Immortal, have mercy on us. **(x3)**

Glory be to the Father, and to the Son, and to the Holy Spirit;

Both now and forever, and unto the ages of ages. Amen.

O Most Holy Trinity, have mercy on us.

O Lord, cleanse us from our sins.

O Master, pardon our iniquities.

O Holy One, visit and heal our infirmities, for Thy names sake.

Lord have mercy. **(x3)**

Glory be to the Father and to the Son and to the Holy Spirit;

Both now and forever, and unto the ages of ages. Amen.

People: *Our Father, Who art in Heaven, hallowed be Thy Name. Thy Kingdom come, Thy will be done, on earth as it is in Heaven. Give us this day our daily bread, and forgive us our trespasses, as we forgive those who trespass against us; and lead us not into temptation, but deliver us from the evil one.*

Priest: For Thine is the Kingdom, and the power, and the glory; of the Father, and of the Son, and of the Holy Spirit, now and ever, and unto the ages of ages.

People: *Amen.*

[Reader chants the Apolytikion of the day and the Kontakion of the Temple.]

Priest: Let us pray to the Lord.

People: *Lord have mercy.*

Priest: O Lord our God, Who through Thy beloved Child, our Lord Jesus Christ, did call us children of God through adoption, and the Grace of Thine All Holy Spirit, and did say, "I shall be to Him a Father, and He shall be to Me a Son." Do Thou, the same King, Loving God, look down from Thy holy dwelling place on high, upon these Thy servants and unite their natures which Thou hast begotten separate from one another according to the flesh, through Your Holy Spirit, into parents and *[son / daughter]*. Confirm them in Thy love; bind them through Thy benediction; bless them to Thy great glory; strengthen them in Thy Faith; preserve them always and renounce them not for that which proceeds from their lips. Be Mediator for their promises, that their love which they have confessed to Thee be not torn asunder even to the evening of their lives; grant that they may be kept sincerely alive in Thee, our only Living and True God, and grant unto them to become heirs of Thy Kingdom, for unto Thee is due all Glory: to the Father, and to the Son, and to the Holy Spirit, both now and forever, and unto the ages of ages.

People: *Amen.*

Priest: Peace be with you all.

People: *And with thy spirit.*

Priest: Let us bow down our heads unto the Lord.

People: *To Thee, O Lord.*

Priest: O Master and Lord, Who art the Maker of all creatures, and by the first Adam did make the bonds of kinship according to the natural flesh, and through Jesus Christ our Lord, Thy beloved Son and our God, by Grace did show us also as Thy kin, now these Thy servants bow their heads before Thee, Who alone know all things before their happenings, and ask of Thee a blessing, that in Thee they may receive that for which they hoped: the bond inscribed in one another, of parents and *[son / daughter]*; and that living worthily in Thee in adoption to *[sonship / daughtership]*, they may keep themselves in due constancy, that as in all things, so in this may be glorified in and to Thine All Holy Name of the Father, and of the Son, and of the Holy Spirit, both now and forever, and to the ages of ages.

People: *Amen.*

[The child returns to, and bows before the parents; who shall place their hands upon the childs head and say:]

Parents: Today you are our child; this day we have begotten you.

[Parents take their child in their arms and kiss one another.]

Dismissal

Priest: Christ our true God, Who was born in a cave and laid in a manger for our salvation, through the intercessions of His pure and spotless Mother, through the power of the precious and life giving Cross, through the protection of the venerable and bodiless heavenly powers, through the prayers of the venerable and glorious prophet Forerunner John the Baptist, of the holy, glorious, all praiseworthy Apostles, of the holy, glorious and; victorious Martyrs, of our venerable God bearing Fathers, of the holy, righteous ancestors of the Lord, Joachim and Anna, and of all the Saints, have mercy on us and save us as our Good and Loving God.

People: *Amen.*

Priest: Through the prayers of our holy Fathers, Lord Jesus Christ, our God, have mercy on us and save us.

People: *Amen.*

Lord, our God, who are seated upon the Cherubim, Thou hast roused Thy power and sent Thine only begotten Son, our Lord Jesus Christ, to save the world through his Cross, Burial and Resurrection. As He drew near to Jerusalem for His voluntary Passion, the people that sat in darkness and the shadow of death, taking the symbols of victory, boughs of trees and branches of palms, foretold His Resurrection. Do Thou, Master, Thyself keep and preserve us also, who, following their example, on this day before the Feast carry palm and branches in our hands and, like those crowds and those children, offer Thee our "Hosanna!", so that with hymns and spiritual songs we may be counted worthy of the life giving Resurrection on the third day day; in Christ Jesus, our Lord, with whom Thou art blessed, together with Thine all holy, good and life giving Spirit, both now and forever and unto the ages of ages. Amen.

The Procession Of The Cross - 1st August
Or nearest Sunday thereafter.
AND
The Exaltation Of The Cross - 14th September.

For:

The Exaltation Of The Cross   – September 14th.

The Adoration Of The Cross   – Third Sunday Of Great Lent.

The Procession Of The Cross   – August 1st.

[The Priest processes around the church carrying the cross on a tray with flowers over his head. The Deacon heads the procession censing the cross all the while. The acolytes next with a candle and one with the processional cross, and the Chorus follow at the rear. The Priest reaches the small table put out for the Cross to be venerated upon and follows the Deacon around it three times.]

[All the while the Chorus chant:]

Chorus: Holy God, Holy Strong, Holy Immortal, have mercy on us.

[The Priest lifts the tray and makes the sign of the cross and says:]

Priest: Wisdom. Stand upright.

[The Priest places the tray and censes around the table three times.]

Priest: O Lord, save Thy people and bless Thine inheritance, granting to Thy people victory over all their enemies, and by the power of Thy Cross preserving Thy commonwealth.

[Then the Chorus repeats this twice.]

Apolytikion Of The Exaltation Of The Holy Cross

Tone 1   Magnificent, happy and earthy.   *C, D, Eb, F, G, A, Bb, C.*

Soson Kyrie ton lao sou, Ke evlogison, tin klironomian sou, Nikas tis Vasilevsii;

Kata varvaron doroumen as Ke to son filaton dia ton stavron sou politev ma.

O Lord, save Thy people and bless Thine inheritance.

Grant victories to the Orthodox Christians over their adversaries.

And by virtue of Thy Cross, preserve Thy commonwealth.

[The Priest lifts aloft the cross and the leaves from the tray.]

Priest: Have mercy on us, O God, according to Thy great mercy, we pray to Thee, hearken and have mercy.

People: *Lord have mercy.* **(x12)**

[During which the Priest makes the sign of the cross above his head, with the cross.
*Still holding it aloft he kneels, stands and moves to the **south** side of the table.]*

Priest: Again we pray for all pious and Orthodox Christians.

People: *Lord have mercy.* **(x12)**

[During which the Priest elevates the cross and blesses it thrice.

*[Still holding it aloft he kneels, stands and moves to the **east** side of the table.]*
Priest: Again we pray for our Archbishop <u>Nikitas</u>. And all our brotherhood in Christ.

People: *Lord have mercy.* **(x12)**

[During which the Priest elevates the cross and blesses it thrice.
*Still holding it aloft he kneels, stands and moves to the **north** side of the table.]*

Priest.   Again we pray mercy, life, peace, health, salvation, visitation and pardon and forgiveness of sins for the servants of God, the parishioners, members of the parish council and organisations, donors and benefactors of this holy house.

People: *Lord have mercy.* **(x12)**

[During which the Priest elevates the cross and blesses it thrice.
*Holding it aloft he kneels, stands and moves to the **west** side of the table and faces east.]*

[If a bishop not present:]
Priest: Again we pray for the souls of all Orthodox Christians, their health, salvation and forgiveness of their sins.

[If a bishop is present:]
Bishop: Again we pray for those who serve in this holy Church Of Christ and the souls of all Orthodox Christians, their health, salvation and forgiveness of their sins.

People: *Lord have mercy.* **(x12)**

[During which the Priest elevates the cross and blesses it thrice.
*Still holding it aloft he kneels, stands to the **west** side of the table and faces east.]*

Kontakion Of The Cross

Tone 4   Festive, joyous and expressing deep piety.   *C, D, Eb, F, G, A, Bb, C.*

Priest: Do Thou, who of Thy good will was lifted up on the Cross, O Christ our God, bestow Thy bounties upon the new nation which is called by Thy name. Make glad in Thy might those who lawfully govern, that with them we may be led to victory over our adversaries, having in Thine aid a weapon of peace and an invincible trophy.

[Priest turns to, and blesses the people.]

[If a bishop is present:]

People: *Many years, master.*

[Priest places the cross upon the tray and:]

Priest: We adore Thy Cross, O Master and we glorify Thy holy resurrection.

Priest prostrates as:

People: *We adore Thy Cross, O Master and we glorify Thy holy resurrection.*

[Clergy re-enter Sanctuary.]

Idiomelon

Tone 2   Majesty, gentleness, hope, repentance and sadness.   *E, F, G, Ab, B, C.*

Come you faithful, let us adore the life giving wood on which Christ the King of glory stretched out his hands of his own free will. To the ancient blessedness he raised us up, whom the enemy had before despoiled through pleasure, making us exiles far from God.

Come you faithful, let us adore the wood, through which we have been made worthy to crush the heads of invisible enemies. Come all you kindred of the nations, let us honour in hymns the cross of the Lord. Rejoice O Cross, complete redemption of fallen Adam.

With thee as their boast our faithful kings laid low by thy might the people of Ishmael. We Christians kiss thee now with fear and, glorifying God who was nailed on thee, we cry: O Lord, who on the cross was crucified, have mercy on us, for Thou art good and love mankind.

Whilst the below is sung the people come forward, prostrate themselves and kiss the cross and receive a flower from the Priest with the antidoron.

Apolytikion Of The Exaltation Of The Holy Cross

Tone 1   Magnificent, happy and earthy.   *C, D, Eb, F, G, A, Bb, C.*

(i,iii)   O Lord, save Thy people and bless Thine inheritance.

Grant victories to the Orthodox Christians over their adversaries.

And by virtue of Thy Cross, preserve Thy commonwealth.

(ii)   Soson Kyrie ton lao sou, Ke evlogison, tin klironomian sou, Nikas tis Vasilevsii;

Kata varvaron doroumen as Ke to son filaton dia ton stavron sou politev ma.

*At the end of the Divine Liturgy, "Blessed be the Name of the Lord" **(twice only)**:*

[Clergy gather on the solea in front of the table where the grapes are placed for blessing.]

The Prayer For The Blessing Of The Grapes / Wine / Honey

Priest: Let us pray to the Lord.

People: *Lord, have mercy.*

[Priest lifts up to the Lord, one of the grape bunches.]

Priest: Bless, O Lord, this new fruit of the vine, which Thou hast graciously been pleased to bring to maturity through temperate seasons, gentle rains, and favourable weather. Let it be for joy to those of us who shall partake of this fruit of the vine for the purification of those who offer it as a gift, through the sacred and holy Body and Blood of Thy Christ, with whom Thou art blessed, together with Thine all holy, good, and life giving Spirit, both now and forever and to ages of ages.

People: *Amen.*

*"Blessed be the Name of the Lord" **(once only)** [and continue the Divine Liturgy.]*

The Making Of A Catechumen - Order Before Holy Baptism

[The Priest divests him that comes to be illuminated of robes and shoes and faces him eastward, barefoot and clad in a single garment, hands down. Then, breathing thrice on his face and signing him thrice on the forehead and breast.]

Priest: In the name of the Father, and of the Son, and of the Holy Spirit.

People: *Amen.*

Priest: Blessed is our God always, both now and ever, and to the ages of ages.

People: *Amen.*

[Laying his hand upon his head, the Priest says:]

Priest: Let us pray to the Lord.

People: *Lord have mercy.*

Priest: In Thy Name, O Lord God of Truth, and in the Name of Thine Only Begotten Son, and of Thy Holy Spirit, I lay my hand upon this Thy servant *[Name],* who has been accounted worthy to flee to Thy Holy Name and to be sheltered under the shadow of Thy wings. Remove far from *[him / her]* that ancient error, and fill *[him / her]* with faith and hope and love that is in Thee, that *[he / she]* may know that Thou alone art the True God, and Thine Only Begotten Son, our Lord Jesus Christ, and Thy Holy Spirit.

Grant *[him / her]* to walk in Thy commandments, and to observe those things that are acceptable before Thee; for if a man does such he shall find life in them. Inscribe *[him / her]* in Thy Book of Life, and unite *[him / her]* to the flock of Thine inheritance. Let Thy Holy Name be glorified in *[him / her]* and that of Thy well beloved Son, our Lord Jesus Christ, and of Thy Life creating Spirit. Let Thine eyes look over *[him / her]* in mercy, and Thine ears be ever attentive unto the voice of *[his / her]* prayer. Let *[him / her]* ever rejoice in the works of *[his / her]* hands, and in all *[his / her]* generation, that *[he / she]* may give thanks to Thee, worshipping and glorifying Thy great and Most High Name, and may ever praise Thee all the days of *[him / her]* life. For all the Powers of Heaven praise Thee, and Thine is the Glory, of the Father, and of the Son, and of the Holy Spirit, both now and forever, and to the ages of ages.

People: *Amen.*

FIRST EXORCISM

Priest: Let us pray to the Lord.

People: *Lord have mercy.*

Priest: The Lord rebukes thee, O devil, He that came into the world and made His dwelling among men, that He might cast down thy tyranny, and deliver men; He that upon the Tree triumphed over the opposing powers, when the sun was darkened, and the earth was shaken, and the tombs were opened, and the bodies of the Saints arose; He that by death destroyed Death, and overcame him that held the might of death, that is, even thou, O devil. I adjure thee by the Living God, Who has shown forth the Tree of Life, and posted the Cherubim, and the flaming sword that turns about to guard this: be rebuked, and depart, for I forbid thee, through Him that walks on the waves of the sea as upon the dry land, Who forbade the storm of the winds,

Whose glance dries up the deep, and Whose threatenings melt the mountains; for it is He Himself that now forbids thee, through us.

Be afraid, and depart, and absent thyself from this creature, and do not come back, neither hide thyself in him, nor encounter him, nor influence him either by night or by day, nor in the morning or at noon; but get thee hence to thine own pit, until the appointed day of Judgement. Fear God, Who sits on the throne of the Cherubim, and looks upon the depths, before Whom tremble Angels, Archangels, Thrones, Principalities, Authorities, Powers, the many eyed Cherubim, and the six winged Seraphim; Whom Heaven and earth fear, the sea, and all that live therein.

Come forth, and depart from the sealed and newly enlisted soldier of Christ our God; for I adjure thee by Him that rides upon the wings of the winds, Who makes His Angels spirits and His Ministers a flame of fire. Come forth, and from this creature which He fashioned depart with all Thy power and might; for glorified is the Name of the Father, and of the Son, and of the Holy Spirit, both now and forever, and to the ages of ages.

People: *Amen.*

SECOND EXORCISM

Priest: Let us pray to the Lord.

People: *Lord have mercy.*

Priest: God, the Holy, the Terrible, and the Glorious, Who concerning all His works and strength is incomprehensible and unsearchable, Who Himself has ordained for thee O devil, the retribution of eternal torment, through us, His unworthy servants, commands thee, and all thy cooperating might to go forth from *[him / her]* that is newly sealed in the Name of our Lord God and Saviour Christ.

Therefore, thou all evil, unclean, abominable, loathsome and alien spirit, I adjure thee by the power of Jesus Christ, Who has all authority in Heaven and on earth, Who says to the deaf and dumb demon, *"Get out of the man, and enter no more into him."* Depart, know the vainness of Thy might, which had not power even over the swine.

Remember Him Who bade thee, at thy request, to enter into the herd of swine. Fear God, at Whose command the earth was established upon the waters; Who has founded the Heavens, and fixed the mountains with a line, and the valleys with a measure; Who has placed the sand for a boundary to the sea, and made safe paths through the waters; Who touched the mountains and they smoked; Who clothed Himself with Light as with a garment; Who has stretched out the Heavens as with a curtain; Who covers His upper rooms with waters; Who has founded the earth on her firm foundations, so that it shall not be moved forever; Who calls up the waters of the seas, and sprinkles it on the face of the earth.

Come out! Depart from *[him / her]* who is now being made ready for Holy Illumination; I adjure thee by the saving Passion of our Lord Jesus Christ, by His Precious Blood and All Pure Body, and by His terrible Coming Again; for He shall come and not tarry, to judge all the earth, and shall punish thee and thy cooperating might in the Gehenna of fire, consigning thee to the outer darkness where the worm does not die and the fire is not quenched; for of Christ is the Might, with the Father and the Holy Spirit, both now and forever, and to the ages of ages.

People: *Amen.*

THIRD EXORCISM

Priest: Let us pray to the Lord.

People: *Lord have mercy.*

Priest: O Lord Sabaoth, the God of Israel, Who heals every sickness and every wound, Look down upon this Thy servant *[Name]*; search out and try *[him / her]*, driving away from *[him / her]* every operation of the devil. Rebuke the unclean spirits and expel them, cleansing the work of Thy hands; and, using Thy trenchant energy, beat down Satan under *[his / her]* feet, giving *[him / her]* victory over him, and over his unclean spirits; so that, obtaining the mercy that comes from Thee, he may be accounted worthy of Thy Immortal and Heavenly Mysteries, and may send up all glory to Thee, to the Father, and to the Son, and to the Holy Spirit, both now and forever, and to the ages of ages.

People: *Amen.*

Prayer

Priest: Let us pray to the Lord.

People: *Lord have mercy.*

Priest: Thou, the Existing Sovereign Master and Lord, Who made man after Thine own image and likeness and gave to him power of eternal life; and when he had fallen through sin did not disdain him, but did provide for him through the Incarnation of Thy Christ, the salvation of the world. Redeeming this Thy creature from the yoke of the enemy, receive him into Thy heavenly Kingdom. Open the eyes of *[his / her]* understanding, so that the Illumination of Thy Gospel may dawn upon *[him / her]*. Yoke to *[his / her]* life a shining Angel to deliver *[him / her]* from every plot directed against *[him / her]* by the adversary, from encounter with evil, from the noon day demon, and from evil dreams.

Three Times:
[And the Priest breathes on his forehead, on his mouth, and on his breast, saying:]
Priest: Drive out from *[him / her]* every evil and unclean spirit, hiding and lurking in *[his / her]* heart.

Priest: The spirit of error, the spirit of evil, the spirit of idolatry and of all covetousness that works according to the teaching of the devil. Make *[him / her]* a reason endowed sheep of the holy Flock of Thy Christ, and honourable member of Thy Church, a hallowed vessel, a child of Light, and heir of Thy Kingdom. So that, having ordered *[his / her]* life according to Thy commandments, and having guarded the Seal and kept it unbroken, and having preserved his garment undefiled, *[he / she]* may attain to the blessedness of the Saints of Thy Kingdom. Through the Grace and Compassion and Love of humanity of Thine Only Begotten Son, with Whom Thou art blessed, together with Thine All Holy, Good, and Life creating Spirit, both now and forever, and to the ages of ages.

People: *Amen.*

[Then the Priest turns him that is to be baptised to face westward, unclothed, barefoot, hands upraised. If the person is a child, the Sponsor holds him faces West.]

Three Times:	
Priest:	Dost thou renounce Satan, and all his works, and all his worship, and all of his angels, and all his pomp?
Catechumen:	I do renounce him.

Three Times:	
Priest:	Hast thou renounced Satan?
Catechumen:	I have renounced him.

Priest: Then breathe and spit upon him.

[Catechumen spits on the ground.]

[The Priest turns the Catechumen to the East with lowered hands.]

Three Times:	
Priest:	Dost thou join Christ?
Catechumen:	I do join Him.

Three Times:	
Priest:	Hast thou joined Christ?
Catechumen:	I have joined Him.

Three Times:	
Priest:	And dost thou believe in Him?
Catechumen:	I believe in Him as King and as God.

The Symbol of Faith - The Nicene Creed

Catechumen: I believe in one God, the Father Almighty, Maker of heaven and earth and of all things visible and invisible.

And in one Lord Jesus Christ, the Son of God, the Only begotten, begotten of the Father before all ages; Light of Light, true God of true God; begotten, not made; of one essence with the Father, by Whom all things were made; Who for us men and for our salvation came down from the heavens, and was incarnate of the Holy Spirit and the Virgin Mary, and became man; And was crucified for us under Pontius Pilate, and suffered and was buried; And arose again on the third day according to the Scriptures; And ascended into the heavens, and sits at the right hand of the Father; And shall come again, with glory, to judge both the living and the dead; Whose kingdom shall have no end.

And in the Holy Spirit, the Lord, the Giver of life; Who proceeds from the Father; Who together with the Father and the Son is worshipped and glorified; Who spoke by the prophets. In One, Holy, Catholic, and Apostolic Church. I confess one baptism for the remission of sins. I look for the resurrection of the dead, And the life of the age to come. Amen.

Three Times:	
Priest:	Hast thou joined Christ?
Catechumen:	I have joined Him.

Priest: Then bow before Him and worship Him.

Catechumen: *[Bows down, saying:]*

             I bow down before the Father, and the Son, and the Holy Spirit; Trinity;

             One in Essence and Undivided.

Priest: Blessed is God Who desires that all people should be saved, and come to the knowledge of the Truth; both now and ever, and to the ages of ages.

People: *Amen.*

Priest: Let us pray to the Lord.

People: *Lord have mercy.*

Priest: Sovereign Master, Lord our God, call this Thy servant *[Name]* to Thine Holy Illumination, and account *[him / her]* worthy of this great Grace and Thy Holy Baptism. Put off from *[him / her]* the old man, and renew *[him / her]* unto everlasting life; fill *[him / her]* with the power of Thy Holy Spirit, unto union with Thy Christ; that *[he / she]* may no longer be a child of the body, but a child of Thy Kingdom; through the good pleasure and Grace of Thine Only Begotten Son, with Whom Thou art blessed, together with Thine All Holy, Good, and Life creating Spirit, both now and forever, and to the ages of ages.

People: *Amen.*

Dismissal

Priest: Glory to Thee, O Christ our God and our Hope, glory to Thee. Christ our true God, through the prayers of His immaculate Mother, of our holy and God bearing fathers, and of all the Saints, have mercy on us and save us, for He is good and the Lover of mankind.

People: *Amen.*

Priest: Through the prayers of our holy Fathers, O Lord Jesus Christ our God, have mercy on us.

People: *Amen.*

The Order For Confessing And Communing The Sick

The Euchologion assumes that the only person to be communed outside the church is one who is near death and unable to come or be brought to the church temple. This is in accordance with Canon XXXVI of St Athanasios the Great, Patriarch of Alexandria (293-373), which states: *"No priest shall carry forth the mysteries and go with them about the streets, except for a sick man, when the end and deaths hour of need draw nigh. And when they carry the mysteries (without), they shall suffer none but the sick to partake. And they shall not do according to favour and give unto one beside the sick, but unto the sick alone. And if any constrain them that they should give him of the mysteries, he shall be unto him as he that hid his lords money in the earth, because that he honoured not the church. Let him go thither and not be sluggish, for there is no need."* While it may be acceptable to commune the sick and / or shut in whether or not they are near death, it remains the practice of the Church that only they (not their relatives or care givers who may be standing by) be communed outside the church temple. The Priest carries upon his breast the portable artophorion in which are the Immaculate Mysteries. Upon arrival at the place where the sick man abides, the Priest blesses and dons his epitrachelion, covers a table with a clean cloth and places upon it the artophorion, the precious Cross and two candles in their stands. With all reverence he opens the artophorion, takes from it a small portion of the Immaculate Mysteries, places that portion into a small chalice, and then carefully pours into the chalice a small amount of sweet, red wine. Then, in the hearing of the sick man, the Priest prays as follows:

Priest: Blessed is our God, always, now and ever, and unto ages of ages. Amen.

O Heavenly King, the Comforter, the Spirit of Truth; who art everywhere present and fillest all things; Treasury of blessings, and giver of life: come and abide in us, and cleanse us from every impurity, and save our souls, O Good One.

The Trisagion Prayers

Holy God, Holy Mighty, Holy Immortal, have mercy on us. **(x3)**

Glory be to the Father, and to the Son, and to the Holy Spirit;
Both now and forever, and unto the ages of ages. Amen.

O Most Holy Trinity, have mercy on us.
O Lord, cleanse us from our sins.
O Master, pardon our iniquities.
O Holy One, visit and heal our infirmities, for Thy names sake.

Lord have mercy. **(x3)**

Glory be to the Father, and to the Son, and to the Holy Spirit;
Both now and forever, and unto the ages of ages. Amen.

People: *Our Father, who art in heaven, hallowed be Thy name. Thy Kingdom come. Thy will be done, on earth as it is in heaven. Give us this day our daily bread; and forgive us our trespasses, as we forgive those who trespass against us; and lead us not into temptation, but deliver us from the evil one.*

Priest: For Thine is the kingdom, the power, and the glory, of the Father, and the Son and the Holy Spirit, both now and forever, and to the ages of ages.

People: *Amen.*

Lord, have mercy. **(x12)**

O come let us worship God our King.

O come let us worship and fall down before Christ, our King and God.

O come let us worship and fall down before Christ Himself, our King and our God.

Psalm 50

Have mercy on me, O God, according to Thy great mercy; and according to the multitude of Thy compassions blot out my transgression. Wash me thoroughly from mine iniquity, and cleanse me from my sin. For I acknowledge mine iniquity, and my sin is ever before me. Against Thee, Thee only have I sinned, and done evil in Thy sight, that Thou mayest be found just when Thou speakest, and victorious when Thou art judged. For behold, I was conceived in iniquity, and in sin my mother bore me. For behold, Thou hast loved truth; Thou hast made known to me the hidden and secret things of Thy wisdom. Thou shalt sprinkle me with hyssop, and I shall be made clean; Thou shalt wash me, and I shall be whiter than snow. Make me to hear joy and gladness; that the humbled bones may rejoice. Turn Thy face away from my sins, and blot out all mine iniquities.

Create in me a clean heart, O God, and renew a steadfast spirit within me. Cast me not away from Thy presence, and take not Thy Holy Spirit from me. Restore to me the joy of Thy salvation, and establish me with Thy governing Spirit. I shall teach transgressors Thy ways, and the ungodly shall turn back to Thee. Deliver me from blood guiltiness, O God, the God of my salvation; my tongue shall joyfully declare Thy righteousness. Lord, open my lips, and my mouth shall declare Thy praise. For if Thou hadst desired sacrifice, I would give it; Thou dost not delight in burnt offerings. A sacrifice to God is a broken spirit; God shall not despise a broken and a humbled heart. Do good, O Lord, in Thy good pleasure to Zion, and let the walls of Jerusalem be builded. Then Thou shalt be pleased with a sacrifice of righteousness, with oblation and whole burned offerings. Then shall they offer bulls on Thine altar.

Little Litany

Priest: In peace let us pray to the Lord.

People: *Lord have mercy.*

Priest: For the peace from above; for the salvation of our souls; let us pray to the Lord.

People: *Lord have mercy.*

Priest: That the Lord shall deliver *N* and us from all tribulation, wrath, danger, and necessity; let us pray to the Lord.

People: *Lord have mercy.*

Priest: Help us; save us; have mercy on us and keep us, O God, by Thy Grace.

People: *Lord have mercy.*

Priest: Calling to remembrance our all; holy, pure, exceedingly blessed and glorious Lady Theotokos and Ever Virgin Mary, with all the Saints; let us commend ourselves and one another and all our life to Christ our God.

People: *Lord have mercy.*

Priest: For to Thee are due all glory, honour, and worship: to the Father and to the Son and to the Holy Spirit, both now and forever, and unto the ages of ages.

People: *Amen.*

The Confession

[All others leave the room so that the Priest may hear the confession of the sick man. Upon completion of the confession, the Priest places the edge of his epitrachelion over the head of the sick man and says the following prayer:]

Priest: O Lord our God, who didst remit the sins of Peter and the harlot through their tears, and didst justify the Publican who acknowledged his iniquities: Accept Thou the confession of Thy servant *N*, and overlook *[his / her]* sins whether voluntary or involuntary, by word or by deed, or thought. Forgive *[him / her]*, O Thou Who art good and lovest mankind, for Thou alone hast power to remit sins, and unto Thee we ascribe glory, together with Thine unoriginate Father and Thine all holy and good and life creating Spirit, now and ever, and unto the ages of ages. Amen.

O Master, Lord Jesus Christ, our Saviour, Who alone hast the power to forgive sins, and are our Loving God, overlook, we beseech Thee, the transgressions of Thy servant *N*, whether of knowledge or ignorance, granting to *[him / her]* to partake without condemnation of Thine immaculate Mysteries, not unto judgement, nor to the increase of sins, but to the cleansing of soul and body, and to the inheritance of Thy Kingdom; for Thou art *[his / her]* help and a firm wall and bulwark against the Adversary, and the purification of *[his / her]* iniquities; for Thou art our merciful and Man befriending God, and to Thee do we send up Glory, to the Father, and to the Son, and to the Holy Spirit, both now and forever, and unto the ages of ages. Amen.

[The Priest then says the following, making the sign of the Cross over the penitent:]

God it was who forgave David through Nathan the Prophet, when he confessed his sins, and Peter weeping bitterly for his denial, and the sinful woman in tears at His feet, and the Publican, and the Prodigal Son: May that same God forgive thee all things, through me a sinner, both in this present world and in that which is to come, and set thee uncondemned before His fearful Judgement Seat. And now, having no further care for the sins which thou hast declared, depart in peace.

[The Priest then removes his epitrachelion from the sick mans head and offers him the precious Cross to kiss. The Priest may now anoint the sick man on his forehead, chin, cheeks, and hands with Holy Oil saying:]

O Holy Father, Physician of our souls and bodies, have mercy, forgive and save Thy servant *N*.

[Laying aside the Cross, the Priest takes up the chalice in his left hand, and the spoon and red communion cloth in his right hand, and says the following pre-communion prayers:]

Fourth Prayer Of St John Chrysostom

I believe, Lord, and I confess that Thou art truly the Christ, the Son of the living God, Who came into the world to save sinners, of whom I am first. Also I believe that this is indeed Thy most pure Body, and this indeed Thy precious Blood. Therefore I beseech Thee, have mercy on me and forgive me my offences, voluntary and involuntary, in word and in deed, in knowledge and in ignorance, and count me worthy to partake uncondemned of Thy most pure Mysteries for forgiveness of sins and for eternal life. Amen.

Lines Of St Symeon The Translator

Of Thy mystical supper, Son of God, receive me today as a communicant; for I shall not tell of the Mystery to Thine enemies; I shall not give Thee a kiss like Judas; but like the thief I confess Thee. Remember me, Lord, in Thy kingdom.

Tremble, O man, when thou seest the deifying Blood, For it is a coal that burns the unworthy. The Body of God both deifies and nourishes; It deifies the spirit and wondrously nourishes the mind.

Not unto judgement nor unto condemnation be my partaking of Thy Holy Mysteries, O Lord, but unto the healing of soul and body.

[The Priest places the red communion cloth under the chin of the sick man and communes him, saying:]

The servant of God, *N*, partakes of the precious and all holy Body and Blood of our Lord and God and Saviour Jesus Christ, unto the forgiveness of sins and unto life everlasting.

[After wiping the lips of the sick man with the red communion cloth, the Priest himself carefully consumes what remains in the chalice of the Immaculate Mysteries, and thoroughly cleanses and dries the chalice and spoon. After laying them aside, he says:]

Prayers Of Thanksgiving

Let Thy holy Body, O Lord, be unto Life Everlasting for me, and Thy precious Blood unto remission of sins. Let this holy Eucharist be a source of joy and gladness for me. At Thy second coming make me worthy of standing at Thy right hand, through the intercessions of Thy holy Mother, the Theotokos, and all Thy Saints. Amen.

Song Of Symeon

Lord, now lettest Thou Thy servant depart in peace, according to Thy word. For mine eyes have seen Thy salvation, which Thou hast prepared before the face of all people, a light to lighten the Gentiles, and the glory of Thy people Israel.

Holy God, Holy Mighty, Holy Immortal: have mercy on us. **(x3)**

> *Glory be to the Father, and to the Son, and to the Holy Spirit;*
> *Both now and forever, and unto the ages of ages. Amen.*

O Most Holy Trinity, have mercy on us.
O Lord, cleanse us from our sins.
O Master, pardon our iniquities.
O Holy One, visit and heal our infirmities, for Thy names sake.

Lord have mercy. **(x3)**

> *Glory be to the Father, and to the Son, and to the Holy Spirit;*
> *Both now and forever, and unto the ages of ages. Amen.*

People: *Our Father, who art in heaven, hallowed be Thy name. Thy Kingdom come. Thy will be done, on earth as it is in heaven. Give us this day our daily bread; and forgive us our trespasses, as we forgive those who trespass against us; and lead us not into temptation, but deliver us from the evil one.*

Priest: For Thine is the kingdom, the power, and the glory, of the Father, and the Son and the Holy Spirit, both now and forever, and to the ages of ages.

People: *Amen.*

[The Priest says the Apolytikion of the day, followed by:]

> *Glory be to the Father, and to the Son, and to the Holy Spirit;*
> *Both now and forever, and unto the ages of ages. Amen.*

Through the intercessions, O Lord, of all Thy saints and of the Theotokos, grant us Thy peace, and have mercy on us, for Thou alone art compassionate.

[After putting everything in its place, the Priest may say this brief prayer of thanksgiving:]

Glory to Thee, O God. **(x3)**

I thank Thee, O Lord my God, that Thou hast not rejected me, a sinner, but hast vouchsafed me to become a communicant of Thy holy things. May Thy holy Body, O Lord Jesus Christ our God, be unto me for life eternal, and Thy precious Blood unto forgiveness of my sins. May this Eucharist be unto me for joy, health and gladness; and at Thy fearful second coming make me, the sinner, worthy to stand at the right hand of Thy glory, through the intercessions of Thine all immaculate Mother and of all Thy saints. Amen.

Prayers In Times Of Trouble

Priest: Let us pray to the Lord.

People: *Lord have mercy.*

Priest: O Lord of Powers, be with us, for in the time of trouble we have no other help but Thee.

People: *Lord have mercy.*

Priest: O Lord, God of Powers, have mercy on us.

People: *Lord have mercy.*

Priest: O God, our help in time of need, Who art just and merciful, and Who inclines to the supplications of His people; look down upon us, miserable sinners, have mercy on us, and deliver us from the trouble which now besets us, for which we acknowledge we are deservedly suffering.

People: *Lord have mercy.*

Priest: We acknowledge and believe, O Lord, that all the trials of this life are disposed by Thee for our chastisement, when we drift away from Thee, and disobey Thy commandments;

People: *Lord have mercy.*

Priest: Deal with us not according to our iniquities, but according to Thy manifold mercies, for we are the works of Thine hands, and Thou knowest our weaknesses:

People: *Lord have mercy.*

Priest: Grant, we beseech Thee, Thy divine helping Grace, and endow us with patience and strength to endure our tribulations with complete submission to Thine Will.

People: *Lord have mercy.*

Priest: Thou knowest our misery and sufferings, and to Thee, our only hope and refuge, we flee for relief and comfort, trusting in Thine infinite love and compassion, that in due time, When Thou knowest best, Thou wilt deliver us from this trouble, and turn our distress into comfort.

People: *Lord have mercy.*

Priest: When we shall rejoice in Thy mercy, and exalt and praise Thine Holy Name O Father, Son and Holy Spirit; both now and forever, and unto the ages of ages.

People: *Amen.*

The Dismissal

Glory to Thee, O Christ our God and our Hope, glory to Thee.

May Christ our true God, through the intercessions of His all immaculate and all blameless holy Mother; of *[Saint of the sick]*; of *[Saint of the temple]*; of the holy and righteous ancestors of God, Joachim and Anna; of *[Saint of the day]* whose memory we celebrate, and of all the saints: have mercy on us, and save us, forasmuch as He is good and loveth mankind.

Through the prayers of our holy fathers, Lord Jesus Christ our God, have mercy on us, and save us. Amen.

The Trisagion Prayers

Deacon: Holy Father, Bless.

Priest: Blessed is our God, always, now and ever, and unto the ages of ages.

People: Amen.

Priest: Glory to Thee, our God, glory to Thee.

O Heavenly King, Comforter, Spirit of Truth, Who art everywhere present and fillest all things, Treasury of blessings and Giver of life: Come and abide in us and cleanse us from every impurity and save our souls, O Good One.

Reader: Holy God, Holy Mighty, Holy Immortal, have mercy on us. **(x3)**

Glory be to the Father, and to the Son, and to the Holy Spirit;
Both now and forever, and unto the ages of ages. Amen.

O Most Holy Trinity, have mercy on us.

O Lord, cleanse us from our sins.

O Master, pardon our iniquities.

O Holy One, visit and heal our infirmities, for Thy name's sake.

Lord have mercy. **(x3)**

Glory be be to the Father and to the Son and to the Holy Spirit;
Both now and forever, and unto the ages of ages. Amen.

People: Our Father, Who art in Heaven, hallowed be Thy Name. Thy Kingdom come, Thy will be done, on earth as it is in Heaven. Give us this day our daily bread, and forgive us our trespasses, as we forgive those who trespass against us; and lead us not into temptation, but deliver us from the evil one.

Priest: For Thine is the kingdom and the power and the glory of the Father and of the Son and of the Holy Spirit; both now and forever and unto the ages of ages.

People: Amen.

Lord, have mercy. **(x3)**

Glory be be to the Father and to the Son and to the Holy Spirit;
Both now and forever and unto the ages of ages. Amen.

The Litany of Peace

Deacon: In peace let us pray to the Lord.

People: *Lord, have mercy.*

Deacon: For the peace from above and the salvation of our souls, let us pray to the Lord.

People: *Lord, have mercy.*

Deacon: For peace in the whole world, the welfare of the holy churches of God, and the union of all men, let us pray to the Lord.

People: *Lord, have mercy.*

Deacon: For this holy Temple, and for those who enter it with faith, reverence and the fear of God, let us pray to the Lord.

People: *Lord, have mercy.*

Deacon: For the Most Holy Orthodox Patriarchs, for His Eminence Nikitas, for the honourable Priesthood, the Diaconate in Christ, and for all the clergy and the people, let us pray to the Lord.

People: *Lord, have mercy.*

Deacon: For our Country, our Royal Family, our Welsh Assembly Government, and all in seats of authority, let us pray to the Lord.

People: *Lord, have mercy.*

Deacon: For this *[city / town / village / monastery]* and for every city and land, and for those who live in them by faith, let us pray to the Lord.

People: *Lord, have mercy.*

Deacon: For seasonable weather, the abundance of the fruits of the earth and peaceful times, let us pray to the Lord.

People: *Lord, have mercy.*

Deacon: For those who are travelling by land, air and water, for the sick, the suffering, for prisoners and captives, and for their salvation, let us pray to the Lord.

People: *Lord, have mercy.*

Deacon: That He shall deliver us from all tribulation, anger, danger, and want, let us pray to the Lord.

People: *Lord, have mercy.*

Deacon: Help us, save us, have mercy on us, and keep us, O God, by Thy grace.

People: *Lord, have mercy.*

Deacon: Calling to remembrance our all holy, immaculate, most blessed and glorious Lady Theotokos and Ever Virgin Mary, with all the saints, let us commend ourselves and each other and all our life unto Christ our God.

People: *To You, O Lord.*

Priest: For unto Thee belongs all glory, honour and adoration, to the Father, and to the Son, and to the Holy Spirit, now and ever, and to the ages of ages.

People: *Amen.*

Troparion Of St Martin Of Tours

Tone 4   *Festive, joyous and expressing deep piety.*   *C, D, Eb, F, G, A, Bb, C.*

In signs and in miracles thou wert renowned throughout Gaul. By grace and adoption thou art a light for the world, O Martin, blessed of God. Alms deeds and compassion filled thy life with their splendours. Teaching and wise counsel were thy riches and treasures, which thou dispensest freely to those who honour thee.

Gospel

Priest: Wisdom, stand upright! Let us listen to the Holy Gospel. Peace be with you all.

People: *And with thy spirit.*

Priest: The Reading is from the Holy Gospel of Matthew

People: *Glory to You, O Lord, glory to You.*

Deacon: Let us attend.

Priest: At that time, when he got into the boat, the disciples followed him. And behold, there arose a great storm on the sea, so that the boat was being swamped by the waves; but he was asleep. And they went and woke him, saying, "Save, Lord, we are perishing." And he said to them, "Why are you afraid, O men of little faith?" Then he rose and rebuked the winds and the sea, and there was a great calm. And the men marvelled saying, "What sort of man is this, that even the winds and the sea obey him?"

People: *Glory to You, O Lord, glory to You.*

The Intercession

Priest: O God, save Thy people, and bless Thine inheritance. Visit Thy world with mercy and compassions. Exalt the horn of Orthodox Christians, and send down upon us Thy rich mercies. Through the intercessions of our all immaculate Lady Theotokos and Ever Virgin Mary; by the might of the precious and life giving Cross, by the protection of the honourable bodiless powers of heaven; at the supplication of the honourable, glorious Prophet, Forerunner and Baptist John; of the holy, glorious, all laudable apostles; of our fathers among the saints, great hierarchs and ecumenical teachers, Basil the Great, Gregory the Theologian and John Chrysostom; Athanasios, Cyril, and John the Merciful, patriarchs of Alexandria; Nicholas of Myra in Lycia, Spyridon of Trimythous and Nektarios of Pentapolis, the Wonder workers and, Raphael, of Brooklyn; of the holy and glorious great martyrs, George the Trophy bearer, Demetrios the Myrrh streaming, Theodore the Soldier, Theodore the General, Menas the Wonder worker; and the soldier saints Phanourios, Mercurios, Artemios, Nikitas the Goth, Victor of Damascus, James the Persian, Eustathios, Sergios and Bacchus, Sebastian, Andrew the General, and the Forty Holy Martyrs of Sevbaste, of the hieromartyrs Ignatios the God bearer of Antioch, Haralambos and Eleftherios; of the holy, glorious great martyrs, Thekla, Barbara, Anastasia, Katherine, Kyriaki, Photini, Marina, Paraskeve and Irene; of the holy, glorious and right victorious martyrs; of our venerable and God bearing fathers, who shone in the ascetic life; of *[Patron saint of the Church]* of the holy and righteous divine ancestors, Joachim and Anna; of *[Saints of the day]* whose memory we celebrate today and of all Thy saints, we beseech thee, O only most merciful Lord, hearken unto the petitions of us sinners who make our supplications unto Thee, and have mercy on us.

People: *Lord, have mercy.* **(x12)**

Priest: Through the mercy and compassions and love for mankind of Thine only begotten Son, with whom Thou art blessed, together with Thine all holy and good and life giving Spirit, both now and forever, and unto the ages of ages.

People: *Amen.*

Ektenia

Deacon: Have mercy on us, O God, according to thy great mercy, we pray thee, hearken and have mercy.

People: *Lord, have mercy.* **(x3)**

Deacon: Again we pray for all pious and Orthodox Christians.

People: *Lord, have mercy.* **(x3)**

Deacon: Again we pray for our Archbishop Nikitas.

People: *Lord, have mercy.* **(x3)**

Deacon: Again we pray for our brethren the priests, hieromonks, deacons, hierodeacons and monastics, and all our brotherhood in Christ.

People: *Lord, have mercy.* **(x3)**

Deacon: Again we pray for mercy, life, peace, health, salvation, and visitation, and pardon and forgiveness of sins, for all Orthodox Christians of true worship, who live and dwell in this community.

People: *Lord, have mercy.* **(x3)**

Deacon: Again we pray for our nation, that the Lord our God may bring us speedily to victory, and that He may establish peace on earth and good will among men.

People: *Lord, have mercy.* **(x3)**

Deacon: Again we pray for our First Minister, the Royal Family, our elected and appointed governmental officials, and all our civil authorities, that the Lord our God would grant them wisdom to rightly pursue justice and peace.

People: *Lord, have mercy.* **(x3)**

Deacon: Again we pray for our relatives, friends, neighbours and fellow countrymen who combat our enemies, and for all who serve in the Armed Forces of our country; that the Lord our God may bring them safely out of every peril and danger, and ever sustain them with the comfort of His mercy.

People: *Lord, have mercy.* **(x3)**

Deacon: Again we pray for all those who have been wounded by the hands of our enemies: for children, the aged, the infirm, the bereaved, and all those whom our enemies have harmed; for all those who labour to bring them comfort and solace in their hour of extreme necessity; that the Lord our God would look upon them with compassion; that He may comfort, strengthen, and preserve them; and that He may deliver them speedily from injury and distress.

People: *Lord, have mercy.* **(x3)**

Deacon: Again we pray for the repose of the souls of all those who have perished at the hands of our enemies, for all those who have given their lives for our country, (especially the Orthodox servant[s] of God N.); and for all our fathers and brethren, the Orthodox who here and in all the world lie asleep in the Lord.

People: *Lord, have mercy.* **(x3)**

Deacon: Again we pray that we may be preserved from wrath, pestilence, earthquake, flood, fire, the sword, foreign invasion, civil war, terrorism, and sudden death; that the Lord our God shall be gracious, favourable, and conciliatory, and turn away and dispel all the wrath stirred up against us and all sickness, and may deliver us from His righteous chastisement which impendeth against us, and have mercy on us.

People: *Lord, have mercy.* **(x40)**

Deacon: Again we pray that the Lord our God shall hearken unto the voice of supplications of us sinners, and have mercy on us.

People: *Lord, have mercy.* **(x3)**

Priest: Hear us, O God our Saviour, the Hope of all the ends of the earth and of those who are afar off on the sea and in the air, and be gracious, be gracious, O Master, upon our sins, and have mercy on us. For Thou art a merciful God and lovest mankind, and unto thee do we ascribe glory, to the Father and to the Son, and to the Holy Spirit, now and ever and unto ages of ages.

People: *Amen.*

Priest: Peace be with you all.

People: *And with thy spirit.*

Deacon: Let us bow down our heads to the Lord.

People: *To Thee, O Lord.*

Priest: O Lord God of hosts, God of our salvation, God who alone doest wonders: In mercy and goodness look upon Thy humble servants, and as the Lover of mankind hear us and have mercy on us. For, behold, our enemies have gathered themselves against us to destroy us and to bring ruin to our sanctuaries. Help us, O God our Saviour, and deliver us, for the glory of Thy name, and grant that we also may say with truth, as did Moses when he spoke to the people of Israel, and said: "Be bold, and stand fast; and you shall see the salvation that comes from the Lord. The Lord shall fight for you." Yea, O Lord God our Saviour, our strength, our hope, and our protection: Remember not the transgressions and unrighteousness of Thy people, and turn not away from us because of thine anger; but in mercy and goodness look upon Thine humble servants who bow down before Thy loving kindness. Rise up to help us, and grant us victory over our enemies in Thy name. Grant forgiveness of sins to those, who in the mystery of Thy dispensation, have lost their lives at the hands of our enemies, and on the day of thy just retribution bestow on them crowns of incorruption. For Thou art the protection, the victory and the salvation of those who hope on thee, and to Thee we ascribe glory: to the Father, and to the Son, and to the Holy Spirit, now and ever and unto the ages of ages.

People: *Amen.*

Hymn To The Virgin

Tone 5 Stimulating, dancing, and rhythmical.   *C, D, Eb, F, G, A, Bb, C.*

Rejoice O Virgin, Theotokos Mary full of grace, the Lord is with thee; blessed art thou among women, and blessed is the fruit of thy womb, for thou hast borne the Saviour of our souls.

The Litany Of Supplication

Deacon: Let us complete our prayer unto the Lord.

People: *Lord, have mercy.*

Deacon: Help us; save us; have mercy on us; and keep us, O God, by thy grace.

People: *Lord, have mercy.*

Deacon: That the whole day may be perfect, holy, peaceful and sinless, let us ask of the Lord.

People: *Grant this, O Lord.*

Deacon: An angel of peace, a faithful guide, a guardian of our souls and bodies, let us ask of the Lord.

People: *Grant this, O Lord.*

Deacon: Pardon and forgiveness of our sins and transgressions, let us ask of the Lord.

People: *Grant this, O Lord.*

Deacon: All things good and profitable for our souls and peace for the world, let us ask of the Lord.

People: *Grant this, O Lord.*

Deacon: That we may complete the remaining time of our life in peace and repentance, let us ask of the Lord.

People: *Grant this, O Lord.*

Deacon: A Christian ending to our life, painless, blameless, peaceful and a good defense before the fearful judgment seat of Christ, let us ask.

People: *Grant this, O Lord.*

Deacon: Calling to remembrance our all holy, immaculate, most blessed and glorious Lady Theotokos and Ever Virgin Mary, with all the saints, let us commend ourselves and each other and all our life unto Christ our God.

People: *To Thee, O Lord.*

Priest: For Thou art a good God and lovest mankind, and unto Thee we ascribe glory to the Father and to the Son and to the Holy Spirit, both now and forever, and unto the ages of ages.

People: *Amen.*

Deacon: Again and again, let us, on bended knees, pray to the Lord.

People: *Lord, have mercy.*

Priest: O Master, Lord God of our fathers, we beseech Thee and we humbly implore thee: Behold mercifully the supplication of us, Thine unworthy servants, and as of yore Thou didst deign to ascend with Moses, Thy well pleasing servant, leading thy people Israel from Egypt to the promised land: so do thou now go with these warriors, and thyself be their Helper and Defender, and preserve them both at day and at night inviolate and unharmed from every evil circumstance, malady, famine and flood and every fear. And as Thou didst strengthen Joshua the son of Nun by the cross wise raising of Moses' hands upon Amalek and upon the Canaanite kingdom warring against them, that waste to Zeb, and Zebee and Salmana, and all their princes; and as thou didst aid Gideon with three hundred chosen men to vanquish the multitudes of Midian: so do thou grant these Thy faithful servants, strength, power and a courageous heart, aid and protection. And like as Thou didst assist the first among Christian sovereigns, Constantine, to conquer Thy defiant foes by a heavenly manifestation: so do Thou now mercifully grant triumph an vigorous vanquishment over enemies to these Thy faithful servants; and encompass them in warfare from all directions with thine Angel; and arm them with the power and defense of the precious and life giving Cross, in the Name of Thee, God the Father, and Thy beloved Only begotten Son, our Lord Jesus Christ, and Thy most holy and life creating Spirit: both now and forever, and unto the ages of ages.

People: *Amen.*

Dismissal

Deacon: Wisdom.

Reader: Holy Father, bless.

Priest: Christ our God, the Existing One, is blessed, always, both now and forever, and unto the ages of ages.

People: *Amen.*

Reader: Preserve, O God, the holy Orthodox faith and all Orthodox Christians, unto the ages of ages.

People: *Amen.*

[Priest bows toward the icon of the Theotokos:]

Priest: Most holy Theotokos, save us.

Reader: More honourable than the Cherubim and more glorious beyond compare than the seraphim, thou who without corruption bearest God the Word and art truly Theotokos: We magnify thee.

[Priest bows toward the icon of Christ:]

Priest: Glory to Thee, O Christ our God and our Hope, glory to Thee.

Reader: *Glory be to the Father, and to the Son, and to the Holy Spirit.*

  Both now and forever, and unto the ages of ages. Amen.

  Lord, have mercy. **(x3)**

  Holy Father, Bless!

Priest: May Christ, Our true God, through the intercessions of His all immaculate and all blameless holy Mother, of the holy and righteous ancestors of God, Joachim and Anna, of *[Saints of the day]* whose memory we celebrate today, *[Patron Saint of the Temple]* and of all the saints; have mercy on us and save us, for He is a good God and loves mankind.

People: *Amen.*

Priest: Through the prayers of our Holy Fathers, Lord Jesus Christ our God, have mercy on us and save us.

People: *Amen.*

House Blessing

All who reside in the household should be present for the Blessing. In anticipation of the arrival of the Priest to the house, the lamps, hand censer and incense in the family icon corner should be prepared. (If there is no icon corner, a small table should be placed on the eastern wall of the main room of the dwelling; the table, covered with a white cloth, should be set with one or more icons standing upright, a candle in a candlestand, a hand censer and incense). A small bowl along with several sprigs of evergreen bound together with a ribbon should also be placed in the icon corner (or on the table), along with a clearly printed list of the Baptismal names of the members of the household.

Upon the arrival of the Priest, he is to be greeted by all of the family members, each of whom asks the Priests blessing and reverences his right hand. Then a family member lights the lamps (or candle) and hand censer and turns off all televisions, radios, etc. Lights should be turned on in all the rooms of the house that are to be blessed. The entire family gathers with the Priest before the icon corner (or table) to begin.

The Priest brings the vessel of Holy Water and a sprinkler, as well as oil in a small vessel, and the censer. On each of the four walls (inside), there should be traced a Cross.

The Priest, vested in rasson, faces the icons, blesses and dons his epitrachelion saying the usual vesting prayer. He puts incense upon the lighted charcoal in the hand censer and blesses it saying the usual prayer. He puts his hand cross on the icon corner (or on the table) and, after pouring Holy Water into the bowl provided by the family, he blesses himself whilst intoning:

The Trisagion Prayers

Priest: Blessed is our God, always, now and ever, and unto the ages of ages.

People: *Amen.*

Priest: Glory to Thee, our God. Glory to Thee.

O Heavenly King, the Comforter, the Spirit of Truth; who art everywhere present and fillest all things; Treasury of blessings, and giver of life: come and abide in us, and cleanse us from every impurity, and save our souls, O Good One.

Reader: Holy God, Holy Mighty, Holy Immortal, have mercy on us. **(x3)**

Glory be to the Father, and to the Son, and to the Holy Spirit;
Both now and forever, and unto the ages of ages. Amen.

O Most Holy Trinity, have mercy on us.

O Lord, cleanse us from our sins.

O Master, pardon our iniquities.

O Holy One, visit and heal our infirmities, for Thy name's sake.

Lord have mercy. (x3)

Glory be to the Father, and to the Son, and to the Holy Spirit;
Both now and forever, and unto the ages of ages. Amen.

People: *Our Father, who art in heaven, hallowed be Thy name. Thy Kingdom come. Thy will be done, on earth as it is in heaven. Give us this day our daily bread; and forgive us our trespasses, as we forgive those who trespass against us; and lead us not into temptation, but deliver us from the evil one.*

Priest: For Thine is the kingdom, the power, and the glory, of the Father, and the Son and the Holy Spirit, both now and forever, and to the ages of ages.

People: *Amen.*

Lord, have mercy. **(x12)**

Glory be to the Father, and to the Son, and to the Holy Spirit;
Both now and forever, and unto the ages of ages. Amen.

Psalm 100

Reader: Of mercy and judgement shall I sing to Thee, O Lord; I shall chant and have understanding in a blameless path. When wilt Thou come unto me? I have walked in the innocence of my heart in the midst of my house. I have no unlawful thing before mine eyes; the workers of transgressions I have hated. A crooked heart hath not cleaved unto me; as for the wicked man who turned from me, I knew him not. Him that privily talked against his neighbour did I drive away from me. With him whose eye was proud and his heart insatiate, I did not eat. Mine eyes were upon the faithful of the land, that they might sit with me; the man that walked in the blameless path, he ministered unto me. The proud doer dwelt not in the midst of my house; the speaker of unjust things prospered not before mine eyes. In the morning I slew all the sinners of the land, utterly to destroy out of the city of the Lord all them that work iniquity.

Litany Of Fervent Supplication

Priest: Have mercy on us, O God, according to Thy great mercy, we pray Thee, hearken and have mercy.

People: *Lord, have mercy.* **(x3)**

Priest: Again we pray that He shall send down His blessing upon this house and upon His servant(s), _____, and everyone that lives in it in piety, and that He shall send unto them His Angel of mercy, who shall preserve and protect them from every evil thing, and shall guide them to the performing of every virtue and the fulfilling of the Holy Commandments of Christ; and that He shall protect them from famine, pestilence, earthquake, flood, fire, the sword, foreign invasion or civil war, and from sudden death; and that He shall grant them health and shall encompass them with length of days, and shall grant them abundance in every good thing, let us all say: O Lord, hear us and have mercy.

People: *Lord, have mercy.* **(x3)**

Priest: Again we pray for all pious and Orthodox Christians.

The Holy Gospel

[The Priest stands facing the east.]

Priest: And that we may be accounted worthy of hearing the Holy Gospel, let us pray to the Lord God.

People: *Lord, have mercy.* **(x3)**

Priest: Wisdom! Let us attend! Let us hear the Holy Gospel!

[Facing the people:]

Priest: Peace be with you all.

People: *And with thy spirit.*

Priest: The Reading from the Holy Gospel according to Luke (19:1-10).

People: *Glory to Thee, O Lord, Glory to Thee.*

Priest: Let us attend.

Priest: At that time, Jesus came to Jericho. And behold, there was a man named Zacchaeus who was a chief tax collector, and he was rich. And he sought to see who Jesus was, but could not because of the crowd, for he was of short stature. So he ran ahead and climbed up into a sycamore tree to see Him, for He was going to pass that way. And when Jesus came to the place, He looked up and saw him, and said to him, "Zacchaeus, make haste and come down, for today I must stay at your house." So he made haste and came down, and received Him joyfully. But when they saw it, they all complained, saying, "He has gone to be a guest with a man who is a sinner." Then Zacchaeus stood and said to the Lord, "Look, Lord, I give half of my goods to the poor; and if I have taken anything from anyone by false accusation, I restore fourfold." And Jesus said to him, "Today salvation has come to this house, because he also is a son of Abraham; for the Son of Man has come to seek and to save that which was lost."

People: *Glory to Thee, O Lord, Glory to Thee.*

Reader: Come, let us worship God, our King.

Come, let us worship and fall down before Christ, our King and our God.

Come, let us worship and fall down before Christ Himself, our King and our God.

Psalm 90

Reader: He who dwells in the secret place of the Most High shall abide under the shadow of the Almighty. I shall say of the Lord, *"He is my refuge and my fortress; My God, in Him I shall trust."* Surely He shall deliver thee from the snare of the fowler and from the perilous pestilence. He shall cover thee with His feathers, and under His wings thou shalt take refuge; His truth shall be thy shield and buckler. You shall not be afraid of the terror by night, nor of the arrow that flies by day, Nor of the pestilence that walks in darkness, nor of the destruction that lays waste at noonday. A thousand may fall at thy side, and ten thousand at thy right hand;

but it shall not come near thee. Only with thine eyes shalt thou look, and see the reward of the wicked. Because thou hast made the Lord, Who is my refuge, even the Most High, thy habitation.

No evil shall befall thee, nor shall any plague come near thy dwelling; For He shall give His angels charge over thee, to keep thee in all thy ways. They shall bear thee up in their hands, lest thou dashest thy foot against a stone. Thou shalt tread upon the lion and the cobra, the young lion and the serpent thou shalt trample under foot. Because he has set his love upon Me, therefore I shall deliver him; I shall set him on high, because he has known My name. He shall call upon Me, and I shall answer him; I shall be with him in trouble; I shall deliver him and honour him. With long life shall I satisfy him, and show him My salvation.

After The Psalm

Glory be to the Father, and to the Son, and to the Holy Spirit;
Both now and forever, and unto the ages of ages. Amen.

Halleluiah, Halleluiah, Halleluiah. Glory to Thee, O God. **(x3)**

Troparion

Tone 8   Humility, tranquillity, repose, suffering, pleading.   C, D, Eb, F, G, A, Bb, C.

As salvation came unto the house of Zacchaeus at Thine entrance, O Christ, and likewise now at the entrance of Thy sacred ministers, and, with them, Thy holy Angels, do Thou grant Thy peace unto this house and mercifully bless it, saving and illumining all that live in it.

[Priest stands, facing east, and says:]
Priest: Let us pray to the Lord,
People: Lord, have mercy.
Priest: O Lord Jesus Christ, our God, Who wast pleased to enter under the roof of Zacchaeus the Publican, and didst bring salvation unto him and all his house: Do Thou Thyself now also preserve unharmed by any evil thing them that have desired to live here, and offer unto Thee prayers and supplications through us who are unworthy, blessing them and this habitation, and keeping their life always free from snares, abundantly granting them, by Thy blessing, every good thing that is profitable for them. For unto Thee are due all glory, honour and worship, together with Thy Father Who is without beginning, and Thy Most holy, Good and Life giving Spirit, now and ever and unto ages of ages.
People: Amen.

[Facing the people:]
Priest: Peace be with you all.
People: And with thy spirit.

Priest: Let us bow down our heads unto the Lord.
People: To Thee, O Lord.

Priest: Let us bow our heads unto the Lord.

People: To Thee, O Lord.

Priest: O Master, Lord our God, Who lives on High and looks down upon the lowly; Who didst bless the house of Laban at the entrance of Jacob, and the house of Potiphar at the coming of Joseph; Who blessed the house of Abinadab with the carrying in of the Ark; and Who, in the days of the Advent in the flesh of Christ, our God, granted salvation to the house of Zacchaeus: Bless also this house, and encompass with the fear of Thee them that live in it, and keep them unharmed by adversaries; and send down Thy blessing from Thy dwelling on High, and bless and increase every good thing in this house. For Thine it is to be merciful and to save us, O our God, and unto Thee do we send up glory: to the Father, and to the Son, and to the Holy Spirit, now and ever, and unto ages of ages.

People: Amen.

[Priest blesses the oil three times with the Sign of the Cross, and says:]

Priest: In the Name of the Father, and of the Son, and of the Holy Spirit. Amen.

Priest: O Lord, our God, look down now with mercy on the prayer of Thy lowly and unworthy servant, and send down the Grace of Thy Most holy Spirit on this oil, and sanctify it, that it may be for the sanctification of this place and on this house that has been constructed, and for the expelling of every contrary power and satanic snare: For Thou art He that blesses and sanctifies all things, O Christ, our God, and unto Thee do we send up glory: to the Father, and to the Son, and to the Holy Spirit, both now and forever, and unto the ages of ages.

People: Amen.

[Priest takes the Holy Water and sprinkles, with it, all the walls of the house in crosswise form, and all its rooms. The members of the household may walk behind the Priest, or they may remain at the icon corner (or table), saying at each:]

Priest: In the Name of the Father, and of the Son, and of the Holy Spirit, by the sprinkling of this Holy Water, let every evil demonic activity be put to flight. Amen.

[Taking the oil, the Priest anoints, with it, the walls of the house where the Cross was traced – in its middle, beginning with the eastern wall of the home, then the western wall, and after this the northern wall, ending with the southern wall, saying at each:]

Priest: This house is blessed through the anointing of this Holy Oil, in the Name of the Father, and of the Son, and of the Holy Spirit. Amen.

[Lit candles are set before each Cross on each wall.]

Sticheron

Tone 5   Stimulating, dancing, and rhythmical.   C, D, Eb, F, G, A, Bb, C.

Bless this house, O Lord, and fill it with Thine earthly good things. And keep unharmed from every evil circumstance them that live in it with piety. And grant unto them every heavenly abundance and Thine earthly blessing. And as Thou art compassionate, have mercy, according to Thy great mercy.

People: *Lord, have mercy.* (**x3**)

Priest: Hearken unto us, O God, our Saviour, the hope of all the ends of the earth, and of them that be far off at sea; and be merciful, be merciful, O Master, regarding our sins, and have mercy on us. For Thou art a merciful God, and the Lover of mankind, and unto Thee do we send up glory, to the Father, and to the Son, and to the Holy Spirit, both now and forever and unto the ages of ages.

People: *Amen.*

The Dismissal

Priest: "He Who Is" is blessed, even Christ our God, always, now and ever and unto ages of ages.

People: *Amen.*

Reader: Confirm, O God, the holy Orthodox faith and Orthodox Christians unto ages of ages.

Priest: Most holy Theotokos, save us.

Reader: Greater in honour than the Cherubim and beyond compare more glorious than the Seraphim; without corruption thou gavest birth to God the Word, truly the Theotokos, we magnify thee.

Priest: Glory to Thee, O Christ our God and our Hope. Glory to Thee.

Reader: *Glory be to the Father, and to the Son, and to the Holy Spirit;*

Both now and forever, and unto the ages of ages. Amen.

Lord, have mercy. (**x3**)

Holy Father, bless.

Priest: May Christ our true God, through the intercessions of His all immaculate and all blameless holy Mother, at the supplications of *[Saint of the Temple]*, of the holy and righteous ancestors of God Joachim and Anna, and of all the saints: have mercy on us, and save us, forasmuch as He is good and loveth mankind.

Through the prayers of our holy Fathers; O Lord Jesus Christ our God; have mercy on us and save us.

People: *Amen.*

Priest: O Lord Jesus Christ, Son of God, for the sake of the prayers of Thy most pure Mother, of our holy and God bearing fathers, of *[Saint of the Temple]*, of _____ (*saints of the day*), of the holy and righteous ancestors of God, Joachim and Anna; and of all the saints, have mercy on us and save us, for Thou art good and the Lover of mankind.

People: *Amen.*

[Facing the holy icons, the Priest holds the hand cross:]

Priest: Grant, O Lord, a peaceful life, health, salvation and furtherance in all good things to Thy servant(s), *[name all those who dwell in the house]* NN., and preserve *him / her / them* for many years.

[Priest turns and blesses the people thrice with the hand-cross as all sing:]

God grant you many years.

God grant you many years.

God grant you many many many many years.

[Householders reverence the hand cross and the Priests hand, and are blessed with the Holy Water.

It is customary for the head of the household to discreetly present the Priest with an envelope containing an honorarium and a list of the Living and Departed for whom the family requests his prayers for the next year.]

Apokries   - The period just before Lent.

As we approach Pascha the number of services greatly increases until, in the final days, they are each day. The length of services increases and we encounter canons that occur one day a week and after a few weeks all the parts are done together. There are great spiritual lessons to be learned, but in this volume we are concerned with the services. Each Reader differs in their needs and 3 or more hours of a service can bring out your weaknesses. It is normal that the people can sit when they are tired, but the Reader is thoroughly expected to stand throughout (medical reasons excepting). Thirst may be an issue. The author keeps a small bottle of water to hand to sip and wet the tubes, however there is one in our chorus who amazes me but not needing any drink for hour after hour.

There is a case for saying that we should not eat or drink on a Sunday morning before the Eucharist. However if, for lack of a sip of water, your throat dries, and your singing degrades into a hacking cough then you are not going to be able to chant for the people anyway. This is a case of "oekonomia", that is; allowances must be made so that the service may be done.

The Trisagion Prayers

Priest: Blessed is our God always, both now and forever and unto the ages of ages. Amen.

People: Amen.

Priest: Glory to Thee, our God, glory to Thee.

Priest: O Heavenly King, the Comforter, the Spirit of Truth; who art everywhere present and fillest all things; Treasury of blessings, and giver of life: come and abide in us, and cleanse us from every impurity, and save our souls, O Good One.

People: Holy God, Holy Mighty, Holy Immortal, have mercy on us. **(x3)**

Glory be to the Father and to the Son and to the Holy Spirit;
Both now and forever, and unto the ages of ages. Amen.

O Most Holy Trinity, have mercy on us.

O Lord, cleanse us from our sins.

O Master, pardon our iniquities.

O Holy One, visit and heal our infirmities, for Thy names sake.

Lord have mercy. **(x3)**

Glory be to the Father and to the Son and to the Holy Spirit;
Both now and forever, and unto the ages of ages. Amen.

People: *Our Father, who art in heaven, hallowed be Thy name. Thy Kingdom come. Thy will be done, on earth as it is in heaven. Give us this day our daily bread; and forgive us our trespasses, as we forgive those who trespass against us; and lead us not into temptation, but deliver us from the evil one.*

Priest: For Thine is the kingdom, and the power, and the glory: of the Father, and of the Son, and of the Holy Spirit; now and ever, and unto ages of ages.

People: *Amen.*

Lord have mercy. **(x12)**

Glory be to the Father and to the Son and to the Holy Spirit;
Both now and forever, and unto the ages of ages. Amen.

Come, let us worship God, our King.

Come, let us worship and fall down before Christ, our King and our God.

Come, let us worship and fall down before Christ Himself, our King and our God.

Psalm 103

Of David. Concerning The Formation Of The World.

Bless the Lord, O my soul. O Lord my God, Thou hast been exceedingly magnified. Confession and majesty hast Thou put on, Who covered Thyself with light as with a garment, Who stretched out the heaven as it were a curtain; Who supports His chambers in the waters, Who appoints the clouds for His ascent, Who walks upon the wings of the winds, Who makes His angels spirits, and His ministers a flame of fire, Who establishes the earth in the sureness thereof; it shall not be turned back for ever and ever. The abyss like a garment is His mantle; upon the mountains shall the waters stand. At Thy rebuke they shall flee, at the voice of Thy thunder shall they be afraid.

The mountains rise up and the plains sink down to the place where Thou hast established them. Thou appointed a boundary that they shall not pass, neither return to cover the earth. He sends forth springs in the valleys; between the mountains shall the waters run. They shall give drink to all the beasts of the field; the wild asses shall wait to quench their thirst. Beside them shall the birds of the heaven lodge, from the midst of the rocks shall they give voice. He waters the mountains from His chambers; the earth shall be satisfied with the fruit of Thy works.

He causes the grass to grow for the cattle, and green herb for the service of men, To bring forth bread out of the earth; and wine makes glad the heart of man. To make his face cheerful with oil; and bread strengthens mans heart. The trees of the plain shall be satisfied, the cedars of Lebanon, which Thou hast planted. There shall the sparrows make their nests; the house of the heron is chief among them. The high mountains are a refuge for the harts, and so is the rock for the hares. He has made the moon for seasons; the sun knows his going down. Thou appointed the darkness, and there was the night, wherein all the beasts of the forest shall go abroad. Young lions roaring after their prey, and seeking their food from God. The sun arises, and they are gathered together, and they lay them down in their dens.

But man shall go forth unto his work, and to his labour until the evening. How magnified are Thy works, O Lord. In wisdom hast Thou made them all; the earth is filled with Thy creation. So is this great and spacious sea, therein are things creeping innumerable, small living creatures with the great. There go the ships; there this dragon, whom Thou hast made to play therein. All things wait on Thee, to give them their food in due season; when Thou gavest it to them, they shall gather it. When Thou opened Thy hand, all things shall be filled with goodness; when Thou turned away Thy face, they shall be troubled. Thou wilt take their spirit, and they shall cease; and to their dust shall they return. Thou wilt send forth Thy Spirit, and they shall be created; and Thou shalt renew the face of the earth.

Let the glory of the Lord be unto the ages; the Lord shall rejoice in His works. Who looks on the earth and makes it tremble, Who touches the mountains and they smoke. I shall sing unto the Lord throughout my life, I shall chant to my God for as long as I have my being. May my words be sweet unto Him, and I shall rejoice in the Lord. O that sinners would cease from the earth, and they that work iniquity, that they should be no more. Bless the Lord, O my soul. The sun knows his going down, Thou appointed the darkness, and there was the night. How magnified are Thy works, O Lord. In wisdom hast Thou made them all.

After The Psalm

Glory be to the Father and to the Son and to the Holy Spirit;

Both now and forever, and unto the ages of ages. Amen.

Halleluia, Halleluia, Halleluia. Glory to Thee, O God. **(x3)**

O our God and our Hope, glory to Thee.

The Great Litany

Deacon: In peace, let us pray to the Lord.

People: *Lord, have mercy.*

Deacon: For the peace from above, and for the salvation of our souls, let us pray to the Lord.

People: *Lord, have mercy.*

Deacon: For the peace of the whole world, for the good estate of the holy churches of God, and for the union of all men, let us pray to the Lord.

People: *Lord, have mercy.*

Deacon: For this Holy House, and for those who with faith, reverence, and fear of God, enter therein, let us pray to the Lord.

People: *Lord, have mercy.*

Deacon: For our father and Archbishop Nikitas, for the venerable Priesthood, the Diaconate in Christ, for all the clergy and the people, let us pray to the Lord.

People: *Lord, have mercy.*

Deacon: For Her Majesty Queen Elizabeth, for the First Minister, for all civil authorities, and for our Armed Forces, let us pray to the Lord.

People: *Lord, have mercy.*

Deacon: That He shall aid them and grant them victory over every enemy and adversary, let us pray to the Lord.

People: *Lord, have mercy.*

Deacon: For this city, and for every city and land, and for the faithful who dwell therein, let us pray to the Lord.

People: *Lord, have mercy.*

Deacon: For healthful seasons, for abundance of the fruits of the earth, and for peaceful times, let us pray to the Lord.

People: *Lord, have mercy.*

Deacon: For travellers by sea, by land, and by air; for the sick and the suffering; for captives and their salvation, let us pray to the Lord.

People: *Lord, have mercy.*

Deacon: For our deliverance from all tribulation, wrath, danger, and necessity, let us pray to the Lord.

People: *Lord, have mercy.*

Deacon: Help us; save us; have mercy on us; and keep us, O God, by Thy grace.

People: *Lord, have mercy.*

Deacon: Calling to remembrance our all holy, immaculate, most blessed and glorious Lady Theotokos and ever virgin Mary, with all the Saints: let us commend ourselves and each other, and all our life unto Christ our God.

People: *To Thee, O Lord.*

Priest: For to Thou art due all glory, honour, and worship: to the Father, and to the Son, and to the Holy Spirit; Both now and forever and unto the ages of ages.

People: *Amen.*

Psalm 140

Choir: Lord, I have cried to Thee: hear me. Hear me, O Lord.

Lord, I have cried to Thee: hear me. Receive the voice of my prayer.

When I call upon Thee, hear me, O Lord. Let my prayer arise as incense in Thy sight,

And let the lifting up of my hands be an evening sacrifice. Hear me, O Lord.

Kekragarion
Sticheroi From Psalm 140

• Set, O Lord, a watch before my mouth, and a door of enclosure round about my lips.

• Incline not my heart to words of evil, to make excuses for sins.

• Those that work iniquity; I shall not join with their number.

• The righteous man shall chasten me with mercy and reprove me; as for the oil of the sinner, let it not anoint my head.

• For yet more is my prayer in the presence of their pleasures; their judges have been swallowed up by the rock.

• They shall hear my words, for they be sweetened; as a clod of earth is broken upon the earth, so have their bones been scattered into hades.

• To Thee O Lord are mine eyes. In Thee have I hoped; take not my soul away.

• Keep me from the snare which they have laid for me, and from the stumbling blocks of them that work iniquity.

• The sinners shall fall into their own net; I am alone until I pass by.

Sticheroi From Psalm 141

• With my voice to the Lord have I cried, with my voice have I made supplication.

• I shall pour out before Him my supplications; my afflictions shall I declare before Him.

• When my spirit was fainting within me, then Thou knewest my paths.

• In this way wherein I have walked they hid for me a snare.

• I looked on my right hand, and beheld, and there was none that knew me.

• Flight has failed me, and there is none that watches out for my soul.

• I cried to Thee, O Lord; I said: Thou art my hope, my portion in the land of the living.

• Attend unto my supplication, for I am brought very low.

- Deliver me from them that persecute me, for they are stronger than I.

- *10. Bring my soul out of prison. That I may confess Thy name.*
I cease not from sin, O Lord, nor do I perceive the love Thou showest me. Vanquish my blindness, for Thou alone art good, and have mercy upon me.

- *9. The righteous shall patiently wait for me until Thou shalt reward me.*
O Lord, from fear of Thee I tremble, yet I cease not from doing evil. When called to trial, who does not fear the judge? What man, desiring to be healed, angers the physician, as I do? Take pity upon my weakness, O forbearing Lord, and have mercy upon me.

Sticheroi From Psalm 129

- *8. Out of the depths have I cried unto Thee, O Lord. O Lord, hear my voice.*
Woe is me, for I am like the barren fig tree, and I fear that I shall also be cursed and cut down. But, O heavenly Husbandman, Christ my God, make my dry and barren soul bear fruit. Receive me as the Prodigal Son, and have mercy upon me.

- *7. Let Thine ears be attentive to the voice of my supplication.*
O Lord born of the Virgin, pass over my manifold transgressions and wipe out all my sins. Grant me the firm intent to turn back unto Thee, for Thou alone lovest mankind, and have mercy upon me.

- *6. If Thou should mark iniquities, O Lord; O Lord, who shall stand? For with Thee there is forgiveness.*
Grant me reverence, estrangement from evil, and perfect discipline, who am now drowned in the passions of the flesh, estranged from Thee, and entirely without hope, O my God, King of all. Save me, thy prodigal son, by the bounty of thy goodness, O Jesus the Almighty, the Saviour of our souls.

- *5. For Thy names sake have I patiently waited for Thee, O Lord; my soul has patiently waited for Thy word, my soul has hoped in the Lord.*
When Moses the wonderful was purified by fasting, he beheld the beloved One. Wherefore, emulate him, my humble soul, and hasten to be purified of evils on the day of abstinence, that the Lord may bestow forgiveness on thee, and that thou mayest behold Him, for He is the Almighty, the good Lord, and the Lover of mankind.

- *4. From the morning watch until night, from the morning watch let Israel hope in the Lord.*
Let us now set out with joy upon the second week of the Fast; and like Elijah the Tishbite let us fashion for ourselves from day to day, O brethren, a fiery chariot from the four great virtues; let us exalt our minds through freedom from the passions; let us arm our flesh with purity and our hands with acts of compassion; let us make our feet beautiful with the preaching of the Gospel; and let us put the enemy to flight and gain the victory.

- 3. *For with the Lord there is mercy, and with Him is plenteous redemption; and He shall redeem Israel out of all his iniquities.*

[daily or seasonal Troparia]

Sticheroi From Psalm 116

- 2. *O praise the Lord, all you nations; praise Him, all you peoples.*

[daily or seasonal Troparia]

- 1. *For He has made His mercy to prevail over us, and the truth of the Lord abides forever.*

[daily or seasonal Troparia]

Glory be to the Father and to the Son and to the Holy Spirit.

Both now and forever, and unto the ages of ages. Amen.

Theotokion

Tone 8   Humility, tranquillity, repose, suffering, pleading.   C, D, Eb, F, G, A, Bb, C.

Tossed in the sea of my many transgressions, I take flight unto the tranquil haven of thy spotless entreaty, O all-holy Mother of God, and I cry: Save thy servant who perisheth; stretch out thy mighty right hand and deliver me, O all-blameless Virgin full of grace.

[Whilst:]

The Holy Entrance

Deacon: *[soto voce]* Let us pray to the Lord. Lord have mercy.

Priest: *[soto voce]* In the evening and in the morning and at noon we praise Thee, we bless Thee, we give thanks unto Thee, and we pray unto Thee, O Master of all, Lord Who lovest mankind; Direct our prayer as incense before Thee, and incline not our hearts unto words of thought of evil, but deliver us from all who seek after our souls. For unto Thee, O Lord, Lord are our eyes, and in Thee have we hoped. Put us not to shame, O our God. For unto Thee are due all glory, honour and worship, to the Father, the Son and the Holy Spirit, both now and forever, and to the ages of ages.

Deacon: Amen.

[Censing]

Deacon: *[soto voce]*   Master, bless the Holy Entrance.

Priest: *[soto voce]*   Blessed is the Entrance to Thy Holy place; both now and forever, and unto the ages of ages. Amen.

Deacon: *[aloud]*   Wisdom. Stand up!

O Gladsome Light

O Gladsome Light of the holy glory of the immortal Father; Heavenly holy, blessed Jesus Christ.

Now that we have come to the setting of the sun, and behold the Evening Light.

We praise God; Father, Son and Holy Spirit.

For meet it is at all time to worship Thee, with voices of praise;

O Son of God and Giver of Life. Therefore all the world doth glorify Thee.

Prokeimenon

Deacon: The Evening Prokeimenon.

Second Lenten Great Prokeimenon

Tone 8   *Humility, tranquillity, repose, suffering, pleading.*   *C, D, Eb, F, G, A, Bb, C.*

Chorus: *Thou hast given an inheritance, O Lord, to them that fear Thy Name.* **(x2)**

Reader: From the ends of the earth I cried unto Thee.

Chorus: *Thou hast given an inheritance, O Lord, to them that fear Thy Name.* **(x2)**

Reader: I shall be protected under the cover of Thy wings.

Chorus: *Thou hast given an inheritance, O Lord, to them that fear Thy Name.* **(x2)**

Reader: I shall praise Thy Name forever.

Chorus: *Thou hast given an inheritance, O Lord, to them that fear Thy Name.* **(x2)**

The Evening Prayer

Reader: Vouchsafe, O Lord, to keep us this evening without sin. Blessed art Thou, O Lord, the God of our fathers, and praised and glorified is Thy name unto the ages. Amen.

Let Thy mercy, O Lord, be upon us, according as we have hoped in Thee.

Blessed art Thou, O Lord, teach me Thy statutes.
Blessed art Thou, O Master, give me understanding of Thy statutes.
Blessed art Thou, O Holy One, enlighten me by Thy statutes.

O Lord, Thy mercy endures forever; disdain not the work of Thy hands. To Thee is due praise, to Thee is due song, to Thee is due glory, to the Father, and to the Son, and to the Holy Spirit; both now and forever, and unto the ages of ages. Amen.

The Litany Of Supplication

Deacon: Let us complete our evening prayer unto the Lord.

People: *Lord, have mercy.*

Deacon: Help us; save us; have mercy on us; and keep us, O God, by Thy grace.

People: *Lord, have mercy.*

Deacon: That the whole evening may be perfect, holy, peaceful and sinless, let us ask of the Lord.

People: *Grant this, O Lord.*

Deacon: An angel of peace, a faithful guide, a guardian of our souls and bodies, let us ask of the Lord.

People: *Grant this, O Lord.*

Deacon: Pardon and remission of our sins and transgressions, let us ask of the Lord.

People: *Grant this, O Lord.*

Deacon: All things good and profitable for our souls and peace for the world, let us ask of the Lord.

People: *Grant this, O Lord.*

Deacon: That we may complete the remaining time of our life in peace and repentance, let us ask of the Lord.

People: *Grant this, O Lord.*

Deacon: A Christian ending to our life, painless, blameless, peaceful, and a good defence before the fearful judgement seat of Christ, let us ask of the Lord.

People: *Grant this, O Lord.*

Deacon: Calling to remembrance our all holy, immaculate, most blessed and glorious Lady Theotokos and ever virgin Mary, with all the Saints: let us commend ourselves and one another, and all our life to Christ our God.

People: *To Thee, O Lord.*

Priest: For Thou art a good God and lovest mankind, and to Thee we ascribe glory: to the Father, and to the Son, and to the Holy Spirit; both now and forever, and to the ages of ages.

People: *Amen.*

Priest: Peace be with you all.

People: *And with thy spirit.*

Deacon: Let us bow our heads unto the Lord.

People: *To Thee, O Lord.*

Priest: [*soto voce*] O Lord our God, Who didst bow the heavens and come down for the salvation of mankind: Look upon Thy servants and Thine inheritance; for unto Thee, the fearful Judge Who yet lovest mankind, have Thy servants bowed their heads and submissively inclined their necks, awaiting not help from men but entreating Thy mercy and looking confidently for Thy salvation. Guard them at all times, both during this present evening and in the approaching night, from every foe, from all adverse powers of the devil, and from vain thoughts and from evil imaginations.

[*soto voce*] Blessed and glorified be the majesty of Thy kingdom, of the Father and of the Son and of the Holy Spirit, now and ever and unto ages of ages.

People: *Amen.*

The Aposticha For Sunday Of Orthodoxy, With The Following Stichoi

Tone 8   Humility, tranquillity, repose, suffering, pleading.   *C, D, Eb, F, G, A, Bb, C.*

Come, let us purify our souls with alms and mercy to the poor, not blowing the trumpet, nor making public what we accomplish in charity, lest the left hand know what the right hand doeth, and vainglory do away with the fruits of alms. Let us, however, plead secretly with Him Who knoweth our secrets, crying: Father, forgive us our trespasses, for Thou art the Lover of mankind.

Choir: *Unto Thee have I lifted up mine eyes, O Thou that dwellest in heaven. Behold, as the eyes of servants look unto the hands of their masters, as the eyes of the handmaiden look unto the hands of her mistress, so do our eyes wait upon the Lord our God, until He take pity upon us.*

Reader: Come, let us purify our souls with alms and mercy to the poor, not blowing the trumpet, nor making public what we accomplish in charity, lest the left hand know what the right hand doeth, and vainglory do away with the fruits of alms. Let us, however, plead secretly with Him Who knoweth our secrets, crying: Father, forgive us our trespasses, for Thou art the Lover of mankind.

Choir: *Have mercy upon us, O Lord, have mercy upon us: for we are utterly humiliated. Let shame come on them that prosper, and abasement on the proud.*

Reader: Every place you sanctify, O martyrs of the Lord, and every sickness you heal. Wherefore, now, intercede with Christ, asking Him to deliver our souls from the traps and snares of the enemy.

Choir: *Glory be to the Father and to the Son and to the Holy Spirit.*
Both now and forever, and unto the ages of ages. Amen.

Theotokion For Sunday Of Orthodoxy

Tone 8   Humility, tranquillity, repose, suffering, pleading.   C, D, Eb, F, G, A, Bb, C.

The celestials do praise thee, O full of grace, the spouseless Mother. We glorify thine inapprehensible birth giving. Wherefore, O Theotokos, intercede for the salvation of our souls.

THE PROCESSION OF THE HOLY ICONS

[The clergy, bearing icons, now make a great entrance around the church. The altar servers carry the processional candles, the holy cross, the fans and the banners. The Procession shall go around the entire church, stopping in each of the four corners.]

Apolytikion Of The First Sunday Of Great Lent

Tone 2   Majesty, gentleness, hope, repentance and sadness.   E, F, G, Ab, B, C.

Thy pure image do we venerate, O good One, asking forgiveness of our sins, O Christ our God; for by Thine own will Thou didst ascend the Cross in Thy body, to save Thy creatures from the bondage of the enemy. Thou hast verily filled all with joy, since Thou didst come, O our Saviour, to save the world.

The Litany (At The First Stop)

Deacon: Have mercy on us, O God, according to Thy great mercy, we pray Thee, hear us and have mercy.

People: *Lord, have mercy.* **(x3)**

Deacon: Again we pray for all pious and Orthodox Christians.

People: *Lord, have mercy.* **(x3)**

Deacon: Again we pray for our father and Archbishop <u>Nikitas</u> and for all our brothers and sisters in Christ.

People: *Lord, have mercy.* **(x3)**

Priest: For Thou art a merciful God and love mankind, and to Thee we ascribe glory: to the Father, and to the Son, and to the Holy Spirit; now and ever, and unto the ages of ages.

People: *Amen.*

[Procession to the West wall.]

Apolytikion Of The Sunday Of Orthodoxy

Tone 2   *Majesty, gentleness, hope, repentance and sadness.*   *E, F, G, Ab, B, C.*

We venerate Thy holy icons, loving Lord, asking forgiveness of our sins, Christ our God. For by Thine own will Thou didst ascend the Cross in Thy body, to save Thy creatures from the bondage of the enemy. Therefore in thanksgiving we sing to Thee: Thou hast truly filled all with joy, our Saviour, when Thou camest to save the world.

The Litany (At The Second Stop)

Deacon: Have mercy on us, O God, according to Thy great mercy, we pray to Thee, hear us and have mercy.

People: *Lord, have mercy.* **(x3)**

Deacon: Again we pray for our brethren: the priests, hieromonks, deacons, hierodeacons and monastics and all our brotherhood in Christ.

People: *Lord, have mercy.* **(x3)**

Deacon: Again we pray for mercy, life, peace, health, salvation and visitation and pardon and remission of sins for *(the servants of God, [Names], and)* all Orthodox Christians of true worship, who live and dwell in this community.

People: *Lord, have mercy.* **(x3)**

Priest: For Thou art the resurrection and the life and the repose of Thy departed servants, Christ our God. And to Thee we give glory, with Thine eternal Father and Thine all holy, good and life giving Spirit, now and ever and to the ages of ages.

People: *Amen.*

[Procession to the South.]

Apolytikion Of The Sunday Of Orthodoxy

Tone 2   *Majesty, gentleness, hope, repentance and sadness.*   *E, F, G, Ab, B, C.*

We venerate Thy holy icons, loving Lord, asking forgiveness of our sins, Christ our God. For by Thine own will Thou didst ascend the Cross in Thy body, to save Thy creatures from the bondage of the enemy. Therefore in thanksgiving we sing to Thee: Thou hast truly filled all with joy, our Saviour, when Thou camest to save the world.

The Litany (At The Third Stop)

Deacon: Have mercy on us, O God, according to Thy steadfast love, we pray to Thee, hear us and have mercy.

People: *Lord, have mercy.* **(x3)**

Deacon: Again we pray for the blessed and ever-memorable founders of this holy church and for *(the departed servants of God, [Names], and)* all our fathers and brethren, the Orthodox departed this life before us, who here and in all the world lie asleep in the Lord.

People: *Lord, have mercy.* **(x3)**

Deacon: Again we pray for those who bear fruit and do good works in this holy and all venerable temple, those who serve and those who sing, and for all the people here present, who await Thy great and rich mercy.

People: *Lord, have mercy.* **(x3)**

Priest: For Thou art a merciful and loving God and to Thee we ascribe glory: to the Father and to the Son and to the Holy Spirit; both now and forever and unto the ages of ages.

People: *Amen.*

[Procession to the East – Centre front.]

Apolytikion Of The Sunday Of Orthodoxy

Tone 2   *Majesty, gentleness, hope, repentance and sadness.*   *E, F, G, Ab, B, C.*

We venerate Thy holy icons, loving Lord, asking forgiveness of our sins, Christ our God. For by Thine own will Thou didst ascend the Cross in Thy body, to save Thy creatures from the bondage of the enemy. Therefore in thanksgiving we sing to Thee: Thou hast truly filled all with joy, our Saviour, when Thou camest to save the world.

The Litany (At The Fourth Stop)

Deacon: Have mercy on us, O God, according to Thy great mercy, we pray Thee, hear us and have mercy.

People: *Lord, have mercy.* **(x3)**

Deacon: Again we pray for the ever-memorable Orthodox patriarchs, kings and rulers, and all our fathers and brethren, the Orthodox departed this life before us, who here and in all the world lie asleep in the Lord.

People: *Lord, have mercy.* **(x3)**

Priest: For Thou art the Resurrection, and the Life, and the Repose of Thy departed servants, O Christ our God, and unto Thee we ascribe glory, together with Thy Father, Who is from everlasting, and Thine All Holy, and good, and life creating Spirit: both now and forever, and unto the ages of ages.

People: *Amen.*

[Procession back to normal positions.]

Apolytikion Of The Sunday Of Orthodoxy

Tone 2   *Majesty, gentleness, hope, repentance and sadness.*   *E, F, G, Ab, B, C.*

We venerate Thy holy icons, loving Lord, asking forgiveness of our sins, Christ our God. For by Thine own will Thou didst ascend the Cross in Thy body, to save Thy creatures from the bondage of the enemy. Therefore in thanksgiving we sing to Thee: Thou hast truly filled all with joy, our Saviour, when Thou camest to save the world.

The Synodicon: The Affirmation Of The Orthodox Faith

Priest: As the Prophets beheld, as the Apostles have taught, as the Church has received, as the Teachers have declared, as the world has agreed, as Grace has shown forth, as Truth has revealed, as falsehood has been dissolved, as Wisdom has presented, as Christ has awarded: thus we declare, thus we assert, thus we preach Christ our true God, and honour His Saints in words, in writings, in thoughts, in sacrifices, in churches, in Holy Icons; on the one hand worshipping and reverencing Christ as God and Lord; and on the other hand honouring the saints as true servants of the same Lord of all, and accordingly offering them proper veneration. This is the Faith of the Apostles; this is the Faith of the Fathers; this is the Faith of the Orthodox; this is the Faith on which the world is established.

The Nicene-Constantinopolitan Creed - The Symbol Of Faith

I believe in one God, Father, Almighty, Maker of heaven and earth, and of all things visible and invisible.

And in one Lord Jesus Christ, the only begotten Son of God, begotten from the Father before all ages; Light from Light, true God from true God; begotten not made; consubstantial with the Father, through Him all things were made. For our sake and for our salvation He came down from Heaven, and was incarnate from the Holy Spirit and the Virgin Mary and became man. He was crucified for us under Pontius Pilate, and suffered and was buried. He rose again on the third day in accordance with the Scriptures, and ascended into Heaven, and is seated at the right hand of the Father. He is coming again in glory to judge the living and the dead. And His kingdom shall have no end.

And in the Holy Spirit, the Lord, the Giver of life; Who proceeds from the Father; Who together with the Father and the Son is worshipped and together glorified; Who spoke through the prophets. In One, Holy, Catholic, and Apostolic Church. I confess one baptism for the forgiveness of sins. I await the resurrection of the dead, And the life of the age to come. Amen.

The Great Prokeimenon

Tone 7   *Manly character and strong melody.*   *F, G, A, A#, C, D, E, F.*

Chorus: *Who is so great a God as our God? Thou alone art the God that doest wonders.*

Reader: Thou hast made known Thy power among the peoples.

Chorus: *Who is so great a God as our God? Thou alone art the God that doest wonders.*

Reader: And I said, now have I begun; these are the charges of the right hand of the Most High.

Chorus: *Who is so great a God as our God? Thou alone art the God that doest wonders.*

Reader: Remembering the works of the Lord; for from the beginning I shall remember Thy wonders.

[The clergy now return to the sanctuary.]

Hymn Of Simeon The God Receiver

Reader: Lord, now lettest Thou Thy servant depart in peace, according to Thy word, for mine eyes have seen Thy salvation, which Thou hast prepared before the face of all peoples; a light of revelation for the Gentiles, and the glory of Thy people Israel.

Trisagion Prayers

Holy God, Holy Mighty, Holy Immortal, have mercy on us. **(x3)**

Glory be to the Father, and to the Son, and to the Holy Spirit;
Both now and forever, and unto the ages of ages. Amen.

O Most Holy Trinity, have mercy on us.

O Lord, cleanse us from our sins.

O Master, pardon our iniquities.

O Holy One, visit and heal our infirmities, for Thy names sake.

Lord have mercy. **(x3)**

Glory be to the Father and to the Son and to the Holy Spirit;
Both now and forever, and unto the ages of ages. Amen.

People: Our Father, Who art in Heaven, hallowed be Thy Name. Thy Kingdom come, Thy will be done, on earth as it is in Heaven. Give us this day our daily bread, and forgive us our trespasses, as we forgive those who trespass against us; and lead us not into temptation, but deliver us from the evil one.

Priest: For Thine is the kingdom, the power, and the glory, of the Father, and the Son and the Holy Spirit, both now and ever, and to the ages of ages.

People: Amen.

Lenten Apolytikia

Tone 5   *Stimulating, dancing, and rhythmical.*   *C, D, Eb, F, G, A, Bb, C.*

Reader: Rejoice, O Virgin Theotokos, Mary full of grace; the Lord is with thee. Blessed art thou among women and blessed is the fruit of thy womb, for thou didst give birth to the Saviour of our souls.

prostration

O Baptiser of Christ, remember our congregation, that we may escape from our iniquities, for to thee was given grace to intercede for us.   **prostration**

Glory be to the Father and to the Son and to the Holy Spirit;

O pure apostles, and all you saints, pray for our sakes, that we escape tribulations and sorrows, for we have taken you as fervent intercessors with the Saviour.   **prostration**

Both now and forever, and unto the ages of ages. Amen.

We have taken refuge under the wing of thy compassion, O Theotokos. Turn not away from our beseechings in tribulation, but save us from distress, O thou who alone art pure and blessed.

People: *Lord, have mercy.* **(x40)**

Glory be to the Father and to the Son and to the Holy Spirit;
Both now and forever, and unto the ages of ages. Amen.

Reader: Greater in honour than the Cherubim and beyond compare more glorious than the Seraphim; without corruption thou gavest birth to God the Word, truly the Theotokos, we magnify thee.

People: *Holy Father, bless.*
Priest: Christ our God, the Existing One, is blessed, always, now and forever, and unto the ages of ages.
People: *Amen.*
Reader: O heavenly King, support our believing kings; confirm their faith; guide the nations; give peace to the world and preserve well this holy church. Grant repose to our departed fathers and brothers, in the dwelling places of the righteous. Receive us in repentance and confession, for Thou art good and the Lover of mankind.
People: *Amen.*

The Prayer Of St Ephraim The Syrian
Priest: O Lord and Master of my life, take from me the spirit of sloth, meddling, lust of power, and idle talk.
prostration
Priest: But give rather the spirit of chastity, humility, patience and love to Thy servant.
prostration
Priest: O Lord and King, grant me to see my own sins and not to judge my brother; for Thou art blessed to the ages of ages. Amen.
prostration

The Dismissal
Priest: Glory to Thee, O Christ, our God and our hope, glory to Thee.
Reader: Glory be to the Father, and to to Son, and to the Holy Spirit, both now and for ever, both and to the ages of ages.
People: *Amen.*
Lord, have mercy. **(x3)**
Holy Father, bless!
Priest: May He who rose from the dead, Christ our true God, through the prayers of His most holy Mother, by the power of the precious and life giving Cross, through the protection of the honoured, Bodiless powers of Heaven, through the intercessions of the honoured, glorious prophet, forerunner and baptist John, of the holy, all praised and glorious Apostles, of the holy, glorious and triumphant Martyrs, of our venerable and God

bearing Fathers and Mothers who have shone forth in the ascetic life, of the holy and righteous ancestors of God, Joachim and Anna, of *[patronal saint(s)]* to whom the church is dedicated, of *[Saint N]* whose memory we celebrate today, and of all the Saints, have mercy on us and save us, for He is good and loves mankind.

People: *Amen.*

Priest: Through the prayers of our holy Fathers; O Lord Jesus Christ our God; have mercy on us and save us.

People: *Amen.*

Lenten Vespers with Ceremony of Mutual Forgiveness

[Saints Change According To The Fixed Calendar. If done on a Sunday, use the Saints for Monday.]

Priest: Blessed is our God, always, now and ever, and unto ages of ages.

Chorus: Amen.

Come, let us worship and fall down before God our King.

Come, let us worship and fall down before Christ, our King and our God.

Come, let us worship and fall down before Christ Himself, our King and God.

Psalm 103

Bless the Lord, O my soul. O Lord my God, Thou hast been exceedingly magnified. Confession and majesty hast Thou put on, Who covered Thyself with light as with a garment, Who stretched out the heaven as it were a curtain; Who supports His chambers in the waters, Who appoints the clouds for His ascent, Who walks upon the wings of the winds, Who makes His angels spirits, and His ministers a flame of fire, Who establishes the earth in the sureness thereof; it shall not be turned back for ever and ever. The abyss like a garment is His mantle; upon the mountains shall the waters stand. At Thy rebuke they shall flee, at the voice of Thy thunder shall they be afraid. The mountains rise up and the plains sink down to the place where Thou hast established them. Thou appointed a boundary that they shall not pass, neither return to cover the earth. He sends forth springs in the valleys; between the mountains shall the waters run. They shall give drink to all the beasts of the field; the wild asses shall wait to quench their thirst. Beside them shall the birds of the heaven lodge, from the midst of the rocks shall they give voice. He waters the mountains from His chambers; the earth shall be satisfied with the fruit of Thy works.

He causes the grass to grow for the cattle, and green herb for the service of men, To bring forth bread out of the earth; and wine makes glad the heart of man. To make his face cheerful with oil; and bread strengthens mans heart. The trees of the plain shall be satisfied, the cedars of Lebanon, which Thou hast planted. There shall the sparrows make their nests; the house of the heron is chief among them. The high mountains are a refuge for the harts, and so is the rock for the hares. He has made the moon for seasons; the sun knows his going down. Thou appointed the darkness, and there was the night, wherein all the beasts of the forest shall go abroad. Young lions roaring after their prey, and seeking their food from God. The sun arises, and they are gathered together, and they lay them down in their dens. But man shall go forth unto his work, and to his labour until the evening. How magnified are Thy works, O Lord. In wisdom hast Thou made them all; the earth is filled with Thy creation. So is this great and spacious sea, therein are things creeping innumerable, small living creatures with the great. There go the ships; there this dragon, whom Thou hast made to play therein. All things wait on Thee, to give them their food in due season; when Thou gavest it to them, they shall gather it. When Thou opened Thy hand, all things shall be filled with goodness; when Thou turned away Thy face, they shall be troubled. Thou wilt take their spirit, and they shall cease; and to their dust shall they return. Thou wilt send forth Thy Spirit, and they shall be created; and Thou shalt renew the face of the earth.

Let the glory of the Lord be unto the ages; the Lord shall rejoice in His works. Who looks on the earth and makes it tremble, Who touches the mountains and they smoke. I shall sing unto the Lord throughout my life, I shall chant to my God for as long as I have my being. May my words be sweet unto Him, and I shall rejoice in the Lord. O that sinners would cease from the earth, and they that work iniquity, that they should be no more. Bless the Lord, O my soul. The sun knows his going down, Thou appointed the darkness, and there was the night. How magnified are Thy works, O Lord. In wisdom hast Thou made them all.

After The Psalm

Glory be to the Father and to the Son and to the Holy Spirit;

Both now and forever, and unto the ages of ages. Amen.

Halleluiah, Halleluiah, Halleluiah. Glory to Thee, O God. **(x3)**

O our God and our Hope, glory to Thee.

The Great Litany

Deacon: In peace, let us pray to the Lord.

People: *Lord, have mercy.*

Deacon: For the peace from above, and for the salvation of our souls, let us pray to the Lord.

People: *Lord, have mercy.*

Deacon: For the peace of the whole world, for the good estate of the holy churches of God, and for the union of all men, let us pray to the Lord.

People: *Lord, have mercy.*

Deacon: For this Holy House, and for those who with faith, reverence, and fear of God, enter therein, let us pray to the Lord.

People: *Lord, have mercy.*

Deacon: For our father and Archbishop Nikitas, for the venerable Priesthood, the Diaconate in Christ, for all the clergy and the people, let us pray to the Lord.

People: *Lord, have mercy.*

Deacon: For Her Majesty, Queen Elizabeth, for the First Minister, for all civil authorities, and for our Armed Forces, let us pray to the Lord.

People: *Lord, have mercy.*

Deacon: That He shall aid them and grant them victory over every enemy and adversary, let us pray to the Lord.

People: *Lord, have mercy.*

Deacon: For this city, and for every city and land, and for the faithful who dwell therein, let us pray to the Lord.

People: *Lord, have mercy.*

Deacon: For healthful seasons, for abundance of the fruits of the earth, and for peaceful times, let us pray to the Lord.

People: Lord, have mercy.

Deacon: For travellers by sea, by land, and by air; for the sick and the suffering; for captives and their salvation, let us pray to the Lord.

People: Lord, have mercy.

Deacon: For our deliverance from all tribulation, wrath, danger, and necessity, let us pray to the Lord.

People: Lord, have mercy.

Deacon: Help us; save us; have mercy on us; and keep us, O God, by Thy grace.

People: Lord, have mercy.

Deacon: Calling to remembrance our all holy, immaculate, most blessed and glorious Lady Theotokos and ever virgin Mary, with all the Saints: let us commend ourselves and each other, and all our life unto Christ our God.

People: To Thee, O Lord.

Priest: For to Thou art due all glory, honour, and worship: to the Father, and to the Son, and to the Holy Spirit; Both now and forever and unto the ages of ages.

People: Amen.

O Lord, I Have Cried.

Chorus: Lord, I have cried to Thee: hear me. Hear me, O Lord.

Lord, I have cried to Thee: hear me. Receive the voice of my prayer,

When I call upon Thee, hear me, O Lord. Let my prayer arise as incense in Thy sight

And let the lifting up of my hands be an evening sacrifice. Hear me, O Lord.

Kekragarion
Sticheroi From Psalm 140

• Set, O Lord, a watch before my mouth, and a door of enclosure round about my lips.

• Incline not my heart to words of evil, to make excuses for sins.

• Those that work iniquity; I shall not join with their number.

• The righteous man shall chasten me with mercy and reprove me; as for the oil of the sinner, let it not anoint my head.

• For yet more is my prayer in the presence of their pleasures; their judges have been swallowed up by the rock.

• They shall hear my words, for they be sweetened; as a clod of earth is broken upon the earth, so have their bones been scattered into hades.

• To Thee O Lord are mine eyes. In Thee have I hoped; take not my soul away.

• Keep me from the snare which they have laid for me, and from the stumbling blocks of them that work iniquity.

• The sinners shall fall into their own net; I am alone until I pass by.

Sticheroi From Psalm 141

- With my voice to the Lord have I cried, with my voice have I made supplication.
- I shall pour out before Him my supplications; my afflictions shall I declare before Him.
- When my spirit was fainting within me, then Thou knewest my paths.
- In this way wherein I have walked they hid for me a snare.
- I looked on my right hand, and beheld, and there was none that knew me.
- Flight has failed me, and there is none that watches out for my soul.
- I cried to Thee, O Lord; I said: Thou art my hope, my portion in the land of the living.
- Attend unto my supplication, for I am brought very low.
- Deliver me from them that persecute me, for they are stronger than I.

The Penitential Stichera

Verse 10. *Bring my soul out of prison, that I may praise Thy Name.*

The angels praise Thee without ceasing, O King and Master, and I fall before Thee crying like the Publican: God be merciful to me and save me.

Verse 9. *The righteous shall wait for me until Thou shalt recompense me.*

Since thou art immortal, O my soul, be not overwhelmed by the waves of life; but return to soberness and cry to thy Benefactor: God be merciful to me and save me.

Sticheroi From Psalm 129

Verse 8. *Out of the depths have I cried to Thee, O Lord. Lord hear my voice.*

Give me tears, O God, as once Thou gavest them to the woman that had sinned, and count me worthy to wash Thy feet that have delivered me from the way of error. As sweet smelling ointment let me offer Thee a pure life, created in me by repentance; and may I also hear those words for which I long: "Thy faith has saved thee, go in peace."

Verse 7. *Let Thy ears be attentive to the voice of my supplication.*

When I call to mind the many evils I have done, and I think upon the fearful day of judgement, seized with trembling I flee to Thee for refuge, O God Who loves mankind. Turn not away from me, I beseech Thee, Who alone art free from sin; but before the end comes, grant compunction to my humbled soul and save me.

Troparion For Forgiveness Sunday

Tone 2   *Majesty, gentleness, hope, repentance and sadness.*   *E, F, G, Ab, B, C.*

Verse 6. *If Thou, O Lord, shouldest mark iniquities, O Lord, who shall stand?*

For with Thee there is forgiveness.

Let us all hasten to the subjugation of the flesh by abstinence, as we approach the divine battlefield, the battlefield of blameless fasting. Let us pray to the Lord, our Saviour, in tears and prayers, turning away completely from sin, and crying, "We have sinned against Thee, O Christ, the King. Save us, therefore, as of old Thou didst save the people of Nineveh; and make us partakers of Thy heavenly kingdom, O compassionate One."

Verse 5.   Because of Thy Name have I waited for Thee, O Lord;

My soul has waited upon Thy word, my soul has hoped in the Lord.

If I were to imagine all my sins deserving all punishment, I would despair of myself, O Lord Saviour; for by them have I disobeyed Thy noble commandment, wasting my life in extravagance. Wherefore, I beseech Thee to purify me with Thy showers of forgiveness, and lighten me with fasting and supplication; for Thou alone art compassionate; and reject me not, O all bountiful and of transcendent goodness.

Verse 4.   From the morning watch until night, from the morning watch let Israel trust in the Lord.

Let us begin the season of fasting with rejoicing, giving ourselves to spiritual strife, purifying soul and body, fasting from passions, as we fast from foods, faring on the virtues of the Spirit, which, if we continue to long for, we shall all be worthy to behold the most solemn Passion of Christ, and the holy Passover, rejoicing with spiritual joy.

Troparia For The Saint Of The Day

Tone 3   *Arrogant, brave, and mature atmosphere.*   *F, G, A, A#, C, D, E, F.*

Verse 3.   For with the Lord there is mercy and with Him is abundant redemption,

And He shall deliver Israel from all his iniquities.

[Troparion for the Saint of the Day here.]

Troparia For The Saint Of The Day

Verse 2.   Praise the Lord, all you nations; praise Him, all you people.

[Troparion for the Saint of the Day here.]

Kontakion For The Saint Of The Day

Verse 1.   For His mercy is great toward us, and the truth of the Lord endures forever.

[Kontakion for the Saint of the Day here.]

Glory be to the Father, and to the Son, and to the Holy Spirit;
Both now and forever, and unto the ages of ages. Amen.

Theotokion From The Menaion

Tone 2   Majesty, gentleness, hope, repentance and sadness.   *E, F, G, Ab, B, C.*

Bridle the digressions of my mind; stay the wayward drift of my senses; O Virgin, wholly blot out all the deadly passions with their sinful images. Grant tranquillity unto me and calm the disturbance of my lowly soul, that I may rightly magnify thy great goodness; for I possess thee as my steadfast succour in weakness and the watchful guardian of all my life.

[Whilst:]

The Holy Entrance

[The following QUIETLY occurs as the clergy make the entrance.]

Deacon: Let us pray to the Lord.

People: *Lord, have mercy.*

Priest: In the evening and in the morning and at noonday we praise Thee, we bless Thee, we give thanks unto Thee, and we pray unto Thee, O Master of all, Lord Who loves mankind: Direct our prayer as incense before Thee, and incline not our hearts to words or thoughts of evil, but deliver us from all who seek after our souls. For to Thee, O Lord, Lord, are our eyes, and in Thee have we hoped. Put us not to shame, O our God. For to Thee are due all glory, honour, and worship: to the Father and to the Son and to the Holy Spirit; Both now and forever, and unto the ages of ages.

Deacon: Amen.

[When the clergy reach the centre of the solea, start the 1st part of the great censing.
After the first part of the great censing is completed, this next QUIETLY occurs.]

Deacon: Bless, Father, the Holy Entrance.

Priest: Blessed is the entrance to Thy Holy Place, always;

         Both now and forever, and to the ages of ages. Amen.

[After the Chorus has finished, the following is said ALOUD.]

Deacon: Wisdom! Let us attend!

O Gladsome Light

O Gladsome Light of the holy glory of the immortal Father;

Heavenly holy, blessed Jesus Christ;

Now that we have come to the setting of the sun, and behold the Evening Light;

We praise God; Father, Son and Holy Spirit.

For meet it is at all time to worship Thee, with voices of praise;

O Son of God and Giver of Life. Therefore all the world doth glorify Thee.

Forgiveness Sunday Prokeimenon

Deacon: The Evening Prokeimenon.

Tone 8   *Humility, tranquillity, repose, suffering, pleading.*   *C, D, Eb, F, G, A, Bb, C.*

Reader: Turn not away Thy face from Thy servant; For I am in trouble: hear me speedily.

Attend to my soul, and deliver it. **(x2)**

Chorus: *Let Thy salvation, O God, help me.*

Reader: Turn not away Thy face from Thy servant; For I am in trouble: hear me speedily.

Attend to my soul, and deliver it. **(x2)**

Chorus: *Let the poor see it and be glad.*

Reader: Turn not away Thy face from Thy servant; For I am in trouble: hear me speedily.

Attend to my soul, and deliver it.

Chorus: *Seek God, and thy soul shall live.*

Reader: Turn not away Thy face from Thy servant; For I am in trouble: hear me speedily.

Attend to my soul, and deliver it.

The Evening Prayer

Reader: Vouchsafe, O Lord, to keep us this evening without sin. Blessed art Thou, O Lord, the God of our fathers, and praised and glorified is Thy Name forever. Amen.

Let Thy mercy be upon us, Lord, even as we have set our hope on Thee.

Blessed art Thou, O Lord; teach me Thy statutes.

Blessed art Thou, O Master; make me to understand Thy statutes.

Blessed art Thou, O Holy One; enlighten me with Thy statutes.

Thy mercy, Lord, endures forever. Despise not the works of Thy hands. To Thee belongs worship, to Thee belongs praise, to Thee belongs glory. To the Father, and to the Son, and to the Holy Spirit; both now and forever and to the ages of ages. Amen.

The Litany Of Supplication

Deacon: Let us complete our evening prayer unto the Lord.

People: *Lord, have mercy.*

Deacon: Help us; save us; have mercy on us; and keep us, O God, by Thy grace.

People: *Lord, have mercy.*

Deacon: That the whole evening may be perfect, holy, peaceful and sinless, let us ask of the Lord.

People: *Grant this, O Lord.*

Deacon: An angel of peace, a faithful guide, a guardian of our souls and bodies, let us ask of the Lord.

People: *Grant this, O Lord.*

Deacon: Pardon and remission of our sins and transgressions, let us ask of the Lord.

People: *Grant this, O Lord.*

Deacon: All things good and profitable for our souls and peace for the world, let us ask of the Lord.

People: *Grant this, O Lord.*

Deacon: That we may complete the remaining time of our life in peace and repentance, let us ask of the Lord.

People: *Grant this, O Lord.*

Deacon: A Christian ending to our life, painless, blameless, peaceful, and a good defence before the fearful judgement seat of Christ, let us ask of the Lord.

People: *Grant this, O Lord.*

Deacon: Calling to remembrance our all holy, immaculate, most blessed and glorious Lady Theotokos and ever virgin Mary, with all the Saints: let us commend ourselves and one another, and all our life to Christ our God.

People: *To Thee, O Lord.*

Priest: For Thou art a good God and lovest mankind, and to Thee we ascribe glory: to the Father, and to the Son, and to the Holy Spirit; both now and forever, and to the ages of ages.

People: *Amen.*

Priest: Peace be with you all.

People: *And with thy spirit.*

Deacon: Let us bow our heads unto the Lord.

People: *To Thee, O Lord.*

Priest: O Lord our God, Who did bow the heavens and come down for the salvation of mankind: Look upon Thy servants and Thine inheritance; for to Thee, the fearful Judge Who yet loves mankind, have Thine servants bowed their heads and submissively inclined their necks, awaiting not help from men but entreating Thy mercy and looking confidently for Thy salvation. Guard them at all times, both during this present evening and in the approaching night, from every foe, from all adverse powers of the devil, and from vain thoughts and from evil imaginations.

Blessed and glorified be the might of Thy kingdom: of the Father, and of the Son, and of the Holy Spirit; both now and forever, and unto the ages of ages.

People: *Amen.*

The Aposticha For Forgiveness Sunday

Tone 4   Festive, joyous and deep piety.   *C, D, Eb, F, G, A, Bb, C.*

Reader: Thy grace has risen, O Lord, the illumination of our souls has shone forth. Now is the acceptable time; the season of repentance has come. Let us cast down the works of darkness, and put on the works of light, that we may pass the great tempest of fasting and reach the summit of the third day Resurrection of our Lord and Saviour Jesus Christ, the Saviour of our souls.

Verse 1.

Chorus: *To Thee have I lifted up mine eyes, O Thou who dwells in heaven. Behold, as the eyes of servants look to the hands of their masters, as the eyes of the handmaiden look to the hands of her mistress, so do our eyes wait upon the Lord our God, until He take pity upon us.*

Reader: Thy grace has risen, O Lord, the illumination of our souls has shone forth. Now is the acceptable time; the season of repentance has come. Let us cast down the works of darkness, and put on the works of light, that we may pass the great tempest of fasting and reach the summit of the third day Resurrection of our Lord and Saviour Jesus Christ, the Saviour of our souls.

Verse 2.

Chorus: *Have mercy upon us O Lord, have mercy upon us: for we are utterly humiliated. Let shame come on them that prosper, and abasement on the proud.*

Reader: O Christ God, glorified in the mention of Thy saints, send us, through their beseechings, Thy Great Mercy.

Chorus: *Glory be to the Father, and to the Son, and to the Holy Spirit;*
            Both now and ever, and unto the ages of ages. Amen.

Theotokion For Forgiveness Sunday

Tone 4   Festive, joyous and deep piety.   *C, D, Eb, F, G, A, Bb, C.*

O most holy Theotokos, the ranks of angels praise thee, for thou didst bear God Who forever is with the Father and the Holy Spirit, by Whose shall the ranks of angels arose from nothing. Wherefore, beseech Him to save and lighten the souls of those who praise thee in Orthodoxy, O most pure one.

The Hymn Of St Simeon The God Receiver

Reader: Lord, now lettest Thou Thy servant depart in peace, according to Thy word; for mine eyes have seen Thy salvation, which Thou hast prepared before the face of all people, a light to lighten the Gentiles and the glory of Thy people Israel.

The Trisagion Prayers

[Chanted, not sung:]

Reader: Holy God, Holy Mighty, Holy Immortal: have mercy on us. **(x3)**

Glory be to the Father, and to the Son, and to the Holy Spirit;
Both now and forever, and unto the ages of ages. Amen.

O Most Holy Trinity, have mercy on us.

O Lord, cleanse us from our sins.

O Master, pardon our iniquities.

O Holy One, visit and heal our infirmities, for Thy names sake.

Lord, have mercy. **(x3)**

Glory be to the Father, and to the Son, and to the Holy Spirit;
Both now and forever, and unto the ages of ages. Amen.

People: *Our Father, Who art in Heaven, hallowed be Thy Name. Thy kingdom come; Thy will be done on earth as it is in Heaven. Give us this day our daily bread; And forgive us our trespasses, as we forgive those who trespass against us. And lead us not into temptation, but deliver us from the evil one.*

Priest: For Thine is the kingdom, and the power, and the glory: of the Father and of the Son and of the Holy Spirit; both now and forever, and to the ages of ages.

People: *Amen.*

[Priest exits Sanctaury whilst:]

Lenten Apolytikia

Tone 5   *Stimulating, dancing, and rhythmical.*   C, D, Eb, F, G, A, Bb, C.

Rejoice, O Virgin Theotokos, Mary full of grace; the Lord is with thee. Blessed art thou amongst women and blessed is the fruit of thy womb, for thou didst give birth to the Saviour of our souls.

Priest: Rejoice, O Virgin Theotokos, Mary full of grace; the Lord is with thee. Blessed art thou amongst women and blessed is the fruit of thy womb, for thou didst give birth to the Saviour of our souls.

prostration

O Baptiser of Christ, remember our congregation, that we may escape from our iniquities, for to Thee was given grace to intercede for us.   **prostration**

Glory be to the Father, and to the Son, and to the Holy Spirit.

O pure apostles, and all you saints, pray for our sakes, that we may escape tribulations and sorrows, for we have taken you as fervent intercessors with the Saviour.   *prostration*

Both now and forever, and to the ages of ages. Amen.

We have taken refuge under the wing of thy compassion, O Theotokos. Turn not away from our beseechings in tribulation, but save us from distress, O thou who alone art pure and blessed.

[Slow chant for people to join in:]
People: *Lord, have mercy.* **(x40)**

Reader: *Glory be to the Father, and to the Son, and to the Holy Spirit;*
Both now and forever, and unto the ages of ages. Amen.

Greater in honour than the Cherubim and beyond compare more glorious than the Seraphim. Without corruption thou gavest birth to God the Word, truly the Theotokos, we magnify thee.

Holy Father Bless.

Priest: Christ our God, the Existing One, is blessed, always, now and forever, and to the ages of ages.
Reader: Amen. O heavenly King, support our believing rulers; confirm their faith; guide the nations; give peace to the world and preserve well this holy church. Grant repose to our departed fathers and brothers, in the dwelling places of the righteous. Receive us in repentance and confession, for Thou art good and the Lover of mankind.

The Prayer Of St Ephraim The Syrian
Priest: O Lord and Master of my life, take from me the spirit of sloth, meddling, lust of power, and idle talk.   *prostration*

Priest: But give rather the spirit of chastity, humility, patience and love to Thy servant.   *prostration*

Priest: O Lord and King, grant me to see my own sins and not to judge my brother; for Thou art blessed to the ages of ages. Amen.   *prostration*

The Dismissal
Priest: Glory to Thee, O Christ our God and our hope, glory to Thee.
Reader: *Glory be to the Father, and to the Son, and to the Holy Spirit;*
Both now and forever, and unto the ages of ages. Amen.

Lord, have mercy. **(x3)**

Holy Father, bless.

Priest: May Christ our true God, through the intercessions of His all immaculate and all blameless holy Mother; by the protection of the honourable Bodiless Powers of Heaven; at the supplication of *[Saint N.,]* the patron and protector of this holy community; of the holy and righteous ancestors of God, Joachim and Anna; and *[N]* whose memories we celebrate today, and of all the saints: have mercy on us and save us, for as much as He is good and loves mankind.

People: *Amen.*

The Ceremony Of Mutual Forgiveness

[As the Chorus very slowly and in low voice sings the Theotokion below, the exchange of mutual forgiveness may now take place, beginning with the clergy.]

Forgiveness Theotokion

Tone 2   Majesty, gentleness, hope, repentance and sadness.   *E, F, G, Ab, B, C.*

O righteous one, Mother of the most high God, defend all those who take refuge in faith in thy precious protection; for we sinners, bowed by the multitude of sins, have no other constant intercessor with God in tribulations and sorrows, save thee. Wherefore, we bow to thee, adoring. Save thy servants from every distress.

- *The priest stands next to the analogion.*
- *The faithful venerate the icon of the Theotokos.*
- *Each of the faithful bow before the priest, who also does the same, each saying to one another,* **"Forgive me, a sinner."** *The response is,* **"God forgives."**
- *The faithful then receive his blessing and kiss his hand. The faithful also ask forgiveness from each other in the same manner, exchanging among themselves the kiss of peace.*
- *When everyone has completed; the priest faces the icon of Christ and says:*

Priest: Through the prayers of our holy fathers, Lord Jesus Christ our God, have mercy upon us and save us.

People: *Amen.*

First Sunday Of Lent
The Procession Of The Holy Icons

(Bring an Icon)

Laymen carry the icons of Christ, the Theotokos and the Saints, preceded by the Altar boys with candles and the Cross, proceed from the Altar area while the Chorus repeatedly sings:

Chorus: Holy God, Holy Strong, Holy Immortal. *[repeat].*

[Procession around the church, stopping first at the North wall.]

Apolytikion Of The Sunday Of Orthodoxy

Tone 2   Majesty, gentleness, hope, repentance and sadness.   *E, F, G, Ab, B, C.*

We venerate Thy holy icons, loving Lord, asking forgiveness of our sins, Christ our God. For by Thine own will Thou didst ascend the Cross in Thy body, to save Thy creatures from the bondage of the enemy. Therefore in thanksgiving we sing to Thee: Thou hast truly filled all with joy, our Saviour, when Thou camest to save the world.

The Litany (At The First Stop)

Deacon: Have mercy on us, O God, according to Thy great mercy, we pray Thee, hear us and have mercy.

People: *Lord, have mercy.* **(x3)**

Deacon: Again we pray for all pious and Orthodox Christians.

People: *Lord, have mercy.* **(x3)**

Deacon: Again we pray for our father and Archbishop Nikitas and for all our brothers and sisters in Christ.

People: *Lord, have mercy.* **(x3)**

Priest: For Thou art a merciful God and love mankind, and to Thee we ascribe glory: to the Father, and to the Son, and to the Holy Spirit; now and ever, and unto the ages of ages.

People: *Amen.*

[Procession to the West wall.]

Apolytikion Of The Sunday Of Orthodoxy

Tone 2   Majesty, gentleness, hope, repentance and sadness.   *E, F, G, Ab, B, C.*

We venerate Thy holy icons, loving Lord, asking forgiveness of our sins, Christ our God. For by Thine own will Thou didst ascend the Cross in Thy body, to save Thy creatures from the bondage of the enemy. Therefore in thanksgiving we sing to Thee: Thou hast truly filled all with joy, our Saviour, when Thou camest to save the world.

The Litany (At The Second Stop)

Deacon: Have mercy on us, O God, according to Thy great mercy, we pray to Thee, hear us and have mercy.

People: *Lord, have mercy.* **(x3)**

Deacon: Again we pray for the blessed memory and eternal repose of Thy departed servants; emperors, patriarchs, hierarchs, priests, hieromonks, deacons, monks and all of our departed faithful and Orthodox Christians everywhere in the world: fathers, brothers, sisters and relatives.

People: *Memory eternal.* **(x3)**

Deacon: For Thou art the resurrection and the life and the repose of Thy departed servants, Christ our God. And to Thee we give glory, with Thine eternal Father and Thine all holy, good and life giving Spirit, now and ever and to the ages of ages.

People: *Amen.*

[Procession to the South.]

Apolytikion Of The Sunday Of Orthodoxy

Tone 2   Majesty, gentleness, hope, repentance and sadness.   *E, F, G, Ab, B, C.*

We venerate Thy holy icons, loving Lord, asking forgiveness of our sins, Christ our God. For by Thine own will Thou didst ascend the Cross in Thy body, to save Thy creatures from the bondage of the enemy. Therefore in thanksgiving we sing to Thee: Thou hast truly filled all with joy, our Saviour, when Thou camest to save the world.

The Litany (At The Third Stop)

Deacon: Have mercy on us, O God, according to Thy steadfast love, we pray to Thee, hear us and have mercy.

People: *Lord, have mercy.* **(x3)**

Deacon: Again we pray for all faithful and Orthodox Christians.

People: *Lord, have mercy.* **(x3)**

Deacon: Again we pray for our Archbishop Nikitas and for all our brothers and sisters in Christ.

People: *Lord, have mercy.* **(x3)**

Priest: For Thou art a merciful and loving God and to Thee we ascribe glory: to the Father and to the Son and to the Holy Spirit; both now and forever and unto the ages of ages.

People: *Amen.*

[Procession to the East – Centre front.]

Apolytikion Of The Sunday Of Orthodoxy

Tone 2   Majesty, gentleness, hope, repentance and sadness.   *E, F, G, Ab, B, C.*

We venerate Thy holy icons, loving Lord, asking forgiveness of our sins, Christ our God. For by Thine own will Thou didst ascend the Cross in Thy body, to save Thy creatures from the bondage of the enemy. Therefore in thanksgiving we sing to Thee: Thou hast truly filled all with joy, our Saviour, when Thou camest to save the world.

The Litany (At The Fourth Stop)

Deacon: Have mercy on us, O God, according to Thy great mercy, we pray Thee, hear us and have mercy.

People: *Lord, have mercy.* (**x3**)

Deacon: Again we pray for the protection of this holy church, this [*city / town / village*] and every city, town and village, from wrath, famine, earthquake, flood, fire, sword, foreign invasions, civil strife and accidental death. That our good and loving God may be merciful, gracious and favourable to us, that He may turn and keep from us all wrath and sickness and deliver us from His just rebuke and have mercy on us.

People: *Lord, have mercy.* (**x3**)

Deacon: Hear us, O God our Saviour, the hope of all those who live everywhere on earth and those far out at sea. Be gracious toward our sins Master, and have mercy on us.

People: *Lord, have mercy.* (**x3**)

Priest: For Thou art a merciful and loving God, and to Thee we ascribe glory; to the Father and the Son and the Holy Spirit; both now and forever, and to the ages of ages.

People: *Amen.*

The Synodicon: The Affirmation Of The Orthodox Faith

Priest: As the Prophets beheld, as the Apostles have taught, as the Church has received, as the Teachers have declared, as the world has agreed, as Grace has shown forth, as Truth has revealed, as falsehood has been dissolved, as Wisdom has presented, as Christ has awarded: thus we declare, thus we assert, thus we preach Christ our true God, and honour His Saints in words, in writings, in thoughts, in sacrifices, in churches, in Holy Icons; on the one hand worshipping and reverencing Christ as God and Lord; and on the other hand honouring the saints as true servants of the same Lord of all, and accordingly offering them proper veneration.

This is the Faith of the Apostles; this is the Faith of the Fathers; this is the Faith of the Orthodox; this is the Faith on which the world is established. Therefore with fraternal and filial love we praise the heralds of the faith, those who with glory and honour have struggled for the faith, and we say: to the champions of Orthodoxy, faithful emperors, most holy patriarchs, hierarchs, teachers, martyrs and confessors: May thy memory be eternal.

People: *Memory eternal.* (**x3**)

Priest: Let us beseech God that we may be instructed and strengthened by the trials and struggles of these saints which they endured for the faith even unto death, and by their teachings, entreating that we may, to the end, imitate their godly life. May we be deemed worthy of obtaining our requests through the mercy and grace of the Great and First Hierarch, Christ our God, through the intercession of our glorious Lady, the Theotokos and ever virgin Mary, the divine angels and all the Saints.

People: *Amen.*

People: *Who is so great a God as our God? Thou art the God who alone performs wonders.* (**x3**)

People: *Today salvation has come to the world. Let us sing and praise Him who rose from the tomb and is the author of life. For having vanquished death by death, He has bestowed upon us victory and great mercy.*

For:

The Exaltation Of The Cross   – September 14th.

The Adoration Of The Cross   – Third Sunday Of Great Lent.

The Procession Of The Cross   – August 1st.

[After the prayer behind the Ambon, the Priest, having placed the Holy Cross on a tray decorated with roses and flowers and three candles, takes the tray and puts it on the Holy Altar and censes the Holy Cross nine times.

*Priest starts the **procession**, preceded by the Altar boys, other clergy with the censer and the Chorus. Exit North Door, go around the Church. Meanwhile:]*

Chorus: Holy God, Holy Strong, Holy Immortal, have mercy on us. *[Many times and slow.]*

[When they reach the Ambon.]

Apolytikion Of The Exaltation Of The Holy Cross

    Tone 1   *Magnificent, happy and earthy.*   C, D, Eb, F, G, A, Bb, C.

(i, iii)   O Lord, save Thy people and bless Thine inheritance.

               Grant victories to the Orthodox Christians over their adversaries.

               And by virtue of Thy Cross, preserve Thy commonwealth.

(ii)   Soson Kyrie ton lao sou, Ke evlogison, tin klironomian sou, Nikas tis Vasilevsii;

               Kata varvaron doroumen as Ke to son filaton dia ton stavron sou politev ma.

*The Priest reaches the small table put out for the Cross to be venerated upon. Whilst the priest and the one who is carrying the censer go **around the table three times**:*

Priest: O Lord, save Thy people, and bless Thine inheritance. Grant victories to Orthodox Christians over their adversaries. And by Thy Cross preserve Thy commonwealth.

People: *O Lord, save Thy people, and bless Thine inheritance. Grant victories to Orthodox Christians over their adversaries. And by Thy Cross preserve Thy commonwealth.*

Priest: We adore Thy Cross, O Master. And glorify Thy Holy Resurrection. **(x3)**

   prostration

Chorus: We adore Thy Cross, O Master. And glorify Thy Holy Resurrection. **(x3)**

   prostration

Chorus: We adore Thy Cross, O Master. And glorify Thy Holy Resurrection. **(x3)**

   All approach in a line for prostration and kiss the Cross

Clergy re-enter Sanctuary. Chorus sings:

Idiomelon

Tone 2   Majesty, gentleness, hope, repentance and sadness.   *E, F, G, Ab, B, C.*

Come you faithful, let us adore the life giving wood on which Christ the King of glory stretched out his hands of his own free will. To the ancient blessedness he raised us up, whom the enemy had before despoiled through pleasure, making us exiles far from God. Come you faithful, let us adore the wood, through which we have been made worthy to crush the heads of invisible enemies. Come all you kindred of the nations, let us honour in hymns the cross of the Lord. Rejoice O Cross, complete redemption of fallen Adam.

With thee as their boast our faithful kings laid low by Thy might the people of Ishmael. We Christians kiss thee now with fear and, glorifying God who was nailed on thee, we cry: O Lord, who on the cross was crucified, have mercy on us, for Thou art good and love mankind.

[The people receive a flower from the Priest with the antidoron]

[With a priest]

The Great Canon of St Andrew, Bishop of Crete, is the longest canon in all of our services, and is associated with Great Lent, since the only times it is appointed to be read in church are the first four nights of Great Lent (Clean Monday through Clean Thursday, at Great Compline, when it is serialised) and at Matins for Thursday of the fifth week of Great Lent, when it is read in its entirety (in this latter service, the entire life of St Mary of Egypt is also read).

There is no other sacred hymn which compares with this monumental work, which St Andrew wrote for his personal meditations. Nothing else has its extensive typology and mystical explanations of the scripture, from both the Old and New Testaments. One can almost consider this hymn to be a "survey of the Old and New Testament". Its other distinguishing features are a spirit of mournful humility, hope in God, and complex and beautiful Trinitarian Doxologies and hymns to the Theotokos in each Ode.

The canon is a dialogue between St Andrew and his soul. The ongoing theme is an urgent exhortation to change ones life. St Andrew always mentions his own sinfulness placed in juxtaposition to Gods mercy, and uses literally hundreds of references to good and bad examples from the OT and NT to "convince himself" to repent.

A canon is an ancient liturgical hymn, with a very strict format. It consists of a variable number of parts, each called an "ode", number from one to nine. Most common canons have eight Odes, numbered from one to nine, with Ode 2 being omitted. The most penitential canons have all nine odes. Some canons have only three Odes, such as many of the canons in the "Triodion" (which means "Three Odes").

In any case, all Odes have the same basic format. An "Irmos" begins each Ode. This is generally sung, and each Irmos has a reference to one of the nine biblical canticles, which are selections from the Old and New Testament, which can be found in an appendix in any complete liturgical Psalter (book of Psalms, arranged for reading in the services). A variable number of "troparia" follow, which are short hymns about the subject of the canon. These are usually chanted, and not sung. After each troparion a "refrain" is chanted. At the end of each Ode, another hymn, called the "Katavasia", either the Irmos previously sung, or one like it is sung. The troparia of the Great Canon in all its twelve Odes are usually chanted by the priest in the centre of the church, with the Chorus singing the Irmos and Katavasia. In Greek "B" and "V" are pretty much interchangeable. Both spellings are used to make the reader feel comfortable with both.

St Andrew, Archbishop of Crete *(Commemorated July 4)*

Born in Damascus of Christian parents, he was dumb until the age of seven. When his parents took him to church for Communion, the power of speech was given to him. Such is the divine power of Communion.

He went to Jerusalem at the age of fourteen and was tonsured in the monastery of St Sava the Sanctified. In his understanding and ascesis, he surpassed many of the older monks and was an example to all. The Patriarch took him as his secretary.

When the Monothelite heresy, which taught that the Lord had no human will but only a divine one, began to rage, the Sixth Ecumenical Council met in Constantinople in 681, in the reign of Constantine IV.

Theodore, Patriarch of Jerusalem, was not able to be present at the Council, and sent Andrew, then a deacon, as his representative. At the Council, Andrew showed his great gifts: his articulateness, his zeal for the Faith and his rare prudence. Being instrumental in confirming the Orthodox faith, Andrew returned to his work in Jerusalem.

He was later chosen and enthroned as archbishop of the island of Crete. As archbishop, he was greatly beloved by the people. He was filled with zeal for Orthodoxy and strongly withstood all heresy. He worked miracles through his prayers, driving the Saracens from the island of Crete by means of them. He wrote many learned books, poems and canons, of which the best-known is the Great Canon of Repentance which is read in full on the Thursday of the Fifth Week of the Great Fast.

Such was his outward appearance that, 'looking at his face and listening to the words that flowed like honey from his lips, each man was touched and renewed'. Returning from Constantinople on one occasion, he foretold his death before reaching Crete. And so it happened. As the ship approached the island of Mitylene, this light of the Church finished his earthly course and his soul went to the Kingdom of Christ, in about the year 740.

From The Prologue From Ochrid by Bishop Nikolai Velimirovich ©1985 Lazarica Press, Birmingham UK

[Monday to Thursday of the First Week of Lent and Great Thursday.]

The Trisagion Prayers

Priest: Blessed is our God, always, now and forever and unto the ages of ages.

Reader: Amen. Glory to Thee, our God, glory to Thee.

O Heavenly King, the Comforter, the Spirit of Truth; who art everywhere present and fillest all things; Treasury of blessings, and giver of life: come and abide in us, and cleanse us from every impurity, and save our souls, O Good One.

Holy God, Holy Mighty, Holy Immortal, have mercy on us. **(x3)**

Glory be to the Father and to the Son and to the Holy Spirit;
Both now and forever, and unto the ages of ages. Amen.

O Most Holy Trinity, have mercy on us.
O Lord, cleanse us from our sins.
O Master, pardon our iniquities.
O Holy One, visit and heal our infirmities, for Thy names sake.

Lord have mercy. **(x3)**

Glory be to the Father and to the Son and to the Holy Spirit;

Both now and forever, and unto the ages of ages. Amen.

People: *Our Father, who art in heaven, hallowed be Thy name. Thy Kingdom come. Thy will be done, on earth as it is in heaven. Give us this day our daily bread; and forgive us our trespasses, as we forgive those who trespass against us; and lead us not into temptation, but deliver us from the evil one.*

Priest: For Thine is the Kingdom and the power, and the glory of the Father and of the Son and of the Holy Spirit; both now and forever and unto the ages of ages.

People: *Amen.*

Reader: Lord have mercy. **(x12)**

Glory be to the Father and to the Son and to the Holy Spirit;

Both now and forever, and unto the ages of ages. Amen.

Come, let us worship God, our King.

Come, let us worship and fall down before Christ, our King and our God.

Come, let us worship and fall down before Christ Himself, our King and our God.

Psalm 69

O God, be attentive to help me; Lord, make haste to help me. Let them be ashamed and confounded who seek after my life. Let them be turned back and be ashamed who desire evil against me. Let them be turned back because of their shame who say to me: "Well done. Well done." Let all those who seek Thee rejoice and be glad in Thee, O God, and let those who love Thy salvation say continually: *"Let the Lord be magnified."* But as for me, I am poor and needy; O God help me. Thou art my help and my deliverer; Lord; do not delay.

[Insert Great Canon Of St Andrew Of Crete here.]

Psalm 4

Answer me when I call, O God of my right. Thou gavest me room when I was in distress. Be gracious to me, and hear my prayer. How long, you people, shall my honour suffer shame? How long shall you love vain words, and seek after lies? But know that the Lord has set apart the faithful for Himself; the Lord hears when I call to Him. When you are disturbed, do not sin; ponder it on your beds, and be silent. Offer right sacrifices, and put your trust in the Lord. There are many who say, *"O that we might see some good. Let the light of Thy face shine on us, O Lord."* Thou hast put gladness in my heart more than when their grain and wine abound. I shall both lie down and sleep in peace; for Thou alone, O Lord, make me to lie down in safety.

Psalm 6

O Lord, do not rebuke me in Thine anger, or discipline me in Thy wrath. Be gracious to me, O Lord, for I am languishing; O Lord, heal me, for my bones are shaking with terror. My soul also is struck with terror, and Thee, O Lord, how long? Turn, O Lord, save my life; deliver me for the sake of Thy steadfast love. For in death there is no remembrance of Thee; in Sheol who can give Thee praise? I am weary with my moaning; every night I flood my bed with tears; I drench my couch with my weeping. Mine eyes waste away because of grief; they grow weak because of all my foes. Depart from me, all you workers of evil, for the Lord has heard the sound of my weeping. The Lord has heard my supplication; the Lord accepts my prayer. All mine enemies shall be ashamed and struck with terror; they shall turn back, and in a moment be put to shame.

Psalm 12

How long, O Lord? Wilt Thou forget me forever? How long wilt Thou hide Thy face from me? How long must I bear pain in my soul, and have sorrow in my heart all the day long? How long shall mine enemy be exalted over me? Consider and answer me, O Lord my God. Give light to mine eyes, or I shall sleep the sleep of death, and mine enemy shall say, "I have prevailed"; my foes shall rejoice because I am shaken. But I trusted in Thy steadfast love; my heart shall rejoice in Thy salvation. I shall sing to the Lord, because He has dealt bountifully with me.

After The Psalm

Glory be to the Father and to the Son and to the Holy Spirit;
Both now and forever and unto the ages of ages. Amen.

Halleluiah, Halleluiah, Halleluiah. Glory to Thee, O God. **(x3)**
Lord, have mercy. **(x3)**

Glory be to the Father and to the Son and to the Holy Spirit;
Both now and forever and unto the ages of ages. Amen.

Psalm 24

Unto Thee, O Lord, have I lifted up my soul. O my God, in Thee have I trusted; let me never be put to shame, nor let mine enemies laugh me to scorn. Yea, let none that wait on Thee be put to shame; let them be ashamed which are lawless without a cause. Make Thy ways, O Lord, known unto me and teach me Thy paths. Lead me in Thy truth and teach me, for Thou art God my Saviour; for on Thee have I waited all the day long. Remember Thy compassions, O Lord, and Thy mercies, for they are from everlasting. The sins of my youth and mine ignorances remember not; according to Thy mercy remember Thou me, for the sake of Thy goodness, O Lord. Good and upright is the Lord; therefore shall He set a law for them that sin in the way. He shall guide the meek in judgement, He shall teach the meek His ways. All the ways of the Lord are mercy and truth, unto them that seek after His covenant and His testimonies. For the sake of Thy name, O

Lord, be gracious unto my sin; for it is great. Who is the man that feareth the Lord? He shall set him a law in the way which he hath chosen. His soul shall dwell among good things, and his seed shall inherit the earth. The Lord is the strength of them that fear Him, and His covenant shall be manifested unto them. Mine eyes are ever toward the Lord, for He it is that shall draw my feet out of the snare. Look upon me, and have mercy on me; for I am one only begotten and poor. The afflictions of my heart are multiplied; bring me out from my necessities. Behold my lowliness and my toil, and forgive all my sins. Look upon mine enemies, for they are multiplied, and with an unjust hatred have they hated me. Keep my soul and rescue me; let me not be put to shame, for I have hoped in Thee. The innocent and the upright have cleaved unto me, for I waited on Thee, O Lord. Redeem Israel, O God, out of all his afflictions.

Psalm 30

In Thee, O Lord, I seek refuge; do not let me ever be put to shame; in Thy righteousness deliver me. Incline Thine ear to me; rescue me speedily. Be a rock of refuge for me, a strong fortress to save me. Thou art indeed my rock and my fortress; for Thy names sake lead me and guide me, take me out of the net that is hidden for me, for Thou art my refuge. Into Thine hand I commit my spirit; Thou hast redeemed me, O Lord, faithful God. Thou hatest those who pay regard to worthless idols, but I trust in the Lord. I shall exult and rejoice In Thy steadfast love, because Thou hast seen mine affliction; Thou hast taken heed of mine adversities, and have not delivered me into the hand of the enemy; Thou hast set my feet in a broad place. Be gracious to me, O Lord, for I am in distress; mine eye wastes away from grief, my soul and body also. For my life is spent with sorrow, and my years with sighing; my strength fails because of my misery, and my bones waste away. I am the scorn of all mine adversaries, a horror to my neighbours, an object of dread to mine acquaintances; those who see me in the street flee from me. I have passed out of mind like one who is dead; I have become like a broken vessel. For I hear the whispering of many *"terror all around"* as they scheme together against me, as they plot to take my life. But I trust in Thee, O Lord; I say, *"Thou art my God."* My times are in Thine hand; deliver me from the hand of mine enemies and persecutors. Let Thy face shine upon Thy servant; save me in Thy steadfast love. Do not let me be put to shame, O Lord, for I call on Thee; let the wicked be put to shame; let them go dumbfounded to Sheol. Let the lying lips be stilled that speak insolently against the righteous with pride and contempt. O how abundant is Thy goodness that Thou hast laid up for those who fear Thee, and accomplished for those who take refuge in Thee, in the sight of everyone. In the shelter of Thy presence Thou hidest them from human plots; Thou holdest them safe under Thy shelter from contentious tongues. Blessed be the Lord, for He has wondrously shown His steadfast love to me when I was beset as a city under siege. I had said in mine alarm, *"I am driven far from Thy sight."* But Thou heardest my supplications when I cried out to Thee for help. Love the Lord, all you His saints. The Lord preserves the faithful, but abundantly repays the one who acts haughtily. Be strong, and let your heart take courage, all you who wait for the Lord.

He who dwells in the secret place of the Most High shall abide under the shadow of the Almighty. I shall say of the Lord, *"He is my refuge and my fortress; My God, in Him I shall trust."* Surely He shall deliver thee from the snare of the fowler and from the perilous pestilence. He shall cover thee with His feathers, and under His wings thou shalt take refuge; His truth shall be thy shield and buckler. You shall not be afraid of the terror by night, nor of the arrow that flies by day, Nor of the pestilence that walks in darkness, nor of the destruction that lays waste at noonday. A thousand may fall at thy side, and ten thousand at thy right hand; but it shall not come near thee. Only with thine eyes shalt thou look, and see the reward of the wicked. Because thou hast made the Lord, Who is my refuge, even the Most High, thy habitation.

No evil shall befall thee, nor shall any plague come near thy dwelling; For He shall give His angels charge over thee, to keep thee in all thy ways. They shall bear thee up in their hands, lest thou dashest thy foot against a stone. Thou shalt tread upon the lion and the cobra, the young lion and the serpent thou shalt trample under foot. Because he has set his love upon Me, therefore I shall deliver him; I shall set him on high, because he has known My name. He shall call upon Me, and I shall answer him; I shall be with him in trouble; I shall deliver him and honour him. With long life shall I satisfy him, and show him My salvation.

After The Psalm

Glory be to the Father and to the Son and to the Holy Spirit;
Both now and forever and unto the ages of ages. Amen.

Halleluiah, Halleluiah, Halleluiah. Glory to Thee, O God. **(x3)**
Lord, have mercy. **(x3)**

Glory be to the Father and to the Son and to the Holy Spirit;
Both now and forever and unto the ages of ages. Amen.

God is with us. The day is now over, Lord: I thank Thee. Let this evening pass without sin, O Saviour, and save me.

Glory be to the Father and to the Son and to the Holy Spirit;

The day is now over, Master: I praise Thee. Let this evening pass undisturbed, O Saviour, and save me.

Both now and forever and unto the ages of ages. Amen.

The day is now over, Holy One: I hymn Thee. Let this evening and night pass without trouble, O Saviour, and save me.

The incorporeal Cherubim glorify Thee with unceasing praise. The Seraphim, the six winged angels, exalt

Thee with tireless voices. And all of the armies of angels praise Thee with the Thrice holy Hymn. Because Thou art, before all else, O Father; and Thy Son, like Thyself, is without beginning. By breathing forth the Spirit of Life, equal in honour to Thee, Thou makest manifest the indivisibility of the Trinity.

Virgin most holy, Mother of God, and you eye witnesses of the Lord, and His servants, intercede for us. All the Chorus' of the prophets and martyrs who are enjoying eternal life, intercede for all of us unceasingly, for we are all in distress. That escaping from the terrors of evil, we may sing the angelic hymn: Holy, holy, holy, O Thrice holy Lord, have mercy on us and save us.

The Symbol Of Faith

I believe in one God, Father, Almighty, Maker of heaven and earth, and of all things visible and invisible.

And in one Lord Jesus Christ, the only begotten Son of God, begotten from the Father before all ages; Light from Light, true God from true God; begotten not made; consubstantial with the Father, through Him all things were made. For our sake and for our salvation He came down from Heaven, and was incarnate from the Holy Spirit and the Virgin Mary and became man. He was crucified for us under Pontius Pilate, and suffered and was buried. He rose again on the third day in accordance with the Scriptures, and ascended into Heaven, and is seated at the right hand of the Father. He is coming again in glory to judge the living and the dead. And His kingdom shall have no end.

And in the Holy Spirit, the Lord, the Giver of life; Who proceeds from the Father; Who together with Father and Son is worshipped and glorified; Who spoke through the prophets. In One, Holy, Catholic, and Apostolic Church. I confess one baptism for the forgiveness of sins. I await the resurrection of the dead, And the life of the age to come. Amen.

The All Holy

Priest: O all holy sovereign Lady, Theotokos, pray for us sinners.

People: *O all holy sovereign Lady, Theotokos, pray for us sinners.*

Priest: O all you heavenly hosts of Angels and Archangels, pray for us sinners.

People: *O all you heavenly hosts of Angels and Archangels, pray for us sinners.*

Priest: O holy John, prophet, and forerunner, and Baptist of our Lord Jesus Christ, pray for us sinners.

People: *O holy John, prophet, and forerunner, and Baptist of our Lord Jesus Christ, pray for us sinners.*

Priest: O holy, glorious apostles, prophets and martyrs, and all saints, pray for us sinners.

People: *O holy, glorious apostles, prophets and martyrs, and all saints, pray for us sinners.*

Priest: O reverend and God fearing fathers, pastors and ecumenical teachers, pray for us sinners.

People: *O reverend and God fearing fathers, pastors and ecumenical teachers, pray for us sinners.*

Priest: O venerable [Father David - *patron of the country*], pray for us sinners.

People: *O venerable [Father David - patron of the country], pray for us sinners.*

Priest: O [patron of the temple], pray for us sinners.

People: *O [patron of the temple], pray for us sinners.*

Priest: O invincible, and ineffable, and divine power of the Honourable and Life giving Cross, do not forsake us sinners.

People: *O invincible, and ineffable, and divine power of the Honourable and Life giving Cross, do not forsake us sinners.*

Priest: O God, cleanse us sinners.

People: *O God, cleanse us sinners.*

Priest: O God, cleanse us sinners, and have mercy on us.

People: *O God, cleanse us sinners, and have mercy on us.*

Reader: Holy God, Holy Mighty, Holy Immortal, have mercy on us. **(x3)**

Glory be to the Father and to the Son and to the Holy Spirit;
Both now and forever and unto the ages of ages. Amen.

Lord, have mercy. **(x3)**

Glory be to the Father and to the Son and to the Holy Spirit;
Both now and forever and unto the ages of ages. Amen.

People: *Our Father, Who art in heaven, hallowed be Thy name. Thy kingdom come. Thy will be done, on earth as it is in heaven. Give us this day our daily bread; and forgive us our trespasses, as we forgive those who trespass against us; and lead us not into temptation, but deliver us from the evil one.*

Priest: For Thine is the Kingdom and the power, and the glory of the Father, and of the Son, and of the Holy Spirit; both now and forever and unto the ages of ages.

People: *Amen.*

Lord, have mercy. **(x12)**

Glory be to the Father and to the Son and to the Holy Spirit;
Both now and forever and unto the ages of ages. Amen.

[Monday, Wednesday, Fifth Wednesday]

Tone 2   Majesty, gentleness, hope, repentance and sadness.   E, F, G, Ab, B, C.

Reader: Illumine mine eyes, O Christ God, that I not sleep unto death;

So that mine enemy cannot say: I have prevailed against him.

Chorus: *Glory be to the Father and to the Son and to the Holy Spirit.*

Reader: O God, be the defender of my soul, for I walk in the midst of a multitude of snares.

Deliver me from them and save me, O Good One. For Thou art the Lover of mankind.

Chorus: *Both now and forever and unto the ages of ages. Amen.*

Theotokion

Seeing that we have no boldness on account of our many sins, do thou beseech Him that was born of thee, O Virgin Theotokos for the supplication of a mother availeth much to win the Masters favour. Disdain not the prayers of sinners, O all pure one, for merciful and mighty to save is He Who deigned also to suffer for our sake.

[End of Monday, Wednesday]

[Tuesday, Thursday, Fifth Wednesday]

Chorus: Lord, I have cried to Thee: hear me. Hear me, O Lord.

Lord, I have cried to Thee: hear me. Receive the voice of my prayer.

When I call upon Thee, hear me, O Lord. Let my prayer arise as incense in Thy sight,

And let the lifting up of my hands be an evening sacrifice. Hear me, O Lord.

Tone 8   Humility, tranquillity, repose, suffering, pleading.   C, D, Eb, F, G, A, Bb, C.

Thou knowest, O Lord my Creator, the sleepless vigilance of mine invisible enemies, and the frailty of my miserable flesh. Into Thine hands, therefore, shall I commit my spirit. Cover me with the wings of Thy goodness, that I not sleep unto death, and enlighten the eyes of my spiritual understanding, that I may delight in Thy divine words. And make me, in a time acceptable unto Thee, to glorify Thee in praise, as the only God Who lovest mankind.

Chorus: *Look upon me, and give ear unto me, O Lord my God.*

Reader: How fearful is Thy judgement, O Lord, When angels stand around about, and men are led before Thee. And the books are opened, and the deeds are tried and all thoughts are searched out. What judgement shall then be awarded unto me, who was conceived in sins? Who shall quench the flame for me? Who shall enlighten my darkness, if not Thee, O Lord, Who showest mercy upon me because of Thy love towards mankind?

Chorus: *Glory be to the Father and to the Son and to the Holy Spirit.*

Reader: Grant me tears, O God, as once to the sinful woman of old. And graciously grant that I may wash Thy feet which delivered me from the path of straying and grant that I may offer unto Thee incense of sweet savour, which is pure life, fashioned by my repentance. And so shall I also hear Thy voice which I long for saying: *"Thy faith has saved thee; go in peace."*

Chorus: *Both now and forever and unto the ages of ages. Amen.*

Reader: In that I have thee, O Theotokos, that hope which makes not ashamed, I shall be saved. In that I possess thine intercession, O all pure One, I shall not fear. I shall pursue mine enemies and drive them away, taking along thy refuge as a breastplate, as an all powerful aid. And fervently imploring I cry unto thee: *"O Lady, save me by thine intercessions, and raise me up again from dark sleep to glorify thee in song. By the might of the Son of God, Who through thee was incarnate."*

[End of Tuesday, Thursday]

The Prayer Of St Basil

Reader: O Lord our Lord. As Thou preserved us this day from the arrows that fly in broad daylight, so now keep us safe from everything that lurks about in the darkness of night. To Thee we raise our hands in prayer: accept this as our evening sacrifice. Count us worthy of sleep free of sin, sheltered from all evil. Keep far from us all the fearful disturbances inspired by the powers of darkness. Fill our souls with reverence and our minds with diligence that we may come to realize the awesome justice of Thy divine decrees. Pierce us through with reverence for Thee. Still our passions, that in the quiet of night Thine instructions may penetrate us with their light. Spare us indecent dreams, all improper desires. Awaken us in time for prayer, strong in faith and ready to observe all Thou hast taught us. Through the loving kindness of Thine only Son, with Whom Thou art blessed, together with Thine all holy good, and life giving Spirit: now and forever, and unto the ages of ages. Amen.

Repentance

Reader: Come, let us worship God, our King.

Come, let us worship and fall down before Christ, our King and our God.

Come, let us worship and fall down before Christ Himself, our King and our God.

Psalm 50

Have mercy on me, O God, according to Thy great mercy; and according to the multitude of Thy compassions blot out my transgression. Wash me thoroughly from mine iniquity, and cleanse me from my sin. For I acknowledge mine iniquity, and my sin is ever before me. Against Thee, Thee only have I sinned, and done evil in Thy sight, that Thou mayest be found just when Thou speakest, and victorious when Thou art judged. For behold, I was conceived in iniquity, and in sin my mother bore me. For behold, Thou hast loved truth; Thou hast made known to me the hidden and secret things of Thy wisdom. Thou shalt sprinkle me with hyssop, and I shall be made clean; Thou shalt wash me, and I shall be whiter than snow. Make me to hear joy and gladness; that the humbled bones may rejoice. Turn Thy face away from my sins, and blot out all mine iniquities.

Create in me a clean heart, O God, and renew a steadfast spirit within me. Cast me not away from Thy presence, and take not Thy Holy Spirit from me. Restore to me the joy of Thy salvation, and establish me with Thy governing Spirit. I shall teach transgressors Thy ways, and the ungodly shall turn back to Thee. Deliver me from blood guiltiness, O God, the God of my salvation; my tongue shall joyfully declare Thy righteousness. Lord, open my lips, and my mouth shall declare Thy praise. For if Thou hadst desired sacrifice, I would give it; Thou dost not delight in burned offerings. A sacrifice to God is a broken spirit; God shall not despise a broken and a humbled heart. Do good, O Lord, in Thy good pleasure to Zion, and let the walls of Jerusalem be built. Then Thou shalt be pleased with a sacrifice of righteousness, with oblation and whole burned offerings. Then shall they offer bulls on Thine altar.

Psalm 101

Hear my prayer, O Lord; let my cry come to Thee. Do not hide Thy face from me in the day of my distress. Incline Thine ear to me; answer me speedily in the day when I call. For my days pass away like smoke, and my bones burn like a furnace. My heart is stricken and withered like grass; I am too wasted to eat my bread. Because of my loud groaning my bones cling to my skin. I am like an owl of the wilderness, like a little owl of the waste places. I lie awake; I am like a lonely bird on the housetop. All day long mine enemies taunt me; those who deride me use my name for a curse. For I eat ashes like bread, and mingle tears with my drink, because of Thine indignation and anger; for Thou hast lifted me up and thrown me aside. My days are like an evening shadow; I wither away like grass. But Thou, O Lord, art enthroned forever; Thy name endures to all generations. Thou wilt rise up and have compassion on Zion, for it is time to favour it; the appointed time has come. For Thy servants dearly hold its stones, and have pity on its dust. The nations shall fear the name of the Lord, and all the kings of the earth Thy glory. For the Lord shall build up Zion; He shall appear in His glory. He shall regard the prayer of the destitute, and shall not despise their prayer. Let this be recorded for a generation to come, so that a people yet unborn may praise the Lord: that He looked down from His holy height, from heaven the Lord looked at the earth, to hear the groans of the prisoners, to set free those who were doomed to die; so that the name of the Lord may be declared in Zion, and His praise in Jerusalem, when peoples gather together, and kingdoms, to worship the Lord. He has broken my strength in mid course; He has shortened my days. *"O my God,"* I say, *"do not take me away at the mid point of my life,*

Thou whose years endure throughout all generations." Long ago Thou laid the foundation of the earth, and the heavens are the work of Thine hands. They shall perish, but Thou endurest; they shall all wear out like a garment. Thou changest them like clothing, and they pass away; but Thou art the same, and Thy years have no end. The children of Thy servants shall live secure; their offspring shall be established in Thy presence.

Prayer Of Manasses

Priest: O Lord Almighty. God of our fathers Abraham and Isaac, of Jacob, and all their children. Who made heaven and earth with all their splendid beauty, Who set the limits of the sea with a word, Who sank the depths and fixed it once and for all by the power of Thine awesome and sublime name. In Thy presence, everything is filled with awe; all things quake and tremble in the face of Thy power. For the magnificence of Thy glory, Thy terrible loathing of evil and the riches of Thy compassion are beyond our power to comprehend. Thou art the Lord most high: tender hearted and patient, ready to accept our atonement for all our wrong doing. In the greatness of Thy mercy, Thou Thyself, Lord, promised to show us the way to repentance and forgiveness, to salvation. Never, Lord, did Abraham or Isaac or Jacob need repentance as we do. Our sins are beyond counting: they outnumber the very fish of the sea. We dare not raise our eyes to heaven, for our sins weigh heavily upon us, they are as heavy as iron chains, and we are near to despair. For we have been offensive not only by doing wrong, but by our stubborn refusal to please Thee, by multiplying one offence after another, in complete indifference, yes even defiance, of Thy commands. But now, Lord, we fall to our knees in our hearts, entreating Thee to pour forth Thy goodness upon us. We are guilty. We know we have done wrong. Who needs Thy mercy more than we? Forgive us, Lord; do not let us perish with our sins. Do not resent our wickedness forever. Do not condemn us to unending punishment. Though we do not deserve it, pour forth Thy mercy on us, for Thou art the God of repentant sinners. In Thy compassion, save us, that we may sing Thy praises with all the powers of heaven, for all glory belongs to Thee, Lord, unto the ages of ages.

People: *Amen.*

Reader: Holy God, Holy Mighty, Holy Immortal, have mercy on us. **(x3)**

Glory be to the Father and to the Son and to the Holy Spirit;
Both now and forever and unto the ages of ages. Amen.

Lord, have mercy. **(x3)**
Glory be to the Father and to the Son and to the Holy Spirit;
Both now and forever and unto the ages of ages. Amen.

People: *Our Father, Who art in heaven, hallowed be Thy name. Thy kingdom come. Thy will be done, on earth as it is in heaven. Give us this day our daily bread; and forgive us our trespasses, as we forgive those who trespass against us; and lead us not into temptation, but deliver us from the evil one.*

Priest: For Thine is the Kingdom and the power, and the glory; of the Father and of the Son and of the Holy Spirit. Both now and forever and unto the ages of ages.

People: *Amen.*

Reader: Lord, have mercy. **(x12)**

Glory be to the Father and to the Son and to the Holy Spirit;
Both now and forever and unto the ages of ages. Amen.

Tone 6   Rich texture, funeral character, sorrowful tone.   D, Eb, F##, G, A, Bb, C##, D

Reader: Have mercy on us, O Lord, Have mercy on us, For laying aside all excuse we sinners offer to Thee, as to our Master, This supplication: Have mercy on us.

Chorus: *Glory be to the Father and to the Son and to the Holy Spirit.*

Reader: O Lord, have mercy on us, for in Thee have we put our trust. Do not be angry with us, nor remember our iniquities, but look down on us even now. Since Thou art compassionate, and deliver us from our enemies; for Thou art our God and we are Thy people. We are all the work of Thine hands, and we call on Thy name.

Chorus: *Both now and forever and unto the ages of ages. Amen.*

Reader: O blessed Theotokos, Open the doors of compassion to us whose hope is in thee, That we may not perish but be delivered from adversity through thee, who art the salvation of the Christian people.

Lord, have mercy. **(x40)**

Glory be to the Father and to the Son and to the Holy Spirit;
Both now and forever and unto the ages of ages. Amen.

Greater in honour than the Cherubim and beyond compare more glorious than the Seraphim; without corruption thou gavest birth to God the Word, truly the Theotokos, we magnify thee.

People: *Holy Father, bless.*

Priest: Through the prayers of our holy fathers and mothers, Lord Jesus Christ our God, have mercy on us and save us.

People: *Amen.*

Reader: O God and Master. Father Almighty, only Son, and Holy Spirit. O unique Power and Divinity. Have mercy on me, a sinner, and in Thine omniscience, save me, Thy servant, unworthy as I am. For Thou art blessed unto the ages of ages. Amen.

The Glorification Of God

Reader: Come, let us worship God, our King.

Come, let us worship and fall down before Christ, our King and our God.

Come, let us worship and fall down before Christ Himself, our King and our God.

Lesser Doxology

Glory to God, Who has shown us the Light. Glory to God in the highest, and on earth, peace, good will toward men. We praise Thee. We bless Thee. We worship Thee. We glorify Thee and give thanks to Thee for Thy great glory. O Lord God, Heavenly King, God the Father Almighty. O Lord, the Only Begotten Son, Jesus Christ, and the Holy Spirit. \

O Lord God, Lamb of God, Son of the Father, Who takes away the sins of the world, have mercy on us. Thou, Who takes away the sins of the world, receive our prayer. Thou, Who sittest at the right hand of God the Father, have mercy on us. /

For Thou alone art holy, and Thou alone art Lord. Thou alone, O Lord Jesus Christ, are most high in the glory of God the Father. Amen. I shall give thanks to Thee every day and praise Thy Name forever and ever. Lord, Thou hast been our refuge from generation to generation. I said, *"Lord, have mercy on me. Heal my soul, for I have sinned against Thee."* \

Lord, I flee to Thee. Teach me to do Thy will, for Thou art my God. For with Thee is the fountain of Life, and in Thy light we shall see light. Continue Thy loving kindness to those who know Thee. Vouchsafe, O Lord, to keep us this day without sin. Blessed art Thou, O Lord, the God of our fathers, and praised and glorified is Thy Name forever. Amen. Let Thy mercy be upon us, O Lord, even as we have set our hope on Thee.

Blessed art Thou, O Master; teach me Thy statutes.

Blessed art Thou, O Lord; enlighten me with Thy commandments.

Blessed art Thou, O Holy One; make me to understand Thy precepts.

Thy mercy endures forever, O Lord. Do not despise the works of Thine hands. To Thee belongs worship, to Thee belongs praise, to Thee belongs glory: to the Father and to the Son and to the Holy Spirit, both now and forever and unto the ages of ages. Amen. \

Prayers Before Sleep

Reader: Holy God, Holy Mighty, Holy Immortal, have mercy on us. **(x3)**

Glory be to the Father and to the Son and to the Holy Spirit;
Both now and forever and unto the ages of ages. Amen.

Lord, have mercy. (x3)

Glory be to the Father and to the Son and to the Holy Spirit;
Both now and forever and unto the ages of ages. Amen.

People: *Our Father, Who art in heaven, hallowed be Thy name. Thy kingdom come. Thy will be done, on earth as it is in heaven. Give us this day our daily bread; and forgive us our trespasses, as we forgive those who trespass against us; and lead us not into temptation, but deliver us from the evil one.*

Priest: For Thine is the Kingdom and the power, and the glory; of the Father and of the Son and of the Holy Spirit. Both now and forever and unto the ages of ages.

People: *Amen.*

Lord, have mercy. (x12)

Reader: *Glory be to the Father and to the Son and to the Holy Spirit;*
Both now and forever and unto the ages of ages. Amen.

Remain with us, O Lord of Hosts.

Lord, have mercy. (x40)

The Prayer Of The Hours

Priest: At all times and in every hour, Thou art worshipped and glorified in heaven and on earth, Christ our God. Long in patience, great in mercy and compassion, Thou lovest the righteous and showest mercy to sinners. Thou callest all to salvation through the promise of good things to come. Lord, receive our prayers at the present time. Direct our lives according to Thy commandments. Sanctify our souls. Purify our bodies. Set our minds aright. Cleanse our thoughts, and deliver us from all sorrow, evil and distress. Surround us with Thy holy angels, that, guarded and guided by their host, we may arrive at the unity of the faith and the understanding of Thine ineffable glory. For Thou art blessed unto the ages of ages.

People: *Amen.*

Reader: Lord, have mercy. (x3)

Glory be to the Father and to the Son and to the Holy Spirit;
Both now and forever and unto the ages of ages. Amen.

Greater in honour than the Cherubim and beyond compare more glorious than the Seraphim; without corruption thou gavest birth to God the Word, truly the Theotokos, we magnify thee.

People: Holy Father, bless.

Priest: God be merciful to us, and bless us, and shine the light of His countenance upon us, and have mercy on us.

People: *Amen.*

The Prayer Of St Ephraim

O Lord and Master of my life. Take from me the spirit of sloth, despair, lust of power, and idle talk.

prostration

But give rather the Spirit of chastity, humility, patience and love to Thy servant.

prostration

Yes, O Lord and King, grant me to see mine own transgressions and not to judge my brother. For blessed art Thou unto the ages of ages. Amen.   ***prostration***

[12 bows, repeating silently:] O God, cleanse me a sinner.

O Lord and Master of my life. Take from me the spirit of sloth, despair, lust of power, and idle talk; but give rather the Spirit of chastity, humility, patience and love to Thy servant. Yes, O Lord and King, grant me to see mine own transgressions and not to judge my brother. For blessed art Thou unto the ages of ages. Amen.

prostration

Reader: Holy God, Holy Mighty, Holy Immortal, have mercy on us. **(x3)**

Glory be to the Father and to the Son and to the Holy Spirit;
Both now and forever and unto the ages of ages. Amen.

O Most Holy Trinity, have mercy on us.
O Lord, cleanse us from our sins.
O Master, pardon our iniquities.
O Holy One, visit and heal our infirmities, for Thy names sake.

Lord, have mercy. **(x3)**

Glory be to the Father and to the Son and to the Holy Spirit;
Both now and forever and unto the ages of ages. Amen.

People: *Our Father, Who art in heaven, hallowed be Thy name. Thy kingdom come. Thy will be done, on earth as it is in heaven. Give us this day our daily bread; and forgive us our trespasses, as we forgive those who trespass against us; and lead us not into temptation, but deliver us from the evil one.*

Priest: For Thine is the Kingdom and the power, and the glory; of the Father, and of the Son, and of the Holy Spirit. Both now and forever and unto the ages of ages.

People: *Amen.*

Reader: Lord, have mercy. **(x12)**

Glory be to the Father and to the Son and to the Holy Spirit;
Both now and forever and unto the ages of ages. Amen.

The Supplicatory Prayer To The Most Holy Theotokos

Paul, The Monk Of The Monastery Of Evergetis.

Priest: Spotless, undefiled, immaculate, unstained, pure Virgin, Lady and Bride of God, by thy wondrous conceiving thou united God the Word with human beings and joined the fallen nature of our race to heavenly things. Thou art the only hope of the hopeless, and the help of those oppressed. Thou art the ready protection of those who flee to thee, and the refuge of all Christians. Do not spurn me an accused sinner, though I have made myself completely useless by my shameful thoughts, words and deeds and through indolence have become a slave to the pleasures of life. But as the Mother of God who loves all people, mercifully have compassion upon me a sinner and a prodigal and receive my prayer though it be offered to thee by unclean lips. Entreat thy Son and our Lord and Master, using thy boldness as a mother, that he may open to me the loving mercy of his goodness, overlook my numberless transgressions, turn me to repentance, and make me an acceptable doer of His commandments. Always be near me, for thou art merciful, compassionate and loving. Be mine ardent help and protection in this present life, defending me from the assaults of adversaries and lead me to salvation. At the hour of my death, care for my miserable soul, and drive the dark visions of evil spirits from it. On the awesome day of judgement, save me from eternal punishment and make me an inheritor of the ineffable glory of thy Son, our God. May this be my lot, my Lady, all Holy Theotokos, through thine intercession and protection, by the grace and love of thine only begotten Son, our Lord and God and Saviour, Jesus Christ, to whom belong all glory, honour and worship, together with his eternal Father, and all holy, righteous, and life creating Spirit, both now and forever, and unto the ages of ages.

People: *Amen.*

A Prayer To Our Lord Jesus Christ

Antiochus, The Monk Of Pandektes.

Priest: Grant us, Master, as we depart for sleep, rest for body and soul. Protect us from the gloom of sinful sleep and from all dark pleasures of the night. Calm the impulses of passion, and quench the fiery darts of evil that are treacherously cast against us. Restrain the turbulence of our flesh and lull all our earthly and mundane thoughts. Grant to us, O God, a watchful mind, prudent reason, a vigilant heart, and tranquil sleep, free from all evil dreams. Raise us up at the hour of prayer, strengthen us in Thy commandments, and keep unshaken within us the remembrance of Thy judgements. Grant us to glorify Thee all night long that we may praise and bless and glorify Thine all honourable and majestic name; of the Father and of the Son and of the Holy Spirit, both now and forever, and unto the ages of ages.

People: *Amen.*

Priest: Most glorious, ever virgin, blessed Theotokos, present our prayers to thy Son and our God, and plead with Him, that through thee, He may save our souls.

My hope is the Father, my refuge the Son, my protection the Holy Spirit: O Holy Trinity, glory to Thee.

Reader: *Glory be to the Father and to the Son and to the Holy Spirit;*
Both now and forever and unto the ages of ages. Amen.

Lord, have mercy. **(x3)**
Holy Father, bless.

[All kneel.]
Priest: O Master rich in mercy, Lord Jesus Christ, our God. By the prayers of our most pure lady, the Theotokos and ever virgin Mary; by the power of the holy and life giving Cross; through the intercessions of the holy bodiless powers of heaven and of the glorious prophet and forerunner, John the Baptist; of the holy, glorious and illustrious apostles; the glorious and victorious martyrs; by the prayers of Thy holy grandparents, Joachim and Anna, as well as those of all Thy saints, make this prayer of Thy servants acceptable and pleasing, and grant us the remission of all our sins; protect us under the shelter of Thy wings, and drive far from us every assault of our enemies: fill our lives with peace, have mercy on us and on this world of Thine, and save us, for Thou art good and full of love for all mankind.

[Priest prostrates himself before the people, saying:]
Priest: Brother and sisters, forgive me a sinner.
People: *May God forgive thee, Father.*

[During these next petitions, slowly chant on the same note.]
Chorus: *Lord, have mercy*
Priest:

• Let us pray for the peace of the world.
• For all pious and Orthodox Christians.
• For our Archbishop *(N)*, the honourable priesthood, the diaconate in Christ, all the clergy and people.

- For all civil authorities and those who serve in the armed forces.
- For those who are absent from us.
- For those who are kind to us and those who minister unto us.
- For those who hate us and those who love us.
- For those who have asked us to pray for them, unworthy as we are.
- For the release of captives.
- For travellers by land, air and sea.
- For those afflicted with sickness.
- Let us pray for abundance of the fruits of the earth.
- And for the soul of every Orthodox Christian.
- For God fearing rulers, Orthodox Bishops, the founders of this holy temple, our parents and teachers, and for all our fathers and brethren departed from this life, who here and everywhere lie asleep in the Lord.
- Let us also say for ourselves:

Chorus: Lord, have mercy. **(x3)**

Priest: O Lord, Lover of mankind, forgive them that hate and wrong us. Do good to them that do good. Grant our brethren and kindred their saving petitions and eternal life; visit the infirm and grant them healing. Guide those at sea. Journey with those who travel. Help Orthodox Christians in their tribulations. To those who serve and are kind to us grant remission of sins. On those who have charged us, the unworthy, to pray for them, have mercy according to Thy great mercy. Remember, Lord, our fathers and the brethren departed before us, and grant them rest where the light of Thy countenance shall shine upon them. Remember Lord, our brethren in captivity, and deliver them from every misfortune. Remember Lord, those who bear fruit and do good works in Thy holy churches and grant them their saving petitions and eternal life. Remember also Lord, us Thy lowly and sinful and unworthy servants, and enlighten our minds with the light of Thy knowledge and guide us in the way of Thy commandments; through the intercessions of our most pure Lady, the Theotokos and ever virgin Mary, and of all Thy saints, for blessed art Thou to the ages of ages.
People: Amen.

Priest: Through the prayers of our holy fathers and mothers; brothers and sisters, Lord Jesus Christ our God, have mercy on us and save us.
People: Amen.

Great Canon Of St Andrew Of Crete, The Jerusalemite

A Work Of Our Holy Father Among The Saints Andrew Of Crete, The Jerusalemite.

Venerable Andrew, thrice blessed father, shepherd of Crete, do not cease to offer prayer for us who sing thine praises, so that we, who honour thy memory with faith, may be delivered from all wrath and affliction and corruption, and released from faults.

Monday	just below
Tuesday	Page 428
Wednesday	Page 442
Thursday	Page 456
Fifth Wednesday	All 4 sections

MONDAY AT GREAT COMPLINE
THE FIRST WEEK OF THE GREAT FAST

Ode 1

Eirmos

Tone 6   Rich texture, funereal character, sorrowful tone.   *D, Eb, F##, G, A, Bb, C##, D.*

He has become Helper and Protector for me unto salvation. He is my God and I glorify Him. God of my fathers and I exalt Him, for He is greatly glorified.
(Exodus 15: 2, 1; Psalms 117: 14)

Refrain: Have mercy on me, O God, have mercy on me.

Where shall I begin to weep for the actions of my wretched life? What first fruit shall I offer, O Christ, in this my lamentation? But in Thy compassion grant me remission of sins.

Refrain: Have mercy on me, O God, have mercy on me.

Come, wretched soul, together with thy flesh, to the Creator of all. Make confession, and abstain henceforth from thy past brutishness; and offer to God tears of repentance.

Refrain: Have mercy on me, O God, have mercy on me.

In transgressions I have rivalled Adam the first formed, and I have found myself stripped naked of God, of the eternal kingdom and its joy, because of my sins.
(Genesis 3)

Refrain: Have mercy on me, O God, have mercy on me.

Woe to thee, miserable soul. How thou art like the first Eve. For thou hast looked in wickedness and were grievously wounded; and thou hast touched the tree and rashly tasted the deceptive food.

Refrain: Have mercy on me, O God, have mercy on me.

Instead of the visible Eve, I have Eve in my mind: the passionate thought in the flesh, showing me what seems sweet; yet whenever I taste I find it bitter.

Refrain: Have mercy on me, O God, have mercy on me.

Adam was justly banished from Eden because he disobeyed one commandment of Thine, O Saviour. What then shall I suffer, for I am always rejecting Thy words of life?
(Hebrews 12: 25; Genesis 3: 23)

Glory be to the Father and to the Son and to the Holy Spirit.

Triadicon

Trinity beyond being, worshipped in unity, take from me the heavy yoke of sin, and in Thy compassion grant me tears of contrition.

Both now and forever and unto the ages of ages. Amen.

Theotokion

O Mother of God, the help and protection of those who sing praise to thee, take from me the heavy yoke of sin, and, pure Lady, accept me in repentance.

Ode 2

Eirmos

Attend, O heaven, and I shall speak and sing in praise of Christ, who took flesh from a Virgin and came to dwell among us.

Refrain: Have mercy on me, O God, have mercy on me.

Attend, O heaven, and I shall speak; give ear, O earth, to the voice of one who repents before God and sings His praise.

Refrain: Have mercy on me, O God, have mercy on me.

Look on me, God my Saviour, with Thy merciful eye, and accept my fervent confession.
(Proverbs 15: 3; Psalms 33: 15)

Refrain: Have mercy on me, O God, have mercy on me.

I have sinned more than all people; I alone have sinned against Thee. But as God take pity on Thy creation, O Saviour.
(1 Timothy 1: 15)

Refrain: Have mercy on me, O God, have mercy on me.

With my lustful desires I have given form to the deformity of the passions and disfigured the beauty of my mind.

Refrain: Have mercy on me, O God, have mercy on me.

A storm of evils surrounds me, O compassionate Lord; but stretch out Thine hand also to me as Thou didst to Peter.
(Matthew 14: 31)

Refrain: Have mercy on me, O God, have mercy on me.

I have stained the garment of my flesh, and defiled what was made in Thine image and likeness, O Saviour.
(Genesis 3: 21)

Refrain: Have mercy on me, O God, have mercy on me.

With the lusts of passion I have darkened the beauty of my soul, and turned my whole mind entirely into dust.

Refrain: Have mercy on me, O God, have mercy on me.

I have now torn the first robe that the Creator wove for me from the beginning, and I lie naked.
(Genesis 3: 21)

Refrain: Have mercy on me, O God, have mercy on me.

I have clothed myself in the torn garment that the serpent wove for me, and I am ashamed.
(Genesis 3: 4-5)

Refrain: Have mercy on me, O God, have mercy on me.

The tears of the harlot I too offer to Thee, O Merciful One. Take pity on me, O Saviour, in Thy compassion.
(Luke 7: 38; 18: 13)

Refrain: Have mercy on me, O God, have mercy on me.

I looked on the beauty of the tree and my mind was deceived; and now I lie naked and ashamed.
(Genesis 3: 7)

Refrain: Have mercy on me, O God, have mercy on me.

All the ruling passions have worked on my back, lengthening their evils on me.
(Psalms 128: 3)

Glory be to the Father and to the Son and to the Holy Spirit.

Triadicon

I sing Thy praises, God of all, one in three Persons, the Father, the Son and the Holy Spirit.

Both now and forever and unto the ages of ages. Amen.

Theotokion

O most pure Virgin Mother of God, alone all praised, intercede fervently for our salvation.

Ode 3

Eirmos

Establish my thoughts on the unshaken rock of Thy commandments, O Christ.

Refrain: Have mercy on me, O God, have mercy on me.

The Lord once rained down fire from the Lord, and consumed the land of Sodom of old.
(Genesis 19: 24)

Refrain: Have mercy on me, O God, have mercy on me.

O soul, save thyself on the mountain like Lot and take refuge in Segor.
(Genesis 19: 22)

Refrain: Have mercy on me, O God, have mercy on me.

O soul, flee from the flames, flee from the burning of Sodom, flee from destruction by the fire of God.
(Deuteronomy 4: 24; Hebrews 12: 29)

Refrain: Have mercy on me, O God, have mercy on me.

I alone have sinned against Thee, I have sinned more than all; O Saviour Christ, do not reject me.

Refrain: Have mercy on me, O God, have mercy on me.

Thou art the Good Shepherd: seek me, the lamb, and, though I have strayed, do not forget me.
(John 10: 11-14)

Refrain: Have mercy on me, O God, have mercy on me.

Thou art the sweet Jesus, Thou art my Creator. In Thee O Saviour, I shall be justified.

Refrain: Have mercy on me, O God, have mercy on me.

I confess to Thee, O Saviour: I have sinned, I have sinned against Thee. But, as Thou art compassionate, absolve and forgive me.

Glory be to the Father and to the Son and to the Holy Spirit.

Triadicon

O Trinity, one God, save us from delusion and temptations and misfortunes.

Both now and forever and unto the ages of ages. Amen.

Theotokion

Rejoice, womb that received God. Rejoice, throne of the Lord. Rejoice, Mother of our Life.

Ode 4

Eirmos

The prophet heard of Thy coming, O Lord, and he was afraid how Thou were to be born of a Virgin and revealed to mankind; and he said: *"I have heard the report of Thee, and I was afraid."* Glory to Thy power, O Lord.

(Hebrews 3:2)

Refrain: Have mercy on me, O God, have mercy on me.

O just Judge, do not despise Thy works; do not forsake Thy creation, even though I alone have sinned as a human more than all people, O Lover of mankind. But as Lord of all Thou hast the power to pardon sins.

(Mark 2: 10)

Refrain: Have mercy on me, O God, have mercy on me.

The end draws near, O soul, it draws near; but thou dost not trouble or prepare. The time grows short, rise up. The Judge is near the doors. As a dream, as a flower, the days of our life pass swiftly. Why do we trouble ourselves in vain?

(Matthew 24: 33; Psalms 38: 7)

Refrain: Have mercy on me, O God, have mercy on me.

Return to sobriety, O my soul. Consider the actions that thou hast done, and set them before thine eyes, and let the drops of thy tears fall. With freedom to speak tell Christ thine actions and thoughts, and be justified.

Refrain: Have mercy on me, O God, have mercy on me.

There has been in life no sin, no deed, no wickedness, that I have not committed, O Saviour. In mind and in word, in intent and in design, in thought and in action, I have sinned as no other has ever done.

Refrain: Have mercy on me, O God, have mercy on me.

For this I am condemned, for this I am convicted in my misery by mine own conscience, which is more forceful than anything in the world. My Judge and Redeemer, who know me, spare and deliver and save me, Thy servant.

Refrain: Have mercy on me, O God, have mercy on me.

The ladder, which of old the great one among the Patriarchs saw, is a sign, O my soul, of beginning an approach through action and succeeding in rising through contemplation. If, therefore, thou wishest to live in action and knowledge and contemplation, then be made new.
(Genesis 28: 12; Romans 12: 2; Titus 3: 5)

Refrain: Have mercy on me, O God, have mercy on me.

In privation the Patriarch endured the burning heat of the day and the frost of the night, making daily gains, shepherding, fighting and serving, so that he might gain his two wives.
(Genesis 29: 16-30; 31-40)

Refrain: Have mercy on me, O God, have mercy on me.

By the two wives, understand action and knowledge in contemplation. Leah is action, for she had many children; and Rachel is knowledge, for she toiled much. For without toil neither action nor contemplation shall succeed, O soul.

Glory be to the Father and to the Son and to the Holy Spirit.

Triadicon
Undivided in Essence, unconfused in Persons, I confess Thee as God: the Trinity in one Godhead, equal in kingship and throne; and I raise to Thee the great threefold song that is sung in the highest.

Both now and forever and unto the ages of ages. Amen.

Theotokion
Thou gave birth and are a virgin, and in both thou remainest by nature Virgin. He who is born makes new the laws of nature, and the womb brings forth without labour pains. When God so wills, the natural order is overcome; for He does whatever He wishes.

Ode 5

Eirmos
From the night I seek Thee early, O Lover of mankind: give me light, I pray Thee, and guide me also in Thy commandments, and teach me, O Saviour, to do Thy will.

Refrain: Have mercy on me, O God, have mercy on me.

I have ever passed my life in night, for the night of sin has been for me darkness and deepest gloom. But show me to be as a child of the day, O Saviour.

(Ephesians 5: 8)

Refrain: Have mercy on me, O God, have mercy on me.

I, the wretched one, imitating Reuben have devised an unlawful and disobedient plan against God Most High, defiling my bed as he did his fathers.

(Genesis 35: 21; 49: 3-4)

Refrain: Have mercy on me, O God, have mercy on me.

I confess to Thee, Christ King: I have sinned, I have sinned like the brothers of Joseph, who once sold the fruit of purity and chastity.

(Genesis 37)

Refrain: Have mercy on me, O God, have mercy on me.

The righteous soul was bound by his kinsmen; the sweet one was sold into slavery as a figure of the Lord; but as for thee, O soul, thou hast sold thyself entirely to thine evils.

(Genesis 37: 27-28)

Refrain: Have mercy on me, O God, have mercy on me.

Wretched and worthless soul, imitate the righteous and pure mind of Joseph, and do not defile thyself with inordinate lusts, for ever sinning.

(Genesis 39: 7-23)

Refrain: Have mercy on me, O God, have mercy on me.

If Joseph was once cast into a pit, O Master and Lord, then it was as a figure of Thy death and Thy rising; but what could I ever offer Thee such as this?

(Genesis 37)

Glory be to the Father and to the Son and to the Holy Spirit.

Triadicon

We glorify Thee, O Trinity, the one God: Holy, holy, holy is the Father, the Son, and the Spirit, simple Essence and Unity, worshipped for ever.

Both now and forever and unto the ages of ages. Amen.

Theotokion

O inviolate Virgin Mother without a husband, from Thee God, the Creator of the ages, was clothed in my shape, and He took human nature to Himself.

Ode 6

Eirmos

With my whole heart I cried to the compassionate God, and He heard me from the lowest depths of hell, and brought my life up from corruption.

Refrain: Have mercy on me, O God, have mercy on me.

I offer to Thee in purity, O Saviour, the tears of mine eyes and groanings from the depths of my heart, crying: I have sinned against Thee, O God. Be merciful to me.
(Luke 18:13)

Refrain: Have mercy on me, O God, have mercy on me.

O soul, like Dathan and Aveiron thou hast become a stranger to God. But from the lowest depths of hell cry out *"Spare me; so that the chasm of the earth may not cover thee."*
(Numbers 16)

Refrain: Have mercy on me, O God, have mercy on me.

O soul, raging like a heifer thou hast become like Ephraim. Rescue thy life, like a deer from the snares, gaining wings for the mind through action and contemplation.
(Hosea 4: 16)

Refrain: Have mercy on me, O God, have mercy on me.

O soul, the hand of Moses shall be our assurance, proving how God can make a leprous life white and clean; and do not be in despair of thyself, even though thou art leprous.
(Exodus 4: 6-8)

Glory be to the Father and to the Son and to the Holy Spirit.

Triadicon

"I am Trinity, simple and undivided, divided in Persons, and I am Unity from the beginning, by Nature one." says the Father and the Son and the divine Spirit.

Both now and forever and unto the ages of ages. Amen.

Theotokion

Thy womb gave birth to God for us, fashioned in our shape. Pray to Him as the Creator of all, O Mother of God, that through thy prayers we may be justified.

Kontakion

My soul, my soul, rise up. Why art thou sleeping? The end draws near, and soon thou wilt be troubled. Watch, then, so that Christ God may spare thee, for He is present everywhere and fillest all things.

Ode 7

Eirmos

We have sinned, we have transgressed, we have done evil before Thee, and neither have we followed, nor have we done, what Thou commanded us. But do not reject us utterly, O God of our fathers.

Refrain: Have mercy on me, O God, have mercy on me.

I have sinned, I have offended, and I have rejected Thy commandments, for I came forth in sins and added bruises to my wounds. But, as Thou Thyself art compassionate, have mercy on me, O God of our fathers.

Refrain: Have mercy on me, O God, have mercy on me.

I have confessed the secrets of my heart to Thee, my Judge. See mine abasement, and see mine affliction, and attend to my judgement now; and, as Thou Thyself art compassionate, have mercy on me, O God of our fathers.

Refrain: Have mercy on me, O God, have mercy on me.

O soul, once when Saul lost his fathers asses, in searching for them he found Himself proclaimed as king. Beware, lest unknown to thyself thou preferest thine animal appetites to the Kingdom of Christ.
(1 Kings 10: 12)

Refrain: Have mercy on me, O God, have mercy on me.

My soul, David, the forefather of God, once sinned doubly, pierced with the arrow of adultery and the point of the spear of vengeful murder. But thou art sick from weightier acts, the impulses of thy will.
(2 Kings 11:12; 12:1-23)

Refrain: Have mercy on me, O God, have mercy on me.

David once joined sin to sin, mixing murder with adultery; yet he then showed at once a twofold repentance. But thee, O soul, have thyself done things more evil, yet thou hast not repented before God.

Refrain: Have mercy on me, O God, have mercy on me.

David once raised a hymn, setting forth, as in an icon, the action he had done, which he condemned, crying: *"Have mercy on me, for I have sinned against Thee alone, O God of all; cleanse me Thyself."*
(Psalm 50)

Glory be to the Father and to the Son and to the Holy Spirit.

Triadicon

Trinity, simple, undivided, consubstantial, and one in Essence, Lights and Light, three Holies and one Holy, God the Trinity is praised in song. So, O soul, praise and glorify Life and Lives, the God of all.

Both now and forever and unto the ages of ages. Amen.

Theotokion

We praise thee, we bless thee, we venerate thee, O Mother of God: for thou hast given birth to Christ God, one of the undivided Trinity; and thou thyself hast opened the heavenly places to us who dwell on earth.

Ode 8

Eirmos

Him, whom the hosts of heaven glorify, and who terrifies the Cherubim and the Seraphim, let everything that has breath and every creature praise, bless, and highly exalt to all the ages.

Refrain: Have mercy on me, O God, have mercy on me.

I have sinned, O Saviour, have mercy. Awaken my mind so that I may be converted; accept me in repentance, have pity as I cry: I have sinned against Thee, save me; I have done evil, have mercy on me.

Refrain: Have mercy on me, O God, have mercy on me.

The charioteer Elijah once mounted a chariot of the virtues, and was carried as if to heaven, high above earthly things. My soul, reflect on his ascent.
(4 Kings 2: 11)

Refrain: Have mercy on me, O God, have mercy on me.

Elisha once took the mantle of Elijah, and received a double portion of grace from the Lord; but thou, O my soul, hast no share in this grace because of thine uncontrolled desires.
(4 Kings 2: 9)

Refrain: Have mercy on me, O God, have mercy on me.

With the mantle of Elijah, Elisha made the stream of the Jordan stand still on either side; but thou, O my soul, have no share in this grace because of thine uncontrolled desires.
(4 Kings 2: 14)

Refrain: Have mercy on me, O God, have mercy on me.

The goodly minded Sonamite woman once entertained the righteous man; but thou, O soul, hast not admitted to thy house either stranger or traveller, and so thou wilt be cast out weeping from the bridal chamber.
(4 Kings 4: 8)

Refrain: Have mercy on me, O God, have mercy on me.

O wretched soul, thou hast always imitated the unclean thoughts of Giëzi. Drive away his love of money, at least in old age. Flee from the fire of Gehenna, turning away from thy sins.

Glory be to the Father and to the Son and to the Holy Spirit.

Triadicon
Father without beginning, Son also without beginning, good Paraclete, Spirit of truth; Begetter of the Word of God, Word of the Father without beginning, Spirit, living and creating: Trinity in Unity, have mercy on me.

Both now and forever and unto the ages of ages. Amen.

Theotokion

As from purple thread, O All Pure, the spiritual royal robe of Emmanuel, His flesh, was woven within thy womb. Therefore we honour thee in truth as Mother of God.

Ode 9

Eirmos

The nativity is past understanding - from a conception without seed; the child bearing is undefiled - from a Mother without a husband; for the birth of God makes the natures new. Therefore with true belief all generations magnify thee as Bride and Mother of God.

Refrain: Have mercy on me, O God, have mercy on me.

The mind is wounded, the body has grown feeble, the spirit is sick, reason is infirm, life is dead; the end is at the doors. What wilt thou do then, my wretched soul, when the Judge comes to examine what thou hast done?

Refrain: Have mercy on me, O God, have mercy on me.

I have put before thee, O soul, Moses' account of the creation of the world, and after that all the recognised Scriptures that tellest to thee the story of the righteous and the wicked. But thou, O soul, have followed the second of these and not the first, and have sinned against God.

Refrain: Have mercy on me, O God, have mercy on me.

The Law is powerless, the Gospel of no effect, and the whole of Scripture is ignored by thee; the Prophets and all the words of the righteous are useless. Thy wounds, O soul, have been multiplied, and there is no physician to heal thee.

Refrain: Have mercy on me, O God, have mercy on me.

O soul, I bringest thee examples from the New Testament, to lead thee to contrition. Follow the examples of the righteous, turn away from the sinful and through prayers and fasting, through chastity and reverence, propitiate Christ.

Refrain: Have mercy on me, O God, have mercy on me.

Christ became man, calling thieves and harlots to repentance. Repent, O soul: the door of the Kingdom is already open - and Pharisees and tax collectors and adulterers pass through it before thee, having changed their lives.
(Matthew 21: 31; 11: 12)

Refrain: Have mercy on me, O God, have mercy on me.

Christ became man, keeping company with me in flesh; and of His own will He fulfilled all that belongs to this nature, except for sin: a model for thee, O soul, and an image illustrating His condescension.
(Matthew 1: 25)

Refrain: Have mercy on me, O God, have mercy on me.

Christ saved the Magi, called the Shepherds, revealed as martyrs a multitude of Infants, and glorified the Elder and the aged Widow. But thou, O soul, hast not followed their actions or their lives. Woe to thee, then, when thou art judged.
(Matthew 2. 12; Luke 2: 9-12; Matthew 2: 16; Luke 2. 25-38)

Refrain: Have mercy on me, O God, have mercy on me.

The Lord fasted for forty days in the wilderness, and afterwards He was hungry, showing His humanity. My soul, do not be dismayed: if the enemy attacks thee, drive him from thy feet through both prayer and fasting.
(Matthew 4: 1-11; 17: 21; Mark 9: 29)

Glory be to the Father and to the Son and to the Holy Spirit.

Triadicon
Let us glorify the Father, let us exalt the Son, and with faith let us worship the divine Spirit: undivided Trinity, Unity in Essence, as Light and Lights, and Life and Lives, giving life and light to the ends of the earth.

Both now and forever and unto the ages of ages. Amen.

Theotokion
Preserve thy city, all pure Mother of God. For by thee she reigns in faith, and by thee she is made strong, and through thee she is victorious; she puts to flight every temptation, and she despoils the enemy, and she administers the subjects.

Refrain: Venerable Father Andrew, pray to God for us.

Venerable Andrew, thrice blessed father, shepherd of Crete, do not cease to offer prayer for us who sing thy praises, so that we, who honour thy memory with faith, may be delivered from all wrath and affliction and corruption, and released from faults.

Katavasia

The nativity is past understanding - from a conception without seed; the child bearing is undefiled - from a Mother without a husband; for the birth of God makes the natures new. Therefore with true belief all generations magnify thee as Bride and Mother of God.

END OF MONDAY

TUESDAY AT GREAT COMPLINE
THE FIRST WEEK OF THE GREAT FAST
Ode 1

Eirmos

Tone 6   *Rich texture, funereal character, sorrowful tone.*   *D, Eb, F##, G, A, Bb, C##, D.*

He has become Helper and Protector for me unto salvation. He is my God and I glorify Him, God of my fathers and I exalt Him, for He is greatly glorified.

(Exodus 15: 2, 1; Psalms 117: 14)

Refrain: Have mercy on me, O God, have mercy on me.

By choice I have shared in the murder by Cain: I have become a murderer of the conscience of my soul, bringing the flesh to life, and making war on the soul by my wicked actions.

(Genesis 4: 8)

Refrain: Have mercy on me, O God, have mercy on me.

O Jesus, I have not been like Abel in his righteousness. I have never offered Thee acceptable gifts, or godly actions, or a pure sacrifice, or an unblemished life.

(Genesis 4: 4)

Refrain: Have mercy on me, O God, have mercy on me.

O wretched soul, like Cain we too have offered together defiled actions and a polluted sacrifice and a worthless life to the Creator of all; and so we are also condemned.

(Genesis 4: 5; Hebrews 11: 4)

Refrain: Have mercy on me, O God, have mercy on me.

As the potter Thou gavest life to the clay, giving me flesh and bones, and breath and life. But accept me in repentance, O my Maker and Deliverer and Judge.

(Genesis 2: 7; Hebrews18: 1-10; Romans 9: 21)

Refrain: Have mercy on me, O God, have mercy on me.

I confess to Thee, O Saviour, the sins that I have committed, the wounds of my soul and body, which murderous thoughts, like bandits, have inflicted inwardly on me.

(Luke 10: 30)

Refrain: Have mercy on me, O God, have mercy on me.

And though I have sinned, O Saviour, yet I know that Thou art a lover of mankind. Thou chastisest with mercy and are fervent in compassion. Thou seest the tears and run to meet me, like the father welcoming back the Prodigal.

(Luke 15: 20)

Glory be to the Father and to the Son and to the Holy Spirit.

Triadicon

Trinity beyond being, worshipped in unity, take from me the heavy yoke of sin, and in Thy compassion, grant me tears of contrition.

Both now and forever and unto the ages of ages. Amen.

Theotokion

O Mother of God, the help and protection of those who sing praise to thee, take from me the heavy yoke of sin, and, pure Lady, accept me in repentance.

Ode 2

Eirmos

Attend, O heaven, and I shall speak and sing in praise of Christ, who took flesh from a Virgin and came to dwell among us.

Refrain: Have mercy on me, O God, have mercy on me.

Sin has sewed for me garments of skin; it has stripped me of the robe that God once wove for me.

(Genesis 3: 21)

Refrain: Have mercy on me, O God, have mercy on me.

I am clothed with the raiment of shame as with fig leaves, as a reproach for my self willed passions.

Refrain: Have mercy on me, O God, have mercy on me.

I am clothed in a garment that is stained and defiled with blood, the product of a life of passion and self indulgence.

Refrain: Have mercy on me, O God, have mercy on me.

I have fallen beneath the pain of passions and the corruption of material things; and from then until now the enemy oppresses me.

Refrain: Have mercy on me, O God, have mercy on me.

Instead of voluntary poverty, O Saviour, I have preferred a life in love with possessions and in love with material things and now I wear the heavy yoke.
(Matthew 5: 3)

Refrain: Have mercy on me, O God, have mercy on me.

I have adorned the human shape of my flesh with the many coloured coat of shameful thoughts, and I am condemned.
(1 John 5: 21)

Refrain: Have mercy on me, O God, have mercy on me.

I have cared only for the outward adornment, and have neglected what is within: a body bearing the divine likeness.
(1 Peter 3: 3-4)

Refrain: Have mercy on me, O God, have mercy on me.

O Saviour, I have discoloured with the passions the first beauty of the image. But, as once with the lost coin: seek it and find it.
(Luke 15: 8)

Refrain: Have mercy on me, O God, have mercy on me.

Like the harlot I cry to Thee: I have sinned, I alone have sinned against Thee. Accept my tears also as sweet ointment, O Saviour.
(Luke 10: 30)

Refrain: Have mercy on me, O God, have mercy on me.

Like the Tax Collector I cry to Thee: Be merciful, O Saviour, be merciful to me. For no child of Adam has ever sinned against Thee as I have sinned.
(Luke 18: 13)

Glory be to the Father and to the Son and to the Holy Spirit.

Triadicon

I sing Thy praises, God of all, one in three Persons: the Father, the Son and the Holy Spirit.

Both now and forever and unto the ages of ages. Amen.

Theotokion

O most pure Virgin Mother of God, alone all praised, intercede fervently for our salvation.

Ode 3

Eirmos

O Lord, establish my wavering heart on the rock of Thy commandments, for Thou alone art holy and Lord.

Refrain: Have mercy on me, O God, have mercy on me.

I have acquired Thee, source of life, the destroyer of death; and from my heart before the end I cry to Thee: I have sinned, be merciful and save me.

Refrain: Have mercy on me, O God, have mercy on me.

I have sinned, O Lord, I have sinned against Thee; be merciful to me, for there is no sinner amongst humans whom I have not surpassed in sins.

Refrain: Have mercy on me, O God, have mercy on me.

O Saviour, I have followed the example of those who lived in wantonness in the time of Noah; I have inherited from them the condemnation to drown in the flood.
(Genesis 6)

Refrain: Have mercy on me, O God, have mercy on me.

O soul, thou hast followed that Ham, who sinned against his father; thou hast not covered thy neighbours shame: walking backwards with averted gaze.

(Genesis 9: 20-27)

Refrain: Have mercy on me, O God, have mercy on me.

My soul, flee like Lot from the burning of sin; flee from Sodom and Gomorrah; flee from every abnormal desire.

(Genesis 19)

Refrain: Have mercy on me, O God, have mercy on me.

Have mercy, O Lord, have mercy on me, I cry to Thee, when Thou comest with Thine angels to give to everyone what is due for their deeds.

Glory be to the Father and to the Son and to the Holy Spirit.

Triadicon

Simple Unity, uncreated Nature without beginning, praised in a Trinity of Persons, save us who in faith worship Thy power.

Both now and forever and unto the ages of ages. Amen.

Theotokion

O Mother of God, strange wonder: without knowing a man thou hast conceived within time the Son, who is from the Father outside time, remaining a Virgin while giving suck.

Ode 4

Eirmos

The prophet heard of Thy coming, O Lord, and he was afraid of how Thou were to be born of a Virgin and revealed to mankind; and he said: *"I have heard the report of Thee, and I was afraid."* Glory to Thy power, O Lord.

(Hebrews 3: 2)

Refrain: Have mercy on me, O God, have mercy on me.

O my soul, be watchful, be courageous, like the great one among the Patriarchs, so that thou mayest acquire action with knowledge, so that thou mayest be called *"mind that sees God,"* and may reach by contemplation the innermost darkness and become a rich merchant.
(Genesis 32: 28; Luke 19: 13-15)

Refrain: Have mercy on me, O God, have mercy on me.

The great one among the Patriarchs had the Twelve Patriarchs as children, mystically setting up for thee, my soul, a ladder of ascent through action, most wisely setting up his children as the rungs, the steps for ascent.

Refrain: Have mercy on me, O God, have mercy on me.

O soul, thou hast rivalled Esau the hated, and given the birthright of thy former beauty to the supplanter and lost the paternal blessing, and in thy wretchedness have been twice supplanted in action and in knowledge. Therefore repent now.
(Genesis 25: 31; 27: 37)

Refrain: Have mercy on me, O God, have mercy on me.

Esau was called Edom because of his madness for women: burning always with unrestrained desires and stained with pleasures. He was named "Edom", which means: the red heat of a soul that loves sin.
(Genesis 25: 30)

Refrain: Have mercy on me, O God, have mercy on me.

O my soul, having heard of Job justified on a dung hill, thou hast not emulated his fortitude. Thou hast had no firmness of purpose in all that thou hast experienced and known and been tempted by, but have shown thyself inconstant.
(Job 1)

Refrain: Have mercy on me, O God, have mercy on me.

He who was once on a throne is now on a dung hill, naked and covered with sores. He who had many children and was admired by all people is suddenly childless and homeless. Yet he counted his dung hill as a palace and his sores as pearls.
(Job 2: 7-8)

Glory be to the Father and to the Son and to the Holy Spirit.

Triadicon

Undivided in Essence, unconfused in Persons, I confess Thee as God: the Trinity in one Godhead, equal in kingship and throne; and I raise to Thee the great threefold song that is sung in the highest.

Both now and forever and unto the ages of ages. Amen.

Theotokion

Thou gavest birth and art a virgin, and in both thou remainest by nature Virgin. He who is born makes new the laws of nature, and the womb brings forth without labour pains. When God so wills, the natural order is overcome; for He does whatever He wishes.

Ode 5

Eirmos

From the night I seek Thee early, O Lover of mankind: give me light, I pray Thee, and guide me also in Thy commandments, and teach me, O Saviour, to do Thy will.

Refrain: Have mercy on me, O God, have mercy on me.

O soul, thou hast heard of Moses, how he was carried of old in the reed basket on the waves of the waters of the river, as in a chamber, escaping the bitter execution of the decree of Pharaoh.
(Genesis 1: 22-2: 3)

Refrain: Have mercy on me, O God, have mercy on me.

O soul, thou hast heard of the wretched midwives who once killed in its infancy the manly action of self control: now like great Moses be suckled on wisdom.
(Genesis 1: 16; 2: 9; Acts 7: 22)

Refrain: Have mercy on me, O God, have mercy on me.

O wretched soul, thou hast not struck and killed the Egyptian mind like Moses the great. Tell me, then, how wilt thou go to dwell through repentance in the desert empty of the passions?
(Exodus 2: 12)

Refrain: Have mercy on me, O God, have mercy on me.

Moses the great went to dwell in the desert. Come, O soul, and follow his way of life, so that thou also mayest attain the vision of God in the bush.

(Exodus 3: 1)

Refrain: Have mercy on me, O God, have mercy on me.

Picture, O soul, the rod of Moses striking the sea and making the deep solid by the sign of the divine Cross, through which thou also can do great things.

(Exodus 14: 16)

Refrain: Have mercy on me, O God, have mercy on me.

Aaron brought to God fire that was blameless and pure, but Hophni and Phineas, like thee, O soul, brought to God a strange fire, a defiled life.

(Leviticus 9: 21-24: 1 Kings 2: 12-34)

Glory be to the Father and to the Son and to the Holy Spirit.

Triadicon

We glorify Thee, O Trinity, the one God: Holy, holy, holy is the Father, the Son, and the Spirit, simple Essence and Unity, worshipped for ever.

Both now and forever and unto the ages of ages. Amen.

Theotokion

O inviolate Virgin Mother without a husband, from Thee God, the Creator of the ages, was clothed in my shape, and He took human nature to Himself.

Ode 6

Eirmos

With my whole heart I cried to the compassionate God, and He heard me from the lowest depths of hell, and brought my life up from corruption.

Refrain: Have mercy on me, O God, have mercy on me.

O Saviour, the billows of my sins have returned and suddenly engulfed me, as once in the Red Sea the billows engulfed the Egyptians and their captains.

(Exodus 14: 7-31)

Refrain: Have mercy on me, O God, have mercy on me.

O soul, thou hast made a foolish choice, like Israel before thee; instead of the divine manna thou hast senselessly preferred the pleasure loving gluttony of the passions.
(Exodus 21: 5; 1 Corinthians 10: 9)

Refrain: Have mercy on me, O God, have mercy on me.

My soul, thou hast valued the wells of Canaanite thoughts more than the veined Rock, from whom torrents of the wisdom of divine knowledge pour forth as from a chalice.
(Genesis 21: 25; Exodus 17: 16)

Refrain: Have mercy on me, O God, have mercy on me.

My soul, thou hast preferred swines meat and cauldrons and Egyptian food to the heavenly, as the ungrateful people did of old in the wilderness.
(Genesis 16: 3, Numbers 11: 4 7)

Refrain: Have mercy on me, O God, have mercy on me.

When Moses Thy servant struck the rock with his rod, he prefigured Thy life giving side, O Saviour, from which we all draw the water of life.
(Numbers 20: 11; 1 Corinthians 10: 4)

Refrain: Have mercy on me, O God, have mercy on me.

O soul, like Jesus son of Navi, search and spy out the nature of the Promised Land, and take up thy dwelling in it through obedience to the Law.
(Jonah 2)

Glory be to the Father and to the Son and to the Holy Spirit.

Triadicon
"I am Trinity, simple and undivided, divided in Persons, and I am Unity from the beginning, by Nature one." says the Father and the Son and the divine Spirit.

Both now and forever and unto the ages of ages. Amen.

Theotokion

Thy womb gave birth to God for us, fashioned in our shape. Pray to Him as the Creator of all, O Mother of God, that through thy prayers we may be justified.

Kontakion

My soul, my soul, rise up. Why art thou sleeping? The end draws near, and soon thou shall be troubled. Watch, then, so that Christ God may spare thee, for He is present everywhere and fills all things.

Ode 7

Eirmos

We have sinned, we have transgressed, we have done evil before Thee, and neither have we followed, nor have we done, what Thou commanded us. But do not reject us utterly, O God of our fathers.

Refrain: Have mercy on me, O God, have mercy on me.

When the Ark was being carried on a cart and the ox stumbled, Zan only touched it, but the wrath of God struck Him. O soul, flee from his presumption and rightly show reverence for the divine things.
(2 Kings 6: 6)

Refrain: Have mercy on me, O God, have mercy on me.

Thou hast heard of Absalom, and how he rebelled against nature; thou knowest the abominable deeds by which he despised the bed of his father David. Yet thou hast followed him in his passionate and pleasure seeking impulses.
(2 Kings 15; 16: 21)

Refrain: Have mercy on me, O God, have mercy on me.

O soul, thou hast subjected thy free dignity to thy body; for thou hast found the enemy, another Ahitophel, and thou hast agreed to his counsels. But Christ Himself has brought them to nothing, so that thou mightest be saved from them all.
(2 Kings 16: 20)

Refrain: Have mercy on me, O God, have mercy on me.

Solomon the wonderful, who was full of the grace of wisdom, once did evil opposing God, and turned away from Him. Thou hast become like Him, O soul, by thine accursed life.
(3 Kings 11; Ecclesiasticus 47: 12-20)

Refrain: Have mercy on me, O God, have mercy on me.

Carried away by the desires of his passions, he had fallen. Alas, the lover of wisdom became a lover of wanton women and a stranger to God. Thou, O soul, have imitated Him in mind through shameful pleasures.
(3 Kings 3: 12; 11: 4-12)

Refrain: Have mercy on me, O God, have mercy on me.

O soul, thou hast emulated Rovoam, who paid no regard to his fathers counsellors, and at the same time also the evil servant, Jeroboam, the rebel of old. But flee from their example and cry to God: I have sinned, take pity on me.
(3 Kings 12: 13-20)

Glory be to the Father and to the Son and to the Holy Spirit.

Triadicon

Trinity, simple, undivided, consubstantial, and one in Essence, Lights and Light, three Holies and one Holy, God the Trinity is praised in song. So, O soul, praise and glorify Life and Lives, the God of all.

Both now and forever and unto the ages of ages. Amen.

Theotokion

We praise thee, we bless thee, we venerate thee, O Mother of God: for thou hast given birth to Christ God, one of the undivided Trinity; and thou thyself have opened the heavenly places to us who dwell on earth.

Ode 8

Eirmos

Him, whom the hosts of heaven glorify, and who terrifies the Cherubim and the Seraphim, let everything that has breath and every creature praise, bless, and highly exalt to all the ages.

Refrain: Have mercy on me, O God, have mercy on me.

O soul, thou hast followed Ozias, and have his leprosy in double form: for thy thoughts are wicked and thine acts unlawful. Leave what thou hast, and hasten to repentance.
(4 Kings 15; 2 Chronicles 26: 19)

Refrain: Have mercy on me, O God, have mercy on me.

O soul, thou hast heard of the Ninevites repenting before God in sackcloth and ashes. Thou hast not followed them, but have shown thyself to be more wicked than all who sinned before the Law and after the Law.
(Jonah 3: 5)

Refrain: Have mercy on me, O God, have mercy on me.

O soul, thou hast heard how Jeremiah in the muddy pit cried out with lamentations for the city of Zion and asked to be given tears. Follow his life of lamentation and be saved.
(Jeremiah 38: 6)

Refrain: Have mercy on me, O God, have mercy on me.

Jonah fled to Tharsis, foreseeing the conversion of the Ninevites; for as a prophet he knew the loving kindness of God, but he was jealous that his prophecy should not be proved false.
(Jonah 1: 3)

Refrain: Have mercy on me, O God, have mercy on me.

O soul, thou hast heard how Daniel in the pit stopped the mouths of wild beasts; and thou knowest how the Youths who were with Azarias quenched the flames of the fiery furnace through faith.
(Daniel 6: 16-22; 3: 23)

Refrain: Have mercy on me, O God, have mercy on me.

O soul, I have set before thee all the people from the Old Testament as examples. Imitate the pious acts of the righteous, but flee rather from the sins of the wicked.

Glory be to the Father and to the Son and to the Holy Spirit.

Triadicon
Father without beginning, Son also without beginning, good Paraclete, Spirit of truth; Begetter of the Word of God, Word of the Father without beginning, Spirit, living and creating: Trinity in Unity, have mercy on me.

Both now and forever and unto the ages of ages. Amen.

Theotokion

As from purple thread, O All Pure, the spiritual royal robe of Emmanuel, His flesh, was woven within thy womb. Therefore we honour thee in truth as Mother of God.

Ode 9

Eirmos

The nativity is past understanding from a conception without seed; the child bearing is undefiled from a Mother without a husband; for the birth of God makes the natures new. Therefore with true belief all generations magnify thee as Bride and Mother of God.

Refrain: Have mercy on me, O God, have mercy on me.

Christ was tempted. The Devil tempted Him, showing Him the stones so that they might be made into bread. He led Him up into a mountain, to see in an instant all the kingdoms of the world. O soul, fear fantasy, be vigilant, pray every hour to God.
(Matthew 4: 3-9; 26: 41)

Refrain: Have mercy on me, O God, have mercy on me.

The Turtle dove who loved the wilderness, the voice of one crying aloud, the Lamp of Christ, was heard preaching repentance. Herod sinned with Herodias. My soul, see that thou art not trapped in the snares of the lawless, but embrace repentance.
(Mark 1: 3; Matthew 14: 3)

Refrain: Have mercy on me, O God, have mercy on me.

The Forerunner of grace went to dwell in the wilderness, and Judea and all Samaria ran to hear Him; they confessed their sins and were baptised eagerly. But thou, O soul, hast not followed them.
(Matthew 3: 5-6)

Refrain: Have mercy on me, O God, have mercy on me.

Marriage is honourable, and the bed undefiled. For on both Christ has given His blessing, eating in the flesh at the wedding in Cana, turning the water into wine and revealing His first miracle, so that thou, O soul, mightest be converted.
(Hebrews 13: 4; John 2: 1-11)

Refrain: Have mercy on me, O God, have mercy on me.

Christ gave strength to the paralysed man, who took up his bed; He raised from the dead a young man, the son of the widow, and the centurions servant; He appeared to the Samaritan woman, and depicted beforehand to thee, O soul, worship in spirit.
(Matthew 9: 2-7; Luke 7: 14; Matthew 8: 6-13; John 4: 26; Jonah 4: 24)

Refrain: Have mercy on me, O God, have mercy on me.

By the touch of the hem of His garment, the Lord healed the woman with an issue of blood; He cleansed lepers and gave sight to the blind and made the lame walk upright; by His word He cured deaf and dumb and the woman bowed to the ground, so that thou, wretched soul, mightest be saved.
(Matthew 9: 20-22; 10: 8; 11: 5; Luke 13: 11-13)

Glory be to the Father and to the Son and to the Holy Spirit.

Triadicon

Let us glorify the Father, let us exalt the Son, and with faith let us worship the divine Spirit: undivided Trinity, Unity in Essence, as Light and Lights, and Life and Lives, giving life and light to the ends of the earth.

Both now and forever and unto the ages of ages. Amen.

Theotokion

Preserve thy city, all pure Mother of God. For by thee she reigns in faith, and by thee she is made strong, and through thee she is victorious; she puts to flight every temptation, and she despoils the enemy, and she administers the subjects.

Refrain: Venerable Father Andrew, pray to God for us.

Venerable Andrew, thrice blessed father, shepherd of Crete, do not cease to offer prayer for us who sing thy praises, so that we, who honour thy memory with faith, may be delivered from all wrath and affliction and corruption, and released from faults.

Eirmos

The nativity is past understanding from a conception without seed; the child bearing is undefiled from a Mother without a husband; for the birth of God makes the natures new. Therefore with true belief all generations magnify thee as Bride and Mother of God.

END OF TUESDAY

Great Canon Of St Andrew Of Crete, The Jerusalemite

WEDNESDAY AT GREAT COMPLINE
THE FIRST WEEK OF THE GREAT FAST

Ode 1

Eirmos

Tone 6   Rich texture, funereal character, sorrowful tone.   D, Eb, F##, G, A, Bb, C##, D.

He has become Helper and Protector for me unto salvation. He is my God and I glorify Him, God of my fathers — and I exalt Him, for He is greatly glorified.
(Exodus 15: 2, 1; Psalms 117: 14)

Refrain: Have mercy on me, O God, have mercy on me.

From my youth, O Saviour, I have rejected thy commandments. Ruled by the passions, I have passed my whole life in heedlessness and sloth. Therefore even at the end I cry to Thee, O Saviour: Save me.

Refrain: Have mercy on me, O God, have mercy on me.

Having cast me out before thy gates, O Saviour, do not, in mine old age, cast me down empty into hell; but before the end, as Thou art the Lover of mankind, grant me remission of sins.

Refrain: Have mercy on me, O God, have mercy on me.

In my hunger I cry: O Saviour, I have wasted all of my substance in riotous living, and I am barren of the fruit of piety. O Father, in thy compassion Thou ran to meet me to take pity on me.
(Luke 15: 13, 17)

Refrain: Have mercy on me, O God, have mercy on me.

I am the one who fell among thieves - mine own thoughts; now I am wounded all over by them, beaten and bruised. But Thou Thyself came to me Christ Saviour, to heal me.
(Luke 10: 30)

Refrain: Have mercy on me, O God, have mercy on me.

Seeing me first, the Priest passed by on the other side, and the Levite, looking in terror, despised my nakedness. But, O Jesus, who sprang from Mary, Thou camest to me to take pity on me.
(Luke 10: 31-33)

Refrain: Venerable Mother Mary, pray to God for us.

Grant me the light of grace, from divine providence on high, to flee from the darkness of the passions and to sing fervently the joyful narrative of thy life, O Mary.

Glory be to the Father and to the Son and to the Holy Spirit.

Triadicon

Trinity beyond being, worshipped in unity, take from me the heavy yoke of sin, and in thy compassion grant me tears of contrition.

Both now and forever and unto the ages of ages. Amen.

Theotokion

O Mother of God, the help and protection of those who sing praise to thee, take from me the heavy yoke of sin, and, pure Lady, accept me in repentance.

Ode 2

Eirmos

Attend, O heaven, and I shall speak and sing in praise of Christ, who took flesh from a Virgin and came to dwell among us.

Refrain: Have mercy on me, O God, have mercy on me.

Like David, I have fallen through incontinence, and I am covered with filth. But with my tears, Thou, O Saviour, hast washed me clean.
(2 Kings 11: 1-4)

Refrain: Have mercy on me, O God, have mercy on me.

I have no tears, no repentance, no contrition. O Saviour, as God, grant them to me Thyself.

Refrain: Have mercy on me, O God, have mercy on me.

I have lost the beauty and dignity with which I was first created, and now I lie naked, and I am ashamed.

Refrain: Have mercy on me, O God, have mercy on me.

Lord, Lord, do not close thy door against me then; but open it to me who repent to Thee.
(Matthew 25: 11)

Refrain: Have mercy on me, O God, have mercy on me.

Give ear to the groaning of my soul, and accept the drops that fall from mine eyes; O Lord, save me.

Refrain: Have mercy on me, O God, have mercy on me.

O Lover of mankind, who desire that all shall be saved, call me back, as Thou art good, and accept me in repentance.
(1 Timothy 2: 4)

Refrain: Most holy Mother of God, save us.

Undefiled Virgin Mother of God, alone all praised, intercede fervently for our salvation.

Eirmos

See, see, that I am God, who of old in the desert rained down manna and made springs of water flow from the rock for my people, by my right hand alone and by my power.

Refrain: Have mercy on me, O God, have mercy on me.

See, see that I am God. Give ear, my soul, to the Lord as He cries, and forsake thy former sin, and fear Him as Avenger and as Judge and God.
(Deuteronomy 23: 35; Hebrews 10: 30)

Refrain: Have mercy on me, O God, have mercy on me.

To whom shall I liken thee, O soul of many sins? Alas, to the first Cain, and to that Lamech. For thou hast stoned thy body to death with evil deeds, and killed thy mind with inordinate lusts.
(Genesis 4; 4: 23)

Refrain: Have mercy on me, O God, have mercy on me.

O soul, call to mind all who were before the Law. Thou hast not been like Seth, or followed Enos or Enoch who wast translated to heaven; but thou art found to be lacking the life of the righteous.
(Genesis 5)

Refrain: Have mercy on me, O God, have mercy on me.

My soul, thou alone hast opened the windows of the wrath of thy God, and thou hast flooded, as the earth, all thy flesh and thy deeds and thy life; and thou hast remained outside the Ark of salvation. *(Genesis 6-8)*

Refrain: Venerable Mother Mary, pray to God for us.

With eagerness and longing thou hast run to Christ, turning from thy former path of sin, and being sustained in the trackless wilderness, and thereby fulfilling in purity the divine commandments.

Glory be to the Father and to the Son and to the Holy Spirit.

Triadicon

Uncreated Trinity without beginning, undivided Unity: accept me in repentance, and save me, a sinner. I am thy creation, do not reject me, but spare me and deliver me from the fire of condemnation.

Both now and forever and unto the ages of ages. Amen.

Theotokion

O most pure Lady, Mother of God, the hope of those who run to thee and the haven of the storm tossed, through thy prayers grant that thy merciful Creator and Son may be merciful even to me.

Ode 3

Eirmos

O Lord, establish my wavering heart on the rock of thy commandments, for Thou alone art holy and Lord.

Refrain: Have mercy on me, O God, have mercy on me.

Wretched soul, thou hast not inherited the blessing of Sem, nor hast thou received, like Japheth, a spacious domain in the land of forgiveness. *(Genesis 9; 26-27)*

Refrain: Have mercy on me, O God, have mercy on me.

My soul, depart from the land of Harran, from sin, and enter into the land that Abraham inherited, which flows with everlasting incorruption. *(Genesis 12: 4)*

Refrain: Have mercy on me, O God, have mercy on me.

My soul, thou hast heard how Abraham of old left the land of his fathers and became a wanderer: follow Him in his choice.
(Genesis 12: 1)

Refrain: Have mercy on me, O God, have mercy on me.

At the oak of Mamvre the Patriarch gave hospitality to the angels; in old age he inherited the rewards of the promise.
(Genesis 18: 1)

Refrain: Have mercy on me, O God, have mercy on me.

My miserable soul, thou knowest how Isaac was mystically presented as a whole burnt offering, a new sacrifice to the Lord: follow Him in his choice.
(Genesis 22: 2)

Refrain: Have mercy on me, O God, have mercy on me.

My soul, be vigilant! Thou hast heard how Ishmael was driven out as the offspring of a slave girl. Watch lest thou sufferest the same because of thy lechery.
(Genesis 21: 10)

Refrain: Venerable Mother Mary, pray to God for us.

O Mother, I am held fast by the tempest and billow of sins; but keep me safe now thyself, and lead me to the haven of divine repentance.

Refrain: Venerable Mother Mary, pray to God for us.

To thee Venerable Mother. We offer now our prayers to the compassionate Mother of God, and through thine intercessions open to me the divine entrances.

Glory be to the Father and to the Son and to the Holy Spirit.

Triadicon

Simple Unity, uncreated Nature without beginning, praised in a Trinity of Persons, save us who in faith worship Thy power.

Both now and forever and unto the ages of ages. Amen.

Theotokion

O Mother of God, strange wonder: without knowing a man thou hast conceived within time the Son, who is from the Father outside time, remaining a Virgin while giving suck.

Ode 4

Eirmos

The prophet heard of Thy coming, O Lord, and he was afraid of how Thou were to be born of a Virgin and revealed to mankind; and he said: *"I have heard the report of Thee, and I was afraid."* Glory to Thy power, O Lord.
(Hebrews 3: 2)

Refrain: Have mercy on me, O God, have mercy on me.

I have defiled my body, I have stained my spirit, and I am all covered with wounds: but as physician, O Christ, heal them both for me through repentance. Wash, purify and cleanse me, my Saviour, and make me whiter than snow.

Refrain: Have mercy on me, O God, have mercy on me.

O Word, when Thou wast crucified Thou offered Thy Body and Thy Blood for the sake of all: Thy Body to refashion me, and Thy Blood to cleanse me; and Thou gavest up the spirit, O Christ, to bring me to Thy Father.

Refrain: Have mercy on me, O God, have mercy on me.

In Thy pity Thou worked salvation in the midst of the earth so that we might be saved. Of Thine own will Thou wert crucified on the Tree; and Eden, closed until then, was opened. Things above and things below, the creation and all nations have been saved and worship Thee.
(Psalms 73: 12)

Refrain: Have mercy on me, O God, have mercy on me.

May the Blood that flows from Thy side be to me a font, and may the Water that flows with it be a drink of forgiveness, so that by them both, O Word, I may be purified, anointed and refreshed, having as chrism and drink Thy words of life.

(John 19: 34; Acts 7: 38)

Refrain: Have mercy on me, O God, have mercy on me.

Our Saviour, the Church has been granted Thy life bearing side as a chalice, from which there flows down to us the two fold stream of forgiveness and knowledge, representing the two Covenants, the Old and the New.

Refrain: Have mercy on me, O God, have mercy on me.

I am deprived of the bridal chamber, and I am deprived of the wedding, and also of the supper; for lack of oil my lamp went out; while I slept the bridal chamber was closed to me, the supper was eaten, and I was cast out, bound hand and foot.

(John 19: 34; Acts 7: 38)

Glory be to the Father and to the Son and to the Holy Spirit.

Triadicon

Undivided in Essence, unconfused in Persons, I confess Thee as God: the Trinity in one Godhead, equal in kingship and throne; and I raise to Thee the great threefold song that is sung in the highest.

Both now and forever and unto the ages of ages. Amen.

Theotokion

Thou gavest birth and art a virgin, and in both thou remainest by nature Virgin. He who is born makes new the laws of nature, and the womb brings forth without labour pains. When God so wills, the natural order is overcome; for He does whatever He wishes.

Ode 5

Eirmos

From the night I seek Thee early, O Lover of mankind. Give me light, I pray Thee, and guide me also in Thy commandments, and teach me, O Saviour, to do Thy will.

Refrain: Have mercy on me, O God, have mercy on me.

As Jannes and Jamvres were grievous to the will of cruel Pharaoh, so have I become in soul and body, and my mind is overwhelmed: but, O Lord, come to mine aid.
(Exodus 7: 11; 2 Timothy 3: 8)

Refrain: Have mercy on me, O God, have mercy on me.

I, the wretched one, have destroyed my mind with mire. Cleanse me in the bath of my tears, I pray Thee, O Master, and make the garment of my flesh as white as snow.

Refrain: Have mercy on me, O God, have mercy on me.

When I examine my works, O Saviour, I see that I have myself gone beyond all mankind in sins, for I knew and understood what I did; I did not sin in ignorance.

Refrain: Have mercy on me, O God, have mercy on me.

Spare, O Lord, spare what Thou hast made. I have sinned, forgive me: for Thou alone art pure by nature, and none except Thee is free from pollution.
(1 Peter 3: 21)

Refrain: Have mercy on me, O God, have mercy on me.

Being God, O Saviour, Thou wert formed like me for my sake. Thou performed wonders, Thou healed lepers, Thou gavest strength to the paralysed, and Thou stopped the issue of blood when the woman touched the hem of Thy garment.
(Philemon 2: 6; Matthew 4: 24; Luke 8: 43-48)

Refrain: Venerable Mother Mary, pray to God for us.

Crossing the stream of Jordan thou foundest peace, escaping from the deadening pleasures of the flesh. Deliver us also from them by thine intercessions, O Venerable Mother.

Glory be to the Father and to the Son and to the Holy Spirit.

Triadicon
We glorify Thee, O Trinity, the one God: Holy, holy, holy is the Father, the Son, and the Spirit, simple Essence and Unity, worshipped for ever.

Both now and forever and unto the ages of ages. Amen.

Theotokion

Inviolate Virgin Mother without a husband, from Thou God, the Creator of the ages, was clothed in my shape, and He took human nature to Himself.

Ode 6

Eirmos

With my whole heart I cried to the compassionate God, and He heard me from the lowest depths of hell, and brought my life up from corruption.

Refrain: Have mercy on me, O God, have mercy on me.

Rise up and make war on the passions of the flesh, like Jesus against Amalek, ever gaining victory over the Gavaonites, thy deceitful thoughts.
(Exodus 17: 8; Jonah 8: 21)

Refrain: Have mercy on me, O God, have mercy on me.

God commands thee, O soul: pass through the flowing nature of time like the Ark of old and take possession of that promised land.
(Jonah 3: 17; Deuteronomy 1: 8)

Refrain: Have mercy on me, O God, have mercy on me.

As Thou saved Peter when he cried out; Save me. Come quickly, O Saviour, and deliver me from the beast. Stretch out Thine hand and lead me up from the deep of sin.
(Matthew 14: 25-31)

Refrain: Have mercy on me, O God, have mercy on me.

O Master, I know Thee as a calm haven: come quickly, O Christ the Master, and deliver me from the lowest depths of sin and despair.

Glory be to the Father and to the Son and to the Holy Spirit.

Triadicon

"I am Trinity, simple and undivided, divided in Persons, and I am Unity from the beginning, by Nature one." says the Father and the Son and the divine Spirit.

Both now and forever and unto the ages of ages. Amen.

Theotokion

Thy womb gave birth to God for us, fashioned in our shape. Pray to Him as the Creator of all, O Mother of God, that through thy prayers we may be justified.

Kontakion

My soul, my soul, rise up. Why art thou sleeping? The end draws near, and soon thou wilt be troubled. Watch, then, so that Christ God may spare thee, for He is present everywhere and fillest all things.

Ode 7

Eirmos

We have sinned, we have transgressed, we have done evil before Thee, and neither have we followed, nor have we done, what Thou commanded us. But do not reject us utterly, O God of our fathers.

Refrain: Have mercy on me, O God, have mercy on me.

By choice thou heaped up the faults of Manasses, O soul, setting up passions as abominations, and multiplying offences. But with fervour imitate his repentance and acquire compunction.
(4 Kings 21; 2 Chronicles 33)

Refrain: Have mercy on me, O God, have mercy on me.

Woe is me, my soul. Thou hast rivalled Ahab in crimes. Thou hast become a lodging for fleshly defilements and a shameful vessel of the passions. But groan from the depths and tell thy sins to God.
(3 Kings 16: 30)

Refrain: Have mercy on me, O God, have mercy on me.

Heaven is closed to thee, O soul, and a famine from God has come upon thee: for thou hast been disobedient, as Ahab was to the words of Elijah the Thesbite. But imitate the woman of Saraphtha, and feed the soul of the prophet.
(3 Kings 17)

Refrain: Have mercy on me, O God, have mercy on me.

Elijah once set fire to twice fifty of Jezebels men, and he slew the prophets of shame, as a rebuke to Ahab. But flee from the examples of them both, O soul, and be strong.
(4 Kings 1: 10-15; 3 Kings 18: 40)

Glory be to the Father and to the Son and to the Holy Spirit.

Triadicon

Trinity, simple, undivided, consubstantial, and one in Essence, Lights and Light, three Holies and one Holy, God the Trinity is praised in song. So, O soul, praise and glorify Life and Lives, the God of all.

Both now and forever and unto the ages of ages. Amen.

Theotokion

We praise thee, we bless thee, we venerate thee, O Mother of God: for thou hast given birth to Christ God, one of the undivided Trinity; and thou thyself hast opened the heavenly places to us who dwell on earth.

Ode 8

Eirmos

Him, whom the hosts of heaven glorify, and who terrifies the Cherubim and the Seraphim, let everything that has breath and every creature praise, bless, and highly exalt to all the ages.

Refrain: Have mercy on me, O God, have mercy on me.

Righteous Judge and Saviour, have mercy on me and deliver me from the fire, and from the punishment that I rightly expect to suffer at the Judgement. Before the end release me through virtue and repentance.

Refrain: Have mercy on me, O God, have mercy on me.

Like the thief I cry to Thee: Remember me; like Peter I weep bitterly; like the Tax Collector I call out: Release me; like the Harlot I shed tears: accept my lamentation as once Thou accepted that of the Canaanite woman.
(Luke 23: 42; Mt 26: 75; Luke 18: 13; Luke 7: 37-38; Matthew 15: 22-28)

Refrain: Have mercy on me, O God, have mercy on me.

O Saviour, the only Physician, heal the putrefaction of my humbled soul; apply plaster to me, and oil and wine; works of repentance and compunction with tears.

(Luke 10: 34)

Refrain: Have mercy on me, O God, have mercy on me.

I too follow the Canaanite woman, and cry: *"Son of David, have mercy on me."* Like the woman with an issue of blood I touch the hem of Thy garment. I weep as Martha and Mary wept for Lazarus.

Glory be to the Father and to the Son and to the Holy Spirit.

Triadicon

Father without beginning, Son also without beginning, good Paraclete, Spirit of truth; Begetter of the Word of God, Word of the Father without beginning, Spirit, living and creating: Trinity in Unity, have mercy on me.

Both now and forever and unto the ages of ages. Amen.

Theotokion

As from purple thread, O All Pure, the spiritual royal robe of Emmanuel, His flesh, was woven within thy womb. Therefore we honour thee in truth as Mother of God.

Ode 9

Eirmos

The nativity is past understanding from a conception without seed; the childbearing is undefiled from a Mother without a husband; for the birth of God makes the natures new. Therefore with true belief all generations magnify thee as Bride and Mother of God.

Refrain: Have mercy on me, O God, have mercy on me.

Christ the Word healed sicknesses, preached the gospel to the poor, cured cripples, ate with tax collectors, and talked with sinners. With the touch of His hand He brought back the departed soul of the daughter of Jairos.

(Matthew 9: 11; Mark 5: 41-42)

Refrain: Have mercy on me, O God, have mercy on me.

The Tax Collector was saved, and the Harlot turned to chastity, but the Pharisee with his boasting was condemned. For the first said *"Be merciful"*; and the second: *"Have mercy on me"*; but the third said, boasting: *"I thank Thee, O God"* and other words of madness.
(Luke 7: 36-50; 18: 9-14)

Refrain: Have mercy on me, O God, have mercy on me.

Zacchaeus was a tax collector, yet he was saved; but Simon the Pharisee went astray; while the Harlot received remission and release from Him who has power to forgive sins. Make haste, O soul, to follow her example.
(Luke 19: 1-10; 7: 36-50)

Refrain: Have mercy on me, O God, have mercy on me.

O my wretched soul, thou hast not acted like the Harlot, who took the alabaster box of ointment, and anointed with tears the feet of the Lord, and wiped them with her hair. And He tore in pieces the record of her previous sins.
(Luke 7: 37-38; Colossians 2: 14)

Refrain: Have mercy on me, O God, have mercy on me.

My soul, thou knowest how the cities were cursed to which Christ gave the Gospel. Fear their example, lest thou becomest like them, for the Master compared them to the men of Sodom, and condemned them to hell.
(Luke 10: 13-15)

Refrain: Have mercy on me, O God, have mercy on me.

My soul, do not be overcome by despair; for thou hast heard of the faith of the woman of Canaan, and how through it her daughter was healed by the Word of God. Cry out from the depth of thy heart, as she did to Christ: *"Save me also, O Son of David."*
(Matthew 15: 22)

Glory be to the Father and to the Son and to the Holy Spirit.

Triadicon

Let us glorify the Father, let us exalt the Son, and with faith let us worship the divine Spirit: undivided Trinity, Unity in Essence, as Light and Lights, and Life and Lives, giving life and light to the ends of the earth.

Both now and forever and unto the ages of ages. Amen.

Theotokion

Preserve thy city, All Pure Mother of God. For by thee she reigns in faith, and by thee she is made strong, and through thee she is victorious; she puts to flight every temptation, and she despoils the enemy, and she administers the subjects.

Refrain: Venerable Father Andrew, pray to God for us.

Venerable Andrew, thrice blessed father, shepherd of Crete, do not cease to offer prayer for us who sing thy praises, so that we, who honour thy memory with faith, may be delivered from all wrath and affliction and corruption, and released from faults.

Katavasia

The nativity is past understanding from a conception without seed; the childbearing is undefiled from a Mother without a husband; for the birth of God makes the natures new. Therefore with true belief all generations magnify thee as Bride and Mother of God.

END OF WEDNESDAY

Great Canon Of St Andrew Of Crete, The Jerusalemite

THURSDAY AT GREAT COMPLINE
THE FIRST WEEK OF THE GREAT FAST

Ode 1

Eirmos

Tone 6   Rich texture, funereal character, sorrowful tone.   *D, Eb, F##, G, A, Bb, C##, D.*

He has become Helper and Protector for me unto salvation. He is my God and I glorify Him, God of my fathers and I exalt Him, for He is greatly glorified.

(Exodus 15: 2, 1; Psalms 117: 14)

Refrain: Have mercy on me, O God, have mercy on me.

O Lamb of God, who takes away the sins of all, take from me the heavy yoke of sin, and as Thou art compassionate give me tears of compunction.

(John 1: 29)

Refrain: Have mercy on me, O God, have mercy on me.

O Jesus, I fall down at Thy feet. I have sinned against Thee: be merciful to me. Take from me the heavy yoke of sin, and as Thou art a compassionate God, accept me in repentance.

Refrain: Have mercy on me, O God, have mercy on me.

Do not enter into judgement with me, bringing before me the things I should have done: examining my words and correcting my impulses. But in Thy pity overlook such things, and save me, O All Powerful.

Refrain: Have mercy on me, O God, have mercy on me.

It is time for repentance: I come to Thee, my Creator. Take from me the heavy yoke of sin, and in Thy compassion give me tears of compunction.

Refrain: Have mercy on me, O God, have mercy on me.

I have wasted the substance of my soul in sin and I am barren of the virtues of piety. In my hunger I cry: Grant mercy to me, O Lord, my Saviour.

(Luke 15: 13, 17)

Refrain: Venerable Mother Mary, pray to God for us.

Bowing before the laws of Christ, thou hast drawn near to Him, forsaking the ungovernable longings of sensual pleasure; and thou hast most reverently accomplished all the virtues as if they were one.

Glory be to the Father and to the Son and to the Holy Spirit.

Triadicon

Trinity beyond being, worshipped in unity, take from me the heavy yoke of sin, and in Thy compassion grant me tears of contrition.

Both now and forever and unto the ages of ages. Amen.

Theotokion

O Mother of God, the help and protection of those who sing praise to thee, take from me the heavy yoke of sin, and, pure Lady, accept me in repentance.

Ode 2

Eirmos

See, see, that I am God, who of old in the desert rained down manna and made springs of water flow from the rock for My people, by My right hand alone and by My power.

Refrain: Have mercy on me, O God, have mercy on me.

"I have killed a man to my bruising and a young man to my hurt." said Lamech, as he cried aloud lamenting. O my soul, dost thou not tremble then, for thou hast defiled thy flesh and stained thy mind?
(Genesis 4: 23)

Refrain: Have mercy on me, O God, have mercy on me.

O soul, thou cleverly planned to build a tower, and to construct a fortress for thy lusts; but the Creator confounded thy plans and dashed thy constructions to the ground.
(Genesis 11: 3-4)

Refrain: Have mercy on me, O God, have mercy on me.

Oh, how I have emulated Lamech, the murderer of old, slaying my body like the man, and my mind like the young man. And with longings for sensual pleasures I have slain my body as a brother, like Cain the murderer.

(Genesis 4: 23)

Refrain: Have mercy on me, O God, have mercy on me.

Roused to anger by their transgression, the Lord once rained down fire from the Lord and burnt up the men of Sodom. And thou, O soul, hast kindled the fire of Gehenna, in which thou wilt burn with them.

(Genesis 19: 24)

Refrain: Have mercy on me, O God, have mercy on me.

I am wounded, I am struck: see the arrows of the enemy which have pierced my soul and my body; see the wounds, the festering sores, and the maimings; cry the blows of my freely chosen passions.

Refrain: Venerable Mother Mary, pray to God for us.

Sunk in the abyss of wickedness, O Mary, thou lifted up thine hands to the merciful God. And as to Peter, in His love for mankind, He stretched out His divine hand to thee, seeking in every way thy conversion.

Glory be to the Father and to the Son and to the Holy Spirit.

Triadicon

Uncreated Trinity without beginning, undivided Unity: accept me in repentance, and save me, a sinner. I am Thy creation, do not reject me, but spare me and deliver me from the fire of condemnation.

Both now and forever and unto the ages of ages. Amen.

Theotokion

O Most pure Lady, Mother of God, the hope of those who run to thee and the haven of the storm tossed, through thy prayers grant that thy merciful Creator and Son may be merciful even to me.

Ode 3

Eirmos

O Lord, establish my wavering heart on the rock of Thy commandments, for Thou alone art holy and Lord.

Refrain: Have mercy on me, O God, have mercy on me.

O soul, thou hast become like Hagar the Egyptian of old: thy free choice has been enslaved and thou hast given birth to a new Ishmael - stubborn wilfulness.
(Genesis 16: 15)

Refrain: Have mercy on me, O God, have mercy on me.

My soul, thou knowest the ladder of Jacob, appearing from earth to heaven. Why dost thou not have a secure step of piety?
(Genesis 28: 12)

Refrain: Have mercy on me, O God, have mercy on me.

Follow the example of the one set apart as Priest of God and King, the symbolic representation of the life of Christ in the world among mankind.
(Hebrew 7: 1-4; Genesis 14: 18)

Refrain: Have mercy on me, O God, have mercy on me.

Turn back, wretched soul, and lament, before the festival of life comes to an end, before the Lord shuts the door to the bridal chamber.

Refrain: Have mercy on me, O God, have mercy on me.

Do not look back, O soul, and become a pillar of salt. May the precedent of Sodom make thee fearful, and mayest thou go up to refuge in Segor.
(Genesis 19: 26)

Refrain: Have mercy on me, O God, have mercy on me.

O Master, do not reject the prayer of those who sing praise to Thee, but, O Lover of mankind, be merciful and grant forgiveness to those who ask with faith.

Glory be to the Father and to the Son and to the Holy Spirit.

Triadicon
Simple Unity, uncreated Nature without beginning, praised in a Trinity of Persons, save us who in faith worship Thy power.

Both now and forever and unto the ages of ages. Amen.

Theotokion

O Mother of God, strange wonder: without knowing a man thou hast conceived within time the Son, who is from the Father outside time, remaining a Virgin while giving suck.

Ode 4

Eirmos

The prophet heard of Thy coming, O Lord, and he was afraid of how Thou wert to be born of a Virgin and revealed to mankind; and he said: *"I have heard the report of Thee, and I was afraid."* Glory to Thy power, O Lord.

(Hebrews 3: 2)

Refrain:　Have mercy on me, O God, have mercy on me.

The time of my life is short, filled with trouble and evil. But accept me in repentance and call me back to knowledge. Do not let me become the possession or the food of the enemy; but, O Saviour, take pity on me Thyself.

(Genesis 47: 9)

Refrain:　Have mercy on me, O God, have mercy on me.

A man of great wealth and righteous, of royal dignity, clothed in diadem and purple, abounding in riches and cattle, became suddenly a beggar, stripped of wealth, glory and kingship.

Refrain:　Have mercy on me, O God, have mercy on me.

If he who was righteous and blameless above all did not escape the snares and pits of the deceiver, what wilt thou do, wretched and sin loving soul, when some unexpected misfortune befalls thee?

Refrain:　Have mercy on me, O God, have mercy on me.

Now I begin to speak boastfully, with rashness of heart, to no purpose and in vain. O just Judge, who alone have pity, do not condemn me with the Pharisee, but grant me the humility of the Tax Collector and number me with Him.

(Luke 18: 9-14)

Refrain:　Have mercy on me, O God, have mercy on me.

O Merciful One, I know that I have sinned, that I have shown contempt for the vessel of my flesh. But accept me in repentance and call me back to knowledge. Do not let me become the possession or the food of the enemy; but, O Saviour, take pity on me Thyself.

Refrain: Have mercy on me, O God, have mercy on me.

I have become mine own idol, utterly defiling my soul with the passions. But accept me in repentance and call me back to knowledge. Do not let me become the possession or the food of the enemy; but, O Saviour, take pity on me Thyself.

Refrain: Have mercy on me, O God, have mercy on me.

I have not listened to Thy voice, I have not heeded Thy Scriptures, O Giver of the Law. But accept me in repentance and call me back to knowledge. Do not let me become the possession or the food of the enemy; but, O Saviour, take pity on me Thyself.

Refrain: Venerable Mother Mary, pray to God for us.

Thou wert brought down into the depth of great iniquities, yet not held fast; but with better intent thou perceptibly ascended to the height of virtue, beyond all expectation; and the angelic nature was amazed, O Mary.

Glory be to the Father and to the Son and to the Holy Spirit.

Triadicon
Undivided in Essence, unconfused in Persons, I confess Thee as God: the Trinity in one Godhead, equal in kingship and throne; and I raise to Thee the great threefold song that is sung in the highest.

Both now and forever and unto the ages of ages. Amen.

Theotokion
Thou gavest birth and art a virgin, and in both thou remainest by nature Virgin. He who is born makes new the laws of nature, and the womb brings forth without labour pains. When God so wills, the natural order is overcome; for He does whatever He wishes.

Ode 5

Eirmos

From the night I seek Thee early, O Lover of mankind: give me light, I pray Thee, and guide me also in Thy commandments, and teach me, O Saviour, to do Thy will.

Refrain: Have mercy on me, O God, have mercy on me.

O soul, imitate the woman who was bowed down to the ground: fall at the feet of Jesus, so that He may make thee straight again, and thou wilt walk uprightly on the paths of the Lord.
(Luke 13: 11)

Refrain: Have mercy on me, O God, have mercy on me.

Since Thou art a deep well, O Master, make springs gush forth for me from Thy pure veins, so that like the woman of Samaria I may drink and thirst no more; for from Thee flowest the streams of life.
(John 4: 13-15)

Refrain: Have mercy on me, O God, have mercy on me.

Master and Lord, may my tears be to me as Siloam, so that I also may wash clean the eyes of my heart, and with my mind behold Thee, the pre-eternal Light.
(John 9: 7; Genesis 1: 2-19)

Refrain: Venerable Mother Mary, pray to God for us.

All blessed one, with a love beyond compare thou longed to venerate the wood of the Cross, and thy desire was granted. Make me also worthy to attain the glory on high.

Glory be to the Father and to the Son and to the Holy Spirit.

Triadicon

We glorify Thee, O Trinity, the one God: Holy, holy, holy is the Father, the Son, and the Spirit, simple Essence and Unity, worshipped for ever.

Both now and forever and unto the ages of ages. Amen.

Theotokion

O inviolate Virgin Mother without a husband, from Thou God, the Creator of the ages, wast clothed in my shape, and He took human nature to Himself.

Ode 6

Eirmos

With my whole heart I cried to the compassionate God, and He heard me from the lowest depths of hell, and brought my life up from corruption.

Refrain: Have mercy on me, O God, have mercy on me.

O Saviour, I am the coin marked with the likeness of the King and which Thou lost of old. But light Thy lamp, Thy Forerunner, O Word, and seek and find Thine image.
(Luke 15: 8)

Refrain: Have mercy on me, O God, have mercy on me.

Rise up and make war on the passions of the flesh, like Jesus against Amalek, ever gaining victory over the Gavaonites, thy deceitful thoughts.
(Exodus 17: 8; Jonah 8: 21)

Refrain: Venerable Mother Mary, pray to God for us.

In order to quench the burning of the passions, O Mary, with thy soul on fire thou hast ever shed streams of tears. Grant the grace of these also to me, thy servant.

Refrain: Venerable Mother Mary, pray to God for us.

O Mother, thou attained heavenly detachment through the excellence of thy way of life on earth. Pray that those who sing praise to thee may be delivered from passions through thine intercessions.

Glory be to the Father and to the Son and to the Holy Spirit.

Triadicon

"I am Trinity, simple and undivided, divided in Persons, and I am Unity from the beginning, by Nature one." says the Father and the Son and the divine Spirit.

Both now and forever and unto the ages of ages. Amen.

Theotokion

Thy womb gave birth to God for us, fashioned in our shape. Pray to Him as the Creator of all, O Mother of God, that through thy prayers we may be justified.

Kontakion

My soul, my soul, rise up. Why art thou sleeping? The end draws near, and soon thou wilt be troubled. Watch, then, so that Christ God may spare thee, for He is present everywhere and fillest all things.

Ode 7

Eirmos

We have sinned, we have transgressed, we have done evil before Thee, and neither have we followed, nor have we done, what Thou commanded us. But do not reject us utterly, O God of our fathers.

Refrain: Have mercy on me, O God, have mercy on me.

My days have vanished like a dream of one awaking; and so, like Hezekiah, I weep on my bed, so that years may be added to my life. But what Esaïas will come to me, O soul, except the God of all?
(4 Kings 20: 3; Ic. 38: 2)

Refrain: Have mercy on me, O God, have mercy on me.

I fall before Thee, and as tears I offer Thee my words. I have sinned as the Harlot never sinned, and I have transgressed as no one else on earth. But take pity on Thy creature, O Master, and call me back.

Refrain: Have mercy on me, O God, have mercy on me.

I have discoloured Thine image and broken Thy commandment. All my beauty is darkened and my lamp is quenched by the passions, O Saviour. But take pity on me, as David sings, and restore to me Thy joy.
(Psalms 50: 14)

Refrain: Have mercy on me, O God, have mercy on me.

Turn back, repent, uncover all that thou hast hidden. Say to God, to whom all things are known: Thou alone knowest my secrets, O Saviour; have mercy on me Thyself, as David sings, according to Thy mercy.

Refrain: Venerable Mother Mary, pray to God for us.

Crying out to the most pure Mother of God, of old thou drovest back the fury of the passions that violently attacked thee, and put to shame the enemy who sought to make thee stumble. But give thy help in trouble also to me, thy servant.

Refrain: Venerable Mother Mary, pray to God for us.

Pray to Him whom thou loved, to Him whom thou desired, for whose sake thou wore out thy flesh, O Venerable Mother; pray now to Christ for thy servants, that He may show mercy on us all, and grant a peaceful existence to those who worship Him.

Glory be to the Father and to the Son and to the Holy Spirit.

Triadicon

Trinity, simple, undivided, consubstantial, and one in Essence, Lights and Light, three Holies and one Holy, God the Trinity is praised in song. So, O soul, praise and glorify Life and Lives, the God of all.

Both now and forever and unto the ages of ages. Amen.

Theotokion

We praise thee, we bless thee, we venerate thee, O Mother of God: for thou hast given birth to Christ God, one of the undivided Trinity; and thou thyself hast opened the heavenly places to us who dwell on earth.

Ode 8

Eirmos

Him, whom the hosts of heaven glorify, and who terrifies the Cherubim and the Seraphim, let everything that has breath and every creature praise, bless, and highly exalt to all the ages.

Refrain: Have mercy on me, O God, have mercy on me.

O Saviour, as ointment I empty on Thine head the alabaster box of my tears. Like the Harlot I cry to Thee, seeking mercy: I bring my prayer and ask to receive forgiveness.
(Matthew 26: 7; Luke 7: 38)

Refrain: Have mercy on me, O God, have mercy on me.

No one has sinned against Thee as I have; yet accept even me, compassionate Saviour, as I repent in fear and cry with longing: I have sinned against Thee alone; I have transgressed, have mercy on me.

Refrain: Have mercy on me, O God, have mercy on me.

O Saviour, spare what Thou hast made Thyself, and as shepherd seek the lost sheep that has gone astray. Snatch me from the wolf and make me a sheep in the pasture of Thy flock.
(Psalms 118: 176; John 10: 11-16)

Refrain: Have mercy on me, O God, have mercy on me.

When Thou, the compassionate Judge, art enthroned and revealest Thy dread glory, O Christ, what fear there shall be then, when the furnace burns with fire, and all shrink back in terror before Thy Judgement seat.
(Matthew 25: 31-46)

Refrain: Venerable Mother Mary, pray to God for us.

The Mother of the Light that never sets illumined thee and freed thee from the darkness of the passions. O Mary, who has received the grace of the Spirit, give light to those who faithfully praise thee.

Refrain: Venerable Mother Mary, pray to God for us.

Godly Zosimas was struck with amazement, beholding in thee, O Mother, a wonder truly strange and new. For he saw an angel in the body and was filled with astonishment, praising Christ to the ages.

Glory be to the Father and to the Son and to the Holy Spirit.

Triadicon
Father without beginning, Son also without beginning, good Paraclete, Spirit of truth; Begetter of the Word of God, Word of the Father without beginning, Spirit, living and creating: Trinity in Unity, have mercy on me.

Both now and forever and unto the ages of ages. Amen.

Theotokion
As from purple thread, O All Pure, the spiritual royal robe of Emmanuel, His flesh, was woven within thy womb. Therefore we honour thee in truth as Mother of God.

Ode 9

Eirmos

The nativity is past understanding: from a conception without seed; the child bearing is undefiled - from a Mother without a husband; for the birth of God makes the natures new. Therefore with true belief all generations magnify thee as Bride and Mother of God.

Refrain: Have mercy on me, O God, have mercy on me.

O Son of David, with a word Thou healed the possessed: be compassionate, save me and have mercy. Let me hear Thy compassionate voice speak to me as to the Thief: *"Amen, I say to thee, thou wilt be with Me in Paradise, when I come in My glory."*
(Luke 9: 38-42; 23: 43)

Refrain: Have mercy on me, O God, have mercy on me.

A thief accused Thee, a Thief acknowledged Thee as God: for both were hanging beside Thee on the Cross. O Greatly compassionate, open to me also the door of Thy glorious kingdom, as once it was opened to Thy Thief, who with faith recognized Thee as God.
(Luke 23: 32-42)

Refrain: Have mercy on me, O God, have mercy on me.

The creation was in anguish when it saw Thee crucified; mountains and rocks were split from fear, and the earth quaked, and hell was despoiled; and the light grew dark in the day, when they beheld Thee, O Jesus, nailed in the flesh.
(Matthew 27: 51-53; Luke 23: 44-45)

Refrain: Have mercy on me, O God, have mercy on me.

Do not demand from me worthy fruits of repentance, for my strength has failed within me. Give me an ever contrite heart and poverty of spirit, so that I may offer these to Thee as an acceptable sacrifice, O only Saviour.
(Matthew 3: 8; 5: 3; Psalms 50: 17)

Refrain: Have mercy on me, O God, have mercy on me.

My Judge, who knows me, when Thou comest again with the angels to judge the whole world, look on me then with Thy merciful eye and spare me; take pity on me, O Jesus, for I have sinned more than the whole nature of mankind.

(Matthew 25: 31-32)

Refrain: Venerable Mother Mary, pray to God for us.

By thy strange way of life thou hast struck all with wonder: the hosts of angels and the assemblies of mortals; for thou surpassed nature and lived as though no longer in the body. Like a bodiless being thou walked on the Jordan with thy feet and crossed over.

Refrain: Venerable Mother Mary, pray to God for us.

Venerable Mother, call down the gracious mercy of the Creator on those who praise thee, that we may be set free from the sufferings and afflictions that beset us round about; so that without ceasing, delivered from temptations, we may magnify the Lord who has glorified thee.

Refrain: Venerable Father Andrew, pray to God for us.

Venerable Andrew, thrice blessed father, shepherd of Crete, do not cease to offer prayer for us who sing thy praises, so that we, who honour thy memory with faith, may be delivered from all wrath and affliction and corruption, and released from faults.

Glory be to the Father and to the Son and to the Holy Spirit.

Triadicon

Let us glorify the Father, let us exalt the Son, and with faith let us worship the divine Spirit: undivided Trinity, Unity in Essence, as Light and Lights, and Life and Lives, giving life and light to the ends of the earth.

Both now and forever and unto the ages of ages. Amen.

Theotokion

Preserve thy city, all pure Mother of God. For by thee she reigns in faith, and by thee she is made strong, and through thee she is victorious; she puts to flight every temptation, and she despoils the enemy, and she administers the subjects.

Katavasia

The nativity is past understanding: from a conception without seed; the child bearing is undefiled. From a Mother without a husband; for the birth of God makes the natures new. Therefore with true belief all generations magnify thee as Bride and Mother of God.

END OF THURSDAY

Instructions:

An icon of the Theotokos is placed on a stand in the middle of the solea.

The candles are lit and the church is semi illumined.

The censer is not needed until the stases of the Akathist Hymn.

The curtain and Holy Doors are closed until the priest begins the scheduled stasis of the Akathist Hymn, and they remain open for the Holy Gospel lection on the first Friday.

The priest wears a blue epitrachelion over his exorasson and starts Little Compline in front of the icon.

The Trisagion Prayers

Priest: Blessed is our God always, both now and forever and unto the ages of ages. Amen.

People: Amen.

Priest: Glory to Thee, our God, glory to Thee

Priest: O Heavenly King, the Comforter, the Spirit of Truth; who art everywhere present and fillest all things; Treasury of blessings, and giver of life: come and abide in us, and cleanse us from every impurity, and save our souls, O Good One.

People: Holy God, Holy Mighty, Holy Immortal, have mercy on us. **(x3)**

Glory be to the Father and to the Son and to the Holy Spirit;
Both now and forever, and unto the ages of ages. Amen.

O Most Holy Trinity, have mercy on us.

O Lord, cleanse us from our sins.

O Master, pardon our iniquities.

O Holy One, visit and heal our infirmities, for Thy names sake.

Lord have mercy. **(x3)**

Glory be to the Father and to the Son and to the Holy Spirit;
Both now and forever, and unto the ages of ages. Amen.

People: Our Father, who art in heaven, hallowed be Thy name. Thy Kingdom come. Thy will be done, on earth as it is in heaven. Give us this day our daily bread; and forgive us our trespasses, as we forgive those who trespass against us; and lead us not into temptation, but deliver us from the evil one.

Priest: For Thine is the kingdom, and the power, and the glory: of the Father, and of the Son, and of the Holy Spirit; now and ever, and unto ages of ages.

People: *Amen.*

Lord have mercy. **(x12)**

Glory be to the Father and to the Son and to the Holy Spirit;
Both now and forever, and unto the ages of ages. Amen.

Come, let us worship God, our King.

Come, let us worship and fall down before Christ, our King and our God.

Come, let us worship and fall down before Christ Himself, our King and our God.

[Priest goes to Readers stand.]

Psalm 50

Have mercy on me, O God, according to Thy great mercy; and according to the multitude of Thy compassions blot out my transgression. Wash me thoroughly from mine iniquity, and cleanse me from my sin. For I acknowledge mine iniquity, and my sin is ever before me. Against Thee, Thee only have I sinned, and done evil in Thy sight, that Thou mayest be found just when Thou speakest, and victorious when Thou art judged. For behold, I was conceived in iniquity, and in sin my mother bore me. For behold, Thou hast loved truth; Thou hast made known to me the hidden and secret things of Thy wisdom. Thou shalt sprinkle me with hyssop, and I shall be made clean; Thou shalt wash me, and I shall be whiter than snow. Make me to hear joy and gladness; that the humbled bones may rejoice. Turn Thy face away from my sins, and blot out all mine iniquities.

Create in me a clean heart, O God, and renew a steadfast spirit within me. Cast me not away from Thy presence, and take not Thy Holy Spirit from me. Restore to me the joy of Thy salvation, and establish me with Thy governing Spirit. I shall teach transgressors Thy ways, and the ungodly shall turn back to Thee. Deliver me from blood guiltiness, O God, the God of my salvation; my tongue shall joyfully declare Thy righteousness. Lord, open my lips, and my mouth shall declare Thy praise. For if Thou hadst desired sacrifice, I would give it; Thou dost not delight in burnt offerings. A sacrifice to God is a broken spirit; God shall not despise a broken and a humbled heart. Do good, O Lord, in Thy good pleasure to Zion, and let the walls of Jerusalem be builded. Then Thou shalt be pleased with a sacrifice of righteousness, with oblation and whole burned offerings. Then shall they offer bulls on Thine altar.

Psalm 69

O God, be attentive to help me; Lord, make haste to help me. Let them be ashamed and confounded who seek after my life. Let them be turned back and be ashamed who desire evil against me. Let them be turned back because of their shame who say to me: "Well done. Well done." Let all those who seek Thee rejoice and be glad in Thee, O God, and let those who love Thy salvation say continually: "Let the Lord be magnified." But as for me, I am poor and needy; O God help me. Thou art my help and my deliverer; Lord; do not delay.

Psalm 142

Lord, hear my prayer; in Thy truth give ear to my supplications; in Thy righteousness hear me. Enter not into judgement with Thy servant, for no one living is justified in Thy sight. For the enemy has pursued my soul; he has crushed my life to the ground. He has made me to dwell in darkness, like those that have long been dead, and my spirit within me is overwhelmed; my heart within me is distressed. I remembered the days of old, I meditated on all Thy works, I pondered on the creations of Thine hands. I stretched forth my hands to Thee; my soul longs for Thee like a thirsty land. Lord, hear me quickly; my spirit fails. Turn not Thy face away from me, lest I be like those who go down into the pit. Let me hear Thy mercy in the morning; for in Thee have I put my trust. Lord, teach me to know the way wherein I should walk; for I lift up my soul to Thee. Rescue me, Lord, from mine enemies, to Thee have I fled for refuge. Teach me to do Thy will, for Thou art my God. Thy good Spirit shall lead me on a level path. Lord, for Thy names sake Thou shalt preserve my life. In Thy righteousness Thou shalt bring my soul out of trouble, and in Thy mercy Thou shalt utterly destroy my enemies. And Thou shalt destroy all those who afflict my soul, for I am Thy servant.

Lesser Doxology

Glory to God, Who has shown us the Light. Glory to God in the highest, and on earth, peace, good will toward men. We praise Thee. We bless Thee. We worship Thee. We glorify Thee and give thanks to Thee for Thy great glory. O Lord God, Heavenly King, God the Father Almighty. O Lord, the Only Begotten Son, Jesus Christ, and the Holy Spirit. \

O Lord God, Lamb of God, Son of the Father, Who takes away the sins of the world, have mercy on us. Thou, Who takes away the sins of the world, receive our prayer. Thou, Who sittest at the right hand of God the Father, have mercy on us. /

For Thou alone art holy, and Thou alone art Lord. Thou alone, O Lord Jesus Christ, are most high in the glory of God the Father. Amen. I shall give thanks to Thee every day and praise Thy Name forever and ever. Lord, Thou hast been our refuge from generation to generation. I said, *"Lord, have mercy on me. Heal my soul, for I have sinned against Thee."* \

Lord, I flee to Thee. Teach me to do Thy will, for Thou art my God. For with Thee is the fountain of Life, and in Thy light we shall see light. Continue Thy loving kindness to those who know Thee. Vouchsafe, O Lord, to keep us this day without sin. Blessed art Thou, O Lord, the God of our fathers, and praised and glorified is Thy Name forever. Amen. Let Thy mercy be upon us, O Lord, even as we have set our hope on Thee.

Blessed art Thou, O Master; teach me Thy statutes.

Blessed art Thou, O Lord; enlighten me with Thy commandments.

Blessed art Thou, O Holy One; make me to understand Thy precepts.

Thy mercy endures forever, O Lord. Do not despise the works of Thine hands. To Thee belongs worship, to Thee belongs praise, to Thee belongs glory: to the Father and to the Son and to the Holy Spirit, both now and forever and unto the ages of ages. Amen. \

The Symbol Of Faith

I believe in one God, Father, Almighty, Maker of heaven and earth, and of all things visible and invisible.

And in one Lord Jesus Christ, the only begotten Son of God, begotten from the Father before all ages; Light from Light, true God from true God; begotten not made; consubstantial with the Father, through Him all things were made. For our sake and for our salvation He came down from Heaven, and was incarnate from the Holy Spirit and the Virgin Mary and became man. He was crucified for us under Pontius Pilate, and suffered and was buried. He rose again on the third day in accordance with the Scriptures, and ascended into Heaven, and is seated at the right hand of the Father. He is coming again in glory to judge the living and the dead. And His kingdom shall have no end.

And in the Holy Spirit, the Lord, the Giver of life; Who proceeds from the Father; Who together with Father and Son is worshipped and glorified; Who spoke through the prophets. In One, Holy, Catholic, and Apostolic Church. I confess one baptism for the forgiveness of sins. I await the resurrection of the dead, And the life of the age to come. Amen.

Reader: [*St Gabriel:* It is truly right to call thee blessed, who gavest birth to God, ever-blessed and God-obedient the Mother of our God.] Greater in honour than the Cherubim and beyond compare more glorious than the Seraphim; without corruption thou gavest birth to God the Word, truly the Mother of God, we magnify thee.

[End Small Compline part 1]

[Fridays 1, 2, 3, 4]

The Canon Of The Akathist
By Saint Joseph The Hymnographer

Ode One

Eirmoз

Tone 4   Festive, joyous and expressing deep piety.   *C, D, Eb, F, G, A, Bb, C.*

Reader: I shall open my mouth and it shall be filled with the Spirit, and I shall speak forth to the Queen and Mother. I shall be seen joyfully singing her praises, and I shall delight to sing of her wonders.

Refrain: *Most Holy Theotokos, save us.*

Troparia

When the great Archangel saw thee, O Immaculate One, thou living book of Christ, sealed by the Spirit, he cried unto thee: Rejoice, vessel of gladness, through whom the curse of our first mother is loosed.

Refrain: *Most Holy Theotokos, save us.*

Rejoice, virgin bride of God, thou uplifter of Adam and death knell of Hades;

Rejoice, O all blameless one, thou palace of the only King;

Rejoice, thou fiery throne of the Almighty.

Glory be to the Father, and to the Son, and to the Holy Spirit.

Rejoice, thou from whom alone didst blossom the Unwithering Rose;

Rejoice, thou who didst bear the fragrant Apple;

Rejoice, immaculate maiden, fragrance of the King of All and salvation of the world.

Both now and forever, and unto the ages of ages. Amen.

Rejoice, thou treasure house of purity, through which we rose up from our fall;

Rejoice, Lady, sweet scented lily perfuming the faithful, thou fragrant incense and most precious myrrh.

Ode Three

Eirmos

Reader: As a living and copious fountain, O Theotokos, do thou strengthen those who hymn thy praises, and are joined together in a spiritual company for thy service; and in thy divine glory make them worthy of crowns of glory.

Refrain: *Most Holy Theotokos, save us.*

Troparia

As a clear and untilled field, thou didst make the Divine Ear of Grain to sprout; Rejoice, thou living table that held the Bread of Life; Rejoice, thou unfailing fountain of Living Water.

Refrain: *Most Holy Theotokos, save us.*

Rejoice, O mystic heifer that didst bear the Spotless Calf;

Rejoice, ewe lamb who didst conceive the Lamb of God that taketh away the sins of the whole world;

Rejoice, thou Fervent Intercessor.

Glory be to the Father, and to the Son, and to the Holy Spirit.

Rejoice, O radiant dawn, which alone dost bear Christ the Sun, the dwelling place of Light;

Rejoice, thou who didst dispel the darkness and reduce to naught the demons of gloom.

Both now and forever, and unto the ages of ages. Amen.

Rejoice, thou only gate, through which the Word alone didst pass;

Rejoice, Lady, for by thy birth giving the bars and gates of Hades were burst asunder;

Rejoice, thou most worthy of all praise, divine entry for the saved.

Ode Four

Eirmos

Reader: He Who sits in clouds of glory upon the throne of the Godhead, Jesus the Most High God, came with mighty hand and saved those who cried out unto Him: Glory to Thy Power, O Christ.

Refrain: *Most Holy Theotokos, save us.*

Troparia

In hymns of faith, O all praised one, we cry out unto thee: Rejoice, thou mountain fertile with the fullness of the Spirit; Rejoice, thou lamp of light and vase of manna, to the senses of the reverent most sweet.

Refrain: *Most Holy Theotokos, save us.*

Rejoice, immaculate Lady, mercy seat of the world;

Rejoice, thou ladder which raised all from earth to grace;

Rejoice, thou bridge which truly leads from death to life all who sing thy praises.

Refrain: *Most Holy Theotokos, save us.*

Rejoice, O Immaculate One, higher than the heavens, thou who didst without pain carry within thee the Foundation of the Earth.

Rejoice, O seashell that didst dip in thy blood the divine purple for the King of the Powers of Heaven.

Glory be to the Father, and to the Son, and to the Holy Spirit.

Rejoice, Lady, who didst truly bear the Lawgiver that freely blotted out the transgressions of all; O Unimaginable Depth, O Height Ineffable, O Maiden Unwedded, through whom we are become divine.

Both now and forever, and unto the ages of ages. Amen.

With hymns we praise thee, O thou who didst weave for the world a crown not woven by hands, and we cry aloud: Rejoice, O Virgin, fortress of all mankind, and rampart, and strength, and refuge divine.

Ode Five

Eirmos

Reader: All creation was amazed at thy divine glory, for thou, O Unwedded Virgin, didst hold within thee the God of All, and didst bear the Eternal Son, Who rewards with salvation all who hymn thy praises.

Refrain: *Most Holy Theotokos, save us.*

Rejoice, O all blameless one, who didst bear the Way of Life and save the world from the deluge of sin;
Rejoice, bride of God, thou of great report and mighty fame;
Rejoice, thou dwelling place of the Master of Creation.

Refrain: *Most Holy Theotokos, save us.*

Rejoice, O Immaculate One, stronghold and fortress of mankind, and place of hallowed glory, death knell of Hades, bridal chamber full of light;
Rejoice, joy of the angels;
Rejoice, help of those who faithfully pray unto thee.

Refrain: *Most Holy Theotokos, save us.*

Rejoice, O Lady, fiery chariot of the Word; living paradise having the Lord, the Tree of Life, in thy midst; His sweetness gives to those who partake in faith, even though they be subject to corruption.

Glory be to the Father, and to the Son, and to the Holy Spirit.

Strengthened by thy might, faithfully we cry unto thee: Rejoice, city of the King of All, great in glory and repute, of whom all these were clearly spoken; O mount unhewn and depth beyond all measure.

Both now and forever, and unto the ages of ages. Amen.

Thou spacious tabernacle of the Word, Rejoice. O Immaculate One, Thou seashell which didst proffer the Divine Pearl, Rejoice. O All wondrous One, Thou art the reconciliation to God, O Theotokos, of all who forever bless thee.

Ode Six

Eirmos

Reader: As we, the Godly minded, celebrate this sacred and all honourable feast of the Mother of God; come, let us clap our hands together and glorify the God Whom she bore.

Refrain: *Most Holy Theotokos, save us.*

Troparia

Immaculate bridal chamber of the Word, and aid to the sanctification of us all, Rejoice. O All pure Maiden, whom the Prophets did proclaim; Rejoice, thou ornament of the Apostles.

Refrain: *Most Holy Theotokos, save us.*

From thee the dew distilled that quenched the flame of polytheism, wherefore we cry out unto thee, O Virgin: Rejoice, O Dewy Fleece which Gideon did foresee.

Glory be to the Father, and to the Son, and to the Holy Spirit.

Behold, we cry out unto thee: Rejoice. Be thou our haven and our port when we voyage on the sea of tribulations and through the snares of the adversary.

Both now and forever, and unto the ages of ages. Amen.

O Cause of Joy, favour us with reason to cry out unto thee: Rejoice, thou bush that burns yet unconsumed, thou light filled cloud which unceasingly shelters the faithful.

Ode Seven

Eirmos

Reader: The Godly minded children worshipped not the creature rather than the Creator, but trampling upon the threat of fire in manly fashion, they rejoiced and sang: O All Praised Lord and God of our Fathers, blessed art Thou.

Refrain: *Most Holy Theotokos, save us.*

Troparia

To thee we sing a hymn and cry: Rejoice. Chariot of the mystic sun, true vine that did produce the ripe cluster of grapes, dripping wine to gladden the souls of those who with faith do glorify thee.

Refrain: *Most Holy Theotokos, save us.*

Rejoice, thou Bride of God, who didst bear the Healer of Mankind; the mystic staff from which blossomed the Unfading Flower; Rejoice, O Sovereign Lady, through whom we are filled with joy, and inherit life.

Refrain: *Most Holy Theotokos, save us.*

The tongue of eloquence has not power to sing thy praises, O Sovereign Lady, for thou wast exalted above the Seraphim when thou didst bear Christ the King; do thou now implore Him to deliver from all harm those who faithfully reverence thee.

Glory be to the Father, and to the Son, and to the Holy Spirit.

The ends of the earth do praise and bless thee, and cry out unto thee: Rejoice, pure Maiden, scroll on which the finger of God did inscribe His Word; do thou now implore Him, O Theotokos, to write down thy servants in the Book of Life.

Both now and forever, and unto the ages of ages. Amen.

We thy servants bend the knee of our hearts and implore thee, O Pure Maiden: incline thine ear and save us, who are engulfed in tribulations; and guard thy city, O Theotokos, from every assault of her enemies.

Ode Eight

Eirmos

Reader: The three holy children in the furnace the Child of the Theotokos saved; then was the type, now is its fulfilment, and the whole world gathers to sing: All you works, praise the Lord, and magnify Him unto all ages.

Refrain: *Most Holy Theotokos, save us.*

Troparia

Thou didst receive the Word within thee, O Pure Maiden, and didst bear Him Who beareth all things; thou didst nourish Him with milk, Who by His nod dost sustain all the universe; to Him we sing: All you works, praise the Lord, and magnify Him unto all ages.

Refrain: *Most Holy Theotokos, save us.*

Moses perceived in the burning bush the great mystery of thy birth giving, O Chaste and Holy Virgin; the children prefigured this most clearly when they stood in the midst of the flame and were unburned; wherefore we praise thee unto all ages.

Refrain: *Most Holy Theotokos, save us.*

We, who of old were made naked by deceit, have been clothed in a garment of incorruption by thy conception; and we who were sitting in the darkness of transgressions have come to see the light, O Maiden who art the dwelling place of Light: wherefore we praise thee unto all ages.

Glory be to the Father, and to the Son, and to the Holy Spirit.

Through thee the dead are made to live, for thou didst bear the Life Essential; those who before were speechless now find useful eloquence, lepers are cleansed, diseases are driven away, and the multitude of aerial spirits are vanquished, O Virgin, salvation of mortals.

Both now and forever, and unto the ages of ages. Amen.

We Rejoice in thee, O all blessed one, who didst bring forth Salvation for the world, through which we have been raised from earth to heights above; O Pure Maiden, thou art shelter and stronghold, bulwark and fortress of all who sing: All you works, praise the Lord, and magnify Him unto all ages.

Ode Nine

Eirmos

Reader: Let all earth born mortals rejoice in spirit, bearing their lamps, and let the nature of bodiless minds celebrate with honour the holy festival of the Mother of God, and cry out: Rejoice, all blessed, pure and ever virgin Theotokos.

Refrain: *Most Holy Theotokos, save us.*

Troparia

Through thee, O Maiden, have we faithful become partakers of joy, so that we may further cry out unto thee: Rejoice. Do thou deliver us from perpetual temptation, from barbaric attack, and from all the multitude of evils which we mortals suffer for the number of our sins.

Refrain: *Most Holy Theotokos, save us.*

Thou hast appeared to enlighten us and be our confirmation, wherefore we cry aloud to thee:
Rejoice, O unsetting star which didst introduce into the world the mighty Sun;
Rejoice, pure maiden, who didst open up fast closed Eden;
Rejoice, fiery pillar, which doth lead mans nature to the life above.

Refrain: *Most Holy Theotokos, save us.*

Let us stand with reverence in the house of our God, and let us cry aloud:
Rejoice, mistress of the world;
Rejoice, Mary, Lady of us all;
Rejoice, thou who alone art blameless among women, and beautiful;
Rejoice, O Vessel, which didst receive into thyself the myrrh which was never before poured out.

Glory be to the Father, and to the Son, and to the Holy Spirit.

Rejoice, O Ever Virgin, thou Dove who didst bring forth Him Who is merciful.

Rejoice, boast of all the righteous saints and crown of those who strive.

Rejoice, Ornament Divine of all the just, and of us the faithful, our salvation as well.

Both now and forever, and unto the ages of ages. Amen.

Spare, O God, Thine inheritance, and overlook now all our sins. For as intercessor in Thy sight, O Christ, there stands before Thee she that on earth conceived Thee without seed, when in Thy Great Mercy Thou hast willed to be shaped in a form that was not Thine own.

[Priest dons phelonion, exits Holy Doors and stands before the icon of the Theotokos in the centre of the solea. The censer is kept near at hand. Whilst:]

Kontakion For The Annunciation

Tone 8   *Humility, tranquillity, repose, suffering, pleading.*   *C, D, Eb, F, G, A, Bb, C.*

To Thee, the Champion Leader, we Thy servants dedicate a feast of victory and of thanksgiving as ones rescued out of sufferings, O Theotokos: but as Thou art one with might, which is invincible, from all dangers that can be, do Thou deliver us, that we may cry to Thee: Rejoice, Thou Bride Unwedded.

[End of Friday 1, 2, 3, 4]

[Friday 1 below.

Friday 2 go to page 483

Friday 3 go to page 485

Friday 4 go to page 487].

FIRST STASIS: FIRST FRIDAY OF GREAT LENT
1. OIKOS

Priest: An angel of supreme rank was sent from heaven to say "Rejoice." unto the Theotokos. **(x3)**

And beholding Thee, O Lord, taking bodily form, he stood rapt in wonder, and with bodiless voice cried aloud to her in this wise:

- Rejoice, thou, through whom joy shall shine forth;
- Rejoice, thou, through whom the curse shall be destroyed.
- Rejoice, thou restoration of fallen Adam;
- Rejoice, thou, redemption of the tears of Eve.
- Rejoice, thou height untrodden by human minds;

- Rejoice, thou depth hard to scan, even for angels' eyes.
- Rejoice, thou that art a kingly throne;
- Rejoice, thou that holdest the Upholder of all.
- Rejoice, thou star that showed the Sun;
- Rejoice, womb of the Divine Incarnation.
- Rejoice, thou through whom Creation is renewed;
- Rejoice, thou through whom the Creator becomes a babe.
- Rejoice, O Bride without bridegroom.

[Priest censes the icon nine times.]

People: *Rejoice, O Bride without bridegroom.*

2. KONTAKION

Priest: Boldly spake the holy maiden unto Gabriel, conscious of her chastity: To my soul thy strange message seems hard to grasp; how speakest thou of a virgin conception, crying aloud: Halleluiah.

[Priest censes the icon nine times.]

People: *Halleluiah.*

3. OIKOS

Priest: Craving to know knowledge unknowable, the Virgin cried out unto him who ministered unto her: From a maiden body, how may a Son be born; tell thou me. To her he spake in fear, and thus only cried aloud:
- Rejoice, thou initiate of the ineffable counsel;
- Rejoice, O faith of those who pray in silence.
- Rejoice, thou beginning of the miracles of Christ;
- Rejoice, thou crown of His decrees.
- Rejoice, heavenly ladder, by which God came down;
- Rejoice, Bridge that leadest us from earth to Heaven.
- Rejoice, thou much talked of wonder of angels;
- Rejoice, thou much lamented damager of demons.
- Rejoice, thou who ineffably didst bear the Light;
- Rejoice, thou who told none how it was done.
- Rejoice, thou, who over-soarest the knowledge of the wise;
- Rejoice, thou who enlightenest the minds of the faithful.
- Rejoice, O Bride without bridegroom.

[Priest censes the icon nine times.]

People: *Rejoice, O Bride without bridegroom.*

4. KONTAKION

Priest: Divine power from on high then overshadowed the maiden, that she might conceive, and showed forth her fruitful womb as a fertile field to all who desire to reap salvation, as they sing: Halleluiah.

[Priest censes the icon nine times.]

People: Halleluiah.

5. OIKOS

Priest: Enshrining God in her womb, the Virgin hastened unto Elizabeth; whose unborn babe at once perceived her Salutation, and rejoiced; and with stirrings as if with voices cried out to the Theotokos:

- Rejoice, Branch of unfading growth;
- Rejoice, Possessor of untouched fruit.
- Rejoice, thou who labourest for Him Whose labour is love;
- Rejoice, thou who tendest Him Who tendeth our life.
- Rejoice, Field with compassions rich harvest;
- Rejoice, Table with abundance of mercies spread.
- Rejoice, thou who revivest the green meadows of joy;
- Rejoice, thou who makest ready a safe haven for souls.
- Rejoice, thou accepted incense offering of intercessions;
- Rejoice, thou oblation of all the world.
- Rejoice, Good will of God towards men;
- Rejoice, Access of mortals to God.
- Rejoice, O Bride without bridegroom.

[Priest censes the icon nine times.]

People: Rejoice, O Bride without bridegroom.

6. KONTAKION

Priest: Floods of doubtful thoughts troubled the wise Joseph within, and he feared a furtive love as he beheld thee unwed, O Blameless One; but when he learned that thy conception was of the Holy Spirit, he said: Halleluiah.

[Priest censes the icon nine times.]

People: Halleluiah.

[End first stasis. Go to Page 489 and sing the Kontakion "To Thee the Champion Leader."]

7. OIKOS

Priest: Gloriously the Angels hymned the incarnate Presence of Christ, and the shepherds heard; and running as to a Shepherd, they beheld Him as an unspotted Lamb, being nurtured at Marys breast, and her they hymned and said:

- Rejoice, Mother of the Lamb and of the Shepherd;
- Rejoice, fold of reason endowed sheep.
- Rejoice, bulwark against foes invisible;
- Rejoice, Opener of the Gates of Paradise.
- Rejoice, for that which all the Heavens and earth Rejoice;
- Rejoice, for all the earth doth dance its joy together with the Heavens.
- Rejoice, never silent Voice of the Apostles;
- Rejoice, invincible courage of those who strive.
- Rejoice, thou firm foundation of the faith;
- Rejoice, thou shining token of grace.
- Rejoice, thou through whom Hades was laid bare;
- Rejoice, thou through whom we are clothed with glory.
- Rejoice, O Bride without bridegroom.

[Priest censes the icon nine times.]

People: Rejoice, O Bride without bridegroom.

8. KONTAKION

Priest: High in the heavens the Magi beheld the Godward pointing star, and they followed its rays; using it as a beacon, they sought the mighty King, and as they approached the Unapproachable, they rejoiced and cried out unto Him: Halleluiah.

[Priest censes the icon nine times.]

People: Halleluiah.

9. OIKOS

Priest: In the Virgins hand the sons of the Chaldees saw Him Whose hand had made man; and knowing Him as Master, even though He had taken on Himself the form of a servant, they hastened with their gifts to worship, and cried out to her who is blessed:

Rejoice, Mother of the unsetting Star;

Rejoice, terror of the mystic Day.

Rejoice, thou who quenchest the fiery furnace of error;

Rejoice, thou who enlightenest the initiates of the Trinity.

Rejoice, thou who cast out the inhuman tyrant of old;

Rejoice, thou who showest forth Christ the Lord Who loveth mankind.

Rejoice, thou who redeemest from barbarous superstitions;

Rejoice, thou who rescuest us from works unclean.

Rejoice, thou who causest the worship of fire to cease;

Rejoice, thou who allayest the flame of suffering.

Rejoice, guide of the wisdom of the faithful;

Rejoice, joy of all generations.

Rejoice, O Bride without bridegroom.

[Priest censes the icon nine times.]

People: *Rejoice, O Bride without bridegroom.*

10. KONTAKION

Priest: Kings messengers did the Magi become, when they returned to Babylon; they fulfilled Thy bidding and preached Thee to all as the Christ, and they left Herod as a trifler who knew not how to sing: Halleluiah.

[Priest censes the icon nine times.]

People: *Halleluiah.*

11. OIKOS

Priest: Lighting in Egypt the lamp of truth, Thou didst cast out the darkness of untruth; for their idols, O Saviour, could not bear Thy strength, and fell down; and those of them who were set free cried out to the Theotokos:

- Rejoice, thou uplifter of mankind;
- Rejoice, thou downfall of demons.
- Rejoice, thou who tramplest upon the wanderings of error;
- Rejoice, thou who refutest the frauds of idols.
- Rejoice, thou sea which drowned the mystic Pharaoh;
- Rejoice, Rock which refreshed those athirst for Life.
- Rejoice, fiery Pillar, guiding those in darkness;
- Rejoice, Shelter of the world, broader than a cloud.
- Rejoice, thou Sustenance in place of manna;
- Rejoice, minister of holy joy.
- Rejoice, thou land of promise;
- Rejoice, thou from whom flow honey and milk.
- Rejoice, O Bride without bridegroom.

[Priest censes the icon nine times.]

People: *Rejoice, O Bride without bridegroom.*

12. KONTAKION

Priest: Most near his transit from this deceitful world was Simeon when Thou wast presented to him as a newborn babe, but Thou wast discerned by him as perfect God; wherefore overcome by Thine ineffable wisdom he cried out: Halleluiah.

[Priest censes the icon nine times.]

People: Halleluiah.

[End second stasis. Go to Page 489 and sing the Kontakion "To Thee the Champion Leader."]

THIRD STASIS: THIRD FRIDAY OF GREAT LENT

13. OIKOS

Priest: New was the Creation which the Creator showed to us His creatures, when He appeared blossoming from a virgin womb; and He preserved her just as she was, in purity, so that we, beholding this marvel, might cry aloud and sing:

- Rejoice, Flower of incorruption;
- Rejoice, Crown of chastity.
- Rejoice, thou who flashest out the type of the Resurrection;
- Rejoice, thou who mirrorest the life of the Angels.
- Rejoice, Tree of goodly fruit, from which the faithful are nourished;
- Rejoice, goodly shade tree, beneath which many are sheltered.
- Rejoice, thou who bearest the Guide of those who stray abroad;
- Rejoice, thou who engenderest the Redeemer of captives.
- Rejoice, thou intercession before the Righteous Judge;
- Rejoice, thou forgiveness for many who stumble.
- Rejoice, Robe of the naked of liberty;
- Rejoice, selfless love that vanquishest all mean desires.
- Rejoice, O Bride without bridegroom.

[Priest censes the icon nine times.]

People: *Rejoice, O Bride without bridegroom.*

14. KONTAKION

Priest: Our minds are brought over into heaven when we behold this strange birth giving, so let us be estranged from the world; for this cause indeed did the most high God appear on earth as humble man, that He might raise on high those who cry out unto Him: Halleluiah.

[Priest censes the icon nine times.]

People: Halleluiah.

15. OIKOS

Priest: Present and complete with those below, and in no wise absent from those above was the Uncircumscribed Word; for there took place indeed a divine Descent and not a simple change of place; and the Birth was from a God chosen Virgin, who heard such words as these:

- Rejoice, Resting place of the uncontained God;
- Rejoice, Door of hallowed Mystery.
- Rejoice, doubtful Rumour of the faithless;
- Rejoice, undoubted Boast of the faithful.
- Rejoice, all holy Chariot of Him Who rideth upon the Cherubim;
- Rejoice, all excellent Chair of Him Who sitteth upon the Seraphim.
- Rejoice, thou who makest things that differ to agree;
- Rejoice, thou who joinest together virginity and motherhood.
- Rejoice, thou whom through transgression is annulled;
- Rejoice, thou whom through Paradise was opened.
- Rejoice, Key of the Kingdom of Christ;
- Rejoice, Hope of eternal good things.
- Rejoice, O Bride without bridegroom.

[Priest censes the icon nine times.]

People: *Rejoice, O Bride without bridegroom.*

16. KONTAKION

Priest: Choruses of Angels were amazed at Thy great work of Incarnation; for they saw the inaccessible God as man accessible to all, dwelling among us and hearing from us all: Halleluiah.

[Priest censes the icon nine times.]

People: *Halleluiah.*

17. OIKOS

Priest: Ready voiced orators we see become voiceless as fish before thee, O Theotokos, and unable to say how thou couldst give birth and yet remain virgin; but we, marvelling at this Mystery, cry out in faith:

- Rejoice, Vessel of the Wisdom of God;
- Rejoice, Treasury of His foreknowledge.
- Rejoice, thou who showest the learned to be fools;
- Rejoice, thou who provest logicians illogical.
- Rejoice, for the subtle disputants are made fools;
- Rejoice, for the makers of myths are made to fade away.
- Rejoice, thou who didst disperse the word webs of the Athenians;
- Rejoice, thou who didst fill the nets of the fishermen.
- Rejoice, thou who drawest us up from the depths of ignorance;
- Rejoice, thou who enlightenest many with knowledge.
- Rejoice, Raft for those who wish to be saved;

- Rejoice, haven for those who swim in the sea of life.
- Rejoice, O Bride without bridegroom.

[Priest censes the icon nine times.]

People: *Rejoice, O Bride without bridegroom.*

18. KONTAKION

Priest: Salvation for the world the Architect of all desired, and to this end by His own will He came; as God from everlasting He is our shepherd, yet as man He appeared among us for our sake, and although called like by like, still as God He hears: Halleluiah.

[Priest censes the icon nine times.]

People: *Halleluiah.*

[End third stasis. Go to Page 489 and sing the Kontakion "To Thee the Champion Leader."]

FOURTH STASIS: FOURTH FRIDAY OF GREAT LENT

19. OIKOS

Priest: Thou, O Virgin Theotokos, art a protecting wall to virgins and to all who run to thee; for the Maker of Heaven and earth prepared thee, O Pure Maiden, and dwelt in thy womb, and taught all to sing out unto thee:

- Rejoice, pillar of virginity;
- Rejoice, gate of salvation.
- Rejoice, source of spiritual reformation;
- Rejoice, leader of divine goodness.
- Rejoice, for thou didst regenerate those conceived in sin;
- Rejoice, for thou didst remind those who were mindless.
- Rejoice, thou who didst annul the corruption of hearts;
- Rejoice, thou who didst bear the Sower of Chastity.
- Rejoice, bridal chamber of a virgin marriage;
- Rejoice, thou who joinest the faithful to the Lord.
- Rejoice, fair nursing mother of virgins;
- Rejoice, bridesmaid of holy souls.
- Rejoice, O Bride without bridegroom.

[Priest censes the icon nine times.]

People: *Rejoice, O Bride without bridegroom.*

20. KONTAKION

Priest: Unworthy is every hymn that seeks to encompass the multitude of Thy many mercies; for if we should offer to Thee hymns of praise as numberless as the sands, O Holy King, we should still have done nothing worthy of that which Thou hast given to us who cry out unto Thee: Halleluiah.

[Priest censes the icon nine times.]

People: Halleluiah.

21. OIKOS

Priest: Verily we behold the holy Virgin as a light giving beacon, shining for those in darkness: for by kindling the supernal Light, she guides us all to divine knowledge; illumining our minds with radiance, she is honoured by this our cry:

- Rejoice, ray of the living Sun; Rejoice, flash of unfading splendour.
- Rejoice, lightning flash, shining upon our souls;
- Rejoice, thou who dost as thunder strike down our enemies.
- Rejoice, for thou didst cause the many starred light to dawn;
- Rejoice, for thou didst cause the richly flowing river to gush forth.
- Rejoice, thou who didst from life describe the type of the baptismal font;
- Rejoice, thou who didst take away the stain of sin.
- Rejoice, laver that dost purify conscience; Rejoice, mixing bowl for the mingling of joy.
- Rejoice, fragrance of the sweetness of Christ; Rejoice, life of mystic festival.
- Rejoice, O Bride without bridegroom.

[Priest censes the icon nine times.]

People: Rejoice, O Bride without bridegroom.

22. KONTAKION

Priest: When He Who pays the ancient debts of all men was minded to give grace, He came of His own will to dwell among those who had departed from His grace; and when He tore asunder the written charge against them. He heard from all in this wise: Halleluiah.

[Priest censes the icon nine times.]

People: Halleluiah.

23. OIKOS

Priest: Yet while we sing to Him Whom thou didst bear, we all hymn thee, O Theotokos, as a living temple; for the Lord, Who holds all things in His hand, by dwelling within thee, hallowed and glorified thee, and taught all to cry out unto thee:

- Rejoice, tabernacle of God, and of the Word;
- Rejoice, holiest of all the holy ones.
- Rejoice, ark made golden by the Spirit;
- Rejoice, inexhaustible treasury of life.
- Rejoice, precious diadem of pious rulers;
- Rejoice, venerable boast of reverent priests.
- Rejoice, steady tower of the Church;
- Rejoice, impregnable wall of the realm.
- Rejoice, thou through whom trophies are set up;

- Rejoice, thou through whom enemies are cast down.
- Rejoice, healing of my body;
- Rejoice, salvation of my soul.
- Rejoice, O Bride without bridegroom.

[Priest censes the icon nine times.]

People: *Rejoice, O Bride without bridegroom.*

24. KONTAKION

Priest: Zealously art thou praised, O Mother who didst bear the most holy Word of all the Saints. **(x3)**
And when thou receivest this present offering, deliver us from every calamity, and deliver from all wrath to come those who cry out unto thee: Halleluiah.

[Priest censes the icon nine times.]

People: *Halleluiah.*

[RESUME ALL HERE]

Small Compline Resumes

Kontakion For The Annunciation

Tone 8   *Humility, tranquillity, repose, suffering, pleading.*   *C, D, Eb, F, G, A, Bb, C.*

To Thee, the Champion Leader, we Thy servants dedicate a feast of victory and of thanksgiving as ones rescued out of sufferings, O Theotokos: but as Thou art one with might, which is invincible, from all dangers that can be, do Thou deliver us, that we may cry to Thee: Rejoice, Thou Bride Unwedded.

[Priest stands before the Holy Doors, facing east.]

THE TRISAGION PRAYERS

Reader: Holy God, Holy Mighty, Holy Immortal, have mercy on us. **(x3)**

Glory be to the Father and to the Son and to the Holy Spirit;
Both now and forever, and unto the ages of ages. Amen.

O Most Holy Trinity, have mercy on us.

O Lord, cleanse us from our sins.

O Master, pardon our iniquities.

O Holy One, visit and heal our infirmities, for Thy names sake.

Lord have mercy. **(x3)**

Glory be to the Father and to the Son and to the Holy Spirit;

Both now and forever, and unto the ages of ages. Amen.

People: *Our Father, who art in heaven, hallowed be Thy name. Thy Kingdom come. Thy will be done, on earth as it is in heaven. Give us this day our daily bread; and forgive us our trespasses, as we forgive those who trespass against us; and lead us not into temptation, but deliver us from the evil one.*

Priest: For Thine is the kingdom, and the power, and the glory: of the Father, and of the Son, and of the Holy Spirit; now and ever, and unto ages of ages.

People: Amen.

On the First Friday of Great Lent

[Plain Reading]

Kontakion Of St Theodore The Tyro Soldier

Thou hast carried as a shield the Faith of Christ within thy heart, and trampled underfoot the power of the enemy, O greatly suffering martyr Theodore; thou hast received a heavenly and eternal crown, for thou wast undefeated in the battle.

[End of First Friday.]

On the Second, Third and Fourth Fridays of Great Lent

[Plain Reading]

Kontakion Of The Martyrs

Reader: Unto Thee, O Lord, the Author of creation, the universe doth offer the God bearing Martyrs as the first fruits of nature. By whose prayers, through the Theotokos, do thou preserve in peace profound Thy Church, O most merciful One.

[End of Second, Third, Fourth Friday.]

People: *Lord, have mercy.* **(x40)**

The Prayer Of The Hours

Reader: At all times and in every hour, Thou art worshipped and glorified in heaven and on earth, Christ our God. Long in patience, great in mercy and compassion, Thou lovest the righteous and showest mercy to sinners. Thou callest all to salvation through the promise of good things to come. Lord, receive our prayers at the present time. Direct our lives according to Thy commandments. Sanctify our souls. Purify our bodies. Set our minds aright. Cleanse our thoughts, and deliver us from all sorrow, evil and distress. Surround us with Thy holy angels, that, guarded and guided by their host, we may arrive at the unity of the faith and the understanding of Thine ineffable glory. For Thou art blessed unto the ages of ages. Amen.

Lord, have mercy. **(x3)**

Glory be to the Father and to the Son and to the Holy Spirit;
Both now and forever, and unto the ages of ages. Amen.

Greater in honour than the Cherubim and beyond compare more glorious than the Seraphim; without corruption thou gavest birth to God the Word, truly the Theotokos, we magnify thee.

People: *Holy Father, bless.*

Priest: May God be merciful unto us and bless us, and cause His face to shine upon us, and be merciful unto us.

People: *Amen.*

Lord, have mercy. **(x12)**

Reader: Most holy Theotokos, save us.

Supplicatory Prayer To The Most Holy Theotokos

Paul, The Monk Of The Monastery Of Evergetis.

Priest or Reader: Spotless, undefiled, immaculate, unstained, pure Virgin, Lady and Bride of God, by thy wondrous conceiving thou united God the Word with human beings and joined the fallen nature of our race to heavenly things. Thou art the only hope of the hopeless, and the help of those oppressed. Thou art the ready protection of those who flee to thee, and the refuge of all Christians. Do not spurn me an accused sinner, though I have made myself completely useless by my shameful thoughts, words and deeds and through indolence have become a slave to the pleasures of life. But as the Mother of God who loves all people, mercifully have compassion upon me a sinner and a prodigal and receive my prayer though it be offered to thee by unclean lips. Entreat thy Son and our Lord and Master, using thy boldness as a mother, that he may open to me the loving mercy of his goodness, overlook my numberless transgressions, turn me to repentance, and make me an acceptable doer of His commandments. Always be near me, for thou art merciful, compassionate and loving. Be mine ardent help and protection in this present life, defending me from the assaults of adversaries and lead me to salvation. At the hour of my death, care for my miserable soul, and drive the dark visions of evil spirits from it. On the awesome day of judgement, save me from eternal punishment and make me an inheritor of the ineffable glory of thy Son, our God. May this be my lot, my Lady, all Holy Theotokos, through thine intercession and protection, by the grace and love of thine only begotten Son, our Lord and God and Saviour, Jesus Christ, to whom belong all glory, honour and worship, together with his eternal Father, and all holy, righteous, and life creating Spirit, both now and forever, and unto the ages of ages. Amen.

[Priest enters the sanctuary through the south door to prepare for the Gospel lection, whilst:]

A Prayer To Our Lord Jesus Christ
Antiochus, The Monk Of Pandektes.

Reader: Grant us, Master, as we depart for sleep, rest for body and soul. Protect us from the gloom of sinful sleep and from all dark pleasures of the night. Calm the impulses of passion, and quench the fiery darts of evil that are treacherously cast against us. Restrain the turbulence of our flesh and lull all our earthly and mundane thoughts. Grant to us, O God, a watchful mind, prudent reason, a vigilant heart, and tranquil sleep, free from all evil dreams. Raise us up at the hour of prayer, strengthen us in Thy commandments, and keep unshaken within us the remembrance of Thy judgements. Grant us to glorify Thee all night long that we may praise and bless and glorify Thine all honourable and majestic name; of the Father and of the Son and of the Holy Spirit, both now and forever, and unto the ages of ages. Amen.

Final Intercessions

Most glorious, ever virgin, blessed Theotokos, present our prayers to thy Son and our God, and plead with him, that through thee, He may save our souls.

Prayer Of Saint Ioannikios *(commemorated 4th November)*

My hope is the Father, my refuge the Son, my protection the Holy Spirit: O Holy Trinity, glory to Thee.

My every hope I place in thee, Mother of God, keep me under thy protection.

THE COMPLINE GOSPEL - FIRST FRIDAY IN GREAT LENT

Deacon: And that we may be accounted worthy to hear the Holy Gospel, let us pray to the Lord.

People: *Lord, have mercy.* **(x3)**

Deacon: Wisdom. Attend. Let us hear the Holy Gospel.

Priest: Peace be with you all.

People: *And with thy spirit.*

Priest: The Reading from the Holy Gospel according to John (15:1-7).

People: *Glory to Thee, O Lord, glory to Thee.*

Deacon: Let us attend.

[Read From The Holy Doors]

Priest: The Lord said: "I am the true vine, and My Father is the vine dresser. Every branch in Me that does not bear fruit He takes away; and every branch that bears fruit He prunes, that it may bear more fruit. You are already clean because of the word which I have spoken to you. Abide in Me, and I in you. As the branch cannot bear fruit of itself, unless it abides in the vine, neither can you, unless you abide in Me. I am the vine, you are the branches. He who abides in Me, and I in him, bears much fruit; for without Me you can do nothing.

If anyone does not abide in Me, he is cast out as a branch and is withered; and they gather them and throw them into the fire, and they are burned. If you abide in Me, and My words abide in you, you shall ask what you desire, and it shall be done for you."

People: *Glory to Thee, O Lord, glory to Thee.*

[End of First Friday Only]

[Priest stands on solea, and faces the icon of Christ:]

THE DISMISSAL

Priest: Glory to Thee, O Christ our God and our hope, glory to Thee.

People: *Glory be to the Father and to the Son and to the Holy Spirit;*
Both now and forever, and unto the ages of ages. Amen.

Lord, have mercy (**x3**).

Holy Father, bless.

[Facing the congregation:]

Priest: May Christ our true God, through the intercessions of His all immaculate and all blameless holy Mother; by the might of the Precious and Life giving Cross; by the protection of the honourable Bodiless Powers of Heaven; at the supplication of the honourable, glorious Prophet, Forerunner and Baptist John; of the holy, glorious and all laudable apostles; of the holy, glorious and right victorious Martyrs; of our venerable and God bearing Fathers; of Saint N., the patron and protector of this holy community; of the holy and righteous ancestors of God, Joachim and Anna; (in the first week, add: of the holy, glorious and right victorious Great martyr Theodore the Soldier); and of all the saints: have mercy on us and save us, forasmuch as He is good and loveth mankind.

People: *Amen.*

[Standing before the Holy Doors, facing east, the priest makes three metanias, saying each time.]

Priest: O God, be gracious unto me, a sinner, and have mercy on me.

[The priest turns west and bows to the people, saying:]

Priest: Forgive me, a sinner.

People: *God forgive thee, holy father.*

Priest: Let us pray for the peace of the world.

People: *Lord, have mercy.*

Priest: And for pious and Orthodox Christians.

People: Lord, have mercy.

Priest: And for our Archbishop Nikitas and for all our brotherhood in Christ.

People: Lord, have mercy.

Priest: And for the civil authorities of this land.

People: Lord, have mercy.

Priest: And for the welfare of our armed forces.

People: Lord, have mercy.

Priest: And for our fathers and brethren absent from among us.

People: Lord, have mercy.

Priest: And for those who hate us, and those who love us.

People: Lord, have mercy.

Priest: And for those who are kind to us and minister unto us.

People: Lord, have mercy.

Priest: And for those who have requested our prayers, unworthy though we be.

People: Lord, have mercy.

Priest: And for the deliverance of captives.

People: Lord, have mercy.

Priest: And for travellers by land, sea and air.

People: Lord, have mercy.

Priest: And for those who lie in sickness.

People: Lord, have mercy.

Priest: And let us pray also for the abundance of the fruits of the earth.

People: Lord, have mercy.

Priest: And for the soul of every Orthodox Christian.

People: Lord, have mercy.

Priest: Let us bless God fearing leaders, Orthodox bishops, the founders of this holy church and our parents and teachers, and all our fathers and brethren gone before us, the Orthodox who here and everywhere lie asleep in the Lord.

People: Lord, have mercy.

Priest: And let us say also for ourselves.

People: Lord, have mercy. **(x3)**

[People come forward to venerate icon of the Theotokos and receive a blessing from the priest; Whilst:]

Troparion

Tone 3   *Arrogant, brave, and mature atmosphere.*   *F, G, A, A#, C, D, E, F.*

Awed by the beauty of thy virginity and the exceeding radiance of thy purity, Gabriel stood amazed and cried to thee, O Mother of God: What praise may I offer thee, that is worthy of thy beauty? By what name shall I call thee? I am lost and bewildered. But I shall greet thee, as I was commanded: Rejoice, Thou that art full of grace.

[Priest faces the icon of Christ and says:]

Priest: Through the prayers of our holy fathers, Lord Jesus Christ our God, have mercy upon us and save us.

People: *Amen.*

Instructions:

An icon of the Theotokos is placed on a stand in the middle of the solea.

The candles are lit and the church is semi illumined.

The censer is not needed until the stases of the Akathist Hymn.

The curtain and Holy Doors are closed until the priest begins the scheduled stasis of the Akathist Hymn, and they remain open for the Holy Gospel lection on the first Friday.

The priest wears a blue epitrachelion over his exorasson and starts Little Compline in front of the icon.

Priest: Blessed is our God always, now and ever, and unto the ages of ages.

Reader: Glory to Thee, our God, glory to Thee.

Priest: O Heavenly King, the Comforter, the Spirit of Truth; who art everywhere present and fillest all things; Treasury of blessings, and giver of life: come and abide in us, and cleanse us from every impurity, and save our souls, O Good One.

Holy God, Holy Mighty, Holy Immortal, have mercy on us. **(x3)**

Glory be to the Father and to the Son and to the Holy Spirit;
Both now and forever, and unto the ages of ages. Amen.

O Most Holy Trinity, have mercy on us.

O Lord, cleanse us from our sins.

O Master, pardon our iniquities.

O Holy One, visit and heal our infirmities, for Thy names sake.

Lord have mercy. **(x3)**

Glory be to the Father and to the Son and to the Holy Spirit;
Both now and forever, and unto the ages of ages. Amen.

People: Our Father, who art in heaven, hallowed be Thy name. Thy Kingdom come. Thy will be done, on earth as it is in heaven. Give us this day our daily bread; and forgive us our trespasses, as we forgive those who trespass against us; and lead us not into temptation, but deliver us from the evil one.

Priest: For Thine is the kingdom, and the power, and the glory: of the Father, and of the Son, and of the Holy Spirit; now and ever, and unto ages of ages.

People: Amen.

Lord have mercy. **(x12)**

Glory be to the Father and to the Son and to the Holy Spirit;
Both now and forever, and unto the ages of ages. Amen.

Come, let us worship God, our King.

Come, let us worship and fall down before Christ, our King and our God.

Come, let us worship and fall down before Christ Himself, our King and our God.

[Priest goes to Readers stand.]

Psalm 50

Have mercy on me, O God, according to Thy great mercy; and according to the multitude of Thy compassions blot out my transgression. Wash me thoroughly from mine iniquity, and cleanse me from my sin. For I acknowledge mine iniquity, and my sin is ever before me. Against Thee, Thee only have I sinned, and done evil in Thy sight, that Thou mayest be found just when Thou speakest, and victorious when Thou art judged. For behold, I was conceived in iniquity, and in sin my mother bore me. For behold, Thou hast loved truth; Thou hast made known to me the hidden and secret things of Thy wisdom. Thou shalt sprinkle me with hyssop, and I shall be made clean; Thou shalt wash me, and I shall be whiter than snow. Make me to hear joy and gladness; that the humbled bones may rejoice. Turn Thy face away from my sins, and blot out all mine iniquities.

Create in me a clean heart, O God, and renew a steadfast spirit within me. Cast me not away from Thy presence, and take not Thy Holy Spirit from me. Restore to me the joy of Thy salvation, and establish me with Thy governing Spirit. I shall teach transgressors Thy ways, and the ungodly shall turn back to Thee. Deliver me from blood guiltiness, O God, the God of my salvation; my tongue shall joyfully declare Thy righteousness. Lord, open my lips, and my mouth shall declare Thy praise. For if Thou hadst desired sacrifice, I would give it; Thou dost not delight in burnt offerings. A sacrifice to God is a broken spirit; God will not despise a broken and a humbled heart. Do good, O Lord, in Thy good pleasure to Zion, and let the walls of Jerusalem be builded. Then Thou shalt be pleased with a sacrifice of righteousness, with oblation and whole burned offerings. Then shall they offer bulls on Thine altar.

Psalm 69

O God, be attentive to help me; Lord, make haste to help me. Let them be ashamed and confounded who seek after my life. Let them be turned back and be ashamed who desire evil against me. Let them be turned back because of their shame who say to me: "Well done. Well done." Let all those who seek Thee rejoice and be glad in Thee, O God, and let those who love Thy salvation say continually: "Let the Lord be magnified." But as for me, I am poor and needy; O God help me. Thou art my help and my deliverer; Lord; do not delay.

Psalm 142

Lord, hear my prayer; in Thy truth give ear to my supplications; in Thy righteousness hear me. Enter not into judgement with Thy servant, for no one living is justified in Thy sight. For the enemy has pursued my soul; he has crushed my life to the ground. He has made me to dwell in darkness, like those that have long been dead, and my spirit within me is overwhelmed; my heart within me is distressed. I remembered the days of old, I meditated on all Thy works, I pondered on the creations of Thine hands. I stretched forth my hands to Thee; my soul longs for Thee like a thirsty land. Lord, hear me quickly; my spirit fails. Turn not Thy face away from me, lest I be like those who go down into the pit. Let me hear Thy mercy in the morning; for in Thee have I put my trust. Lord, teach me to know the way wherein I should walk; for I lift up my soul to Thee. Rescue me, Lord, from mine enemies, to Thee have I fled for refuge. Teach me to do Thy will, for Thou art my God. Thy good Spirit shall lead me on a level path. Lord, for Thy names sake Thou shalt preserve my life. In Thy righteousness Thou shalt bring my soul out of trouble, and in Thy mercy Thou shalt utterly destroy my enemies. And Thou shalt destroy all those who afflict my soul, for I am Thy servant.

Lesser Doxology

Glory to God, Who has shown us the Light. Glory to God in the highest, and on earth, peace, good will toward men. We praise Thee. We bless Thee. We worship Thee. We glorify Thee and give thanks to Thee for Thy great glory. O Lord God, Heavenly King, God the Father Almighty. O Lord, the Only Begotten Son, Jesus Christ, and the Holy Spirit. \

O Lord God, Lamb of God, Son of the Father, Who takes away the sins of the world, have mercy on us. Thou, Who takes away the sins of the world, receive our prayer. Thou, Who sittest at the right hand of God the Father, have mercy on us. /

For Thou alone art holy, and Thou alone art Lord. Thou alone, O Lord Jesus Christ, are most high in the glory of God the Father. Amen. I shall give thanks to Thee every day and praise Thy Name forever and ever. Lord, Thou hast been our refuge from generation to generation. I said, *"Lord, have mercy on me. Heal my soul, for I have sinned against Thee."* \

Lord, I flee to Thee. Teach me to do Thy will, for Thou art my God. For with Thee is the fountain of Life, and in Thy light we shall see light. Continue Thy loving kindness to those who know Thee. Vouchsafe, O Lord, to keep us this day without sin. Blessed art Thou, O Lord, the God of our fathers, and praised and glorified is Thy Name forever. Amen. Let Thy mercy be upon us, O Lord, even as we have set our hope on Thee.

Blessed art Thou, O Master; teach me Thy statutes.

Blessed art Thou, O Lord; enlighten me with Thy commandments.

Blessed art Thou, O Holy One; make me to understand Thy precepts.

Thy mercy endures forever, O Lord. Do not despise the works of Thine hands. To Thee belongs worship, to Thee belongs praise, to Thee belongs glory: to the Father and to the Son and to the Holy Spirit, both now and forever and unto the ages of ages. Amen. \

The Symbol Of Faith

I believe in one God, Father, Almighty, Maker of heaven and earth, and of all things visible and invisible.

And in one Lord Jesus Christ, the only begotten Son of God, begotten from the Father before all ages; Light from Light, true God from true God; begotten not made; consubstantial with the Father, through Him all things were made. For our sake and for our salvation He came down from Heaven, and was incarnate from the Holy Spirit and the Virgin Mary and became man. He was crucified for us under Pontius Pilate, and suffered and was buried. He rose again on the third day in accordance with the Scriptures, and ascended into Heaven, and is seated at the right hand of the Father. He is coming again in glory to judge the living and the dead. And His kingdom shall have no end.

And in the Holy Spirit, the Lord, the Giver of life; Who proceeds from the Father; Who together with Father and Son is worshipped and glorified; Who spoke through the prophets. In One, Holy, Catholic, and Apostolic Church. I confess one baptism for the forgiveness of sins. I await the resurrection of the dead, And the life of the age to come. Amen.

Reader: [*St Gabriel:* It is truly right to call thee blessed, who gavest birth to God, ever-blessed and God-obedient the Mother of our God.] Greater in honour than the Cherubim and beyond compare more glorious than the Seraphim; without corruption thou gavest birth to God the Word, truly the Mother of God, we magnify thee.

Kontakion For The Annunciation

Tone 8   Humility, tranquillity, repose, suffering, pleading.   *C, D, Eb, F, G, A, Bb, C.*

To Thee, the Champion Leader, we Thy servants dedicate a feast of victory and of thanksgiving as ones rescued out of sufferings, O Theotokos: but as Thou art one with might, which is invincible, from all dangers that can be, do Thou deliver us, that we may cry to Thee: Rejoice, Thou Bride Unwedded.

[After the Kontakion, the Priest begins the relevant Stasis. At the words "Rejoice, O Bride without Bridegroom." and "Halleluiah," he censes the Icon nine times.]

FIRST STASIS OF THE AKATHIST HYMN

1. OIKOS

Priest: An angel chieftain was sent from heaven to say "Rejoice" unto the Theotokos. **(x3)**

And beholding Thee, O Lord, taking bodily form, he stood rapt in wonder, and with bodiless voice cried aloud to her in this wise:

- Rejoice, thou, through whom joy shall shine forth;
- Rejoice, thou, through whom the curse shall be destroyed.
- Rejoice, thou restoration of fallen Adam;
- Rejoice, thou, redemption of the tears of Eve.
- Rejoice, thou height untrodden by human minds;

- Rejoice, thou depth hard to scan, even for angels' eyes.
- Rejoice, thou that art a kingly throne;
- Rejoice, thou that holdest the Upholder of all.
- Rejoice, thou star that showed the Sun;
- Rejoice, womb of the Divine Incarnation.
- Rejoice, thou through whom Creation is renewed;
- Rejoice, thou through whom the Creator becomes a babe.
- Rejoice, O Bride without bridegroom.

[Priest censes the icon.]

People: *Rejoice, O Bride without bridegroom.*

2. KONTAKION

Priest: Boldly spake the holy maiden unto Gabriel, conscious of her chastity: To my soul thy strange message seems hard to grasp; how speakest thou of a virgin conception, crying aloud: Halleluiah.

[Priest censes the icon.]

People: Halleluiah.

3. OIKOS

Priest: Craving to know knowledge unknowable, the Virgin cried out unto him who ministered unto her: From a maiden body, how may a Son be born; tell thou me. To her he spake in fear, and thus only cried aloud:

- Rejoice, thou initiate of the ineffable counsel;
- Rejoice, O faith of those who pray in silence.
- Rejoice, thou beginning of the miracles of Christ;
- Rejoice, thou crown of His decrees.
- Rejoice, heavenly ladder, by which God came down;
- Rejoice, Bridge that leadest us from earth to Heaven.
- Rejoice, thou much talked of wonder of angels;
- Rejoice, thou much lamented damager of demons.
- Rejoice, thou who ineffably didst bear the Light;
- Rejoice, thou who told none how it was done.
- Rejoice thou, who over soarest the knowledge of the wise;
- Rejoice, thou who enlightenest the minds of the faithful.
- Rejoice, O Bride without bridegroom.

[Priest censes the icon.]

People: *Rejoice, O Bride without bridegroom.*

4. KONTAKION

Priest: Divine power from on high then overshadowed the maiden, that she might conceive, and showed forth her fruitful womb as a fertile field to all who desire to reap salvation, as they sing: Halleluiah.

[Priest censes the icon.]

People: *Halleluiah.*

5. OIKOS

Priest: Enshrining God in her womb, the Virgin hastened unto Elizabeth; whose unborn babe at once perceived her Salutation, and rejoiced; and with stirrings as if with voices cried out to the Theotokos:

- Rejoice, Branch of unfading growth;
- Rejoice, Possessor of untouched fruit.
- Rejoice, thou who labourest for Him Whose labour is love;
- Rejoice, thou who tendest Him Who tendeth our life.
- Rejoice, Field with compassions harvest rich;
- Rejoice, Table with abundance of mercies spread.
- Rejoice, thou who revivest the green meadows of joy;
- Rejoice, thou who makest ready a safe haven for souls.
- Rejoice, thou accepted incense offering of intercessions;
- Rejoice, thou oblation of all the world.
- Rejoice, Good will of God towards men;
- Rejoice, Access of mortals to God.
- Rejoice, O Bride without bridegroom.

[Priest censes the icon.]

People: *Rejoice, O Bride without bridegroom.*

6. KONTAKION

Priest: Floods of doubtful thoughts troubled the wise Joseph within, and he feared a furtive love as he beheld thee unwed, O Blameless One; but when he learned that thy conception was of the Holy Spirit, he said: Halleluiah.

[Priest censes the icon.]

People: *Halleluiah.*

The Canon Of The Akathist – Part 1

Tone 4　　*Festive, joyous and expressing deep piety.*　　　　　　　*C, D, Eb, F, G, A, Bb, C.*

Ode One

Reader: I shall open my mouth and it shall be filled with the Spirit, and I shall speak forth to the Queen and Mother. I shall be seen joyfully singing her praises, and I shall delight to sing of her wonders.

Refrain: *Most Holy Theotokos, save us.*

When the great Archangel saw thee, O Immaculate One, thou living book of Christ, sealed by the Spirit, he cried unto thee: Rejoice, vessel of gladness, through whom the curse of our first mother is loosed.

Refrain: *Most Holy Theotokos, save us.*

Rejoice, virgin bride of God, thou uplifter of Adam and death knell of Hades;
Rejoice, O all blameless one, thou palace of the only King;
Rejoice, thou fiery throne of the Almighty.

Glory be to the Father, and to the Son, and to the Holy Spirit.

Rejoice, thou from whom alone didst blossom the Unwithering Rose;
Rejoice, thou who didst bear the fragrant Apple;
Rejoice, immaculate maiden, fragrance of the King of All and salvation of the world.

Both now and forever, and unto the ages of ages. Amen.

Rejoice, thou treasure house of purity, through which we rose up from our fall;
Rejoice, Lady, sweet scented lily perfuming the faithful, thou fragrant incense and most precious myrrh.

Ode Three

Reader: As a living and copious fountain, O Theotokos, do thou strengthen those who hymn thy praises, and are joined together in a spiritual company for thy service; and in thy divine glory make them worthy of crowns of glory.

Refrain: *Most Holy Theotokos, save us.*

As a clear and untilled field, thou didst make the Divine Ear of Grain to sprout; Rejoice, thou living table that held the Bread of Life; Rejoice, thou unfailing fountain of Living Water.

Refrain: *Most Holy Theotokos, save us.*

Rejoice, O mystic heifer that didst bear the Spotless Calf;
Rejoice, ewe lamb who didst conceive the Lamb of God that taketh away the sins of the whole world;
Rejoice, thou Fervent Intercessor.

Glory be to the Father, and to the Son, and to the Holy Spirit.
Rejoice, O radiant dawn, which alone dost bear Christ the Sun, the dwelling place of Light;
Rejoice, thou who didst dispel the darkness and reduce to naught the demons of gloom.

Both now and forever, and unto the ages of ages. Amen.

Rejoice, thou only gate, through which the Word alone didst pass;

Rejoice, Lady, for by thy birth giving the bars and gates of Hades were burst asunder;

Rejoice, thou most worthy of all praise, divine entry for the saved.

[Priest stands before the icon of the Theotokos in the centre of the solea. The censer is kept near at hand. Whilst:]

Kontakion For The Annunciation

Tone 8   Humility, tranquillity, repose, suffering, pleading.   *C, D, Eb, F, G, A, Bb, C.*

To Thee, the Champion Leader, we Thy servants dedicate a feast of victory and of thanksgiving as ones rescued out of sufferings, O Theotokos: but as Thou art one with might, which is invincible, from all dangers that can be, do Thou deliver us, that we may cry to Thee: Rejoice, Thou Bride Unwedded.

SECOND STASIS OF THE AKATHIST HYMN
7. OIKOS

Priest: Gloriously the Angels hymned the incarnate Presence of Christ, and the shepherds heard; and running as to a Shepherd, they beheld Him as an unspotted Lamb, being nurtured at Marys breast, and her they hymned and said:

- Rejoice, Mother of the Lamb and of the Shepherd;
- Rejoice, fold of reason endowed sheep.
- Rejoice, bulwark against foes invisible;
- Rejoice, Opener of the Gates of Paradise.
- Rejoice, for that which all the Heavens and earth Rejoice;
- Rejoice, for all the earth doth dance its joy together with the Heavens.
- Rejoice, never silent Voice of the Apostles;
- Rejoice, invincible courage of those who strive.
- Rejoice, thou firm foundation of the faith;
- Rejoice, thou shining token of grace.
- Rejoice, thou through whom Hades was laid bare;
- Rejoice, thou through whom we are clothed with glory.
- Rejoice, O Bride without bridegroom.

[Priest censes the icon.]

People: *Rejoice, O Bride without bridegroom.*

8. KONTAKION

Priest: High in the heavens the Magi beheld the Godward pointing star, and they followed its rays; using it as a beacon, they sought the mighty King, and as they approached the Unapproachable, they rejoiced and cried out unto Him: Halleluiah.

[Priest censes the icon.]

People: *Halleluiah.*

9. OIKOS

Priest: In the Virgins hand the sons of the Chaldees saw Him Whose hand had made man; and knowing Him as Master, even though He had taken on Himself the form of a servant, they hastened with their gifts to worship, and cried out to her who is blessed:

Rejoice, Mother of the unsetting Star;

Rejoice, terror of the mystic Day.

Rejoice, thou who quenchest the fiery furnace of error;

Rejoice, thou who enlightenest the initiates of the Trinity.

Rejoice, thou who cast out the inhuman tyrant of old;

Rejoice, thou who showest forth Christ the Lord Who loveth mankind.

Rejoice, thou who redeemest from barbarous superstitions;

Rejoice, thou who rescuest us from works unclean.

Rejoice, thou who causest the worship of fire to cease;

Rejoice, thou who allayest the flame of suffering.

Rejoice, guide of the wisdom of the faithful;

Rejoice, joy of all generations.

Rejoice, O Bride without bridegroom.

[Priest censes the icon.]

People: *Rejoice, O Bride without bridegroom.*

10. KONTAKION

Priest: Kings messengers did the Magi become, when they returned to Babylon; they fulfilled Thy bidding and preached Thee to all as the Christ, and they left Herod as a trifler who knew not how to sing: Halleluiah.

[Priest censes the icon.]

People: *Halleluiah.*

11. OIKOS

Priest: Lighting in Egypt the lamp of truth, Thou didst cast out the darkness of untruth; for their idols, O Saviour, could not bear Thy strength, and fell down; and those of them who were set free cried out to the Theotokos:

• Rejoice, thou uplifter of mankind;

• Rejoice, thou downfall of demons.

• Rejoice, thou who tramplest upon the wanderings of error;

- Rejoice, thou who refutest the frauds of idols.
- Rejoice, thou sea which drowned the mystic Pharaoh;
- Rejoice, Rock which refreshed those athirst for Life.
- Rejoice, fiery Pillar, guiding those in darkness;
- Rejoice, Shelter of the world, broader than a cloud.
- Rejoice, thou Sustenance in place of manna;
- Rejoice, minister of holy joy.
- Rejoice, thou land of promise;
- Rejoice, thou from whom flow honey and milk.
- Rejoice, O Bride without bridegroom.

[Priest censes the icon.]

People: *Rejoice, O Bride without bridegroom.*

12. KONTAKION

Priest: Most near his transit from this deceitful world was Simeon when Thou wast presented to him as a newborn babe, but Thou wast discerned by him as perfect God; wherefore overcome by Thine ineffable wisdom he cried out: Halleluiah.

[Priest censes the icon.]

People: *Halleluiah.*

The Canon Of The Akathist – Part 2

Tone 4   *Festive, joyous and expressing deep piety.*   *C, D, Eb, F, G, A, Bb, C.*

Ode Four

Reader: He Who sits in clouds of glory upon the throne of the Godhead, Jesus the Most High God, came with mighty hand and saved those who cried out unto Him: Glory to Thy Power, O Christ.

Refrain: *Most Holy Theotokos, save us.*

In hymns of faith, O all praised one, we cry out unto thee: Rejoice, thou mountain fertile with the fullness of the Spirit; Rejoice, thou lamp of light and vase of manna, to the senses of the reverent most sweet.

Refrain: *Most Holy Theotokos, save us.*

Rejoice, immaculate Lady, mercy seat of the world;
Rejoice, thou ladder which raised all from earth to grace;
Rejoice, thou bridge which truly leads from death to life all who sing thy praises.

Refrain: *Most Holy Theotokos, save us.*

Rejoice, O Immaculate One, higher than the heavens, thou who didst without pain carry within thee the Foundation of the Earth.

Rejoice, O seashell that didst dip in thy blood the divine purple for the King of the Powers of Heaven.

Glory be to the Father, and to the Son, and to the Holy Spirit.

Rejoice, Lady, who didst truly bear the Lawgiver that freely blotted out the transgressions of all; O Unimaginable Depth, O Height Ineffable, O Maiden Unwedded, through whom we are become divine.

Both now and forever, and unto the ages of ages. Amen.

With hymns we praise thee, O thou who didst weave for the world a crown not woven by hands, and we cry aloud: Rejoice, O Virgin, fortress of all mankind, and rampart, and strength, and refuge divine.

Ode Five

Reader: All creation was amazed at thy divine glory, for thou, O Unwedded Virgin, didst hold within thee the God of All, and didst bear the Eternal Son, Who rewards with salvation all who hymn thy praises.

Refrain: *Most Holy Theotokos, save us.*

Rejoice, O all blameless one, who didst bear the Way of Life and save the world from the deluge of sin;
Rejoice, bride of God, thou of great report and mighty fame;
Rejoice, thou dwelling place of the Master of Creation.

Refrain: *Most Holy Theotokos, save us.*

Rejoice, O Immaculate One, stronghold and fortress of mankind, and place of hallowed glory, death knell of Hades, bridal chamber full of light;
Rejoice, joy of the angels;
Rejoice, help of those who faithfully pray unto thee.

Refrain: *Most Holy Theotokos, save us.*

Rejoice, O Lady, fiery chariot of the Word; living paradise having the Lord, the Tree of Life, in thy midst; His sweetness gives to those who partake in faith, even though they be subject to corruption.

Glory be to the Father, and to the Son, and to the Holy Spirit.

Strengthened by thy might, faithfully we cry unto thee: Rejoice, city of the King of All, great in glory and repute, of whom all these were clearly spoken; O mount unhewn and depth beyond all measure.

Both now and forever, and unto the ages of ages. Amen.

Thou spacious tabernacle of the Word, rejoice. O Immaculate One, Thou seashell which didst proffer the Divine Pearl, rejoice. O All wondrous One, Thou art the reconciliation to God, O Theotokos, of all who forever bless thee.

Ode Six

Reader: As we, the Godly minded, celebrate this sacred and all honourable feast of the Mother of God; come, let us clap our hands together and glorify the God Whom she bore.

Refrain: *Most Holy Theotokos, save us.*

Immaculate bridal chamber of the Word, and aid to the sanctification of us all, rejoice. O All pure Maiden, whom the Prophets did proclaim; Rejoice, thou ornament of the Apostles.

Refrain: *Most Holy Theotokos, save us.*

From thee the dew distilled that quenched the flame of polytheism, wherefore we cry out unto thee, O Virgin: Rejoice, O Dewy Fleece which Gideon did foresee.

Glory be to the Father, and to the Son, and to the Holy Spirit.

Behold, we cry out unto thee: Rejoice. Be thou our haven and our port when we voyage on the sea of tribulations and through the snares of the adversary.

Both now and forever, and unto the ages of ages. Amen.

O Cause of Joy, favour us with reason to cry out unto thee: Rejoice, thou bush that burns yet unconsumed, thou light filled cloud which unceasingly shelters the faithful.

[Priest stands before the icon of the Theotokos in the centre of the solea. The censer is kept near. Whilst:]

Kontakion For The Annunciation

Tone 8   Humility, tranquillity, repose, suffering, pleading.   C, D, Eb, F, G, A, Bb, C.

To Thee, the Champion Leader, we Thy servants dedicate a feast of victory and of thanksgiving as ones rescued out of sufferings, O Theotokos: but as Thou art one with might, which is invincible, from all dangers that can be, do Thou deliver us, that we may cry to Thee: Rejoice, Thou Bride Unwedded.

THIRD STASIS OF THE AKATHIST HYMN
13. OIKOS

Priest: New was the Creation which the Creator showed to us His creatures, when He appeared blossoming from a virgin womb; and He preserved her just as she was, in purity, so that we, beholding this marvel, might cry aloud and sing:

- Rejoice, Flower of incorruption;
- Rejoice, Crown of chastity.
- Rejoice, thou who flashest out the type of the Resurrection;
- Rejoice, thou who mirrorest the life of the Angels.
- Rejoice, Tree of goodly fruit, from which the faithful are nourished;
- Rejoice, goodly shade tree, beneath which many are sheltered.
- Rejoice, thou who bearest the Guide of those who stray abroad;
- Rejoice, thou who engenderest the Redeemer of captives.
- Rejoice, thou intercession before the Righteous Judge;
- Rejoice, thou forgiveness for many who stumble.
- Rejoice, Robe of the naked of liberty;
- Rejoice, selfless love that vanquishest all mean desires.
- Rejoice, O Bride without bridegroom.

[Priest censes the icon.]

People: *Rejoice, O Bride without bridegroom.*

14. KONTAKION

Priest: Our minds are brought over into heaven when we behold this strange birth giving, so let us be estranged from the world; for this cause indeed did the most high God appear on earth as humble man, that He might raise on high those who cry out unto Him: Halleluiah.

[Priest censes the icon.]

People: *Halleluiah.*

15. OIKOS

Priest: Present and complete with those below, and in no wise absent from those above was the Uncircumscribed Word; for there took place indeed a divine Descent and not a simple change of place; and the Birth was from a God chosen Virgin, who heard such words as these:

- Rejoice, Resting place of the uncontained God;
- Rejoice, Door of hallowed Mystery.
- Rejoice, doubtful Rumour of the faithless;
- Rejoice, undoubted Boast of the faithful.
- Rejoice, all holy Chariot of Him Who rideth upon the Cherubim;
- Rejoice, all excellent Chair of Him Who sitteth upon the Seraphim.
- Rejoice, thou who makest things that differ to agree;
- Rejoice, thou who joinest together virginity and motherhood.
- Rejoice, thou whom through transgression is annulled;

- Rejoice, thou whom through Paradise was opened.
- Rejoice, Key of the Kingdom of Christ;
- Rejoice, Hope of eternal good things.
- Rejoice, O Bride without bridegroom.

[Priest censes the icon.]

People: *Rejoice, O Bride without bridegroom.*

16. KONTAKION

Priest: Choirs of Angels were amazed at Thy great work of Incarnation; for they saw the inaccessible God as man accessible to all, dwelling among us and hearing from us all: Halleluiah.

[Priest censes the icon.]

People: *Halleluiah.*

17. OIKOS

Priest: Ready voiced orators we see become voiceless as fish before thee, O Theotokos, and unable to say how thou couldst give birth and yet remain virgin; but we, marvelling at this Mystery, cry out in faith:

- Rejoice, Vessel of the Wisdom of God;
- Rejoice, Treasury of His foreknowledge.
- Rejoice, thou who showest the learned to be fools;
- Rejoice, thou who provest logicians illogical.
- Rejoice, for the subtle disputants are made fools;
- Rejoice, for the makers of myths are made to fade away.
- Rejoice, thou who didst disperse the word webs of the Athenians;
- Rejoice, thou who didst fill the nets of the fishermen.
- Rejoice, thou who drawest us up from the depths of ignorance;
- Rejoice, thou who enlightenest many with knowledge.
- Rejoice, Raft for those who wish to be saved;
- Rejoice, haven for those who swim in the sea of life.
- Rejoice, O Bride without bridegroom.

[Priest censes the icon.]

People: *Rejoice, O Bride without bridegroom.*

18. KONTAKION

Priest: Salvation for the world the Architect of all desired, and to this end by His own will He came; as God from everlasting He is our shepherd, yet as man He appeared among us for our sake, and although called like by like, still as God He hears: Halleluiah.

[Priest censes the icon.]

People: *Halleluiah.*

The Canon Of The Akathist – Part 3

Tone 4   *Festive, joyous and expressing deep piety.*   *C, D, Eb, F, G, A, Bb, C.*

Ode Seven

Reader: The Godly minded children worshipped not the creature rather than the Creator, but trampling upon the threat of fire in manly fashion, they rejoiced and sang: O All Praised Lord and God of our Fathers, blessed art Thou.

Refrain: *Most Holy Theotokos, save us.*

To thee we sing a hymn and cry: Rejoice. Chariot of the mystic sun, true vine that did produce the ripe cluster of grapes, dripping wine to gladden the souls of those who with faith do glorify thee.

Refrain: *Most Holy Theotokos, save us.*

Rejoice, thou Bride of God, who didst bear the Healer of Mankind; the mystic staff from which blossomed the Unfading Flower; Rejoice, O Sovereign Lady, through whom we are filled with joy, and inherit life.

Refrain: *Most Holy Theotokos, save us.*

The tongue of eloquence has not power to sing thy praises, O Sovereign Lady, for thou wast exalted above the Seraphim when thou didst bear Christ the King; do thou now implore Him to deliver from all harm those who faithfully reverence thee.

Glory be to the Father, and to the Son, and to the Holy Spirit.

The ends of the earth do praise and bless thee, and cry out unto thee: Rejoice, pure Maiden, scroll on which the finger of God did inscribe His Word; do thou now implore Him, O Theotokos, to write down thy servants in the Book of Life.

Both now and forever, and unto the ages of ages. Amen.

We thy servants bend the knee of our hearts and implore thee, O Pure Maiden: incline thine ear and save us, who are engulfed in tribulations; and guard thy city, O Theotokos, from every assault of her enemies.

Ode Eight

Reader: The three holy children in the furnace the Child of the Theotokos saved; then was the type, now is its fulfilment, and the whole world gathers to sing: All you works, praise the Lord, and magnify Him unto all ages.

Refrain: *Most Holy Theotokos, save us.*

Thou didst receive the Word within thee, O Pure Maiden, and didst bear Him Who beareth all things; thou didst nourish Him with milk, Who by His nod dost sustain all the universe; to Him we sing: All you works, praise the Lord, and magnify Him unto all ages.

Refrain: *Most Holy Theotokos, save us.*

Moses perceived in the burning bush the great mystery of thy birth giving, O Chaste and Holy Virgin; the children prefigured this most clearly when they stood in the midst of the flame and were unburned; wherefore we praise thee unto all ages.

Refrain: *Most Holy Theotokos, save us.*

We, who of old were made naked by deceit, have been clothed in a garment of incorruption by thy conception; and we who were sitting in the darkness of transgressions have come to see the light, O Maiden who art the dwelling place of Light: wherefore we praise thee unto all ages.

Glory be to the Father, and to the Son, and to the Holy Spirit.

Through thee the dead are made to live, for thou didst bear the Life Essential; those who before were speechless now find useful eloquence, lepers are cleansed, diseases are driven away, and the multitude of aerial spirits are vanquished, O Virgin, salvation of mortals.

Both now and forever, and unto the ages of ages. Amen.

We Rejoice in thee, O all blessed one, who didst bring forth Salvation for the world, through which we have been raised from earth to heights above; O Pure Maiden, thou art shelter and stronghold, bulwark and fortress of all who sing: All you works, praise the Lord, and magnify Him unto all ages.

Ode Nine

Reader: Let all earth born mortals rejoice in spirit, bearing their lamps, and let the nature of bodiless minds celebrate with honour the holy festival of the Mother of God, and cry out: Rejoice, all blessed, pure and ever virgin Theotokos.

Refrain: *Most Holy Theotokos, save us.*

Through thee, O Maiden, have we faithful become partakers of joy, so that we may further cry out unto thee: Rejoice. Do thou deliver us from perpetual temptation, from barbaric attack, and from all the multitude of evils which we mortals suffer for the number of our sins.

Refrain: *Most Holy Theotokos, save us.*

Thou hast appeared to enlighten us and be our confirmation, wherefore we cry aloud to thee:
Rejoice, O unsetting star which didst introduce into the world the mighty Sun;
Rejoice, pure maiden, who didst open up fast closed Eden;
Rejoice, fiery pillar, which doth lead mans nature to the life above.

Refrain: *Most Holy Theotokos, save us.*

Let us stand with reverence in the house of our God, and let us cry aloud:
Rejoice, mistress of the world;
Rejoice, Mary, Lady of us all;
Rejoice, thou who alone art blameless among women, and beautiful;
Rejoice, O Vessel, which didst receive into thyself the myrrh which was never before poured out.

Glory be to the Father, and to the Son, and to the Holy Spirit.

Rejoice, O Ever virgin, thou Dove who didst bring forth Him Who is merciful.
Rejoice, boast of all the righteous saints and crown of those who strive.
Rejoice, Ornament Divine of all the just, and of us the faithful, our salvation as well.

Both now and forever, and unto the ages of ages. Amen.

Spare, O God, Thine inheritance, and overlook now all our sins. For as intercessor in Thy sight, O Christ, there stands before Thee she that on earth conceived Thee without seed, when in Thy Great Mercy Thou hast willed to be shaped in a form that was not Thine own.

[Priest stands before the icon of the Theotokos in the centre of the solea. The censer is kept near at hand. Whilst:]

Kontakion For The Annunciation

Tone 8   *Humility, tranquillity, repose, suffering, pleading.*   *C, D, Eb, F, G, A, Bb, C.*

To Thee, the Champion Leader, we Thy servants dedicate a feast of victory and of thanksgiving as ones rescued out of sufferings, O Theotokos: but as Thou art one with might, which is invincible, from all dangers that can be, do Thou deliver us, that we may cry to Thee: Rejoice, Thou Bride Unwedded.

FOURTH STASIS OF THE AKATHIST HYMN

19. OIKOS

Priest: Thou, O Virgin Theotokos, art a protecting wall to virgins and to all who run to thee; for the Maker of Heaven and earth prepared thee, O Pure Maiden, and dwelt in thy womb, and taught all to sing out unto thee:

- Rejoice, pillar of virginity;
- Rejoice, gate of salvation.
- Rejoice, source of spiritual reformation;
- Rejoice, leader of divine goodness.
- Rejoice, for thou didst regenerate those conceived in sin;
- Rejoice, for thou didst remind those who were mindless.
- Rejoice, thou who didst annul the corruption of hearts;
- Rejoice, thou who didst bear the Sower of Chastity.
- Rejoice, bridal chamber of a virgin marriage;
- Rejoice, thou who joinest the faithful to the Lord.
- Rejoice, fair nursing mother of virgins;
- Rejoice, bridesmaid of holy souls.
- Rejoice, O Bride without bridegroom.

[Priest censes the icon.]

People: *Rejoice, O Bride without bridegroom.*

20. KONTAKION

Priest: Unworthy is every hymn that seeks to encompass the multitude of Thy many mercies; for if we should offer to Thee hymns of praise as numberless as the sands, O Holy King, we should still have done nothing worthy of that which Thou hast given to us who cry out unto Thee: Halleluiah.

[Priest censes the icon.]

People: *Halleluiah.*

21. OIKOS

Priest: Verily we behold the holy Virgin as a light giving beacon, shining for those in darkness: for by kindling the supernal Light, she guides us all to divine knowledge; illumining our minds with radiance, she is honoured by this our cry:

- Rejoice, ray of the living Sun;
- Rejoice, flash of unfading splendour.

- Rejoice, lightning flash, shining upon our souls;
- Rejoice, thou who dost as thunder strike down our enemies.
- Rejoice, for thou didst cause the many starred light to dawn;
- Rejoice, for thou didst cause the richly flowing river to gush forth.
- Rejoice, thou who didst from life describe the type of the baptismal font;
- Rejoice, thou who didst take away the stain of sin.
- Rejoice, laver that dost purify conscience;
- Rejoice, mixing bowl for the mingling of joy.
- Rejoice, fragrance of the sweetness of Christ;
- Rejoice, life of mystic festival.
- Rejoice, O Bride without bridegroom.

[Priest censes the icon.]

People: *Rejoice, O Bride without bridegroom.*

22. KONTAKION

Priest: When He Who pays the ancient debts of all men was minded to give grace, He came of His own will to dwell among those who had departed from His grace; and when He tore asunder the written charge against them. He heard from all in this wise: Halleluiah.

[Priest censes the icon.]

People: *Halleluiah.*

23. OIKOS

Priest: Yet while we sing to Him Whom thou didst bear, we all hymn thee, O Theotokos, as a living temple; for the Lord, Who holds all things in His hand, by dwelling within thee, hallowed and glorified thee, and taught all to cry out unto thee:
- Rejoice, tabernacle of God, and of the Word;
- Rejoice, holiest of all the holy ones.
- Rejoice, ark made golden by the Spirit;
- Rejoice, inexhaustible treasury of life.
- Rejoice, precious diadem of pious rulers;
- Rejoice, venerable boast of reverent priests.
- Rejoice, steady tower of the Church;
- Rejoice, impregnable wall of the realm.
- Rejoice, thou through whom trophies are set up;
- Rejoice, thou through whom enemies are cast down.
- Rejoice, healing of my body;
- Rejoice, salvation of my soul.
- Rejoice, O Bride without bridegroom.

[Priest censes the icon.]

People: *Rejoice, O Bride without bridegroom.*

24. KONTAKION

Priest: Zealously art thou praised, O Mother who didst bear the most holy Word of all the Saints; when thou receivest this present offering, deliver us from every calamity, and deliver from all wrath to come those who cry out unto thee: Halleluiah.

[Priest censes the icon.]

People: *Halleluiah.*

1. OIKOS

Priest: An angel chieftain was sent from heaven to say "Rejoice." unto the Theotokos. **(x3)**

And beholding Thee, O Lord, taking bodily form, he stood rapt in wonder, and with bodiless voice cried aloud to her in this wise:

- Rejoice, thou, through whom joy shall shine forth;
- Rejoice, thou, through whom the curse shall be destroyed.
- Rejoice, thou restoration of fallen Adam;
- Rejoice, thou, redemption of the tears of Eve.
- Rejoice, thou height untrodden by human minds;
- Rejoice, thou depth hard to scan, even for angels' eyes.
- Rejoice, thou that art a kingly throne;
- Rejoice, thou that holdest the Upholder of all.
- Rejoice, thou star that showed the Sun;
- Rejoice, womb of the Divine Incarnation.
- Rejoice, thou through whom Creation is renewed;
- Rejoice, thou through whom the Creator becomes a babe.
- Rejoice, O Bride without bridegroom.

[Priest censes the icon.]

People: *Rejoice, O Bride without bridegroom.*

Kontakion For The Annunciation

Tone 8   Humility, tranquillity, repose, suffering, pleading.   *C, D, Eb, F, G, A, Bb, C.*

To Thee, the Champion Leader, we Thy servants dedicate a feast of victory and of thanksgiving as ones rescued out of sufferings, O Theotokos: but as Thou art one with might, which is invincible, from all dangers that can be, do Thou deliver us, that we may cry to Thee: Rejoice, Thou Bride Unwedded.

[Priest stands before the Holy Doors, facing east.]

The Trisagion Prayers

Reader: Holy God, Holy Mighty, Holy Immortal, have mercy on us. **(x3)**

Glory be to the Father and to the Son and to the Holy Spirit;

Both now and forever, and unto the ages of ages. Amen.

O Most Holy Trinity, have mercy on us.

O Lord, cleanse us from our sins.

O Master, pardon our iniquities.

O Holy One, visit and heal our infirmities, for Thy names sake.

Lord have mercy. **(x3)**

Glory be to the Father and to the Son and to the Holy Spirit;

Both now and forever, and unto the ages of ages. Amen.

People: Our Father, who art in heaven, hallowed be Thy name. Thy Kingdom come. Thy will be done, on earth as it is in heaven. Give us this day our daily bread; and forgive us our trespasses, as we forgive those who trespass against us; and lead us not into temptation, but deliver us from the evil one.

Priest. For Thine is the kingdom, and the power, and the glory: of the Father, and of the Son, and of the Holy Spirit; now and ever, and unto ages of ages.

People: Amen.

[Plain chant]

Kontakion Of Akathist Saturday

Reader: With mystic apprehension of the divine commandment, the bodiless angel quickly appeared in the dwelling place of Joseph and said to the unwed Virgin: Lo, He Who in His Descent did bow the Heavens is housed unchanged and whole in thee; as I behold Him in thy womb taking on the form of a servant, I marvel and I cry unto thee: Rejoice, Thou Bride Unwedded.

People: *Lord, have mercy.* **(x40)**

The Prayer Of The Hours

Reader: At all times and in every hour, Thou art worshipped and glorified in heaven and on earth, Christ our God. Long in patience, great in mercy and compassion, Thou lovest the righteous and showest mercy to sinners. Thou callest all to salvation through the promise of good things to come. Lord, receive our prayers at the present time. Direct our lives according to Thy commandments. Sanctify our souls. Purify our bodies. Set our minds aright. Cleanse our thoughts, and deliver us from all sorrow, evil and distress. Surround us with Thy holy angels, that, guarded and guided by their host, we may arrive at the unity of the faith and the understanding of Thine ineffable glory. For Thou art blessed unto the ages of ages. Amen.

Lord, have mercy. **(x3)**

Glory be to the Father and to the Son and to the Holy Spirit;

Both now and forever, and unto the ages of ages. Amen.

Greater in honour than the Cherubim and beyond compare more glorious than the Seraphim; without corruption thou gavest birth to God the Word, truly the Theotokos, we magnify thee.

People: *Holy Father, bless.*

Priest: May God be merciful unto us and bless us, and cause His face to shine upon us, and be merciful unto us.

People: *Amen.*

Lord, have mercy. **(x12)**

Reader: Most holy Theotokos, save us.

Supplicatory Prayer To The Most Holy Theotokos

Paul, The Monk Of The Monastery Of Evergetis.

Priest or Reader: Spotless, undefiled, immaculate, unstained, pure Virgin, Lady and Bride of God, by thy wondrous conceiving thou united God the Word with human beings and joined the fallen nature of our race to heavenly things. Thou art the only hope of the hopeless, and the help of those oppressed. Thou art the ready protection of those who flee to thee, and the refuge of all Christians. Do not spurn me an accused sinner, though I have made myself completely useless by my shameful thoughts, words and deeds and through indolence have become a slave to the pleasures of life. But as the Mother of God who loves all people, mercifully have compassion upon me a sinner and a prodigal and receive my prayer though it be offered to thee by unclean lips. Entreat thy Son and our Lord and Master, using thy boldness as a mother, that he may open to me the loving mercy of his goodness, overlook my numberless transgressions, turn me to repentance, and make me an acceptable doer of His commandments. Always be near me, for thou art merciful, compassionate and loving. Be mine ardent help and protection in this present life, defending me from the assaults of adversaries and lead me to salvation. At the hour of my death, care for my miserable soul, and drive the dark visions of evil spirits from it. On the awesome day of judgement, save me from eternal punishment and make me an inheritor of the ineffable glory of thy Son, our God. May this be my lot, my Lady, all Holy Theotokos, through thine intercession and protection, by the grace and love of thine only begotten Son, our Lord and God and Saviour, Jesus Christ, to whom belong all glory, honour and worship, together with his eternal Father, and all holy, righteous, and life creating Spirit, both now and forever, and unto the ages of ages. Amen.

A Prayer To Our Lord Jesus Christ

Antiochus, The Monk Of Pandektes.

Priest or Reader: Grant us, Master, as we depart for sleep, rest for body and soul. Protect us from the gloom of sinful sleep and from all dark pleasures of the night. Calm the impulses of passion, and quench the fiery darts of evil that are treacherously cast against us. Restrain the turbulence of our flesh and lull all our earthly and mundane thoughts. Grant to us, O God, a watchful mind, prudent reason, a vigilant heart, and tranquil sleep, free from all evil dreams. Raise us up at the hour of prayer, strengthen us in Thy commandments, and keep unshaken within us the remembrance of Thy judgements. Grant us to glorify Thee all night long that we may praise and bless and glorify Thine all honourable and majestic name; of the Father and of the Son and of the Holy Spirit, both now and forever, and unto the ages of ages. Amen.

Final Intercessions

Reader: Most glorious, ever virgin, blessed Theotokos, present our prayers to thy Son and our God, and plead with him, that through thee, He may save our souls.

Prayer Of Saint Ioannikios *(commemorated 4th November)*

My hope is the Father, my refuge the Son, my protection the Holy Spirit: O Holy Trinity, glory to Thee. My every hope I place in thee, Mother of God, keep me under thy protection.

[Priest stands on solea, and faces the icon of Christ:]

THE DISMISSAL

Priest: Glory to Thee, O Christ our God and our hope, glory to Thee.

People: *Glory be to the Father and to the Son and to the Holy Spirit;*
Both now and forever, and unto the ages of ages. Amen.
Lord, have mercy. **(x3)**.
Holy Father, bless.

[Facing the congregation:]

Priest: May Christ our true God, through the intercessions of His all immaculate and all blameless holy Mother; by the might of the Precious and Life giving Cross; by the protection of the honourable Bodiless Powers of Heaven; at the supplication of the honourable, glorious Prophet, Forerunner and Baptist John; of the holy, glorious and all laudable apostles; of the holy, glorious and right victorious Martyrs; of our venerable and God bearing Fathers; of Saint N., the patron and protector of this holy community; of the holy and righteous ancestors of God, Joachim and Anna; (in the first week, add: of the holy, glorious and right victorious Great martyr Theodore the Soldier); and of all the saints: have mercy on us and save us, forasmuch as He is good and loveth mankind.

People: *Amen.*

[Standing before the Holy Doors, facing east, the priest makes three metanias, saying each time.]

Priest: O God, be gracious unto me, a sinner, and have mercy on me.

[The priest turns west and bows to the people, saying:]

Priest: Forgive me, a sinner.

People: *God forgive thee, holy father.*

Priest: Let us pray for the peace of the world.

People: *Lord, have mercy.*

Priest: And for pious and Orthodox Christians.

People: *Lord, have mercy.*

Priest: And for our Archbishop Nikitas and for all our brotherhood in Christ.

People: *Lord, have mercy.*

Priest: And for the civil authorities of this land.

People: *Lord, have mercy.*

Priest: And for the welfare of our armed forces.

People: *Lord, have mercy.*

Priest: And for our fathers and brethren absent from among us.

People: *Lord, have mercy.*

Priest: And for those who hate us, and those who love us.

People: *Lord, have mercy.*

Priest: And for those who are kind to us and minister unto us.

People: *Lord, have mercy.*

Priest: And for those who have requested our prayers, unworthy though we be.

People: *Lord, have mercy.*

Priest: And for the deliverance of captives.

People: *Lord, have mercy.*

Priest: And for travellers by land, sea and air.

People: *Lord, have mercy.*

Priest: And for those who lie in sickness.

People: *Lord, have mercy.*

Priest: And let us pray also for the abundance of the fruits of the earth.

People: *Lord, have mercy.*

Priest: And for the soul of every Orthodox Christian.

People: *Lord, have mercy.*

Priest: Let us bless God fearing leaders, Orthodox bishops, the founders of this holy church and our parents and teachers, and all our fathers and brethren gone before us, the Orthodox who here and everywhere lie asleep in the Lord.

People: *Lord, have mercy.*

Priest: And let us say also for ourselves.

People: *Lord, have mercy.* **(x3)**

[People come forward to venerate icon of the Theotokos and receive a blessing from the priest; Whilst:]

Troparion

Tone 3   Arrogant, brave, and mature atmosphere.   F, G, A, A#, C, D, E, F.

Awed by the beauty of thy virginity and the exceeding radiance of thy purity, Gabriel stood amazed and cried to thee, O Mother of God: What praise may I offer thee, that is worthy of thy beauty? By what name shall I call thee? I am lost and bewildered. But I shall greet thee, as I was commanded: Rejoice. Thou that art full of grace.

[After all have venerated:]

[Plain chant]

THE SYNAXARION

Reader: On the fifth Saturday of the Great Fast, we celebrate the praise of our Most holy Lady, the Theotokos and Ever virgin Mary, during which "it is not permitted to sit."

Verses

Tone 1   Magnificent, happy and earthy.   C, D, Eb, F, G, A, Bb, C.

The city in thanksgiving and watchfulness doth praise Her who upholdeth and constantly watcheth in wartime, giving the victory.

[speaking voice]

In 626, when the Emperor Heraclius of Constantinople was away with the majority of his army fighting the Persians, the Khan sent forces to attack the Imperial City by land and by sea. Patriarch Sergius urged the people not to lose heart, but to trust in God. They made a procession around the city with the Cross of the Lord, the robe of the Virgin, the Icon of the Saviour "not made by hands," and the Hodigitria ("She who shows the Way") Icon of the Mother of God. The Patriarch dipped the Virgins robe in the sea, and the citys defenders beat back the Khans forces. The sea became very rough and many boats sank. The invaders retreated and the people of Constantinople gave thanks to God and to His Most pure Mother. On two other occasions, in 673 and on the eve of the Annunciation in 718, the Theotokos saved the city and destroyed the Saracen invaders. On the latter occasion, the hymn "To thee, the Champion Leader" was composed, most likely by Saint Germanus, Patriarch of Constantinople. A feast day dedicated to the Laudation of the Virgin was established to commemorate these victories, although the Akathist Service to the Mother of God was already in use for the Feast of the Annunciation, together with the hymn "With mystic apprehension." Use of this Akathist has spread from Constantinople to other Orthodox lands where it holds prominence and honour.

The icon before which this Akathist was sung was given to the Dionysiou Monastery on Mount Athos by Emperor Alexius Comnenos. There, it began to flow with myrrh. This icon shows the Mother of God seated on a throne, surrounded by the Prophets, holding scrolls, who foretold of the Annunciation and the Incarnation of our Lord. Most authorities agree that this Akathist Hymn is the work of Saint Romanos the Melodist (October 1st) in the sixth century. He was born in Homs, Syria and served as a deacon in Beirut, Lebanon before going to Constantinople. Scholars consider this Akathist one of the greatest achievements in ecclesiastical poetry. Orthodox Christians cherish it as one of the most beloved hymns of praise to the Theotokos.

Tone 1   *Magnificent, happy and earthy.*   *C, D, Eb, F, G, A, Bb, C.*

Wherefore, through the intercessions of thy combating Mother who combateth not, O Christ God, deliver us from all afflictions that encompass us, and have mercy upon us, for Thou alone art the Lover of mankind. Amen.

[After all have passed, the Priest faces the icon of Christ and says:]

Priest: Through the prayers of our holy fathers, Lord Jesus Christ our God, have mercy upon us and save us.

People: *Amen.*

The Liturgy Of The Presanctified Gifts
By Saint Basil The Great

The Presanctified is conducted 15 to 18 times a year:

1) Wednesday and Friday of the first six weeks of Lent.

2) Thursday of the fourth week of Lent.

3) Monday, Tuesday and Wednesday of Holy Week.

The Sacrificial / Resurrection Liturgy is celebrated on all Saturdays and Sundays in Lent, on the Feast of the Annunciation, and on Holy Thursday.

Good Friday is a liturgical day.

Preparation Of The Presanctified Gifts

On the preceding Sunday, at the Prothesis, after dedicating the principal Amnos, or "Lamb", to be distributed in Holy Communion that day, the Priest prepares as many additional "Lambs" as there will be Liturgies of the Presanctified during that week, saying for each the same dedicatory prayers as for the first. However, at the Consecration of the Gifts all the "Lambs" are presented as one, for Christ is one. Similarly, at the elevation, all the "Lambs" are elevated together. At the fraction, the Priest breaks only that Amnos which he dedicated first at the Prothesis. As for the others, he takes them one by one in his left hand, and with the spoon in his right pours a small amount of the Holy and Precious Blood of the Lord crosswise on the underside incised with the Cross, then places them in the tabernacle.

Vesperal Liturgy Of The Presanctified Gifts

Deacon: Master, Bless.

Priest: Blessed is the Kingdom of the Father and of the Son and of the Holy Spirit;

Both now and forever and unto the ages of ages.

People: *Amen.*

Reader: Come, let us worship God, our King.

Come, let us worship and fall down before Christ, our King and our God.

Come, let us worship and fall down before Christ Himself, our King and our God.

Priest *(sote voce whilst Psalm 103):* O Lord our God, Who upholdest all things in the all pure hollow of Thy hand; Who showest long suffering upon us all, and repentest Thee at our calamities: remember Thy bounties and Thy mercy. Visit us with loving kindness; and grant that, though the remainder of the day, by Thy grace, we may avoid the diverse subtle snares of the Evil One, and preserve our lives unassailed; through the grace of Thine Only begotten Son, with Whom Thou are blessed, together with Thine all holy, good and life giving Spirit; both now and forever and unto the ages of ages. Amen.

O God, great and wonderful, Who with wisdom inscrutable and great riches of providence orderest all things, and bestowest upon us earthly good things; Who hast given us a pledge of The Promised Kingdom through the good things already bestowed upon us, and hast made us to shun all evil during that part of the day which is past; Grant that we may also fulfil the remainder of this day without reproach before Thy holy glory, and hymn Thee, the Only Good One, our God, Who lovest mankind. For Thou art our God and unto Thee we ascribe glory, to the Father and to the Son and to the Holy Spirit; both now and forever, and unto the ages of ages. Amen.

O great and most high God, Who alone hast immortality, and dwellest in light unapproachable; Who hast made all creation in wisdom; Who hast divided the light from the darkness, and hast appointed the sun to rule the day, the moon and stars also to rule the night; Who hast vouchsafed unto us sinners at this present hour also to come before Thy presence with confession, and to offer unto Thee our evening sacrifice of praise: Do Thou Thyself, Who lovest mankind, direct our prayer as incense before Thee, and accept it for a savour of sweet incense and grant that we may pass this present evening and the coming night in peace. Endow us with the armour of light. Deliver us from the terror of the night, and from everything that walketh in darkness; and grant that the sleep, which Thou hast appointed for the repose of our weakness, may be free from every machination of the Devil. Yes, O Master, Bestower of all good things, may we, being moved to compunction upon our beds, call to remembrance Thy Holy Name in the night season: that, enlightened in my meditation on Thy statutes, we may rise up in joyfulness of soul to glorify Thy goodness, offering up prayers and supplications unto Thy tender love for our own sins and for those of all Thy people, whom do Thou visit in mercy: through the intercessions of the Holy Theotokos. For Thou art a gracious God, and lovest mankind, and unto Thee do we ascribe glory: to the Father and to the Son and to the Holy Spirit; both now and forever and unto the ages of ages. Amen.

Psalm 103

Of David. Concerning The Formation Of The World.

Reader: Bless the Lord, O my soul. O Lord my God, Thou hast been exceedingly magnified. Confession and majesty hast Thou put on, Who covered Thyself with light as with a garment, Who stretched out the heaven as it were a curtain; Who supports His chambers in the waters, Who appoints the clouds for His ascent, Who walks upon the wings of the winds, Who makes His angels spirits, and His ministers a flame of fire, Who establishes the earth in the sureness thereof; it shall not be turned back for ever and ever. The abyss like a garment is His mantle; upon the mountains shall the waters stand. At Thy rebuke they shall flee, at the voice of Thy thunder shall they be afraid.

The mountains rise up and the plains sink down to the place where Thou hast established them. Thou appointed a boundary that they shall not pass, neither return to cover the earth. He sends forth springs in the valleys; between the mountains shall the waters run. They shall give drink to all the beasts of the field; the wild asses shall wait to quench their thirst. Beside them shall the birds of the heaven lodge, from the midst of the rocks shall they give voice. He waters the mountains from His chambers; the earth shall be satisfied with the fruit of Thy works.

He causes the grass to grow for the cattle, and green herb for the service of men, To bring forth bread out of the earth; and wine makes glad the heart of man. To make his face cheerful with oil; and bread strengthens mans heart. The trees of the plain shall be satisfied, the cedars of Lebanon, which Thou hast planted. There shall the sparrows make their nests; the house of the heron is chief among them. The high mountains are a refuge for the harts, and so is the rock for the hares. He has made the moon for seasons; the sun knows his going down. Thou appointed the darkness, and there was the night, wherein all the beasts of the forest shall go abroad. Young lions roaring after their prey, and seeking their food from God. The sun arises, and they are gathered together, and they lay them down in their dens.

But man shall go forth unto his work, and to his labour until the evening. How magnified are Thy works, O Lord. In wisdom hast Thou made them all; the earth is filled with Thy creation. So is this great and spacious sea, therein are things creeping innumerable, small living creatures with the great. There go the ships; there this dragon, whom Thou hast made to play therein. All things wait on Thee, to give them their food in due season; when Thou gavest it to them, they shall gather it. When Thou opened Thy hand, all things shall be filled with goodness; when Thou turned away Thy face, they shall be troubled. Thou wilt take their spirit, and they shall cease; and to their dust shall they return. Thou wilt send forth Thy Spirit, and they shall be created; and Thou shalt renew the face of the earth.

Let the glory of the Lord be unto the ages; the Lord shall rejoice in His works. Who looks on the earth and makes it tremble, Who touches the mountains and they smoke. I shall sing unto the Lord throughout my life, I shall chant to my God for as long as I have my being. May my words be sweet unto Him, and I shall rejoice in the Lord. O that sinners would cease from the earth, and they that work iniquity, that they should be no more. Bless the Lord, O my soul. The sun knows his going down, Thou appointed the darkness, and there was the night. How magnified are Thy works, O Lord. In wisdom hast Thou made them all.

After The Psalm

Glory be to the Father and to the Son and to the Holy Spirit;
Both now and forever and unto the ages of ages. Amen.

Halleluiah, Halleluiah, Halleluiah, glory to Thee, O God. **(x3)**
Glory to Thee, our Lord and our hope, glory to Thee.

The Litany of Peace

Deacon: In peace let us pray to the Lord.

People: *Lord, have mercy.*

Deacon: For the peace from above and the salvation of our souls, let us pray to the Lord.

People: *Lord, have mercy.*

Deacon: For the peace of the whole world, the welfare of the holy churches of God, and for the union of all, let us pray to the Lord.

People: *Lord, have mercy.*

Deacon: For this holy house, and for those who enter it with faith, reverence and the fear of God, let us pray to the Lord.

People: *Lord, have mercy.*

Deacon: For all devout and Orthodox Christians, let us pray to the Lord.

People: *Lord, have mercy.*

Deacon: For our Archbishop <u>Nikitas</u>, for the honoured order of presbyters, for the diaconate in Christ, for all the clergy and the people, let us pray to the Lord.

People: *Lord, have mercy.*

Deacon: For our Sovereign Lady, <u>Queen Elizabeth</u>, the Royal family, our Welsh Assembly Government, and all in authority, let us pray to the Lord.

People: *Lord, have mercy.*

Deacon: For this *[city/town/village]*, and for every city, town and village, and for the faithful who dwell in them, let us pray to the Lord.

People: *Lord, have mercy.*

Deacon: For favourable weather, an abundance of the fruits of the earth and temperate seasons, let us pray to the Lord.

People: *Lord, have mercy.*

Deacon: For those who travel by land, air or water, for the sick, the suffering, for those in captivity, and for their safety and salvation, let us pray to the Lord.

People: *Lord, have mercy.*

Deacon: For our deliverance from all affliction, wrath, danger and constraint, let us pray to the Lord.

People: *Lord, have mercy.*

Deacon: Help us, save us, have mercy on us, and keep us, O God, by Thy grace.

People: *Lord, have mercy.*

Deacon: Commemorating our all holy, pure, most blessed and glorious Lady, Mother of God and Ever Virgin Mary, with all the Saints, let us entrust ourselves and one another, and our whole life to Christ our God.

People: *To Thee, O Lord.*

Priest: O Lord, bountiful and compassionate, long suffering and plenteous in mercy, give ear to our prayer, and attend to the voice of our supplication. Work upon us a sign of good. Lead us in Thy way, that we may walk in Thy truth. Make glad our hearts, that we may fear Thy Holy Name. For Thou art great and doest wonders. Thou along art God, and among all the gods there is none like unto Thee, O Lord, mighty in mercy, gracious in strength, to aid and comfort and save all those who put their trust in Thy Holy Name.

Priest: For to Thee belongs all glory, honour and worship, to the Father, the Son, and the Holy Spirit, both now and forever, and unto the ages of ages.

People: *Amen.*

The Prayer Of The First Antiphon

Priest: *[soto voce]* Gracious and merciful Lord, forbearing and generous in mercy, hear our prayer and heed the voice of our entreaty. Give us a sign of Thy favour. Lead us in Thy way, that we may walk in Thy truth; gladden our hearts, that we may be in awe of Thy holy name, for Thou art great in the wonders Thou performest. Thou alone art God, and among all deities none is like Thee, O Lord: mighty in mercy and benevolent in might, helping and comforting and saving all who trust in Thy holy name.

Priest: *[aloud]* For all glory, honour and worship are Thine due, Father, Son and Holy Spirit, both now and forever and to the ages of ages.

People: Amen.

[Holy Doors are closed and Reader sings the Psalter, whilst:]

Priest: *prostration* (x3)

[Wash hands.

Kiss Gospel and put on stand.

Opens the Tabernacle (Artophorion).

Censes the gifts.

Places the paten (diskarion) on the open Antimension on the Holy Altar.

Places a "Lamb" thereon.

Cover it with the veil, and led by the censer, he proceeds to the Prothesis.

Pours wine and water into the chalice in the usual way, covers it with the second veil, then both vessels with the aer. During which:]

Priest: *[soto voce]* Through the prayers of the Holy Fathers, Lord Jesus Christ, have mercy on us and save us.

First Stasis
Psalm 119

Reader: In my distress, I cried out to the Lord, and he answered me. O Lord, save me from lying lips, and from a treacherous tongue. What shall be given thee and what more shall be done to thee, thou deceitful tongue? The sharpened arrows of a warrior with firebrands made of the broom tree. Woe is me that my exile has been so long; that I have set up tent in the camp of Kedar. Too long have I stayed among those who hate peace. I was peaceable, but when I spoke to them, they warred against me without cause.

Psalm 120

I lifted up my eyes to the hills whence help shall come to me. My help is from the Lord who made heaven and earth. He shall not suffer thy foot to stumble; nor shall the Guardian fall asleep. Behold, he shall neither sleep nor slumber, the Watcher over Israel. The Lord shall keep watch over thee; the Lord is thy shade at thine right hand. The sun shall not scorch thee by day, nor shall the moon fail thee by night. The Lord shall preserve thee from every evil, the Lord shall safeguard thy life. The Lord shall guard thy coming and thy going henceforth and for evermore.

Psalm 121

I was happy when they said to me: *"Let us go to the house of the Lord."* Our feet stood within thy courts, Jerusalem. Jerusalem built as a city whose people are as one. For there did the tribes go up, the tribes of the Lord as it was decreed to Israel to give thanks to the name of the Lord. For there have been placed thrones for judgement, thrones for the house of David. Pray, then, for the peace of Jerusalem, and may prosperity be with those who love thee. May peace be within thy walls, and prosperity upon thy towers. For the sake of my brethren and my friends, I have indeed asked peace for thee; for the sake of the house of the Lord our God, I have earnestly sought thy good.

Psalm 122

I have lifted up my eyes to Thee who dwell in heaven. As the eyes of the servants are on the hands of their masters, as the eyes of a maid are on the hands of her mistress, so our eyes are on the Lord our God until he has mercy on us. Have mercy on us, O Lord, have mercy on us; for we have had more than our fill of contempt: yes, our soul has been more than glutted. May disgrace fall on the prosperous, and contempt on the proud.

Psalm 123

Had not the Lord been with us, let Israel now say, had not the Lord been with us at the time men rose against us, truly, they would have swallowed us alive when their fury was inflamed against us; truly, the water would have drowned us, the torrent would have swept over us. Truly, the raging waters would have overwhelmed us. Blessed be the Lord who has not abandoned us as prey to their teeth. Like a bird of passage we were rescued from the fowlers net. The snare was torn asunder, and we escaped. Our help is in the name of the Lord who made heaven and earth.

After The Psalm

Glory be to the Father and to the Son and to the Holy Spirit;
Both now and forever and unto the ages of ages. Amen.

Halleluiah, Halleluiah, Halleluiah, glory to Thee, O God. **(x3)**
Lord, have mercy. **(x3)**

Reader: **a)** *Glory be to the Father and to the Son and to the Holy Spirit;*

Short Litany

Deacon: Again and again, in peace let us pray to the Lord.
People: *Lord, have mercy.*
Deacon: Help us, save us, have mercy on us and keep us, O God, by Thy grace.
People: *Lord, have mercy.*
Deacon: Commemorating our all holy, pure, most blessed and glorious Lady, Mother of God and Ever Virgin Mary, with all the Saints, let us entrust ourselves and one another, and our whole life to Christ our God.
People: *To Thee, O Lord.*

The Prayer Of The Second Antiphon

Priest: *[soto voce]* O Lord, do not rebuke us in Thine anger; do not chastise us in Thy wrath; but deal with us according to Thy loving kindness, as Healer and Physician of our souls. Guide us to the harbour of Thy will; enlighten the eyes of our hearts that we may know Thy truth; and grant that the rest of this day may be peaceful and without sin, as may our whole life, through the prayers of the Theotokos and of all tile saints.

Priest: *[aloud]* For Thine is the dominion and the kingdom and the power and the glory; Father, Son and Holy Spirit. Both now and forever and to the ages of ages.

People: Amen.

Reader: **b)** *Both now and forever and unto the ages of ages. Amen.*

Second Stasis
Psalm 124

Those who trust in the Lord are like Mount Zion which cannot be moved, which shall stand forever. Mountains are all around Jerusalem, as the Lord is around his people, now and forever. For the Lord shall not let the sceptre of the wicked rule over the land of the just, lest the just themselves apply their hands to iniquities. Do good, O Lord, to those who are good, and to those whose heart is upright. But those who stray into crooked ways, the Lord shall expel with evildoers. Peace upon Israel.

Psalm 125

When the Lord returned the captives of Zion, we were like men dreaming. Then our mouth was filled with laughter, and our tongue with rejoicing. Then it was said among the Gentiles, *"The Lord has done great things for them."* The Lord has done great things for us: we have been made to rejoice. O Lord, return our captives as streams return to the south. Those who weep as they sow shall rejoice as they reap. Though they went forth shedding tears as they scattered their seeds, they shall return rejoicing, bearing with them their sheaves.

Psalm 126

Unless the Lord build the house, in vain do the builders toil; unless the Lord guard the city, in vain does the watchman keep watch. In vain dost thou rise early: thou arisest after rest only to eat the bread of grief, for he provides for his beloved while they sleep. Behold, the Lords inheritance is his children, and his reward, the fruit of the womb. As arrows in the hand of a mighty warrior, so are the children of the exiles. Blessed the man who shall be able to fill his quiver with them: they shall never be put to shame when they meet their foes at the gates.

Psalm 127

Blessed are all who fear the Lord, who walk in his ways. Thou shalt eat of thy hands labour: blessed art thou, and it shall be well with thee. Thy wife shall be like a fruitful vine in the recesses of thy house: thy children like olive shoots around thy table. Behold, in this way shall be blessed the man who fears the Lord. May the Lord bless thee from Zion, and may thou seest the wealth of Jerusalem all the days of thy life. And may thou seest thy childrens children. Peace upon Israel.

Psalm 128

Often have they assailed me since my youth: let Israel say it! Often have they assailed me since my youth, but they have not prevailed over me. The wicked ploughed my back: they increased their iniquity. But the righteous Lord has cut asunder the neck of the sinners. Let them all be confounded and turned back, those who hate Zion: let them become like grass on the house-tops which withers before it can sprout; with which the reaper fills not his hand, nor the binder of sheaves his arms, while those who pass by do not say, *"The blessing of the Lord be upon thee!"* We have blessed thee in the name of the Lord.

After The Psalm

Glory be to the Father and to the Son and to the Holy Spirit;
Both now and forever and unto the ages of ages. Amen.

Halleluiah, Halleluiah, Halleluiah, glory to Thee, O God. **(x3)**
Lord, have mercy. **(x3)**

Reader: a) *Glory be to the Father and to the Son and to the Holy Spirit;*

Short Litany

Deacon: Again and again, in peace let us pray to the Lord.

People: *Lord, have mercy.*

Deacon: Help us, save us, have mercy on us and keep us, O God, by Thy grace.

People: *Lord, have mercy.*

Deacon: Commemorating our all holy, pure, most blessed and glorious Lady, Mother of God and Ever Virgin Mary, with all the Saints, let us entrust ourselves and one another, and our whole life to Christ our God.

People: *To Thee, O Lord.*

Prayer Of The Third Antiphon

Priest: *[soto voce]* Lord our God, be mindful of us sinners and Thine unfit servants, even as we call upon Thine holy name; and do not put us to shame for having placed our hope in Thine mercy; but grant, O Lord, all that we ask for our salvation; and make us worthy to love and fear Thee with all our heart and in all things to do Thy will.

Priest: *[aloud]* For Thou art a good and loving God, and unto Thee we offer the glory, to the Father, and to the Son and to the Holy Spirit, both now and forever and unto the ages of ages.

People: *Amen.*

Reader: b) *Both now and forever and unto the ages of ages. Amen.*

Third Stasis

Psalm 129

Out of the depths I have cried out to Thee: Lord, Lord, hear my voice! Let Thine ears be attentive to the voice of my plea. If Thou retainest sins, Lord, O Lord, who can stand? With Thee there is forgiveness. For Thy names sake, O Lord, I have waited for Thee. My soul has waited for Thy promise, my soul has hoped in the Lord. My soul has trusted in the Lord, from the morning watch till night. Let Israel hope in the Lord, for with the Lord there is steadfast love and in him is full redemption, and he shall redeem Israel from all his iniquities.

Psalm 130

O Lord, my heart is not uplifted, nor are my eyes upraised. I have not busied myself with lofty pursuits, nor with wonders too great for me. If I have failed to remain humble, but instead have exalted my soul, as a weaned child is treated by its mother, so shall Thou dealest with my soul. Let Israel hope in the Lord, henceforth and forever.

Psalm 131

O Lord, remember David and all his forbearance, how he swore to the Lord, and made a vow to the God of Jacob: *"I shall not enter the tent, my abode, nor get up on the couch of my repose; I shall give no sleep to my eyes, nor to my eyelids any slumber, nor to my temples any rest, until I find a place for the Lord, a tabernacle for the God of Jacob."* Behold, I have heard of it in Ephratha: we found it in the forest clearings. Let us enter into his tabernacles, let us worship where his feet once stood. Arise, O Lord, and go to Thy rest, Thou and the ark of Thine holiness. May Thy priests be clothed in righteousness, and Thy faithful ones rejoice. For the sake of David Thy servant, turn not away the face of Thine anointed one. The Lord swore to David a promise which he shall not retract: *"One of Thine own flesh I shall place on Thy throne. If Thy sons shall keep my covenant and the revelations I shall offer them, their sons also shall be seated upon Thine throne for evermore."* For the Lord has elected Zion, he has chosen it for his dwelling: *"This is my home for ever and ever; here I shall dwell because I have chosen it. I shall bless abundantly her provisions; I shall feed her poor with bread; I shall clothe her priests with salvation, and the faithful shall exult with joy. There shall I raise the pride of David; I have readied a lamp for my anointed one. I shall clothe his enemies with shame, but on him my crown shall shine."*

Psalm 132

Behold how good and pleasant it for brothers to dwell in unity. It is as ointment upon the head, which runs down over the beard, the beard of Aaron, runs down to the hem of his garment. It is like the dew of Hermon which falls on the mountains of Zion, for there the Lord has ordained the blessing: life for evermore.

Psalm 133

Behold now, bless the Lord all thou servants of the Lord who stand in the house of the Lord, in the courts of the house of our God. By night, lift up thy hands to the holy places and bless the Lord. May the Lord who made heaven and earth bless thee out of Zion.

After The Psalm

Glory be to the Father and to the Son and to the Holy Spirit;
Both now and forever and unto the ages of ages. Amen.

Halleluiah, Halleluiah, Halleluiah, glory to Thee, O God. **(x3)**
O Lord our hope, glory to Thee.

Short Litany

Deacon: Again and again, in peace let us pray to the Lord.

People: *Lord, have mercy.*

Deacon: Help us, save us, have mercy on us and keep us, O God, by Thy grace.

People: *Lord, have mercy.*

Deacon: Commemorating our all holy, pure, most blessed and glorious Lady, Mother of God and Ever Virgin Mary, with all the Saints, let us entrust ourselves and one another, and our whole life to Christ our God.

People: *To Thee, O Lord.*

The Prayer Of The Fourth Antiphon

Priest: *[soto voce]* Praised by the heavenly powers with hymns that are never silent and doxologies that never cease, fill our lips with praise of Thee, that we may fitly magnify Thine holy name. And grant us a portion and share with all who truly fear Thee and keep Thy commandments; at the intercession of the holy Theotokos and of all the saints.

Priest: *[aloud]* For Thou art our God, a God who shows mercy and saves, and to Thee we offer up glory, to the Father and to the Son and to the Holy Spirit, both now and forever and to the ages of ages.

People: *Amen.*

[Priest opens curtains, hat, bless incense.]

Priest *(blesses the incense):* Blessed is our God always, both now and forever, and unto the ages of ages.

[Censing, Prothesis, exit North doors, enter South doors.]

[Deacon censes in the usual manner.]

Psalm 140 - De Profundis Clamo Ad Te Domine.

Reader: Lord, I have cried to Thee: hear me. Hear me, O Lord.

Lord, I have cried to Thee: hear me. Receive the voice of my prayer.

When I call upon Thee, hear me, O Lord.

Let my prayer arise as incense in Thy sight,

And let the lifting up of my hands be an evening sacrifice. Hear me, O Lord.

Kekragarion

Sticheroi From Psalm 140

- Set, O Lord, a watch before my mouth, and a door of enclosure round about my lips.

- Incline not my heart to words of evil, to make excuses for sins.

- Those that work iniquity; I shall not join with their number.

- The righteous man shall chasten me with mercy and reprove me; as for the oil of the sinner, let it not anoint my head.

- For yet more is my prayer in the presence of their pleasures; their judges have been swallowed up by the rock.

- They shall hear my words, for they be sweetened; as a clod of earth is broken upon the earth, so have their bones been scattered into hades.

- To Thee O Lord are mine eyes. In Thee have I hoped; take not my soul away.

- Keep me from the snare which they have laid for me, and from the stumbling blocks of them that work iniquity.

- The sinners shall fall into their own net; I am alone until I pass by.

Sticheroi From Psalm 141

- With my voice to the Lord have I cried, with my voice have I made supplication.

- I shall pour out before Him my supplications; my afflictions shall I declare before Him.

- When my spirit was fainting within me, then Thou knewest my paths.

- In this way wherein I have walked they hid for me a snare.

- I looked on my right hand, and beheld, and there was none that knew me.

- Flight has failed me, and there is none that watches out for my soul.

- I cried to Thee, O Lord; I said: Thou art my hope, my portion in the land of the living.

- Attend unto my supplication, for I am brought very low.

- Deliver me from them that persecute me, for they are stronger than I.

- Bring my soul out of prison. That I may confess Thy name.

- The righteous shall patiently wait for me until Thou shalt reward me.

Fourth Week Of Great Lent

Fifth Week Of Great Lent

Sixth Week Of Great Lent

Seventh Week Of Great Lent

First Week Of Great Lent – Wednesday Evening
Sticheroi From Psalm 129

- Out of the depths have I cried unto Thee, O Lord. O Lord, hear my voice.
- Let Thine ears be attentive to the voice of my supplication.
- If Thou should mark iniquities, O Lord; O Lord, who shall stand? For with Thee there is forgiveness.

Chorus: *5) For Thy names sake have I patiently waited for Thee, O Lord; my soul has patiently waited for Thy word, my soul has hoped in the Lord.*

Tone 8   Humility, tranquillity, repose, suffering, pleading.   C, D, Eb, F, G, A, Bb, C.

Reader: While physical fasting, brethren, let us also fast spiritually. Let us loose every knot of iniquity; let us tear up every unrighteous bond; let us distribute bread to the hungry and welcome into our homes those who have no roof over their heads, so that we may receive great mercy from Christ our God.

Chorus: *4) From the morning watch until night, from the morning watch let Israel hope in the Lord.*

Reader: Fame and praise befits the saints, for they bowed their necks beneath the sword. To Thee who didst bow the heavens and come down. They shed blood for Thee who didst empty Thyself and take the form of a servant. By emulating Thy poverty they too humbled themselves even unto death. By their prayers have mercy on us, O God. According to the abundance of Thy mercies.

Chorus: *3) For with the Lord there is mercy, and with Him is plenteous redemption; and He shall redeem Israel out of all his iniquities.*

Tone 2   Majesty, gentleness, hope, repentance and sadness.   E, F, G, Ab, B, C.

Reader: Jesus, the spiritually radiant sun, has sent you into the world as shining flashes of lightening, O Apostles and eye witnesses of God. By the rays of your divine doctrines the error of darkness was swept away, enlightening those who were held in the ignorant gloom. Entreat Him to grant us enlightenment and great mercy.

Sticheroi From Psalm 116

Chorus: *2) O praise the Lord, all you nations; praise Him, all you peoples.*

Reader: Elijah was enlightened through fasting, he mounted he chariot of good works and was taken up to the heights of heaven. Emulate him, O humble soul; abstain from every evil and jealousy, from every fleeting pleasure, so that you might be cleansed of corrupting disease, the fires of Gehenna. Crying to Christ: O Lord, glory to Thee.

Chorus: *1) For He has made His mercy to prevail over us, and the truth of the Lord abides forever.*

    Tone 5   Stimulating, dancing, and rhythmical.   *C, D, Eb, F, G, A, Bb, C.*

Reader: O divine intercessors for the world, defenders of the Orthodox. You have the authority to entreat Christ our God with boldness. We entreat you to pray for us, O honourable ones, that we might spend the good time of fasting in joyousness, and receive the grace of the Consubstantial Trinity. Pray for our souls, O great and glorious preachers.

Theotokion

    Tone 1   Magnificent, happy and earthy.   *C, D, Eb, F, G, A, Bb, C.*

Caught in the storm of transgressions. I have run to a calm haven in praying to you, O Birth giver of God. Stretch forth your mighty hand to your servant, O Immaculate One.

[End of First week of Great Lent, Wednesday Evening] – jump to page 556.]

First Week Of Great Lent – Friday Evening
Sticheroi From Psalm 129

- Out of the depths have I cried unto Thee, O Lord. O Lord, hear my voice.
- Let Thine ears be attentive to the voice of my supplication.
- If Thou should mark iniquities, O Lord; O Lord, who shall stand? For with Thee there is forgiveness.

Chorus: *5) For Thy names sake have I patiently waited for Thee, O Lord; my soul has patiently waited for Thy word, my soul has hoped in the Lord.*

    Tone 5   Stimulating, dancing, and rhythmical.   *C, D, Eb, F, G, A, Bb, C.*

Reader: Come, O faithful, let us perform the works of God in the Light. Let us walk with honesty as in the day. Let us rid ourselves of unjust accusations against our neighbours, so that we place no stumbling blocks in their way. Let us put aside the pleasures of the flesh so that we may increase the gifts to our souls. Let us give bread to those in need. Let us draw near to Christ in repentance and say: O our God, have mercy on us.

Chorus: *4) From the morning watch until night, from the morning watch let Israel hope in the Lord.*

    Tone 2   Majesty, gentleness, hope, repentance and sadness.   *E, F, G, Ab, B, C.*

Reader: Come all lovers of the martyrs, let us be glad in spirit and celebrate. Today the martyr Theodore offers the Mystical Banquet making us glad in the Feast that we might sing to him:

Rejoice, unconquerable bearer of suffering, victor over torturers.

Rejoice, for you gave your body over to torture for Christ God.

Rejoice, for by many trials you were revealed as a true soldier of the heavenly army.

O beauty of martyrs, pray for our souls.

Chorus: *3) For with the Lord there is mercy, and with Him is plenteous redemption; and He shall redeem Israel out of all his iniquities.*

Reader: You extend the Divinely granted grace of your miracles to all who run to you in faith, O martyr Theodore. Therefore we praise you in song: you release the captives, heal the sick, reward the poor, and save those who are drowning. You intercede for all who honour your sacred memory. Entreat Christ to grant mercy even to us, who praise your suffering, 'O sacred martyr.

Sticheroi From Psalm 116

Chorus: *2) O praise the Lord, all you nations; praise Him, all you peoples.*

Reader: You were revealed as the highest gift of God, O martyr Theodore. Even after your end you grant help to those who run to you. When the widow came to your temple in tears, you appeared in mercy and returned her son who had been taken into captivity by alien soldiers. You did not cease doing wonders. Entreat Christ God that our souls may be saved.

Chorus: *1) For He has made His mercy to prevail over us, and the truth of the Lord abides forever*

Reader: I honour you as the true gift to God, O thrice blessed Theodore. You were revealed as an unfailing candle of the Divine Light. Your sufferings illumined the creation. More powerful than fire, you quenched the flames, and crushed the head of the evil serpent. When you went to your suffering Christ place the crown on your divine head. Since you have boldness before God, O great martyr, fervently pray for our souls.

The Little Entrance

Chorus: *Glory be to the Father and to the Son and to the Holy Spirit;*

    Tone 6   *Rich texture, funeral, sorrowful.*   *D, Eb, F##, G, A, Bb, C##, D.*

Reader: The devil used the apostate as a vessel of evil filling him with foul thoughts of polluting the food of the people who were fasting. But you overcame his craftiness with wiser reasoning; you appeared to the Archbishop in a dream and revealed the wicked plot to him. For this we give thanks to you, O martyr Theodore, and honour you as a helper and deliverer, remembering this miracle every year in this season. By your intercession to God, may we be delivered from the reasoning of the evil one.

Chorus: *Both now and forever and unto the ages of ages. Amen.*

Theotokion

Tone 1   Magnificent, happy and earthy.   *C, D, Eb, F, G, A, Bb, C.*

Let us praise the Virgin Mary the gate of heaven, the glory of the world, the song of angels, the beauty of the faithful. She was born of man, yet gave birth to God. She became the heaven, the temple of the God head. She destroyed the wall of enmity, She opened the kingdom. Since she is the foundation of our faith, our defender is the Lord whom she bore. Courage, courage, O People of God. For Christ shall destroy our enemies, since He is all powerful.

[End of First week of Great Lent, Friday Evening] – jump to page 556.]

Second Week Of Great Lent – Wednesday Evening
Sticheroi From Psalm 129

- Out of the depths have I cried unto Thee, O Lord. O Lord, hear my voice.
- Let Thine ears be attentive to the voice of my supplication.
- If Thou should mark iniquities, O Lord; O Lord, who shall stand? For with Thee there is forgiveness.

Chorus: *5) For Thy names sake have I patiently waited for Thee, O Lord; my soul has patiently waited for Thy word, my soul has hoped in the Lord.*

Tone 1   Magnificent, happy and earthy.   *C, D, Eb, F, G, A, Bb, C.*

Reader: Having undertaken the spiritual fast, brothers, let us speak no lies with our tongues, nor give each other a cause for scandal. But illumining the light of our souls through repentance. Let us cry to Christ with tears: remit our falls in sin, O lover of man.

Chorus: *4) From the morning watch until night, from the morning watch let Israel hope in the Lord.*

Reader: O most laudable martyrs, the earth did not hide you for heaven received you. The gate of Paradise was opened to you, where you now delight in the tree of life. Entreat Christ that peace and great mercy be granted to our souls.

Chorus: *3) For with the Lord there is mercy, and with Him is plenteous redemption; and He shall redeem Israel out of all his iniquities.*

Tone 3   Arrogant, brave, and mature atmosphere.   *F, G, A, A#, C, D, E, F.*

Reader: Through the prayers of Thy divine apostles, O Lord, enable us to perform a proper fast with compunction of mind. That, being saved by Thee, we may glorify Thee, O gracious and merciful God.

Sticheroi From Psalm 116

Chorus: *2) O praise the Lord, all you nations; praise Him, all you peoples.*

Reader: Thy coming shall be great and fearful, O Lord, when Thou wilt come in righteous judgement. Do not condemn me, though I stand condemned. But spare me as the compassionate God, through the acceptable prayers of Thine apostles.

Chorus: *1) For He has made His mercy to prevail over us, and the truth of the Lord abides forever.*

Tone 6   Rich texture, funeral, sorrowful.   *D, Eb, F##, G, A, Bb, C##, D.*

Reader: O apostles of Christ, the lights of those born on earth and treasuries for the world of the knowledge of God. Through your prayers, deliver those who praise you, from temptation. Enable us to pass the time of fasting in peace, as children. So that having attained the passions of Christ, with boldness we may offer songs of praise to our God.

Theotokion

Tone 2   Majesty, gentleness, hope, repentance and sadness.   *E, F, G, Ab, B, C.*

The Word, equal in honour to the Father and the Holy Spirit, has shone in these latter days as a mighty sun from the virgin handmaid of God. He has sent you, O glorious apostles, to illumine all men who were in the gloom of delusion with the light of faith, and by your divine doctrines to bring them to her.

[End of Second week of Great Lent, Wednesday Evening] – jump to page 556.]

Second Week Of Great Lent – Friday Evening
Sticheroi From Psalm 129

- Out of the depths have I cried unto Thee, O Lord. O Lord, hear my voice.
- Let Thine ears be attentive to the voice of my supplication.
- If Thou should mark iniquities, O Lord; O Lord, who shall stand? For with Thee there is forgiveness.
- For Thy names sake have I patiently waited for Thee, O Lord; my soul has patiently waited for Thy word, my soul has hoped in the Lord.
- From the morning watch until night, from the morning watch let Israel hope in the Lord.

For with the Lord there is mercy, and with Him is plenteous redemption; and He shall redeem Israel out of all his iniquities.

Sticheroi From Psalm 116

- O praise the Lord, all you nations; praise Him, all you peoples.

Chorus: *1) For He has made His mercy to prevail over us, and the truth of the Lord abides forever.*

Tone 4   Festive, joyous and expressing deep piety.   *C, D, Eb, F, G, A, Bb, C.*

Reader: Now is the acceptable time. Now is the day of salvation. Visit my soul in the abundance of Thy mercy. Take away the heavy burden of my transgressions, O only lover of man.

Theotokion

Tone 2   Majesty, gentleness, hope, repentance and sadness.   *E, F, G, Ab, B, C.*

The shadow of the law passed when Grace came. As the bush burned, yet was not consumed, so the virgin gave birth, yet remained a virgin. The sun of righteousness has risen instead of a pillar of flame. Instead of Moses, Christ the Salvation of our souls.

[End of Second week of Great Lent, Friday Evening] – jump to page 556.]

Sticheroi From Psalm 129

- Out of the depths have I cried unto Thee, O Lord. O Lord, hear my voice.
- Let Thine ears be attentive to the voice of my supplication.
- If Thou should mark iniquities, O Lord; O Lord, who shall stand? For with Thee there is forgiveness.

Chorus: **5)** *For Thy names sake have I patiently waited for Thee, O Lord; my soul has patiently waited for Thy word, my soul has hoped in the Lord.*

Tone 4   Festive, joyous and expressing deep piety.   *C, D, Eb, F, G, A, Bb, C.*

Reader: I have blindly squandered my fathers riches. I am now empty, living in a land of evil man. In my foolishness, I have become like the senseless beasts, and am now stripped of every Divine grace. So in my return, I cry to Thee, O merciful and compassionate Father: I have sinned, O God, receive me in repentance and have mercy on me.

Chorus: **4)** *From the morning watch until night, from the morning watch let Israel hope in the Lord.*

Reader: O martyrs of the Lord, inspired sacrifices, perfect victims for God, sheep who know God and are known by Him, whose pasture cannot be trespassed by wolves, pray that we too may graze with you near peaceful waters.

Chorus: **3)** *For with the Lord there is mercy, and with Him is plenteous redemption; and He shall redeem Israel out of all his iniquities.*

Tone 6   Rich texture, funeral, sorrowful.   *D, Eb, F##, G, A, Bb, C##, D.*

Reader: You were revealed as the rays of the spiritual sun, O apostles who behold our God. Entreat Him to illumine our souls and deliver us from the darkness of passions, so that we may behold the saving day. By your intercessions and prayers may our hearts be purified, the hearts wounded by the evil one. And we shall honour you in faith forever, for you saved the world by your wise preaching.

Sticheroi From Psalm 116

Chorus: **2)** *O praise the Lord, all you nations; praise Him, all you peoples.*

Reader: I, the prodigal, have wandered away into a land of evil, and I have squandered the riches which Thou hadst given me. Now I am pining with hunger, O compassionate Father. Clothed in the shame of transgression, I am now stripped of righteous deeds and grace. I cry to Thee: I have sinned, but I know Thy goodness. Receive me as one of Thy servants, O compassionate Christ, Through the prayers of the apostles who loved Thee.

Chorus: **1)** *For He has made His mercy to prevail over us, and the truth of the Lord abides forever.*

Reader: O apostles of the Saviour, lights and benefactors and saviours of the world, seers of Gods glory and heaven, adorned with miracles and signs of healing, fervently pray to the Lord for us so that our prayers may be accepted. May we all be made worthy of seeing and kissing the Life bearing Cross with fear. In worshipping it, send down on us Thy mercy, O Saviour, as the lover of sins.

Theotokion

Tone 3   Arrogant, brave, and mature atmosphere.   *F, G, A, A#, C, D, E, F.*

The power of your miracles is great, O pure one. You deliver us from sorrows and save us from death. You free us from attacks, remove our pains, and take away the transgressions of men.

[End of Third week of Great Lent, Wednesday Evening] – jump to page 556.]

Third Week Of Great Lent – Friday Evening

Sticheroi From Psalm 129

- Out of the depths have I cried unto Thee, O Lord. O Lord, hear my voice.
- Let Thine ears be attentive to the voice of my supplication.
- If Thou should mark iniquities, O Lord; O Lord, who shall stand? For with Thee there is forgiveness.
- For Thy names sake have I patiently waited for Thee, O Lord; my soul has patiently waited for Thy word, my soul has hoped in the Lord.
- From the morning watch until night, from the morning watch let Israel hope in the Lord.
- For with the Lord there is mercy, and with Him is plenteous redemption; and He shall redeem Israel out of all his iniquities.

Sticheroi From Psalm 116

- O praise the Lord, all you nations; praise Him, all you peoples.

Chorus: *1) For He has made His mercy to prevail over us, and the truth of the Lord abides forever.*

Tone 4   Festive, joyous and expressing deep piety.   *C, D, Eb, F, G, A, Bb, C.*

Reader: Now is the acceptable time. Now is the day of salvation. Visit my soul in the abundance of Thy mercy. Take away the heavy burden of my transgressions, O only lover of man.

Theotokion

Tone 3   Arrogant, brave, and mature atmosphere.   *F, G, A, A#, C, D, E, F.*

How shall we but marvel at your Divine-human giving of birth, most holy Lady? For without knowing a man, you gave birth to a fatherless Son in the flesh, O Immaculate Virgin. The Son born of the Father before eternity was born of you at the fullness of time. He underwent no mingling, no change, no division, but preserved the fullness of each Nature, entreat Him to save the souls, O Lady and Virgin and Mother, of those who confess you in the Orthodox manner to be the Theotokos.

[End of Third week of Great Lent, Friday Evening] – jump to page 556.]

Sticheroi From Psalm 129

Chorus: **8)** *Out of the depths have I cried unto Thee, O Lord. O Lord, hear my voice.*

Tone 4   *Festive, joyous and expressing deep piety.*   *C, D, Eb, F, G, A, Bb, C.*

Reader: The fast, the means of receiving blessings has now led us half way though its course. Pleasing God with the days that are past and proposing purposeful tasks for the the days ahead, for the increase of blessings produces a greater number of good deeds. Therefore let us cry to Christ, the Giver of all blessings: O Thou who didst fast and endure the cross for our sake, enable us to partake uncondemned of Thy Divine Pascha, to lead our lives in peace, worthily glorifying Thee with the Father and the Spirit.

Chorus: **7)** *Let Thine ears be attentive to the voice of my supplication.*

Tone 5   *Stimulating, dancing, and rhythmical.*   *C, D, Eb, F, G, A, Bb, C.*

Reader: Those who thirst for spiritual blessings perform their good deeds in secret, not noising them abroad in markets, but cherishing and keeping them in their hearts. For He who sees all that is done in secret shall reward us for our abstinence. Let us fulfil the fast without sad faces, but ceaselessly praying in the depths of our hearts: Our Father, who art in heaven, lead us not into temptation, but deliver us from the evil one.

Chorus: **6)** *If Thou should mark iniquities, O Lord; O Lord, who shall stand? For with Thee there is forgiveness.*

Reader: With boundless love in your souls, O holy martyrs, you did not forsake Christ. Enduring the various wounds of suffering, you laid low the torturers' impudence. Preserving unbending and unshakeable faith you were translated to heaven. Since you received boldness before Him, entreat Him to grant peace to the world, and for our souls great mercy.

Chorus: **5)** *For Thy names sake have I patiently waited for Thee, O Lord; my soul has patiently waited for Thy word, my soul has hoped in the Lord.*

Tone 1   *Magnificent, happy and earthy.*   *C, D, Eb, F, G, A, Bb, C.*

Reader: Let us clean our souls with the water of the fast. Let us draw near to the precious and pure cross of the Lord, venerating it in faith and drawing Divine enlightenment, even now obtaining eternal salvation, peace and great mercy.

Chorus: **4)** *From the morning watch until night, from the morning watch let Israel hope in the Lord.*

Tone 5   *Stimulating, dancing, and rhythmical.*   *C, D, Eb, F, G, A, Bb, C.*

Reader: O Cross, boast of apostles, surrounded by Principalities, Powers and Archangels. Save those who bow before You from all harm, and enable us to fulfil well the Divine course of abstinence, to attain to the saving Day, by which we are saved.

Chorus: **3)** *For with the Lord there is mercy, and with Him is plenteous redemption; and He shall redeem Israel out of all his iniquities.*

Tone 7   *Manly character and strong melody.*   *F, G, A, A#, C, D, E, F.*

Reader: Today, as we bow before the Cross of the Lord, let us cry:
- Rejoice, O Tree of life, the tormentor of hell.
- Rejoice, O Joy of the world, the destroyer of corruption.
- Rejoice, O Power which drives out demons.
- Rejoice, O confirmation of the faithful, Invincible weapon. Preserve and sanctify those who kiss you.

Sticheroi From Psalm 116

Chorus: **2)** *O praise the Lord, all you nations; praise Him, all you peoples.*

Tone 8   *Humility, tranquillity, repose, suffering, pleading.*   *C, D, Eb, F, G, A, Bb, C.*

Reader: Today the unapproachable by nature approaches me, and frees me from passions by enduring the Passion. The Light of the blind is spat upon by sinful men, and gives His back to scourging for the sake of the captives. When the pure Virgin Mother beheld Him on the Cross she cried out in pain: *"Woe to me. What is this Thou hast done, O my child? Thou, whose beauty was fairer than that of any man, appearest lifeless, with no form nor comeliness."*

Chorus: **1)** *For He has made His mercy to prevail over us, and the truth of the Lord abides forever*

Reader: Woe to me, O my Light, I cannot bear to look upon Thee sleeping. By being wounded for a sword has pierced my heart. But I praise Thy Passion, I bow before Thy compassion. O Long suffering Lord, glory to Thee.

The Little Entrance

Chorus: *Glory be to the Father and to the Son and to the Holy Spirit;*

Tone 7   *Manly character and strong melody.*   *F, G, A, A#, C, D, E, F.*

Reader: By my passions I have ruined my souls nobility. Like a beast, I cannot look up to Thee, O most High. But bowing low, O Christ, I pray like the Publican, crying: *"Have mercy on me, O God, and save me."*

Chorus: *Both now and forever and unto the ages of ages. Amen.*

Theotokion

Tone 4   *Festive, joyous and expressing deep piety.*   *C, D, Eb, F, G, A, Bb, C.*

Deliver us from our wants, O Mother of Christ our God, who gave birth to the Creator of all. Rejoice, O only mediatrix, for our souls.

[End of Fourth week of Great Lent, Wednesday Evening] – jump to page 556.]

Sticheroi From Psalm 129

- Out of the depths have I cried unto Thee, O Lord. O Lord, hear my voice.

- Let Thine ears be attentive to the voice of my supplication.

- If Thou should mark iniquities, O Lord; O Lord, who shall stand? For with Thee there is forgiveness.

- For Thy names sake have I patiently waited for Thee, O Lord; my soul has patiently waited for Thy word, my soul has hoped in the Lord.

- From the morning watch until night, from the morning watch let Israel hope in the Lord.

- For with the Lord there is mercy, and with Him is plenteous redemption; and He shall redeem Israel out of all his iniquities.

Sticheroi From Psalm 116

- O praise the Lord, all you nations; praise Him, all you peoples.

Chorus: **1)** *For He has made His mercy to prevail over us, and the truth of the Lord abides forever.*

Tone 7   Manly character and strong melody.   F, G, A, A#, C, D, E, F

Reader: By my passions I have ruined my souls nobility. Like a beast, I cannot look up to Thee, O most High. But bowing low, O Christ, I pray like the Publican, crying: Have mercy on me, O God, and save me.

Theotokion

Tone 4   Festive, joyous and expressing deep piety.   C, D, Eb, F, G, A, Bb, C.

The prophet David, the ancestor of God, sang to God who glorified you: *"At Thy right hand stood the queen."* He showed you as Mother, giving us life, since God was freely born of you without a father. Desiring to renew His fallen Image, made corrupt in passion. He took the lost sheep upon His shoulder and brought it to His Father joining it to the heavenly powers, Christ, who has great and rich mercy, has saved the world, O Theotokos.

Hymns To The Martyrs

Tone 1   Magnificent, happy and earthy.   C, D, Eb, F, G, A, Bb, C.

Through the prayers of all the Saints and the Theotokos, O Lord, grant us Thy peace and have mercy on us, as the only Bountiful One.

Your confession in the courts, O Saints, spat upon the strength of Demons and delivered men from delusion. And as you were being beheaded, you cried: "Let the sacrifice of our souls, O Lord, be well pleasing before Thee. In loving Thee, we have not cared for this temporal life, O lover of man."

Tone 2   Majesty, gentleness, hope, repentance and sadness.   E, F, G, Ab, B, C.

By the holy martyrs praying for us, and singing the praises of Christ, every delusion has come to an end, and mankind is being saved by faith.

The choirs of martyrs faced their torturers, saying: "We fight for Lord Sabaoth. Even if you deliver us to fire and tortures, we shall not deny the Power of the Trinity."

Tone 3   *Arrogant, brave, and mature atmosphere.*   *F, G, A, A#, C, D, E, F.*

The power of Thy Cross is great, O Lord. Set in one place, it acts throughout the world. It made fishermen into apostles, and the nations into martyrs. May they always pray for our souls.

The prophets, apostles and martyrs of Christ, taught us to sing the praises of the Consubstantial Trinity. They enlightened the nations which had gone astray, and made the sons of men companions of the angels.

Tone 4   *Festive, joyous and expressing deep piety.*   *C, D, Eb, F, G, A, Bb, C.*

O martyrs of the Lord, inspired sacrifices, rational offerings, perfect victims for God, sheep who know God and are known by Him, whose pasture cannot be trespassed by wolves, pray that we too may graze with you near peaceful waters.

Since you have boldness before the Saviour, O Saints, pray unceasingly for us sinners, entreating remission of our sins and great mercy for our souls.

Tone 5   *Stimulating, dancing, and rhythmical.*   *C, D, Eb, F, G, A, Bb, C.*

Behold the shield of faith, armed with the sign of the Cross, Thy Saints, O Lord, bravely marched forth to tortures and destroyed the devils pride and baseness. By their prayers, as the Almighty God, send down peace to the world and to our souls great mercy.

O most laudable martyrs, not rejoicing in earthly things, going bravely to tortures, you did not fail in your blessed hopes and inherited the kingdom of heaven. Since you now have boldness before God, the lover of man, entreat peace for the world and great mercy for our souls.

Tone 6   *Rich texture, funeral, sorrowful.*   *D, Eb, F##, G, A, Bb, C##, D.*

Thy martyrs, O Lord, did not forsake Thee, nor did they turn from Thy commandments. By their prayers have mercy on us.

On this earth the martyrs endured many sufferings, and became citizens of heaven. By their prayers and entreaties, O Lord, preserve us all.

Tone 7   *Manly character and strong melody.*   *F, G, A, A#, C, D, E, F.*

Glory to Thee, O Christ God, praise of apostles and gladness of martyrs, whose preaching was the Consubstantial Trinity.

O holy martyrs, who fought the good fight and have received the crown. Entreat the Lord that our souls may be saved.

Tone 8   *Humility, tranquillity, repose, suffering, pleading.*   C, D, Eb, F, G, A, Bb, C.

O martyrs of the Lord, you sanctify every place and heal every ill. And now we entreat you to deliver our souls from the snares of the enemy.

Fame and praise befits the Saints, for they bowed their necks beneath the sword to Thee who didst bow the heavens and come down. They shed blood for Thee who didst empty Thyself and take the form of a servant. By emulating Thy poverty they too humbled themselves even unto death. By their prayers have mercy on us, O God, according to the abundance of Thy mercy.

Glory be to the Father, and to the Son, and to the Holy Spirit;
Both now and forever, and to the ages of ages. Amen.

[End of Fourth week of Great Lent, Friday Evening] – jump to page 556.]

[End of Fourth week of Great Lent, Friday Evening] – jump to page 556.]

Fifth Week Of Great Lent – Wednesday Evening

Sticheroi From Psalm 129

- Out of the depths have I cried unto Thee, O Lord. O Lord, hear my voice.
- Let Thine ears be attentive to the voice of my supplication.
- If Thou should mark iniquities, O Lord; O Lord, who shall stand? For with Thee there is forgiveness.

Chorus: *5) For Thy names sake have I patiently waited for Thee, O Lord; my soul has patiently waited for Thy word, my soul has hoped in the Lord.*

Tone 8   *Humility, tranquillity, repose, suffering, pleading.*   C, D, Eb, F, G, A, Bb, C.

Reader: I fell amongst thieves by my reasoning, I was robbed by my wretched mind. Greatly stricken and wounded in soul, naked of grace I lie upon the road of life. The priest saw my hopeless wounds and passed me by, the Levite knew my disease and turned away. But in Thy love for man Thou wast pleased to stoop down to me, O Christ God, not by the road of Samaria, but from the flesh of Mary. Grant me healing by pouring out on me Thy great mercy.

Chorus: *4) From the morning watch until night, from the morning watch let Israel hope in the Lord.*

Reader: Fame and praise befit the saints. For they bowed their necks beneath the sword to Thee who didst bow the heavens and come down. They shed blood for Thee who didst empty Thyself and take the form of a servant. By emulating Thy poverty they too humbled themselves even unto death. By their prayers have mercy on us, O God, according to the abundance of Thy mercies.

Chorus: *3) For with the Lord there is mercy, and with Him is plenteous redemption; and He shall redeem Israel out of all his iniquities.*

Reader: O Lord, Thou hast revealed Thy sacred disciples as an understandable heaven. By their saved meditations deliver me from earthly pains, by abstinence always elevating my reasoning above wandering to passions, since Thou art bountiful and the lover of man.

Sticheroi From Psalm 116

Chorus: **2)** *O praise the Lord, all you nations; praise Him, all you peoples.*

Reader: O most laudable apostles, intercessors for the world, physicians of the sick, protectors of health, preserve us who are passing the time of fasting. So that, making peace with each other in Divine Fashion, preserving our minds unsullied by passions, we may sing a song of victory to the risen Christ.

Chorus: **1)** *For He has made His mercy to prevail over us, and the truth of the Lord abides forever.*

    Tone 4   Festive, joyous and expressing deep piety.   C, D, Eb, F, G, A, Bb, C.

Reader: What great condescension, what wonder of Nativity. The Virgin carries Thee, her Creator and God, in her arms. O benefactor, who willed to receive flesh from her, save me before I perish to the end, O Lord.

Theotokion

    Tone 5   Stimulating, dancing, and rhythmical.   C, D, Eb, F, G, A, Bb, C.

Rejoice, O seal of the prophets and preaching of the apostles. Beyond reason and understanding you gave birth to the truly existing God in the flesh. In Him we have received our first nobility and enjoy the food of paradise, O Pure One. We honour you as the mediatrix of this joy and a well pleasing intercessor. We have been made right by you, O Most Pure One, made worthy of the everlasting life of your Son, Who bounteously grants great mercy.

[End of Fifth week of Great Lent, Wednesday Evening] – jump to page 556.]

Fifth Week Of Great Lent – Thursday Evening
Sticheroi From Psalm 129

- Out of the depths have I cried unto Thee, O Lord. O Lord, hear my voice.
- Let Thine ears be attentive to the voice of my supplication.
- If Thou should mark iniquities, O Lord; O Lord, who shall stand? For with Thee there is forgiveness.

Chorus: **5)** *For Thy names sake have I patiently waited for Thee, O Lord; my soul has patiently waited for Thy word, my soul has hoped in the Lord.*

    Tone 8   Humility, tranquillity, repose, suffering, pleading.   C, D, Eb, F, G, A, Bb, C.

Reader: I have forsaken the splendour of virtues by my own will through my first sin. But by Thy condescension, O Word of God, I am now clothed in that splendour again. Thou didst not despise me, even when I was wounded by evil passions, and trampled on the way as a transgressor. Thou didst keep me safe by Thy mighty strength. Thou hast granted me Thy protection, O merciful Lord.

Chorus: **4)** *From the morning watch until night, from the morning watch let Israel hope in the Lord.*

Reader: O martyrs of the Lord, you sanctify every place and heal every ill. Now we entreat you to deliver our souls from the snares of the enemy.

Chorus: **3)** *For with the Lord there is mercy, and with Him is plenteous redemption; and He shall redeem Israel out of all his iniquities.*

> Tone 1   *Magnificent, happy and earthy.*   *C, D, Eb, F, G, A, Bb, C.*

Reader: Thou didst destroy the curse on Adam, O Lord, by Thy crucifixion. Destroy my bonds, O Word, that I may offer Thee a sacrifice of praise, in joy and faith during this acceptable time of fasting, which Thou hast revealed for the salvation of all.

Sticheroi From Psalm 116

Chorus: **2)** *O praise the Lord, all you nations; praise Him, all you peoples.*

Reader: When Moses shone with the grace of fasting, he beheld the glory God. Emulate him, O humble soul, in prayer and abstinence, for the One who graciously stretched out His hands on the Cross. Do this to receive Divine enjoyment.

Chorus: **1)** *For He has made His mercy to prevail over us, and the truth of the Lord abides forever.*

> Tone 6   *Rich texture, funeral, sorrowful.*   *D, Eb, F##, G, A, Bb, C##, D.*

Reader: Venerating Thy Life creating Cross, granted us by Thy boundless goodness, with enlightened souls we always sing Thy praise, O Christ. Enable us to complete the course of the fast with joy, in wholeness of heart, so that we may sing the praises of Thy Passion, by which Thou hast saved us.

[End of Fifth week of Great Lent, Thursday Evening] – jump to page 556.]

Fifth Week Of Great Lent – Friday Evening
Sticheroi From Psalm 129

- Out of the depths have I cried unto Thee, O Lord. O Lord, hear my voice.
- Let Thine ears be attentive to the voice of my supplication.

Chorus: **6)** *If Thou should mark iniquities, O Lord; O Lord, who shall stand? For with Thee there is forgiveness.*

> Tone 6   *Rich texture, funereal character, sorrowful tone.*   *D, Eb, F##, G, A, Bb, C##, D*

Reader: I now lie wounded and lifeless, as if I had left Jerusalem, the way of Thy Divine Commandments, and had reached the Passions of Jericho, revelling in the impious glory of earthly pursuits. As if my reasonings had become thieves and robbed me of my garments of sonship by grace. The priest came by and, seeing my corpse, passed my by: the Levite too saw and departed. But do Thou, O Lord, unspeakably Incarnate of the virgin, bind up the wounds as if with healing ointment, O Christ God, by the flood of blood and water which streamed Salvation from Thy side. Join me to the heavenly choir, since Thou are tender hearted.

Chorus: *5) For Thy names sake have I patiently waited for Thee, O Lord; my soul has patiently waited for Thy word, my soul has hoped in the Lord.*

Reader: Thy martyrs, O Lord, did not forsake Thee, nor did they turn from Thy commandments. By their prayers have mercy on us.

Chorus: *4) From the morning watch until night, from the morning watch let Israel hope in the Lord.*

Reader: Revealing the pre-eternal council to you, O handmaid, Gabriel came and in greeting announced:

- Rejoice, O virgin earth.
- Rejoice, O unconsumable bush.
- Rejoice, O unseeable depth.
- Rejoice, O bridge to heaven.
- Rejoice, O lofty ladder which Jacob beheld.
- Rejoice, O divine manna.
- Rejoice, O lifter of the curse.
- Rejoice, I recall of Adam. The Lord is with you.

Chorus: *3) For with the Lord there is mercy, and with Him is plenteous redemption; and He shall redeem Israel out of all his iniquities.*

Reader: "You appear as a man," replied the undefiled handmaid to the commander of the hosts. "And so how can you utter words higher than man? You have said: "God shall be with me, and shall dwell in my womb." And how, tell me, shall I be the abided of sanctification for the One upborne by Cherubim?"

Sticheroi From Psalm 116

Chorus: *2) O praise the Lord, all you nations; praise Him, all you peoples.*

Reader: "Do not deceive me, for I have not known sweetness, remaining unwedded. How then can I bear a child?"

Chorus: *1) For He has made His mercy to prevail over us, and the truth of the Lord abides forever.*

Reader: Where God so wills the order of nature s overruled, answered the bodiless leader. And that which is above man is accomplished. Believe my words of truth, O all holy and most undefiled. She cried out: let it be to me according to your word, and I shall give birth to the Bodiless God, who shall assume flesh from me, and by His sufferings shall exalt man to his first nobility, for He alone is mighty.

The Little Entrance

Chorus: *Glory be to the Father and to the Son and to the Holy Spirit;*

Tone 2   *Majesty, gentleness, hope, repentance and sadness.*   *E, F, G, Ab, B, C.*

Reader: The mystery of all eternity is revealed today, the Son of God becomes the Son of Man. Accepting the lowest, He grants me the Highest. Of old, Adam was deceived into desiring to become God and did not. God becomes man, so that He might make Adam a god. Let creation be glad and let nature sing for joy. The

Archangel stands in fear before the virgin and announces the greeting: Rejoice, O opposite of sorrow. Becoming man through the tender heartedness of Thy mercy, O our God, glory to Thee.

Chorus: *Both now and forever and unto the ages of ages. Amen.*

Theotokion

Tone 5   *Stimulating, dancing, and rhythmical.*   *C, D, Eb, F, G, A, Bb, C.*

In the Red Sea of old, a type of the virgin bride was figured. There Moses divided the waters; here Gabriel assisted in the miracle. There Israel crossed the sea without getting wet; here the virgin gave birth to Christ without seed. After Israels passage the sea remained impassable; after Emmanuels birth the virgin remained a virgin. O ever existing God, who appeared as man, O Lord, have mercy on us.

[End of Fifth week of Great Lent, Friday Evening] – jump to page 556.]

Sixth Week Of Great Lent – Wednesday Evening
Sticheroi From Psalm 129

- Out of the depths have I cried unto Thee, O Lord. O Lord, hear my voice.
- Let Thine ears be attentive to the voice of my supplication.
- If Thou should mark iniquities, O Lord; O Lord, who shall stand? For with Thee there is forgiveness.

Chorus: *5) For Thy names sake have I patiently waited for Thee, O Lord; my soul has patiently waited for Thy word, my soul has hoped in the Lord.*

Reader: I am rich in passions. I am clothed in vile garments of hypocrisy. Through lack of abstinence, I delight in foul deeds, and show a boundless lack of tender heartedness. Cast before the gates of repentance, I despise my mind, thirsting for every blessing but ill from lack of concentration. Make me, O Lord, like Lazarus, who was poor in sin, lest I receive no answer when I pray: The finger dipped in water to relieve my burning tongue. Make me dwell in the bosom of Abraham, as the lover of man,

Chorus: *4) From the morning watch until night, from the morning watch let Israel hope in the Lord.*

Reader: With boundless love in your souls, O holy martyrs, you did not forsake Christ, enduring the various wounds of suffering you laid low the torturers impudence. Preserving unbending and unshakeable faith, you were translated to heaven. Since you received boldness before Him, entreat Him to grant peace to the world, and for our souls great mercy.

Chorus: *3) For with the Lord there is mercy, and with Him is plenteous redemption; and He shall redeem Israel out of all his iniquities.*

Reader: Jesus told those who were with Him when he walked in the flesh by the river Jordan: my great friend Lazarus is already dead, given over for burial. But I rejoice for your sake, O friends, for by his death you shall learn that I know all, for I am God. Even though I have appeared as man. Let us go and bring him to life, so that death may really feel its utter destruction, and the victory I shall win, granting the world great mercy.

Sticheroi From Psalm 116

Chorus: *2) O praise the Lord, all you nations; praise Him, all you peoples.*

Reader: Imitating Martha and Mary, O Faithful, let us offer Divine works to the Lord as they did, that He might come and raise our minds, which now lie dead in the Tomb of carelessness, feeling no fear of God, and deprived of any living action. Behold, O Lord, who of old didst raise Thy friend Lazarus by Thy coming. Give life to us also, O Bountiful One, granting us great mercy.

Chorus: *1) For He has made His mercy to prevail over us, and the truth of the Lord abides forever.*

Reader: Lazarus is in the tomb two days, seeing the dead of all ages, beholding strange sights of terror, a great crowd held by the bonds of hell. His relatives grieve bitterly, looking at his tomb. But Christ is coming to bring His friend to life, so that one harmonious song may be sung by all: Blessed art Thou, O Savour, have mercy on us.

Theotokion

Tone 6   Rich texture, funeral, sorrowful.   *D, Eb, F##, G, A, Bb, C##, D.*

The evil adversary, jealous of your flock, O most pure one, always battles and desires us as food for himself. But deliver us from this danger, O Theotokos.

[End of Sixth week of Great Lent, Wednesday Evening] – jump to page 556.]

Sixth Week Of Great Lent – Friday Evening
Sticheroi From Psalm 129

Chorus: *8) Out of the depths have I cried unto Thee, O Lord. O Lord, hear my voice.*

Tone 8   Humility, tranquillity, repose, suffering, pleading.   *C, D, Eb, F, G, A, Bb, C.*

Reader: Account us worthy of beholding the week of Thy Passion, O lover of Man, for we have finished the forty days of the fast, that we may glorify Thy greatness, Thy dispensation for our sake. O Lord, glory to Thee.

Chorus: *7) Let Thine ears be attentive to the voice of my supplication.*

Reader: Entreat our God, O martyrs of the Lord, and beseech great bounties for our souls, and purification of our many transgressions.

Chorus: *6) If Thou should mark iniquities, O Lord; O Lord, who shall stand? For with Thee there is forgiveness.*

Tone 6   Rich texture, funereal character, sorrowful tone.   *D, Eb, F##, G, A, Bb, C##, D*

Reader: O Lord, desiring to see the tomb of Lazarus, Thou who voluntarily didst desire to dwell in the tomb, didst ask: *"Where have you laid him?"* After learning that which Thou didst already know, Thou didst call out to him who Thou didst love: *"Lazarus, come forth!"* The dead man listened to the Living God, To Thee, The Saviour of our souls.

Chorus: *5) For Thy names sake have I patiently waited for Thee, O Lord; my soul has patiently waited for Thy word, my soul has hoped in the Lord.*

Reader: O Lord, coming to the place of Lazarus' burial Thou didst weep at the tomb of Thy friend, resurrecting hum who was dead four days. Therefore, death was bound by a voice. Grave clothes were loosed by a hand. Then a multitude of disciples was filled with joy, and one harmony was heard by all: Blessed art Thou, O Saviour, have mercy upon us.

Chorus: *4) From the morning watch until night, from the morning watch let Israel hope in the Lord.*

Reader: O Lord, Thy voice destroyed the kingdom of hell. The Word of Thy Might raised the dead one from the tomb. Lazarus became the saving foretaste of eternal life. All is possible for Thee, O Master, King of all. Grant Thy servants purification and great mercy.

Chorus: *3) For with the Lord there is mercy, and with Him is plenteous redemption; and He shall redeem Israel out of all his iniquities.*

Reader: O Lord, desiring to confirm to Thy disciples Thy resurrection from the dead, Thou didst come to the tomb of Lazarus, calling him. Hell was bound. The man dead four days cried out: "Glory to Thee, O Blessed Lord."

Sticheroi From Psalm 116

Chorus: *2) O praise the Lord, all you nations; praise Him, all you peoples.*

Reader: O Lord, Thou didst come to Bethany to raise Lazarus. As a man Thou didst weep; as God Thou didst raise him who was dead four days. Glory to Thee, O Blessed Lord.

Chorus: *1) For He has made His mercy to prevail over us, and the truth of the Lord abides forever.*

Tone 8   *Humility, tranquillity, repose, suffering, pleading.*   C, D, Eb, F, G, A, Bb, C.

Reader: Standing by the tomb of Lazarus, O Saviour, Thou didst call Thy friend, who was dead, resurrecting hum as from sleep. Mortality was shaken by immortality. By a word the bound was unbound. All is possible, all serves, all submits to Thee, O lover of Man. O our Saviour, glory to Thee.

The Little Entrance

Chorus: *Glory be to the Father and to the Son and to the Holy Spirit;*

Reader: Having complete the edifying forty days, let us sing: Rejoice O Bethany, home of Lazarus. Rejoice, O Martha and Mary, his sisters. On the morrow, Christ shall come to raise your brother, who was dead. Hearing his voice, bitter and unsatisfied hell, shaking and groaning, shall release bound Lazarus. The assembly of the Hebrews was amazed by this. With palms and branches they shall greet Him. Blessed is the King of Israel, who comes in the Name of the Lord.

Chorus: *Both now and forever and unto the ages of ages. Amen.*

Theotokion

Tone 6   Rich texture, funeral, sorrowful.   *D, Eb, F##, G, A, Bb, C##, D.*

Who shall not bless you, O most holy virgin? Who shall not sing of your most pure Child? The Only begotten Son shone timelessly from the Father, but from you He was ineffably Incarnate. God by Nature, He became man for our sake, not divided into two persons, but manifested as One in two Natures. Entreat Him, O pure and all blessed Lady, to have mercy on our souls.

[End of Sixth week of Great Lent, Friday Evening] – jump to page 556.]

Great And Holy Monday
Sticheroi From Psalm 129

- Out of the depths have I cried unto Thee, O Lord. O Lord, hear my voice.
- Let Thine ears be attentive to the voice of my supplication.
- If Thou should mark iniquities, O Lord; O Lord, who shall stand? For with Thee there is forgiveness.

Chorus: **5)** *For Thy names sake have I patiently waited for Thee, O Lord; my soul has patiently waited for Thy word, my soul has hoped in the Lord.*

Tone 1   Magnificent, happy and earthy.   *C, D, Eb, F, G, A, Bb, C.*

Reader: When the Lord was going to His voluntarily Passion He said to His disciples on the way: "Behold, we go up to Jerusalem where the Son of Man shall be delivered, as it is written." Come, therefore, let us accompany Him with minds purified from the pleasures of life. Let us be crucified and die with Him that we may live with Him and hear Him say: "I go now not to the earthly Jerusalem to suffer, but unto my Father and your Father, to my God and your God. I shall raise you to the higher Jerusalem, into the kingdom of heaven."

Chorus: **4)** *From the morning watch until night, from the morning watch let Israel hope in the Lord.*

Tone 5   Stimulating, dancing, and rhythmical.   *C, D, Eb, F, G, A, Bb, C.*

Reader: We have now come near, O faithful, to the saving passion of Christ God. Let us glorify His ineffable forbearance so that by His compassion He may raise us up who were dead. For He is good and the lover of man. While going to Thy passion, O Lord, Thou didst reassure Thy disciples, saying: "How do you not remember the words I have spoken? That in the prophets all things are not written, but that I, in Jerusalem, must be put to death. Now is the time of which I told you. Now I turn myself over to the hands of sinners to be mocked, so that they may raise me upon the cross, buying me as a dead man enduring corruption. Then take courage, for on the third day I shall arise for the joy of the faithful and for life everlasting.

Chorus: *3) For with the Lord there is mercy, and with Him is plenteous redemption; and He shall redeem Israel out of all his iniquities.*

Reader: The ineffable mystery of Thy dispensation, O Lord, was incomprehensible to the mother of Zebedees children. And she asked the honour of a temporal kingdom for her sons. But instead Thou didst promise to Thy friends that they too should drink the cup of death. Thou didst say that Thou wouldst drink this cup for them for the purification of sins. O Salvation of our souls: glory to Thee.

Sticheroi From Psalm 116

Chorus: *2) O praise the Lord, all you nations; praise Him, all you peoples.*

Reader: When Thou wast giving Thy last instruction to Thy disciples, O Lord, Thou didst teach them so that they would not be like the Gentiles. And exercise dominion over the weakest. It shall not be so with you, O disciples, since I desire poverty. So let the first amongst you be the servant of all. And he that rules shall be like those he rules. And he that is first shall be like the last. For truly I have come to Adam in his need, to serve and to give my soul as a ransom for the many who sing: glory to Thee.

Chorus: *1) For He has made His mercy to prevail over us, and the truth of the Lord abides forever.*

Tone 8   Humility, tranquillity, repose, suffering, pleading.   *C, D, Eb, F, G, A, Bb, C.*

Reader: The fig tree was withered because of its barrenness. Let us, O brothers shun a like sentence and bring to Christ fruits worthy of repentance, who grants us great mercy.

The Little Entrance

Chorus: *Glory be to the Father and to the Son and to the Holy Spirit;*

Reader: Finding the Egyptian woman another eye, the tempter tried by flattery to cause Joseph to fall. But Joseph left his garment and fled from sin. And nakedness did not cause him shame, even as to Adam before the fall. Through his prayers, O Christ, have mercy on us.

Chorus: *Both now and forever and unto the ages of ages. Amen.*

Theotokion

Tone 7   Manly character and strong melody.   *F, G, A, A#, C, D, E, F.*

Bear the entreaties of your servants to your Son, O all pure one, that He might save all, whom He made.

[End of Great Monday] – jump to page 556.]

Sticheroi From Psalm 129

- Out of the depths have I cried unto Thee, O Lord. O Lord, hear my voice.

- Let Thine ears be attentive to the voice of my supplication.

Chorus: **6)** *If Thou should mark iniquities, O Lord; O Lord, who shall stand? For with Thee there is forgiveness.*

Tone 1   *Magnificent, happy and earthy.*   C, D, Eb, F, G, A, Bb, C.

Reader: How can I, the unworthy one, enter into the radiance of Thy sanctuary? If I dare to enter into the bridal chamber my garments betray me, for they are not beautiful. And so I will be cast out by the angels. Cleanse the filth of my soul, O Lord and save me, O lover of man.

Chorus: **5)** *For Thy names sake have I patiently waited for Thee, O Lord; my soul has patiently waited for Thy word, my soul has hoped in the Lord.*

Tone 2   *Majesty, gentleness, hope, repentance and sadness.*   E, F, G, Ab, B, C.

Reader: O Christ the Bridegroom I have let my soul slumber in laziness. I have no torch aflame with virtue, and like the foolish virgins I relax when it is time for work. But do not close Thy compassionate heart to me. Rouse me and shake off my heavy sleep, O Master. Lead me into the bridal chamber with the wise virgins, where the voice of those that feast unceasingly is heard, Singing: O Lord, glory to Thee.

Chorus: **4)** *From the morning watch until night, from the morning watch let Israel hope in the Lord.*

Tone 4   *Festive, joyous and capable of expressing deep piety.*   C, D, Eb, F, G, A, Bb, C

Reader: You have heard the condemnation, O soul, of the man who hid his talent, so do not likewise hide the Word of God. Proclaim His miracles, increase the gift of grace, and enter into the Joy of your Lord.

Chorus: **3)** *For with the Lord there is mercy, and with Him is plenteous redemption; and He shall redeem Israel out of all his iniquities.*

Tone 6   *Rich texture, funeral, sorrowful.*   D, Eb, F##, G, A, Bb, C##, D.

Reader: Come, O faithful, let us work zealously for the Master, for He distributes His wealth to His servants. Let each of us, according to his ability increase the talent of grace. Let one grow in wisdom, through good works; let another fashion works of beauty; let some communicate the word to those who ignore it; let others distribute their wealth to the poor, for thus we increase what is entrusted to us. And as faithful stewards of grace we shall be accounted worthy of the Masters joy. Of this make us worthy O Christ God, as the lover of man.

Sticheroi From Psalm 116

Chorus: **2)** *O praise the Lord, all you nations; praise Him, all you peoples.*

Reader: When Thou shalt come in glory with the angelic hosts, O Jesus, and shalt sit upon the throne of judgement, drive me not away, O good Shepherd. For Thou hast the love of those on Thy right side; but those on the left have gone astray. Do not let me, a sinner perish; but number me in Thy faithful flock on Thy right hand and save me, O lover of man.

Chorus: *1) For He has made His mercy to prevail over us, and the truth of the Lord abides forever.*

Reader: Exceeding all men in beauty, O Bridegroom, Thou hast called us to the spiritual banquet of Thy bridal chamber. By participation in Thy suffering let the absurd raiment of my sins disappear. Adorn me with the glorious robe of Thy beauty. Make me a radiant guest of Thy kingdom, O Merciful One.

The Little Entrance

Chorus: *Glory be to the Father and to the Son and to the Holy Spirit;*

   Tone 7   *Manly character and strong melody.*   F, G, A, A#, C, D, E, F

Reader: The Master has entrusted you with a talent, O soul, receive this gift with fear. Lend to Him who gave and distribute to the poor. Acquire for yourself your Lord as a friend, so that when He shall come in glory you may stand on His right hand and hear His blessed Voice: "Enter, my servant, into the joy of your Lord." Of this make me worthy who have gone astray, by Thy great mercy, O Saviour.

Chorus: *Both now and forever and unto the ages of ages. Amen.*

Theotokion

   Tone 7   *Manly character and strong melody.*   F, G, A, A#, C, D, E, F.

Beyond nature you became a mother, O Theotokos, and you remained a virgin beyond reason and understanding. No tongue can explain the wonder of your child bearing. You conceived marvellously, and incomprehensibly gave birth, O pure one. When God wills, the order of nature is over ruled. Therefore, knowing you to be the Mother of God, devoutly we pray to you. Beseech Him to save our souls.

[End of Great Tuesday] – jump to page 556.]

Great And Holy Wednesday
Sticheroi From Psalm 129

• Out of the depths have I cried unto Thee, O Lord. O Lord, hear my voice.

Chorus: *7) Let Thine ears be attentive to the voice of my supplication.*

   Tone 1   *Magnificent, happy and earthy.*   C, D, Eb, F, G, A, Bb, C.

Reader: When the harlot knew Thee as God, O Son of a virgin, she cried: "I have committed acts worthy of tears. Loose my debt as I have loosed my hair. Love her who loves Thee." As the companion of Publicans, I proclaim Thee: "O benefactor and lover of man." The harlot mixed the costly myrrh with her tears, pouring it upon Thy precious feet and kissing them. At once Thou didst forgive her. Grant us forgiveness also and save us.

Chorus: *6) If Thou should mark iniquities, O Lord; O Lord, who shall stand? For with Thee there is forgiveness.*

Reader: While the harlot poured the myrrh the disciple schemed with lawless men. She rejoiced in pouring costly myrrh, he hurried to sell the priceless one. She recognised the Master, but he left His company. She was set free, but Judas become a slave to the enemy. How cruel his apathy; how great her repentance. Grant us repentance, O Saviour, and save us.

Chorus: 5) *For Thy names sake have I patiently waited for Thee, O Lord; my soul has patiently waited for Thy word, my soul has hoped in the Lord.*

Tone 1   *Magnificent, happy and earthy.*   *C, D, Eb, F, G, A, Bb, C.*

Reader: Oh, the wretchedness of Judas. He saw the harlot kissing Christs' footsteps. But deceitfully contemplated the kiss of betrayal. She loosed her hair, but he unleashed his wrath. Instead of myrrh he offered his rotten wickedness. Envy does not know how to honour what is valuable. Oh, the wretchedness of Judas. Deliver our souls from it, O God.

Chorus: 4) *From the morning watch until night, from the morning watch let Israel hope in the Lord.*

Tone 2   *Majesty, gentleness, hope, repentance and sadness.*   *E, F, G, Ab, B, C.*

Reader: The sinful woman hurried to buy the costly myrrh and anoint the Saviour. She cried: "Sell me some so that even I may anoint the One who has cleansed all my sins."

Chorus: 3) *For with the Lord there is mercy, and with Him is plenteous redemption; and He shall redeem Israel out of all his iniquities.*

Tone 6   *Rich texture, funeral, sorrowful.*   *D, Eb, F##, G, A, Bb, C##, D.*

Reader: The sinful harlot found Thee a haven of salvation. She poured myrrh with tears and cried: "Look upon me, O Master who accepts the repentance of sinners, and save me from the tempest of sin by Thy great mercy."

Sticheroi From Psalm 116

Chorus: 2) *O praise the Lord, all you nations; praise Him, all you peoples.*

Reader: The harlot stretched her hair to Thee, O Master, but Judas stretched his hand to the lawless men. She in order to receive forgiveness, he in order to receive some silver. We cry to Thee who wast sold, yet didst set us free: "O Lord, glory to Thee." The filthy and defiled woman drew near to Thee, O Saviour, pouring tears upon Thy precious feet, so proclaiming Thy passion. How can I look at Thee, O Master? Yet Thou hast come to save the harlot, so raise me who am dead in sin as Thou didst raise Lazarus after he was in the tomb four days. Receive me and save me.

Chorus: 1) *For He has made His mercy to prevail over us, and the truth of the Lord abides forever.*

Reader: The woman was in despair for her life and her evil charms were known. Yet she brought costly myrrh and cried: "Do not forsake me, even though I am a harlot. Do not turn away from my tears, O Son of a virgin. Receive me in repentance, O joy of angels. For Thou didst not cast me, a sinner, aside, by Thy great mercy.

The Little Entrance

Chorus: *Glory be to the Father and to the Son and to the Holy Spirit;*

Tone 8   Humility, tranquillity, repose, suffering, pleading.   *C, D, Eb, F, G, A, Bb, C.*

Reader: The woman had fallen into many sins, O Lord, yet when she perceived Thy Divinity she received the dignity of a myrrh bearer. She lamented at Thy feet and cried: "Great is Thy tribulation. For the love of sin and adultery makes my every night dark and without light. Accept my fountain of tears. Incline to the sighing of my heart. I shall kiss Thy pure and Sacred feet. Who can measure my many sin? Yet who can measure the love in Thy judgements? Do not turn away from me, Thy handmaid, O most merciful Saviour."

Chorus: *Both now and forever and unto the ages of ages. Amen.*

Theotokion

Tone 8   Humility, tranquillity, repose, suffering, pleading.   *C, D, Eb, F, G, A, Bb, C.*

Behold the sighs of my broken heart, O Bride of God. Accept the lifting up of my hands, O pure Virgin Mary. In your love for man do not cast me away, O immaculate One, that I may praise and magnify you, who magnified man.

[End of Great Wednesday] – continue straight.

[Continue all from here.]

Continue After Stichera

[Start procession by Deacon and Priest with Holy Gospel - if a feast of a Great Saint, Monday, Tuesday or Wednesday of Great Week. Otherwise just with censer.]

Chorus: *Both now and forever and unto the ages of ages. Amen.*

Deacon: Wisdom. Attend.

O Gladsome Light

O Gladsome Light of the holy glory of the immortal Father;

Heavenly holy, blessed Jesus Christ.

Now that we have come to the setting of the sun, and behold the Evening Light.

We praise God; Father, Son and Holy Spirit.

For meet it is at all time to worship Thee, with voices of praise;

O Son of God and Giver of Life. Therefore all the world doth glorify Thee.

Deacon: The evening Prokeimenon.

[Then find your day from this list:]

First Week Of Great Lent – Wednesday Evening

Tone 5   *Stimulating, dancing, and rhythmical.*   *C, D, Eb, F, G, A, Bb, C.*

Reader: Thou, O Lord, shalt keep us and shalt preserve us from this generation, and for evermore.

People: *Thou, O Lord, shalt keep us and shalt preserve us from this generation, and for evermore.*

Reader: Save me, O Lord, for a righteous man is no more.

People: *Thou, O Lord, shalt keep us and shalt preserve us from this generation, and for evermore.*

Reader: Thou, O Lord, shalt keep us and shalt preserve us from this generation | and for evermore.

The First Reading

[Readings during Lent are from the Old Testament.]

Priest or Reader: The reading is from the book of Genesis (1:24 – 2:3).

Deacon: Let us attend.

Priest or Reader: And God said, "Let the earth bring forth the living creature according to kind: quadrupeds and creeping things and wild animals of the earth according to kind." And it became so. And God made the wild animals of the earth according to kind and the cattle according to kind and all the creeping things of the earth according to their kind. And God saw that they were good. Then God said, "Let us make humankind according to our image and according to likeness, and let them rule the fish of the sea and the birds of the sky and the cattle and all the earth and all the creeping things that creep upon the earth." And God made humankind; according to divine image he made it; male and female he made them. And God blessed them, saying, "Increase, and multiply, and fill the earth, and subdue it, and rule the fish of the sea and the birds of the sky and all the cattle and all the earth and all the creeping things that creep upon the earth." And God said, "See, I have given to you all sowable herbage, propagating seed that is atop the whole earth, and every tree that has in itself fruit of sowable seed – you shall have it a for food, and to all the wild animals of the earth and to all the birds of the sky and to every creeping thing that creeps on the earth that has in itself the animating force of life, even all green herbage for food." And it became so. And God saw all the things that he had made, and see, they were exceedingly good. And it came to be evening, and it came to be morning, a sixth day. And the heaven and the earth were finished, and all their arrangement. And on the sixth day God finished his works that he had made, and he left off on the seventh day from all his works that he had made. And God blessed the seventh day and hallowed it, because on it he left off from all his works that God had begun to make.

Deacon: The evening Prokeimenon.

Tone 6   Rich texture, funeral, sorrowful.   *D, Eb, F##, G, A, Bb, C##, D.*

Reader: Look upon me, hear me, O Lord my God.

People: Look upon me, hear me, O Lord my God.

Reader: How long, O Lord, wilt Thou utterly forget me? How long wilt Thou turn Thy face away from me?

People: Look upon me, hear me, O Lord my God.

Reader: Look upon me, hear me | O Lord my God.

The Second Reading

[Readings during Lent are from the Old Testament.]

Reader: Command!

[People kneel:]

Priest: Wisdom. Attend! The Light of Christ illumines all.

[People stand.]

Priest or Reader: The reading is from the book of Proverbs (2:1-22).

Deacon: Let us attend.

Priest or Reader: My son, if, when you accept the saying of my commandment, you hide it with yourself, your ear shall be attentive to wisdom, and you shall incline your heart to understanding; yes, you shall incline it to the admonition of your son. For if you call upon wisdom and raise your voice for understanding, as well as seek perception with a loud voice, and if you seek it like silver and search for it like treasures, then you shall understand the fear of the Lord, and you shall find divine knowledge. Because the Lord gives wisdom, also from his presence come knowledge and understanding, and he stores up salvation for those who succeed; he shall shield their journey to guard the ways of righteous deeds, and he shall protect the way of the ones who revere him. Then you shall understand righteousness and judgement, and you shall make all good courses straight. For if wisdom comes into your mind and perception seems pleasing to your soul, good counsel shall guard you, and holy insight shall protect you in order that it can rescue you from an evil way and from a man who speaks nothing reliable. Oh, those who abandon straight ways, to walk in ways of darkness, who rejoice in evil and are happy about evil perverseness, whose paths are crooked and their courses are bent in order to remove you far from the straight way and to make you a stranger to a righteous opinion. My son, do not let bad counsel overtake you, that which forsakes the teaching of youth and has forgotten the divine covenant; for it has set her house near death and its courses by Hades with the shades; all those who walk in her shall not come back, nor shall they seize straight paths, for they are not being seized by years of life. For if they were walking good paths, they would have found the smooth paths of righteousness. The kind shall be inhabitants of the earth, and the innocent shall be left in it, because the upright shall encamp on the earth and the holy shall be left in it; the ways of the impious shall perish from the earth, and the transgressors shall be banished from it.

[End of First week of Great Lent, Wednesday Evening] – jump to page 585.]

First Week Of Great Lent – Friday Evening

Tone 5 *Stimulating, dancing, and rhythmical.* *C, D, Eb, F, G, A, Bb, C.*

Reader: The Lord hear thee in the day of affliction.

People: *The Lord hear thee in the day of affliction.*

Reader: The name of the God of Jacob defend thee.

People: *The Lord hear thee in the day of affliction.*

Reader: The Lord hear thee | in the day of affliction.

The First Reading

[Readings during Lent are from the Old Testament.]

Priest or Reader: The reading is from the book of Genesis (2:23 – 3:20).

Deacon: Let us attend.

Priest or Reader: And Adam said, "This now is bone of my bones and flesh of my flesh; this one shall be called Woman, for out of her husband she was taken." Therefore a man shall leave his father and mother and shall be joined to his wife, and the two shall become one flesh. And the two were naked, both Adam and his wife, and were not ashamed. Now the snake was the most sagacious of all the wild animals that were upon the earth, which b the Lord God had made. And the snake said to the woman, "Why is it that God said, 'You shall not eat from any tree that is in the orchard'?" And the woman said to the snake, "We shall eat of the fruit of the tree of the orchard, but of the fruit of the tree that is in the middle of the orchard, God said, 'You shall not eat of it nor shall you even touch it, lest you die.' " And the snake said to the woman, "You shall not die by death, for God knew that on the day you eat of it, your eyes would be opened, and you would be like gods knowing good and evil." And the woman saw that the tree was good for food and that it was pleasing for the eyes to look at and it was beautiful to contemplate, and when she had taken of its fruit she ate, and she also gave some to her husband with her, and they ate. And the eyes of the two were opened, and they knew that they were naked, and they sewed fig leaves together and made loincloths for themselves. And they heard the sound of the Lord God walking about in the orchard in the evening, and both Adam and his wife hid themselves from the presence of the Lord God in the midst of the timber of the orchard. And the Lord God called Adam and said to him, "Adam, where are you?" And he said to him, "I heard the sound of you walking about in the orchard, and I was afraid, because I am naked, and I hid myself." And he said to him, "Who told you that you are naked, unless you have eaten from the tree of which I commanded you, of this one alone, not to eat from it?" And Adam said, "The woman, whom you gave to be with me, she gave me of the tree, and I ate." And God said to the woman, "What is this you have done?" And the woman said, "The snake tricked me, and I ate." And the Lord God said to the snake, "Because you have done this, cursed are you from all the domestic animals and from all the wild animals of the earth; upon your chest and belly you shall go, and earth you shall eat all the days of your life. And I shall put enmity between you and between the woman and between your offspring and between her offspring; he shall watch your head, and you shall watch his heel." And to the woman he said, "I shall increasingly increase your pains and your groaning; with pains you shall bring forth children. And your recourse shall be to your husband, and he shall dominate you." Then to Adam he said, "Because you have listened to the voice of your wife and have eaten from the tree of which I commanded you, of this one alone, not to eat from it, cursed is the earth in your labours; with pains you shall eat it all the days of your life; thorns and thistles it shall cause to grow up for you, and you shall eat the herbage of the field. By the sweat of your face you shall eat your bread until you return to the earth from which you were taken, for you are earth and to earth you shall depart." And Adam called the name of his wife Life, because she is the mother of all the living. And the Lord God made leather tunics for Adam and for his wife and clothed them.

Deacon: The evening Prokeimenon.

Tone 6   *Rich texture, funeral, sorrowful.*   *D, Eb, F##, G, A, Bb, C##, D.*

Reader: Be Thou exalted, O Lord, in Thy strength; we shall sing and chant of Thy mighty acts.

People: *Be Thou exalted, O Lord, in Thy strength; we shall sing and chant of Thy mighty acts.*

Reader: O Lord, in Thy strength the king shall be glad.

People: *Be Thou exalted, O Lord, in Thy strength; we shall sing and chant of Thy mighty acts.*

Reader: Be Thou exalted, O Lord, in Thy strength; we shall sing and chant | of Thy mighty acts.

The Second Reading

[Readings during Lent are from the Old Testament.]

Reader: Command!

[People kneel:]

Priest: Wisdom. Attend! The Light of Christ illumines all.

[People stand.]

Priest or Reader: The reading is from the book of Proverbs (3:19-34).

Deacon: Let us attend.

Priest or Reader: God by wisdom founded the earth, and he prepared the heavens by prudence. By perception the deeps were broken open, and the clouds poured dew. My son, do not break away, but keep my counsel and insight so that your soul may live and that there may be grace round your neck. And it shall be healing to your flesh and treatment for your bones, that you may walk all your ways confidently in peace and that your foot shall not stumble. For if you sit down, you shall be without fear, and when you lie down, you shall pleasantly sleep.

[End of First week of Great Lent, Friday Evening] – jump to page 585.]

Second Week Of Great Lent – Wednesday Evening

Tone 6   Rich texture, funeral, sorrowful.   *D, Eb, F##, G, A, Bb, C##, D.*

Reader: Be glad in the Lord and rejoice, you righteous, and glory all you that are upright of heart.

People: *Be glad in the Lord and rejoice, you righteous, and glory all you that are upright of heart.*

Reader: Blessed are they whose iniquities are forgiven.

People: *Be glad in the Lord and rejoice, you righteous, and glory all you that are upright of heart.*

Reader: Be glad in the Lord and rejoice, you righteous | and glory all you that are upright of heart.

The First Reading

[Readings during Lent are from the Old Testament.]

Priest or Reader: The reading is from the book of Genesis (4:16-26).

Deacon: Let us attend.

Priest or Reader: Then Cain went away from the presence of God and lived in the land of Naid over against Edem. And Cain knew his wife, and after she had conceived she bore Enoch, and he was building a city and named the city after the name of his son Enoch. Then to Enoch was born Gaidad, and Gaidad was the father of Maiel, and Maiel the father of Mathousala, and Mathousala the father of Lamech. And Lamech took for himself two wives; the name of the one was Ada, and the name of the second was Sella. And Ada bore Iobel; he was the ancestor of cattle raisers living in tents. And his brothers name was Ioubal; he was the one who introduced the harp and lyre. As for Sella, she also bore Thobel, and he was a smith, a forger of bronze and iron, and the sister of Thobel was Noahma. Now Lamech said to his own wives: "Ada and Sella, hear my voice; you wives of Lamech, listen to my words, because I have killed a man for a wound to me, and a young man for a welt to me, because seven times vengeance has been exacted by Kain, but by Lamech seventy times seven." Now Adam knew his wife Eve, and after she had conceived she bore a son and named his name Seth, saying, "For God has raised up for me another offspring instead of Habel, whom Cain killed." And to Seth a son was born, and he named his name Enos. He hoped to invoke the name of the Lord God.

Deacon: The evening Prokeimenon.

Tone 1   Magnificent, happy and earthy.   *C, D, Eb, F, G, A, Bb, C.*

Reader: Let Thy mercy, O Lord, be upon us, according as we have hoped in Thee.

People: *Let Thy mercy, O Lord, be upon us, according as we have hoped in Thee.*

Reader: Rejoice in the Lord, O you righteous, praise is meet for the upright.

People: *Let Thy mercy, O Lord, be upon us, according as we have hoped in Thee.*

Reader: *Let Thy mercy, O Lord, be upon us | according as we have hoped in Thee.*

The Second Reading

[Readings during Lent are from the Old Testament.]

Reader: Command!

[People kneel:]

Priest: Wisdom. Attend! The Light of Christ illumines all.

[People stand.]

Priest or Reader: The reading is from the book of Proverbs (5:15 – 6:3).

Deacon: Let us attend.

Priest or Reader: Drink water from your vessels and from the cisterns of your well. Let not the waters out of your well overflow for you; rather let your waters flow into your streets. Let them be at the disposal of you alone, and let no stranger share with you. Let your well of water be solely your own, and rejoice with the woman from your youth. Let the fawn of your love and the foal of your favours consort with you, and let her be considered your very own and be with you on every occasion, for while indulging in her love you shall be increased immeasurably. Do not be for long with a strange woman, nor be held in the arms of someone not your own; for the ways of a man are before the eyes of God, and he observes all their courses. Transgressions ensnare a man, and each one is bound by the ropes of his own sins. He comes to an end with the uninstructed, and he was cast forth from the abundance of his own sustenance and perished through folly. My son, if you stand security for your friend, you shall surrender your hand to an enemy, for a mans own lips are a strong snare, and he is caught by the lips of his own mouth. My son, do what I command you and save yourself, for through your friend you have fallen into the hands of evil; go; do not falter; rather spur on even your friend for whom you stood security.

[End of Second week of Great Lent, Wednesday Evening] – jump to page 585.]

Second Week Of Great Lent – Friday Evening

Tone 4   Festive, joyous and capable of expressing deep piety.   C, D, Eb, F, G, A, Bb, C

Reader: Let Thy mercy and Thy truth continually help me.

People: *Let Thy mercy and Thy truth continually help me.*

Reader: With patience I waited patiently for the Lord, and He was attentive unto me;

And He hearkened unto my supplication.

People: *Let Thy mercy and Thy truth continually help me.*

Reader: Let Thy mercy and Thy truth | continually help me.

The First Reading

[Readings during Lent are from the Old Testament.]

Priest or Reader: The reading is from the book of Genesis (5:32 – 6:8).

Deacon: Let us attend.

Priest or Reader: And Noah was five hundred years of age, and Noah became the father of three sons: Sem, Cham, Japeth. And it came about when humans began to become numerous on the earth, that daughters also were born to them. Now when the sons of God saw the daughters of humans, that they were fair, they took wives for themselves of all that they chose. And the Lord God said, "My spirit shall not abide in these humans forever, because they are flesh, but their days shall be one hundred twenty years." Now the giants were on the earth in those days and afterwards. When the sons of God used to go in to the daughters of humans, then they produced offspring for themselves. Those were the giants that were of old, the renowned humans. And when the Lord God saw that the wicked deeds of humans were multiplied on the earth and that all think attentively in their hearts on evil things all the days, then God considered that he had made humankind on the earth, and he thought it over. And God said, "I shall wipe out from off the earth humankind which I have made, from human to domestic animal and from creeping things to birds of the sky, for I have become angry that I have made them." Yet Noah found favour before the Lord God.

Deacon: The evening Prokeimenon.

Tone 6   Rich texture, funeral, sorrowful.   *D, Eb, F##, G, A, Bb, C##, D.*

Reader: I said: "O Lord, have mercy on me, heal my soul, for I have sinned against Thee."

People: I said: "O Lord, have mercy on me, heal my soul, for I have sinned against Thee."

Reader: Blessed is the man that hath understanding for the poor man and the pauper.

People: I said: "O Lord, have mercy on me, heal my soul, for I have sinned against Thee."

Reader: I said: "O Lord, have mercy on me, heal my soul | for I have sinned against Thee."

The Second Reading

[Readings during Lent are from the Old Testament.]

Reader: Command!

[People kneel:]

Priest: Wisdom. Attend! The Light of Christ illumines all.

[People stand.]

Priest or Reader: The reading is from the book of Proverbs (6:20 – 7:1).

Deacon: Let us attend.

Priest or Reader: My son, keep your fathers laws, and do not forsake your mothers precepts. But always bind them upon your soul, and make them a collar on your neck. When you walk, bring it, and let it be with you, and when you lie down, let it watch over you in order that it may communicate with you when you awake, for the laws commandment is a lamp and a light and a way of life, reproof and discipline, to keep you from a married woman and from the slander of a strange tongue. Let not her desire for beauty conquer you, nor be captured by your eyes; neither be captivated by her eyelashes, for the price of a prostitute is just about as much as a loaf of bread and a mens lady hunts for precious souls. Can anyone put fire in his lap and not burn his clothes? Or can anyone walk on coals of fire and not scorch his feet? So is he who goes in to a married woman. He shall not be held guiltless, nor anyone who touches her. It is not to be marvelled at if someone is caught stealing, for he steals in order to fill himself when he is hungry. Yet, if he is caught, he shall pay sevenfold, and he shall rescue himself by surrendering all his possessions. But the adulterer procures destruction to himself through lack of sense. He experiences both pain and disgrace, and his dishonour shall never be wiped out; for filled with jealousy is the anger of her husband; he shall show no constraint in the day of judgement; neither shall he take any compensation as exchange for his hate, nor shall he at all be reconciled by many gifts. My son, keep my words, and hide my commandments with yourself.

[End of Second week of Great Lent, Friday Evening] – jump to page 585.]

Third Week Of Great Lent – Wednesday Evening

Tone 4   Festive, joyous and capable of expressing deep piety.   *C, D, Eb, F, G, A, Bb, C*

Reader: I have hoped in the mercy of God for ever, and unto the ages of ages.

People: *I have hoped in the mercy of God for ever, and unto the ages of ages.*

Reader: Why dost thou boast in evil, O mighty man, and in iniquity all the day long?

People: *I have hoped in the mercy of God for ever, and unto the ages of ages.*

Reader: I have hoped in the mercy of God for ever | and unto the ages of ages.

The First Reading

[Readings during Lent are from the Old Testament.]

Priest or Reader: The reading is from the book of Genesis (7:6 - 9).

Deacon: Let us attend.

Priest or Reader: Now Noah was six hundred years of age, and the flood of water came on the earth. And Noah and his sons and his wife and his sons' wives went with him into the ark because of the water of the flood. And some of the birds and of the clean domestic animals and of the domestic animals that are not clean and of all the creeping things that are on the earth, two by two, male and female, went into the ark to Noah, as God had commanded him.

Deacon: The evening Prokeimenon.

Tone 4   Festive, joyous and capable of expressing deep piety.   *C, D, Eb, F, G, A, Bb, C*

Reader: When God hath turned back the captivity of His people; Jacob shall rejoice and Israel shall be glad.

People: *When God hath turned back the captivity of His people; Jacob shall rejoice and Israel shall be glad.*

Reader: The fool hath said in his heart: "There is no God."

People: *When God hath turned back the captivity of His people; Jacob shall rejoice and Israel shall be glad.*

Reader: When God hath turned back the captivity of His people, |
              Jacob shall rejoice and Israel shall be glad.

The Second Reading

[Readings during Lent are from the Old Testament.]

Reader: Command!

[People kneel:]

Priest: Wisdom. Attend! The Light of Christ illumines all.

[People stand.]

Priest or Reader: The reading is from the book of Proverbs (9:12 - 18).

Deacon: Let us attend.

Priest or Reader: My son, if you become wise for yourself, you shall be wise for your neighbours as well; however, if you turn out evil, you shall bear the evil alone. He who supports himself with lies shall as well herd winds, and the same person shall pursue flying birds, for he has forsaken the ways of his vineyard and has caused the axles on his own farm to go astray. Yes, he travels through an arid wilderness and a land destined to drought and gathers barrenness with his hands. A foolish and audacious woman who knows no shame comes in need of a morsel of food. She sat at the doors of her own house, on a seat, openly in the streets, inviting those who are passing by and who are keeping straight in their ways. "He of you who is most foolish, let him turn aside to me, and to those that are in need of prudence I urge, saying, 'Take secret bread gladly, and sweet water of theft.'" But he does not know that the dead perish with her, and he meets up with a springboard of Hades. On the contrary, run away; do not linger in the place; neither fix your eye upon her, for so you shall cross strange water and pass through a strange river. However, abstain from strange water, and do not drink from a strange well, that you may live for a long time and years of life may be added to you.

[End of Third week of Great Lent, Wednesday Evening] – jump to page 585.]

Third Week Of Great Lent – Friday Evening

Tone 4   *Festive, joyous and capable of expressing deep piety.*   C, D, Eb, F, G, A, Bb, C.

Reader: Give us help from affliction, for vain is the salvation of the selfish man.

People: *Give us help from affliction, for vain is the salvation of the selfish man.*

Reader: O God, Thou hast cast us off and hast destroyed us;
Thou hast been wroth and hast had pity upon us.

People: *Give us help from affliction, for vain is the salvation of the selfish man.*

Reader: Give us help from affliction, for vain is the salvation | of the selfish man.

The First Reading

[Readings during Lent are from the Old Testament.]

Priest or Reader: The reading is from the book of Genesis (8:4 - 21).

Deacon: Let us attend.

Priest or Reader: And in the seventh month, on the twenty-seventh of the month, the ark settled on the mountains of Ararat. Now the water, as it was proceeding, was diminishing until the tenth month; then in the eleventh month, on the first of the month, the tops of the mountains appeared. And it came about after forty days that Noah opened the window of the ark that he had made and sent out the raven to see if the water had subsided, and after it had gone out it did not return until the water was dried up from the earth. And he sent out the dove after it to see if the water had subsided from the face of the earth. And the dove, because it could not find a resting place for its feet, returned to him into the ark, for water was on the whole face of the whole earth, and extending his hand he took it and brought it into the ark to himself. And when he had waited yet another seven days, again he sent forth the dove from the ark, and the dove went back to him toward evening, and it had an olive leaf, a dry twig, in its mouth, and Noah knew that the water had subsided from the earth. And when he had waited yet another seven days, again he sent forth the dove, and it did not continue to turn back to him any more. And it came about in the six hundred first year in the life of Noah, the first month, on the first of the month, that the water disappeared from the earth, and Noah uncovered the roof of the ark that he had made, and he saw that the water had disappeared from the face of the earth. Then in the second month, on the twenty-seventh of the month, the earth was dry. And the Lord God spoke to Noah, saying, "Go out of the ark, you and your wife and your sons and your sons' wives with you, and bring out with yourself all the wild animals that are with you, and all flesh from birds to domestic animals and every creeping thing that moves on the earth, and increase, and multiply on the earth." And Noah went out, and his wife and his sons and his sons' wives with him, and all the wild animals and all the domestic animals and every bird and every creeping thing that moves on the earth went out of the ark according to their kind. And Noah built an altar to God and took of all the clean domestic animals and of all the clean birds and offered whole burnt offerings on the altar. And the Lord God smelled an odour of fragrance, and the Lord God, when he had given it thought, said, "I shall not proceed hereafter to curse the earth because of the deeds of humans, for the mind of humankind applies itself attentively to evil things from youth; so I shall not proceed hereafter to smite all living flesh, as I have done.

Deacon: The evening Prokeimenon.

Tone 6   *Rich texture, funeral, sorrowful.*   *D, Eb, F##, G, A, Bb, C##, D.*

Reader: Hearken, O God, unto my supplication, attend unto my prayer.

People: *Hearken, O God, unto my supplication, attend unto my prayer.*

Reader: So shall I chant unto Thy name unto ages.

People: *Hearken, O God, unto my supplication, attend unto my prayer.*

Reader: Hearken, O God, unto my supplication, | attend unto my prayer.

The Second Reading

[Readings during Lent are from the Old Testament.]

Reader: Command!

[People kneel:]

Priest: Wisdom. Attend! The Light of Christ illumines all.

[People stand.]

Priest or Reader: The reading is from the book of Proverbs (10:31 – 11:12).

Deacon: Let us attend.

Priest or Reader: The mouth of the righteous drips wisdom, but the tongue of the unjust shall perish. The lips of the righteous drip charm, but the mouth of the impious turns people away. False balances are an abomination before the Lord, but a just weight is acceptable to him. Where pride enters, there shall also be disgrace, but the mouth of the humble attends to wisdom. When a righteous person died, he left regret, but destruction of the impious is at hand, and joyous. Righteousness cuts out blameless paths, but impiety is beset with injustice. The righteousness of upright men rescues them, but transgressors are taken captive by their destruction. When a righteous man dies, hope does not perish, but the boast of the impious perishes. A righteous person eludes from a chase, and the impious is handed over in his stead. In the mouth of the impious is a snare to citizens, but the perception of the righteous is free from difficulties. By the good deeds of the righteous a city succeeded, but by the mouths of the impious it was levelled. A person who lacks sense scorns citizens, but an intelligent man keeps quiet.

[End of Third week of Great Lent, Friday Evening] – jump to page 585.]

[End of Third week of Great Lent, Friday Evening] – jump to page 585.]

Fourth Week Of Great Lent – Wednesday Evening

Tone 8   *Humility, tranquillity, repose, suffering, pleading.*   *C, D, Eb, F, G, A, Bb, C.*

Reader: Blessed is the Lord, the God of Israel, Who alone doest wonders.

People: *Blessed is the Lord, the God of Israel, Who alone doest wonders.*

Reader: O God, give Thy judgement to the king, and Thy righteousness to the son of the king.

People: *Blessed is the Lord, the God of Israel, Who alone doest wonders.*

Reader: Blessed is the Lord, the God of Israel | Who alone doest wonders.

The First Reading

[Readings during Lent are from the Old Testament.]

Priest or Reader: The reading is from the book of Genesis (9:18 – 10:1).

Deacon: Let us attend.

Priest or Reader: Now the sons of Noah who went out of the ark were Sem, Cham, Japheth; Cham was the father of Chanaan. These three are the sons of Noah; from these they were scattered abroad over the whole earth. And Noah was the first soil tilling person, and he planted a vineyard. And he drank some of the wine and became drunk, and he was stripped naked in his house. And Cham, the father of Chanaan, saw the nakedness of his father, and after he had gone out he told his two brothers outside. And Sem and Japheth, when they had taken the garment, laid it on their two backs and walked backward and covered the nakedness of their father, and their face was looking backward, and they did not see their fathers nakedness. Then Noah sobered up from the wine, and he knew what his younger son had done to him, and he said, "Cursed be Chanaan; a slave, a domestic, shall he be to his brothers." He also said, "Blessed be the Lord, the God of Sem, and Chanaan shall be his slave. May God make space for Japheth, and let him live in the houses of Sem, and let Chanaan become their slave." Now after the flood Noah lived three hundred fifty years. And all the days of Noah amounted to nine hundred fifty years, and he died. Now these are the generations of Noahs sons, Sem, Cham, Japheth, and sons were born to them after the flood.

Deacon: The evening Prokeimenon.

Tone 4   *Festive, joyous and capable of expressing deep piety.*   *C, D, Eb, F, G, A, Bb, C.*

Reader: But it is good for me to cleave unto God, to put my hope in the Lord.

People: *But it is good for me to cleave unto God, to put my hope in the Lord.*

Reader: How good is God to Israel, to them that are upright of heart.

People: *But it is good for me to cleave unto God, to put my hope in the Lord.*

Reader: But it is good for me to cleave unto God | to put my hope in the Lord.

The Second Reading

[Readings during Lent are from the Old Testament.]

Reader: Command!

[People kneel:]

Priest: Wisdom. Attend! The Light of Christ illumines all.

[People stand.]

Priest or Reader: The reading is from the book of Proverbs (12:23 – 13:9).

Deacon: Let us attend.

Priest or Reader: An intelligent man is a seat of perception, but the heart of fools shall meet with curses. The hand of the elected shall easily govern, but the deceitful shall become a prey. Terrifying news troubles the heart of a just man, but a good message cheers him up. A just arbiter shall be his own friend, but the opinions of the impious are unfair. Evil shall pursue those that sin, and the way of the impious shall lead them astray. The deceitful shall obtain no game, but a pure man a valuable possession. In the ways of justice there is life, but the ways of those who bear grudges lead to death. A smart son is obedient to his father, but a disobedient son is on course to destruction. A good person shall eat of the fruits of justice, but the souls of transgressors shall perish untimely. He who guards his own mouth keeps his own life, but he who is rash with his lips shall bring terror upon himself. Every lazy person has desires, but the hands of the courageous are diligent. A just person hates an unjust word, but the impious is ashamed and shall have no confidence. Justice guards the innocent, but sin makes the impious worthless. There are some who, while having nothing, enrich themselves, and there are others who humble themselves in much wealth. A mans own wealth is the ransom of his soul, but the poor does not experience threat. The just always have light, but the light of the impious is extinguished.

[End of Fourth week of Great Lent, Wednesday Evening] – jump to page 585.]

Fourth Week Of Great Lent – Friday Evening

Tone 4   *Festive, joyous and capable of expressing deep piety.*   *C, D, Eb, F, G, A, Bb, C.*

Reader: Thou that sittest upon the cherubim, manifest Thyself.

People: *Thou that sittest upon the cherubim, manifest Thyself.*

Reader: O Shepherd of Israel, attend. Thou that leadest Joseph like a sheep.

People: *Thou that sittest upon the cherubim, manifest Thyself.*

Reader: Thou that sittest upon the cherubim | manifest Thyself.

The First Reading

[Readings during Lent are from the Old Testament.]

Priest or Reader: The reading is from the book of Genesis (12:1 - 7).

Deacon: Let us attend.

Priest or Reader: And the Lord said to Abram, "Go forth from your country and from your kindred and from your fathers house to the land that I shall show you. And I shall make you into a great nation, and I shall bless you and make your name great, and you shall be one blessed. And I shall bless those who bless you, and those who curse you I shall curse, and in you all the tribes of the earth shall be blessed." And Abram went, as the Lord had told him to, and Lot left with him. Now Abram was seventy-five years of age when he departed from Charran. And Abram took his wife Sara and his brothers son Lot and all their possessions that they had acquired and every person whom they had acquired in Charran, and they departed to go to the land of Chanaan, and they came to the land of Chanaan. And Abram passed through the land in its length as far as the place Sychem, at the high oak. Now at that time the Chananites used to inhabit the land. And the Lord appeared to Abram and said to him, "To your offspring I shall give this land." And Abram built there an altar to the Lord who had appeared to him.

Deacon: The evening Prokeimenon.

Tone 2   *Majesty, gentleness, hope, repentance and sadness.*   *E, F, G, Ab, B, C.*

Reader: Rejoice in God our helper, shout with joy to the God of Jacob.

People: *Rejoice in God our helper, shout with joy to the God of Jacob.*

Reader: Take up a psalm, and bring the timbrel.

People: *Rejoice in God our helper, shout with joy to the God of Jacob.*

Reader: Rejoice in God our helper, shout with joy | to the God of Jacob.

The Second Reading

[Readings during Lent are from the Old Testament.]

Reader: Command!

[People kneel:]

Priest: Wisdom. Attend! The Light of Christ illumines all.

[People stand.]

Priest or Reader: The reading is from the book of Proverbs (14:15 - 26).

Deacon: Let us attend.

Priest or Reader: The innocent believes every word, but the smart comes to a change of mind. A wise man feared and turned away from evil, but the fool trusts in himself and associates with the lawless. A passionate person acts with thoughtlessness, but a sensible man endures many things. Fools shall partake of evil, but the smart shall lay hold of perception. The evil shall fall down before the good, and the impious shall serve at the gates of the just. Friends shall hate poor friends, but the friends of the rich are many. He who dishonours the needy sins, but one who pities the poor is deemed most happy. They who go astray devise evil, but the good devise pity and truth. The planners of evil do not understand pity and loyalty, but acts of mercy and of loyalty are with planners for good. With everyone who is careful there is abundance, but the hedonist and indolent shall have want. A crown for the wise is a smart man, but the pastime of fools is evil. A faithful witness shall rescue a soul from evil, but a deceitful person kindles falsehoods. In the fear of the Lord is hope in strength, and he leaves his children support.

[End of Fourth week of Great Lent, Friday Evening] – jump to page 585.]

Fifth Week Of Great Lent – Wednesday Evening

Tone 4   *Festive, joyous and capable of expressing deep piety.*   *C, D, Eb, F, G, A, Bb, C.*

Reader: The Lord is the God of vengeance, the God of vengeance hath openly spoken.

People: *The Lord is the God of vengeance, the God of vengeance hath openly spoken.*

Reader: Be Thou exalted, O Thou that judgest the earth; render the proud their due.

People: *The Lord is the God of vengeance, the God of vengeance hath openly spoken.*

Reader: The Lord is the God of vengeance | the God of vengeance hath openly spoken.

The First Reading

[Readings during Lent are from the Old Testament.]

Priest or Reader: The reading is from the book of Genesis (17:1 - 9).

Deacon: Let us attend.

Priest or Reader: Now Abram came to be ninety-nine years of age, and the Lord appeared to Abram and said to him, "I am your God; be well pleasing before me, and become blameless, and I shall set my covenant between me and between you and shall make you very numerous." And Abram fell face down, and God spoke to him, saying, "And as for me, see, my covenant is with you, and you shall be an ancestor of a multitude of nations. And no longer shall your name be called Abram, but your name shall be Abraham, for I have made you an ancestor of many nations. And I shall increase you very, very much, and I shall make you into nations, and kings shall come from you. And I shall establish my covenant between me and between you and between your offspring after you throughout their generations for an everlasting covenant, to be your God and your offspring after you. And I shall give to you and to your offspring after you the land that you inhabit as a resident alien, all the land of Canaan, for a perpetual holding, and I shall be a God to them." And God said to Abraham, "Now as for you, you shall keep my covenant, you and your offspring after you throughout their generations.

Deacon: The evening Prokeimenon.

Tone 6   Rich texture, funeral, sorrowful.   *D, Eb, F##, G, A, Bb, C##, D.*

Reader: O sing unto the Lord a new song, sing unto the Lord all the earth.

People: *O sing unto the Lord a new song, sing unto the Lord all the earth.*

Reader: Sing unto the Lord, bless His name.

People: *O sing unto the Lord a new song, sing unto the Lord all the earth.*

Reader: O sing unto the Lord a new song | sing unto the Lord all the earth.

The Second Reading

[Readings during Lent are from the Old Testament.]

Reader: Command!

[People kneel:]

Priest: Wisdom. Attend! The Light of Christ illumines all.

[People stand.]

Priest or Reader: The reading is from the book of Proverbs (15:20 - 16:9).

Deacon: Let us attend.

Priest or Reader: A wise son gladdens his father, but a foolish son scorns his mother. The paths of the foolish are void of sense, but the prudent man proceeds in a straight course. They who do not honour councils delay deliberations, but counsel prevails in the hearts of those giving advice. The evil person shall not heed it; neither shall he say anything appropriate or good for the public. The thoughts of the intelligent person are ways of life in order that one turn aside and escape from Hades. The Lord tears down the homes of the insolent, but he established the border of the widow. An unjust thought is an abomination to the Lord, but the sayings of the pure are solemn. A receiver of bribes destroys himself, but he who hates the receiving of bribes is saved. By acts of mercy and by faithfulness sins are purged, but by the fear of the Lord everyone turns away from evil. The hearts of the righteous ponder faithfulness, but the mouth of the impious answers evil things. The ways of righteous persons are acceptable to the Lord, and through them even enemies become friends. God is far from the impious, but he hears the prayers of the righteous. Better is a small intake with righteousness than abundant produce with injustice. Let the heart of a man think righteous things, that his steps may be directed by God. The eye that observes good things rejoices the heart, and good news refreshes the bones. He who rejects discipline hates himself, but he who heeds rebukes loves his soul. Fear of God is discipline and wisdom, and the beginning of glory shall respond to it. All the works of the humble are manifest with God, but the impious shall perish in an evil day. Everyone who is arrogant is impure with God, and he who unjustly joins hands shall not be deemed innocent. The beginning of a good way is to do righteous things, and they are more acceptable with God than to bring sacrifices. He who seeks the Lord shall find knowledge with righteousness, and they who seek him rightly shall find peace. All the works of the Lord are done with righteousness, but the impious is kept for an evil day.

[End of Fifth week of Great Lent, Wednesday Evening] – jump to page 585.]

Fifth Week Of Great Lent – Thursday Evening

Tone 7   *Manly character and strong melody.*   *F, G, A, A#, C, D, E, F.*

Reader: Exalt you the Lord our God and worship the footstool of His feet; for His is holy.

People: *Exalt you the Lord our God and worship the footstool of His feet; for His is holy.*

Reader: The Lord is king, let the people rage.

People: *Exalt you the Lord our God and worship the footstool of His feet; for His is holy.*

Reader: Exalt you the Lord our God and worship the footstool of His feet | for His is holy.

The First Reading

[Readings during Lent are from the Old Testament.]

Priest or Reader: The reading is from the book of Genesis (18:20 - 33).

Deacon: Let us attend.

Priest or Reader: The the Lord said, "The outcry concerning Sodom and Gomorra has been increased, and their sins are very great! So when I go down I shall see whether they are perpetrating according to the outcry concerning them that is coming to me, but if not - that I may know." And after the men had turned away from there, they went to Sodom, but Abraham was still standing before the Lord. Then when Abraham had come near, he said, "Surely you shall not destroy the righteous with the ungodly, and the righteous shall be as the ungodly? If there should be fifty righteous in the city, shall you destroy them? Shall you not let the whole place go free on account of the fifty righteous, if they should be in it? By no means shall you do anything like this thing, to slay the righteous with the ungodly, and the righteous shall be like the ungodly! By no means! Shall not you, the one who judges all the earth, do what is just?" Then the Lord said, "If I find in Sodom fifty righteous in the city, I shall forgive the whole place for their sake." And Abraham said in reply, "Now I have begun to speak to the Lord, though I am earth and ashes. But if the fifty righteous should be diminished by five, shall you destroy the whole city on account of the five?" And he said, "I shall not destroy it, if I find forty-five there." And he continued still to speak to him and said, "But if forty should be found there?" And he said, "On account of the forty I shall not destroy it." And he said, "Pardon, Lord, if I should speak. But if thirty should be found there?" And he said, "I shall not destroy it, if I find thirty there." And he said, "Since I am compelled to speak to the Lord - and if twenty should be found there?" And he said, "On account of the twenty I shall not destroy it." And he said, "Pardon, Lord, if I should speak once more. But if ten should be found there?" And he said, "On account of the ten I shall not destroy it." Then the Lord went away, when he had left off speaking to Abraham, and Abraham returned to his place.

Deacon: The evening Prokeimenon.

Tone 6   *Rich texture, funeral, sorrowful.*   *D, Eb, F##, G, A, Bb, C##, D.*

Reader: Shout with jubilation unto God, all the earth.

People: *Shout with jubilation unto God, all the earth.*

Reader: Serve the Lord with gladness; come before His presence with rejoicing.

People: *Shout with jubilation unto God, all the earth.*

Reader: Shout with jubilation unto God | all the earth.

The Second Reading

[Readings during Lent are from the Old Testament.]

Reader: Command!

[People kneel:]

Priest: Wisdom. Attend! The Light of Christ illumines all.

[People stand.]

Priest or Reader: The reading is from the book of Proverbs (16:17 – 17:17).

Deacon: Let us attend.

Priest or Reader: The paths of life turn away from evil, and the ways of righteousness are length of existence. He who receives discipline shall prosper, and he who heeds rebukes shall become wise. He who heeds his ways preserves his own soul, and he who loves his life shall spare his mouth. Pride goes before ruin, and malice before a fall. Better is a person of gentle mind with humility than he who divides spoils with the proud. One who is capable in business is a discoverer of good things, but he who trusts in God is most fortunate. Some call the wise and intelligent worthless, but they who are pleasant in speech shall be heard more. Insight is a fountain of life to its possessors, but the discipline of fools is evil. The heart of the wise shall consider what comes from his own mouth, and on his lips he shall bear prudence. Noble words are honeycombs, and its sweetness a healing for the soul. There are ways that seem to be right for a man, but their ends look towards Hades' depth. A man at labour labours for himself and fences off his own destruction, but the crooked carries destruction in his own mouth. A foolish man digs up evil for himself, and treasures fire on his own lips. A crooked man spreads evil and shall kindle with evil a torch of deceit, and he separates friends. A man who transgresses makes trial of friends and leads them in ways that are not good. He who fixes his eyes considers perverse things, and he marks out with his lips all evil; he is a furnace of evil. Old age is a crown of boasting; however, it is gained in the ways of righteousness. A man who is slow to anger is better than the mighty, and he who controls his temper better than one who captures a city. All things come upon the unrighteous into their laps, but all righteous things come from the Lord. Better is a morsel with pleasure in peace than a house full of many good things and unjust sacrifices with strife. An intelligent domestic shall rule over foolish masters and shall divide portions among brothers. As silver and gold are tried in a furnace, so are choice hearts with the Lord. A bad person listens to the tongue of transgressors, but a righteous person does not give heed to false lips. He who laughs at the poor provokes his maker, and he who rejoices at one being destroyed shall not go unpunished. But he who has compassion shall find mercy. Childrens children are a crown for the aged, and their fathers are the boast of children. The faithful has the whole world full of money, but the faithless not even a farthing. Faithful lips shall not suit a fool, nor false lips the righteous. Discipline is a gracious wage to them that use it, and wherever it turns, it shall prosper. He who conceals wrongdoings seeks friendship, but he who hates to conceal them separates friends and family. A threat shatters the heart of a prudent person, but a fool, though whipped, does not comprehend. Every bad person stirs up controversies, but the Lord shall send out against him a cruel messenger. Care shall befall a man of understanding, but fools shall consider evil. He who requites evil for good - evil shall not be moved from his house. Righteous rule gives power to words, but sedition and strife precede want. He who judges the unjust just and the just unjust is unclean and abominable with God. Why should fools have money? For the heartless shall not be able to buy wisdom. He who makes his own house high is looking for ruin, and the one who is too crooked to learn shall fall into evil. You should have a friend for every season, but let brothers be supportive in distress, for on this account are they born.

[End of Fifth week of Great Lent, Thursday Evening] – jump to page 585.]

Fifth Week Of Great Lent – Friday Evening

Tone 4	*Festive, joyous and capable of expressing deep piety.*	C, D, Eb, F, G, A, Bb, C.

Reader: Compassionate and merciful is the Lord, long suffering and plenteous in mercy.

People: *Compassionate and merciful is the Lord, long suffering and plenteous in mercy.*

Reader: Bless the Lord, O my soul, and all that is within me bless His holy name.

People: *Compassionate and merciful is the Lord, long suffering and plenteous in mercy.*

Reader: Compassionate and merciful is the Lord | long suffering and plenteous in mercy.

The First Reading

[Readings during Lent are from the Old Testament.]

Priest or Reader: The reading is from the book of Genesis (22:1 - 18).

Deacon: Let us attend.

Priest or Reader: And it came about after these matters that God tested Abraham and said to him, "Abraham, Abraham!" And he said, "Here I am." And he said, "Take your beloved son Isaac, whom you love, and go into the high land, and offer him as a whole burnt offering on one of the mountains, whichever I mention to you." And when Abraham had risen in the morning, he saddled his donkey. Now he took along with himself two servants and his son Isaac, and after he had split wood for a whole burnt offering and risen, he went and came to the place that God had mentioned to him, on the third day. And when Abraham looked up with his eyes, he saw the place far away. Then Abraham said to his servants, "Sit right here with the donkey, and the youngster and I shall go through hither, and after we have done obeisance, we shall come back to you." And Abraham took the wood of the whole burnt offering and laid it on his son Isaac; then he took both the fire and the knife in hand, and the two walked on together. And Isaac spoke to his father Abraham (when he had said, "Father!" and he had said, "What is it, child?"), saying, "Look, the fire and the wood! Where is the sheep for a whole burnt offering?" And Abraham said, "God shall see to a sheep as a whole burnt offering for himself, child." And as both walked on together they came to the place that God had mentioned to him. And Abraham built the altar there and laid on the wood, and when he had bound his son Isaac hand and foot, he laid him on the altar atop the wood. Then Abraham reached out his hand to take the knife to slay his son. And the Lords angel called him from heaven and said to him, "Abraham, Abraham!" And he said, "Here I am." And he said, "Do not lay your hand on the youngster nor do anything to him. For now I know that you do fear God, and for my sake you have not spared your beloved son." And as Abraham looked up with his eyes he saw, and see, a ram held fast in a sabek plant by the horns. And Abraham went and took the ram and offered it up as a whole burnt offering instead of his son Isaac. And Abraham called the name of that place "The-Lord-saw," that they might say today, "On the mountain the Lord appeared." And the Lords angel called Abraham a second time from heaven, saying, "By myself I have sworn, says the Lord: Inasmuch as you have carried out this matter and for my sake have not spared your beloved son, I shall indeed bless you with blessings, and I shall make your offspring as numerously numerous as the stars of heaven and as the sand that is by the seashore, and your offspring shall possess the cities of their adversaries, and in your offspring shall all the nations of the earth be blessed, because you have obeyed my voice."

Deacon: The evening Prokeimenon.

Tone 4   Festive, joyous and capable of expressing deep piety.   *C, D, Eb, F, G, A, Bb, C.*

Reader: How magnified are Thy works, O Lord. In wisdom hast Thou made them all.

People: *How magnified are Thy works, O Lord. In wisdom hast Thou made them all.*

Reader: Bless the Lord, O my soul. O Lord my God, Thou hast been exceedingly magnified.

People: *How magnified are Thy works, O Lord. In wisdom hast Thou made them all.*

Reader: How magnified are Thy works, O Lord. | In wisdom hast Thou made them all.

The Second Reading

[Readings during Lent are from the Old Testament.]

Reader: Command!

[People kneel:]

Priest: Wisdom. Attend! The Light of Christ illumines all.

[People stand.]

Priest or Reader: The reading is from the book of Proverbs (17:17 – 18:5).

Deacon: Let us attend.

Priest or Reader: You should have a friend for every season, but let brothers be supportive in distress, for on this account are they born. A foolish man applauds and rejoices over himself; as well, he who pledges himself ought to answer for his own friend. A lover of sin rejoices in fights, but the hard hearted does not meet up with good things. A man who is fickle of tongue shall fall into evil, and the heart of a fool is grief to its possessor. A father does not rejoice over an uninstructed son, but a prudent son gladdens his mother. A cheerful heart promotes well being, but the bones of a depressed man dry up. The ways of one who unjustly receives bribes in his pocket do not prosper, and the impious perverts the ways of righteousness. The face of a wise person is intelligent, but the eyes of the fool are on the ends of the earth. A foolish son is a cause of anger to his father and a grief to her who bore him. It is not good to punish a righteous man, nor is it pious to plot against righteous rulers. He who is careful to utter a harsh word is discreet, and a patient man is sensible. Wisdom shall be imputed to a silly person who asks after wisdom, but someone who keeps himself speechless shall seem to be sensible. A man who wishes to separate from friends looking for excuses, but shall be liable to reproach at all times. A person lacking in sense feels no need for wisdom, for he is much more led by folly. When the impious comes into a depth of evils, he shows contempt, but disgrace and reproach come upon him. A word in the heart of a man is deep water, and a river and a fountain of life spring forth. It is not good to respect the person of the impious, nor is it pious to pervert justice in judgement.

[End of Fifth week of Great Lent, Friday Evening] *– jump to page 585.]*

Sixth Week Of Great Lent – Wednesday Evening

Tone 4	*Festive, joyous and capable of expressing deep piety.*	*C, D, Eb, F, G, A, Bb, C.*

Reader: I shall be well pleasing before the Lord in the land of the living.

People: *I shall be well pleasing before the Lord in the land of the living.*

Reader: I am filled with love, for the Lord shall hear the voice of my supplication.

People: *I shall be well pleasing before the Lord in the land of the living.*

Reader: I shall be well pleasing before the Lord | in the land of the living.

The First Reading

[Readings during Lent are from the Old Testament.]

Priest or Reader: The reading is from the book of Genesis (43:26 – 31; 45:1 - 16).

Deacon: Let us attend.

Priest or Reader: And Joseph came into the dwelling, and they brought to him the presents that they had in their hands - into the house - and did obeisance to him face down on the ground. And he asked them, "How are you?" And he said to them, "Is your father well, the old man of whom you spoke? Is he still alive?" And they said, "Your servant our father is well; he is still alive." And he said, "Blessed be that man to God." And bending forward they did obeisance to him. Then looking up with his eyes, he saw his brother Benjamin, born of the same mother, and said, "Is this your younger brother, whom you said you would bring to me?" And he said, "May God show mercy to you, child!" And Joseph was troubled, for his insides were twisting up over his brother, and he was seeking to weep. And going into the chamber he wept there. Then washing his face and coming out he controlled himself and said, "Serve bread loaves."

And Joseph could not bear with all those who were standing by him, but said, "Send all away from me." And no one stood by Joseph any longer when he was making himself known to his brothers. And he let go his voice with weeping; now all the Egyptians heard it, and it came to be heard in the household of Pharaoh. And Joseph said to his brothers, "I am Joseph. Is my father still alive?" And his brothers could not answer him, for they were troubled. Then Joseph said to his brothers, "Come near to me." And they came near. And he said, "I am your brother Joseph, whom you sold into Egypt. Now therefore do not be distressed nor let it seem hard to you that you sold me here, for God sent me before you for life. For famine is on the earth this second year, and there are still five years remaining in which there shall be neither ploughing nor harvest. For God sent me before you, to leave behind a remnant of you on the earth and to nourish a great posterity of you. Now therefore it is not you who have sent me here, but rather God, and he made me as a father to Pharaoh and lord of all his house and ruler over all the land of Egypt. So hurry, go up to my father, and say to him, 'This is what your son Joseph says, God made me lord of all the land of Egypt; so come down to me, and do not remain. And you shall settle in the land of Gesem of Arabia, and you shall be near me, you and your sons and your sons sons, your sheep and your cattle and as much as you have, and I shall nourish you there - for there is famine for five more years – lest you be annihilated, you and your sons and all your possessions.' Look, your eyes and the eyes of Benjamin my brother see that it is my mouth that speaks to you. So report to my father all my glory in Egypt and how much you have seen and make haste; bring my father down here." And falling upon his brother Benjamins neck, he wept on him, and Benjamin wept on his neck. And kissing all his brothers, he wept on them, and after that his brothers spoke to him. And the utterance was proclaimed in Pharaohs house - they were saying - "Josephs brothers have come." And Pharaoh and his retinue were delighted.

Deacon: The evening Prokeimenon.

Tone 4   *Festive, joyous and capable of expressing deep piety.*   *C, D, Eb, F, G, A, Bb, C.*

Reader: My vows unto the Lord shall I pay in the presence of all His people.

People: *My vows unto the Lord shall I pay in the presence of all His people.*

Reader: I believed, wherefore I spake, I was exceedingly humbled.

People: *My vows unto the Lord shall I pay in the presence of all His people.*

Reader: My vows unto the Lord shall I pay | in the presence of all His people.

The Second Reading

[Readings during Lent are from the Old Testament.]

Reader: Command!

[People kneel:]

Priest: Wisdom. Attend! The Light of Christ illumines all.

[People stand.]

Priest or Reader: The reading is from the book of Proverbs (21:23 – 22:4).

Deacon: Let us attend.

Priest or Reader: He who guards his mouth and tongue keeps his soul out of trouble. The bold and audacious and pretentious is called a pest, and he who contemplates evil is a transgressor of the law. Desires kill the lazy, for his hands choose not to do anything. The impious longs for wicked desires all day long, but the righteous has compassion and pity unsparingly. The sacrifice of the impious is an abomination to the Lord, for they even offer them unlawfully. A false witness shall perish, but an obedient man shall speak cautiously. An impious man impudently resists with his face, but the upright - he understands his ways. There is no wisdom; there is no courage; there is no counsel against the impious. A horse is prepared for the day of battle, but assistance is from the Lord. A good name is a better choice than great wealth, and good favour is above silver and gold. The rich and the poor have encountered each other, but the Lord has made them both. When the clever sees the wicked severely punished, he himself is being educated, but the fools passed by and were penalised. The offspring of wisdom is the fear of the Lord as well as riches and honour and life.

[End of Sixth week of Great Lent, Wednesday Evening] – jump to page 585.]

Sixth Week Of Great Lent – Friday Evening

Tone 6   Rich texture, funeral, sorrowful.   *D, Eb, F##, G, A, Bb, C##, D.*

Reader: Our help is in the name of the Lord; Who hath made heaven and the earth.

People: *Our help is in the name of the Lord; Who hath made heaven and the earth.*

Reader: You that stand in the house of the Lord, in the courts of the house of our God.

People: *Our help is in the name of the Lord; Who hath made heaven and the earth.*

Reader: Our help is in the name of the Lord | *Who hath made heaven and the earth.*

The First Reading

[Readings during Lent are from the Old Testament.]

Priest or Reader: The reading is from the book of Genesis (49:33 – 50:26).

Deacon: Let us attend.

Priest or Reader: And Jacob ceased issuing orders to his sons, and lifting his feet onto the bed he breathed his last and was added to his people. And Joseph, falling on his fathers face, wept over him and kissed him. And Joseph ordered his servants, the undertakers, to prepare his father for burial, and the undertakers prepared Israel for burial. And they completed his forty days, for so the days of burial are reckoned. And Egypt mourned for him seventy days. Then after the days of mourning had passed, Joseph spoke to the chief men of Pharaoh, saying, "If I have found favour before you, speak into the ears of Pharaoh, saying: My father made me swear an oath, saying, 'In the tomb that I dug out for myself in the land of Canaan, there you shall bury me.' Now then I shall go up and bury my father, and I shall return." And Pharaoh said, "Go up; bury your father, as he made you swear." And Joseph went up to bury his father, and together with him went up all the servants of Pharaoh and the elders of his house and all the elders of the land of Egypt and the whole entire household of Joseph and his brothers and all his paternal household. And their kindred and their sheep and their cattle they left behind in the land of Gesem. And both chariots and horsemen went up together with him, and the company was very great. And they arrived at the threshing floor of Atad, which is beyond the Jordan, and they lamented him with a very great and strong lamentation, and he made mourning for his father seven days. And the inhabitants of the land of Canaan saw the mourning on the threshing floor of Atad and said, "This is a great mourning to the Egyptians." Therefore one called the name of the place Mourning-of-Egypt, which is beyond the Jordan. And his sons did thus for him just as he had commanded them, and they buried him there. And his sons took him up into the land of Canaan and buried him in the double cave over against Mamvre, which cave Abraham acquired in acquisition of a tomb from Ephraim the Hittite. And Joseph returned to Egypt, he and his brothers and those who had gone up together to bury his father. Now when Josephs brothers saw that their father had died, they said, "Perhaps Joseph may bear a grudge against us and requite us a requital for all the evils that we showed him." And approaching Joseph they said, "Your father administered an oath before he expired, saying, 'Say thus to Joseph: Forgive them their injustice and fault, seeing that they showed you painful things.' And now accept the injustice of the attendants of the God of your father." And Joseph wept as they were speaking to him. And coming to him they said, "We here are your domestics." And Joseph said to them, "Do not be afraid, for I am Gods. You deliberated against me for painful things, but God deliberated concerning me for good things in order that a numerous people might be sustained, so that it might come to be as today." And he said to them, "Have no fear; it is I who shall sustain you and your households." And he reassured them and spoke to their heart. And Joseph dwelt in Egypt, he and his brothers and his fathers whole entire household. And Joseph lived one hundred ten years. And Joseph saw the children of Ephraim to the third generation, and the sons of Machir the son of Manasseh were born on Joseph's thighs. And Joseph spoke to his brothers, saying, "I am about to die, but with a visitation God shall visit you and bring you up out of this land to the land that God swore to our fathers Abraham and Isaac and Jacob." And Joseph made the sons of Israel swear, saying, "In the time of the visitation with which God shall visit you, you shall also carry up my bones from here together with you." And Joseph expired at one hundred ten years of age, and they honoured him with funeral rites and placed him in the coffin in Egypt.

Priest: Peace be with thee who readest.
Reader: And with thy spirit.

Reader: The Prokeimenon.
    Tone 4   *Festive, joyous and capable of expressing deep piety.*   *C, D, Eb, F, G, A, Bb, C.*

Reader:	They that trust in the Lord shall be as Mount Zion.
People:	*They that trust in the Lord shall be as Mount Zion.*
Reader:	Had it not been that the Lord was with us, let Israel now say.
People:	*They that trust in the Lord shall be as Mount Zion.*
Reader:	They that trust in the Lord	*shall be as Mount Zion.*

The Second Reading

[Readings during Lent are from the Old Testament.]

Reader: Command!

[People kneel:]

Priest: Wisdom. Attend! The Light of Christ illumines all.

[People stand.]

Priest or Reader: The reading is from the book of Proverbs (31:8 - 31).

Deacon: Let us attend.

Priest or Reader: Open your mouth with a divine word, and judge all fairly. Open your mouth, and judge justly, and plead the cause of the poor and weak. Who can find a courageous wife? Yes, such a one is more precious than valuable jewels. The heart of her husband is confident about her; such a one shall have no need of good spoils, for she toils for the benefit of her husband all her life. After spinning wool and flax, she made it useful with her hands. She became like a ship that sails from afar, and it is she who gathers a livelihood. And she got up in the night and supplied food for her household and work for her attendants. After considering a field, she bought it, and with the fruits of her hands she planted the purchase. After strongly girding her loins, she strengthened her arms for work. She experienced that it was good to work, and her lamp is not extinguished the whole night. She extends her forearms to what is profitable, and she strengthens her hands at the spindle. And she opens her hands to the needy and reaches out her wrist to the poor. Her husband has no concern for his household, when he spends time somewhere, for all that are hers are being clothed. She duplicated cloaks for her husband, and for herself clothes of fine linen and purple. And her husband is admired in the gates, when he sits in the council with elderly inhabitants of the land. She made linen garments and sold them, and girdles for the Canaanites. She opened her mouth cautiously and legitimately and reined in her tongue. She is clothed in strength and dignity, and she was happy in her last days. The way she ran her household was careful, and she did not eat the bread of idleness. And she opens her mouth wisely and lawfully, and her compassion built up her children, and they became rich, and her husband praised her: "Many daughters have obtained wealth; many did mighty things, but you, you have surpassed and transcended all." Allurements are false, and the beauty of a woman is vain, but an intelligent woman is spoken well of; yes, let her praise the fear of the Lord. Give her of the fruits of her hands, and let her husband be praised in the gates.

Theotokion

| *Tone 8* | *Humility, tranquillity, repose, suffering, pleading.* | *C, D, Eb, F, G, A, Bb, C.* |

The King of heaven, because of His love for man, appeared on earth and dwelt with men, for He took flesh from the pure virgin and He came forth from her as a man. He is One Son, two Natures, but not two persons. Therefore, proclaiming His as perfect God and perfect man, we confess Christ our God. Entreat Him, O unwedded Mother, to have mercy on our souls.

[End of Sixth week of Great Lent, Friday Evening] – jump to page 585.]

Seventh Week Of Great Lent – Holy and Great Monday Evening

Tone 6   *Rich texture, funeral, sorrowful.*   *D, Eb, F##, G, A, Bb, C##, D.*

Reader: The Lord bless thee out of Zion;

And mayest thou see the good things of Jerusalem all the days of thy life.

People: *The Lord bless thee out of Zion;*

And mayest thou see the good things of Jerusalem all the days of thy life.

Reader: Blessed are all they that fear the Lord, that walk in His ways.

People: *The Lord bless thee out of Zion;*

And mayest thou see the good things of Jerusalem all the days of thy life.

Reader: The Lord bless thee out of Zion; and mayest thou see the good things of Jerusalem |

all the days of thy life.

The First Reading

[Readings during Lent are from the Old Testament.]

Priest or Reader: The reading is from the book of Exodus (1:1 - 20).

Deacon: Let us attend.

Priest or Reader: These are the names of the sons of Israel who had entered into Egypt with Jacob their father. Each with their whole household went in: Rouben, Symeon, Leui, Ioudas, Issachar, Zaboulon and Benjamin, Dan and Nephthali, Gad and Aser. But Joseph was in Egypt. Now all souls from Jacob were seventy-five. Then Joseph died, and all his brothers and all that generation. But the sons of Israel increased and multiplied and became common and were growing very, very strong. Now the land kept multiplying them. Now another king arose over Egypt, who did not know Joseph. Now he said to his nation, "Look, the race of the sons of Israel is a great multitude and is becoming stronger than we. Come then, let us deal shrewdly with them, lest it be multiplied, and, whenever war happens to us, these also shall be added to the opponents, and after going to war against us, they shall depart from the land." And he set over them overseers of tasks in order to afflict them in the tasks. And they built fortified cities for Pharaoh, both Pithom and Ramesses and On, which is Heliopolis. But as much as they were humbling them, by so much the more they kept becoming more numerous and stronger, and the Egyptians were disgusted with the sons of Israel. And the Egyptians were oppressing the sons of Israel forcefully and were grievously afflicting their life by the hard tasks in clay and brick making and all the tasks in the plains, according to all the tasks in which they were enslaving them with force. And the king of the Egyptians spoke to the Hebrews' midwives, to one of them whose name was Sepphora, and the name of the second was Phoua, and he said, "Whenever you act as midwives to the Hebrew women and they should be at the birthing stage, if then it be male, kill it, but if female, preserve it alive." But the midwives feared God, and they did not do as the king of Egypt instructed them and tried to keep the males alive. Then the king of Egypt summoned the midwives and said to them, "Why is it that you have done this thing and tried to keep the males alive?" The midwives then said to Pharaoh, "The Hebrew women are not like the women of Egypt, for they give birth before the midwives go in to them," and they were already giving birth. Now God was dealing well with the midwives, and the people kept on multiplying and becoming very strong.

Deacon: The evening Prokeimenon.

Tone 8   *Humility, tranquillity, repose, suffering, pleading.*   *C, D, Eb, F, G, A, Bb, C.*

Reader: We have blessed you in the name of the Lord.

People: *We have blessed you in the name of the Lord.*

Reader: Many a time have they warred against me from my youth, let Israel now say.

People: *We have blessed you in the name of the Lord.*

Reader: We have blessed you | in the name of the Lord.

The Second Reading

[Readings during Lent are from the Old Testament.]

Reader: Command!

[People kneel:]

Priest: Wisdom. Attend! The Light of Christ illumines all.

[People stand.]

Priest or Reader: The reading is from the book of Job (1:1 - 12).

Deacon: Let us attend.

Priest or Reader: There was a certain man in the land of Ausitis, whose name was Job, and that man was genuine, blameless, righteous, religious, staying away from every evil thing. Now there were born to him seven sons and three daughters. And his live stock was: seven thousand sheep, three thousand camels, five hundred yoke of oxen, five hundred she donkeys at pasture; as well he had very many servants and extensive activities in the land, and that man was well-born among those of the east. Now his sons used to gather with one another and hold a feast each day; they used to take along their three sisters as well, to eat and drink with them. And when the feast days had run their course, Job used to send and purify them, rising early in the morning, and he used to offer a sacrifice on their behalf, according to their number, and one bull calf as a sin offering for their souls - for Job said, "Perhaps my sons thought bad things in their mind toward God." So this is what Job would always do. And when the set day came, then, look, the angels of God came to present themselves before the Lord, and the slanderer came with them. And the Lord said to the slanderer, "Where have you come from?" And the slanderer answered the Lord, "I have come, after going round the earth and walking about what lies beneath heaven." And the Lord said to him, "Did you give thought to your disposition against my servant Job – because there is no one of those on the earth like him, a man who is blameless, genuine, religious, staying away from every evil thing?" Then the slanderer answered and said before the Lord, "Does Job really worship the Lord for nothing? Have you not put a fence around things external to him, both what is within his household as well as what is outside of all that belongs to him, all around? You blessed the works of his hands, and his livestock you increased on the earth. But stretch out your hand, and touch all that he has; surely he shall bless a you to your face!" Then the Lord said to the slanderer, "Look, all that he has I am giving into your power, but do not touch him." So the slanderer went out from the Lord.

[End of Seventh week of Great Lent, Holy and Great Monday Evening] – jump to page 585.]

Seventh Week Of Great Lent – Holy and Great Tuesday Evening

Tone 6   *Rich texture, funeral, sorrowful.*   *D, Eb, F##, G, A, Bb, C##, D.*

Reader: Arise, O Lord, into Thy rest, Thou and the ark of Thy holiness.

People: *Arise, O Lord, into Thy rest, Thou and the ark of Thy holiness.*

Reader: Remember, O Lord, David and all his meekness.

People: *Arise, O Lord, into Thy rest, Thou and the ark of Thy holiness.*

Reader: Arise, O Lord, into Thy rest, | Thou and the ark of Thy holiness.

The First Reading

Priest or Reader: The reading is from the book of Exodus (2:5 - 10).

Deacon: Let us attend.

Priest or Reader: Now Pharaohs daughter came down to the river to bathe, and her attendants were walking beside the river. And when she saw the basket in the marsh, she sent her attendant, and she picked it up. Now when she opened it, she saw a child crying in the basket, and Pharaohs daughter spared it and said, "This is one of the Hebrews' children." And his sister said to Pharaohs daughter, "Do you wish that I summon for you a nursing woman from the Hebrews, and she shall suckle the child for you?" Then she, Pharaohs daughter, said to her, "Go!" But the girl went and summoned the childs mother. And Pharaohs daughter said to her, "Take care of this child for me, and suckle it for me, and I shall give you your pay." Then the woman took the child and kept suckling it. Now when the child grew up, she brought it to Pharaohs daughter, and it became to her for a son. And she named his name Moses, saying, "I drew him out of the water."

Deacon: The evening Prokeimenon.

Tone 4   *Festive, joyous and expressing deep piety.*   *C, D, Eb, F, G, A, Bb, C.*

Reader: Behold now, what is so good or so joyous as for brethren to dwell together in unity?

People: *Behold now, what is so good or so joyous as for brethren to dwell together in unity?*

Reader: It is like the oil of myrrh upon the head, which runneth down upon the beard,
        upon the beard of Aaron.

People: *Behold now, what is so good or so joyous as for brethren to dwell together in unity?*

Reader: Behold now, what is so good or so joyous as for brethren | to dwell together in unity?

The Second Reading

[Readings during Lent are from the Old Testament.]

Reader: Command!

[People kneel:]

Priest: Wisdom. Attend! The Light of Christ illumines all.

[People stand.]

Priest or Reader: The reading is from the book of Job (1:13 - 22).

Deacon: Let us attend.

Priest or Reader: So it was, when it was the set day, Jobs sons and daughters were drinking wine in their eldest brothers house. And, look, a messenger came to Job and said to him, "The yokes of oxen were ploughing, and the she donkeys were feeding beside them, and marauders came and carried them off, and they killed the servants with daggers, but when I alone escaped, I came to tell you." While he was still speaking, a further messenger came and said to Job, "Fire fell from heaven and burned up the sheep, and it likewise consumed the shepherds, and when I alone escaped, I came to tell you." While he was still speaking, a further messenger came and said to Job, "Horsemen formed three columns against us, and they encircled the camels and carried them off and killed the servants with daggers, but I alone escaped, and I came to tell you." While he was still speaking, another messenger came, saying to Job, "As your sons and daughters were eating and drinking at their elder brothers, suddenly a great wind came from the wilderness and struck the four corners of the house, and the house fell on your children, and they died, but I alone escaped, and I came to tell you." So Job arose, tore his clothes and shaved the hair of his head and fell on the ground and did obeisance and said, "I came naked from my mothers womb; naked also shall I return there; the Lord gave; the Lord has taken away; as it seemed good to the Lord, so it turned out; blessed be the name of the Lord." In all these things that happened to him Job did not sin at all before the Lord, and he did not charge God with folly.

[End of Seventh week of Great Lent, Tuesday Evening] – jump to page 585.]

Seventh Week Of Great Lent – Holy and Great Wednesday Evening

Tone 4   Festive, joyous and expressing deep piety.   *C, D, Eb, F, G, A, Bb, C.*

Reader: O give thanks unto the God of heaven; for His mercy endureth for ever.

People: *O give thanks unto the God of heaven; for His mercy endureth for ever.*

Reader: O give thanks unto the God of gods; for His mercy endureth for ever.

People: *O give thanks unto the God of heaven; for His mercy endureth for ever.*

Reader: O give thanks unto the God of heaven; | for His mercy endureth for ever.

The First Reading

[Readings during Lent are from the Old Testament.]

Priest or Reader: The reading is from the book of Exodus (2:11 - 22).

Deacon: Let us attend.

Priest or Reader: Now it came to pass in the course of those many days, when he had fully grown, Moses went out to his brothers, the sons of Israel. And as he observed their toil, he saw an Egyptian man beating some Hebrew from his own brothers, the sons of Israel. Now when he looked around this way and that, he saw no one, and he struck the Egyptian and hid him in the sand. Now when he went out on the next day, he saw two Hebrew men fighting, and he said to the one who was in the wrong, "Why do you beat your fellow?"

But he said, "Who appointed you ruler and judge over us? You do not intend to kill me, do you, in the same way you killed the Egyptian yesterday?" Then Moses was afraid and said, "Has this matter perhaps become so well known?" Now Pharaoh heard about this matter, and he was seeking to kill Moses. Then Moses withdrew from Pharaohs presence and settled in the land of Madian. Now when he came into the land of Madian, he sat upon the well. Now the priest of Madian had seven daughters who were tending their fathers sheep. So when they arrived, they were drawing water until they filled the receptacles in order to water their fathers sheep. But when the shepherds arrived, they were driving them away. But Moses got up and rescued them and drew water for them and watered their sheep. Now they arrived back to Ragouel, their father, and he said to them, "Why is it that you were quick to arrive today?" And they said, "An Egyptian man rescued us from the shepherds and drew water for us and watered the sheep." And he said to his daughters, "And where is he? And for what reason have you left this man behind like this? Invite him then in order that he might eat bread." Now Moses stayed with the man, and he gave Sepphora, his daughter, to Moses for a wife. Now when she became pregnant, the woman bore a son, and Moses called his name Gersam, saying, "Because I am a resident alien in a foreign land."

Deacon: The evening Prokeimenon.

Tone 4   Festive, joyous and expressing deep piety.   *C, D, Eb, F, G, A, Bb, C.*

Reader: Thy mercy endureth for ever; disdain not the work of Thy hands.

People: *Thy mercy endureth for ever; disdain not the work of Thy hands.*

Reader: I shall confess Thee, O Lord, with my whole heart; and before angels shall I chant unto Thee.

People: *Thy mercy endureth for ever; disdain not the work of Thy hands.*

Reader: Thy mercy endureth for ever; disdain not the work | of Thy hands.

The Second Reading

[Readings during Lent are from the Old Testament.]

Reader: Command!

[People kneel:]

Priest: Wisdom. Attend! The Light of Christ illumines all.

[People stand.]

Priest or Reader: The reading is from the book of Job (2:1 - 10).

Deacon: Let us attend.

Priest or Reader: Now it happened, when it was the set day and the angels of God came to present themselves before the Lord, the slanderer also came among them. to present himself before the Lord. And the Lord said to the slanderer, "Where are you coming from?" Then the slanderer said before the Lord, "I have come, after traversing what lies beneath heaven and walking about everything." Then the Lord said, "So did you notice my attendant Job - that there is no one of those on the earth like him, an innocent, genuine, blameless, religious man, staying away from all wrong? And he still maintains his innocence, though you said to destroy his possessions for no reason." Then the slanderer continued and said to the Lord, "Skin for skin;

whatever a person has he shall use to pay for his life. However, stretch out your hand, and touch his bones and his flesh; surely he shall bless you to your face!" Then the Lord said to the slanderer, "Very well, I am handing him over to you; only spare his life." So the slanderer went out from the Lord, and he struck Job with a grievous festering sore from his feet to his head. And he took a potsherd, so that he could scrape away the pus, and sat on the rubbish heap outside the city. Then after a long time had passed, his wife said to him, "How long shall you persist and say, 'Look, I shall hang on a little longer, while I wait for the hope of my deliverance?' For look, your legacy has vanished from the earth - sons and daughters, my wombs birth pangs and labours, for whom I wearied myself with hardships in vain. And you? You sit in the refuse of worms as you spend the night in the open air. As for me, I am one that wanders about and a hired servant – from place to place and house to house, waiting for when the sun shall set, so I can rest from the distresses and griefs that now beset me. Now say some word to the Lord and die!" But Job looked up and said to her, "You have spoken like one of the foolish women. If we received the good things from the Lords hand, shall we not bear the bad?" In all these things that happened to him Job did not sin at all with his lips before God.

[End of Seventh week of Great Lent, Holy and Great Wednesday Evening] – continue straight.]

All Days Continue From Here

[Priest to front of Holy Table and censes whilst:]

Priest: Let my prayer arise as incense in Thy sight, and let the lifting up of my hands be an evening sacrifice.

[Using the tune as for the full hymn above]

Chorus: *Let my prayer arise as incense in Thy sight, and let the lifting up of my hands be an evening sacrifice.*

[Priest to south of Holy Table and censes whilst:]

Priest: Lord, I have cried to Thee: hear me. Hear me, O Lord.

Lord, I have cried to Thee: hear me. Receive the voice of my prayer.

Reader: Let my prayer arise as incense in Thy sight,

And let the lifting up of my hands be an evening sacrifice.

[Priest to east of Holy Table and censes whilst:]

Priest: Set, O Lord, a watch before my mouth; and a door of enclosure round about my lips.

Reader: Let my prayer arise as incense in Thy sight,

And let the lifting up of my hands be an evening sacrifice.

[Priest to north of Holy Table and censes whilst:]

Priest: Incline not my heart to words of evil, to make excuses for sins.

Those that work iniquity; I shall not join with their number.

Reader: Let my prayer arise as incense in Thy sight,

And let the lifting up of my hands be an evening sacrifice.

[Priest to west of Holy Table and censes whilst:]

Priest: Glory be to the Father and to the Son and to the Holy Spirit;
Both now and forever and unto the ages of ages. Amen.

Reader: Let my prayer arise as incense in Thy sight,
And let the lifting up of my hands be an evening sacrifice.

[Priest stands before the Holy Table:]

Priest: Let my prayer arise as incense in Thy sight.

[Priest through Holy Doors and censes the icon of Christ whilst:]

Priest: Let my prayer arise as incense in Thy sight.

[Priest censes the remaining icons and the faithful whilst:]

Reader: And let the lifting up of my hands be an evening sacrifice. Hear me, O Lord.

[Deacon exits the north door (or the Priest before the Holy table) and:]

Prayer Of St Ephraim The Syrian

Priest: O Lord and Master of my life, a spirit of idleness, despondency, ambition, and idle talking give me not. ***prostration***

Priest: But rather a spirit of chastity, humble mindedness, patience, and love bestow upon me Thy servant. ***prostration***

Priest: Yea, O Lord King, grant me to see my own failings and not condemn my brother; for blessed art Thou unto the ages of ages. Amen. ***prostration***

Gospel On A Saints Day *(variables required)*   just below
Gospel On Holy And Great Monday   Page 587
Gospel On Holy And Great Tuesday   Page 589
Gospel On Holy And Great Wednesday   Page 591

The Gospel On A Saints Day
The Apostle

Deacon: Let us attend.

Priest: Peace be with you all.

People: *And with thy spirit.*

Deacon: Wisdom!

Reader: *[The Prokeimenon]*

Deacon: Wisdom!

Reader:	The Reading is from the book of ...
Deacon:	Let us attend.
Reader:	*[Reads the Apostle.]*
Priest:	Peace be with you who read.
Reader:	And with thy spirit.

Halleluiarion

People:	*Halleluiah, Halleluiah, Halleluiah.*
Reader:	[Response of the week.]
People:	*Halleluiah, Halleluiah, Halleluiah.*
Reader:	[Response of the week.]
People:	*Halleluiah, Halleluiah, Halleluiah.*

The Gospel

Deacon:	*(softly)* Bless, Father, the reader of the Gospel of the holy Apostle and Evangelist *N.*
Priest:	*(softly)* May God, through the intercessions of the holy and glorious Apostle and Evangelist, *N.*, grant thee to announce the glad tidings with great power, for the fulfilment of the Gospel of His beloved Son, our Lord Jesus Christ.
Deacon:	Amen.
Priest:	Wisdom, stand upright! Let us listen to the Holy Gospel. Peace be with you all.
People:	*And with thy spirit.*
Deacon:	The Reading is from the Holy Gospel according to *N.*
People:	*Glory to Thee, O Lord, glory to Thee.*
Priest:	Let us attend.
Deacon:	*[reads the Gospel.]*
People:	*Glory to Thee, O Lord, glory to Thee.*
Priest:	Peace be with you who read.
Reader:	And with thy spirit.

[End of Saints day]

The Gospel On Holy and Great Monday

Deacon:	*(softly)* Bless, Father, the reader of the Gospel of the holy Apostle and Evangelist *N.*
Priest:	*(softly)* May God, through the intercessions of the holy and glorious Apostle and Evangelist, *N.*, grant thee to announce the glad tidings with great power, for the fulfilment of the Gospel of His beloved Son, our Lord Jesus Christ.
Deacon:	Amen.
Priest:	Wisdom, stand upright! Let us listen to the Holy Gospel. Peace be with you all.
People:	*And with thy spirit.*

Deacon: The Reading is from the Holy Gospel according to Matthew (24:3 – 35).

People: *Glory to Thee, O Lord, glory to Thee.*

Priest: Let us attend.

Deacon: And as he sat upon the mount of Olives, the disciples came unto him privately, saying, Tell us, when shall these things be? and what shall be the sign of thy coming, and of the end of the world? And Jesus answered and said unto them, Take heed that no man deceive you. For many shall come in my name, saying, I am Christ; and shall deceive many. And you shall hear of wars and rumours of wars: see that you be not troubled: for all these things must come to pass, but the end is not yet. For nation shall rise against nation, and kingdom against kingdom: and there shall be famines, and pestilences, and earthquakes, in divers places. All these are the beginning of sorrows. Then shall they deliver you up to be afflicted, and shall kill you: and you shall be hated of all nations for my names sake. And then shall many be offended, and shall betray one another, and shall hate one another. And many false prophets shall rise, and shall deceive many. And because iniquity shall abound, the love of many shall wax cold. But he that shall endure unto the end, the same shall be saved. And this gospel of the kingdom shall be preached in all the world for a witness unto all nations; and then shall the end come. When you therefore shall see the abomination of desolation, spoken of by Daniel the prophet, stand in the holy place, (whoso readeth, let him understand:) Then let them which be in Judea flee into the mountains: Let him which is on the housetop not come down to take any thing out of his house: Neither let him which is in the field return back to take his clothes. And woe unto them that are with child, and to them that give suck in those days! But pray you that your flight be not in the winter, neither on the Sabbath day: For then shall be great tribulation, such as was not since the beginning of the world to this time, no, nor ever shall be. And except those days should be shortened, there should no flesh be saved: but for the elects sake those days shall be shortened. Then if any man shall say unto you, Lo, here is Christ, or there; believe it not. For there shall arise false Christs, and false prophets, and shall shew great signs and wonders; insomuch that, if it were possible, they shall deceive the very elect. Behold, I have told you before. Wherefore if they shall say unto you, Behold, he is in the desert; go not forth: behold, he is in the secret chambers; believe it not. For as the lightening cometh out of the east, and shineth even unto the west; so shall also the coming of the Son of man be. For wheresoever the carcase is, there shall the eagles be gathered together. Immediately after the tribulation of those days shall the sun be darkened, and the moon shall not give her light, and the stars shall fall from heaven, and the powers of the heavens shall be shaken: And then shall appear the sign of the Son of man in heaven: and then shall all the tribes of the earth mourn, and they shall see the Son of man coming in the clouds of heaven with power and great glory. And he shall send his angels with a great sound of a trumpet, and they shall gather together his elect from the four winds, from one end of heaven to the other. Now learn a parable of the fig tree; When his branch is yet tender, and putteth forth leaves, you know that summer is nigh: So likewise ye, when you shall see all these things, know that it is near, even at the doors. Verily I say unto you, This generation shall not pass, till all these things be fulfilled. Heaven and earth shall pass away, but my words shall not pass away.

People: *Glory to Thee, O Lord, glory to Thee.*

Priest: Peace be with you who read.

Reader: And with thy spirit.

[End of Holy and Great Monday of the seventh week of Great Lent] – jump to page 591.]

The Gospel On Holy and Great Tuesday

Deacon: *(softly)* Bless, Father, the reader of the Gospel of the holy Apostle and Evangelist *N.*

Priest: *(softly)* May God, through the intercessions of the holy and glorious Apostle and Evangelist, *N.,* grant thee to announce the glad tidings with great power, for the fulfilment of the Gospel of His beloved Son, our Lord Jesus Christ.

Deacon: Amen.

Priest: Wisdom, stand upright! Let us listen to the Holy Gospel. Peace be with you all.

People: *And with thy spirit.*

Deacon: The Reading is from the Holy Gospel according to Matthew (24:36 – 26:2).

People: *Glory to Thee, O Lord, glory to Thee.*

Priest: Let us attend.

Deacon: But of that day and hour knoweth no man, no, not the angels of heaven, but my Father only. But as the days of Noah were, so shall also the coming of the Son of man be. For as in the days that were before the flood they were eating and drinking, marrying and giving in marriage, until the day that Noah entered into the ark, And knew not until the flood came, and took them all away; so shall also the coming of the Son of man be. Then shall two be in the field; the one shall be taken, and the other left. Two women shall be grinding at the mill; the one shall be taken, and the other left. Watch therefore: for you know not what hour your Lord doth come. But know this, that if the goodman of the house had known in what watch the thief would come, he would have watched, and would not have suffered his house to be broken up. Therefore be you also ready: for in such an hour as you think not the Son of man cometh. Who then is a faithful and wise servant, whom his lord hath made ruler over his household, to give them meat in due season? Blessed is that servant, whom his lord when he cometh shall find so doing. Verily I say unto you, That he shall make him ruler over all his goods. But and if that evil servant shall say in his heart, My lord delayeth his coming; And shall begin to smite his fellow servants, and to eat and drink with the drunken; The lord of that servant shall come in a day when he looketh not for him, and in an hour that he is not aware of, And shall cut him asunder, and appoint him his portion with the hypocrites: there shall be weeping and gnashing of teeth. Then shall the kingdom of heaven be likened unto ten virgins, which took their lamps, and went forth to meet the bridegroom. And five of them were wise, and five were foolish. They that were foolish took their lamps, and took no oil with them: But the wise took oil in their vessels with their lamps. While the bridegroom tarried, they all slumbered and slept. And at midnight there was a cry made, Behold, the bridegroom cometh; go you out to meet him. Then all those virgins arose, and trimmed their lamps. And the foolish said unto the wise, Give us of your oil; for our lamps are gone out. But the wise answered, saying, Not so; lest there be not enough for us and you: but go you rather to them that sell, and buy for yourselves. And while they went to buy, the bridegroom came; and they that were ready went in with him to the marriage: and the door was shut. Afterward came also the other virgins, saying, Lord, Lord, open to us. But he answered and said, Verily I say unto you, I know you not. Watch therefore, for you know neither the day nor the hour wherein the Son of man cometh. For the kingdom of heaven is as a man travelling into a far country, who called his own servants, and delivered unto them his goods. And unto one he gave five talents, to another two, and to another one; to every man according to his several ability; and straightaway took his journey. Then he that had received the five talents went and traded with the same, and made them other five talents. And likewise he that had received two, he also gained other two. But he that had received one went and dug in the earth, and hid his lords money. After a long time the lord of those servants cometh, and reckoneth with them. And so he that had received five talents came and brought other five talents, saying, Lord, thou deliveredst unto me five talents: behold, I have gained beside them five talents more. His lord said unto him, Well done, thou good and faithful servant: thou hast been faithful over a few things, I shall make thee ruler over many things: enter thou into the joy of thy lord. He also that had received two talents came and said, Lord, thou deliveredst unto me two talents: behold, I have gained two other talents beside them. His lord said unto him, Well done, good and faithful servant; thou hast been faithful over a few things, I shall make thee ruler over many things: enter thou into the joy of thy lord. Then he which had received the one talent came and said, Lord, I knew thee that thou art an hard man, reaping where thou hast not sown, and gathering where thou hast not sowed: And I was afraid, and went and hid thy talent in the earth: lo, there thou hast that is thine. His lord answered and said unto him, Thou wicked and slothful servant, thou knewest that I reap where I sowed not, and gather where I have not sowed: Thou oughtest therefore to have put my money to the exchangers, and then at my coming I should have received mine own with usury. Take therefore the talent from him, and give it unto him which hath ten talents. For unto every one that hath shall be given, and he shall have abundance: but from him that hath not shall be taken away even that which he hath. And cast you the unprofitable servant into outer darkness: there shall be weeping and gnashing of teeth. When the Son of man shall come in his glory, and all the holy angels with him, then shall he sit upon the throne of his glory: And before him shall be gathered all nations: and he shall separate them one from another, as a shepherd divideth his sheep from the goats: And he shall set the sheep on his right hand, but the goats on the left. Then shall the King say unto them on his right hand, Come, you blessed of my Father, inherit the kingdom prepared for you from the foundation of the world: For I was hungry, and you gave me meat: I was thirsty, and you gave me drink: I was a stranger, and you took me in: Naked, and you clothed me: I was sick, and you visited me: I was in prison, and you came unto me. Then shall the righteous answer him, saying, Lord, when saw we thee hungry, and fed thee or thirsty, and gave thee drink? When saw we thee a stranger, and took thee in? or naked, and clothed thee? Or when saw we thee sick, or in prison, and came unto thee? And the King shall answer and say unto them, Verily I say unto you, Inasmuch as you have done it unto one of the least of these my brethren, you have done it unto me. Then shall he say also unto them on the left hand, Depart from me, you cursed, into everlasting fire, prepared for the devil and his angels: For I was hungry, and you gave me no meat: I was thirsty, and you gave me no drink: I was a stranger, and you took me not in: naked, and you clothed me not: sick, and in prison, and you visited me not. Then shall they also answer him, saying, Lord, when saw we thee a hungry, or athirst, or a stranger, or naked, or sick, or in prison, and did not minister unto thee? Then shall he answer them, saying, Verily I say unto you, Inasmuch as you did it not to one of the least of these, you did it not to me. And these shall go away into everlasting punishment: but the righteous into life eternal. And it came to pass, when Jesus had finished all these sayings, he said unto his disciples, You know that after two days is the feast of the passover, and the Son of man is betrayed to be crucified.

People:	Glory to Thee, O Lord, glory to Thee.
Priest:	Peace be with you who read.
Reader:	And with thy spirit.

[End of Holy and Great Tuesday of the seventh week of Great Lent] – jump to page 591.]

The Gospel On Holy and Great Wednesday

Deacon: *(softly)* Bless, Father, the reader of the Gospel of the holy Apostle and Evangelist *N*.

Priest: *(softly)* May God, through the intercessions of the holy and glorious Apostle and Evangelist, *N*., grant thee to announce the glad tidings with great power, for the fulfilment of the Gospel of His beloved Son, our Lord Jesus Christ.

Deacon: Amen.

Priest: Wisdom, stand upright! Let us listen to the Holy Gospel. Peace be with you all.

People: *And with thy spirit.*

Deacon: The Reading is from the Holy Gospel according to Matthew (26:6 - 16).

People: *Glory to Thee, O Lord, glory to Thee.*

Priest: Let us attend.

Deacon: Now when Jesus was in Bethany, in the house of Simon the leper, There came unto him a woman having an alabaster box of very precious ointment, and poured it on his head, as he sat at meat. But when his disciples saw it, they had indignation, saying, "To what purpose is this waste? For this ointment might have been sold for much, and given to the poor." When Jesus understood it, he said unto them, "Why trouble you the woman? for she hath wrought a good work upon me. For you have the poor always with you; but me you have not always. For in that she hath poured this ointment on my body, she did it for my burial. Verily I say unto you, Wheresoever this gospel shall be preached in the whole world, there shall also this, that this woman hath done, be told for a memorial of her." Then one of the twelve, called Judas Iscariot, went unto the chief priests, And said unto them, "What shall you give me, and I shall deliver him unto you?" And they covenanted with him for thirty pieces of silver. And from that time he sought opportunity to betray him.

Priest: Peace be with you who read.

People: *Glory to Thee, O Lord, glory to Thee.*

[End of Holy and Great Wednesday of the seventh week of Great Lent] – continue straight:]

The Litany Of Fervent Supplication

Deacon: Let us say with our whole heart and our whole mind, let us say.

People: *Lord, have mercy.* (**x3**)

Deacon: Lord Almighty God of our fathers, we pray Thee, hear us and have mercy.

People: *Lord, have mercy.* (**x3**)

Deacon: Have mercy on us, O God, in Thy great goodness; we pray Thee, hear us and have mercy.

People: *Lord, have mercy.* (**x3**)

Deacon: Again we pray for pious and Orthodox Christians.

People: *Lord, have mercy.* (**x3**)

Deacon: Again we pray for our Archbishop Nikitas, for Priests, for Deacons, for Monks and Nuns, and for all of our brethren in Christ.

People: *Lord, have mercy.* (**x3**)

Deacon: Also we pray for mercy, life, peace, health, salvation, visitation, pardon and forgiveness of sins for the servants of God and for the pardon and remission of their sins.

People: *Lord, have mercy.* (**x3**)

Deacon: Also we pray for the blessed and ever remembered founders of this holy church, and for all our brothers and sisters who have gone to their rest before us, and who lie asleep in the true faith; and for the departed Orthodox everywhere *[and the servants of God N and N – (names given before the service)]* and that they may be pardoned all their offences, both voluntary and involuntary.

People: *Lord, have mercy.* (**x3**)

Deacon: Also we pray for those who bring offerings, those who care for the beauty of this holy and venerable house, for those who labour in its service, for those who sing, and for the people here present, who await Thy great and rich mercy.

People: *Lord, have mercy.* (**x3**)

Priest *[soto voce]*: O God, our God, the Creator and Maker of all things, Who willest that all men should be saved and should come unto the knowledge of truth, look upon Thy servants the catechumens, and deliver them from their ancient errors and from the wiles of the adversary, and call them unto eternal life, illumining their souls and bodies and numbering them with Thy reason endowed flock, which is called by Thy name. That with us they may magnify Thine all honourable and majestic name of the Father, and of the Son, and of the Holy Spirit, both now and forever and unto the ages off ages.

[Priest makes the sign of the Cross over the Antimension with the Gospel.]

Priest: *[aloud]*: For Thou, O God, art merciful and love mankind, and to Thee we givest glory, to the Father, the Son and the Holy Spirit, both now and forever, and unto the ages of ages.

People: *Amen.*

The Litany For The Catechumens

Deacon: You who are Catechumens, pray to the Lord.

People: *Lord, have mercy.*

Deacon: You faithful, let us pray for the Catechumens.

People: *Lord, have mercy.*

Deacon: That the Lord shall show them mercy.

People: *Lord, have mercy.*

Deacon: That He shall instruct them in the word of His truth.

People: *Lord, have mercy.*

Deacon: That He shall reveal to them the Gospel of righteousness.

People: *Lord, have mercy.*

Deacon: That He shall unite them to His Holy, Catholic and Apostolic Church.

People: *Lord, have mercy.*

Deacon: Help them, save them, have mercy on them and keep them; O God, by Thy grace.

People: *Lord, have mercy.*

Deacon: You who are Catechumens, bow your heads to the Lord.

People: *To Thee, O Lord.*

Prayer For The Catechumens

Priest: *[soto voce]* O God, our God, Author and Creator of all things, it is Thy will that all should be saved and come to the knowledge of the truth. Look upon Thy servants the Catechumens, and free them of ancient error and from the wiles of the enemy. Call them to eternal life, illuminating their souls and bodies, and numbering them among Thy reasoning flock, on which Thy holy name is invoked.

Priest: *[aloud]*   That with us they too may glorify Thy most noble and majestic name, of the Father and of the Son and of the Holy Spirit, both now and forever and to the ages of ages.

People: *Amen.*

Deacon: All Catechumens, depart. As many as are Catechumens, depart. Let none of the Catechumens remain.

[from Wednesday of the fourth week of Great Lent:]

Deacon: Pray unto the Lord, you who are preparing for Illumination.

People: *Lord, have mercy.*

Deacon: You faithful, pray unto the Lord for these brethren who are preparing for Holy Illumination and for their salvation.

People: *Lord, have mercy.*

Deacon: That the lord our God shall establish them and strengthen them.

People: *Lord, have mercy.*

Deacon: That He shall illumine them with the light of wisdom and of piety.

People: *Lord, have mercy.*

Deacon: That He shall grant unto them, in His own good time, the laver of regeneration, the remission of sins, and the garment of incorruption.

People: *Lord, have mercy.*

Deacon: That He shall beget them with water and the Spirit.

People: *Lord, have mercy.*

Deacon: That He shall grant unto them the perfection of faith. Let us pray to the Lord.

People: *Lord, have mercy.*

Deacon: That He shall number them with His holy and chosen flock.

People: *Lord, have mercy.*

Deacon: Help them; save them; have mercy upon them; and keep them, O God, by thy grace.

People: *Lord, have mercy.*

Deacon: You who are ready for Illumination, bow your heads unto the Lord.

People: *To Thee, O Lord.*

Priest: *[soto voce]* Show the light of Thy countenance, O God, upon those who are preparing for Holy Illumination, and who desire to put away the defilement of sin. Enlighten their understanding. Establish them in the Faith. Strengthen them in hope. Perfect them in love. Make them honourable members of Thy Christ, who gave Himself for our souls.

[aloud] For Thou art our Illumination, and unto Thee do we ascribe glory; to the Father, and to the Son, and to the Holy Spirit; both now and forever and unto the ages of ages.

People: *Amen.*

Deacon: As many as are preparing for Illumination, depart. Depart, you who are preparing for Illumination. Let none of them preparing for Illumination remain.

[End of Wednesday of the fourth week of Great Lent.]

[Continue all days:]

Deacon: All we faithful once again in peace let us pray to the Lord.

People: *Lord, have mercy.*

Deacon: Help us, save us, have mercy on us, and keep us, O God, in Thy grace.

People: *Lord, have mercy.*

Deacon: Wisdom!

The First Prayer Of The Faithful

Priest: *[soto voce]* O God, great and praised, through the life giving death of Thy Christ, Thou hast borne us from corruption to immortality. Liberate all our senses from killing passion, setting over them as a benevolent sovereign our inner reason. Let the eye be averted from every evil sight, and the ear be deaf to idle talk. May the tongue be purged of unseemly speech. Purify these lips that praise Thee, Lord. Make our hands abstain from wicked deeds, doing only such things as are pleasing to Thee, thus sealing with Thy grace all our members, and our mind.

Priest: *[aloud]* For all glory, honour and worship are Thy due: Father, Son and Holy Spirit, both now and forever and unto the ages of ages.

People: *Amen.*

Deacon: Again in peace let us pray to the Lord.

People: *Lord, have mercy.*

Deacon: Help us, save us, have mercy on us and keep us, O God, in Thy grace.

People: *Lord, have mercy.*

Deacon: Wisdom!

The Second Prayer Of The Faithful

Priest: *[soto voce]* Holy Master, infinitely good, we entreat Thee, rich in mercy, to be gracious to us sinners, and to make us worthy to receive Thine only Son and our God, the King of Glory. For behold, His spotless body and life giving blood are about to make their entrance at this hour, to be laid on this mystical table, invisibly attended by a multitude of the heavenly host. Grant that we may receive them in blameless communion, so that as the eyes of our understanding see the light, we may become children of the light and of the day.

Priest: *[aloud]* Through the gift of Thy Christ with Whom Thou art blessed, together with Thine all holy, good and life giving Spirit, Both now and forever and to the ages of ages.

People: *Amen.*

Cherubikon

a) Chorus: Now the Powers of Heaven minister invisibly with us. For, behold, the King of Glory enters.

[In silence the Gifts are carried around and into the Soleas by the priest whose head is covered by the Aer, then into the Sanctuary, and placed on the Holy Altar. As these are the Presanctified Gifts, already consecrated, the people **kneel** *during their Entrance.]*

Priest: *[soto voce]* Through the prayers of our Holy Fathers, Lord Jesus Christ, have mercy on us and save us. Amen.

The Entrance With The Holy Gifts

b) Chorus: *Behold, the mystical sacrifice, fully accomplished, is ushered in. Let us with faith and love draw near, that we may become partakers of life everlasting, Halleluiah, Halleluiah, Halleluiah.*

Priest: Now the Powers of Heaven minister invisibly with us. For, behold, the King of Glory enters. Behold, the mystical sacrifice, fully accomplished, is ushered in.

Deacon or Priest: Let us with faith and love draw near, that we may become partakers of life everlasting, Halleluiah, Halleluiah, Halleluiah.

Priest: Forgive me, my brothers and sisters, my offences.

Prayer Of St Ephraim The Syrian

Priest: O Lord and Master of my life, a spirit of idleness, despondency, ambition, and idle talking give me not. ****prostration****

Priest: But rather a spirit of chastity, humble mindedness, patience, and love bestow upon me Thy servant. ****prostration****

Priest: Yea, O Lord King, grant me to see my own failings and not condemn my brother; for blessed art Thou unto the ages of ages. Amen. ****prostration****

[Priest half closes the curtain.]

The Completion Litany

Deacon: Let us complete our evening prayer to the Lord.

People: *Lord, have mercy.*

Deacon: For the Precious Gifts here set forth and presanctified, let us pray to the Lord.

People: *Lord, have mercy.*

Deacon: That our loving God, having received them at His holy and mystical and celestial altar as a sweet spiritual fragrance, shall in turn send upon us His divine grace and the gift of the Holy Spirit, let us pray.

People: *Lord, have mercy.*

Deacon: That we may be spared all affliction, violence, danger and want, let us pray to the Lord.

People: *Lord, have mercy.*

Deacon: Help us, save us, have mercy on us and keep us, O God, in Thy grace.

People: *Lord, have mercy.*

Deacon: That this whole evening may be perfect, holy, peaceful and without sin, let us ask of the Lord.

People: *Grant this, O Lord.*

Deacon: An angel of peace, a faithful guide, a guardian of our souls and bodies, let us ask of the Lord.

People: *Grant this, O Lord.*

Deacon: Forgiveness of our sins and offences let us ask of the Lord.

People: *Grant this, O Lord.*

Deacon: All that is good and profitable for our souls, and peace in the world, let us ask of the Lord.

People: *Grant this, O Lord.*

Deacon: That we may live out our lives in peace and repentance, let us ask of the Lord.

People: *Grant this, O Lord.*

Deacon: A Christian end to our lives, peaceful, free of suffering and shame, and a good defence at the dread judgement seat of Christ, let us ask.

People: *Grant this, O Lord.*

Deacon: Having prayed for the unity of the faith, and for the communion of the Holy Spirit, let us commend ourselves and one another, and our life to Christ our God.

People: *To Thee, O Lord.*

Priest: O God of ineffable and unseen mysteries, in Thou art hidden the treasures of wisdom and knowledge, yet Thou hast revealed to us this Liturgy and, in Thy great love for mankind, appointed us sinners to offer gifts and sacrifices to Thee, for our sins and for the failings of the people. Invisible King, Thou performest works great and inscrutable, glorious and extraordinary, beyond number. Look upon us Thine undeserving servants as we stand, as at Thy throne of the Cherubim at this Thine holy altar, where Thine only begotten Son, our God, rests in the awesome mysteries here offered. Freeing us all, and Thy faithful people, of all uncleanness, sanctify all of us, soul and body, with a sanctification that cannot be taken away. Thus, partaking of these divine Blessings with pure conscience, faces unblushing, hearts enlightened, and being quickened by them, we may be united to Thy Christ Himself, our true God. For He said: "He who eats my flesh and drinks my blood, abides in me and I in him." Having Thy Word indwelling and moving within us, we may thus become the temple of Thine all holy and worshipful Spirit, free of every wile of the evil one affecting our acts, our words, our thoughts, and so obtain the blessings promised to us as to Thy Saints who have pleased Thee through the ages.

Priest: *[aloud]* And make us worthy, Master, with confidence and without fear of reproach, to make bold to call Thee, the heavenly God, Father, and to say:

The Lords Prayer

People: *Our Father who art in heaven, hallowed by Thy name. Thy kingdom come, Thy will be done, on earth as it is in heaven. Give us this day our daily bread, and forgive us our trespasses as we forgive those who trespass against us; and lead us not into temptation, but deliver us from the evil one.*

Priest: For Thine is the kingdom and the power and the glory, of the Father and of the Son and of the Holy Spirit, both now and forever and to the ages of ages.

People: *Amen.*

Priest: Peace be to all.

People: *And with thy spirit.*

Deacon: Let us bow our heads to the Lord.

People: *To Thee, O Lord.*

Priest: *[soto voce]* O God, Thou alone art compassionate and good. Dwelling on high, yet looking upon the lowly, regard Thy people with a tender eye and safeguard them. Count us all worthy to partake without reproach of these Thy life giving Mysteries. For it is to Thee that we bow our heads, in the hope of Thy rich mercy.

[Lifting the Asterisk from the Paten:]

Priest: *[aloud]* Through the grace, mercy and love for us of Thine only begotten Son, with Whom Thou art blessed, together with Thine all holy, good and life giving Spirit, both now and forever and to the ages of ages.

People: *Amen.*

Priest: *[soto voce]* Lord Jesus Christ, hear us from Thine holy dwelling place and from the throne of glory of Thy kingdom and come to sanctify us. Though enthroned with the Father on high, yet present here in our midst, unseen, deign by Thy mighty hand to give us a share of Thy Pure Body and Precious Blood, and through us to all Thy people.

Priest: *[soto voce]* O God, be gracious unto me a sinner and have mercy upon me. **(x3)**

[The Holy Gifts still covered by the veil, Priest touches the consecrated "Lamb ".]

Deacon: Let us attend.

Priest: The Presanctified Holy Gifts for the holy people of God.

People: *One is holy, one is Lord, Jesus Christ, to the glory of God the Father. Amen.*

The Fraction And Communion

[Priest uncovers the Gifts and performs the fraction.]

Deacon: Master, break the Holy Bread.

Priest: *[soto voce]* The Lamb of God is broken and shared, broken but not divided; forever eaten yet never consumed, but sanctifying those who partake of Him.

[Priest breaks the Amnos into four quarters thus:]

         IC

    NI   KA

      XC

[Whilst:]

Priest: *[soto voce]* Through the prayers of our Holy Fathers, Lord Jesus Christ, have mercy on us and save us. Amen.

[Priest places the portion marked IC (Jesus) in the chalice, saying:]

Priest: *[soto voce]* Through the prayers of our Holy Fathers, Lord Jesus Christ, have mercy on us and save us. Amen.

Deacon: Master, fill the Cup.

[Priest blesses hot water and (Deacon if present) pours it into the chalice whilst:]

Priest: The fullness of the Holy Spirit.

Deacon: Amen.

Deacon: Master, bless the Zeon. *(hot water)*

Priest: Blessed is the fervour of Thy Saints, now and for evermore. Amen.

[Priest pours the Zeon into the chalice, whilst:]

Deacon: The fervour of faith, full of the Holy Spirit. Amen.

The Prayers Before Communion

Priest: **1.** I believe, Lord, and I confess that Thou art truly the Christ, the son of the living God, who came into the world to save sinners, of whom I am first. Also I believe that this is indeed Thy most pure Body, and this indeed Thy precious Blood. Therefore I beseech Thee, have mercy on me and forgive me my offences, voluntary and involuntary, in word and in deed, in knowledge and in ignorance, and count me worthy to partake uncondemned of Thy most pure Mysteries for forgiveness of sins and for eternal life. Amen.

2.   Of Thy mystical supper, Son of God, receive me today as a communicant; for I shall not tell of the Mystery to Thine enemies; I shall not give Thee a kiss like Judas; but like the thief I confess Thee. Remember me, Lord, in Thy kingdom.

3.   Let not the Communion of Thy holy Mysteries, Lord, be to me for judgement or condemnation, but for healing of soul and body.

[Priest makes three prostrations before the altar:]

Priest: *[soto voce]* Lo, I draw near unto Christ, our immortal King and our God.

[Priest bows to the people in a gesture of mutual forgiveness, he then turns to the altar to receive, saying to the Deacon:]

Priest: Brother and con-celebrant, forgive me the unworthy Priest.

Deacon: May the Lord forgive both thee and us.

Priest: May the Lord forgive me a sinner, and have mercy on me. **(x3)**

[Priest then takes the portion of the Lamb sealed XC, saying:]

Priest: Behold, I approach Christ, our immortal King and God. The precious and most holy Body of our Lord God and Saviour Jesus Christ is given to me *(N.)* the unworthy Priest, for the forgiveness of sins and life everlasting.

[Priest wipes fingers on the sponge, takes up the chalice and says:]

Priest: *[soto voce]* Behold, again I approach Christ, our immortal King and God. The precious and most holy, pure and life giving Blood of our Lord God and Saviour Jesus Christ is given to me *(N.)* the unworthy Priest, for forgiveness of sins and life everlasting.

[Priest drinks from the chalice. Then wipes the rim and reverences it, whilst:]

Priest: *[soto voce]* This has touched my lips; it takes away my iniquities and cleanses me of my sins.

[Deacon receives according to the established order.]

[Priest divides NI and KA into small portions and places them in the chalice, whilst:]

Priest: *[soto voce]* Through the prayers of our Holy Fathers, Lord Jesus Christ, have mercy on us and save us. Amen.

[Covers chalice with aer.]

Prayers Said Before Communion.

[In Place Of A Communion Hymn, Chant the following. Deep and slow.]

Reader:

1. I believe, Lord, and I confess that Thou art truly the Christ, the son of the living God, who came into the world to save sinners, of whom I am first. Also I believe that this is indeed Thy most pure Body, and this indeed Thy precious Blood. Therefore I beseech Thee, have mercy on me and forgive me my offences, voluntary and involuntary, in word and in deed, in knowledge and in ignorance, and count me worthy to partake uncondemned of Thy most pure Mysteries for forgiveness of sins and for eternal life. Amen.

2. See, to divine Communion I draw near; My Maker, burn me not as I partake. For Thou art fire, consuming the unworthy; But therefore make me clean from every stain.

3. Of Thy mystical supper, Son of God, receive me today as a communicant; for I shall not tell of the Mystery to Thine enemies; I shall not give Thee a kiss like Judas; but like the thief I confess Thee. Remember me, Lord, in Thy kingdom.

4. Master, lover of mankind, Lord Jesus Christ, my God, let not these Holy Mysteries be for my condemnation because of my unworthiness, but rather for the cleansing and sanctification of both soul and body, and as a pledge of the life and kingdom to come. It is good for me to cleave to God, to place in the Lord the hope of my salvation.

5.   Let not the Communion of Thy holy Mysteries, Lord, be to me for judgement or condemnation, but for healing of soul and body.

[Then sing Psalm 32. The refrain is:
People: *For he spoke, and it was done; he commanded, and it stood fast.]*

[Priest opens curtains.]

The Communion Of The Faithful

Deacon: With the fear of God, with faith and with love, draw near.

People: *Blessed is He that comes in the name of the Lord. God is the Lord and has revealed Himself to us.*

[Followed by the Communion Hymn:]

People: *Taste and see that the Lord is good. Halleluiah, Halleluiah, Halleluiah.*

[After all have received the Holy Eucharist, the Priest holds the chalice aloft whilst:]

Priest: O God, save Thy people and bless Thine inheritance.

[In place of the customary "We have seen the light... ":]

People: *I shall bless the Lord at all times; his praise shall be ever on my lips. Taste the heavenly bread and the cup of life, and see how good is the Lord. Halleluiah, Halleluiah, Halleluiah.*

[Priest puts Asterisk, Covers and spoon on the Diskos censes the chalice three times, whilst:]

Priest: *[soto voce]* Be exalted, O, above the heavens, and let Thy glory be over all the earth. **(x3)**

[Deacon receives the Paten from the Priest and takes it to the Prothesis.]

[Priest lifts the Chalice before the Holy Table, whilst:]

Priest: *[soto voce]* Blessed is our God.

[Priest holds the Chalice aloft, covered, he faces the people, whilst:]

Priest: *[aloud]*   Always, now and ever and to the ages of ages.

People: Amen. *Let our mouth be filled with Thy praise, O Lord, that we may sing of Thy glory, For Thou hast counted us worthy to partake of Thine Holy Mysteries. Keep us in Thy holiness that we may meditate on Thy righteousness all the day long. Halleluiah. Halleluiah. Halleluiah.*

[Priest returns Holy Vessels to the Prothesis and folds the Antimension.]

Deacon: Let us be attend! Having received the divine, holy, pure, immortal, life giving and awesome Mysteries of Christ, let us give fitting thanks to the Lord.

People: *Lord have mercy.*

Deacon: Help us, save us, have mercy on us, and keep us, O God, in Thy grace.

People: *Lord have mercy.*

Deacon: Having asked that this whole evening may be perfect, holy, peaceful and free of sin, let us commend ourselves and one another, and our whole life to Christ our God.

People: *To Thee, O Lord.*

Priest: We give thanks unto Thee, O God, the Saviour of all men, for all the good things which Thou hast vouchsafed unto us, and for the Communion of the holy Body and Blood of Thy Christ. And we beseech Thee, O Lord, who lovest mankind, to keep us under the shelter of Thy wings. And grant that, even unto our last breath, we may worthily partake of Thy Holy Things, unto the illumination of the kingdom of heaven.

[Priest makes the sign of the Cross with the Gospel over the now folded Antimension, whilst:]

Priest: For Thou art our sanctification, and to Thee we give the glory: Father, Son and Holy Spirit; both now and forever and unto the ages of ages.

People: *Amen.*

Priest: Let us depart in peace.

Deacon: Let us pray to the Lord.

People: *Lord, have mercy.*

Prayer Behind The Ambo

[Priest stands before the icon of Christ.]

Priest: Almighty Lord, Thou hast created all things in wisdom. In Thine inexpressible providence and great goodness Thou hast brought us to these saving days, for the cleansing of our souls and bodies, for control of our passions, in the hope of the Resurrection. After the forty days Thou delivered into the hands of Thy servant Moses the tablets of the law in characters divinely traced. Enable us also, O benevolent One, to fight the good fight, to complete the course of the fast, to keep the faith inviolate, to crush underfoot the heads of unseen tempters, to emerge victors over sin and to come, without reproach, to the worship of Thine Holy Resurrection. For blessed and glorified is Thy most honourable and majestic name, of the Father, the Son and the Holy Spirit, now and for evermore.

People: *Amen.*

Blessed be the Name Of The Lord, from this time forth and for evermore. **(x3)**

[Priest goes to the Prothesis, saying:]

Priest: Lord our God, Thou hast guided us to these most holy days, and admitted us as participants to Thine awesome Mysteries. Unite us to Thy spiritual flock and declare us heirs to Thy kingdom, now and forever. Amen.

Deacon: Let us pray to the Lord.

People: *Lord, have mercy.*

Priest: May the blessing of the Lord and His mercy come upon ye; through His divine grace and love, always, now and for evermore.

People: *Amen.*

The Dismissal

Priest: Glory to Thee, O God, our hope, glory to Thee.

Reader: *Glory be to the Father and to the Son and to the Holy Spirit;*

Both now and forever and unto the ages of ages. Amen.

Lord have mercy. **(x3)**

Holy Father, bless.

Priest: May Christ our true God, through the intercessions of His most pure and holy Mother; the power of the precious and life giving Cross; the protection of the honourable, bodiless heavenly powers; the supplications of the honourable, glorious Prophet and Forerunner John the Baptist; the holy, glorious and victorious Martyrs; our venerable and godly Fathers; the holy and righteous ancestors Joachim and Anna; of Saint *(of this church)* of Saint *(of the day)* whose memory we keep today; and of all the Saints, have mercy on us and save us, for He is a good God and loves mankind.

People: *Amen.*

[As the faithful receive the antidoron:]

Psalm 33

Reader. I shall bless tho Lord at all times; his praise shall be ever on my lips. My soul shall glory in the Lord: let the meek hear and rejoice. Magnify the Lord with me, and let us exalt his name together. I sought the Lord, and he heard me, and delivered me from all my fears. Approach the Lord and be enlightened, and thy face shall never be shamed. This wretched man cried out, and the Lord heard him, and delivered him from all his afflictions. The angel shall stand guard around those who fear the Lord and save them. Taste and see how good the Lord is. Blessed is the man who hopes in him. Fear the Lord, all you his faithful ones, for those who fear him shall want for nothing. The rich have become poor and hungry, but those who seek the Lord shall not lack any good. Come, children, hear me: I shall teach you the fear of the Lord. Which of you desires life, and loves to see the good days? Keep thy tongue from wickedness, and thy lips from deceitful speech; turn away from evil, and do good; seek peace and pursue it. The eyes of the Lord are upon the just and his ears are open to their pleas; the face of the Lord is turned against sinners, to erase their memory from the earth. The just cried out and the Lord heard them, and he delivered them from all their trials. The Lord is close to the broken-hearted, and he shall save the humble in spirit. Many are the trials of the righteous, but out of them all the Lord shall deliver them. He protects every bone in their body: not a single one of them shall be broken. The death of sinners is painful; those who hate justice shall be damned. The Lord shall redeem the souls of his servants, and none of those who hope in him shall be lost.

Psalm 144

Reader: I shall exalt Thee, my God and my king, and bless Thy name for ever and ever. Every day I shall bless Thee, and praise Thy name for ever and ever. The Lord is great and greatly to be praised, and to his greatness there is no end. Age after age shall praise Thine works, and proclaim Thine might. They shall tell the glorious splendour of Thy holiness, they shall recount Thy wondrous works; they shall speak of the power of Thine awesome deeds, they shall declare Thine greatness. They shall recall Thine abundant goodness and shall exult in Thy righteousness. The Lord is gracious and merciful: he is long-suffering and abounding in love. The Lord is good towards everyone, and his grace extends over all his works. Let all Thine works give thanks to Thee, Lord, and all Thy faithful ones bless Thee. They shall speak of the glory of Thy kingdom and tell of Thy power, to make known Thy might to the children of men, and the glorious splendour of Thy kingdom. Thy kingdom is a kingdom for all ages and Thy dominion is for all generations. The Lord keeps faith in all his promises and is hallowed in all his works. The Lord supports all who are failing, and raises up all who are bowed down. The eyes of all look up to Thee, and Thou givest them their food in due season. Thou openest Thine hands and satisfy all living beings; the Lord is just in all his ways, and faithful in all his works. The Lord is close to all who pray to him, those who call upon him in truth. He shall meet the desire of those who fear him, and hear their pleas and save them. The Lord keeps watch over those who love him, but the wicked he shall utterly destroy. My mouth shall speak the praise of the Lord, and let all flesh bless his holy name, for ever and to all eternity.

Priest: Through the prayers of our Holy Fathers, Lord Jesus Christ our God, have mercy on us and save us.

People: *Amen.*

1st Sunday Of The Triodion. Publican & Pharisee. No fasting this week.

First Antiphon

Reader: The Lord is King, and hath clothed Himself with majesty.

The Lord is robed; He is girded with strength.

For He hath established the world so that it shall never be moved.

People: *At the prayers of the Mother of God, O Saviour, save us.*

Reader: Who can utter the mighty acts of the Lord?

Who can cause all his praises to be heard? Let the redeemed of the Lord say so;

Whom He hath redeemed from the hand of the enemy.

People: *At the prayers of the Mother of God, O Saviour, save us.*

Reader: Glory be to the Father and to the Son and to the Holy Spirit.

Both now and forever and unto the ages of ages. Amen.

People: *At the prayers of the Mother of God | O Saviour, save us.*

Second Antiphon

Reader: Let them praise the Lord for His mercies, and for His wonderful works to the children of men.

People: *Save us, O Son of God, risen from the dead; Save us who sing to Thee: Halleluia.*

Reader: Let them exalt Him in the congregation of the people, and praise Him in the seat of the elders.

People: *Save us, O Son of God, risen from the dead; Save us who sing to Thee: Halleluia.*

Reader: The eyes of the Lord are upon them that fear Him; upon them that hope in His mercy.

To hear the groaning of the prisoners, to loose the sons of the slain.

People: *Save us, O Son of God, risen from the dead; Save us who sing to Thee: Halleluia.*

Reader: Glory be to the Father and to the Son and to the Holy Spirit.

Choir: Both now and forever and unto the ages of ages. Amen.

Third Antiphon – Little Entrance

Let the heavens and the earth praise Him. This is the day which the Lord hath made; let us rejoice and be glad in it. O Lord my God, I shall give thanks unto Thee forever.

+++

Hymn Of The Triodion

Tone 8   Humility, tranquillity, repose, suffering.   *C, D, Eb, F, G, A, Bb, C.*

Open the gates of repentance to me, O Giver of Life, for my spirit rises early in the morning to Thy holy temple, bearing a temple of the body all defiled. But as Thou art full of pity, cleanse it by Thy compassionate mercy.

+++

Apolytikion Of First Sunday Of Great Lent

Tone 2   Majesty, gentleness, hope, repentance and sadness.   *E, F, G, Ab, B, C.*

Thy pure image do we venerate, O good One, asking forgiveness of our sins, O Christ our God; for by Thine own will Thou didst ascend the Cross in Thy body, to save Thy creatures from the bondage of the enemy. Thou hast verily filled all with joy, since Thou didst come, O our Saviour, to save the world.

+++

Troparion Of The Publican And Pharisee

Tone 6   Rich texture, funereal character, sorrowful.   *D, Eb, F##, G, A, Bb, C##, D.*

Have mercy on me, O God, according to Thy great mercy; and according to the multitude of Thy compassions, blot out my transgression. When I think of the multitude of ghastly things I have done, wretch that I am, I tremble at the fearful day of judgement. But trusting in the mercy of Thy loving kindness; like David I cry to Thee: Have mercy on me, O God, according to Thy great mercy.

Troparion Of St Theodore The Tyro

Tone 2   Majesty, gentleness, hope, repentance and sadness.   *E, F, G, Ab, B, C.*

Great are the achievements of faith. In the fountain of flame as in refreshing water, the holy Martyr Theodore rejoiced. He was made a whole burnt offering in the fire and was offered as bread to the Trinity. By his prayers, O Christ our God, save our souls.

Κοντακιον Of St Theodore The Tyro

Tone 8   Humility, tranquillity, repose, suffering.   *C, D, Eb, F, G, A, Bb, C.*

Thou didst receive the Faith of Christ in thy heart as a breastplate and trample upon the enemy hosts, O great Champion St Theodore. thou hast been crowned with a heavenly, eternal crown, for thou art invincible.

Κοντακιον For The Pharisee And Publican

Tone 4   Festive, joyous and expressing deep piety.   *C, D, Eb, F, G, A, Bb, C.*

Let us flee the Pharisees conceited vaunting; let us learn the Publicans humility, and cry with groans unto the Saviour: Thou Who alone art swiftly reconciled, be gracious unto us.

2nd Sunday Of The Triodion. Prodigal son. Normal fasting this week.

Troparion Of The Prodigal Son

Tone 3   Arrogant, brave, and mature atmosphere.   *F, G, A, A#, C, D, E, F.*

Having foolishly abandoned Thy paternal glory, I have squandered on vices the wealth Thou gavest me. Therefore I cry to Thee, O compassionate Father, receive me who repent, and treat me as one of Thy hired servants.

Κοντακιον For The Prodigal Son

Tone 3   Arrogant, brave, mature.   *F, G, A, A#, C, D, E, F.*

Foolishly I sprang away from Thy great fatherly glory, and dispersed in wicked deeds the riches that Thou didst give me. With the Prodigal I therefore cry unto Thee now: I have sinned against Thee, O compassionate Father. But receive me in repentance; make me as one of Thy hired servants, O Lord.

Meat Fare Or Relatives' Saturday

Troparion For Meat Fare Saturday

Tone 8   Humility, tranquillity, repose, suffering, pleading.   *C, D, Eb, F, G, A, Bb, C.*

O Thou Who with wisdom profound orderest all things with love, and Who givest to all what is needful, O only Creator, give rest, O Lord, to the souls of Thy servants, for on Thee they have set their hope, our Maker and Builder, and our God.

Κοντακιον For Meat Fare Saturday

Tone 8   Humility, tranquillity, repose, suffering, pleading.   *C, D, Eb, F, G, A, Bb, C.*

With the Saints give rest, O Christ, to the souls of Thy servants, where there is no pain, no sorrow, no sighing, but life everlasting.

3rd Sunday Of The Triodion. Last Judgement. Meat Sunday.

Troparion For Meat Fare Saturday

Tone 8   Humility, tranquillity, repose, suffering, pleading.   *C, D, Eb, F, G, A, Bb, C.*

O Thou Who with wisdom profound orderest all things with love, and Who givest to all what is needful, O only Creator, give rest, O Lord, to the souls of Thy servants, for on Thee they have set their hope, our Maker and Builder, and our God.

Κοντακιον For Meat Fare Saturday

Tone 8   Humility, tranquillity, repose, suffering, pleading.   *C, D, Eb, F, G, A, Bb, C.*

With the Saints give rest, O Christ, to the souls of Thy servants, where there is no pain, no sorrow, no sighing, but life everlasting.

Κοντακιον For Meat Sunday

Tone 1   Magnificent, happy, earthy.   *C, D, Eb, F, G, A, Bb, C.*

When Thou comest, O God, to earth with glory, and all creatures tremble before Thee, and the river of fire flows before the Altar, and the books are opened and sins revealed, deliver me then from that unquenchable fire, and make me worthy to stand at thy right hand, O righteous Judge.

Konoinikon:

For Third Sunday Of The Triodion

Tone 8   Humility, tranquillity, repose, suffering.   C, D, Eb, F, G, A, Bb, C.

The light of Thy countenance is marked upon us, O Lord. Halleluia.

Saturday Of Cheese Fare

Troparion For Cheese Fare Saturday

Tone 4   Festive, joyous and expressing deep piety.   C, D, Eb, F, G, A, Bb, C.

O God of our Fathers, ever dealing with us according to Thy gentleness, take not Thy mercy from us, but by their prayers guide our life in peace.

Κοντακιον For Cheese Fare Saturday

Tone 8   Humility, tranquillity, repose, suffering, pleading.   C, D, Eb, F, G, A, Bb, C.

Thou hast made the company of our God-bearing Fathers illustrious as preachers of piety and silencers of impiety, O Lord, and they light up the world. By their intercessions keep in perfect peace those who magnify and glorify Thee, that they may praise Thee and sing to Thee: Alleluia.

4ᵗʰ Sunday Of The Triodion. Forgiveness & Cheese Sunday . Full Fast..

Kathisma of Matins, Clean Monday

Let us joyfully begin the all hallowed season of abstinence; and let us worship with the bright radiance of the holy commandments of Christ our God, with the brightness of love and the splendour of prayer, with the purity of holiness and the strength of good courage. So, clothed in raiment of light, let us hasten to the Holy Resurrection on the third day, which shines upon the world with the glory of eternal life.

Κοντακιον For Forgiveness Sunday

Tone 6   Rich, funereal, sorrowful.   D, Eb, F##, G, A, Bb, C##, D.

O Thou Who guidest to wisdom, and givest understanding and intelligence, the Instructor of the ignorant, and Helper of the poor, strengthen my heart and grant it understanding, O Master. Give me word, O Word of the Father; for behold, I shall not refrain my lips from crying to Thee, O merciful One, have mercy upon me who am fallen.

Κοντακιον For Cheese Fare Saturday

Tone 8   Humility, tranquillity, repose, suffering, pleading.   C, D, Eb, F, G, A, Bb, C.

Thou hast made the company of our God bearing Fathers illustrious as preachers of piety and silencers of impiety, O Lord, and they light up the world. By their intercessions keep in perfect peace those who magnify and glorify Thee, that they may praise Thee and sing to Thee: Alleluia.

[For The Sunday Of Forgiveness]

The Reading Is From The Blessed Apostle Pauls Letter To The Romans 13:11-14:4.

Brethren, salvation is nearer to us now than when we first believed; the night is far gone, the day is at hand. Let us then cast off the works of darkness and put on the armour of light; let us conduct ourselves becomingly as in the day, not in revelling and drunkenness, not in debauchery and licentiousness, not in quarrelling and jealousy. But put on the Lord Jesus Christ, and make no provision for the flesh, to gratify its desires. As for the man who is weak in faith, welcome him, but not for disputes over opinions. One believes he may eat anything, while the weak man eats only vegetables. Let not him who eats despise him who abstains, and let not him who abstains pass judgement on him who eats; for God hath welcomed him. Who art thou to pass judgement on the servant of another? It is before his own master that he stands or falls. And he shall be upheld, for the Master is able to make him stand.

[For The Sunday Of Forgiveness]

The Reading Is From The Holy Gospel According To Matthew 6:14-21.

The Lord said to His Disciples: If thou forgive men their trespasses, thy heavenly Father also shall forgive you; but if thou do not forgive men their trespasses, neither shall thy Father forgive thy trespasses. And when thou fast, do not look dismal, like the hypocrites, for they disfigure their faces that their fasting may be seen by men. Truly, I say to you, they have received their reward. But when thou fast, anoint thy head and wash thy face, that thy fasting may not be seen by men but by thy Father Who is in secret; and thy Father Who sees in secret shall reward you. Do not lay up for thyselves treasures on earth, where moth and rust consume and where thieves break in and steal, but lay up for thyselves treasures in heaven, where neither moth nor rust consumes and where thieves do not break in and steal. For where thy treasure is, there shall thy heart be also.

[The following prayer for the Hours of <u>Wednesday</u> and <u>Friday</u> of Cheese Fare Week;
and in <u>all services</u> of the Great Fast, <u>except</u> those of <u>Saturday</u> and <u>Sunday</u>.]

The Prayer Of St Ephraim The Syrian

O Lord and Master of my life, give me not a spirit of idleness, despondency, ambition or vain talking.

prostration

But rather a spirit of purity, humility, patience and love, bestow on me Thy servant.

prostration

Yea, O Lord and King, grant me to see my own faults and not to judge my brother, for blessed art Thou to the ages of ages. Amen.

prostration

O God, cleanse me, a sinner. *[cross and bow]* **(x12)**

O Lord and Master of my life, give me not a spirit of idleness, despondency, ambition or vain talking. But rather a spirit of purity, humility, patience and love, bestow on me Thy servant. Yea, O Lord and King, grant me to see my own faults and not to judge my brother, for blessed art Thou to the ages of ages. Amen.

prostration

First Week Of The Great Fast

Κοντακιον For The First Week Of The Great Fast

Tone 6   Rich texture, funereal character, sorrowful tone.   D, Eb, F##, G, A, Bb, C##, D.

My soul, my soul, arise! Why are you sleeping? The end is drawing hear, and you shall be confounded. Awake, then, and be watchful, that Christ our God may spare you, Who is everywhere present and fills all things.

5th Sunday Of The Triodion. Sunday Of Orthodoxy. Casting Out Of Paradise..
Liturgy Of St Basil of Cappadocia – Lent 5th to 9th.

The priest uses longer prayers. There are no changes for the people and the choir except:

Instead of "It is truly right ... "

Third Antiphon – Little Entrance

Hymns From The Lenten Triodion

Tone 8   Humility, tranquillity, repose, suffering.   C, D, Eb, F, G, A, Bb, C.

Adam was driven out of Paradise, because in disobedience he had eaten food; but Moses was granted the vision of God, because he had cleansed the eyes of his soul by fasting. If then we long to dwell in Paradise, let us abstain from all needless food; and if we desire to see God, let us like Moses fast for forty days. Let us set out with joy upon the season of the Fast, and prepare ourselves for spiritual combat. Let us purify our soul and cleanse our flesh; and as we fast from food, let us abstain also from every passion. Rejoicing in the virtues of the Spirit may we persevere with love, and so be counted worthy to see the solemn Passion of Christ our God, and with great spiritual gladness to behold His holy Passover. Let us joyfully begin the all-hallowed season of abstinence; and let us worship with the bright radiance of the holy commandments of Christ our God, with the brightness of love and the splendour of prayer, with the purity of holiness and the strength of good courage. So clothed in raiments of light, let us hasten to the Holy Resurrection on the third day that shines upon the world with the glory of eternal life.

+++

Troparion For The Sunday Of Orthodoxy

Tone 2   Majesty, gentleness, hope, repentance and sadness.   E, F, G, Ab, B, C.

We worship Thine immaculate Image, O Good One, and ask forgiveness of our sins, O Christ God; for of Thy own will Thou wast pleased to ascend the Cross in the flesh, to deliver from slavery to the enemy those whom Thou hadst created. Therefore we thankfully cry to Thee: Thou hast filled all things with joy, O our Saviour, by coming to save the world.

Troparion Of Great Martyr St Theodore The Tyro

Tone 2   Majesty, gentleness, hope, repentance and sadness.   *E, F, G, Ab, B, C.*

Great are the triumphs of faith. In a fountain of flame the holy martyr Theodore rejoiced as in refreshing water. For having been made a whole burned offering by fire, he was offered as sweet bread to the Trinity. By his prayers, O Christ our God, save our souls.

Κοντακιον Of Great Martyr St Theodore The Tyro

Tone 8   Humility, tranquillity, repose, suffering, pleading.   *C, D, Eb, F, G, A, Bb, C.*

Having received the faith of Christ in thy heart as an inner shield, thou didst overcome all the opposing forces, O great champion, and thou hast been crowned with a heavenly crown, O Theodore, for thou art eternally invincible.

Κοντακιον For The Sunday Of Orthodoxy

Tone 8   Humility, tranquillity, repose, suffering.   *C, D, Eb, F, G, A, Bb, C.*

The illimitable Word of the Father accepted limitations by incarnation from thee, O Mother of God; and He transformed our defiled image to its original state and transfused it with the divine beauty. But we confess and give thanks for our salvation, and we proclaim it by deed and word.

Κοντακιον For The First Week Of The Great Fast

Tone 6   Rich texture, funereal character, sorrowful.   *D, Eb, F##, G, A, Bb, C##, D.*

My soul, my soul, arise! Why art thou sleeping? The end is drawing hear, and thou wilt be confounded. Awake, then, and be watchful, that Christ our God may spare thee, Who art everywhere present and fillest all things.

The Procession Of The Holy Icons.

Sundays Of The Triodion – 5th to 9th.

Instead of "It is truly right ... "

The Megalynarion Of St Basil

Tone 1   Magnificent, happy, earthy.   *C, D, Eb, F, G, A, Bb, C.*

In thee rejoiceth, O full of grace, all creation: the angelic hosts, and the race of men, O hallowed Temple and super sensual paradise, glory of Virgins, of whom God was incarnate and became a little child, even our God Who is before all the ages; for He made thy womb a throne, and thy body He made more spacious than the heavens. In thee rejoiceth, O full of grace, all creation; and it glorifieth thee.

6th Sunday Of The Triodion. St Gregory Palamas.

Liturgy Of St Basil of Cappadocia – Lent 5th to 9th.

The priest uses longer prayers. There are no changes for the people and the choir except:
Instead of "It is truly right ... "

Troparion Of St Gregory Palamas

Tone 8   Humility, tranquillity, repose, suffering.   *C, D, Eb, F, G, A, Bb, C.*

Light of Orthodoxy, pillar and doctor of the Church, adornment of monks, invincible champion of theologians, O Gregory the wonder worker, praise of Thessalonika, preacher of grace, ever pray that our souls may be saved.

Κοντακιον Of St Gregory Palamas

Tone 2   Majesty, gentleness, hope, repentance and sadness.   *E, F, G, Ab, B, C.*

Organ of wisdom, holy and divine, bright clarion of theology, we praise thou in harmony, O divine speaker Gregory: But as a mind standing before the First Mind, direct our mind to Him, father, that we may cry: Rejoice, preacher of grace.

Κοντακιον Of St Gregory Palamas

Tone 4   Festive, joyous and expressing deep piety.   *C, D, Eb, F, G, A, Bb, C.*

Now is the time for action, judgement is at our doors. So let us rise and fast, and let us offer tears of compunction with alms giving, crying: *"We have sinned more than the grains of sand of the sea."* Forgive us all, O Creator, that we may receive incorruptible crowns.

Sundays Of The Triodion – 5th to 9th.

Instead of "It is truly right ... "

The Megalynarion Of St Basil

Tone 1   Magnificent, happy, earthy.   *C, D, Eb, F, G, A, Bb, C.*

In thee rejoiceth, O full of grace, all creation: the angelic hosts, and the race of men, O hallowed Temple and super sensual paradise, glory of Virgins, of whom God was incarnate and became a little child, even our God Who is before all the ages; for He made thy womb a throne, and thy body He made more spacious than the heavens. In thee rejoiceth, O full of grace, all creation; and it glorifieth thee.

7th Sunday Of The Triodion. Veneration Of The Cross.

Liturgy Of St Basil of Cappadocia – Lent 5th to 9th.

The priest uses longer prayers. There are no changes for the people and the choir except:

Instead of "It is truly right ... "

First Antiphon

Reader: The light of Thy countenance is marked upon us.

Thou hast given a sign to them that fear Thee, so that they may flee from the bow.

People: *At the prayers of the Mother of God, O Saviour, save us.*

Reader: Thou hast ascended on high, Thou hast led captivity captive.

Thou hast given an inheritance to those that fear Thy Name, O Lord.

People: *At the prayers of the Mother of God, O Saviour, save us.*

Reader: Glory be to the Father and to the Son and to the Holy Spirit.

Both now and forever and unto the ages of ages. Amen.

People: *At the prayers of the Mother of God | O Saviour, save us.*

Second Antiphon

Reader: All the ends of the earth have seen the salvation of our God.

Let us worship at the place where His feet stood.

People: *Save us, O Son of God, risen from the dead; Save us who sing to Thee: Halleluia.*

Reader: God is our King before the ages, He hath wrought salvation in the midst of the earth.

People: *Save us, O Son of God, risen from the dead; Save us who sing to Thee: Halleluia.*

Reader: I shall be exalted among the heathen; I shall be exalted in the earth.

People: *Save us, O Son of God, risen from the dead; Save us who sing to Thee: Halleluia.*

Reader: Glory be to the Father and to the Son and to the Holy Spirit.

Choir: Both now and forever and unto the ages of ages. Amen.

Third Antiphon – Little Entrance

Exalt ye the Lord our God, and worship at His footstool. O Lord, save Thy people and bless Thine inheritance. Feed them, and lift them up forever.

+++

Apolytikion Of The Holy Cross

Tone 1   Magnificent, happy, earthy.   C, D, Eb, F, G, A, Bb, C.

(i) (iii)   O Lord, save Thy people, and bless Thine inheritance.

Grant victories to Orthodox Christians over their adversaries.

And by Thy Cross preserve Thy commonwealth.

(ii)   Soson Kyrie ton lao sou. Ke evlogison, tin klironomian sou

Nikas tis Vasilevsii. Kata varvaron doroumen as ke to son filaton.

Dia ton stavron sou politev ma.

Κοντακιον Of Sunday Of The Cross

Tone 4   Festive, joyous and expressing deep piety.   C, D, Eb, F, G, A, Bb, C.

O Christ our God, Who wast voluntarily lifted up on the Cross, grant Thy mercies to Thy new people named after Thee. Gladden with Thy power Orthodox Christians and give them victory over their enemies. May they have as an ally that invincible trophy, Thy weapon of peace.

Κοντακιον Of Sunday Of The Cross

Tone 7   Manly character and strong melody.   F, G, A, A#, C, D, E, F.

No longer does the flaming sword guard the gate of Eden, for a glorious extinction hath come upon it, the wood of the Cross. The sting hath been drawn from death and the victory from hell. And Thou, my Saviour, didst come and shout to those in hell: Enter Paradise again.

Instead of "**Holy God ...**" **BB 13:**

The Anti-Trisagion Hymn

We adore Thy Cross, O Master. And we glorify Thy Resurrection. **(x3)**

Glory be to the Father, and to the Son, and to the Holy Spirit;

Both now and forever, and unto ages of ages. Amen.

And we glorify Thy Holy Resurrection.

Deacon: Dynamis.

We adore Thy Cross, O Master. And we glorify Thy Resurrection.

Konoinikon:

Tone 8   *Humility, tranquillity, repose, suffering.*   C, D, Eb, F, G, A, Bb, C.

The light of Thy countenance is marked upon us, O Lord. Halleluia.

Post-Communion Instead of "We have seen the true light..."

Apolytikion Of The Holy Cross

Tone 1   *Magnificent, happy, earthy.*   C, D, Eb, F, G, A, Bb, C.

(i) (iii)   O Lord, save Thy people, and bless Thine inheritance.

Grant victories to Orthodox Christians over their adversaries.

And by Thy Cross preserve Thy commonwealth.

(ii)   Soson Kyrie ton lao sou. Ke evlogison, tin klironomian sou

Nikas tis Vasilevsii. Kata varvaron doroumen as ke to son filaton.

Dia ton stavron sou politev ma.

Sundays Of The Triodion – 5th to 9th.

Instead of "It is truly right ... "

The Megalynarion Of St Basil

Tone 1   *Magnificent, happy, earthy.*   C, D, Eb, F, G, A, Bb, C.

In thee rejoiceth, O full of grace, all creation: the angelic hosts, and the race of men, O hallowed Temple and super sensual paradise, glory of Virgins, of whom God was incarnate and became a little child, even our God Who is before all the ages; for He made thy womb a throne, and thy body He made more spacious than the heavens. In thee rejoiceth, O full of grace, all creation; and it glorifieth thee.

[After 2nd "Blessed be the Name of the Lord" **Procession Of The Holy Cross.***]*

Liturgy Of St Basil of Cappadocia – Lent 5th to 9th.

The priest uses longer prayers. There are no changes for the people and the choir except:

Instead of "It is truly right ... "

Third Antiphon – Little Entrance

Troparion From The Triodion

Apolytikion Of St John Climacus.

Tone 4   Festive, joyous and expressing deep piety.   *C, D, Eb, F, G, A, Bb, C.*

With the streams of thy tears thou cultivated the barren desert, and with deep sighing from the heart thou made thy toils bring forth fruit a hundredfold, and thou became a beacon, shining in all the world by thy wonders, our venerable Father John; intercede with Christ God that our souls may be saved.

+++

Troparion Of St John Of The Ladder

Tone 3   Arrogant, brave, mature.   *F, G, A, A#, C, D, E, F.*

Thou hast set up a holy ladder by thy words and hast shone forth as a teacher of monks; thou dost lead us, O John, from the purification that comes from discipline to the light of the Divine Vision. O righteous Father, pray to Christ our God to grant us His great mercy.

+++

Troparion Of St John Climacus.

Tone 1   Magnificent, happy, earthy.   *C, D, Eb, F, G, A, Bb, C.*

Thou didst prove to be a freeman of the desert, an angel in a body, and a wonder worker, O our God bearing Father John. By fasting, vigil and prayer thou didst obtain heavenly gifts, and thou healest the sick and the souls of those who have recourse to thee with faith. Glory to Him Who gave thee strength, glory to Him Who crowned thee, glory to Him Who works through thee healings for all.

Κοντακιον Of St John Climacus.

Tone 1   Magnificent, happy, earthy.   *C, D, Eb, F, G, A, Bb, C.*

Offering ever-blossoming fruits of learning from thy book, O wise one, thou delightest the hearts of those who study it seriously, O blessed one. For it is a ladder which leads up from the earth to the heavenly and abiding glory souls who with faith honour thee.

Κοντακιον Of St John Climacus.

Tone 1   Magnificent, happy, earthy.   *C, D, Eb, F, G, A, Bb, C.*

From thy book thou dost offer teachings as everlasting fruits, O wise one, and dost sweeten the hearts of those who watchfully attend to them, O blessed one. For it is a ladder that from earth to heavenly glory leads souls who honour thee with faith.

Another Κοντακιον Of St John Climacus.

Tone 8   Humility, tranquillity, repose, suffering.   *C, D, Eb, F, G, A, Bb, C.*

We have found thy God-given virtues to be a divine ladder to heaven. For thou, O holy Father John, wast a model of the virtues.

Sundays Of The Triodion – 5th to 9th.

Instead of "It is truly right ... "

The Megalynarion Of St Basil

Tone 1   Magnificent, happy, earthy.   *C, D, Eb, F, G, A, Bb, C.*

In thee rejoiceth, O full of grace, all creation: the angelic hosts, and the race of men, O hallowed Temple and super sensual paradise, glory of Virgins, of whom God was incarnate and became a little child, even our God Who is before all the ages; for He made thy womb a throne, and thy body He made more spacious than the heavens. In thee rejoiceth, O full of grace, all creation; and it glorifieth thee.

Saturday Of The Fifth Week

Troparion Of The Mother Of God

Tone 8   Humility, tranquillity, repose, suffering, pleading.   *C, D, Eb, F, G, A, Bb, C.*

Having mystically received knowledge of the divine order, the Bodiless One flew with haste and stopped at the house of Joseph, and said to the Virgin: Lo, He Who bowed the heavens by His descent is contained wholly and unchanged in thee. And as I beheld Him in thy womb taking the form of a servant, I marvel and cry to thee: Rejoice, unwedded Bride.

Κοντακιον Of The Mother Of God

Tone 8   Humility, tranquillity, repose, suffering, pleading.   *C, D, Eb, F, G, A, Bb, C.*

Queen of the Heavenly Host, defender of our souls, we thy servants offer to thee songs of victory and thanksgiving, for thou, O Mother of God, hast delivered us from terrors. But as thou hast invincible power, free us from conflicts of all kinds that we may cry to thee: Rejoice, unwedded Bride!

9th Sunday Of The Triodion. St Mary Of Egypt
Liturgy Of St Basil of Cappadocia – Lent 5th to 9th.

The priest uses longer prayers. There are no changes for the people and the choir except:

Instead of "It is truly right ... "

Apolytikion Of St Mary Of Egypt

Tone 8   Humility, tranquillity, repose, suffering.   *C, D, Eb, F, G, A, Bb, C.*

The image of God, was faithfully preserved in you, O Mother. For thou took up the Cross and followed Christ. By thine actions thou taught us to look beyond the flesh for it passes, rather to be concerned about the soul which is immortal. Wherefore, O Holy Mary of Egypt, thy soul rejoices with the angels.

Troparion Of St Mary Of Egypt

Tone 5   Stimulating, dancing, and rhythmical.   *C, D, Eb, F, G, A, Bb, C.*

Enlightened by the grace of the Cross, Thou wert seen to be a bright light of repentance, dispelling the darkness of passions, O all holy one. thou didst appear as an angel in the flesh to holy Zosimas in the wilderness. Intercede with Christ for us, O Mary our righteous Mother.

Κοντακιον Of St Mary Of Egypt

Tone 3   Arrogant, brave, mature.   *F, G, A, A#, C, D, E, F.*

Thou who wert once obsessed with fornication by repentance are now the Bride of Christ. Thou did lovingly imitate the life of the Angels and annihilate demonic hosts by the Cross; thou art now a Bride in the Kingdom of heaven, O most chaste Mary.

Κοντακιον Of The Great Canon Of St Andrew Of Crete

Tone 6   Rich texture, funereal character, sorrowful.   *D, Eb, F##, G, A, Bb, C##, D*

My soul, my soul, arise! Why art thou sleeping? The end is drawing hear, and thou wilt be confounded. Awake, then, and be watchful, that Christ our God may spare thee, Who art everywhere present and fillest all things.

Κοντακιον Of St Mary Of Egypt

Tone 4   Festive, joyous and expressing deep piety.   *C, D, Eb, F, G, A, Bb, C.*

Having escaped the fog of sin, and having illumined thy heart with the light of penitence, O glorious one, thou didst come to Christ and didst offer to Him His immaculate and holy Mother as a merciful intercessor. Hence thou, St Mary, hast found remission for transgressions, and with the angels thou ever rejoicest.

Sundays Of The Triodion – 5th to 9th.

The Megalynarion Of St Basil *Instead of "It is truly right ... "*

Tone 1   Magnificent, happy, earthy.   *C, D, Eb, F, G, A, Bb, C.*

In thee rejoiceth, O full of grace, all creation: the angelic hosts, and the race of men, O hallowed Temple and super sensual paradise, glory of Virgins, of whom God was incarnate and became a little child, even our God Who is before all the ages; for He made thy womb a throne, and thy body He made more spacious than the heavens. In thee rejoiceth, O full of grace, all creation; and it glorifieth thee.

Lazarus Saturday

Troparion Of Lazarus (Lenten Triodion 492)

Tone 1   Magnificent, happy, and earthy.   *C, D, Eb, F, G, A, Bb, C.*

O Christ God, when Thou didst raise Lazarus from the dead, before Thy Passion, Thou didst confirm the universal resurrection. Wherefore, we, like babes, carry the insignia of triumph and victory, and cry to Thee, O Vanquisher of death, Hosanna in the highest. Blessed is he that cometh in the Name of the Lord.

Troparion For Lazarus Saturday

Tone 1   *Magnificent, happy and earthy.*   *C, D, Eb, F, G, A, Bb, C.*

Thou didst give a pledge of the general resurrection before Thy Passion, O Christ our God, by raising Lazarus from the dead. Therefore, we too, like the children, carry the symbols of victory and cry to Thee, the Vanquisher of death: Hosanna in the Heights! Blessed is He Who comes in the Name of the Lord.

Κοντακιον For Lazarus Saturday

Tone 2   *Majesty, gentleness, hope, repentance and sadness.*   *E, F, G, Ab, B, C.*

Christ, the joy of all, the truth, the light, the life, the resurrection of the world, in His goodness appeared to those on earth, and He became an image of the Resurrection and grants to all divine forgiveness.

10th Sunday Of The Triodion. Palm Sunday. St John Chrysostom.

First Antiphon

Reader: I am filled with joy, for the Lord shall hear the voice of my supplication.

        The anguish of death encompassed me, the perils of hell beset me.

People: *At the prayers of the Mother of God, O Saviour, save us.*

Reader: I found tribulation and anguish, and I called upon the Name of the Lord.

        I shall walk acceptably before the Lord in the land of the living.

People: *At the prayers of the Mother of God, O Saviour, save us.*

Reader: Glory be to the Father and to the Son and to the Holy Spirit.

        Both now and forever and unto the ages of ages. Amen.

People: *At the prayers of the Mother of God | O Saviour, save us.*

Second Antiphon

Reader: I believed, and therefore have I spoken: but I was deeply humiliated.

        What shall I render unto the Lord, for all His benefits unto me?

People: *Save us, O Son of God, Who didst sit upon the foal of a donkey;*

        Save us who sing to Thee: Halleluia.

Reader: I shall take the cup of Salvation, and call upon the Name of the Lord.

People: *Save us, O Son of God, Who didst sit upon the foal of a donkey;*

        Save us who sing to Thee: Halleluia.

Reader: I shall pay my vows unto the Lord in the presence of all His people.

People: *Save us, O Son of God, Who didst sit upon the foal of a donkey;*

        Save us who sing to Thee: Halleluia.

Reader: Glory be to the Father and to the Son and to the Holy Spirit.

Choir: *Both now and forever and unto the ages of ages. Amen.*

O give thanks unto the Lord, for He is good;	For His mercy endureth forever.
Let the house of Israel now confess that He is good;	For His mercy endureth forever.
Let the house of Aaron confess that He is good;	For His mercy endureth forever.
Let them now who fear the Lord confess that He is good;	For His mercy endureth forever.

+++

Troparion Of The Mother Of God

Tone 8   Humility, tranquillity, repose, suffering, pleading.   *C, D, Eb, F, G, A, Bb, C.*

Having mystically received knowledge of the divine order, the Bodiless One flew with haste and stopped at the house of Joseph, and said to the Virgin: Lo, He Who bowed the heavens by His descent is contained wholly and unchanged in thee. And as I beheld Him in thy womb taking the form of a servant, I marvel and cry to thee: Rejoice, unwedded Bride.

The Entrance Hymn (Eisodikon)

Reader: Blessed is He Who cometh in the Name of the Lord. The Lord is God and hath appeared unto us.

People: *Save us, O Son of God, Who didst sit upon the foal of a donkey;*

  Save us who sing to Thee: Halleluia.

Apolytikion Of Palm Sunday

Tone 1   Magnificent, happy, and earthy.   *C, D, Eb, F, G, A, Bb, C.*

Assuring us before Thy Passion of the general resurrection, Thou raised Lazarus from the dead, O Christ God: therefore, like the Children, we also carry tokens of victory, and we cry to Thee, the Conqueror of death: Hosanna in the highest. Blessed is He who cometh in the name of the Lord.

Troparion Of Palm Sunday

Tone 4   Festive, joyous and expressing deep piety.   *C, D, Eb, F, G, A, Bb, C.*

O Christ God, when we were buried with Thee in Baptism, we became deserving of Thy Resurrection to immortal life. Wherefore, we praise Thee, crying, Hosanna in the highest, blessed is he that cometh in the Name of the Lord.

Κοντακιον Of The Mother Of God

Tone 8   Humility, tranquillity, repose, suffering, pleading.   *C, D, Eb, F, G, A, Bb, C.*

Queen of the Heavenly Host, defender of our souls, we thy servants offer to thee songs of victory and thanksgiving, for thou, O Mother of God, hast delivered us from terrors. But as thou hast invincible power, free us from conflicts of all kinds that we may cry to thee: Rejoice, unwedded Bride!

The Megalynarion For Palm Sunday   *Instead of "It is truly right ... "*

Tone 4   Festive, joyous and expressing deep piety.   C, D, Eb, F, G, A, Bb, C.

God the Lord hath appeared unto us; let us celebrate the Feast, and let us rejoice and magnify Christ; and with palms and branches let us raise our voices unto Him with praise, saying, "Blessed is He that comes in the Name of the Lord our Saviour."

Konoinikon:

Tone 8   Humility, tranquillity, repose, suffering.   C, D, Eb, F, G, A, Bb, C.

Blessed is He Who cometh in the Name of the Lord. Halleluia.

Post-Communion   Instead of *"We have seen the true light..."*
Troparion Of Lazarus (Lenten Triodion 492)

Tone 1   Magnificent, happy, and earthy.   C, D, Eb, F, G, A, Bb, C.

Seated upon Thy throne in heaven and upon a foal on earth, O Christ God, Thou didst receive the praise of the angels and the hymns of the children: Blessed is He that cometh to recall Adam.

After "Blessed be the Name of the Lord" Procession Around The Church *[alternative below]*
Rejoice, O Bethany

Tone 6   Rich, funereal, sorrowful.   D, Eb, F##, G, A, Bb, C##, D.

Rejoice, rejoice, O Bethany. On this day God came to thee. And in Him the dead are made alive.
As it is right for He is the Life. He is the Life. He is the Life. He is the Life.

When Martha went to receive Him, loudly grieving with bitter tears.
She poured out the sorrow of her heart to Him.
With great sadness, wailing her lament. Wailing her lament. Wailing her lament.

She at once cried out unto Him: *"My most compassionate Lord.*
At the great loss of my brother Lazarus. My heart is broken, help me. Help me. Help me."

Jesus said to her, *"Cease thy weeping, cease thy grieving and sad lament. Sad lament. Sad lament.*
For thy brother, My most beloved friend, Lazarus, shall soon live again. Shall soon live again. Shall soon live again."

Then He, the faithful Redeemer, made His way unto the tomb.
Where he cried unto him who was buried four days, Calling him forth, saying *"Lazarus, arise. Lazarus, arise."*

Come with haste, ye two sisters, and behold a wondrous thing:
For thy brother from the tomb hath returned to life. hath returned to life. hath returned to life. hath returned to life.

To the beloved Redeemer now give thanks. To Thee, O Lord of creation.

We kneel down in reverence profound, for all we who are dead in sin.

In Thee, O Jesus, are made alive. Made alive. Made alive. Made alive. Made alive.

Rejoice, rejoice, O Bethany. On this day God came to thee. And in Him the dead are made alive.

As it is right for He is the Life. He is the Life. He is the Life. He is the Life.

At the Great Dismissal we say:

Seated upon thy throne in heaven and upon a foal on earth, O Christ God, thou didst receive the praise of the angels and the hymns of the children: Blessed is he that cometh to recall Adam.

[alternative below]

[It is customary to hold a Procession after the Divine Liturgy during which we sing:]

Troparion Of Palm Sunday

    Tone 4   Festive, joyous and expressing deep piety.   *C, D, Eb, F, G, A, Bb, C.*

O Christ God, when we were buried with Thee in Baptism, we became deserving of Thy Resurrection to immortal life. Wherefore, we praise Thee, crying, Hosanna in the highest, blessed is he that cometh in the Name of the Lord.

    And as many times as needed:

        Holy God, Holy Strong, Holy Immortal. Have mercy on us.

Doubting Thomas Sunday

Troparion Of Doubting Thomas

    Tone 8   Humility, tranquillity, repose, suffering.   *C, D, Eb, F, G, A, Bb, C.*

With his meddling right hand Thomas explored thy life giving side, Christ God, for the doors being shut when thou entered, he cried out to thou with the rest of the Apostles; "Thou art my Lord and My God."

Instead of "It is truly right ... "

Megalynarion For Thomas Sunday

    Tone 1   Magnificent, happy, earthy.   *C, D, Eb, F, G, A, Bb, C.*

O most radiant lamp, the Theotokos, the immeasurable honour, which is more exalted than all creatures, with praises do we magnify thee.

Konoinikon Of Thomas Sunday (Psalm 147:1)

    Tone 8   Humility, tranquillity, repose, suffering.   *C, D, Eb, F, G, A, Bb, C.*

Praise the Lord, O Jerusalem; praise thy God, O Zion. Halleluia.

Megalynarion For Paralytic Sunday

Tone 1   Magnificent, happy, earthy.   *C, D, Eb, F, G, A, Bb, C.*

We believers in unison bless you, O Virgin, crying: Rejoice, O gate of the Lord. Rejoice, O living city. Rejoice, O thou from whom did rise upon us from the dead the Light of Resurrection, He Who were born of you.

Megalynarion For Sunday Of The Samaritan Woman *(Instead of "It is truly meet...")*

Tone 1   Magnificent, happy, earthy.   *C, D, Eb, F, G, A, Bb, C.*

Choir: *The angel spake to her that is full of grace, saying, O pure Virgin, rejoice; and I say also, Rejoice; for thy Son is risen from the tomb on the third day.*

Reader: Rejoice and be glad, O gate of the divine Light; for Jesus Who disappeared in the tomb hath risen with greater radiance than the sun, illuminating all believers, O Lady Mary favoured of God.

Apolytikion Of Mid-Pentecost

Tone 8   Humility, tranquillity, repose, suffering.   *C, D, Eb, F, G, A, Bb, C.*

In the midst of this Feast, O Saviour, give Thou my thirsty soul to drink of the waters of true worship; for Thou didst call out to all, saying: Whosoever is thirsty, let him come to Me and drink. Wherefore, O Christ our God, Fountain of life, glory to Thee.

Sunday After Ascension (Ascension is always a Thursday).

First Antiphon

Reader: O clap thy hands, all ye peoples; shout unto God with the voice of exultation.

People: *At the prayers of the Mother of God, O Saviour, save us.*

Reader: For the Lord Most High is terrible; He is a great King over all the earth.

    He hath subdued the peoples under us, and the nations under our feet.

People: *At the prayers of the Mother of God, O Saviour, save us.*

Reader: Glory be to the Father, and to the Son, and to the Holy Spirit.

    Both now and to the ages of ages. Amen.

People: *At the prayers of the Mother of God | O Saviour, save us.*

Second Antiphon

Reader: Great is the Lord, and greatly to be praised in the city of our God; In His holy mountain.

People: *Save us, O Son of God, Who did rise from us in glory to the heavens.*

    Save us who sing to Thee. Halleluia.

Reader: God is known in her palaces when He cometh to our aid.

People: *Save us, O Son of God, Who did rise from us in glory to the heavens.*

    Save us who sing to Thee. Halleluia.

Reader: For lo, the kings of the earth were assembled; they came together.

People: *Save us, O Son of God, Who did rise from us in glory to the heavens.*

Save us who sing to Thee. Halleluia.

The Entrance Hymn (Eisodikon):

Reader: O come let us worship and fall down before Christ.

People: *Save us, O Son of God, Who did rise from us in glory to the heavens.*

Save us who sing to Thee. Halleluia.

• *Do NOT sing the apolytikion of the patron saint or feast of the temple [for Ascension].*

Apolytikion Of The Ascension

Tone 4   Festive, joyous and expressing deep piety.   C, D, Eb, F, G, A, Bb, C.

Thou hast ascended in glory, O Christ our God, and gladdened Thy Disciples with the promise of the Holy Spirit, having become confident of the blessing. Verily, Thou art the Son of God, and Deliverer of the world.

Apolytikion For The Ascension

Tone 6   Rich, funereal, sorrowful.   D, Eb, F##, G, A, Bb, C##, D.

When Thou hadst fulfilled Thy dispensation for us, and united things on earth with things in heaven, Thou wert taken up in glory, Christ our God, in no way divided, but remaining inseparable, Thou cried to those who loved Thee: *"I am with ye, and there is no one against ye."*

Megalynarion Of The Ascension *(Instead of "It is truly meet...")*

Tone 5   Stimulating, dancing, and rhythmical.   C, D, Eb, F, G, A, Bb, C.

In unison we believers do magnify thee, because thou didst give birth in time to the Word not bound by time; and in manner transcending every mind and utterance, thou became the Theotokos.

Konoinikon For The Ascension

Tone 8   Humility, tranquillity, repose, suffering.   C, D, Eb, F, G, A, Bb, C.

God hath ascended in jubilation, the Lord with the voice of the trumpet. Halleluia.

+++

Konoinikon:

Apolytikion For The Ascension

Papadikon

When Thou hadst fulfilled Thy dispensation for us, and united things on earth with things in heaven, Thou wert taken up in glory, Christ our God, in no way divided, but remaining inseparable, Thou cried to those who loved Thee: *"I am with ye, and there is no one against ye."*

Post-Communion:

Instead of "We have seen the true Light ...":

Apolytikion For The Ascension

   Tone 6   Rich, funereal, sorrowful.   *D, Eb, F##, G, A, Bb, C##, D.*

When Thou hadst fulfilled Thy dispensation for us, and united things on earth with things in heaven, Thou wert taken up in glory, Christ our God, in no way divided, but remaining inseparable, Thou cried to those who loved Thee: "I am with ye, and there is no one against ye."

Volumes in this series may be purchased as below.

A Compendium Of Orthodox Services – Volume 1.
www.amazon.co.uk/dp/1976973724

A Compendium Of Orthodox Services – Volume 2.
www.amazon.co.uk/dp/1977049265

The Divine Liturgy Of St John Chrysostom In Ancient Greek, English and Welsh.
www.amazon.co.uk/dp/1973516462

The Relationship Between Jewish And Christian Understandings Of "The Word Of God".
www.amazon.co.uk/dp/1549794280

The Time Travelling Saints Of Wales.
www.amazon.co.uk/dp/

END

Made in the USA
Monee, IL
04 February 2020